THE PSYCHOLOGY OF HUMAN DIFFERENCES

THE CENTURY PSYCHOLOGY SERIES

Richard M. Elliott, Gardner Lindzey & Kenneth MacCorquodale

EDITORS

The Psychology of Human Differences

By LEONA E. TYLER

UNIVERSITY OF OREGON

THIRD EDITION

Prentice-Hall, Inc., Englewood Cliffs, New Jersey

Printed in the United States of America

ISBN: 0-13-734939-X

Library of Congress Catalog Card Number: 65-19221

10 9 8 7 6 5 4 3 2 1

PRENTICE-HALL INTERNATIONAL, INC., *London*
PRENTICE-HALL OF AUSTRALIA, PTY. LTD., *Sydney*
PRENTICE-HALL OF CANADA, LTD., *Toronto*
PRENTICE-HALL OF INDIA PRIVATE LIMITED, *New Delhi*
PRENTICE-HALL OF JAPAN, INC., *Tokyo*

PREFACE

For textbook writers the rapid and accelerating rate at which research findings accumulate is not an unmixed blessing. As more and more new evidence on old questions becomes available, the author becomes more and more uncomfortable in the realization that successive groups of students are being led to conclusions and generalizations that are not quite sound. This is a possible, even a probable, outcome because of the fact that continuing research does more than fill in details of pictures whose general outlines are already clear. Its effect in many instances is to make drastic changes in those outlines themselves.

There are special practical reasons for making available all that we know about human differences at the present moment in history. Perhaps never before has there been so great an opportunity to apply such knowledge in the formulation of public policies and action programs. Testing in the schools has become a matter of public concern. Informed citizens need to know what measured differences in intelligence, achievement, and special abilities do and do not mean. Considered attempts to enlarge the scope of women's activities will be more likely to succeed if they are based upon everything research has revealed about sex differences. To wage the "war on poverty" effectively, persons designing and carrying out policies and programs should be familiar with all the complex findings about differences related to race and social class. Any number of other examples could be cited of social reforms being undertaken in our time to which material in one or more of the following chapters is directly or indirectly related.

Turning from application to theory, the most stimulating outgrowth of advancing knowledge is that differential psychology is beginning to emerge from the tight chrysalis in which previous thoughtways had wrapped it. A variety of new research methods is being employed to reveal kinds of individual differences that were not apparent when correlational procedures constituted almost the only technique of investigation. Instead of being content to represent an individual by a score or set of scores, one can now push on to analyze the behavior, the central processes, or the developmental sequences behind such scores. While it is not quite possible to see as yet just what kind of a new science of human individuality will spread its wings when this metamorphosis has been completed, it is exciting to watch it take place. Chapter 19 presents the author's synthesis of these developments. The reader is invited to share in this search for new directions, new organizing principles, new ways of conceptualizing what is one of the most remarkable aspects of the world of living things—the uniqueness of individuals.

L. E. T.

University of Oregon

CONTENTS

Part Four

FACTORS PRODUCING DIFFERENCES

Part One

THE FIELD OF DIFFERENTIAL PSYCHOLOGY

CHAPTER 1

Philosophical and Historical Considerations

THE UNIQUENESS OF INDIVIDUALS is one of the most fundamental characteristic facts of life. Plants raised in the same garden from apparently identical seeds grow into different sizes and shapes and produce different numbers of blossoms. Puppies, even those from the same litter, become dogs clearly distinguishable from one another in appearance and behavior. Children in the same family differ from one another even in infancy, and as they grow they develop different talents and interests, different moods and manners, different ways of reacting to success and failure, reward and punishment. Individual uniqueness was an impressive phenomenon in the ancient world whose total population (at the beginning of the Christian era) was 250,000,000. Its impressiveness is even greater today when the world's population is more than 3,000,000,000.

At all periods of human history men have observed and described differences between individuals. From Homer to Hemingway, literature contains thousands of portrayals of memorable persons. The faces of unique men and women look out at us from the canvases of Rembrandt and Franz Hals. Writers, painters, sculptors, and actors have been content to capture and express the essential quality of each person they portray. But educators, politicians, and administrators have felt a need for some way of organizing or systematizing the many-faceted complexity of individual differences. Philosophers and, in recent periods, psychologists have attempted to produce such systems.

Two kinds of ideal for mankind have played some part in these efforts to deal with human differences. Both are represented not only in the writings of eminent men of all historical periods, but in the accepted opinions of persons whom we know. For one kind of person the important thing, to be stressed above all others, is the equality of men. Such persons prefer to think that in every human being lie the potentialities for almost unlimited development. They hold that the reason for the great differences in individual traits which we observe is that opportunities for the development of full human potentialities have always been anything but equal. The task before us, as they see it, is to hold high the ideal of equality and to work unceasingly at the task of making *opportunities* for all men truly equal. This way of thinking fits in very well with our American democratic philosophy. Back of the delight we all take in stories of the poor boy's rise to fame and fortune lies the tacit belief that any one of us could, if he wished, achieve the same success. Our great faith in the power of education to overcome all handicaps and inequalities is related to this belief. The statement, "All men are created equal," accepted without qualification, satisfies a basic emotional need for many people, even if their own achievements have clearly been mediocre.

The line of approach taken by the other group of persons starts with the assumption that differences between men are basic and ineradicable, biological facts which cannot be ignored. The ideal that such a belief generates is of a society fully utilizing these varied gifts for the enrichment of the common life. The caste system of India, in its ideal aspect, is based on such a philosophy. Plato, in the *Republic,* discusses the problem of variation in individual endowments and even proposes a sort of aptitude test to select persons who are particularly well qualified for military careers. The philosophy back of the educational systems in most European countries is based on this type of thinking. After their elementary schooling in the basic skills, only those individuals who show special intellectual gifts are selected for secondary and higher education along academic lines. Even in democratic Britain, the unlimited educability of every individual has never been assumed.

It is well to admit at the beginning that neither of these assumptions with regard to human individuality can be either proved or disproved. Many workers in social-science fields do, in fact, look at their data now from one point of view, now from the other. Until we have equal opportunity for all, we can never know with certainty that inequalities would persist in spite of it. It is also true that each view carries with it the possibility that some one may draw from it unwarranted conclusions. The philosophy that differences are basic and ineradicable lends itself very conveniently to those who need a rationalization for the existence of the privileged classes. Hindu upper-caste leaders, pre-Civil War slaveowners, modern industrialists and business leaders—all have found it easy to adopt this system of thinking without scrutinizing it too carefully to make sure that it fits all the facts.

The equalitarian philosophy, while it avoids this type of warped reasoning, may lead to another difficulty. If one believes that all normal human beings are creatures of unlimited possibilities, then one is almost certain to be greatly disappointed in the achievements of many of them who have failed to measure up to the opportunities they have had. The result of this disappointment is that wives nag their husbands, teachers prod their slower students, and many men and women live out their lives in the shadow of a haunting feeling of failure. Both tolerance toward others and a frank admission of one's own limitations are encouraged by an acceptance of human differences at their face value.

The viewpoint to be adopted in this book is that while all individuals may be considered to have equal *value,* they are not alike in how they think and feel and act. We assume that for all practical purposes of individual placement and group planning the fact that there are differences between people must be taken into consideration. Our first need is to understand what the differences are.

TYPES *VERSUS* TRAITS

In their efforts to impose some order on the enormously complicated subject matter of individual differences, the first strategy that occurred to mankind was to classify people into *types.* Various ways of doing this were proposed, even in antiquity, and type concepts serve a useful function in personality research even today. As early as the fifth century B.C., Hippocrates gave us a two-fold system based on body build, the *habitus apoplecticus* and *habitus phthisicus.* The later famous Greek physician, Galen, proposed a four-fold classification based on the predominance of different "humors" or biochemical fluids in the body. His four main types were the sanguine, the choleric, the phlegmatic, and the melancholic. Variations of these classifications have appeared under many names right down to our own century, and have been supplemented by typologies based on other aspects of observable personality. Spranger, basing his analysis on literature, analyzed the basic *values* men seem to live by, and elaborated six fundamental types: the theoretical, economic, aesthetic, social, political, and religious. Jaensch, basing his system on observations of eidetic imagery, described what he called a T-type, or integrated person, as opposed to a B-type or disintegrated person. Kretschmer attempted to relate a physical typology not too different from the early one of Hippocrates to a classification of temperaments, and tied the system in with the two major varieties of psychosis, schizophrenia and the manic-depressive states. William James sorted people out into the tough-minded and the tender-minded. But more popular than any of these systems has been the Jung classification into extraverted and introverted types. The fact that such typologies have appeared to many thinkers in many centuries to be a way of bringing some order into the complex realm of personality differences has kept us from dismissing them too lightly. The fact that they are so various and so confusing has led us to look beyond the verbal formulations for evidence that can enable us to sift out the convincing from the merely plausible and to locate the unities underlying the diversity.

During the twentieth century, psychologists, especially American psychologists, became very critical of type concepts. For one thing, the word *type* proved to be an ambiguous term. Because different theorists attached different meanings to it, they often failed to communicate clearly. In their dictionary of psychological terms English and English (1958) specify nine distinguishable meanings. It is obvious that some persons who talk and write about human "types," are assuming "that the word means a real . . . or an ideal or fictitious individual embodying the characteristics of a category in fullest measure." But such persons are not really talking about the same concept as those who assume that "type" means "the peak instances of a bimodal distribution of a single variable: *a normal type* vs. *a pigmy type*."

A second basis for objecting to particular typologies, such as Jung's extravert-introvert classification, arose from research attempts to appraise people's characteristics and assign them to one or the other category. It usually turned out that most persons fell in an in-between category. They would be, for example, introverts in some respects, extraverts in others. The way they were classified would depend on the particular questions about themselves they had been asked to answer.

However, type concepts never entirely disappeared, even from American psychology, and in Europe they have been influential all along. In the 1960's psychologists in the United States are showing an increasing willingness to return to typological systems of organization, at least for some purposes. The Myers-Briggs Type Indicator (1962), for example, is a far more sophisticated effort to give objective form to Jung's complex typology than previous attempts to assess extraversion-introversion have been. Cognitive styles, constitutional types, interest patterns—these are all essentially typological concepts. They play a significant part in research on human differences in the 1960's.

The other main strategy for imposing order upon individual differences was to study traits, one at a time and in combination with one another. Instead of attempting to assign individuals to classes, as type psychologists do, we can direct our attention to the qualities or traits that become evident in their behavior. In our common everyday affairs, a natural way to describe a person is to mention his salient characteristics. A teacher may say, for example, that John is a handsome, athletic, somewhat shy boy, with only average verbal intelligence but exceptional mechanical ability. He may then characterize Bill as not so goodlooking or athletic, less shy, more intelligent, and not so adept at mechanical reasoning. That is, he can, if he wishes, evaluate different individuals on the same traits. The strategy of describing many individuals in terms of the same traits serves to express the differences between them in quantitative rather than qualitative form.

Trait concepts have dominated American differential psychology for half a century or more, and most of the research reported in this book is based on acceptance of this way of thinking. As time has passed, however, some difficulties have arisen in its application. The principal one is the sheer magnitude of the task of identifying all of the separate ways in which individuals can differ from one another and developing techniques for assessing these traits. Instead of the unitary quality early differential psychologists had in mind when they began to develop tests for intelligence, present-day workers are accumulating evidence for many distinct intellectual abilities. J. P. Guilford (1959) concludes that there are probably 120 different varieties of intelligence. Allport and Odbert (1936) showed that there are from 3,000 to 5,000 words used in the languages of civilized people to describe personal qualities. While personality tests for all sorts of traits have proliferated during our century, it is clear that it is never going to be feasible to administer several thousand of them to one individual as a means of understanding and describing him. We shall consider in later sections of this book the attempts psychologists have made to reduce trait complexity by combining related traits through factor analysis, efforts that have brought about a partial but not a complete solution to the problem.

The other major objection to trait psychology arises from the question whether it is really meaningful to describe individuals in terms of traits they all have in common. Allport (1937) raised this question in his discussion of the difference between *nomothetic* and *idiographic* methods of studying individuals. When we administer the same tests to all members of a group or rate all of them on the same set of rating scales we are using the nomothetic approach. Underlying it is the assumption that the uniqueness of individuals is a matter of quantitative variation in characteristics they all share. In contrast to this, we use the idiographic approach when we look for characteristics peculiar to the one person we seek to understand or describe—the quality of his voice that distinguishes it from all others, for example, or his style of walking, writing, or thinking. These unique differentiating attributes are important aspects of individuality, and an overemphasis on trait concepts has perhaps prevented us from giving them the research attention they deserve.

THE DEVELOPMENT OF QUANTITATIVE METHODS

One of the most prominent features of the work psychologists have done on individual differences is an emphasis on quantitative methods. In the long history of man's attempts to understand human individuality, this is a fairly recent development. It is still not accepted completely, to judge by the many books and magazine articles in which mental testing and testers are attacked.

Until about a century ago, the whole idea of *measuring* any aspect of human mental life was unthinkable. Mind was generally held to be an order of reality to which figures were just not applicable. The discovery of the possibility of numerical description of the way an individual's nervous system functions was made by accident, and by an astronomer, not a psychologist. Bessel, looking over a history of the Greenwich Astronomical Observatory in 1816, was struck by an incident recorded there. A young assistant had been dismissed in 1796 for continually reporting the time of the apparent transit of stars across a hair line in the telescope's field of view nearly a second later than his master did. Bessel asked himself why the young man should have been so slow, even when his job was at stake. He began to try out his fellow-astronomers, and discovered that there was considerable variation among individuals in the speed with which they reacted to a visual stimulus. He called this the personal equation. Its importance to psychology was its demonstration that at least one mental characteristic could be measured.

At about the same time, work was in progress on the development of methods of dealing with the numerical quantities obtained in the measurement of any human trait, physical or mental. Quetelet, the Belgian mathematician, was the first to discover that the mathematical theory of probability could be applied to human measurements. Sir Francis Galton, explorer, meteorologist, biologist, one of the most brilliant and versatile men of the nineteenth century, made great contributions to the science of handling such data. He was interested primarily in the problem of heredity, but found that he needed to measure human characteristics in order to get evidence. He set up an anthropometric laboratory in London and made physical measurements of thousands of persons who volunteered to serve as subjects. In order to get at their mental characteristics, he developed some ingenious methods of his own, such as the Galton whistle for determining degree of sensitivity to high pitches and the famous breakfast-table test for determining the strength of an individual's imagery (Galton, 1883). Many of the methods we shall take up in later chapters are based on Galton's pioneering research activities.

During the latter half of the nineteenth century the rise of psychology as a science and the founding of the great psychological laboratories brought about a tremendous increase in the number of measurable human traits. Much research was done on sensation, and exact measurements were made of various aspects of vision, hearing, and the skin senses. Some workers were concerned with discrimination processes and measured the accuracy with which subjects could judge differences in weights and brightnesses and lengths of lines. Others worked on memory and developed methods for measuring how quickly the individual learned and how much he remembered. Processes of attention, observation, aesthetic judgment, and even thinking itself came under the scrutiny of these indefatigable workers.

Most of the early psychologists were far more interested in discovering general laws of human nature, which would hold for everybody, than in exploring differences between people. For each experiment, they would use enough subjects so that they could be fairly confident that the average of the group was a dependable index of the trait they were considering. But one of the early students in the laboratory of the great German psychologist, Wundt, became interested in the *differences between* the subjects and in the possible significance of these differences. He was James McKeen Cattell, an American. By thus changing the emphasis, he initiated the mental-test movement, which has become increasingly important from 1890 on to the present time. Though Cattell seems to have been the first to use the term *mental test,* others at about the same time were initiating similar projects. In Germany, Oehrn (1889) published the results he had obtained using a series of tests of perception, memory, association, and motor functions. Kraepelin (1895) also attempted to work out a set of tests for several traits. Ebbinghaus (1897), whose research on memory has made him famous, developed some tests at the request of the Breslau school authorities, among them the completion test which has become a permanent part of our test repertory. In America, J. McK. Cattell (1890), Cattell and Farrand (1896), Jastrow (1891), Münsterberg (1891), Bolton (1892), J. A. Gilbert (1897), Sharp (1899), Woodworth (1910), and a number of others were all attacking the problem in various ways. Most of this early work, however, failed to produce any significant results. Later research showed that this was because it was based on a false premise. The aim of these early test-makers was to measure intelligence. They were assuming that if you could measure all aspects of sensation, perception, attention, discrimination, and speed of reaction in the individual, the total efficiency index would be an index to his general intelligence. This seemed a reasonable inference, because the accepted psychological theory of the time held that all of mental life was built up of units of sensory experience, just as the physical world is made up of atoms. Unfortunately, when the early mental-testers checked up on the measurements they had made, they found that there was something wrong with the idea. Persons who were quick, accurate, and skillful at simple tasks did not necessarily turn out to be highly intelligent.

The most famous name in mental testing is that of Alfred Binet, who in 1905, with the collaboration of Simon, published the first mental test that really worked. In the course of his work he developed assumptions quite different from those of his orthodox colleagues. He held that the complex mental abilities we classify under the term *intelligence* are not made up of simple abilities. If we are to measure them at all, we must do it directly. If judgment in a complex situation is what we wish to evaluate, we must give the individual a complex situation to work on and see how he handles it. If his ability to solve problems of various sorts is in question, we must give him those problems to grapple with. It seemed to many psychologists at the turn of the century that this approach to mental measurement could never be practical because of the simple fact that you could never *measure* such complex traits in seconds or millimeters or any other meaningful numerical unit. Binet got around this difficulty when, in the 1908 revision of the scale first published in 1905, he arranged the tests in groups according to difficulty and introduced the concept of *mental age*. Although this is not the same kind of measuring unit as inches or seconds, it proved to be a very satisfactory method for treating different performance levels quantitatively. It was the standard method of scoring intelligence tests for children for half a century. Stern in Germany and Terman in this country supplemented the mental-age concept with the additional idea of dividing the obtained mental age by the actual chronological age in order to get an index of the *rate* at which mental growth occurs in a given individual. Terman called this the *intelligence quotient* and used it in the 1916 Stanford-Binet scale. The term immediately became popular both with psychologists and with the general public until, at present, there is scarcely a person who does not know something about IQ tests—whether or not what he knows is correct.

For the student of individual differences, perhaps the most significant aspect of all this early research on mental tests is the indication it gives us of the great *demand* for such tools. As school attendance became more universal, the problem of the slow-learning child became acute. Both Ebbinghaus and Binet, it is to be remembered, were working on definite assignments from the school authorities to develop some technique by which the children who *could* not master the work of their grade might be distinguished from those who *would* not. With the professionalization of social services, the need arose for instruments by means of which the dependent individual's capacity for adjustment could be measured. The earliest work on Binet tests in the United States was done by Goddard, one of whose chief interests was the relationship of feeble-mindedness to delinquency. With all their flaws, mental tests made it possible to handle the problems created by individual differences more intelligently than they had ever been handled before. It is this plain fact that has kept research alive and flourishing.

THE SHAPING OF THE NEW SCIENCE

At about the turn of the century when all this activity centering around the attempt to measure individual differences was going on, two comprehensive statements about the aims and methods of the new science were published. Binet and Henri (1895) began their article, "We broach here a new subject, difficult and as yet very meagerly explored." They then proposed as the two chief aims of this undertaking: first, the study of the *nature and extent* of individual differences in psychological processes; and second, the discovery of the *interrelationships* of mental processes within the individual so as to arrive at a classification of traits and determine which are the more basic functions. Stern's text (1900) outlined a threefold problem: (1) What is the nature and extent of differences in the psychological life of individuals and groups? (2) What factors determine or affect these differences? and (3) How are the differences manifested? To what extent can we use handwriting, facial conformation, and other signs to help us analyze them?

These goals have remained primary from their day to ours, but a number of special emphases have become prominent in different periods. The first of these was the search for group tests which was given great impetus during World War I. Individual intelligence tests are obviously impractical when large numbers of people are to be classified. It seemed that it should be quite feasible to use some of the same types of material that had proved so useful in individual testing but to put them together in a form in which the answers to the questions would be short and definite enough to be accurately scored. This was successfully accomplished at the time of World War I. Five psychologists, under the direction of Robert M. Yerkes, undertook to see if they could produce something that would work in the army situation. Otis put at their disposal several types of test upon which he had been working. The results of their efforts were Army Alpha, a verbal test, and Army Beta, a nonverbal test, both of which could be given to large groups and scored by clerical workers with no psychological training. Since the mental-age concept was of little value in classifying *adult* soldiers, new ways of scoring had to be worked out, based on group norms. The fact that the research workers were provided by the army draft with a large and fairly representative sample of the American population on which to base their derived scores facilitated the solution of the problem. Work on the development of various types of derived scores based on norms for different populations has continued up to the present. A great number of group tests of intelligence have been constructed since 1918 to meet the almost unlimited demand in schools, from kindergarten to college and graduate school.

The second line of research had as its aim the development of *nonverbal* tests of intelligence. For many purposes, tests of either the Binet type or the ordinary group type were found to be useless. If the individual to be tested is deaf, he cannot, of course, hear the questions in an individual test. If he is illiterate, he cannot answer questions requiring that he read and write. If he is deficient in his knowledge of the language of the country in which he lives, he cannot be expected to distinguish himself on a vocabulary test. Furthermore, many psychologists felt that tests depending on some school knowledge were inherently not valid as measures of basic native mental capacity. Psychologists who devoted their efforts to this problem brought forth a wide variety of performance and nonverbal tests, including form boards, puzzles, mazes, block-design problems, and many others. There are both individual and group tests of this sort, and they form an important set of tools for the applied psychologist. It has become increasingly evident as time has passed that such tests do not measure exactly the same mental capacity as the verbal tests do, but once this fact is understood their usefulness is in no way diminished. If they are worth less to us than we expected as *substitutes* for the typical verbal intelligence test, they are worth more as *supplements*. With an increasing amount of statistical knowledge and clinical experience, we have become clearer as to what traits various types of tests measure and what situations call for these traits.

Thus a third direction that research has taken is a turning away from the search for *universal* intelligence tests suitable for all human beings under all circumstances. Test-makers have found that it is impractical if not impossible to develop tests which will be equally valid for preschool children, college students, and illiterate adults. Separate tests are needed. It has also become increasingly apparent that intelligence itself has many aspects. Much of the work of recent years has been concerned with identifying these aspects and developing separate tests for characteristics such as spatial judgment, numerical ability, and verbal ability. The relationship between these separate *factors,* as they are called, and general intellectual ability is still a very live issue. It is discussed in some detail in Chapter 4.

A fourth and related direction of research has been toward the development of tests of special abilities and talents. A great deal of work has been done on mechanical, clerical, and musical aptitudes, somewhat less on talent in the field of art and on the capacity for understanding social situations and handling people. Achievement tests for all branches and levels of knowledge have been constructed. Most of this work has had a strong practical orientation. Its aim has been the production of tools that would be really useful in the selection, placement, education, and guidance of individuals in accordance with their special characteristics and needs. These findings will be discussed in Chapters 5 and 6.

The fifth line of research has been toward the measurement, or at least the rather precise evaluation, of the *nonintellectual* traits of the individual, such as interests, adjustment patterns, and personality traits. E. K. Strong devoted his long research career to vocational interests. There are numerous inventories of traits related to maladjustment and tendencies toward mental illness. In the 1930's an entirely new approach to the problems involved in personality measurement made its appearance, the so-called projective technique, in which the subject by interpreting some material such as an ink blot or an ambiguous picture furnishes an indication of his basic attitudes, motives, and problems. These methods are further removed than the others from the quantitative techniques we have been discussing, but any survey of research on individual differences cannot ignore them entirely. In order to delimit the field with which this book is concerned, we shall not try to cover the vast literature on these clinical techniques except for studies in which some clear-cut *quantitative* method of evaluating the responses of subjects has been worked out. To be familiar with studies where results are reported as verbal descriptions rather than numerical scores is indispensable to our grasp of individual differences in the broad sense. The clinical psychologist, the teacher, and the social worker need such familiarity. But the task before us here is the synthesis of *research* findings, and the quantitative methods have proved more serviceable for testing hypotheses, exploring relationships, and drawing conclusions.

Still a sixth research emphasis had begun to take definite shape by the late 1940's. It was the use of objective laboratory methods to investigate differences in personality and temperament. This was not really an innovation. Hartshorne and May (1928), many German psychologists throughout the 1920's and 1930's, and scattered research workers in Britain and America had all seen the advantages in analyzing personality differences by means of accurately measurable perceptual or motor responses rather than by means of self-reports obtained on personality inventories. By 1950, however, several large-scale research programs were oriented in this direction, and some challenging new ideas had been launched upon the mainstream of our thinking about personality. One of the main contributions this work has made consists of some new *variables* to work with, characteristics that cut across the traditional line between ability and motivation, thought processes and emotions. This has opened up new horizons.

It is not easy to formulate precisely the nature of the change in our thinking that is occurring as the result of these new kinds of concepts, such as Witkin's *field dependence*, Gardner's *equivalence range*, or Bruner's *strategies of problem solving*. What they seem to be doing is to enable us to break out of the rigid molds set for us by the type and trait formulations of the past by revealing another *kind* of way in which individuals differ from one another. Because of unique aspects of a person's developmental history, he acquires preferred ways of dealing with complex situations. Research of the 1950's and 1960's produced ingenious new test and experimental situations and new methods of analyzing data to facilitate the exploration of such differences. We shall be considering these in some detail later in this book.

In attacking all these types of problems, both old and new, there has been increasing emphasis, especially in the period since World War II, on large-scale, coordinated research programs rather than isolated studies. Results have been coming in from longitudinal studies that have been in progress for a long time—Terman's decades of work with a group originally selected as gifted children, for example, and the California Guidance Study. Other programs consist of groups of related experiments organized around an important theoretical issue or practical need. The work of Eysenck and his associates at the Institute of Psychiatry in London and the work of the Committee on Human Development in Chicago are examples.

What this trend toward large research programs means is that we now have far more dependable evidence to use in answering the basic questions of differential psychology than we have ever had before. In many instances we need no longer piece together scraps of information obtained from a host of small and inadequate studies but can make a thorough examination of a reasonable amount of sound evidence. This makes it less possible than it once was to argue for a favorite theory and support one's position by dismissing the evidence against it. A whole body of data obtained by a reputable research institute cannot be ignored or ruled out as can a single questionable study based on a nonrepresentative sample. Arguments about the ill effects of acceleration on bright children, for example, are obsolete since Terman and Oden's careful analysis of the problem became available (see Chapter 15). Arguments that heredity has nothing to do with psychological differences lose much of their weight when confronted with Kallman's impressive accumulation of facts and figures (see Chapter 18). The details about these and other issues will be discussed in later sections of this book. Many psychologists would certainly insist that none of these complex problems is *settled* as yet. The only point here, one that perhaps is not sufficiently appreciated by workers in these vineyards, is that the raw material out of which conclusions and generalizations are now being produced is vastly superior to the best we had thirty years ago.

Perhaps because of this, the present period is marked by a number of rapprochements or syntheses by means of which conclusions once thought to be squarely in opposition to one another have been reconciled. For example, the question about whether or not the IQ is constant has been rephrased. Studies at the University of California and at the Fels Institute have shown that IQ's do change, but in orderly ways that can to a considerable extent be predicted if we have the necessary information about the age of each child when tested, the educational level of his family, and the period of time intervening between examinations. Hereditarians and environmentalists no longer divide themselves into two hostile camps. Increasing knowledge about what is inherited, how learning processes change various mental characteristics, and what kinds of environmental situations have favorable influences on mental growth has changed the whole pattern of the controversy.

The participation of laboratory workers in research on individual differences in personality, discussed as the sixth trend above, may mark an even more significant rapprochement. For many years, experimental psychologists constituted one distinct group, mental-testers another. Experimental workers were familiar with complicated types of apparatus, controlled as many variables as possible, and thought in terms of stimulus and response, independent and dependent variables. Mental measurement specialists used tests consisting of questions or simple tasks, worked in natural settings rather than laboratories, and developed statistical procedures based on correlation rather than dependency analysis. Most of these distinctions have become blurred in the years since World War II. One of the clearest landmarks pointing to this particular synthesis was Cronbach's presidential address to the American Psychological Association (Cronbach, 1957), entitled "The Two Disciplines of Scientific Psychology." In it he argued cogently that the time had come for experimental psychology and correlational psychology to combine forces. The monograph by Cronbach and Gleser (1957) presented some techniques to use in research of this combined sort. For example, it makes good sense to combine research on selection (a problem in correlational or differential psychology) with research on training (a problem in experimental psychology) and try to find out what variety of training procedure works best for each of several sorts of people.

With all this emphasis on progress we must recognize that the science of human differences is still immature. The most interesting questions are still unanswered, perhaps even unasked. Meanwhile, human life goes on. Somehow, we must all adjust ourselves right now to those around us in some fashion and plan as intelligently as possible for ourselves and for each other. It is well that in doing this we use the best information that we have. The more complicated our world becomes, the more essential it is that we avoid any attempt to found human institutions on ideas about human nature that we know to be false. To proceed on the basis of tested evidence when such evidence can be obtained, to suspend judgment in cases where no conclusion is warranted, to formulate tentative courses of action in areas where doubt exists—these are the skills needed by the social scientist and applied psychologist. It is to be hoped that the study of what now is known about individual and group differences will contribute to the development of such skills.

SUMMARY

Differences between individuals are a fundamental phenomenon. Artists have portrayed them; philosophers and psychologists have developed classification systems and concepts to deal with them. Some thinkers see as an ideal the eradication of all differences in the name of equality; others cherish the differences and wish to use them for the enrichment of man's common life.

Classification systems dividing mankind into a limited number of types have existed from the early days of human history to our own day. Psychologists have preferred classification systems based on traits. Both systems have strengths and weaknesses.

Psychological research on individual differences began when quantitative methods came into use during the latter years of the nineteenth century. Many psychologists participated in this development. Its culmination was the work of Binet and the first intelligence test.

Other developments followed: group tests, nonverbal tests, specific tests for different groups and purposes, tests of special aptitudes and achievements, and personality tests. Laboratory methods have come into increasing use. Large-scale research programs have been designed to explore particular areas or problems.

Rapprochements and syntheses have to a large extent superseded the controversies and divisions of the past. Hereditarians and environmentalists no longer line up in opposing camps. The merging of correlational and experimental psychology now seems possible.

CHAPTER 2

General Principles and Concepts

VARIABILITY AMONG INDIVIDUALS—A UNIVERSAL PHENOMENON

This is a book about *human* differences. But before we examine these human differences in detail, it may be instructive to consider briefly what we know about variability in other forms of animal life. Ordinary observation demonstrates again and again that one animal of a species differs in many ways—in behavior as well as appearance—from other animals of the same species. Dog-lovers never tire of stories about some dog's unusual intelligence, resourcefulness, or devotion. Farmers recognize and deal appropriately with temperamental differences in cows. Horses differ in intellectual achievements as well as running speed.

As experimental psychologists have observed animals in their laboratories, a body of scientific knowledge about individual differences has accumulated. It can be concluded with some certainty that individual variability characterizes all species—from the highest to the lowest.

It is not surprising that monkeys differ in behavioral characteristics. Any zoo visitor can observe this for himself. A study by Fjeld (1934) contributes some quantitative evidence as to just how marked the differences between individual monkeys are in a kind of problem-solving capacity somewhat analogous to what we call intelligence in human beings. Figure 1 shows the sort of performance required.

To get the food box open, each animal was required to depress one or more of the plates in the floor. In Problem 1, the easiest problem, all he had to do was to depress Plate 1 and the door would open. In Problem 2, he must depress Plates 1 and 2 in turn, then the door opened; in Problem 3, Plates 1, 2, and 3. Problem 4 required him to depress 1, 2, and 3, reverse his direction, and step on 2 again. In Problem 7 the order was Plate 1, 2, 3, 2, 1, 2, 3. Out of a group of fifteen rhesus monkeys who served as subjects

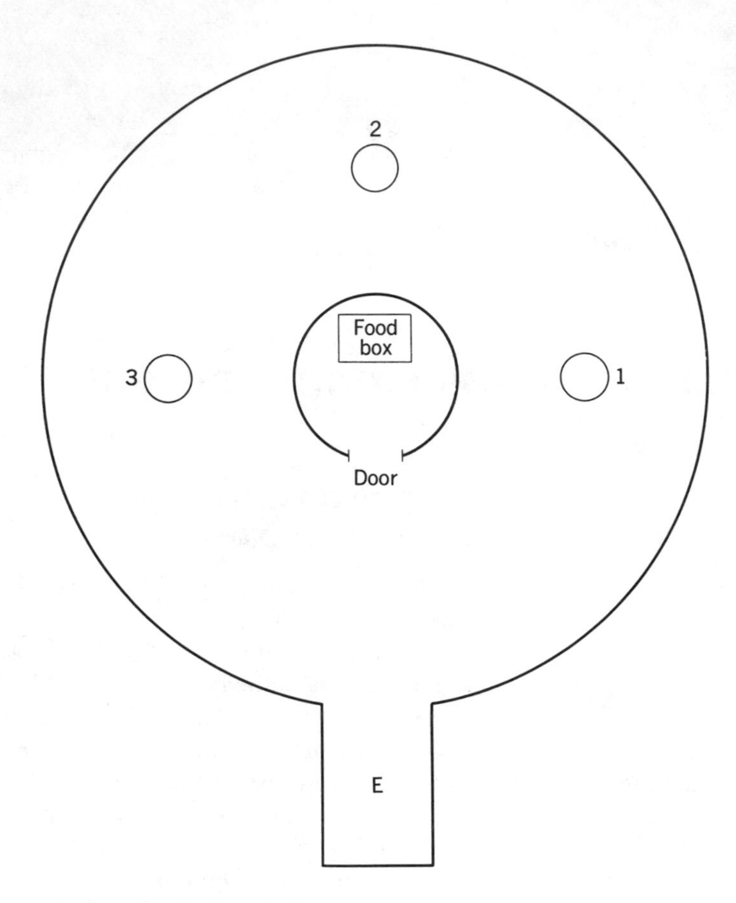

FIGURE 1

Design of Problem Box Used in Fjeld Experiment

(Fjeld, 1934)

through the whole experiment, one was unable to learn more than 2 problems, whereas one learned 22. The rest varied all the way from 3 to 13. A similar study by Koch (1935) on Cebus monkeys gave similar results with somewhat less variability in performance from animal to animal.

A good demonstration of individual differences in cats is a study by Warren (1961). What he required each animal to do in order to obtain food in this kind of experiment was to choose one of two small objects presented to him simultaneously. The "right" object was distinguished from the "wrong" one in different ways in different experiments. In some experiments, it was the *position* that mattered—for example, the left-hand one was always correct. In other experiments it was the shape of the object that was the clue, and the animal had to notice whether it was a square, triangle, circle, trapezoid, or some other geometrical form. The problem was made more difficult for the animal by arranging things in such a way that he must take *size,* as well as position or shape, into consideration. Thus in the position experiments, he was rewarded for choosing the left-hand object when the stimuli were small and for choosing the right-hand object when the stimuli were large. In the shape discrimination experiments, he was to choose one of the pair (e.g., square) when the stimuli were large and the other (e.g., semicircle) when the stimuli were small. It was the task of each cat to discover through a series of trials just what he was expected to do. Once he "caught on" he would choose correctly every time.

It turned out that discriminations on the basis of shape were more difficult than discriminations on the basis of position, but that there were very large differences between animals. The most "brilliant" of the 21 cats Warren tested required only 54 trials to solve the shape-size problem. The "dullest" one required 760 trials. The others ranged somewhere in between.

Because rats have been a favorite kind of experimental subject in psychological laboratories, a considerable amount of information about individual differences in this species has accumulated. They differ widely in maze-running ability (Tryon, 1942), and in temperamental traits such as wildness (C. S. Hall, 1951). Geier, Levin, and Tolman (1941) carried out an elaborate study in which they identified four different traits upon which their rat subjects differed from one another, two of them "intellectual" traits and two "emotional" or "motivational" traits.

What is more surprising than these findings, however, is the report by J. Hirsch that there are individual differences in the behavior of fruit flies (Hirsch, 1962). The object of Hirsch's research program has been to find out more about the genetic bases of behavior, and we will consider it in some detail in a later chapter. But it is worth noting here that individual differences have been demonstrated in what biologists call *taxes,* such as phototaxes and geotaxes—the tendency to approach or to withdraw from light, and the tendency to move upward (against gravity) or to move downward (with gravity). Figure 2 shows graphically the percentages of trials on which different individuals in one experimental population moved *up* in an ingeniously contrived geotactic maze (Hirsch, 1959). Its resemblance to the kind of distribution we often obtain from testing human subjects is obvious.

But individual differences in behavior have been found in species lower than the fruit fly, even in one-celled animals. There is evidence, for instance, that protozoa show changes in behavior with continued experience in a situation, a form of learning that seems to be an elementary sort of conditioned response. Razran (1933) reported that whereas the average protozoon took 138.5 trials to "learn" this, the range from fastest to slowest

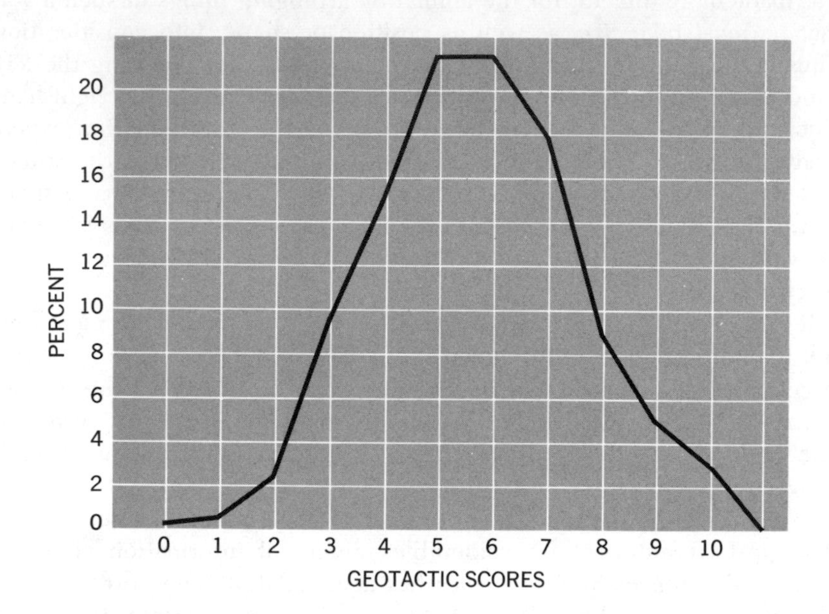

FIGURE 2

Distribution of Geotactic Scores for Male Fruit Flies in a Particular Breeding Population

(Hirsch, J., 1959)

was from 79 to 284 trials. Some experiments by French (1940), using paramecia as subjects, supplied evidence on two other traits or characteristics. One is the tendency to form groups. By an ingenious method, French separated the "groupers" from the "free-swimmers," kept them separate and in clear water for a half hour, and then put them back into separate food solutions to see if the grouping tendency persisted. It did, to a striking extent. Similar experiments were run to see whether tendencies to enter or not to enter solutions in which a small amount of some foreign chemical had been placed would persist. Again, differences turned out to be fairly large in some of the experiments and statistically significant in all.

Examples based on many other types of performance in many other species might be given, but enough have probably been cited to convince the student of human psychology that variation in mental characteristics is far from being an exclusively human phenomenon. Such studies are important for us in that they suggest that differences are universal and usually ineradicable. If this is the case we must learn to understand them, accept them, and use them in the building of our common society.

HUMAN CHARACTERISTICS IN WHICH DIFFERENCES HAVE BEEN MEASURED

Many types of measurement have been made on human beings. First, it is obvious to all of us that human individuals are not the same in size and shape. We have learned to expect and to make at least some provision for this kind of variation, though the army still sometimes has trouble fitting out the new recruit whose shoes are size 13, and women find that both the 8's and the 46's are sometimes hard to obtain at dress shops. Much first-rate work has been done in the field of anthropometric measurements. Not only gross height and weight, but the exact sizes of most of the individual parts of the body have been measured. Second, measurements have been made of the physiological processes, or the way various organ systems of the body function. Basal metabolism, the amount of calcium, sugar, acid, and hemoglobin in the blood, respiratory rate, pulse rate, and concentrations of acid and of urea in the urine are physiological characteristics in which individuals have been found to show definite, measurable differences.

The extensive research work of Williams (1956) has provided an impressive amount of evidence about this variability in physical and physiological characteristics. The organs of the body, such as the stomach and the heart, differ markedly in size and shape. The chemical composition of the various fluids of the body show a similar variability. Take saliva, for example (Williams, 1956, p. 59). The amount of uric acid secreted in saliva by nine different individual subjects varied from 2.5 μg. per ml. in one case to 150 μg. per ml. in another. The amino acids, serine, glycine, alanine, and lysine, were not present at all in some cases but occurred in appreciable amounts in others. Each person's saliva is probably as unique as his appearance, voice, or disposition.

In successive chapters, Williams summarizes evidence with regard to individual differences in enzymic patterns, endocrine activities, excretion patterns, pharmacological manifestations, and nutrition, all of which he considers to be genetically determined. We shall return to his ideas in later chapters. Here we simply take notice that all these kinds of differences exist.

There is even more abundant evidence for individual differences in all sorts of psychological characteristics. There is much variability with regard to motor capacities, such as reaction time, speed of tapping, steadiness, and swiftness of blow. Individuals differ markedly in sensory and perceptual characteristics such as keenness of vision, hearing, and sense of smell. Some are better than others at analyzing and remembering complex patterns of lines, colors, or sounds. Differences in intelligence and the more narrowly-defined intellectual processes, such as memory, judgment, and problem solving, have been demonstrated in hundreds of surveys at all age levels. Among persons who have had equal amounts of schooling there are wide discrepancies in how much they know. People differ in aptitudes and talents, in interests, values, and attitudes, in personality assets and liabilities. In short, research on human beings corroborates the conclusion from animal studies—individual differences in measurable characteristics constitute a universal phenomenon.

THE EXTENT OF HUMAN VARIABILITY

One group of questions falls in a different category from those that psychologists usually attempt to answer, because it touches on the realm of values and basic assumptions about human nature. How large are human differences, in general, in comparison with the magnitudes we have found ways to measure in the external world? Is there a difference in variability from one *trait* to another? Do men differ more with regard to intelligence, for example, than they do in stature or pulse rate? Such questions are connected with broad philosophical issues, and the answers one gives to them may be related to his religious, social, and political convictions. Many psychologists doubt, however, whether there is any way to attack them by research methods.

The one person who has made a serious attempt to do so is Wechsler. In his book *The Range of Human Capacities* (1952), he collected all the distributions he could find of various kinds of measurable characteristics. As an index of variability he used what he called the *range ratio*. Since he was only interested in the variability to be found in the healthy, nonpathological segment of the human race, he left out of his computations the highest and the lowest thousandth of each distribution. This would remove, for example, the measurements of dwarfs and giants, circus fat men and living skeletons, but would leave the great mass of people whose height and weight fall within the normal range. For each of these slightly curtailed distributions, he divided its highest by its lowest figure to obtain his range ratio.

Wechsler was impressed with the fact that differences between human beings, expressed in this way, are relatively small. When we think of the enormous difference in size between the smallest and the largest living creatures, to say nothing of the objects in the inorganic world, a range ratio of 1.27:1 for human stature seems quite insignificant. When we think of the immense superiority of human intelligence over that of any of the lower animals, a ratio of 2.30:1 for mental age appears trifling. His conclusion was that the very large differences we find in income and social prestige certainly do not follow from natural differences, but are man-made exaggerations of those differences. Those who champion an equalitarian philosophy can take considerable comfort in these findings.

The most serious difficulty we encounter, however, when we attempt to draw any such general conclusion about human psychological differences, is that a whole class of measurements must be left out. Unless a measuring scale has a true zero-point it is not legitimate to divide one number by another as one must to get range ratios. There is no question about the fact that 200 cubic inches of lung capacity is twice as much as 100 cubic inches. The person whose reaction time is 200 seconds is just twice as slow as the person who reacts in 100 seconds. As long as our scores are expressed in inches or seconds or pounds, we are on safe ground when we make such statements. But intelligence measurements cannot be handled in this way. The individual with an IQ of 140 is not twice as bright as the one with an IQ of 70. Each IQ point represents no definite unit to which a division on some measuring rod corresponds. We do not know what zero intelligence is. Any ratio we could set up between high and low performances would be misleading.

Certain questions in the field of differential psychology are thus unanswerable at present and will perhaps remain so forever. Questions involving comparisons of variability in different traits are of this nature, if the traits have to be measured by mental tests. Do people differ *more* in intelligence than they do in sheer memory, for instance? Do adults differ more than children? Is artistic talent or emotional stability or integrity of character a more variable trait than intelligence? The fact that IQ's run from zero to 200 and art-judgment scores from 50 to 125 means nothing at all, so far as these problems are concerned. Neither the IQ nor the art score represents an exact amount of anything. Zero does not mean that the individual has absolutely none of the ability involved. Five IQ points are not the equivalent of five points of difference in art score. Wechsler realized this limitation and left out the complex characteristics that cannot be measured in physical units except for Binet mental age, Otis IQ, and a hard-learning test, all of which are subject to the criticism of not being measurements to which a ratio should be applied. But it is just these complex characteristics that are of most importance in human life.

Another objection that has been made to Wechsler's conclusions is that even when measurements can be made in physical units such as inches or seconds, the *psychological* units to which these correspond may be quite different in their magnitude and their significance. A runner whose speed on the hundred-yard dash is 15 seconds at the beginning of the practice season can cut this down by one second with relative ease. But when he has reached the point where he is doing it in 10 seconds, a difference of one second represents a tremendous improvement—a step so great, in fact, that nobody has ever taken it. In factory production the fastest worker in a department may work at only twice the speed of the slowest, but the advantage this gives him in income and the standard of living that goes with it makes it appear that the ratio in psychological units would be considerably larger than 2:1. Because we cannot measure these psychological units in such a way as to make range ratios possible we must not conclude that we should ignore them.

The thing that we *can* do with psychological measurements of many kinds is to arrange all the scores in order, express each individual's score in terms that will show how he compares with other people, and accumulate information as to the practical significance in human affairs of derived scores of various levels of magnitude. This is probably a more fruitful procedure than the attempt to describe in any absolute terms the variability of the human race.

If we cannot state how many times as bright as the village idiot Einstein is, we can say with some assurance what kind of contribution to human progress each is likely to make. If we cannot say that the aviation cadet with a score of 9 on the qualifying examination is nine times as talented as the man with a score of 1, our statistical data allow us to state with some assurance that he has *sixteen* times as good a chance to get through his elementary training. If we cannot say that the student with a college aptitude score of 120 is four times as bright as her classmate with a score of 30, we do know that the one is almost certain to pass, the other almost certain to fail in college competition. It may not be philosophically satisfying to express the situation in these terms, but still it answers our practical needs fairly well.

THE NATURE OF DISTRIBUTION

As measurements of various human characteristics became available, it was necessary to work out methods of handling the data so as to bring order into them, make it possible to study them systematically, and provide for comparisons between the individual and the norms for his group. The first step in this procedure is to arrange the measurements or scores in an orderly table called a *frequency distribution.* The method is simply to tally all scores falling within each specified range of score points. This method is illustrated in Table 1.

It is easier to comprehend the significance of such arrays of figures if they are then portrayed in graphic form. Figure 3 shows how this distribution looks when graphed.

A graphic presentation of the sort shown in Figure 3 is called a *histogram* and is the most common, most generally satisfactory way of graphing a frequency distribution. Measurements are always indicated as *distances* along the horizontal base line. Any convenient scale that will include the full range of obtained measures may be used. In the present example, each unit of base-line distance represents an interval of 20 cubic inches of lung capacity. Bars are then erected showing how many individuals in the group obtained scores falling within that interval, and the scale

TABLE 1
Frequency Distribution of Lung Capacity (White soldiers 66.5 to 67.5 inches in height)

(Gould's data as reported by Wechsler, 1952, p. 28)

CUBIC INCHES	NUMBER OF MEN
Below 96	19
96-115	52
116-135	81
136-155	136
156-175	271
176-195	319
196-215	330
216-235	160
236-255	85
256-275	22
Above 275	16
	N = 1,491

along the side indicates how many *individuals* are represented by each bar. In this figure, each unit of height stands for 30 cases.

A person who has never seen any sort of pictured distribution before, if asked to describe the shape of Figure 3, could not help noticing the short bars at the ends and the long bars in the middle. He would probably comment also on the fact that the height of the bars shows a gradual increase up to the middle and from there on a gradual decrease, giving a step-like effect similar to an old-fashioned stile over a fence. Again and again, as they worked with sets of physical or psychological measurements of all the types listed in the preceding section, investigators encountered distributions of this same shape, high in the middle, tapering off at both ends. Almost all intelligence tests in common use, for example, show a pattern similar to Figure 4. This most common type of distribution is often uncritically called the *normal curve*. It is not really correct to give it that designation unless a mathematical test has been made to see whether the relationship between x and y (base-line distance and height) satisfies a certain mathematical equation. "Normal curve" is a mathematical rather than a psychological term. It is important to recognize this fact in order to get away from unwarranted connotations of the word "normal." There is nothing abnormal about other distributions of human characteristics, as Figure 5 shows.

However, many biological, anatomical, and psychological measurements do seem to distribute themselves in a fairly close approximation to the mathematical normal distribution. That is because this is the form of curve one obtains for repeated determinations of any datum produced by

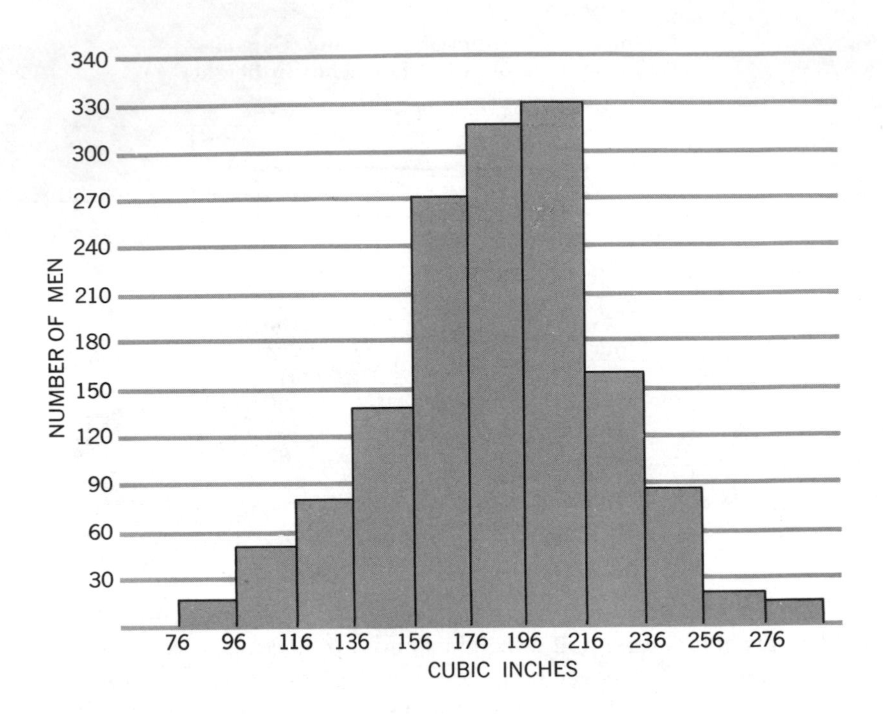

FIGURE 3
Histogram Showing Frequency Distribution of Lung Capacity in 1,491 White Soldiers
(Wechsler, 1952)

an event due to what the mathematicians call pure chance. Chance, in this sense, does not mean that what is being studied is something outside the natural order in which cause-and-effect principles operate, but simply that it is a phenomenon with multiple causes so complex that they have never been isolated. Thus when one tosses ten coins at a time again and again, there is a very complicated interplay of forces which produce at each throw heads for some, tails for others. The most *probable* result in this situation is a combination of five heads and five tails. If the coins are tossed a thousand times, the distribution representing the frequency with which each number of heads, from zero to ten, is obtained, will closely approximate the normal curve. Measurements of physical and mental traits are also determined by a large number of independent factors, many of them at present unanalyzable. So it is natural that when large numbers of subjects are measured, we get an approximation of the normal or chance distribution.

Because non-normal distributions are fairly common, sweeping gen-

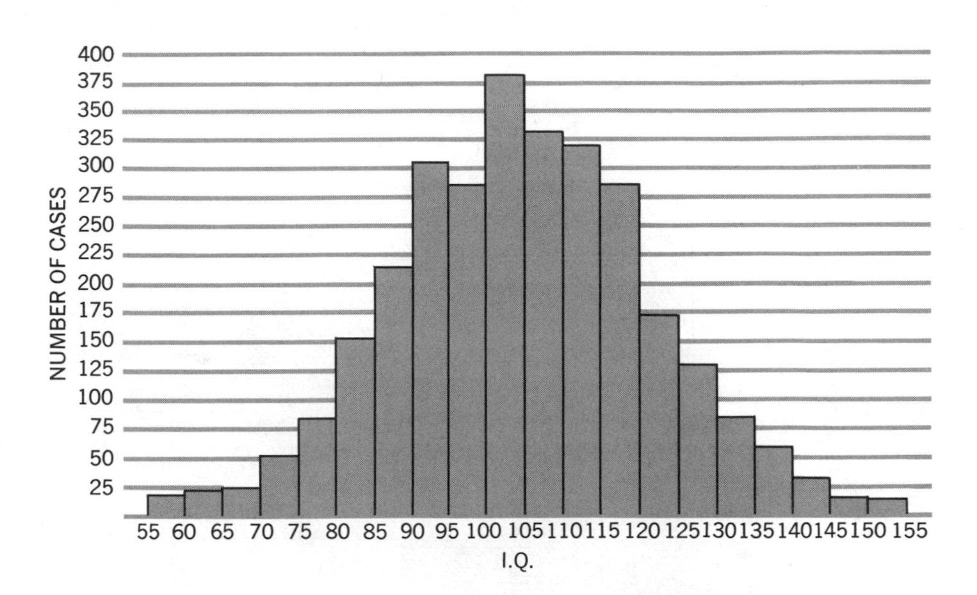

FIGURE 4

Frequency Distribution of IQ's on Form L. Stanford-Binet Test, Ages Two and One-half to Eighteen

(McNemar, 1942)

eralizations which were the rule in earlier stages of research on human differences have had to be abandoned or revised. This is especially true with regard to *mental* characteristics that must be evaluated by means of tests. It is quite possible to change a skewed [1] distribution into a normal one simply by making the test on which it is based a little harder or a little easier, depending upon the direction of the skewness. A test that produces a skewed distribution when given to a representative group of ten-year-olds may give a normal distribution for twelve-year-olds. A test that gives a skewed distribution on a population of college students may give a normal distribution for new recruits at an induction center. We know now that test scores can be manipulated to give us any sort of distribution that we want. Because there are definite mathematical advantages to be obtained from normal distributions, one of the aims of present-day test-builders is the construction of tests that will *give* normal distributions for the types of population in which they are to be used.

Because of these facts about test scores and what we can do with them, it is impossible to determine whether or not most mental traits are actually distributed normally in the population as a great many physical character-

[1] A *skewed* distribution is one that shows a piling up of cases in the direction of either the low or the high end rather than in the middle. Figure 5 is an example.

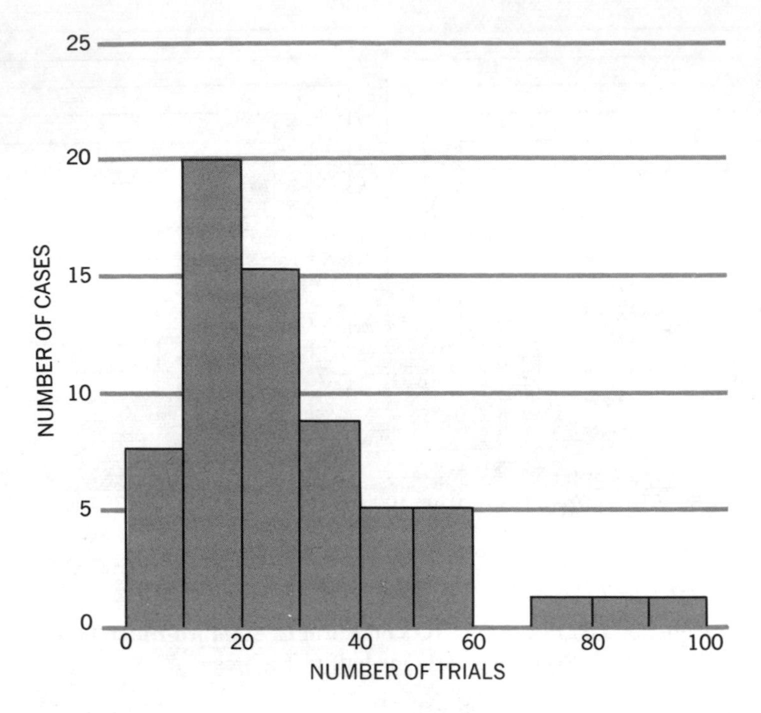

FIGURE 5

Frequency Distribution Showing Individual Differences in the Ease with Which Conditioned Eyelid Responses Are Formed

(Campbell and Hilgard, 1936)

istics seem to be. But there is a great deal of evidence that many if not all distributions of both physical and mental traits are *continuous,* and this finding is of the highest importance. In continuous distributions there are no separate classes, no types. Any classifications we set up are for convenience only and *do not completely represent the facts.* Students are familiar with this idea as it applies to examinations on which grades in courses depend. It is necessary that a class be divided into A, B, C, D, and F groups at the end of a course, but there is always some unfortunate B man who is almost as high as the lowest person in the A group, and some fortunate soul who just barely obtains a D rather than an F. The same holds true in many other classifications. Thus we probably should not say that one person has musical talent and another none, that one person is selfish and another unselfish, that one is rigid, another flexible. Sensitive measuring devices for appraising musical talent, selfishness, and rigidity demonstrate that scores on such traits range from low to high, with no real breaks anywhere in the distributions.

It was the apparent universality of continuous distributions that led psychologists to turn away from typological thinking and concentrate instead on the identification and measurement of traits. This led to progress in research and probably had desirable effects on people's thinking about individual differences. Instead of dividing people into the wicked and the righteous, the stupid and the intelligent, the beautiful and the ugly, or the neat and the slovenly, we learned to pay attention to the common human qualities in which we differ only in amount. In short, we learned to think of differences as quantitative, not qualitative. It may be that differential psychologists have devoted their attention too exclusively to quantitative trait differences and thus have ignored some more elusive aspects of individuality not susceptible to this kind of description. (Tyler, 1959). Work on cognitive styles, interests, temperament, and various other types of problem has been suggesting that we try out formulations better characterized as differences in *structures* or in *directions of development* than as *amounts* of specific traits. Type concepts are being scrutinized again with new interest. We shall return to these problems in the final chapter. For the present it is sufficient to say that by far the largest portion of the research findings in differential psychology is organized around concepts of trait and distribution, so that it is with these we shall be chiefly concerned.

The trait concept itself, however, has undergone changes as time has passed. Increasingly the word *dimension* has been used in place of the word *trait* to signify some measurable aspect of human individuality. The score a person makes on a test is considered to represent a *distance* along some scale rather than an *amount* of knowledge or ability. If we look at Figure 3 or Figure 4 we can see how natural this interpretation is. The first thing we do in making a histogram is to arrange all the scores in order along a horizontal base line. On this line we can measure the distance that separates an IQ of 60, for example, from an IQ of 110. The difference of 50 IQ points is given a *spatial* representation.

This dimensional reformulation of the trait concept has been especially useful when we attempt to combine measurements of several traits. It provides a method for describing the uniqueness of an individual in spatial terms. If, for example, we administer three tests to a group, vocabulary, mechanical aptitude, and arithmetic, we can set up a three-dimensional system to represent combinations of scores made by individual testees. Lucille makes a score of 6 on vocabulary, 3 on mechanical aptitude, 7 on arithmetic. Henry makes 7 on vocabulary, 10 on mechanical aptitude, and 2 on arithmetic. Figure 6 shows how each of them could be located in the space represented by three dimensions corresponding to the three tests. It is a convenient and economical way of combining the available information about individuals and has made for considerable progress in the technology of psychological measurement.

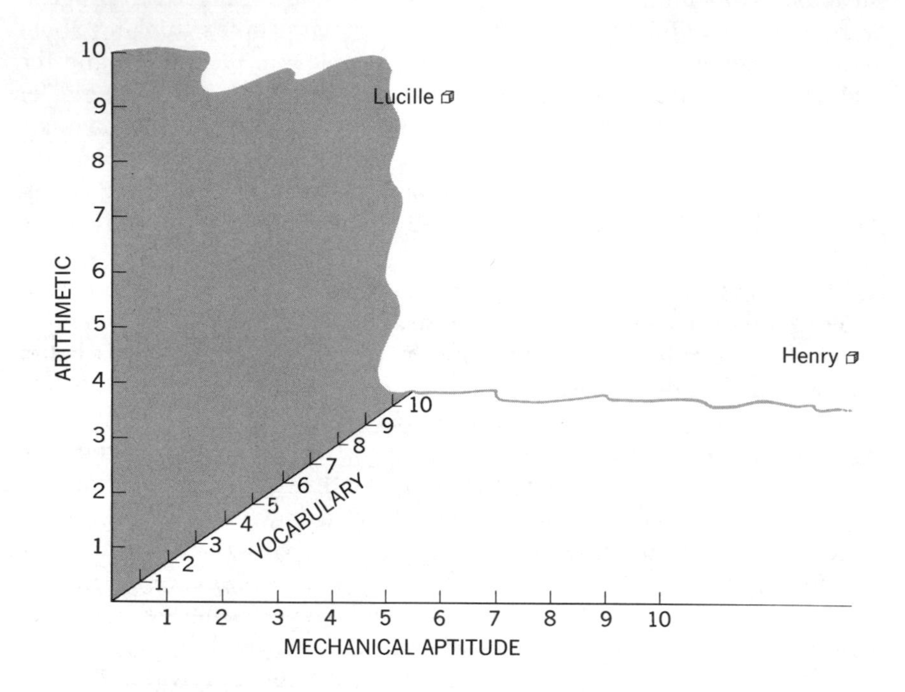

FIGURE 6

Hypothetical Three-dimensional System to Represent Positions of Individuals on Measures of Vocabulary, Mechanical Aptitude, and Arithmetic

Methods like factor analysis and multidimensional scaling rest on dimensional thinking.

Of course, when more than three test scores are obtained for each individual it is no longer possible to denote his position on an actual graph, as has been done in Figure 6. We must think in terms of *n*-dimensional space instead of the three-dimensional space with which we are familiar. But the reasoning and the methematical formulation are the same, regardless of the number of dimensions. In the chapters to come, the reader will encounter again and again this dimensional approach to the measurement of human characteristics.

USE OF STATISTICAL METHODS IN DIFFERENTIAL PSYCHOLOGY

It was an important landmark in the early exploration of human differences when Galton decided that normal curve theory, which Quetelet in

Belgium had been applying to vital and social statistics—what Galton called "the very curious theoretical law of 'deviation from an average'"—could also be applied to measurements of individual ability and achievement (Galton, 1870). It became the basic strategy for imposing order upon psychological measurements of all kinds. Since Galton's time, the field of statistics has been enlarged in many directions and has taken on a complex organization of its own. Anyone who hopes to achieve a thorough understanding of differential psychology must be familiar with at least the most basic varieties of statistical reasoning. We shall not go into these in this book, but simple explanations are available elsewhere for those whose background does not include statistics (Tyler, 1963; Hammond and Householder, 1962). Here we shall simply summarize the principal purposes for which the main varieties of statistical concepts are used.

DESCRIPTIVE STATISTICS

The most fundamental distinction that can be made between kinds of statistical reasoning is the distinction between *descriptive* and *inferential* statistics. As suggested by the name, the main purpose of descriptive statistics is to *describe* in an ordered and economical way the main characteristics of a group of measurements. If a distribution of scores is normal—and as indicated above, test-makers try to guarantee that it will be—the mean and standard deviation of any set of scores summarize for us two kinds of essential information about the group on which the scores were obtained: (1) How high on the average, is this group, or what is its *central tendency?*; and (2) How much do the individual members of the group, tend to differ or what is the group *variability?* Figures 7, 8, and 9 illustrate these concepts of central tendency and variability. If we were to compute the means and standard deviations for the pair of distributions pictured in each of these diagrams, we would find that for Figure 7 we would get different means but the same standard deviation in both cases. For Figure 8, the means would be the same, but one standard deviation would turn out to be much larger than the other. For Figure 9, the distribution to the right would show a higher mean but a lower standard deviation than the one at the left. Thus the use of the mean and standard deviation serves as a convenient shorthand method of communicating information about the characteristics of groups on which measurements have been made.

The mean and standard deviation serve another very useful purpose in descriptive statistics. They enable us to translate scores on different tests into the same language. The reason this is possible is that in a normal distribution there is a fixed relationship between the standard deviation and the total range of scores in a group. Figure 10 shows what this relationship is. In working with actual data, the horizontal base line is num-

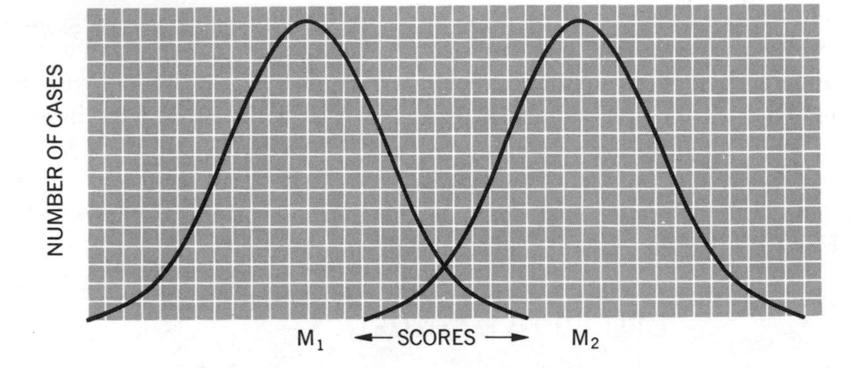

FIGURE 7

Two Distributions Which Differ in Central Tendency

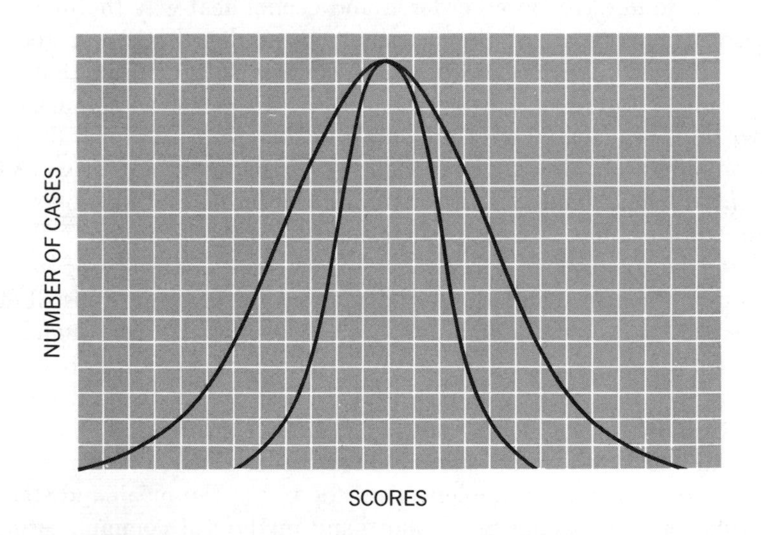

FIGURE 8

Two Distributions Which Differ in Variability

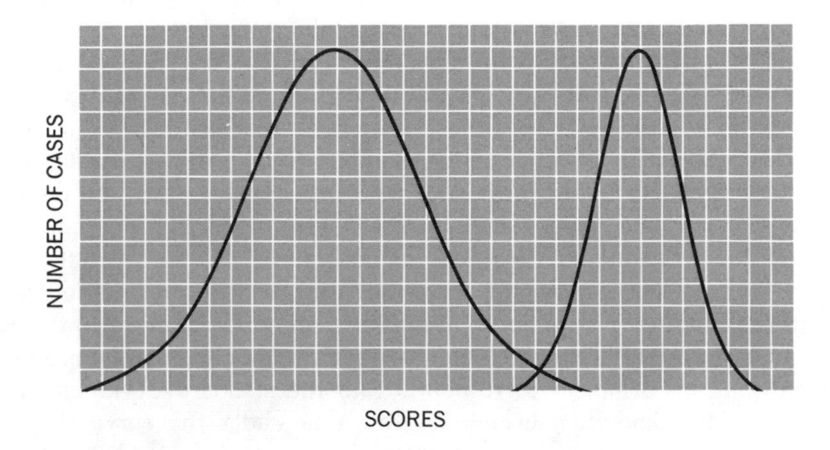

FIGURE 9
Two Distributions Which Differ in Both Central Tendency and Variability

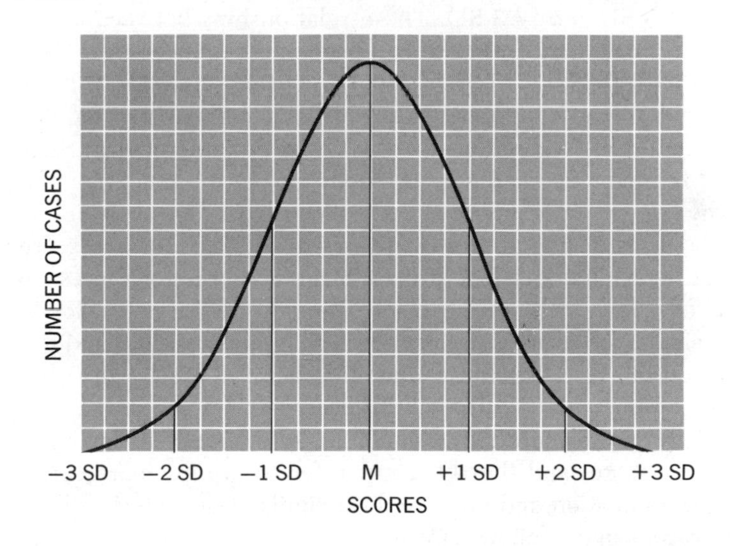

FIGURE 10
The Significance of the Mean and Standard Deviation in a Normal Distribution

bered off to represent the total range of scores in the group represented in the graph. The units of distance along this line may represent one score point each, 5 score points each, or 21 score points each, or any other number of score points, and the total distance along this line may represent a distance of 24 points, 120 points, 504 points, or any other number of points. But whatever the numerical magnitudes involved are, if we measure off along this base line starting from M, the point representing the numerical value of the mean, a distance corresponding to the standard deviation we have computed from the individual scores themselves, we reach the positions shown by the points labeled + 1 SD and — 1 SD. If we examine the curve above the line between these points, and the area between the curve and the base line, which represents the number of persons getting scores within this range, we can see that approximately the middle two-thirds of the group fall into these two middle sections. If we continue the process of measuring off distances corresponding to the standard deviations along the base line and then examining the area under the curve that corresponds to the distance measured from the mean in both directions, we can see that approximately 95 per cent of the area is above the range between — 2 SD and + 2 SD, and the whole distribution is included between — 3 SD and + 3 SD. These relationships between area under the curve and distances from the mean along the X-axis have been worked out mathematically with great accuracy. Many varieties of derived scores are based on this constant relationship. An example or two will illustrate how useful this "translation tool" is. Take the case of Sam Selby, just released from the Service, who is discussing with a counselor the question of whether or not he qualifies for college work. The only information he has about his mental ability is that his Army Classification score was 125. He has heard that an IQ of at least 115 is required for success in the kind of college he is considering. Does he qualify? The counselor knows that the mean of the Army Classification Test scores was 100 and the standard deviation 20. He knows also that the mean of the IQ distribution upon which statements about the ability necessary for success in various kinds of colleges are usually based is 100 and the standard deviation 15. Both the Army scores and the IQ scores refer to groups representative of the general population and are based on similar test material. The counselor then reasons in the following way:

> Sam is about 1¼ standard deviations above the mean of the general population.
> The college seeks students who are at least one standard deviation above the mean of the population.
> Therefore Sam is within the college range. He does qualify.

Another statistical tool that is widely used in describing the characteristics of groups and traits is the *correlation coefficient*. We know very little about what any one set of measurements means until we have related it to some other set of measurements. Whether this search for meaningful relationships takes the form of relating test scores to criterion measurements, as, for example, in the validation of a mechanical aptitude test, or whether it involves complex methods for analyzing a whole network of correlations of test scores with one another, as in factor analysis, the basic question is always to what extent each individual occupies the same position in a group with regard to two or more measured characteristics. In other applications of correlation, the relationship is between persons rather than between traits, as, for example, the correlation between identical twins on intelligence and personality measures, a line of research to be explored in detail in a later chapter.

For descriptive statistics, then, the three basic concepts are *central tendency*, *variability*, and *correlation*. There are many specific statistical techniques available for analyzing various kinds of measurements in various kinds of groups, but the details of these need not concern us here.

INFERENTIAL STATISTICS

Besides the descriptive use of statistics to summarize in a convenient way the information contained in a whole distribution of scores, there is another use which involves some additional logical processes. In our attempts to create a science of human differences we cannot be content with simply a description of the groups of individuals we happened to test. When we compare the scores 50 boys and 50 girls make on an interest test, we hope to be able to draw some general conclusion about masculine and feminine interests. When we correlate a particular set of scores on a musical talent test with achievement in music courses, we hope to be able to draw some conclusions about what the relationship will be in other groups besides this one. We must necessarily carry on our research using only *samples* of the total population of human beings about which we wish to make inferences. And we know from experience that if we carry out exactly the same procedures on another sample of subjects chosen in exactly the same manner as the first sample, the measures of central tendency, variability, and relationship we obtain may not be identical in the two cases. The first thing any investigator must demonstrate, then, in order to prove that a difference between group averages or a correlation between traits really means something, is that it is too large to be accounted for by the random variation in samples from the same population which we call *chance error*.

The term the statistician uses to convey the idea that a result is outside the range of those which sampling fluctuation alone is likely to produce is *statistically significant*. It is expressed as a probability figure. The researcher, for example, may say that the difference or the correlation he is reporting is significant at the 5 per cent level ($P = .05$), at the 1 per cent level ($P = .01$) or even perhaps at the .1 per cent level ($P = .001$). Applied to a difference between the means of two groups, such as middle-class and working-class men, for example, the statement $P = .05$ or $P < .05$ indicates that the statistical procedures one has carried out allow him to infer that, were it possible for him to test a hundred random pairs of samples from the same population, there would be not more than five comparisons out of the hundred in which the difference between means turned out to be as great as the difference he actually obtained in the one comparison he actually made. Thus he feels safe in concluding that the difference he is reporting applies to middle-class and working-class men *as a whole* and not just to the two particular groups he happened to test.

If a person is to achieve a clear understanding of what the results that have been reported in differential psychology mean and to show good judgment in applying them, he needs to understand precisely what the concept of statistical significance means in order to be aware of what it does *not* mean. Around this point much confusion centers, probably because the word "significant" as we use it in our common speech carries a rich freight of connotations. It is a symbol of value as well as fact. What we do when we place the word "statistically" in front of it is to strip it of all this cargo it is carrying. The statement that a result is statistically significant means *nothing but* the fact that it is not accounted for by sampling fluctuations. The facts reported as a result of the research may be unimportant, the conclusion may have no practical application whatever, and the researcher may have wasted his own and our time. It takes far more than statistically significant results to constitute a brilliant contribution to knowledge. But no amount of brilliance in planning a study and interpreting its findings can *make up* for the failure to check first on statistical significance. Unless a researcher does this he runs the risk of expending all his brilliance in efforts to interpret differences or relationships that simply are not there.

SUMMARY

Variability from individual to individual seems to be a universal phenomenon. As far down in the scale of life as it has been possible to go, individual organisms differ in the extent to which they show certain rudimentary psychological traits. One-celled animals differ in the readiness with which they modify their behavior with experience, and consistent individual tendencies toward such behavior as swimming in groups or tolerating chemicals in the water have been noted. Individual rats differ from one another in both learning ability and temperamental traits. Monkeys differ markedly in the complexity of problems they are able to solve.

In human subjects, measurable differences have been shown to exist in physical size and shape, physiological functions, motor capacities, sensory and perceptual sensitivity, intelligence, achievement and knowledge, interests, attitudes, and personality traits.

An ambitious attempt to assess the total amount of human variability and show how it varies from trait to trait was made by Wechsler, using range ratios, or the ratio of the next-to-the-highest to the next-to-the-lowest individual scores in a thousand randomly selected cases. His conclusion is that variability in human capacities covers a relatively narrow range. The criticisms that the ratio method cannot be used on mental-test scores, and that for psychological traits measured in physical units the psychological units may not correspond to the physical ones, throw some doubt on the conclusion. At any rate, the more important task for differential psychologists is to gather information about what measured differences mean in life situations. Thus we can avoid arguments over questions that are at present unanswerable and discover the facts that are really significant in human affairs.

When a set of measurements of any of these characteristics has been obtained, the first thing that is done is to arrange them in order of magnitude in a frequency distribution which can be presented graphically as a histogram. Most measurable traits give us continuous distributions, with no breaks between groups. The majority of the distributions show some resemblance to the mathematical normal curve, and it is usually possible to transform the data in some way for those that do not, so that normal curve statistics may be used. The two summary figures usually computed in analyzing a distribution are the mean and standard deviation, which constitute measures of central tendency and variability. Relationships between traits or between individuals are expressed by means of correlation coefficients. The three principal concepts of *descriptive* statistics are central tendency, variability, and correlation.

Inferential statistics make it possible to draw conclusions about populations from measurements made on samples. To say that a difference or a correlation is statistically significant means that there is only a small probability that it could have been produced by chance variations in samples drawn from the same population.

CHAPTER 3

Research Strategies

As explained in the previous chapters, most of the research on human differences has been based on the concepts of *trait* and *dimension.* The first step in any such investigation is to identify some trait that can be measured and to show that different individuals do possess the trait in different degrees. Sometimes, as in the case of intelligence, the trait is one that has become apparent to everyone who observes children or adults in the situations of everyday life. The task then is to construct some measuring instruments that will enable us to score subjects in sample situations. Sometimes a hypothesis with regard to a trait that ought to be measurable arises out of clinical work with individuals, as in the case of "rigidity" which a number of workers have been attempting to pin down. Sometimes the conclusion that a measurable trait exists is reached by pure accident when marked individual differences show up among subjects who had been expected to give uniform results in an experiment.

There are hundreds of traits in which measurable individual differences have been shown to exist. There is little we can do with such information, however, until we have gone beyond reporting that variability is present. Our concern in this book will be with traits for which research has been carried through one or more further stages, until we have actually learned something significant about it. A complete catalog of all the characteristics upon which human subjects differ, with references to the tests or experiments upon which the list is based, would be a valuable reference for research workers, but it would be of little value to students trying to organize their knowledge, or to teachers, social workers, and clinicians trying to apply what they have learned in real situations. The facts and principles that have been most useful have been based on research that did more than to present a distribution, or a mean and standard deviation for a group.

The methods that have been devised to produce this additional knowledge we need if trait measurements are to be useful in human affairs can be classified under three main headings: (1) correlational studies; (2) studies of group differences; and (3) developmental studies.

CORRELATIONAL RESEARCH

In order to satisfy himself that he is measuring something more than chance behavior, an investigator who is exploring a new technique is likely first of all to compute some sort of *self-correlation*—what is ordinarily called a reliability coefficient. Even if his new test has resulted in a perfectly normal distribution when tried out on a large group of subjects he still cannot be sure that anything except "pure chance" has produced the differences between individual scores. It is likely, for example, that if we gave only the answer sheets for one of our standard intelligence tests to 1,000 persons, and asked them to select a response for each item without ever seeing the questions at all, the distribution of the scores obtained in this way would be approximately normal. (This is not to deny, of course, that the scores would undoubtedly run lower than they do when the test is given in the ordinary way!) To some degree all test scores and measurements are determined by chance factors which it is impossible for anyone to analyze. The investigator must first of all find out how much of the variability in scores is to be attributed to chance, and how much can be assumed to reflect the particular trait he has attempted to measure.

One can assess the importance of some of these chance determiners by correlating scores based on some part of the test with scores based on another part. For example, scores based on the odd items alone can be correlated with scores based on even items alone. If two equivalent forms of the test are being constructed at the same time, scores based on Form A can be correlated with scores based on Form B. Correlations of this type (there are many other specific varieties within the classification) are what Cronbach (1960) has called *equivalence* coefficients. If it is satisfactorily high, such a reliability coefficient indicates that the parts of the test are consistent with one another—that they measure the same characteristic or combination of characteristics.

The other principal way of finding out whether a test is measuring something over and above chance is to give it twice to the same group of subjects and correlate the two sets of scores. This produces what Cronbach calls a *stability* coefficient. When it is satisfactorily high, it indicates that the test measures an aspect of individuality that possesses some permanence.

If the time interval between test and retest is longer than a week or two, a low correlation may indicate either that the test is unreliable or that the trait it measures changes as time passes, and that different individuals change at different rates. Many interesting questions arise as to how stable various traits are at different life stages. Bloom (1964) made a careful analysis of all the evidence he could find in answer to these questions for certain physical characteristics, intelligence, some kinds of achievement, interests, attitudes, and personality. It is clear that some traits are more stable than others and that the shape of the growth curve determines how early a trait becomes stabilized. It is clear also that environmental factors help to determine whether stability or change will predominate. Bloom's book has prepared the way for new research designed specifically to investigate stability and change.

During the first two or three decades of research on mental measurement, little distinction was made between different kinds of self-correlations—coefficients of equivalence, coefficients of stability over short intervals, coefficients of stability over long intervals. They were all lumped together under the term *reliability*. As time passed, it became evident that they provide answers to different questions about any trait under consideration. A careful analysis of what one wishes to find out about whatever he proposes to measure is an indispensable foundation for intelligent decisions about what should be correlated with what.

It may be that the term *reliability* has served its purpose and that we could now dispense with it. Cronbach, et. al. (1963) has proposed that a more useful concept would be *generalizability*. This would suggest questions like: What is the evidence that I can generalize from scores on this particular test to scores on another test made up of similar questions? What is the evidence that I can generalize from scores on this test given now to scores to be expected from these same testees next month? next year? ten years from now? The time is past when we can look at one reliability coefficient and make an overall evaluation of a test. To interpret scores in a variety of situations, one needs a variety of kinds of information.

Even more enlightening than the information we gain by correlating two sets of scores obtained from the same test is what we learn by correlating these test scores with measurements of something else. Most often such correlational studies are undertaken in order to find out how *valid* a test is as an indicator of the trait it was designed to measure. In such cases, the variable with which the scores are correlated is called a *criterion*. One of the commonest examples of this sort of research is to validate an intelligence test by correlating it with grades or other evaluations of academic performance in school or college. In other instances, scores on an established test like the Stanford-Binet are used as a criterion in validating a new test.

In thinking about validity, as well as reliability, psychologists have come to distinguish between situations they once lumped together. We use the term *concurrent validity* if the evidence consists of a correlation between test and criterion measurements obtained at about the same time.

We use the term *predictive validity* if the criterion measures were obtained some time later than the test scores. Which method a research worker chooses to employ depends, again, upon what he wishes to know. If he hopes to develop a new and satisfactory substitute for the Stanford-Binet intelligence test, the most important question for him is whether or not it really measures the same trait as the Stanford-Binet test does. Here a concurrent validity coefficient is indicated. If he is developing a new test he hopes will serve to identify promising candidates for training in computer technology, it is the ability before training he needs to assess, and the predictive validity of the test becomes the important consideration.

During the 1950's and 1960's there has been increasing emphasis on a type of correlational research that does not involve any concrete empirical criteria of the traits under consideration. This variety of data about tests has been classified under the general title *construct validity*. As psychologists explored the complex field of personality measurement, they discovered that their straightforward methods of validating tests by correlating them with criteria were not usually applicable. Take, for example, the problem Adorno et al. (1950) faced when they set out to investigate the authoritarian personality. They were not attempting to produce just a new test to measure a generally recognized characteristic like intelligence. Rather they were trying to develop a new way of understanding the differences in personality underlying political and social attitudes and behavior. What is required in such an undertaking is a careful analysis of the relationships one would expect to find between different sets of measurements if one's theoretical formulation is correct. A *construct* is a product of one's thinking about a theoretical issue. A test has *construct validity* if the relationships between scores obtained on it and various other measures entering into the theoretical formulation turn out to be significant and in the predicted direction. There is no *one* validity coefficient for a test like the F-scale used in the research on the authoritarian personality. Its construct validity rests on the whole body of evidence reported in the book by Adorno et al. (1950) and in the many other research reports that have followed it.

Our discussion of procedures used in validating psychological tests would not be complete without some mention of *content* validity. This term refers to evidence of various sorts that the items or tasks of which a test is composed really represent an adequate sample of the body of knowledge or the kind of skill the test is designed to measure. In this sort of demonstration, correlational procedures are not necessary. To insure a test's content validity one must exercise care in the selection of materials that go into it. It has been in the area of achievement testing that content validity has had the widest application.

These four varieties of validity study—concurrent, empirical, construct, and content—make up a large part of the work done in investigating individual differences in measurable traits. But to consider this work as purely a matter of validating particular kinds of tests is to miss what it all adds up to. Each research program designed to produce new information about what a certain test is measuring also enables us to formulate a clearer, more precise definition of the human characteristic under consideration and the aspect of human personality of which it forms a part. Psychologists have come to realize that the unraveling of strands from the complex fabric of human individuality is a highly complex task. At an earlier stage of our thinking about these matters the order of procedure to be followed seemed obvious: (1) formulate a clear definition of what you intend to measure; (2) construct a test out of items that can be considered a sample of the behavior in which you are interested; and (3) evaluate the success of your efforts. On the basis of their experience in trying to do this, researchers now know that it is seldom if ever possible to achieve a precise definition of any human trait until many kinds of evidence about it have accumulated.

Work on the measurement of intelligence began more than half a century ago, but we are still modifying and clarifying our concept of what intelligence is. The provisional definitions, with which Binet and other early workers began, have been reformulated again and again. As psychological measuring techniques have been applied to each new area—achievement, aptitudes, interests, personality, and others—the same kind of process has repeatedly occurred. Definitions are changed, traits are reclassified, and new theories are developed about the way in which personality is organized. It is this *precipitate* from research on the validation of tests, these general conceptions of the dimensions of variation in human beings that chiefly concern us in this book.

Correlational research has not been limited to the analysis of the relationships between *two* sets of measurements. By considering *several* sets of scores and the correlations between them, psychologists have been able to make inferences, or at least to formulate hypotheses, about what it is that produces these correlations. This mathematical analysis of correlation matrices (rectangular tables of correlation coefficients) is called *factor analysis*. Its purpose is to discover the factors that cause the test scores to correlate.

The kind of reasoning on which the factor-analysis methods are based is an indirect or roundabout process. It is more like what an astronomer does as he tries to reach an understanding of conditions on a distant planet, or what a geologist does when he tries to describe what the earth was like a million years ago, than it is like the customary activity of the laboratory scientist. It is largely this indirectness or deviousness in the original reasoning that confuses the beginning student. The necessity for it arises from the fact that the process we are interested in cannot be observed directly. The mental-tester can no more see the abilities he is tapping than the geologist can look in on the events of a million years ago. Both must somehow contrive to make inferences from the data they have and to check the correctness of these inferences without ever seeing their basic variables at all.

What a scientist does when confronted with a problem like this is to construct a *model* (though not necessarily a concrete physical one) the workings of which would serve to account for the facts he is trying to explain. If the model really accounts for everything, it becomes an accepted explanation. If there are certain facts it cannot account for, eventually someone devises a better model which takes precedence over the old one.

We shall not try to explain here the elaborate computational procedures that are required for a modern factor analysis. It is enough that the reader, the consumer of factor-analytic research, be familiar with the end results that he is likely to encounter, so that he will know what to make of a table of factor loadings and how to avoid pitfalls that arise in their interpretation.

Table 2 is an example of the sort of final results a factor analysis gives

TABLE 2

Rotated Factor Matrix Based on Centroid Analysis of 21 Tests

(Thurstone and Thurstone, 1941, p. 91)

	I (*P*)	*II* (*N*)	*III* (*W*)	*IV* (*V*)	*V* (*S*)	*VI* (*M*)	*VII* (*R*)	RESIDUALS
1. Identical Numbers	.42	.40	.05	−.02	−.07	−.06	−.06	.08
2. Faces	.45	.17	−.06	.04	.20	.05	.02	−.12
3. Mirror Reading	.36	.09	.19	−.02	.05	−.01	.09	.12
4. First Names	−.02	.09	0.2	.00	−.05	.53	.10	.02
5. Figure Recognition	.20	−.10	.02	−.02	.10	.31	.07	−.17
6. Word-Number	.02	.13	−.03	.00	.01	.58	−.04	.04
7. Sentences	.00	.01	−.03	.66	−.08	−.05	.13	.07
8. Vocabulary	−.01	.02	.05	.66	−.04	.02	.02	.05
9. Completion	−.01	.00	−.01	.67	.15	.00	−.01	−.11
10. First Letters	.12	−.03	.63	.03	−.02	.00	−.00	−.08
11. Four-Letter Words	−.02	−.05	.61	−.01	.08	−.01	.04	−.05
12. Suffixes	.04	.03	.45	.18	−.03	.03	−.08	.10
13. Flags	−.04	.05	.03	−.01	.68	.00	.01	−.07
14. Figures	.02	−.06	.01	−.02	.76	−.02	−.02	.07
15. Cards	.07	−.03	−.03	.03	.72	.02	−.03	.13
16. Addition	.01	.64	−.02	.01	.05	.01	−.02	−.03
17. Multiplication	.01	.67	.01	−.03	−.05	.02	.02	.01
18. Three-Higher	−.05	.38	−.01	.06	.20	−.05	.16	−.12
19. Letter Series	−.03	.03	.03	.02	.00	.02	.53	.02
20. Pedigrees	.02	−.05	−.03	.22	−.03	.05	.44	−.02
21. Letter Grouping	.06	.06	.13	−.04	.01	−.06	.42	.06

us. It shows the *loading* each factor has in each test. (The concept of *loading* is a sort of metaphor. Each test is thought of as a vehicle carrying a certain amount of one or more of the abilities. Another way of explaining it is that the loading of a certain factor in a certain test shows us the extent to which this factor determines the scores individuals make on the test.) The mathematical work that produces these loadings does not tell us *what* the factors are. The names that get attached to them are based on a careful scrutiny of the pattern of loadings shown in the table (or "matrix" in technical factor-analytic language). Let us see how this works by examining Table 2.

In the first place, since these loadings are on the correlation scale running from .00 to 1.00, and since they too are subject to sampling errors, it is customary to pay no attention to those which are near zero. The identification of the factor rests primarily on loadings of .30 or higher. When we look at Column I, where the loadings for the first factor are found, we find loadings above .30 for only three tests—Identical Numbers, Faces, and Mirror Reading. What is it that these three tests have in common? Thurstone decided that perceptual speed was the one ability they all required, so he called this factor P. Next we examine the higher loadings for Factor II. The tests on which they occur are Identical Numbers, Addition, Multiplication, and Three-Higher. Even without looking at the test papers themselves, the nature of this factor seems obvious. Thurstone called it N, because working with numbers is what these four tests require. We shall have more to say about the "primary mental abilities" represented in this table in a later chapter.

The reader who has never studied the mathematical theory and the computational procedures of factor analysis must necessarily take the loadings he is given in a table like this one without questioning their numerical accuracy. He has the right, however, to make up his own mind as to what they show about the abilities or personality characteristics being investigated. The description and naming of the factors is a matter of psychological judgment, not mathematical skill. Instead of uncritically accepting the names that a factor analyst has given his factors, it is always a good plan to examine the factor loadings for oneself. There is often room for a considerable difference of opinion as to just what it is that several tests have in common. Sometimes these differences can stimulate important new research activity.

Even if one does not know anything about the mathematical procedures by means of which the "factor matrix" comes into existence, there are certain limitations and defects in it of which he should be aware. It is not as precise and rigid as many nonmathematical readers believe it to be. At several stages in the complicated sequence of steps that must be taken, estimates or informed guesses are required. Mathematically, the *loadings* constitute distances measured along geometrical reference axes, and there is often room for some disagreement among skilled workers as to just where these reference axes should be placed with respect to the points that represent the tests. The encouraging thing is that in spite of the uncertainties that are an ineradicable part of the factor-analytic methods, a great deal of agreement has been achieved. Another equally skillful person working independently from Thurstone's data would probably not produce *precisely* the same set of factor loadings that we find in Table 2. But the loadings would be similar enough so that they would warrant exactly the same *conclusions* about the factor composition of the tests. It is these conclusions that we are working for. There is nothing sacrosanct about the exact loadings themselves. Let us then think of factor analysis as an *aid* to psychological judgment, a methodological tool designed to help us construct a useful body of theory about how traits determine test scores and the other measurements of individuals.

RESEARCH ON GROUP DIFFERENCES

The second main variety of research strategy used in differential psychology is the comparison of groups to determine whether there is a significant difference between them on some measured psychological characteristic. This general method can be divided into two submethods: (1) the comparison of some existing groups, and (2) the comparison of groups that have been constituted especially for the experiment on the basis of their performance in some test or experimental situation. The comparison of naturally occurring groups is the simpler procedure. It came into use very early in the development of differential psychology. The comparison of specially selected experimental groups has come into increasing prominence during recent periods.

On first glance, the setting up of a study to show whether two groups in the population differ with regard to some psychological trait looks easy. This is probably one of the reasons why we have had so many of such studies comparing the intelligence, for example, of boys and girls, whites and Negroes, or farm- and city-dwellers. Actually such studies involve a number of problems and difficulties. One must plan what he does carefully if he expects to be able to draw clear-cut conclusions from his results.

The first of these complexities has to do with the task of getting representative samples, a problem that will be discussed more fully in a later section. When two or more groups are chosen on the basis of convenience, it can often happen that each of them is in a different way *un*representative of the population from which it comes. Measured differences between them, in such cases, may do nothing more than to reflect these combined biases. Suppose, for example, we wish to try out a new algebra test. A college freshman mathematics class is an easy place to get subjects. When we average the scores we find to our amazement that the average for the girls in this class is ten points higher than that for the boys. How shall we account for this result in view of the almost universal finding that the sex difference in mathematics is in the direction of male superiority. First of all, we should realize that neither college boys nor college girls are really representative of the population in general. Furthermore, in a freshman mathematics class, the two sexes may very well have selected themselves on an entirely different basis. The girls here may be students who did unusually well in this subject in high school and decided to take more of it in spite of the fact that most of their sorority sisters shudder at the thought of math. The boys may be those who dodged mathematics in high school because they had less than the average amount of interest and ability in it and only face up to it now because they have learned that it is a prerequisite for later courses in other areas. The special selective factors are such as to wipe out the customary sex difference and produce a difference in the opposite direction. The important point is that such a comparison shows us nothing about differences between males and females in general. If we expected to be able to draw any such general conclusion, we have wasted our time in working with this particular group.

There is much discussion of such selective factors in the literature of differential psychology. As psychologists have become more aware of them, they have made determined efforts to minimize them. Where it is impossible to avoid them because of practical difficulties in getting good representative samples, we can often resist being led astray by them if we try out hypotheses about group differences in various diverse settings. When several studies have been reported, a reasonable conclusion can often be drawn even if all of them are biased one way or another. It helps with such interpretation if the research worker reports what kinds of biases he thinks his sample may represent.

Another problem in comparing groups is making sure the tests or measurements used are suitable for the purpose. Intelligence tests have often been criticized in this connection. They were developed expressly for the purpose of comparing each person with the others in the group to which he belongs. An eight-year-old can be compared with other eight-year-olds because we can make the assumption that all these children have had an approximately equal opportunity to develop the mental skills the test requires. All have been to school for at least two years. All have seen books, heard radios, gone to movies. When we shift over to a comparison of the averages of different groups of children, there is a basis for considerable doubt as to what the differences mean. We cannot immediately conclude that one group is brighter than the other. The difference may represent some discrepancy in the opportunity they have had to develop these mental qualities. The complexity of the problem is increased by the fact that different varieties of intelligence test—even different types of questions within the same test—do not correlate perfectly with one another, so that some may be affected in one way, others in another, by whatever influences differentiate the groups we are comparing.

This basic doubt as to what group differences in intelligence test scores and similar "measurements" mean has led some psychologists, sociologists, and anthropologists to the conclusion that we would be better off to give up completely any attempt to use such tests for group comparisons. However, the fact that we already have the results of hundreds of such studies "in the record," so to speak, and that they are constantly being cited by writers and speakers bent on proving such and such a point, suggests that it might be wiser to analyze what they do show than to try to suppress them. There are by now so many studies comparing boys with girls, Negroes with whites, and high-status with low-status groups, that it is possible to draw much sounder conclusions from the sum of them than could have been drawn from any one alone. Instead of phrasing the question, "Do these groups really differ from one another in intelligence and other mental traits?" we can ask simply, "What do the well-documented differences between groups on mental tests mean?" Then we can proceed to pull together all the pieces of evidence that may enable us to answer the question.

A demonstration that two or more identifiable groups in the population differ significantly with regard to some measured ability or personality trait should constitute the beginning of a *research program* of related studies through which the meaning of the difference can be clarified. Unless this supplementary work is carried out, the report that a difference between groups exists is without much practical value. It may even lead to unwise or harmful policy decisions on the part of persons who do not understand its limitations.

The second main type of group comparison, setting up special groups on the basis of some experimental procedure, and then analyzing various ways in which they differ from one another, has many applications. It has been used extensively in the development of measuring devices, especially achievement tests, personality inventories, and attitude scales. If, for example, an investigator wishes to construct a scale to measure radicalism-conservatism, he may first collect a set of items he thinks are related to this trait, and then administer the collection to a suitable group of subjects. Assuming that his initial evaluation of the general import of these items was sound, he can use the scores on this try-out inventory as a basis for selecting a group of high-scoring subjects and a group of low-scoring subjects, usually about the top 25 per cent and the bottom 25 per cent of the distribution. He then tabulates, item by item, the responses persons in these two groups gave. Any item on which these tabulations do not distinguish between high scorers and low scorers is thrown out. Thus the attitude scale is "purified" of extraneous elements and made into a more accurate indicator of whatever it is that it measures. (The apparent ambiguity of the last clause is deliberate. When this method is used, the resulting test or scale can only be as *valid* as the investigator's first judgment about what its items have in common. It is always advisable to seek further evidence of validity before resting important theoretical formulations on such measurements.)

In other research investigations, especially in the field of personality, the groups to be compared are experimentally determined *types* of persons. For example, in the study by Vogel, Raymond, and Lazarus (1959) on the effects of psychological stress, one of the kinds of comparison the experimenters made was between a group of *achievement-oriented* subjects and a group of *affiliation-oriented* subjects. They selected these groups of 20 each by obtaining a variety of kinds of information about motivation from 185 persons and then looking for "pure" cases—that is, subjects clearly high in achievement motives and below average in affiliation and subjects who showed the opposite combination.

Research of this sort, comparing groups selected experimentally on the basis of some initial theoretical hypothesis about individual differences, constitutes an important methodological development. It is a feature of the increasing convergence of experimental and differential psychology. We shall come back to it in later chapters in discussions of special areas.

DEVELOPMENTAL RESEARCH

Another way of increasing our knowledge about the sources and significance of human differences is to trace them back to their origins in childhood or to follow their vicissitudes through the adult years. Developmental research began with *cross-sectional* studies, comparison of different age groups at one point in time. But it was soon apparent that if in 1950, for example, one compared the performance of ten-year-olds and twenty-year-olds, he would not get unambiguous evidence about the changes associated with this ten-year developmental span. He could not be sure that the 1950 ten-year-olds would in 1960 be acting like the 1950 twenty-year-olds. The processes of history and social change, changes in educational practices, technological innovations such as television, for example—all these things make for variations from period to period in the development of individuals.

Thus the emphasis has been placed increasingly on *longitudinal* studies in which the same persons are observed at successive ages. The most dependable evidence we have about how intelligence develops and changes in children and in adults has come from such studies. More recently, personality characteristics have been scrutinized in this way. Longitudinal studies enable us to explore individual differences in not only the *rate* of growth and ultimate *level* of development of a trait, but also in the *shape* of the growth curve itself. Thus one child may obtain high scores on an intelligence test while he is a preschooler, drop to an average position during the grade school years and show a sudden growth spurt at fourteen. Another may start low but show consistent increases each time he is tested.

Longitudinal studies have their own hazards and difficulties. One can use as subjects only persons or families who are willing to cooperate for a considerable length of time. Thus certain kinds of persons usually do not get studied by this method—the ignorant, the geographically mobile, the antisocial. The inevitable loss of subjects along the way may change the character of the sample one starts with, introducing unknown biases into the evidence from which general conclusions are drawn. The research design and measuring instruments one decides upon at the beginning often limit what can be done at later periods when the advancing knowledge has made available more satisfactory techniques. Nevertheless, these systematic long-range programs of research on the same individuals, such as Terman's study of gifted children, and the infancy-to-maturity studies at the University of California and at Fels Institute have produced a rich harvest of knowledge about human lives—a harvest obtainable by no other means.

Cross-sectional developmental studies have also been useful in several ways. They have led to hypotheses about the origins or causes of observed differences between persons, hypotheses which could be tested by longitudinal or experimental research. For example, Gordon's (1923) report about the increasing intellectual retardation of successive age groups of canal-boat children in England led to many kinds of research on environmental influences that inhibit and facilitate mental growth. In collecting evidence about the construct validity of a new test, it is often enlightening to compare two different age groups for which differences are hypothesized. The study of human development and the study of individuality are linked together in an especially close way. Development is basically an individual phenomenon.

SPECIAL PROBLEMS—OBTAINING REPRESENTATIVE SAMPLES

In attempting to gather evidence on the kinds of research questions that have been outlined many problems have arisen, and we have gradually worked out acceptable ways of solving them. Perhaps the most fundamental of these is the problem of *sampling*. It is essential that the consumer as well as the producer of research data understand just what this problem is.

It is obvious when anyone begins to consider the matter that the pronouncements of psychologists about such things as, for example, the differences between males and females in dominance, the intellectual level of ten-year-old children, or the vocational interests of engineers are not based on a thorough study of all the individuals in the class they are describing. No one has ever given any test to all the 90 million males and 90 million females even in this country alone, to say nothing of the rest of the world. No one has tested all the ten-year-old children or all the engineers. What assurances have we that the sample we have tested is typical of all the rest?

If no attention is paid to this at all, subtle kinds of bias are introduced into the conclusions we draw, and this bias may vary from one study to another. Persons who are working with children aged six through fourteen often obtain a fairly adequate sample of the population by accident, since our compulsory school laws insure that practically all the children within the age range will be in school. While no single grade school would be completely typical of all schools in the community, the state, or the nation, a combination of several of them in different geographical locations can often be used for research purposes. But with older or with younger populations, the problem of obtaining an adequate sample is far more difficult. Even at the high-school level, many students have left school to go to work. Unless we seek them out and test them along with the rest, our generalizations about adolescent characteristics will be in error to an unknown extent. Particular care must be taken not to generalize to the rest of the population from studies of college subjects, since college students are a selected group, both brighter and economically better off than the average. There is no one organization to which one can turn for representative samples of the adult population. Neither the luncheon club nor the labor union is typical of the whole world of adult men. We cannot find all the kinds of women we should like to study in a Ladies' Aid Group, a PTA meeting, or a Business and Professional Women's Club. A group of Negroes in a little southern town where policies of repression and discrimination have been applied for generations is not typical of the whole Negro race. But neither is a group of Negro children brought up under highly favorable educational conditions by parents who through unusual ability and determination have been able to lift themselves far above the general level. If a graduate student sends out questionnaires to 1,000 people and 532 of them are returned, nobody knows just what kind of sample those 532 constitute. There is obviously some psychological difference between persons who cooperated and persons who did not. One important question that a student must learn to ask is, "On what sort of sample of the population are these reported results based?"

Technical means are now available for solving the sampling problem in a completely satisfactory manner. The mathematical concept to which all our statistical reasoning is related is the *random* sample. If we could take the names of all persons living in the United States, write them on little round discs so that they could be thoroughly mixed up, place them in an enormous hat, and then, blindfolded, draw out one name after another, we could secure a random sample of the U.S. population. Needless to say, such a procedure is impractical. Fortunately, we do not often attempt to draw conclusions (at least in quantitative form) for the whole U.S. population, so that it is not really necessary either. But it constitutes a sort of mathematical ideal which other sampling methods approximate as nearly as they can. The essential feature of random sampling is that any one individual in the population from which a sample is drawn has exactly the same chance of being included as another.

It is in the field of public-opinion research that the greatest effort has been made to develop practical methods for obtaining samples that represent the population adequately. Most of us are aware that, in spite of some embarrassing exceptions, in general these polls give much more accurate results than they used to in years gone by. Many special techniques for obtaining representative samples have been invented. For example, each part of the country can be divided and subdivided until the pointer falls on a certain address in a certain block on a certain street. The interviewer goes to this place and asks his questions about soap or politics of the person who answers his knock. A reasonable substitute, much easier to work out, is the stratified sample. One first studies the census reports which show the proportions of different income groups, different age groups, males and females, farm dwellers and city dwellers, Republicans and Democrats, Easterners, Westerners, and Southerners, in the population. Then he selects the right number of individuals in each category and thus puts together a group which, in the aggregate, will have exactly the same proportions of all these characteristics as the whole population does. In this way a few thousand will accurately represent a hundred million.

In studies using mental tests and other kinds of measurements that require a considerable amount of time from each subject, it has not usually been possible to be as careful and thorough about the sampling as the public-opinion pollsters are. Each study in the field of individual differences constitutes a unique challenge to work out some original way of making the sample to be studied as representative as possible. For questionnaire research, follow-up letters after the first appeal is made can often serve to increase the response very markedly. Toops (1926) in a classical study of this sort found that six follow-up letters, each using a different kind of appeal, brought 100 per cent replies in a study where response to the original questionnaire was only 52.7 per cent. Psychologists in Scotland in 1935 and again in 1947 gave individual intelligence tests to a completely representative sample of one age group by testing every child who had been born on February 1, May 1, August 1, and November 1, of a certain year (Scottish Council for Research in Education, 1939, 1949). Jones and Conrad (1933) gave free movies in order to draw in practically the whole population of the New England villages in which they were working. They then made home visits to obtain data from the individuals whose scores were still missing, thus including in their final sample about 90 per cent of the total population of the place within the desired age range. Enough ingenious approaches to the sampling problem are now on record to serve as suggestions and sources of ideas to researchers launching out into new and unknown waters.

If we were to pay attention *only* to studies that have been based on adequate representative samples, a book on differential psychology would be a very thin volume. Fortunately, if we have enough different research reports to draw on, we can make use of much information that has come from patently nonrepresentative samples. By considering the results from several such biased groups simultaneously, we can often come up with a reasonable conclusion that accounts for them all. If, for example, a certain kind of sex difference shows up in separate studies of ten-year-old children in one locality, college men and women in another, and husbands and wives at a PTA meeting in still a different spot, we are led to the conclusion that, at least in our culture, this *is* a sex difference not peculiar to the kind of group we happened to test. Or, if correlations of about the same magnitude between motor skill and intelligence are reported by all investigators whose subjects are mentally retarded children but not by those whose subjects are of better than average intelligence, this combination of facts makes possible a meaningful conclusion.

Furthermore, even findings about limited groups may have a great deal of practical usefulness. If there are important differences between high-school boys and high-school girls, that fact will have implications for education, whether or not the differences would be found in males and females generally. What we find out about the relationships between separate abilities in mentally retarded children can be useful in testing them, educating them, and placing them in employment whether or not we can expect to find such relationships in other groups. We must not generalize beyond our results. On the other hand, we must make use of everything we have. Some knowledge is better than no knowledge at all, and a conclusion with the weight of probability on its side is much better than complete ignorance.

What can be said with certainty about this problem of representative sampling is that it must *always* be kept in mind. The person doing research needs to concentrate on obtaining as satisfactory a sample as possible, considering the practical limits within which he operates. The person reading, evaluating, and applying research conclusions must take into consideration all the information he has been given about the group or groups upon which results were obtained.

SPECIAL PROBLEMS—SEPARATING CAUSES FROM EFFECTS

Neither the correlation methods nor the group-difference methods automatically tell us anything about the causes of the differences between individuals. Experience has shown that we must be constantly on guard against jumping to conclusions about causation from such evidence. Take, for example, the low positive correlation which has consistently shown up between socio-economic level and IQ. This may mean, as some have contended, that the more favorable environments produce more intelligent individuals, that is, that the socio-economic condition is the cause, the IQ the effect. But it may just as easily mean that more intelligent individuals are more successful in the competition for this world's goods, that is, that IQ is the cause and socio-economic status the effect. Causal factors may be working in both directions, that is, the IQ may to some extent determine the economic level, which in turn may influence the IQ. Still another possibility is that some third variable such as education is actually the causal factor and that the apparent relationship between IQ and socio-economic level arises from the fact that they are both related to this "something else." The point is that there is no way we can extract from the correlation coefficient itself decisive information as to which of these hypotheses is correct.

Many psychologists realize this ambiguity in the causal interpretation of correlations, but fail to recognize similar pitfalls when they are dealing with differences between groups. Suppose it is found, for example, that children known to have been weaned early are significantly more unstable emotionally than those known to have had a longer nursing period. Does this prove that early weaning produces or causes neurotic tendencies? Not necessarily. It is quite possible that both the early weaning and the emotional difficulties in the children are caused by neurotic tendencies in their mothers, leading them to reject unconsciously the responsibilities of motherhood. The children may have inherited such neurotic tendencies, or they may have reacted to many other evidences of them besides the early weaning. Again the point is that such a study as this simply cannot tell us what the causal relationships are.

Problems of causation are especially complex and intricate, as many philosophers have pointed out. In one sense, everything in the universe is the cause of each event which occurs. In another sense, nothing can be known with certainty to be the *cause* of what happens since all that we can ever observe is some invariable *sequence* of the type: Event A is followed by Event B. Observations never show the link between them. What we have are correlations, coming to us without any guarantee that the relationships they show will always be maintained. For practical purposes, however, we can and certainly do isolate factors which appear to exercise a determining influence on succeeding events. We mix certain chemicals and an explosion takes place. We predict when an eclipse will occur. We change our tariff laws, and certain economic consequences appear. We deny our child the evidences of our affection which are rightly due him, and he becomes refractory. We administer the proper treatment, and the sick man recovers.

It is the *time* factor characterizing these situations that makes it possible for us to refer to one as the cause of the other. Whether we say that the child's crying is the cause or the effect of the spanking that he gets depends on which comes first. It is this time factor that we must get into our experiments in differential psychology if we are to explore causes. The independent variables must be introduced prior to the time we measure the dependent variable. The experimental method requires that we: (1) measure, (2) introduce the new factor or factors, and (3) measure again. If we wish to know, for example, whether vitamin-B deficiency has an unfavorable effect upon school achievement, the thing to do is to test a representative group of children, put them on a diet deficient in vitamin B, and test again at the end of the experimental period. We might, of course, proceed in the opposite way by testing a group of children known to be deficient in vitamin B, putting them on a diet rich in this substance, and then testing them again. R. F. Harrell (1943, 1947) has in fact carried out an excellent study on this problem using an adaptation of this plan.

In order to make such studies in time at all conclusive, however, some supplementary steps must be taken. In the example given above, how do we know that improved scores on the second test are not simply practice effects? How do we know that they do not reflect some of the innumerable other influences to which children are exposed at home, in school, on the playground, or at the movies? How can we be sure that it is the nutritional factor rather than some of these others which has brought about the change?

The customary way of handling this difficulty is to use a *control* group. Subjects in this group are selected in exactly the same way as those who are to take part in the experiment. In some research designs, a control subject is *paired* with each experimental subject in respect to age, race, sex, IQ, and other characteristics that might influence results. Only the experimental subjects are exposed to the influence whose effect is being investigated. The question at the end of the experiment is then, "Do the experimental subjects differ from the controls?" In Harrell's vitamin study, only half the orphanage children who were subjects were given the supplementary rations. All were tested before and after the experimental period. Since they had all been exposed to the same general environmental influences during that time, the difference between the treated and untreated groups could be definitely tied in with the vitamin supplementation.

The use of a control group in an experiment is a universally recognized essential of scientific procedure. Our problems in psychology have centered around the difficulty of making experimental and control groups truly comparable. To pair subjects is one method, but it is hard when we are investigating a new kind of trait to be sure that we have paired them for everything that may be related to it. Investigations of the effects of counseling, for example, have run into the difficulty that if a control group is set up by matching a noncounseled student with each student who voluntarily seeks a counselor's aid, the two individuals in each pair will not be alike in the characteristic most crucial for counseling success, namely, motivation for change or improvement. If persons in any experimental group think that they are being given special help or attention, increased motivation may lead to more improvement in performance than individuals in the control group show, no matter how carefully they have been equated in the first place.

There is no single best method to overcome these control-group difficulties. Whenever it is practically feasible, *randomization* in the choice of individuals for the experimental and control groups should be carried out. That is, names or numbers of all persons available for the experiment should be placed in one pool and assigned to the separate groups by tossing a coin or using a table of random numbers. Whenever it is possible, both experimental and control groups should be given some treatment that *appears* to be the same, so that no subject knows whether or not he is being exposed to the special experimental influence. In the Harrell vitamin study, for example, each child received an identical-appearing capsule each day. Not even the personnel of the orphanage knew which capsules contained the extra nourishment. It is always important when tests are to be given and scored that the examiners be kept in ignorance of which subjects are in the experimental and which in the control groups. Hard as they may try to be objective, examiners and raters tend to slant their judgments slightly in the direction of what they hope will be the outcome of the experiment.

With the rise of analysis of variance methods, which permit comparisons between more than two groups at a time, problems very difficult to attack by the old methods have been brought under experimental scrutiny. There are numerous problems in psychology for which it appears to be impossible to isolate the effects of one variable alone, controlling everything else. It is in just such instances that complex experimental designs based on analysis of variance are most helpful. (To maximize the student's confusion, such research plans in which the effects of several independent variables on a dependent variable are examined simultaneously are called *factorial* designs, though they have absolutely nothing to do with the *factor*-analysis methods for analyzing correlations. They grow out of quite different statistical soil. In spite of the similarity in the labels, it is necessary that one keep them separate in his thinking.)

Besides making possible research on problems where causal factors cannot be unraveled and examined one by one, the experimental designs based on analysis of variance have another advantage. By setting a study up in this way, the investigator obtains considerably more information for the same expenditure of time, money, and effort. It would be quite possible, for example, to plan a vitamin experiment in which one used the same group of subjects to test out the effects of as many as six or eight different kinds of treatment. Such a study would be planned so that a few subjects would get vitamin A alone, a few B, a few C, a few D, and so on through the vitamin alphabet. Some would get a combination of A and B, some A and C, some B and D, and so on through all possible combinations. At the end, the total amount of variation in test gains would be broken down into the parts associated with the different kinds of treatment, and the statistical significance of each treatment determined. Instead of answering one question, the experiment would have been made to answer several. If it should happen that vitamin B supplementation improves mental functioning only when accompanied by increases in vitamin C intake, this research plan would enable us to find this out, whereas simple comparisons of experimental and control groups might never have brought it to light. These combination effects are what is meant by the term *interaction* among variables.

In view of the fact that controlled experiments make it possible to draw conclusions about the causes of individual differences that cannot be drawn from correlational investigations, why are they not universally used in research on these problems? The answer is that in a great many important areas of human life it is not practically feasible or ethically justifiable to manipulate conditions in order to discover what the results will be. It is necessary that workers in some fields of knowledge, if they are to be cultivated at all, use less powerful tools. Careful observation of "natural experiments" and thoughtful study of relationships between variables in different groups and under different conditions will always be indispensable in the human sciences. Kagan and Moss (1962, p. 4) have commented on this point and emphasized the special value of longitudinal studies of development as a substitute for experiments.

> Many aspects of personality development are not subject to experimental manipulation. Aggressive children can not be transferred to loving homes; mothers can not be told to adopt a pattern of reinforcements so that the psychologist can have an aesthetically pleasing design.
>
> A longitudinal investigation, however, might be viewed as a substitute for the powerful strategy inherent in experimental manipulation—a halfway house between the correlational and experimental investigation. One can hypothesize antecedent-consequent relations, and assess, through continuous observation of the mother and child, the validity of the prediction.

It is only through a combination of all these research methods that we can hope to build up a dependable body of knowledge to draw upon in our efforts to make wise decisions about individual human lives and about social policies.

SUMMARY

Research in any specific area of differential psychology usually begins with the identification or postulation of a trait and a demonstration that measurable differences between individuals with regard to it can be found. From here on there are three general methods of procedure—correlation, differences between groups, and developmental observation.

Correlational studies are of many varieties. Reliability coefficients are self-correlations obtained by correlating a set of scores with another set based on the same measuring instrument administered to the same group. Validity coefficients are of several kinds. Concurrent and predictive validity both involve correlating scores with criterion measures of the trait in question. Construct validity rests on the relationship of scores to other variables as they are suggested by some comprehensive theory. Factor analysis is a method for analyzing a number of correlations simultaneously in a search for the basic variables involved in all of them.

In using group difference methods, existing groups in the population, such as males and females, may be compared. Caution is necessary in interpreting the findings because of the possibility that one's samples may be biased or the measuring instrument not equally appropriate for the groups. In another variety of research on group differences one selects the groups to be compared on the basis of some experimental situation set up in accordance with some theoretical hypothesis.

Developmental studies are of two kinds—cross-sectional and longitudinal. While longitudinal studies have been more productive, cross-sectional comparisons are also useful, especially in suggesting hypotheses to be tested by other methods.

In carrying out research on individual differences, the investigator tries to secure as representative a sample as possible of the population in which he is interested. Statistically, a random sample is the ideal, but because of practical difficulties in achieving this, various methods have been devised for selecting individuals in such a way that the proportions of the sample falling into various subgroups—age, income, sex, and so forth—will be the same as they are for the total population. In interpreting the results of studies that have been made, selective factors in the samples studied must always be taken into consideration.

In analyzing causes and effects, an experiment of some sort is necessary because time relationships must be manipulated. The control group for such an experiment must be carefully chosen if results are to be meaningful. It is through a combination of these research methods that a useful body of knowledge accumulates.

Part Two

MAJOR DIMENSIONS OF INDIVIDUAL DIFFERENCES

CHAPTER 4

Individual Differences in Intelligence

FOR MANY YEARS the psychology of human differences was essentially the study of intelligence. After Binet demonstrated that a human trait of major importance could be measured, and American military psychologists showed that adults as well as children could be classified by such measurements, the ground was prepared for rapid development of many varieties of intelligence test. Psychologists proceeded for a time as though these differences in intelligence were the only differences between human beings that had any relevance to decisions that must be made about them. When this assumption proved unsound the methods used in constructing intelligence tests were applied in constructing tests for other abilities and personality traits.

Out of each attempt to construct an intelligence test or to use an existing one in a new situation came an increment of new knowledge about intelligence, the abstract quality itself, as it operates in human affairs. In one sense we can see the whole body of work on intelligence measurement, covering almost a century if we consider Sir Francis Galton's contribution as its beginning, as a huge *construct validation* project, not yet completed. But certainly we can now give a more precise answer to the question, "What *is* intelligence?" than could have been given in 1950, 1930, or 1910.

It was not realized until fairly recently that in the study of psychological differences, clear and precise definitions of a trait to be measured *follow* rather than *precede* research on it. Early mental-testers attempted at the outset of their work to define intelligence. But it soon became apparent that there was a good deal of disagreement among them. Some definitions emphasized adaptability to new circumstances; some focused on abstractness and complexity; some considered that facility in the use of symbols was the essence of the trait. The general term "learning ability" was often used as a synonym for intelligence, but it never constituted a really satisfactory definition. While many psychologists defined intelligence as a unitary trait, others were convinced that it must be considered as the sum or average of a great many separate abilities.

The thing that saved psychology from bogging down in a mire of semantic confusion was the predominantly practical orientation of mental-testers. Binet thought deeply and wrote wisely about the meaning of intelligence, but the tests that he developed justified themselves not so much by this "thinking about thinking" as by the success with which they identified mentally deficient children in schools. From his time on to the present, test development has been geared to practical problems. Illogical as it seemed at first, psychologists found that it was not necessary to define intelligence in order to measure it. Experience in two world wars and many research undertakings showed that men with quite different theories about the nature of intellectual activity could work together amicably on test-construction projects. The underlying aim was to produce tools that people could use to make with more precision the judgments about individual mental capacities that they were already making on some basis.

Out of this procedure and in accordance with a point of view that became very popular in science during the 1930's came the so-called "operational" definition of intelligence—"intelligence is what these tests measure" (Boring, 1923). Logically there are some difficulties with this approach. An intelligence test, if we consider its construction as well as its administration, is hard to describe in terms of a clearly definable set of operations, and no two tests involve exactly the same ones. The thinking that psychologists did along these lines, however, was of considerable value. It clarified the distinction between *intelligence,* the broad and somewhat ambiguous term of common speech, and "intelligence," the narrower, more limited trait with which tests were concerned. Although a psychometrist thoroughly familiar with tests such as the Binet and the Wechsler might not be able to give a simple definition of the trait measured, he did have a fairly clear conception of what it did and did not include. In practical situations the increasing clarity and precision with which we could describe "what our tests test" constituted real progress.

The varieties of research we have discussed in the previous chapter have all been brought to bear on the problem of intelligence. We shall now consider in some detail what each of these approaches has contributed to our understanding of what individual differences in this trait mean.

DEVELOPMENTAL RESEARCH

One obvious fact that gave psychologists a means of attacking the intelligence-testing problem is that in an absolute sense children become more intelligent as they grow older. With the best teaching in the world the average five-year-old will not master counterpoint nor the average ten-year-old symbolic logic. What Binet and his successors tried to work out was a pool of items, questions, and tasks that sampled mental abilities typical of the various age levels. *Any* task of an intellectual nature that can be evaluated and scored has been considered a suitable item for intelligence testing if it can be shown that older children are significantly better at it than younger children. Intelligence as measured in children is first and foremost a matter of developmental level.

Thus if we plot total score on any such group of items against chronological age for a representative group of children, we obtain a rising curve often referred to as a mental-growth curve. For example, the Otis Quick-Scoring Mental Ability Test for children in the primary grades gives us the curve shown in Figure 11. We can see at a glance that older children get

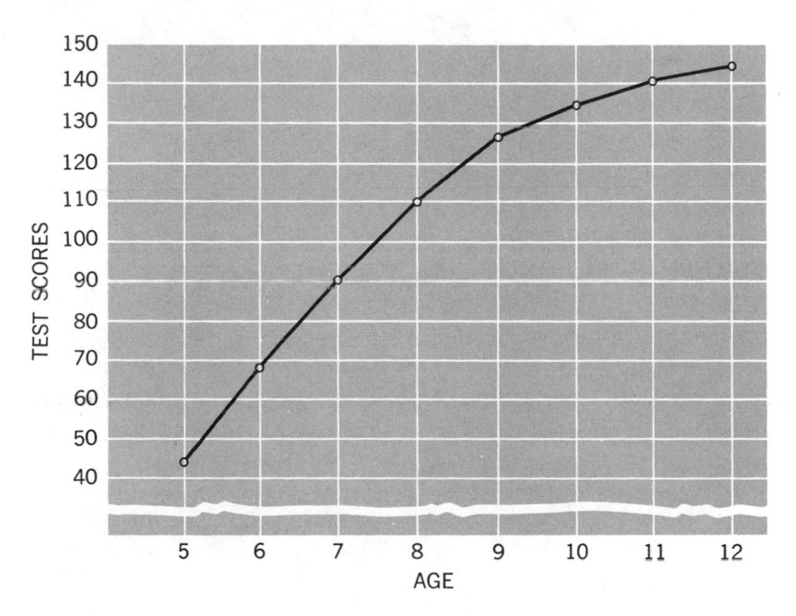

FIGURE 11

Graph Showing Average Scores of Successive Age Groups on Otis Quick-Scoring Test

(Alpha, 1939)

higher scores than younger ones. The exact nature of the relationship between age and intellectual capacity cannot, however, be evaluated from such a diagram. The trouble is that we have no information as to the meaning of the units in which the test scores are plotted. Is each question the equivalent of every other question? Does the difference between scores of 50 and 60 have the same meaning as the difference between 90 and 100? We do not know. Thus the shape the curve should take is not determined.

If we use the mental-age scores usually obtained from Binet-type individual tests as our units, we still are in no better position to describe the course of mental growth in children. For a test standardized in this way, the average achievement of a representative group of children at a given age becomes the standard. Thus for each change in chronological age, the standardized test results show us exactly the same amount of change in mental age, as long as we are considering group averages rather than individual scores. For this reason, the "curve" of mental growth appears always to be a straight line like that shown in Figure 12, up to the

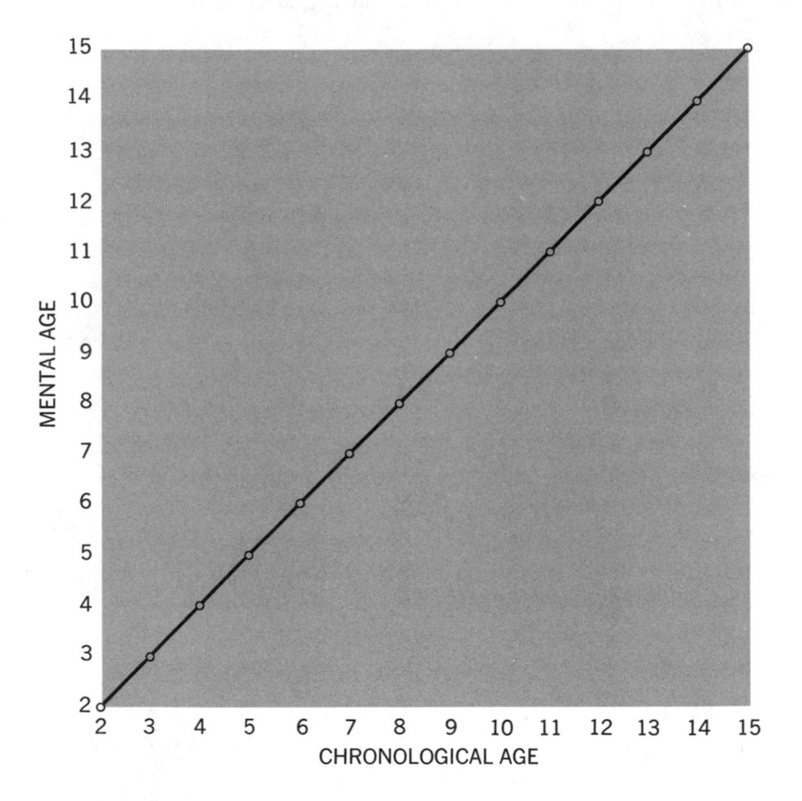

FIGURE 12

Graph Showing Average Mental Age for Each Chronological-age Group on Any Mental-age Scale

age at which intellectual maturity is reached. It still does not tell us anything about what the real course of mental development is like.

During an earlier period of mental testing a number of psychologists were interested in finding some statistical technique that would get around these difficulties and enable them to plot a curve that would really picture the course of mental development in children. It is quite obvious that this should not be a straight line indicating the *same* amount of change each year from early childhood to maturity. Any observation of the way children change as they grow older shows that a year makes more difference in the younger ones than in the older ones. The difference between the problems and tasks that can be mastered by average five-year-olds and by average six-year-olds, for example, appears to be far greater than the difference between the abilities of thirteen-year-olds and fourteen-year-olds.

Several mathematical procedures for what is called "absolute scaling" of intelligence tests have been worked out. (An absolute scale is one that starts from zero and proceeds by equal steps to its highest value.) It is not necessary that we go into detail about these scaling procedures and the mental-development curves they generate. It has become apparent as time has passed that this whole search for a universal mental-growth curve was an unprofitable undertaking. Various assumptions had to be made as a basis for the mathematical treatments that were given the scores, and these are now seen to be untenable, or at least unprovable.

Several lines of research have led to the conviction now generally held that mental-growth curves are of doubtful validity. One has to do with differences in the patterns of the curves obtained using different varieties of test item. Figure 13 illustrates this point. The curve for the maze test rises rapidly and reaches a plateau at about eleven. The curve for vocabulary rises evenly and slowly. At one stage in the history of mental testing, research workers believed that these differences in rate of improvement on different kinds of task were not too important, since each specific task was thought to be only an indicator of the general and innate quality we call intelligence. The factor-analytic studies we will turn to later have shown that the relationships between kinds of test material are much more complex than this, so that we cannot consider them interchangeable indicators of one general ability. Thus we are not justified in piecing together a single over-all growth curve from these specific curves of different shapes. It seems now that if there are such things as general laws of mental development that can be expressed as mathematical functions of age, they are more likely to be separate equations for separate processes than a single equation for the process as a whole.

A second reason for abandoning the search for a universal mental-growth curve is tied up with our increasing awareness of the interaction between native capacities and environmental influences. If we think of a general mental-growth curve as a way of portraying the natural development of pure native capacity, we know now that it cannot be achieved even as an abstraction. At every stage, development itself depends upon the opportunities for learning available at that stage. Later development is always an outgrowth of what the *interaction* of orig-

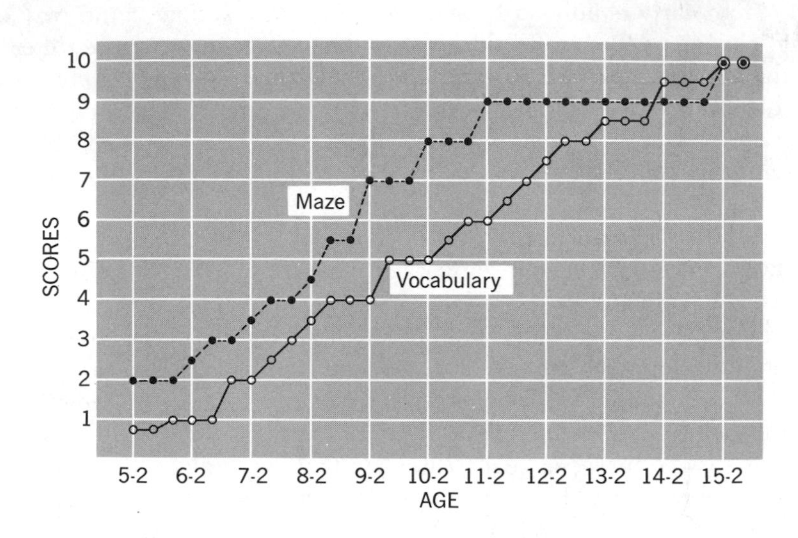

FIGURE 13

Age Trends on Two Subtests of the Wechsler Intelligence Scale for Children

(Wechsler, 1950a)

inal capacity and learned changes have made of the person up to that time. This becomes especially clear when we consider a specific question that has stimulated much discussion and controversy among "growth-curve" thinkers: "At what age is the development of intelligence completed?" Early test-makers, basing their judgments on their standardization data, chose sixteen as the point where increases with age ceased. Many users of the tests became convinced that fourteen was nearer to the true figure. As more different special groups were compared, it became clear that intelligence-test scores increased with age beyond fourteen *if schooling continued* but remained constant or declined slightly in groups no longer in school. R. L. Thorndike (1948b), for example, showed that average scores for 1,000 students increased consistently year by year up to the age of twenty-one and one-half. P. E. Vernon (1951) reported an analysis of scores made by recruits of different ages in the British armed services. Decline in average score set in earlier for those in nonintellectual jobs than for those in intellectual jobs. The effect of this longer period of mental growth in persons remaining at school was clearly demonstrated in a study by Lorge (1945). He went back to the records of 131 boys who as eighth-graders in 1921–22 had been given a number of psychological tests. Twenty years later he gave them the Otis intelligence test. For subjects whose initial intelligence level was the same, the later score varied according to the amount of schooling. Those who had gone to college averaged considerably higher than those who had dropped out during the high-school years. The numbers in most of the subgroups were small, but the trend was unmistakable. Husen (1951) showed that the same sort of relationship held in Sweden. Such findings make it appear unlikely that we shall ever be able to give a single answer to the question, "At what age age does mental growth cease?" We shall always have to say, "That depends."

Another source of dissatisfaction with generalized growth curves has been the constantly accumulating evidence that growth is an *individual* matter and that curves based on group averages tend to mask more than they reveal. One of the special questions about which controversy and research have centered is, "How constant is the IQ?" Carefully analyzed results from several child development centers have produced a complex answer to this simple question.

Practically speaking, there are a number of reasons why a child's obtained IQ may vary considerably from year to year, even if his intellectual status has not changed. One is the fact already mentioned that different tests do not draw on exactly the same kinds of ability. Even when the same measuring instrument, such as the Stanford-Binet, is used on different occasions, the items on which his score depends may not tap exactly the same aspects of intelligence. Nonverbal tests have a greater influence on scores at the lower age levels; educational deficiencies become more of a handicap at the upper age levels. Another problem in evaluating IQ constancy is that *variability* differs for different tests, or even for the same test at different age levels. This can be true even when the test has been standardized so as to give an *average* IQ of 100 at every age. An example will perhaps make this effect clear. If a six-year-old takes a test for which the standard deviation is 10 IQ points in the standardization group, and three years later takes another test for which the standard deviation is 16 IQ points, an IQ of 148 on the second test is actually the equivalent of an IQ of 130 on the first. On both occasions the child has scored three standard deviations above the mean, at or near the top of a normal distribution. What looks at first like a considerable improvement in IQ is only a statistical artifact. There has been no real change at all in intellectual status relative to his age group. Pinneau (1961) made a thorough study of the differences in the variability of the distribution of Stanford-Binet IQ's in different age groups, differences that made it appear that individual IQ's are less constant than they really are. On the basis of his suggestions, a new index of brightness was used in the most recent revision of the Stanford-Binet Test (Terman and Merrill, 1960), one that retains the same meaning from age to age.

Very often teachers and clinical workers are called upon to make inferences about the course of an individual's mental development from what the record tells them about his scores on different tests given at successive periods of his life. To do this they must make allowance for the two sources of error we have discussed, the fact that different tests do not measure exactly the same aspects of intelligence, and the fact that some distributions are more variable than others. Unless one has some definite information about these two matters it is probably better not to try to interpret a series of IQ's.

After we have allowed for these sources of error, however, we find that there is apparently some real fluctuation in intelligence from age to age. Some children become brighter as they grow older, some become less bright in comparison with their age-mates, and some move up and down on the intelligence scale in an apparently random manner. Changes that frequently occur do not by any means cover the whole IQ range. The probability that a six-year-old retarded child will develop into a gifted sixteen-year-old is negligible, but there is a real possibility that a boy who in the first grade appears to be only slightly above the average of his classmates will be leading his class when he reaches high school.

One principal source of our knowledge about these IQ changes is a study that has been going on at the University of California for a long period of time. Forty children, representative of the Berkeley population (considerably above the national average in mental ability, however) were followed through from infancy to adulthood, with tests at frequent intervals. Reports by Bayley (1949) and by Honzik, Macfarlane, and Allen (1948) threw considerable light on the problem of IQ constancy. The findings can be summarized under a few principal headings. Most of them were later corroborated by results from other less extended investigations.

In the first place, infant tests, those given during the first year or year and a half of life, are useless for predicting later intellectual status. It is a curious fact that the correlations of first-year tests with later intelligence measures, though very close to zero, tend to be *negative* rather than positive. The persons destined to reach the highest ultimate level average slightly lower in scores reflecting rate of early development than do those who will later not reach this level. This negative correlation is so slight, however, that it is not worth speculating about. The important point is that indices of the rapidity of infant development give us no clues at all from which we can predict later IQ. (This generalization does not hold for extremely feeble-minded children or for those with gross organic defects. An idiot who makes no progress at all during the first few months of life may be recognized as abnormal long before he reaches the age when valid predictive tests can be given.)

The second general finding is that the degree of relationship between intelligence tests given at different age levels depends upon both the age at first testing and the length of the time interval between tests. Figure 14 illustrates the way in which correlation with a later test rises as both these

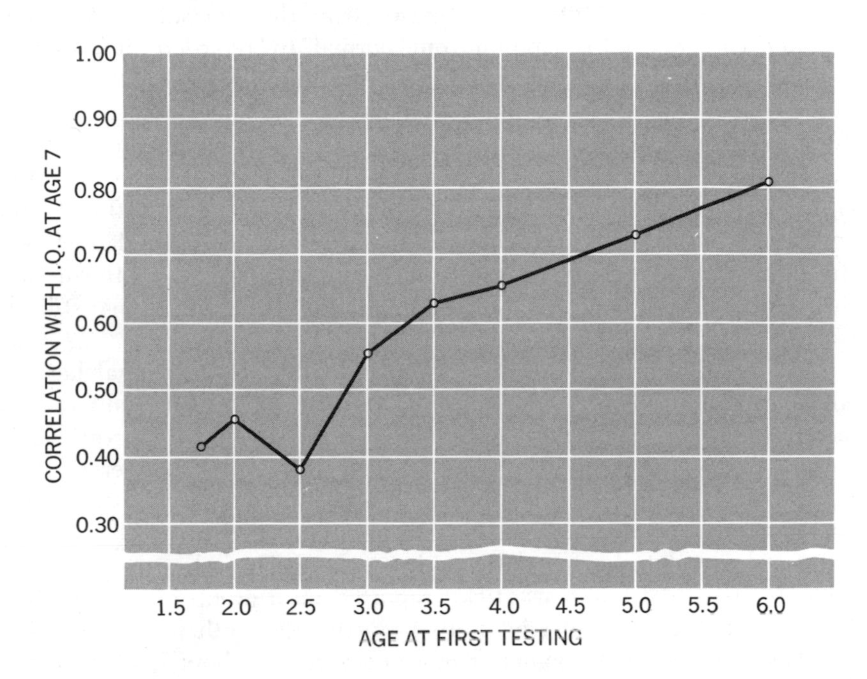

FIGURE 14

Correlations of Preschool Tests Given at Different Ages with Stanford-Binet Intelligence-test Scores at Age Seven

(Honzik, 1938)

factors are changed. A test given at two has very little predictive value. One given at four has considerably more. If later test scores are related to those obtained at the age of six or older, correlations of .7 or .8 are the rule. Six, the customary age for entering school, seems to represent a sort of turning point. From this age on there is enough IQ constancy to give intelligence tests definite predictive value, at least over limited periods of time. Husen (1953) reported test-retest correlations of .7 or higher for a number of Scandinavian groups. Bradway and Thompson (1962) reported a similar pattern of correlations from a follow-up study of subjects used in the standardization of the 1937 Stanford-Binet test.

The third important finding, much more evident in the later California studies than in those reported earlier, is that even a dependable correlation of .8 leaves room for marked fluctuations in individual cases. Honzik, Macfarlane, and Allen (1948) showed that it is *possible* for a change of as much as 50 IQ points to occur during the school years. Changes of 30 or more points were noted in 9 per cent of the cases, changes as great as 15 points in 58 per cent of the cases. Only 15 per cent of the California group showed less than 10 points of IQ change. While a change of 15 to 20 IQ points is not great enough to lift a person from the "normal" to the "very superior" category or to drop him from "normal" to "retarded," it is enough to make an appreciable difference in the evaluation of his potentialities that teachers and others are likely to make. As explained earlier, some of these reported IQ shifts are explained by differences in the variability of the IQ distribution at different age levels. The Stanford-Binet test (Form L) has a standard deviation of 12.5 points at age six and of 20.0 points at age twelve, according to Terman and Merrill's standardization data (1937). But even when all IQ's were transformed into standard scores to rule out this source of variation, much of the fluctuation from age to age still remained.

This variation in growth curves from individual to individual has become apparent wherever longitudinal studies have been undertaken. Several of these long-range studies have been set up at institutions in various parts of the country. Some of them have been in operation for many years. Kagan (1964) has provided a useful summary of the design and objectives of ten of them. Not all are concerned primarily with intelligence, but data having to do with IQ change have been reported by several. Ebert and Simmons (1943) reported on a group of 181 children who were tested at regular intervals from the age of three to the age of ten. Changes of ten IQ points or more occurred in about half the cases. These children (mainly from superior socio-economic levels) were more likely to gain than to lose. Hilden (1949) reported on a group of 30 Colorado children who were tested annually from early childhood to maturity. Variations in individual scores from time to time ranged from 7 to 46 IQ points. Hilden cited some evidence that such changes could not be accounted for by practice effects alone, and that a person's final IQ could be predicted more accurately from the *highest* IQ he obtained before the age of twelve than from the *average* of all his scores up to that time.

The California investigators made a special effort to identify influences in individual lives that might help to account for IQ changes. Case studies of children with unusually regular or unusually irregular growth trends do show that there is a tendency for irregularity to go with life histories characterized by unusual variations in disturbing as against stabilizing factors. The connection is far from clear, however. Some persons with disturbing experiences show very stable mental growth trends. The most clear-cut relationship the California study demonstrated is that between a child's final level of mental development and the educational level of his family. The child from a well-educated family is more likely to increase than to decrease in IQ as time passes. The correlations between parents' and children's intellectual status become higher as children get older (Bayley, 1954). Such findings fit in with those already cited, the Lorge study (1945), for example, which show that test scores are related to educational influences.

Another longitudinal study carried out at the Fels Institute in Ohio (Sontag, et al., 1958) focused particular attention on the question of *what kinds* of children tend to increase their IQ's over the years and what kinds tend to decrease them. Growth curves for 140 children tested at yearly intervals from three to ten were ranged in order from those showing the greatest increase to those showing the greatest decrease. Then the children in the top and bottom quarters of this distribution of IQ changes were selected for special study. One interesting difference between the groups was immediately apparent. In the "ascending" group, boys predominated; in the "descending" group, girls. When the information available in the case folders was examined, certain personality differences between "ascenders" and "descenders" showed up. Ascenders had been rated higher for such traits as independence, aggressiveness, initiative, and competition. Results of the projective testing corroborated these differences (Kagan, et al., 1958). The results suggest that children with an active, independent approach to the world are likely to grow intellectually at a rate faster than normal, whereas passive, dependent children tend to develop at a slower than normal rate.

In spite of the qualifications brought to our attention by the longitudinal studies, a mental-test score is as good an indicator as it ever was of the level a child *has already reached* in his intellectual development. As such it is an enormously useful tool. Perhaps the cautions recently expressed with regard to the IQ will lead us back toward a greater emphasis on the *mental age,* or some statistical equivalent, as a way of emphasizing present status rather than permanent endowment. Those responsible for the guidance of children need to realize that a single intelligence test can never be used as a basis for a definite judgment about what a child will be able to do several years later. Each new decision, at successive stages of development, calls for a recheck. Although extreme changes occur only very rarely, changes from "average" to "superior" and vice versa are relatively frequent. We must remember, however, that we do not know how to *produce* such changes in an individual, and that the older he is the less likely it is that a marked shift will occur. To seize on the evidence accumulated in mental-growth studies as proof that anyone can be a genius if he wants to (or his parents want him to) is fully as unwarranted as to cling to the belief that a person's general level of intelligence is inalterably fixed for all time by the age of six. The fact that the IQ is not completely constant does not make it completely meaningless.

Besides their implications for practical judgments that must be made in the schoolroom and in the clinic, these facts we have been discussing are important in planning and interpreting other research. Whenever the effects of some special influence are to be determined—vitamins, teaching methods, foster homes, or play therapy, for example—it must always be remembered that many children show marked increases in IQ without any identifiable special treatment at all. Therefore the study must be designed to show that in the experimental group either the average shift in an upward direction is greater or a larger number of individuals show upward shifts, than in a comparison group not exposed to the influence being investigated. Too often a few extreme cases showing a striking amount of change are cited as evidence for the effectiveness of a certain method of treatment. Taken by themselves they prove nothing, since we know that such extreme cases occasionally occur regardless of circumstances.

Logically a complete discussion of the relationship of intelligence measurements to age requires a consideration of early and later maturity as well as childhood. When large groups of adults first became available for testing at the time of World War I, psychologists were struck with the fact that the curve of mental development from the early twenties on appeared to be a *falling* one. The older a group was the lower its average turned out to be, and this decrement with advancing years became more and more noticeable throughout middle and old age. As psychological work with adults continued, however, the true relationships were seen to be more complex. The pattern or organization of abilities shifts with the years, and some kinds of capacity show much greater age differences than others. As results of longitudinal studies on the same individuals at different ages became available, the meaning of the group differences previously found became still more doubtful. Able subjects tested on different occasions did not show the decline during their forties that the group difference studies had led us to expect (see Chapter 11). Since all these findings can be brought together more clearly after we have taken up the subject of the patterning of mental abilities, the detailed facts about age trends in adults will be presented in a later chapter rather than here.

CORRELATIONAL RESEARCH—PREDICTIVE VALIDITY

If we were to rest our conclusions about what intelligence tests measure on evidence with regard to their predictive validity, our verdict would be that they are primarily tests of "scholastic aptitude," or what it takes to succeed in school. From the beginning, intelligence measurement has been more or less closely tied in with school situations. The judgments teachers naturally make about the relative brightness of individual pupils has constituted a readily available criterion by means of which test items could be evaluated. If the teachers' judgments were accurate and infallible, we should of course need no tests for children. But if, on the other hand, our tests showed no relationship to these judgments, we should certainly question their validity. What we would expect to find, and what we get when we try it out, is a moderately high but far from perfect correlation between teachers' judgments and test scores.

One thing that the research with tests has shown is that the variation in intellectual level in any one age or grade group is much greater than the average teacher assumes it to be (Cook, 1947). In a typical schoolroom where no grouping on the basis of ability has occurred, the range of mental ages is five years at the primary level, six years at the intermediate level, and eight or more years at the secondary level. When we put test scores into mental age terms we find that the dullest child in a sixth-grade class may be functioning at the level of an average nine-year-old, the brightest at the level of the average fifteen-year-old. School assignments requiring that a child understand abstract terms or reason about complex processes are easy enough for those near the top of this group, but for those at the bottom they may be completely meaningless.

The *correlation* between measures of general intelligence and grades given for school achievement, though it is only moderately high, is remarkably consistent over the whole range of school situations. Either individual or group tests chosen so as to be suitable for the age group where they are used regularly correlate from .4 to .6 with school marks. Various qualifications can be appended to this statement. Tests calling for verbal reasoning tend to give higher correlations than those of the nonverbal or performance type. Predictions of grades over long periods of time are not nearly so accurate as predictions over short periods. Some school subjects are more closely related to measured intelligence than others are. But even when we consider these complications and the variation they produce in the size of the reported correlations from study to study, the general consistency of the correlations from first grade through graduate school constitutes impressive evidence that our tests are revealing some general intellectual factor upon which success in school depends.

Correlations of this magnitude are of considerable value in making predictions that will help students chart their courses. Examination of Figure 15 shows us that while we cannot hope to predict very accurately just what grade-point average any individual student will make, we can determine the range within which his grades are likely to fall and thus answer various specific questions that may arise. It is plain, for example, that the majority of students with stanine ratings of 1, 2, or 3 do not achieve the grade-point average of 2.00 or higher that the university requires. The great majority of students with stanine ratings of 8 and 9, on the other hand, show averages above 2.5 and thus probably qualify for special honors programs. About students in the middle ranges with stanines of 4, 5, and 6, less definite statements can be made. It appears that they are much more likely than not to achieve the 2.00 minimum, but

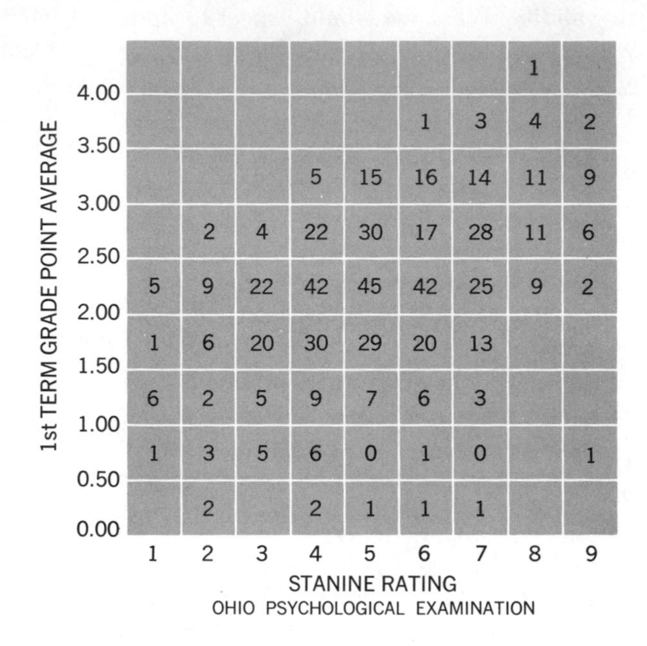

FIGURE 15
Scatter Diagram Showing Relationship of Scholastic Aptitude Test Scores to College Success for 589 University of Oregon Freshmen (r = .43)

a fair proportion of them attain honors level, and a few fail completely.

One of the things that keeps correlations between intelligence and scholarship from being any higher than they are is that failure can occur at all levels of brightness. Figure 15, for example, shows that one of the students with a stanine of 9 made a GPA of less than 1.00, and GPA's at or near zero went with stanines ranging all the way from 2 to 7. Some reasons for such outcomes are obvious. Success in school calls for effort and participation in the work of the class, and bright students as well as dull ones can be lacking in these essentials. It is a curious fact, however, pointed out by Fisher (1959), that in predicting all sorts of criteria, non-adaptive or inadequate forms of behavior can be predicted more accurately than good or superior performance. One possible explanation may be that the behavior of the adaptive, functioning organism is so complex that it is only under circumstances creating some unusual limitation, as in the case of school demands too complex to be mastered by a person of a certain degree of intellectual complexity, that we can predict it with any accuracy at all. Figure 16 is Fisher's graphic representation of the "twisted pear" phenomenon.

When instead of grades based on teachers' judgments, scores on tests of

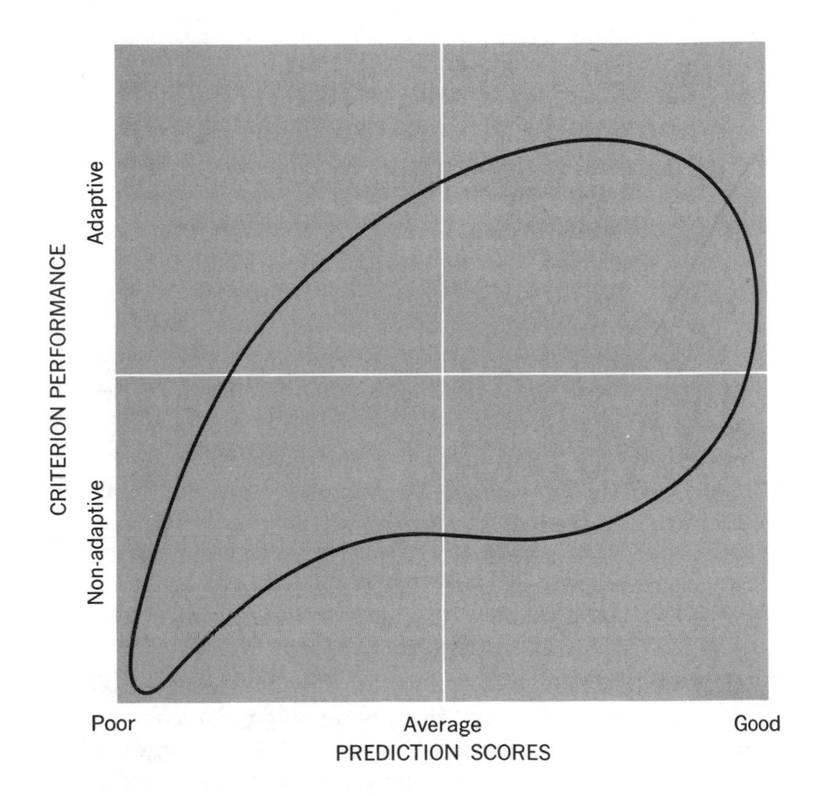

FIGURE 16
Schematic Model of the Twisted Pear Phenomenon in Prediction
(After Fisher, 1959)

school achievement are correlated with intelligence-test scores, somewhat higher coefficients are usually obtained. Correlations reported between group intelligence tests (more dependent on reading skill than individual tests) and standardized measures of school achievement often run as high as .8. This fairly close relationship between intelligence, especially as evaluated by means of group tests, and school-achievement tests, has at times led psychologists to conclude that intelligence tests were *nothing but* tests of schooling. It should always be remembered, however, that within any group made up of individuals who have had *equal* educational opportunities, whether it be a group of first-graders or a group of graduate students, there are marked *individual* differences in both variables—measured achievement and tested intelligence. Equal education does not tend to eradicate these differences. Thus the test score would seem to reflect something more basic than the influence of schooling. There are individual differences in the capacity for profiting by education, and it is these differences that intelligence-test scores reflect.

Long-term predictions from intelligence-test scores also lend some support to the conclusion that the tests measure basic educational aptitude. A number of studies have shown that if school attendance laws are such as to permit students to drop out after their fourteenth or even their sixteenth birthdays, intelligence tests given in grade school will predict with a fair degree of success how far up the educational ladder different students will go. Those who drop out at the ninth-grade level average lower than those who reach the twelfth grade. Those who attend college average higher than those who stop with high-school graduation.

It is useful for anyone who must interpret test scores to know something about the intellectual requirements of the higher educational levels. Studies by Embree (1948) and by Wrenn (1949) indicated that the average Stanford-Binet IQ for college entrants was 118, for bachelor's degree recipients 123, and for advanced degree recipients 126. Persons receiving Ph.D.'s averaged 141. A more recent summary of evidence from a number of separate studies (Plant and Richardson, 1958) concluded that for college students as a whole, the average IQ on the Wechsler test would be 120. For freshmen the average would be 116. All these reports stress the fact that there is much variation in the groups represented by these averages. The *range* of IQ's for degree recipients in Embree's sample was from 95 to 180. In a supplementary study he showed that colleges vary widely in their intelligence requirements. In some, the average IQ of the student is as low as 100, in others as high as 133. In Wrenn's study, 10 per cent of those ultimately receiving Ph.D's scored below the average of entering freshmen at the colleges they attended. Thus the interpretations we make must always be in terms of probabilities. It is *unlikely* that a boy with an IQ below 100 will be able to graduate from college. It is *improbable* that a person with an IQ below 125 will succeed at a first-rate graduate school. In making such judgments we must always keep in mind also the qualifications already discussed with regard to IQ constancy over long periods of time.

Intelligence tests show consistent, dependable relationships to occupational level as well as to educational level. We are accustomed to rank jobs on a prestige scale with the professions at the top and unskilled labor at the bottom. This ranking is not identical with what it would be for income or for social utility, but it is made by various groups of people quite consistently (Deeg and Paterson, 1947). Ball (1938) in 1937 determined the rating on one of these standardized occupational-level scales for each of 219 men who had taken a group test of intelligence as children in 1918 or in 1923. For the 1923 group, who were the younger ones at the time of the follow-up, the correlation between test scores and occupational level rating turned out to be .57. For the older 1917 group, it was .71. This would suggest that there is some tendency for individuals to gravitate toward an occupational level in keeping with their measured intelligence.

Results of the tests given to large numbers of men in the Armed Forces during both world wars pointed in the same direction (see Chapter 13). The professions, probably because they require long periods of advanced education, rank highest in test scores. Business and white-collar occupations rank next highest, then skilled labor, then semiskilled labor, and finally unskilled labor at the bottom. Needless to say, here too there is a great deal of variability within groups. Some unskilled laborers actually score as high as any of the professional men.

These relationships with educational level and with the aspects of occupational placement that depend upon schooling are the clearest evidence we have as to what intelligence tests are measuring. But they in turn require clarification before we can glibly characterize the tests as measures of learning ability. What is it *about* learning that depends upon intelligence? Do the bright learn more *rapidly* than the dull, do they keep on learning *longer,* or do they learn *different things*? These are urgent questions when we wish to use tests for such purposes as the selection of workers. For a job requiring a preliminary training period, is it advisable to choose applicants with the highest score? Just what does "learning ability," often used as a synonym or euphemism for intelligence, mean?

Fortunately there has been enough research centered around these issues so that we can differentiate between what intelligence tests do show and what they do not. In the first place, if what we mean by learning ability is the *rapidity* with which a person improves with practice on any motor or intellectual skill, then we can say quite definitely that intelligence tests do *not* measure it. The most complete evidence on the point came from a series of studies by Woodrow (1938, 1939, 1940) in which a group of students were given a number of practice periods on a variety of different tasks. Before and after this series of practice trials they took intelligence and special aptitude tests. The analysis of the correlations showed that there was no one general learning ability accounting for improvement on all the tasks. Some subjects made faster progress on one, some on another. Thus there was no basis for an identification of intelligence with general learning ability. Furthermore there was no significant relationship between any of the scores representing *gain* with practice and intelligence. In a later study, Woodrow (1946) analyzed correlations between IQ and gains from year to year in the scores obtained by school children on standardized achievement tests. In general, these results also showed almost no relationships between gain and intelligence, although the period from fourth to fifth grade did produce a few significant correlations. Another study done by Simrall (1947) showed that even when the types of material the subjects worked with in practice periods were highly similar to the types of material in the intelligence test, gains during practice were still not significantly related to test scores. Such findings fit in with our common observation that average and dull students often progress as rapidly as bright students in football, automobile driving, accordion-playing, or using an adding machine.

During the 1950's and 1960's a special kind of experimental research has produced some evidence about the nature of the relationship between measured intelligence and learning ability. This is the work on programmed learning—the so-called "teaching machine." This evidence is not entirely consistent. For example, some studies, like that of McNeil and Keisler (1961), report sizable correlations between the amount learned through automated teaching and intelligence. Others, like that of Porter (1959) report near-zero correlations between measured intelligence and amount learned. Stolurow (1960, 1961) has most thoroughly discussed this problem—the way in which intellectual characteristics of the learner are related to various aspects of his performance in a programmed learning situation. While some parts of the picture are not yet clear, most of the findings seem to fit in with Woodrow's conclusions cited above. Neither the amount gained nor the rate at which it is acquired show any consistent relationship to measured intelligence. There may be differences, however, in the type of program and the type of reward most likely to facilitate learning in persons of different intelligence levels, and there may be limits as to what can be taught by means of any program to persons below some minimal level. The McNeil and Keisler study, for example, was an attempt to teach molecular physics to first graders. Perhaps this subject matter is just too complex and difficult to be mastered by the duller children under any program.

If intelligence tests do not measure "learning ability," how do the consistent and fairly high correlations between IQ and school achievement come about? Tilton (1949) has called our attention to another factor that must be considered when we speak of "learning ability." School success involves not just increasing skill in the performance of simple tasks but continuous progress from the simple to the more complex. In arithmetic, for example, we are not content to have children practice, year after year, the simple addition of two-place numbers. If we were, we should probably find that the dull child showed as much improvement as his brilliant classmate. But what we do in our schools is to lead students on from addition to subtraction, multiplication, division, fractions, decimals, and square root. The more rapidly a child's mental capacity is *growing* the better he is able to keep up with the constantly increasing complexity of what is to be learned. The child with an IQ of 80 is handicapped all through school not because he is slow or inept at learning things which are within the capacity of all the children at his age level, but because he is never *ready* to grasp new and more complex ideas at the time when they are ordinarily presented to children of his age. Tilton's study (1949) shows that one obtains substantial correlations between intelligence and gains in school achievement if this difficulty factor is allowed to operate. He obtained a correlation of .49 between intelligence rating and gains on a history test by omitting from the test all the easier items, those answered correctly by 45 per cent or more of the group at the beginning. It seems then that if a test is designed so that a person must learn the more difficult things in order to improve his score on it, the advantage goes to persons with higher IQ's. The fact that gains from fourth to fifth grade were correlated with IQ in the Woodrow study (1946) cited above becomes intelligible from this viewpoint. The achievement test was one designed for the fourth grade and up. Thus it was undoubtedly more difficult for the fourth-graders than for any of the other grade groups. At the level where it was difficult, correlations between intelligence and gains appeared. Another study by Tilton (1953) showed that at the fourth- and fifth-grade level gains in all the school subjects were positively correlated. The same difficulty factor may be involved in a more recent study by Tempero and Ivanoff (1960) which showed that scores on the Cooperative School and College Ability Test were correlated with gains as well as with end-of-the-year achievement scores in various courses after a television correspondence study program. In general, the correlations with gains were lower than those with achievement, but for one course, beginning algebra, the r was .50 for boys, .49 for girls.

It may be that the euphemism "slow *learner*" is not really an accurate characterization of the dull child. "Slow *developer*" would be closer to the true state of affairs during the elementary-school period. If he seems to have taken two years to master what his brighter classmates mastered in one, this is not because he learned more slowly but because it took him longer to reach the level of mental development at which these things could be learned at all. This change in interpretation fits in with the fact, quite familiar to teachers, that at the high-school and college ages which correspond to the leveling-off period in mental growth no amount of time spent by the dull on the same materials which the bright grasp with ease seems to produce mastery of them. There probably is a fair proportion of the adult population who are incapable of understanding integral calculus, Platonism, or international finance. One hesitates to be overly dogmatic about such a negative conclusion, however, since a change in the way problems and materials are formulated, organized, and presented sometimes reduces the level of complexity enough to bring them within the range of much more limited minds. To develop ways of doing this is a constant challenge to educators, in and out of schools. Much of the current research on programmed learning has this explicit purpose, and evidence is accumulating that a good program makes it possible for persons of limited intellectual ability to learn concepts and principles that they would probably have been unable to grasp under ordinary teaching techniques (Stolurow, 1961).

It is possible, also, that there are different ways of learning new concepts and principles and that intelligence is related to this qualitative difference in procedure. Osler and Fivel (1961) studied concept formation in groups of average and superior children at the six-, ten-, and fourteen-year levels. Among the high IQ group at the ten- and fourteen-year levels they found a larger proportion of *sudden* learners than they found in the average groups. They interpreted the differences to mean that the very intelligent children were proceeding by a process of hypothesis formation and testing, whereas the less intelligent were simply accumulating stimulus-response associations. Osler and Trautman (1961) put this interpretation to a test by presenting the average and superior children with a variety of stimulus materials of such a nature that persons proceeding by means of hypothesis testing would be thrown off the track, as it were, by irrelevant characteristics. As the experimenters predicted, the bright children actually made more errors under these circumstances.

Around the kinds of relationships we have been considering can be grouped a large number of miscellaneous studies reporting correlations between adult scores on intelligence tests and a variety of criteria. Tests correlate with occupational level, but not with degrees of success within an occupation. (See Wells, Williams, and Fowler, 1938.) In the military selection and training programs, tests correlate with grades given by instructors, which probably depend somewhat upon grasp of abstract concepts, but not with more "practical" criteria. (See Jenkins, 1946). That this is not simply a matter of "book learning" is suggested by H. A. Smith (1949) who found that intelligence was correlated with gains on a standardized biology test in both an experimental group taught by the use of films and a control group taught in the customary way.

It seems to be clear, then, that there is no simple way of characterizing the relationship between measured intelligence and learning, but it is possible to get rid of a number of minconceptions about it. In school or out, intelligence tests cannot be expected to tell us how quickly individuals will "catch on" or how much they will improve their performance if the task is one they are all clearly capable of doing. Tests do provide an index of the level of complexity and difficulty in the manipulation of symbols to which any individual may be expected to advance under ordinary circumstances, but the research on programmed learning is suggesting that it may be possible to break down complex symbolic processes into smaller steps and thus bring them within the grasp of less intelligent persons. Finally, intelligence tests may be related to the manner in which individuals learn rather than to the amount or the speed of learning. We will consider the question of qualitatively different stages of intellectual development in more detail in a later section of the chapter.

One practical conclusion can be emphasized. We should never underestimate the *learning ability* of persons at the low end of the IQ scale. Some of the research that has been done with the mentally retarded as subjects will be discussed in a later chapter, but it is well to remind ourselves at this point that such persons can learn things within their range of mental ability very effectively, and there is a good deal of evidence that this range is broader than we once considered it to be.

VARIETIES OF INTELLIGENCE—THE ANALYSIS OF RELATIONSHIPS BETWEEN TESTS

Studies of mental growth and of the relationship of test scores to school success have taught us much about the meaning of individual differences in measured intelligence. The other principal pillar upon which our understanding of intelligence tests rests consists of research on the relationships *between* various intelligence tests. The idea that each person is endowed with a fixed quantity of mental ability, and that it will show up however we choose to measure it, has faded with the years. Mental organization has turned out to be vastly more complex than the early mental-testers suspected. Several kinds of evidence force us to recognize that intelligence is neither a single unitary quality nor a simple summation of separate, unrelated traits. Let us examine this evidence.

The first type of results which bear on the problem consists of correlations which have been obtained when both verbal and performance tests of intelligence have been given to the same subjects. If the individuals in the group are all of approximately the same age so that large differences based on maturity level alone are ruled out, the correlations between the two varieties of test seldom run higher than .5 or .6. Gaw's (1925) study on children of about thirteen found correlations of .41 for boys and .49 for girls between Binet IQ and scores on fourteen unselected performance tests. Verbal and performance halves of the Wechsler-Bellevue test correlate .67 with each other when used with representative groups of adult subjects comprising the whole intelligence range (Wechsler, 1950b). For the Wechsler Intelligence Scale for Children, the reported correlations between verbal and performance sections are .60 at age seven and one-half, .68 at age ten and one-half, and .56 at age thirteen and one-half.

In general we can say that the correlations between verbal and performance tests are of about the same magnitude as the correlations between verbal tests and school marks. (Performance tests characteristically show a somewhat lower correlation with measures of school success than verbal tests do.) In interpreting both correlations we recognize that only a part of what is being measured is a common trait represented by the scores we have correlated. Verbal intelligence is not identical with performance intelligence. Neither is identical with brightness in school.

There is a common core of something underlying all of them, but it is only a *core*. Each has also some ingredients not contained in the others.

Another signpost pointing to the conclusion that intelligence is not a unitary trait is the finding that some types of test which are highly correlated with one another during childhood differ greatly in the extent to which they are affected by advancing age or illness. For example, vocabulary is an excellent indicator of *general* intelligence in children, as it correlates highly with most other types of intellectual activity. If a single test must be given to a child in order to ascertain the mental level at which he is functioning, a vocabulary test is more satisfactory than any other. But in adults past middle age and patients suffering from brain injury and schizophrenia, vocabulary is not closely related to various other assessments of intellectual level (Wechsler, 1950b). Performance tests show more impairment of mental functioning in such cases than do verbal tests; memory tests show more than information tests; analogies items show more than comprehension items. There are many more such differences. In order to account for them we must assume some degree of independence in the functions measured. If intelligence were a single unitary quality it would decline as a whole.

Another striking demonstration that intelligence is not a unitary quality is provided by the so-called *idiots savants*, feebleminded persons with one highly-developed talent of some sort. This may be mechanical aptitude, musical talent, proficiency in arithmetic, phenomenal memory, or marked skill in drawing or painting. Of recent years, since tests have been available, it has been possible to make thorough studies of such persons so that actual documentation rather than just hearsay evidence testifies to the enormous discrepancy between the low general level of ability and the marked skill along some special line. Scheerer, Rothmann, and Goldstein (1945) reported on one of these children whom they studied intensively between 1937 and 1943.

In 1937 this eleven-year-old boy, L., was brought to these writers by his mother, for neuropsychiatric and psychological consultation. The complaints about L. summed up to this: he could never follow the regular school curriculum like a normal child, or learn by instruction. His general information was alarmingly substandard; he had made progress in only a few school subjects, and even in these, his achievements were very limited. His motivational and behavior peculiarities had been an early concern of his parents. He had never shown interest in his social surroundings or in normal childhood activities. On the other hand he had always excelled in certain performances.

> The first impression on meeting L. is that of an erratic and hyperkinetic child, driven by an urge to keep in constant motion. He seems to be governed by an ever recurring impulse to move all four fingers of each hand rapidly in a definite beat, rubbing them against the thumbs (in a snapping-like

> motion without the snaps). Alternating with extreme inattentiveness, self-preoccupation and restlessness he displays a friendly poise and stereotyped politeness, as when responding to or addressing people. Most of the time L. appears motorically or otherwise self-absorbed and socially aloof. However, he shows one unique interest in his human surroundings—an amazing phenomenon exhibited in the first minutes of the examination. Spontaneously the boy asks each of us, "When is your birthday?" Given the date, he answers in a fraction of a minute, "Dr. G.'s birthday was on Saturday last year and Dr. S.'s birthday was on Wednesday." A glance at the calendar proves him correct. We call others to the scene, and with amazing swiftness, L. gives correctly the day of the week of every person's birthday. Moreover, he can tell at once exactly which day of the week a person's birthday was last year or 5 years ago, and on what day it will fall in 1945, etc. More closely examined, L. proves capable of telling the day of the week for any given date between about 1880 and 1950. Conversely, he can also give the date for any given week-day in any year of that period, e.g. the date of the first Saturday in May 1950, or of the last Monday in January 1934, etc. As much as we could determine he makes no mistakes in his calendar answers. Though L. unquestionably takes delight in the recognition of his feat, he never seems aware of its extraordinary character in the same sense as a normal person (e.g., the reader of this, if he could master such a task). On the other hand, it is known that, since his seventh year, he had developed a persistent interest in the birthdays of everyone he meets. For some time he has been surprising people he met only once by volunteering their birthdays "on sight." This, of course, happened to the writers on many occasions. In conjunction with this specific memory he almost inevitably will know the day and date of his first visit to a place and usually the names and birthdays of all the people he met there. He never fails to look for the date when he sees a newspaper, which otherwise does not interest him in the least. (Scheerer, Rothmann, & Goldstein, 1945).

The authors go on to describe other aspects of L.'s peculiar talents; his impressive skill in remembering and manipulating numbers without any general superiority in arithmetic, his excellent spelling ability, but lack of knowledge of or interest in the meaning of the words, his interest in opera and ability to play by ear coupled with a complete inability to profit from musical instruction. His IQ on the Binet test was 50.

As has been explained in the previous chapter, our understanding of what the complex interrelationships among tests mean has been greatly facilitated by a statistical technique called factor analysis. It enables us to deal with large numbers of correlation coefficients at the same time and to erect mathematically a structure that serves to account for the varying sizes of these coefficients in terms of hypothetical factors or abilities required by different tests to different extents. In the case of a simple problem, it is easy to see without using any mathematical procedures the kind of reasoning that it involves. For example, one correlation coefficient between an arithmetical reasoning test and a reading test does not tell us much about the ability the tests measure. This correlation could reflect general intelligence or simply reading skill, since problems must be read to be solved. But let us add to the initial battery of two tests two others—an intelligence test that requires no reading and an arithmetic test that requires no reasoning but only simple manipulation of numbers. Then let us study all the correlations between the four tests and we may be able to decide between the different possible hypotheses. If they all show correlations of about the same magnitude, we shall have to postulate the presence of some general ability. If the correlation between intelligence, arithmetical reasoning, and reading are all much higher than those between simple arithmetic and the other tests, it will look as though the manipulation of numbers constitutes a separate ability.

The necessity for mathematical factor-analytic methods in the carrying out of this type of thinking about abilities arises because a relatively small number of tests produces a large number of correlations and they cannot all be kept in mind at once. We can manage well enough with four tests and the six correlations we obtain from them, but for twenty tests we have 190 correlations and for fifty tests 1,225 correlations. Factor analysis does part of the work for us and simplifies the material before we attempt to interpret it.

If we remember always that factor analysis is only an extension of the method we find it quite natural to use when we wish to make an inference about mental traits on the basis of correlation coefficients, we may find the whole process less strange and difficult. We will also be reminded of the limitations of the method. As has been explained previously, it does not give us unequivocal mathematical statements informing us what the basic abilities are. It simply rearranges the information contained in the correlation coefficients. The psychologist doing the study must still name or identify the factors—name them in such a way that they fit the pattern obtained from the correlations. There is nothing mathematical at all about this naming process. And there is nothing *unique* about the mathematical solution. Another sort of rearrangement might fit the data just as well. Thus the factor analyst can only say, "This is *one* combination of traits which would serve to account for the relationships we have found between these tests." Another research worker may propose another set of traits based on equally sound mathematical and psychological reasoning, which will account for the relationships equally well. The choice between them must be made on the grounds of simplicity, usefulness, and congruence with the whole body of psychological knowledge. This is why there are so many arguments among factor analysts and why there is as yet no completely satisfactory account of the way mental abilities are organized.

In spite of these limitations of factor analysis as a method, however, factor analysts approaching the problem of mental organization from very different directions have found themselves meeting on common ground. By now the differences in interpretation are much less striking than the similarities. The most basic of the differences still not completely resolved has to do with types of solution of the factor problem preferred by American and British psychologists, respectively.

The British workers were the ones who initiated this line of research. Since the early years of the century Spearman, and later his students and colleagues, have been working on various aspects of a theory centered around the idea that mental tests all measure to some extent one basic intellectual ability. In *The Abilities of Man* (1927), Spearman summarized a vast amount of significant research. He showed that the intercorrelations for many test batteries containing a wide variety of materials and types of items *could* be accounted for in terms of the one characteristic he called "g." To him it seemed to represent the total *mental energy* available to an individual, while the various kinds of "s" or specific factors in different tests stood for the engines through which this energy was applied. The data showed that "g" is most efficiently measured by questions and items we should ordinarily label "reasoning" tests, where the individual is asked to discover the relationship between two things or to identify something from its relationship to something else. For this kind of thinking Spearman coined the term *noegenesis*.

However, Spearman himself, and others using the methods he developed, encountered some test batteries in which not all of the correlation between certain tests could be adequately accounted for in terms of "g" alone. This seemed to occur in studies where several tests of somewhat similar content were included in the battery to be factor-analyzed. If there were, for example, two tests of vocabulary, or two tests of the formboard type, the correlations between the two members of each pair were higher than their "g" loadings indicated that they should be. Out of this discrepancy grew the idea of "group" factors representing abilities less broad than "g" but broader than "s." Thus has developed the *hierarchical* theory of mental organization.

A clear statement of this rather complex theory as to what intelligence consists of can be found in *The Structure of Mental Abilities* by P. E. Vernon (1950). What the theory means is illustrated in Vernon's diagram as reproduced in Figure 17. We can apply this kind of theory both to tests and to persons being tested. If it is tests we are classifying in accordance with the system represented in Figure 17, we would evaluate them first with regard to their "g" loadings. (The factor loadings, derived from the correlations, answer the question, "How necessary is the ability under consideration for success with this test?") After this we can sort them out into two principal categories according to whether they require in addition to "g" the verbal-educational abilities important in all kinds of school work (v:ed) or the practical knack of understanding concrete things im-

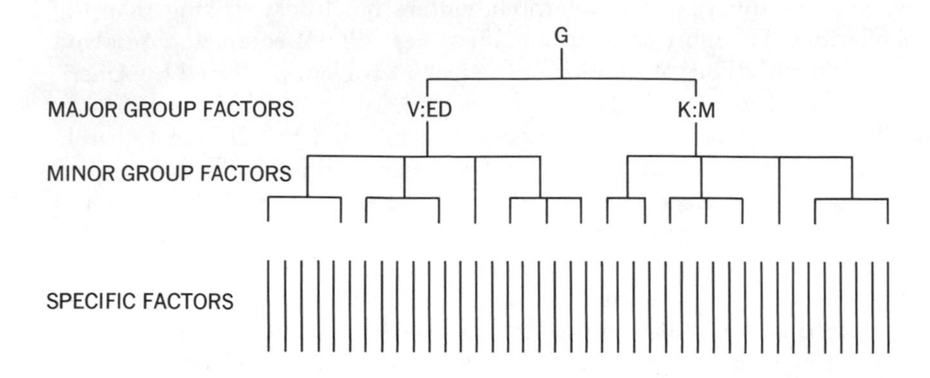

FIGURE 17
Diagram Illustrating the Hierarchical Theory of Mental Organization
(Vernon, 1950, p. 22)

portant in various mechanical jobs (k:m). We may if we wish make a still finer classification of tests by further subdividing the group that falls into each of the two main categories. Within the "v:ed" group, separate verbal and numerical abilities can be distinguished and tests of course differ in the extent to which they draw upon them. Within the "k:m" group, spatial and mechanical abilities can be separated.

It is doubtful, however, how useful these finer differentiations of ability are. Vernon presents statistical evidence that in the school, military, or industrial situations where applied psychologists work, the relevant criteria can be predicted fairly well by using only the "g," "v:ed," and "k:m" ratings. The other narrower group factors contribute so little to the total variance in test and criterion scores that they can safely be ignored. Specific factors, including such things as temperamental and character traits, background and experience, as well as specific talents and aptitudes, are of more importance in job situations than are the abilities at the minor group-factor level in Figure 17. Moursy (1952) presented evidence for the suitability of the hierarchical scheme in accounting for correlations among twenty tests for a group of ten- and eleven-year-olds.

The point of view of the British factor analysts can be summed up in this rule: try always to keep the pattern of abilities you are postulating as *simple* as you can. Measure "g" first and account for as much of the test variance as you can in terms of "g" alone. Supplement this with the measurement of broad educational and practical abilities. Separate out narrow factors of lesser scope only when you need them in the solution of some special research or personnel problem.

In America L. L. and T. G. Thurstone, in an important series of publications beginning in the 1930's, became the principal spokesmen for a different point of view. The question they raised was, "Why must we necessarily postulate any *general* mental ability at all? Would it not be possible to account for correlations between tests in terms of group factors alone, factors which inevitably overlap to some extent?" To put their idea into common-sense terms, it is easy to conceive of five numerical tests that correlate with one another simply because they all require an ability to manipulate figures, not because of "g." But one of them may also correlate with a reading test because the problems to be worked have to be read. Another may correlate with a test calling for the sorting of geometrical figures into categories because in both cases rapid perception of details is involved. Such tie-ups make it possible for all the correlations to be positive even if there is no one ability common to all tests. L. L. Thurstone worked out the mathematical techniques for what he called multiple factor analysis. By these methods it is possible to find a *set* of separate factors that account for the correlations in a battery of tests. (Remember that no mathematical system can guarantee that this is the *only* way the correlations can be explained. Solutions are not *unique.*) The multiple factor methods have been so successful that they have constituted the basis for the vast majority of American factor-analytical work done since they were formulated.

In his first large-scale study L. L. Thurstone (1938) assembled a battery of fifty-six psychological tests, including as wide a variety as possible. Some had to do with seeing relationships between geometrical figures in space. Some were concerned with mechanical relationships such as are found in arrangements of gears and pulleys. Some required computation, some reasoning from syllogisms. The subjects were 240 volunteer college students. Nine "primary abilities" were identified from the tables of factor loadings. Later 1,154 eighth-grade children were given a similar battery of tests in a research undertaking designed to find out whether the same "primary abilities" would turn up in a group that was younger and less highly selected. Seven of them did (Thurstone and Thurstone, 1941). Still later evidence was presented (T. G. Thurstone, 1941) for the differentiation of six of the same factors in kindergarten children.

The primary mental abilities appearing in both college and eighth-grade studies were as follows:

S (space). Visualization of geometrical figures in different positions in space.
P (perceptual speed). Quick noting of details. (The interpretation of the loadings of different tests in this factor is somewhat less certain than for S.)
N (number). Quickness in making arithmetical computations of all sorts.
V (verbal meanings). Grasp of ideas and meanings of words.
W (word fluency). Speed in manipulating single and isolated words.

M (rote memory). Facility in memorizing words, numbers, letters, and other materials.

I (induction). Ability to extract a rule common to the materials of a problem or test.

Many other investigators have confirmed Thurstones' findings for factors V, N, S, and M. The distinction between the two verbal factors V and W was an unanticipated finding, and the meaning of W is still not completely clear. British psychologists have for a long time been interpreting a similar fluency factor they encountered in their studies as a temperamental rather than an intellectual characteristic (Eysenck, 1952). For both the perception and the reasoning factors, correlations were low enough in these original studies to suggest the existence of several factors rather than a single factor. Goodman (1943) noted, for example, that the average correlation of the various perceptual tests in the Primary Mental Abilities battery he was using with a group of engineering freshmen was only .36.

One of the lines of development most prominent during and after World War II was the breaking down of Thurstone's "primary" abilities into others more homogeneous and narrower in their scope. If we analyze a battery of tests all of which have something to do with a single one of the primary abilities, we find that this ability splits up into others still more "primary." Thus Carroll (1941) identified nine verbal abilities in place of the two Thurstone had reported. L. L. Thurstone (1944a) found ten perceptual factors, eight of them represented in enough tests so that they could be identified with special aspects of perception such as "speed and strength of closure" or "susceptibility to illusions." (These will be discussed in some detail in Chapter 9.)

It was a sustained program of research by J. P. Guilford that brought order into the chaos of partially independent factors that had developed out of many such analyses. His work with the Army Air Force (Guilford, 1947) had produced evidence for at least twenty-seven identifiable factors representing different aspects of spatial ability, reasoning, and memory. After the war, Guilford initiated a thorough study of cognitive and thinking abilities, the Aptitudes Project at the University of Southern California. Year after year he and his associates mapped out separate areas of judgment, evaluation, reasoning, and creative thinking. As the number of separate factors increased, Guilford saw that they could be related to one another in a three-dimensional system analogous to the periodic table of elements in chemistry. Figure 18 shows this system graphically.

It indicates that there are three main ways of classifying mental abilities. If we use the kind of process or operation the thinker performs as the basis for the breakdown we find that there are five classes: (1) *cognition* (rediscovery or recognition); (2) *memory* (retention of what is cognized);

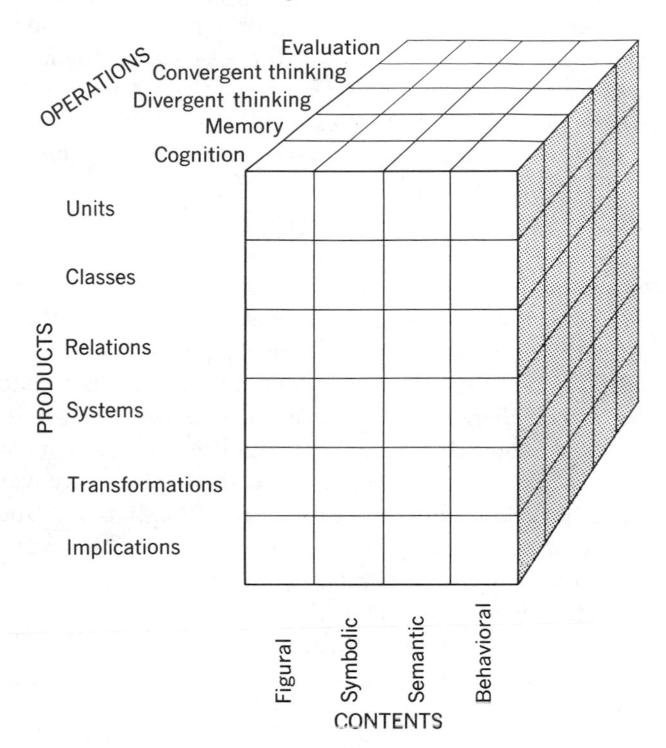

FIGURE 18

A Cubical Model Representing the Structure of Intellect

(From Guilford, J. P., *Personality*. Copyright, 1959, McGraw-Hill Book Co. Used by permission)

(3) *divergent thinking* (searching for different ideas or various solutions to a problem); (4) *convergent thinking* (processing information in a way that leads to the correct or best answer); and (5) *evaluation* (reaching decisions as to how correct, or adequate the results of one's thinking have been).

If we use the contents or material to be thought about as the basis for classifying abilities we come out with the four classes shown at the base of the cube in Figure 18: (1) *figural* (concrete material, such as sizes, forms, colors, or textures); (2) *symbolic* (letters, digits, etc.); (3) *semantic* (verbal meanings and ideas); and (4) *behavioral* (social situations of various kinds, so far not explored to any extent in intelligence testing).

If we use the kind of answer the subject is asked to produce as the basis for our classification, the six classes along the vertical axis of Figure 18 cover the possible forms of response.

This system (Guilford, 1959a, 1959b) makes a place for 120 factors of intellect, since all combinations of operations, products, and contents are theoretically possible (5 x 4 x 6). Not all of these factors have actually shown up in factor analyses done so far, but a large proportion of them have, especially since the formulation of the system has made it possible to design new tests to fit vacant cells. We have the least adequate knowledge of the behavioral class of abilities. While attempts to measure social intelligence have a long history, no satisfactory technology has ever been achieved. Guilford hopes that his theoretical system will suggest operations and products to be tried out in measuring abilities in the behavioral domain.

Of all the distinctions embodied in the Guilford theoretical system, it has been the distinction between convergent and divergent thinking that has had the most important research consequences so far. Most intelligence tests, until this difference was pointed out, were made up of questions for which there is only one correct answer. When it became apparent that tests could be designed in such a way as to evoke many different answers that could be accurately evaluated, the way was cleared for research on individual differences in *creativity*. It is the abilities involved in thinking of *new* answers and *different* possible solutions to a problem in which the creative person excels. We shall consider this line of research in some detail in Chapter 15.

Along with the increase in the number of "primary mental abilities" and the efforts to organize them in a meaningful way has come an increasing realization that not all these abilities are really *independent* of one another. If subjects in a study are scored on the factors themselves, these sets of scores correlate positively. This state of affairs leads to a factor analysis of *factors* and the identification of what are usually called *second-order* factors. When this fact first came to their attention psychologists on both sides of the Atlantic, including Thurstone (1944b), were quick to point out that we had here a basis for "rapprochement" between British and American viewpoints. A second-order general factor might well be the "g" on which Spearman had been insisting. The fact that Spearman's methods made it rise to the top first and Thurstone's picked it up at the bottom last would be more or less immaterial if its *existence* had been demonstrated both ways. Subsequent work has complicated this problem by producing evidence for not just one but *several* second-order factors that often show up when intelligence tests are factor analyzed. In this connection Rimoldi's (1948, 1951) analysis of scores made on a large number of tests by a group of Argentine school children aged eleven to fourteen is pertinent. Three second-order general factors were indicated. The first of them seemed to be much like Spearman's "g" in that it showed up most strongly in tests requiring "noegenesis," or perception of relationships. The nature of the other two second-order factors was less clear.

For the practical worker attempting to apply the results of research to the problems he faces in school or industry, the importance of these second-order factors is that they extend and support the idea that has been prominent since the early days of applied psychology—that abilities are positively correlated and that there is such a thing as general *level* of intellectual competence upon which special talents and skills are superimposed. A person high in one kind of intellectual performance is quite likely to be average or above in others.

It was thought for a time that the generality or specificity of mental abilities was primarily a function of age, but later evidence has made this hypothesis doubtful. McNemar (1942) demonstrated that a large general factor underlay the various problems and materials in the 1937 Stanford-Binet test for children, but L. V. Jones (1949) showed that the correlations could be accounted for just as well in terms of several primary abilities. (Both were probably right. An analysis in terms of second-order factors would probably have given evidence for a general factor as well as for the separate ones.) The Thurstones (1941) stated that factors were more highly correlated with one another in the eighth grade than in the college group. Garrett (1938, 1946), reanalyzing two previous studies, found higher correlations between factors for younger than for older children. Studies by Garrett, Bryan, and Perl (1935) and by Asch (1936) seemed to support this conclusion. However, later studies by Curtis (1949), by Chen and Chow (1948), and by Doppelt (1950) indicated that age was not the variable that determined how important the general factor was. The Curtis study pointed to something else instead. Here a representative group of nine-year-old boys and a similar group of twelve-year-old boys were given ten tests designed to measure N, S, and V as well as "g," in two different *difficulty* levels. Holzinger's factor-analysis method which takes out a "g" factor before analyzing group factors made it possible to compare "g" loadings directly in the two age groups and at the two levels of difficulty. The age groups did not differ with regard to the "g" component in their scores, but the difficulty levels did. The easy form produced a larger general factor than the difficult form did.

This difference in the difficulty of tests used in different age groups, something that was not controlled in the earlier studies, probably accounts for some of the difference in the generality or specificity of traits which was at first thought to arise from age differences. Another possible variation is *selection* in the groups tested. The fact that college populations are much more highly selected on an intellectual basis than grade-school or high-school groups are would tend to produce lower correlations between different intellectual abilities and thus suggest less generality. This conclusion fits in with facts summarized by Anastasi (1948) showing that in the Army group of young adults, similar in age but not in selection to Thurstone's college population, substantial correlations between traits were the rule rather than the exception.

Because of the potential usefulness of differentiated tests in guidance and educational planning there has been considerable research interest in the questions: *How early* can a pattern of differentiated mental abilities be identified in young children and *how stable* are such patterns during childhood and adolescence? As mentioned above, the Thurstones discovered patterned abilities in five-year-olds. The most comprehensive and careful work on this problem, however, is the study by Meyers, Orpet, Atwell, and Dingman (1962). Their subjects were a group of 100 normal children who were tested individually within three months of their sixth birthday, and a group of hospitalized retarded patients whose average mental age was about six. Tests were carefully chosen to represent all of the domains in which previous research had suggested that special abilities might lie (Meyers and Dingman, 1960). The same factors showed up in both the normal and the retarded group: (1) Hand-Eye Psychomotor Ability; (2) Perceptual Speed; (3) Linguistic Ability; (4) Reasoning (Spatial). Digit Span showed up as an additional separate factor represented by a single test. This structure is very similar to that found by T. G. Thurstone in kindergartners in 1941.

Before we can base different treatments or educational plans on this evidence that young children differ in their *patterns* of mental abilities as well as in their general intellectual level, we need additional kinds of evidence. One important question is: How stable or lasting are such patterns? A study by L. E. Tyler (1958) indicated that the separate primary mental ability scores of fourth-graders could be predicted no more accurately from the corresponding scores they had made three years earlier than from the general, over-all scores they had made as first-graders. Individual patterns of high and low scores did not retain their shape over this period. When their eighth-grade PMA scores were compared with their fourth-grade scores, however, (Tyler, 1958) more constancy of pattern was indicated, at least for factors V, N, and S. In a later study, Meyer (1960) made the same kind of comparisons for a group who had taken the PMA tests in the eighth grade and again at the end of the eleventh grade. Over this age range there was even more of a tendency for patterns of high and low abilities to persist. The general conclusion is that patterns of special ability become more consistent over time during the years of development.

There is considerable doubt, however, as to whether these patterns are consistent *enough* so that important life decisions should be based on them. The three-year longitudinal study by Doppelt and Bennett (1951), using the Differential Aptitude Tests, and the similar study by Meyer and Bendig (1961) using the Primary Mental Abilities Test, indicate that the stability coefficients for *differences* between subtest scores are rather low. In the Doppelt and Bennett study, these ranged from .20 (Numerical Ability minus Space Relations) to .74 (Mechanical Reasoning minus Spelling). In the Meyer and Bendig study they ranged from .14 (V-S) to .42 (V-R). What such results mean in practical terms is that if we encourage a ninth-grader to make educational and career plans based on the assumption that he has less talent for verbal than for spatial reasoning (and suggest, for example, that architecture would suit him better than law as a profession) there is only a very low probability that his test results three years later will support this conclusion.

There is another reason for caution in the use of these tests based on factor analysis. Separate scores often do not seem to correlate highly with the school criteria we would expect them to predict. Shaw (1949), for example, using as his subjects 591 high-school students, shows that only V (verbal) of the Primary Mental Abilities battery produced consistently high correlations with school grades in most courses. There were in addition some moderately high correlations with R (reasoning) and a few that were significant with N (number). The other special scores did not correlate with grades in any course. It is to be noted that even the coefficients that showed a significant relationship were not always in the subject areas where we would expect them. "N," for example, correlated to the extent of .43 with writing correctness, .19 with science, and .32 with quantitative thinking. We must not jump to conclusions about what an individual is best at from his factor scores.

What is needed most is more research relating factors to various criteria. Eysenck (1952) has worked out a method for doing this. Since most of his work has been on attitude and personality variables rather than intelligence, it will be discussed in a later chapter. Michael (1949) reported an important study of Army Air Force tests given to two groups of fliers, 815 West Point Cadets, and 356 Negro cadets of much lower socioeconomic background. He included the pass-fail criterion among the variables to be factor-analyzed. By doing this he was able to discover that even though most of the factors were the same for the two groups, their relationship to flying success was quite different. For the West Point group, success was most closely connected with pilot interest, spatial ability, and psychomotor coordination. For the Negro group it was connected with kinesthesis, perceptual speed, and spatial ability. It was apparent that only one of the three factors most closely related to the criterion was common to the two groups. Thus it appears that even if we knew what factors predicted what for a certain kind of people, we still could not be sure that the relationship would hold for another kind.

At this point perhaps we can pull together what all these studies representing both the British and American viewpoints have taught us about the nature of what we loosely call intelligence. The type of theory fitting all the facts best is a hierarchical system similar to the one Vernon proposes. Intelligence is *both* one thing and many things. When we attempt to measure its general component we always leave some portion of the intellectual performance of our subjects unaccounted for. When we attempt to measure narrower abilities separately—verbal, spatial, perceptual

—we always find that something they have in common makes scores on the separate traits correlate positively with one another. To describe an individual's mentality accurately we need to specify both *level* and *pattern*.

Authorities do not agree completely on the reasons for this hierarchical structure. P. E. Vernon (1950) attributes the partial breakdown of general intelligence into more specialized things to the influence of education. Because verbal and numerical abstract materials constitute most of the school curriculum, the specialized cluster of mental traits he calls "v:ed" develops. Children who take well to school work become high in the cluster as a whole; those who are less influenced by school rank lower. (The standard individual and group intelligence tests which have been used most in this country measure a mixture of "g" and "v:ed" and thus correlate well with school criteria, as the previous section has shown.)

Burt (1949) explains the hierarchy of abilities in a somewhat different way. To him the place of any kind of ability in the hierarchy depends upon its simplicity or complexity. Simple sensory processes, at one extreme, are almost completely specific. (An individual with unusually keen vision shows no tendency to excel in hearing, tasting, or smelling.) Work of persons like tea-tasters, for example, reminds us that there are highly specialized sensitivities and skills bearing little if any relationship to one another. Perceptual and motor processes produce factors of a little broader scope, such as perceptual speed and steadiness. The comprehension of relationships or "noegenesis," the process represented by "g," is at the other extreme from the sensory processes with regard to complexity, and it is a unitary trait that can be measured as a whole in each individual. Such a view does fit in well with what we have found to be true in life situations. If we wish to select workers for some highly specialized assembly-line task, we find it necessary to measure specific dexterity at certain kinds of arm and hand movements. If we wish to select college students who will do superior work in any field, a general intelligence test will serve about as well as a specialized test in one field alone.

One aspect of this hierarchical theory of intelligence has a bearing on a variety of problems in differential psychology—race differences, social class differences, and intelligence trends from generation to generation, for example. Much work that was done *before* we developed this theory now needs to be rethought in terms of it. As we have seen, it appears that there is a general intellectual ability in which individuals differ, but it also appears that we are never able to measure it in its pure state by means of any single test. As we encounter "g" in the individual, it is always combined with some of the "primary" and "specific" abilities, abilities which seem to be based in part on schooling and incidental learning. This fact makes group differences on test scores (or IQ's based on them) difficult to interpret. Is it "g" in which the groups differ or is it one of these other things? We shall consider the detailed evidence on this point in later chapters. Here we simply point out the existence of the problem.

Where group-difference studies have a bearing on the nature-nurture problem, it is especially important that we consider carefully what our results really show. P. E. Vernon (1951) speaks for a considerable number of psychologists when he advocates that we stop trying to use intelligence tests for research in eugenics. The fact that "g" is inextricably bound up with other factors makes comparisons of scores for families of different sizes or children from different regions ambiguous. He has concluded that we cannot hope to use our present tests to tell us whether one *group* is more intelligent than another. R. B. Cattell (1944) represents another point of view. He has attempted to develop a culture-free intelligence test which by being equally fair to all groups tested will control the "non-g" factors. His way of doing this has been to construct the test out of perceptual materials unfamiliar to all subjects. The available evidence on this test is still insufficient to permit us to be sure that it is in fact equally fair to all groups regardless of cultural background. It seems likely that dealing with perceptual materials of the paper-and-pencil variety requires a response set more easily developed in some cultures than in others. Some consideration of this problem will be included in the chapter on race differences.

SOME THEORETICAL ISSUES

As psychologists developed techniques for measuring intelligence and used intelligence tests for many purposes in many settings, certain questions about intelligence itself arose again and again. What is the *physiological* basis of intellectual differences? Is intelligence a purely cognitive trait or does it include motivational aspects? Is the intelligence we measure at one age essentially the same trait as the intelligence we measure at a later age, or are there distinguishable stages that must be described as differences in kind or *quality* rather than in amount? And finally, what is the relationship of intelligence to logic, as taught in philosophy?

Research attempts to identify the physiological basis of intelligence have not brought definitive answers. One puzzling fact that has stimulated some of this research is that tests of the types we have been considering, the descendents of Binet's first scale, do not indicate in any consistent way the effects of even quite extensive damage to the brain. Since there is general agreement that the brain is the organ upon which intelligent behavior depends, this fact has led some physiologists and psychologists to doubt their adequacy as intelligence measures. A number of investigators have applied themselves directly to the problem of what the effects of brain damage on mental characteristics are.

One of the most influential of these was K. Goldstein. In a monograph by Goldstein and Scheerer (1941) the important distinction between *abstract* and *concrete* behavior was elaborated. This is a difference that shows up in its most marked form on sorting tests or other tests of concept formation. The person who is high in abstract ability is able to think of individual things in categories and is able to shift easily from one system of classification to another. Given a miscellaneous collection of little toy objects to sort, for example, he can place all the cars in one box, all the pieces of furniture in another, all the animals in a third. If asked to sort them in some other way, he may decide to place all wooden objects in one pile and all metal ones in another, or he may classify them on the basis of size, color, or some other attribute. In contrast to this, the person who is limited to a highly concrete kind of mental activity may be almost helpless faced with such a task. He may be able to place together the things which he has used at one time, such as a knife and fork or a pencil and paper, or he may be able to put two red objects side by side if their color is almost identical. But he cannot think in categories. The fact that such conceptual thinking does differentiate between unimpaired and brain-damaged persons gives it a sort of *biological* validity. It raises the question, "Could this process of abstraction *be* intelligence?" If we assumed that it is we could develop tests that would measure it more accurately and directly than our present standard tests do. The composite of subtests of which they are now composed includes many items that call for abstraction but many others that do not.

Halstead (1947, 1951) also worked with brain-injured subjects. His findings led him to contrast "biological" with "psychometric" intelligence (the ability measured by our standard tests). He made factor analyses of the correlations between some specifically devised tests in both normal and brain-injured groups. He found evidence for four factors, the first resembling Goldstein and Scheerer's abstract ability:

A. The *ability to categorize* and form concepts of wide generality on some rational basis.
B. *Cerebral power.* This shows up especially in flicker-fusion tests where persons high in the factor can distinguish between a steady and an unsteady light at much higher rates of alternation than can those in whom the ability is low.
C. *Direction or modality.* This has to do with the avenue or special talent through which intelligence is manifested.
D. *Memory* or organized experience of the individual.

Using such a system of thinking about intelligence results in a different kind of description of an individual from the one we would formulate using such factors as Thurstone's. We would have to include an evaluation of (a) his abstract or conceptual ability, (b) the power he can bring to bear on a problem, (c) the directions in which his intellect has been developed, and (d) the reservoirs of knowledge he possesses.

A Swiss psychologist, Meili (1946, reported in Myers, 1947), found factors of this sort in an analysis of the performance of well-educated adults and children. He interpreted these not as special abilities but rather as separate *aspects* of intelligence. They can all be expected to appear in every intellectual performance, but their relative importance varies from one situation to another and from one person to another. The factors are:

1. *Plasticity*—the ability to break up a structure and organize it in a different way.
2. *Complexity*—the ability to grasp complex structures clearly and precisely.
3. *Fluency*—the ability to pass rapidly from one idea to another.
4. *Globalization*—the ability to bring separate ideas into a single whole.

In a later paper, Meili (1949) argued against the naming of factors obtained from factor analysis on the basis of the apparent composition of the tests in which they appear. He holds that an analysis of the type of mental process involved is a sounder basis for identification. Goldstein's and Halstead's work would suggest that perhaps differences in these *processes* will show a closer relationship to neurological differences than differences in level and pattern of abilities have shown.

The most systematic attempt to develop a physiological theory of intelligence is that of Krech and his associates at the University of California. Livson and Krech (1956) presented a set of postulates constituting the basic framework for such a theory. The basic unit of analysis is the *dynamic system,* which may combine with other dynamic systems into a higher order organization. How much of such combination will occur depends upon the degree of *cortical conductivity.* The more complex the organization, the higher the person's intelligence. Thus the neurological substrate of intelligence is assumed to be this cortical conductivity, rather than any structural characteristic of the brain. From their theory it was possible to make predictions as to the correlation to be expected between the perception of designs of different degrees of complexity and tested intelligence. Livson and Krech in this paper reported a correlation of —.54 between the number of errors made in the design test and Wechsler vocabulary score for 22 college students, age eighteen to forty-two. The significant correlation confirmed their hypothesis. While there has been some contradictory evidence from other studies (DeSoto and Leibowitz, 1956; Pickrel, 1957) most of the other studies based on the Krech hypotheses have supported them. (Krech and Calvin, 1953; Calvin, and others, 1958.) Perhaps the main question now is whether other sorts of theoretical formulation would lead to the same predictions. The idea that differences in cortical conductivity constitute the physical basis of intelligence is plausible, but more evidence is needed. Another kind of evidence that Krech and his associates have obtained in animal studies will be reported in Chapter 16.

Some evidence bearing on two of the questions stated above—"Are there qualitative differences between developmental stages?" and "Are there motivational components in what we measure as intelligence?"—was contributed by Hofstaetter's (1954) factor analysis of the scores obtained on the same test at different times by the subjects in the California developmental study. The results give rather clear-cut evidence for three factors characterizing different *periods* during early life. Number one, with heavy loadings on tests given during infancy, he called sensori-motor alertness. Number two, with its heavy loadings on tests given in the preschool years, he called persistence or rigidity. Number three, with heavy loadings on tests given during the school years, might be called "g." Thus it would seem that the trait measured by "intelligence" tests may gradually shift over from one sort of thing in very young children to a quite different sort of thing in school-age boys and girls. Motivational aspects of intelligence are most likely to determine children's scores at the preschool ages. Wechsler (1950b) has always maintained that intelligence is a manifestation of the personality as a whole and that emotional and motivational characteristics are among the ingredients out of which it is made.

By far the most comprehensive body of research dealing with stages in intellectual development and linking children's intelligence to adult logic is the work of Piaget. (See Piaget, 1947, for a brief discussion of the theory.) His method is to make careful observations of the kind of adaptive behavior young children spontaneously engage in, and then to devise experiments that enable him to analyze the mental processes they use. The two basic processes are *assimilation,* the incorporation of new experience into an existing "schema" or pattern, and *accommodation,* the modification of existing schemata in response to the impact of the environment. These are present from the beginning. At the earliest stage, however, when the baby turns his head toward the nipple, thus demonstrating the existence of a simple schema, Piaget would not call his mental process intelligence. It is only when the child achieves the power of detaching himself from the pattern and thinking about it from different points of view that genuine intelligence can be said to be operating.

In his book *Intelligence and Experience,* Hunt (1961) analyzes Piaget's thinking and research in detail, showing how they link up with concepts based on research of other sorts, such as Hebb's emphasis on early perceptual learning (Hebb, 1949), Harlow's concept of learning sets (Harlow, 1949) and the more recent concept of cognitive activity as systems for information processing (Newell, Shaw, and Simon, 1958). It would appear that the foundation has been laid for a sound, coherent theory of the development of intelligence. If it becomes an established structure, it will require measuring techniques somewhat different from those we have used heretofore, tests that will show *at what stage* of intellectual development an individual is operating rather than *how much* of some hypothetical trait he possesses. Only a beginning has been made in this direction.

SUMMARY

Over the period of years since Binet published the first scale, research on intelligence measurement has led to increasingly clear concepts about the trait itself. Developmental studies have shown that growth curves differ from person to person. Except for infant tests, correlations between scores at different stages of development are positive, and during the school years, fairly high. Some children, as they get older, however, show sizable gains or losses. Gains are associated with family educational background, and with active, independent personality characteristics.

Predictive validity studies have shown that at all levels intelligence test scores are significantly correlated with school success. Occupational level is another criterion intelligence test scores can be used to predict. They do not constitute good predictors of the speed or efficiency with which any kind of material can be learned but rather of the complexity or difficulty of the material a learner can handle.

Factor analytic studies have shown that intelligence is neither pure "g" nor a combination of completely independent special abilities. Both level and pattern of abilities must be assessed for a complete picture. The number of separate "primary" mental abilities is much larger than it was once thought to be.

Some progress has been made in work on theoretical problems related to the physiological bases of intellectual differences, the nature of the different qualitative stages that occur during intellectual development, and the relationship of cognitive to motivational aspects of intellect.

CHAPTER 5

Individual Differences in School Achievement

IT HAS BEEN in our schools more than in any other one place that individual differences have come forcefully to our attention. There they raise many questions and create many problems. They complicate the teacher's task and challenge her skills in ways that go far beyond the making of assignments and grading of papers. They make it possible for newspaper reporters to come up with "shocking" exposures of ignorance in students who have spent many years in our public schools. They create difficulties for curriculum planners, forcing them to recognize that however sound the objectives for any one age or grade level may be, some pupils will achieve them and others will not. Perhaps their greatest importance lies in the fact that as each person during his own schooldays comes up against the realities of individual differences, he develops feelings of pride or inferiority, anxiety or defensiveness, which he will carry the rest of his life.

THE EXTENT OF THE DIFFERENCES

Teachers and students alike have always been aware that differences exist, but it is only since the development of standardized achievement tests that we have realized how great they are. These achievement tests constitute a development and refinement of the traditional examinations on school subject matter. For research purposes they have a number of advantages. Their content in a particular area is based upon a wide sampling of material that a number of well-qualified teachers agree should be included rather than upon any one person's judgment. Their form is objective and definite so that the student can understand the questions and the scorer can mark the answers right or wrong without ambiguity. Their norms are as representative as possible of all students of the age or grade level for which the test is intended.

One of the commonest ways for publishers to provide this normative information is to give the score on the test that corresponds to the *average* score for each grade. Then each individual's score can be interpreted in terms of the grade placement to which it corresponds. If William makes an arithmetic score of 6–3 in this notation, it means that he knows as much about this subject as the average child who has finished three months in the sixth grade.

Such grade-norm scores make us aware of the tremendous differences between children in any one grade or class. Hildreth (1950) summarized some of these results. In one group of seven-year-olds scores ranged from the first- to the sixth-grade level. For a group of ten-year-olds the range was from the first- to the ninth-grade level. In one study using age norms rather than grade norms the range of educational ages in a group of children all of whom had spent three and a half years in school was from six to fifteen. In other words, the lowest in the group knew no more than the average child just beginning school, whereas the highest was already at the level of high-school students.

Tables 3, 4, and 5 give some figures taken from the norm tables furnished with two tests in common use, the Metropolitan Achievement Tests and the Iowa Every-Pupil Battery. Both tests were standardized on several thousand children fairly typical of the school population. In addition to the sort of information cited in the previous paragraph about the extremes of school accomplishment in any one grade, these tables show how wide the "middle half" is, the group between the 25th and the 75th percentiles which we would probably consider average for each grade. Table 3 shows that for English achievement at the eighth-grade level the distance from the 25th to the 75th percentile represents almost a three-year range. Table 4 shows that for reading comprehension this middle-half distance is one and one-half years for the third-graders, two and one-half for the fifth-graders. In general, the higher up the educational ladder we go, the greater this spread becomes, at least until we reach the level at which compulsory school laws no longer apply and selection cuts off the bottom portion of the distribution. This increase at the higher levels is shown in Table 5 for arithmetic. The middle-half range is about a year for fifth-graders, over two years for ninth-graders. Similarly, the distance from the 10th to the 90th percentiles is less than two years for fifth-graders but more than three and one-half years for ninth-graders.

Figure 19 represents some similar data at the college freshman level. Even though some unofficial selection has occurred because students very low in verbal skills ordinarily do not apply for admission to college, there is still a vast difference in facility with written language among those who have entered. We can appreciate just what this means in practical terms

TABLE 3

Selected Percentile Norms for Metropolitan Achievement Test in English Usage, Grade 8

(Hildreth, Bixler, *et al.*, 1948)

PERCENTILE	SCORE	GRADE EQUIVALENT
98	258	Above 11
90	244	11.4
75	233	9.6
50	222	8.2
25	209	6.9
10	197	5.9
2	179	4.8

TABLE 4

Selected Percentile Norms for Iowa Every-Pupil Test of Silent Reading Comprehension

(Spitzer *et al.*, 1947)

3rd Grade		*5th Grade*	
PERCENTILE	GRADE EQUIVALENT	PERCENTILE	GRADE EQUIVALENT
99	8-2	99	9-8
90	6-0	90	8-4
75	4-9	75	7-2
50	3-9	50	5-9
25	3-3	25	4-8
10	2-6	10	4-0
1	1-9	1	2-9

TABLE 5

Selected Percentile Norms for Iowa Every-Pupil Test of Arithmetic

(Spitzer *et al.*, 1947)

5th Grade		*9th Grade*	
PERCENTILE	GRADE EQUIVALENT	PERCENTILE	GRADE EQUIVALENT
99	7-2	99	11-6
90	6-5	90	11-0
74	6-2	74	10-6
50	5-9	50	9-9
25	5-3	25	8-4
10	4-9	10	7-5
1	4-2	1	6-5

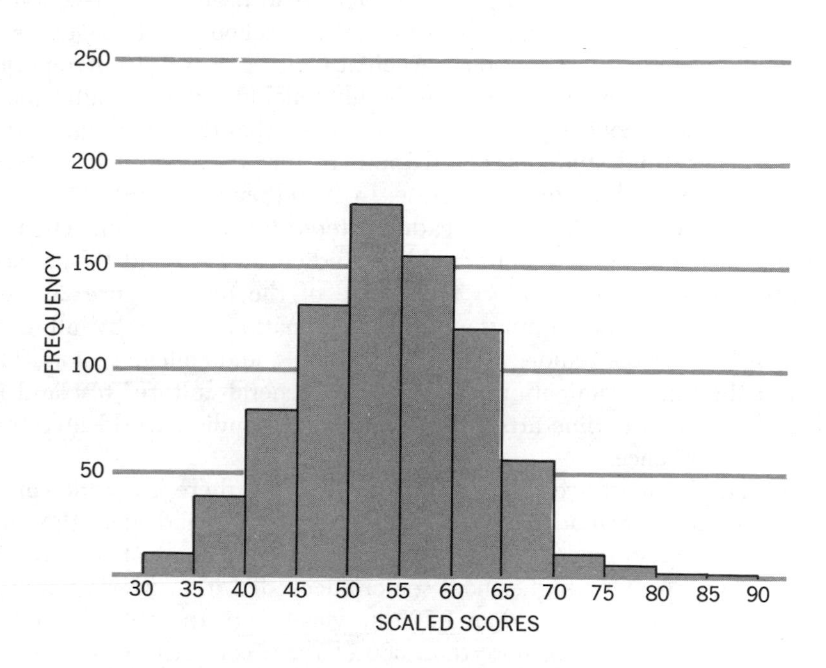

FIGURE 19

Distribution of Scores on Cooperative English Test (Effectiveness of Expression) for 795 University of Oregon Entering Freshmen

when we realize that a scaled score of 50 represents the performance of the average high-school graduate who has had an average amount of training in the subject and that the standard deviation of this scaled-score distribution for average high-school students is set at 10. Thus a score of 34, which would be found in the lowest interval shown on Figure 19, is almost two standard deviations below the mean and corresponds to the average for the seventh grade, according to the norms furnished by Cooperative Test Service. On the other hand a scaled score of 80, near the top of the Oregon freshman distribution, is three standard deviations above the mean and corresponds to a percentile rank of 97 on the norms for college graduates.

These are samples of the sort of variability in school accomplishment, we must stress, that are the *rule*, not the exception, in schools where the problem has been investigated. One of the most exhaustive and thorough of such investigations was a study carried on in Pennsylvania colleges and high schools from 1928 to 1932 and reported in detail in the monograph by Learned and Wood (1938). The purpose of their undertaking was to evaluate the educational system of the state in terms of what students who came through it actually knew. Their examinations were carefully designed and questions were organized under broad headings representative of the objectives of general education in any school—such headings as "Tools of Scientific Investigation," "Ancient Cultures," and "Contemporary Western Civilization." The tests were highly reliable and gave high enough correlations with college grades to make it clear that they were measuring what teachers think students should know. In 1928 they were administered to college seniors throughout the state. In 1930 they were given to college sophomores. In 1932 they were readministered to the same subjects, now seniors in college, so that gains could be studied. In 1933 and 1934 a large number of high-school seniors took some of the tests. Figure 20 summarizes some of the findings on the examinations taken by all three groups—high-school seniors, college sophomores, and college seniors. This part of the total examination was called a "general culture" test and included questions on fine arts, history and social studies, world literature, and natural science.

This graph shows two things very plainly. First, there is a wide spread of scores within each of these groups of students who had spent the same amount of time in school. Second, there is a large amount of overlapping *between* groups. One high-school senior succeeded in answering only 25 questions out of the more than 1,200 he was asked. In contrast, another twelfth-grader answered more than 600 of them correctly. In the sophomore group scores ranged from 25 to 755 points, in the senior group from 45 to 805. It is perhaps a little unfair to judge variability from the exceptional cases at the extremes of the distributions, but even if we look at the middle half of each, the spread within each group is still considerably greater than the average differences between them. There *is* an average difference, obviously. In general we can say that the median for each of the higher groups falls at about the 75th percentile of the group below it. But this means that roughly a quarter of the lower group of students is made up of persons who already know more than the average person with two years more of schooling. As many as 10 per cent of the high-school seniors are above the college senior average.

Learned and Wood analyzed the variability in a number of ways. There were large differences between colleges and between majors within the same college. In general, engineering students averaged highest, candidates for Bachelor of Arts and Bachelor of Science degrees in liberal arts colleges only slightly lower, and business and education students considerably lower. Nondegree students in teachers' colleges stood at the bottom of the list with an average score *below* the average for high-school seniors. These findings were not uniform for all colleges within each classification, however. Engineering schools and liberal arts colleges differed considerably from one another. In one liberal arts college, 85 per cent of the sophomores were above the statewide mean for college seniors; in another, 75 per cent of the sophomores were below the statewide sophomore aver-

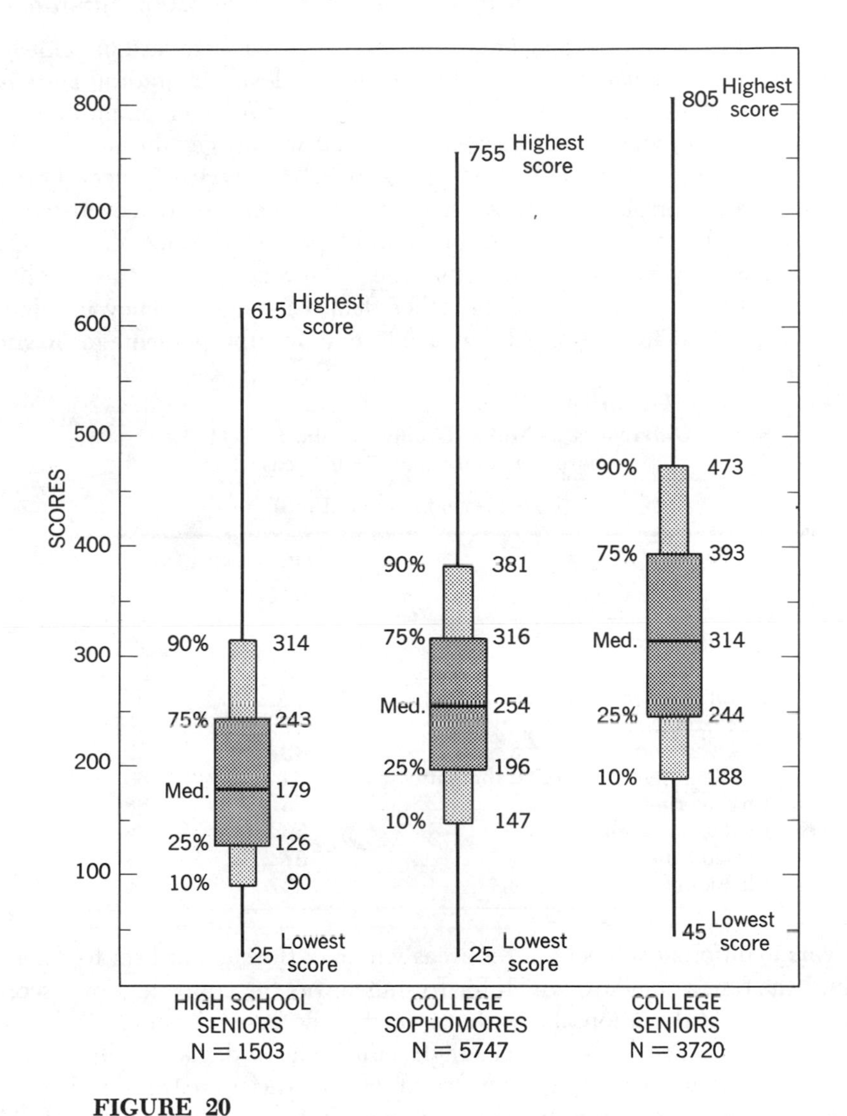

FIGURE 20

Distribution of Scores on a General Culture Test for Pennsylvania Students in Three Groups—High-school Seniors, College Sophomores, and College Seniors

(Learned and Wood, 1938, p. 18)

age. The inescapable conclusion is that there is no one standard of achievement that is "normal" for a certain educational level. If grading systems and course standards assume that there is, they are founded on an illusion.

The testing program which was conducted in colleges throughout the country during 1951 and 1952 using the Selective Service College Qualification Test corroborated these findings about the differences between colleges and between major groups almost perfectly. Since the SSCQT was an intelligence test rather than an achievement test, this parallel suggests that it is student ability rather than teaching efficiency in which the groups and institutions differ. Table 6 shows the percentage of students in different subject-matter areas who met the standard set for "passing" the test, a standard which for freshmen was the equivalent of a score one standard deviation above the mean for the general population. It is clear that science students were high, education students low. In a summary by Chauncey (1952), the extent of the variation from college to college was made clear. In some colleges as few as 35 per cent of the students taking the test received a passing grade; in others the per-cent passing was as high as 98. Thus the students in the lower half of their classes in some institutions, so far as grades are concerned, are actually more capable than the students in the upper half of their classes in other institutions.

TABLE 6
Differences in Major Groups on the SSCQT Test
(based on more than 74,000 cases)

(ETS Developments, 1953)

MAJOR	PER CENT PASSING 1951	PER CENT PASSING 1952
General Arts	48	49
Humanities	52	54
Social Sciences	57	55
Education	27	30
Business and Commerce	42	35
Physical Science and Mathematics	64	69
Engineering	68	68
Biological Sciences	59	62
Agriculture	37	44
All Fields	53	54

To return to some of the other findings of the Learned and Wood study: one was that within any single school or class, the youngest students averaged highest, the oldest lowest. (Selection and promotion policies during the 1920's had something to do with this, since it was customary for brighter students to progress faster and reach any given level at an earlier age than duller students did. Under a policy that discourages the "skipping" of grades the results might not be so striking.) The authors of the monograph illustrated their point about the lack of relationship between the time spent in school and the amount of knowledge gained by analyzing what the composition of a college graduating class would have been if individuals had been awarded diplomas on the basis of tested knowledge rather than hours and credits. Assuming that the top fifth of the student body was ready for graduation, Learned and Wood showed that this group would have consisted of 28 per cent of the senior class, 21 per cent of the juniors, 19 per cent of the sophomores, and 15 per cent of the freshmen. The mean age of this group would have been 20.6, nearly two years lower than that of the seniors. In place of the 3½ per cent who graduated before they were twenty-one under the traditional system, 52 per cent of the group graduated on the basis of knowledge would have been below this age.

Having the college seniors retake the examination they had taken as sophomores made it possible for the investigators to examine *gains* as well as ultimate attainments. Great variability showed up here also. Some individuals gained more than others; some colleges increased their average score more than did others; some subject-matter areas showed more increase than others. However, correlations between scores obtained on the two occasions were consistently high. Although there were some shifts in the positions of individual students in the distributions, they were not large or numerous. For the total score on the test, the correlation over the two-year period was .90. The lowest correlation was .70 (fine arts), the highest .92 (grammar and vocabulary). There is an overwhelming probability that a student who is superior as a sophomore will still be superior as a senior.

A survey of the talents and achievements of American youth far more comprehensive than anything previously carried out was initiated in 1960. Project Talent involved the administration of a two-day battery of tests to almost half a million boys and girls, the entire ninth-, tenth-, eleventh-, and twelfth-grade classes in a carefully selected sample of secondary schools, representative of all regions and types of school in the United States. Besides providing information about the total pool of abilities that constitute a country's principal natural resource, Project Talent plans to follow up the subjects one year, five years, ten years, and 20 years after the original testing to investigate relationships between talents and life achievements (Flanagan, et al., 1962). Preliminary reports provide further evidence for many of the generalizations to which the Learned and Wood study pointed. It is clear, for one thing, that differences *within* a grade are far greater than the average differences *between* grades. If we look at the means and standard deviations as they are reported in the tables (Flanagan, et al., 1964) we find that the standard deviations are usually much larger than the differences between the means for successive years. What this tells us about the distributions is that a considerable number of ninth-graders are scoring above the tenth grade average, a considerable number of tenth-graders are scoring above the eleventh-grade average, and so on. In fact the figures suggest that a sizable proportion of ninth-graders score higher than the twelfth-grade average in each area of subject matter knowledge.

Another finding of Project Talent which corroborates the results of previous studies is that the younger students in a grade make the highest scores, the oldest students the lowest. The superiority of the accelerated students and the inferiority of the retarded students are less apparent in reasoning tests than in reading and information tests, however. Sex differences show the pattern that has appeared in numerous other studies. Boys excel in such tests as information about mechanics, electricity, and outdoor sports; girls excel in such tests as home economics information and social sensitivity. Background factors such as father's and mother's education, and the student's plans for future education and career are also related to the scores.

SOURCES OF THE VARIATION IN SCHOOL ACHIEVEMENT

Why do some students have at their command so much more knowledge than others at the end of any specified length of time in school? The need for answers to this question has initiated thousands of research studies and stimulated endless discussion among educators. Yet despite all effort, we can still supply only a partial answer. The best predictions we can make of an individual's probable achievement are of limited accuracy. We have accounted for only about half the variance; the other half still eludes us. The importance of knowing even as much as we do know about the factors and influences affecting school success must not, however, be minimized in a society like ours that places a great deal of emphasis on education.

In the first place, there is abundant evidence for a consistent dependable relationship between school achievement and intelligence. In the previous chapter we have cited this relationship as evidence for the validity of the intelligence tests. It must be admitted that there is some circularity in the reasoning if we now use the same figures to prove that school success depends upon intelligence. This criticism of the whole mental-testing movement was once more cogent than it is now. As we have shown, our understanding of what intelligence tests are measuring no longer rests exclusively on the correlations with school criteria. Other lines of research—growth studies, factor analyses, and observations of abnormal groups—have helped to determine our present views. We know too from school-prediction studies that intelligence tests do not tell the whole story. Intelligence is related to academic achievement but not synonymous with it.

Correlations between the two vary somewhat from study to study but the bulk of them range between .30 and .80. The median would be about .5. This is not pure random variation. High correlations are typically obtained under some circumstances, low ones under others. There is, first of all, the purely statistical factor of selection in the group for which predictions are made. If the variability of the distribution has been curtailed through the elimination of low-scoring individuals, high-scoring individuals, or both, all correlations will run lower than they otherwise would. If this were the only factor affecting them, we would expect intelligence-achievement correlations to be lower for high-school than for grade-school groups, and lower for college than for high-school groups. They would naturally be lower also in colleges practicing rigorous selection than in those admitting all applicants. While there is a tendency for this differentiation to characterize reported correlations, it is not as marked as it might have been had not more highly discriminating tests been developed for the more highly selected groups. We do not use the Stanford-Binet or the Army General Classification Test for predicting college scholarship. Instead we develop difficult intelligence tests expressly for this purpose, tests which make as many accurate discriminations within the selected group as the easier ones did within wide-range groups. In evaluating reports of relationships between intelligence and scholastic achievement, the suitability of the tests used for the particular intellectual level and range of the groups tested must always be taken into consideration.

Another general finding is that intelligence tests are more highly correlated with scores on achievement *tests* than they are with grades given by teachers. We can summarize in a rough way the trends shown in many studies by stating that correlations with grades are usually below .5, those with achievement-test scores above .5. Is this because teachers are not very good judges of school accomplishment and tend to award marks too much on the basis of cooperativeness, agreeableness, and effort, or is it because intelligence measures are not independent enough of learned information and thus have a good deal of common content with achievement tests? Both reasons probably operate. Teachers do judge pupils partly on the basis of characteristics other than mastery of subject matter. Many authorities hold that it is right that they should. On the other hand, scores on verbal intelligence tests are based to some extent on schooling. It is a well-known fact that performance tests give consistently lower correlations with school criteria than verbal tests do.

It is interesting to note, however, that achievement tests based on quite different philosophies with regard to the aims and methods of education correlate about equally well with verbal intelligence. Beginning about 1930 there was a protest among educational psychologists against the current methods for the selection of content used in school examinations, both standardized and informal. This led to important changes in some achievement tests put on the market for wide distribution and use. Instead of being made up of items on disconnected facts, the questions focused on knowledge more closely related to the basic objectives of education, things like the understanding of concepts and the application of principles to new situations. R. W. Tyler (1936) reported that the correlations between scores obtained on these tests and on those of the traditional type were not high (.31 to .58). T. R. McConnell (1940), however, obtained much higher coefficients, averaging .87, between information and application sections of examinations in the same subject-matter areas. Probably no general statement can be made as to how closely related the two types of test are. It would all depend upon methods of teaching and on specific characteristics of the tests. But it seems clear that both types of test do correlate about equally well with intelligence measures. Lorge (1949) summarized the evidence from several studies on this problem.

Although type of achievement test is not a factor producing differences in correlations with intelligence, subject-matter *area* is. Such correlations tend to be highest for reading and English, somewhat lower for science and the social studies, lower still for mathematics, especially geometry, and negligible for music and the arts. Table 7 from the Learned and

TABLE 7

Correlations of Achievement Test Scores in Various Subjects with Scores in the Otis Intelligence Test

(Learned and Wood, 1938, p. 143)

SUBJECT	r
English	.74
Algebra	.68
General Science	.64
Civics	.62
Biology	.52
American History	.50
Physics	.48
French	.46
Plane Geometry	.43
European History	.42
Ancient History	.42
Trigonometry	.34
Chemistry	.33
Latin	.30
German	.28

Wood study (1938) shows these trends for high-school groups in one large city.

One further factor upon which the magnitude of the correlation between intelligence and school achievement seems to depend is the length of the time interval between the obtaining of the two measures. As one might expect, short-range predictions from intelligence-test scores are more efficient than long-range ones. Bailey (1949) reported correlations of from .53 to .80 for random samples of lower-grade students when intelligence and achievement tests were given during the same school year. The figures were lower (.47 and .67) when first-grade intelligence tests were correlated with fourth-grade achievement. (Correlations of the different group tests used with the Binet would suggest that the test giving the .67 coefficient was a better measure of intelligence than the one giving the .47.) There was still a substantial relationship, however, over the three-year period. Travers (1949), summarizing predictions made over still longer intervals, reported correlations of from .21 to .58 between intelligence as measured in the lower schools and *college* scholarship. The .21 was based on the longest time interval, that from first grade to college. Plainly it would be an unsound procedure for lower-grade teachers to make definite predictions about the aptitude of individual children for advanced education.

Along with the interest American psychologists have shown in breaking down general intelligence into a number of more limited mental abilities have come parallel attempts to predict success in specific school subjects on the basis of special abilities. Two types of research can be distinguished here. In one type, an achievement test in one academic field is used as the basis for prediction in the same field—mathematics tests to predict subsequent mathematics grades, social science tests to predict social science grades, or foreign language tests to predict foreign language grades. In the other type, scores on "primary" mental abilities identified through factor analysis are used to predict grades in subject-matter areas one might logically expect to be related to them—V to predict English grades, S to predict geometry grades, N to predict arithmetic grades, for example. So far the first type of research has been the more successful.

Tests of the first variety, the so-called "prognostic" tests of achievement in various subject-matter areas, do seem to produce somewhat higher correlations with grades than intelligence tests do, especially at the college level. They are not, however, outstandingly high, seldom running above .7. (See Travers, 1949, p. 162.) There are many college personnel problems in connection with which the increase in predictive accuracy from the .5 which is about the maximum for intelligence tests to the .7 obtainable from these batteries has real practical value. One study reported by Olander, Van Wagenen, and Bishop (1949) showed that prognostic tests for arithmetic could be developed even at the first-grade level. These tests correlated to the extent of about .5 with achievement in arithmetic three years later. It is doubtful, however, whether this represents a significantly better prediction than could have been made by means of an intelligence test alone. In any case, there seems to have been little interest in predicting success of specific kinds in young school children.

Specialized prognostic achievement batteries are time-consuming and expensive. Many educators have hoped that as the tests based on factor analysis came into common use they would accomplish the same purpose more efficiently and economically. It seemed reasonable to expect that some kinds of school work would be related most closely to verbal ability, others to memory, and others to facility with numbers. As has been explained in the previous chapter, these hopes have not been supported by the correlational findings. Most of the work has been done with the Thurstone Primary Mental Abilities battery at the college level, but what evidence there is from high-school studies corroborates the conclusion. Verbal and Reasoning factors are the only ones giving consistently significant correlations with scholastic achievement, and they correlate about equally well with *everything*.

The most extensive and thorough research program designed to develop tests to predict *differential* achievement in college-major fields has been that of Horst (1957). A battery of these tests is administered each year to high-school graduates in the state of Washington. A report is given to each student showing how successful he is likely to be in several different kinds of college courses. Testing programs of this sort are rare, and there is still considerable doubt among educators as to how useful they are. French (1963) reported a large-scale study of the value of three types of test in differential prediction. Almost 5,000 students, entering freshmen at eight different colleges, were given 16 short tests of "pure" factors of aptitude, 14 short measures of interest in different kinds of subject matter, and 12 short personality scales. The criteria were grades obtained in general courses during the freshman year and grades obtained in the more specialized major courses during the junior and senior years. It proved possible to make differential predictions of success in *unlike* fields, such as physical science and history, but not in similar fields, such as history and English. The interest tests contributed most to these differential predictions, whereas the aptitude tests were better indicators of the general level of achievement. The personality tests contributed very little to either sort of prediction.

While attempts to make differential predictions of student achievement in many different special fields have been scarce and not altogether successful, it is common practice to construct tests of scholastic aptitude that yield separate verbal and quantitative scores. As one examines tables of validity coefficients, one gets the impression that V (verbal) scores have some advantage in predicting achievement in English and social studies, and Q (quantitative) scores have some advantage in predicting achievement in mathematics. But the difference is not very great, and it varies from sample to sample. Table 8, for example, shows some of the results

TABLE 8

Validity Coefficients for SCAT

(from 1958 SCAT-STEP Supplement, Educational Testing Service, Princeton, N.J.)

				COURSE			
Grade	*School*	*N*	*SCAT Score*	*Eng.*	*Math.*	*Sci.*	*Soc. St.*
7	A	53	V	.67	.78	.85	.78
			Q	.64	.86	.72	.67
7	B	86	V	.69	.52	.61	.64
			Q	.64	.69	.59	.62
9	A	54	V	.59	.64	.71	.71
			Q	.63	.82	.70	.73
9	B	293	V	.55	.37	.56	.42
			Q	.52	.52	.55	.44
11	A	75	V	.64	.47	.51	.61
	(Coll. Prep.)		Q	.44	.55	.40	.40
	A	62	V	.41	.01	.38	.48
	(Bus. & Gen.)		Q	.32	.37	.29	.30
11	B	34	V	.32	.25	.16	.25
	(Coll. Prep.)		Q	.51	.49	.18	.24
	B	32	V	.50	—	—	.62
	(Bus.)		Q	.52	—	—	.38

obtained with the School and College Ability Tests. It is clear that both types of scores tend to correlate with all types of school grades. While there is a reasonably high probability that a student with a high Q score will do well in mathematics classes, the probability is almost as high that he will succeed in English and social studies. Science grades are related to both V and Q scores to about the same extent.

One of the best summaries of the possibilities and pitfalls in the use of tests of special abilities in guidance was published by the American Personnel and Guidance Association in 1957. The conclusion one reaches after studying the evidence on the eight test batteries analyzed in this monograph is that any predictions one is tempted to make about the fields of study in which a student is likely to be most successful must be extremely tentative. Individuals are not very specialized in their educational talents, and each academic discipline draws on a number of abilities rather than on a single way of thinking.

While a few of the reported correlations between scholastic aptitudes and school achievement have been as high as .8, most of them range considerly lower than this. A correlation of .5 leaves 75 per cent of the variance unaccounted for, and as we have seen, measuring special abilities does not reduce it very much. British psychologists have attacked the problem of what these differences in school success mean in a somewhat different way from American psychologists. As indicated in the previous chapter, they have preferred to keep their postulated factor structures as simple as possible. The evidence summarized by P. E. Vernon (1950) indicates that a considerable part of the differences between individuals in school achievement can be accounted for in terms of differences in "g." Another part of the variation arises from differences in the "v:ed" factor, which could be characterized as aptitude in "book learning," and which can be measured by tests of vocabulary, arithmetic, spelling, or general information. There is also a third, *non*intellectual factor which Vernon labels X, a complex of personality traits, interests, and background characteristics. Except in groups so selected or specialized that they are high in all three of these main factors determining school achievement, Vernon feels that it is hardly worth while to look for special aptitudes that may have something to do with scholarship in one area alone. Their effects are so small in comparison with the main factors that measuring them can add very little to the accuracy of our judgments. Attempts to identify separate rote memory and reasoning abilities in school tasks or to differentiate various reading skills from one another have not produced convincing evidence that these traits can be broken down into independent abilities. The idea of basing our judgments of students on the best evaluations we can get of "g," "v:ed," and the X-factor is appealing in its simplicity, and it is in accord with the correlational data obtained so far.

PREDICTIVE STUDIES OF MOTIVATIONAL FACTORS

American psychologists who have attempted to predict academic performance in college have tried in various ways to incorporate measures of X, the motivational factor. One of the most obvious indications that it is operating is the fact that with few exceptions, investigators repeatedly find college grade-point averages to be more closely correlated with marks received in high school than with any sort of test scores. In Garrett's summary (1949) of a large number of such studies, the median correlation with scholastic aptitude test scores was .47, and the median correlation with high-school grades .56. A weighted combination of the two has turned out to be a consistently better predictor of college grades than either taken separately. Evidently something in addition to scholastic aptitude is represented in the grades students make. Cooperativeness, agreeableness, persistence, and willingness to work could all be involved. Another set of facts pointing in the same direction is the almost universal tendency for girls to get better school marks than boys. No higher in measured intelligence, girls do seem to average somewhat higher than boys in these nonintellectual traits making for success in school.

How much can tests of personality or motivational characteristics improve our prediction of school success? The first attempts to include scores on personality inventories in predictive equations were not encouraging. The summary of such studies in Donahue, et al. (1949, pp. 171–172) showed near-zero correlations between scholarship and every conceivable variety of adjustment inventory at all educational levels. The only relationship that appeared with any consistency at all throughout these studies was a small positive correlation between introversion and grades. Introversion scores on personality inventories usually show *negative* correlations with adjustment scores. Thus if items representing the two kinds of trait are included in the same test, as they often are, the tendency for introversion and scholarship to be *positively* related may counteract any slight tendency there may be for general adjustment and scholarship to be *negatively* related. The only conclusion that is at all important for practical purposes is that any degree of adjustment or maladjustment, as measured in personality inventories, may occur with any degree of success or lack of success in school work.

Interest inventories produced results somewhat more impressive than did adjustment inventories, but reported correlations were still too low to be of much practical consequence. A few such correlations have turned out to be as high as .4 or .5 (Super, 1949, Chs. 17 and 18), but the great majority are in the .30's or lower. It is interesting to note that the highest relationships reported for both the Kuder and the Strong tests are in science fields. This suggests the possibility that interests have more effect upon achievement in some areas than in others. Some workers have been of the opinion that correlational procedures are not the most suitable means for exploring whatever relationship there is between interests and achievement. Interests could be very important in determining whether a person chooses a course of study and persists in it, and still have little to do with the grades he obtains in the course. A certain ambiguity with regard to the meaning of scores obtained on either the Strong or the Kuder blanks also complicates the problem of interpreting correlations obtained with them. Neither of these instruments measures the *intensity* of the person's interest in a kind of activity and this may be the very factor upon which school achievement depends.

After projective tests came into common use for the evaluation of personality characteristics numerous attempts were made to relate their findings to school achievement. One of the most successful of these was the study reported by Munroe (1945). Using a check list to register the number of indicators of maladjustment each Rorschach record showed she obtained a correlation of .49 between adjustment scores and college grades. Since the adjustment scores were correlated to only a negligible extent with intelligence-test scores, they enabled the advisers responsible for helping individual students to make a considerably better judgment about each person's prospects for college success than could have been made from the ability test alone. Cronbach (1950) in another college did not get a correlation of this magnitude between Rorschach adjustment levels and grades. In this instance adding Rorschach scores to intelligence scores raised the overall correlation from .45 to only .49. Such an increase in predictive power is not enough to justify the use of the personality test. Why these two studies using similar methods should differ in their results is still an unanswered question, one that calls our attention to the complexity of this field of research and the necessity for caution in generalizing from one group of students to another. Colleges differ in their educational goals and in the bases upon which grades are given. Students are selected differently by different institutions and have different attitudes toward their school tasks. All these things are likely to affect the correlation between grades and personality factors to a greater extent than the correlation between grades and intelligence.

When instead of working with personality tests designed for other purposes, investigators attempted to develop special inventories of motivational characteristics required for school success or special "achievement" scoring keys for such tests as the Rorschach or MMPI, the results were more promising. The basic technique in such studies is item analysis. The standard procedure is to identify by some means a group of *over*achievers, students who make better academic records than their intelligence test scores taken by themselves, would have predicted, and a group of *under*-achievers, those whose record turns out to be poorer than the predicted one. The responses of the individuals in the two groups to each item of a biographical questionnaire, personality inventory, projective technique, or interest blank can then be tabulated. Items on which difference between the two groups is large enough to be statistically significant can then be combined into a scholarship prediction inventory.

An essential feature of this type of research is the procedure called *cross-validation.* We cannot prove that a test constructed in this way is really a valid instrument unless we try it out on a new group of students whose responses were not used in the development of the special scoring key. The reason for this is that the groups initially selected may differ from one another in a variety of *chance* ways as well as in the fact that one group is made up of better students than the other. Therefore some of the items we select will reflect these chance differences rather than the trait we are attempting to measure. But because they are chance differences they will not characterize new groups composed of different individuals. Thus, the correlation we obtain between test scores and scholarship in a new group shows us the extent to which we have identified real differences between good and poor students in general rather than chance differences between the persons who served as subjects in the initial tryout of the test.

Using such methods, it has been repeatedly demonstrated that a set of items correlating with criteria of school success can be selected, and that some of the relationships stand up under cross-validation. Gough (1949a) developed an achievement scale for the MMPI. It correlated .25 with grades and — .02 with intelligence in a high school group different from the one on which it was derived. Because of the low correlation between these scores and intelligence, the multiple correlation of the two together with the achievement criterion was .68 as compared with the correlation of .62 between grades and intelligence alone.

Still better results have been obtained by selecting items from an item pool made up especially for the purpose instead of using items from a standard instrument designed for other purposes, such as the MMPI. Borow (1945) worked out a set of items giving a correlation of .30 with college grades in a cross-validation sample. Gough (1953) located a set of sixty-four items that correlated more than .5 with scholarship. While these scores are also related to some extent to IQ (about .3) they add enough new information about students so that prediction of grades is significantly improved by their use. Even more striking success with the identification of motivational factors related to grades obtained in college was reported by Holtzman and Brown (1953). Their inventory correlated .57 with scholarship in a group of men and .56 in a group of women. Using it along with scores on the ACE test produced multiple *r*'s of .63 for women and .73 for men in the cross-validation sample.

Over the years Gough has continued his search for valid predictors of good school achievement. After the publication of the California Psychological Inventory (Gough, 1957) he used items and scales from this instrument in several large-scale research studies. Evidence has accumulated that for students of many levels of scholastic ability and at various educational levels ranging from junior high school to the upper years of college it is possible to obtain cross-validated correlations of .50 or higher between academic achievement and relevant personality variables. What these consistent results tell us about which personal qualities are relevant is summarized by Gough and Fink (1964) as follows:

> Three themes would appear to be discernible. One has to do with the internalization of value and sensitivity to issues involving precept and code. A second has to do with achievement motivation in its form-manifesting and

> form-enhancing variants. The third would seem to involve a preference for order and stability . . . but with freedom from undue conventionality and deference. . . The pattern is one of positive personal effectiveness coupled with diligence, perseverance, and restraint. It is not a pattern of creativity or innovation, but rather that of constructive adaptation to a world in which one's circumstances are modest and one's destiny limited.

This description is not greatly different from those which teachers give of their good students. The research studies corroborate our convictions that these qualities of character and personality are important, but so far they tell us nothing about the sources of such qualities or the methods that will develop them. If we wish simply to predict who will succeed, it is useful to have this information. But if we wish to change conditions and introduce methods that will improve scholarship, we need to know more.

Other kinds of items besides those pertaining to personality characteristics and motivation have come in for some study. R. C. Myers (1952) and Anastasi et al. (1960) used biographical information. Neidt and Merrill (1951) obtained a correlation of .36 between favorable attitudes toward education and scholarship. Havighurst and Taba (1949) and Hieronymus (1951) analyzed the aspects of social status that work for and against school success. It is middle-class children who characteristically show the highest motivation in school and the most anxiety about school achievement. Hieronymus showed also that, at least for boys, *expectation*—or whatever complex of attitudes makes for upward mobility—is more closely related to achievement-test scores than is present status. We shall consider some of these problems arising from social class differences in more detail in a later chapter.

For one particular group, college students of very high scholastic ability, a comprehensive research program under the auspices of the National Merit Scholarship organization has produced some definitive answers to questions about the relationship of motivation to high achievement. Holland and Nichols (1964) reported a comprehensive study designed to test all the hypotheses suggested by a long series of previous studies. Besides using grades in college courses as criteria, they developed six achievement scales for such main areas as science, writing, and leadership, using such items as "Received a research grant" and "Won one or more debate contests." Out of a large number of correlations between these criteria and the motivational measures developed in previous studies, they selected the most promising predictors, constructed regression equations, and cross-validated them on a separate sample. One outstanding feature of this research undertaking was the large number of cases in each sample. The predictive sample was made up of 1,000 cases and the cross-validation sample of 437.

The results were a little surprising in their simplicity. Two kinds of predictors clearly surpassed all the rest. First, actual achievement of a particular kind in high school predicted achievement of the same kind in college. For example, science achievements leading to special recognition in high school predicted science achievement in college. The second predictor consisted of measures of interests, self-conceptions, and goals. The investigators constructed a special-interest test they labeled *potential achievement,* consisting of the items about activities, preferences, reading habits, etc. that distinguished between high and low achievers in each of the six special areas at the high-school level. This was one of the best predictors at the college level also. In this group where all the members were unusually intelligent, individual differences in scholastic ability turned out not to be predictive of differences in achievement.

A conclusion suggested by this research and compatible with all the previous work in this and other settings is that the differences in motivation leading to differences in school achievement are not those that personality theorists, with their background in the clinic and the hospital, tend to think of first. They are not differences in basic drives but in *learned habits of work.* They are not differences in the degree to which negative qualities like anxiety and neurotic traits are present but rather the degree to which strong and well organized positive qualities such as interests, commitment, or enthusiasm about some line of endeavor characterize an individual. Translating somewhat crudely into Freudian terms, it is the nature of the *ego,* not the *id* that makes the difference between high and low school achievement.

SOURCES OF UNDERACHIEVEMENT

With the resurgence of public interest in education that occurred during the 1950's, research on the problem of achievement differences took on a somewhat different character. The emphasis shifted from questions related to prediction and selection to questions related to diagnosis and treatment. Why do many students, often those who score at the upper levels of our intelligence scales, fail in school? Why do others accumulate distinguished scholastic records, even though they appear to have only average scholastic aptitude?

A typical design for research on these questions is to select from some school population two groups of students differing in the nature of the relationship of their achievement to their measured intelligence. In addition to these groups of underachievers and overachievers, some investigators include also a group of normal achievers, those whose school record is about what one would expect from their intelligence scores. Many kinds of test and interview techniques are then employed in a search for the personality or situational factors involved in deviant achievement.

This kind of research design has many weaknesses, as R. L. Thorndike (1963) has pointed out. Can we assume that the "overachiever" differs from the "underachiever" quantitatively on all the factors we measure, or may there not be qualitative differences that do not show up when we analyze personality variables in this way? Can we assume that the relationship between each measured personality variable and school achievement is *linear* so that the higher the score on the one, the higher we would expect it to be on the other? Can we assume that if we compare our groups on one hundred personality variables and ten of the differences turn out to be significant at the .05 level that this small yield represents real and not chance difference? One would expect five out of a hundred differences to appear significant by chance alone.

In addition to these and other matters Thorndike discusses, there is a further consideration to which too little attention has so far been given. Some researchers working on the problem of underachievement have used the grades or marks given by teachers as their criterion while others have used the scores on standardized achievement tests. These are related but by no means identical variables. They should be differentiated. It is quite possible for a student failing all of his college courses to get high scores on a test of actual knowledge in the areas that these courses covered. It would seem highly doubtful whether such a student should be labeled an "underachiever." He may be a "self-educator," one who obtains his knowledge through reading and independent thinking rather than by carrying out assignments.

With all these limitations, the many studies of this sort have produced a considerable fund of information about the characteristics of high- and low-achieving students, information that is suggestive if not conclusive. Much of it has been summarized by R. G. Taylor (1964). Seven varieties of trait have repeatedly shown up in these studies. Table 9, taken from

TABLE 9

Hypothesized Personality Traits Related to High and Low Achievement

(from Taylor, 1964)

DIRECTION *Low Achiever*	*Trait*	DIRECTION *High Achiever*
Free-floating	Academic Anxiety	Directed
Negative	Self-value	Positive
Hostility toward Authority	Authority Relations	Acceptance of Authority
Negative	Interpersonal Relations	Positive
High Conflict	Independence-Dependence Conflict	Low Conflict
Socially Oriented	Activity Patterns	Academically Oriented
Unrealistic	Goal Orientations	Realistic

Taylor's summary, shows what they are. Not all investigations support all these hypotheses, but the great majority of them point in these directions.

Another source of hypotheses about low and high achievers has been Rotter's social learning theory (Rotter, 1954). The aspect of this theory most pertinent to this topic is the way it ties motivation to needs, goals, and expectations. Following this lead, we might expect underachievement to develop from *needs* of a character that are not satisfied by school success, *goals* that are unsuitable or unclear, or simply the *expectation* that one is not likely to succeed in school—perhaps from a combination of these conditions. Starting with hypotheses based on this line of reasoning, Uhlinger and Stephens (1960), studying high ability students at a midwestern university, found that the high and low achievers were not differentiated by the strength of their needs for recognition and affection, but that the high achievers did have a greater expectancy of success and higher goals so far as grades were concerned. These trends were much clearer for boys than for girls. Todd, Terrell, and Frank (1962) also working with high-ability university students, found significant differences supporting all their hypotheses. There were differences in the strength of needs for recognition and affection, in vocational goals, and in the expectation of doing well in school.

Another important aspect of the problem of underachievement in school is suggested by the report of M. C. Shaw and McCuen (1960). Their subjects were public-school students who scored above the 75th percentile on an intelligence test given in the eighth grade. Two groups were compared—persons whose scholastic average in grades 9, 10, and 11 was above the class mean, and those whose average was below the class mean. The records were examined for evidence as to how well these students had done in their *previous* school careers, Grades 1 through 8. In the case of the boys, those classified as low achievers in high school had made poorer records than the other group, even in first grade. There were *significant* differences in the groups from Grade 3 on, increasing year by year. The pattern for the girls was different. Low achievers could not have been distinguished from the high achievers in the first five grades. The low achievers were "low" only from sixth grade on. What this study suggests is that the habits and attitudes producing inadequate achievement begin at an early age, especially in boys.

SCHOOL ACHIEVEMENT AND SUCCESS IN LATER LIFE

The exhortations of teachers and assembly speakers emphasizing the value of a good school record in the world outside the schoolroom rest on all too little dependable evidence, as the more cynical of the student listeners seem to feel intuitively. A summary of much of the information that is available on the subject was made by Trout (1949).

The most thoroughgoing studies have been made on groups of college graduates. Here there does seem to be a fairly high relationship between academic achievement and later success, particularly at the upper intelligence levels. Of the men who have qualified for inclusion in *Who's Who,* more than three-quarters are college graduates and more than one-quarter hold doctor's degrees. When follow-up studies are made of college graduating classes, the persons rated most successful turn out to be predominantly honor students. Phi Beta Kappa members are more successful than the general run of college students when success is evaluated either by inclusion in *Who's Who* or by size of salary. Such studies do not of course separate intelligence from grade-getting. It is quite possible that the success of honor students is a reflection primarily of their high ability and has little to do with what they learned in college or with nonintellectual qualities contributing to their high scholarship. There is one piece of follow-up research, however, that permits us to differentiate the effects of school achievement from those of intelligence alone. It is the analysis of the later careers of gifted children, by Terman and Oden (1947), which will be reported in some detail in a later chapter. This study does point out the fact that even among persons of outstanding intellectual ability there are wide variations in life success, and that some of the sources of the variations are identifiable in the school record. But the findings of Jepsen (1951) with regard to male graduates of Fresno State College should make us cautious about drawing general conclusions, since no relationship was found in this case between income and grades, for the whole group or within the separate professions.

Probably the most extensive and thorough study of factors related to different criteria of success in a professional group is to be found in one investigation of physicians (Price, et al., 1963). Great care was used in formulating meaningful criteria of success for each of the four main types of medical career—urban general practice, rural general practice, specialty practice, teaching and research. When medical school course grades and other criteria of success in training were correlated with these measures of career success, only a small number of significant correlations emerged —small enough to fall easily within the range of what would be expected by chance. The conclusion appears inescapable that these two variables—success in medical school and success in medical careers—are essentially uncorrelated. It is of course true that the subjects in this study, all of them M.D.'s, were highly selected on the basis of general scholastic ability. The results of the study cannot be interpreted to mean that all students who might *wish* to enter medicine have equal prospects of success. Studies of this nature for other professions would be of great value. We still know far too little about the factors upon which achievement in the world outside the schoolroom depends.

SUMMARY

At all school levels enormous differences exist with regard to what individual students know. At ten, some fifth-graders have learned more than the average high-school students know at sixteen. In a typical group of high-school students, some will be reading and writing at a fourth-grade level while others will know more than the average college sophomore. Changes in educational procedures or in methods of testing and grading have not eradicated such differences. Intelligence, particularly in its verbal aspects, seems to account for the largest single portion of this variability, somewhere from 20 to 50 per cent, depending upon methods of selection in the group. What the other 50 to 80 per cent of the variability in students means is far from clear. To a slight extent it reflects differences in specialized mental abilities, verbal, numerical, spatial, and so forth, but they seem to be important mainly in groups already selected on the basis of general intelligence. Some research attempts to predict differential success in college fields of study by means of test batteries designed especially for this purpose have produced promising results.

Research on over- and underachievement has pointed to characteristic kinds of differences in personality and motivation between students of the two types—differences relating to academic anxiety, self-value, authority relations, interpersonal relations, conflict over independence *vs.* dependence, activity patterns, and goal orientations.

There is some evidence that for college students, already selected to a considerable extent on the basis of intellectual ability, a good academic record gives a favorable prognosis for success in later life. But in the case of one profession, medicine, a thorough study failed to turn up any evidence of a relationship between career success and success in medical training. The question of the relationship of life success to school success is still an open one.

CHAPTER 6

Individual Differences in Special Aptitudes and Talents

SPECIAL ABILITIES AND HUMAN NEEDS

INTELLIGENCE IS NOT ALL THAT is needed to keep complex human societies running smoothly. As we look around us at the people we know, it often seems more natural to characterize them according to *what they are good at* than to evaluate overall intellectual capacity. Take Phil, for example, an outstanding athlete. His talents were recognized even before he entered high school, and he has continued throughout his high school and college years to make a name for himself and win recognition for his school in several competitive sports. Chris is a musician. Able to carry a tune at the age of two, he started violin lessons and was well on his way to a concert career at an age when many boys begin to learn an instrument for the sole purpose of playing in the school band. Henry is a mechanic. He could take an automobile engine apart and put it together again long before he was old enough to qualify for a driver's license. Milly Stevens is a community leader. Since her school days, she has been elected president of every club she has joined because of her apparently effortless skill in organizing all kinds of group work and in smoothly intervening if signs of conflict appear.

How much emphasis is to be placed on such special abilities, especially in school, is a question to which no one definitive answer can be given. Policies in this matter have changed with changing circumstances. At some times and places educators have stressed general development and attempted through remedial programs to provide special training for each student in his weakest fields. At other times and places they have stressed individualized development and encouraged specialized work in areas of a student's greatest strength. More often an educational system represents a compromise between these two viewpoints. But to some extent the ideal of the all-round man always competes for people's approval and support with the ideal of many individuals, each specialized in his own field of excellence but limited in other ways, pooling their efforts for the common good.

In the 1960's, the swing of the pendulum made it seem very important to discover and develop the special talents of individuals. As the demand for unskilled laborers decreases and the demand for highly trained professional workers increases, it is evident that there simply are not enough persons at the high end of the intelligence distribution to man all the posts in the complex socio-economic system we have created. We are being forced to reconsider our concepts of high ability or "giftedness" and pay more attention to persons who are only average in intelligence but outstanding in some other way. Thus we increase the number of persons who qualify for various kinds of advanced education. For example, DeHaan and Havighurst (1957) selected as participants in the Quincy youth development study the children who ranked in the top 10 per cent in intelligence. Adding to this group other boys and girls who ranked in the top 10 per cent in leadership and the top 2 per cent in drawing ability increased their "gifted" group to 16 per cent of the total population. The authors estimated that their group of talented children would have included 20 to 25 per cent of the school population had they also included those who ranked in the top 10 per cent in music, dramatic ability, creative writing, and mechanical ability. Measures of all these kinds of special talent are correlated with one another, and the coefficients often turn out to be fairly high. But the correlations are far from perfect, and a sizable number of individuals are much better at some of these things than at others.

The best concise discussion of diversity of talent and its implications is an article by Wolfle (1960). He argues that in our kind of society it is more desirable to stimulate uneven than well-rounded development.

> Suppose that a given individual has 1000 units of ability . . . and let us suppose that he can distribute these 1000 units in any way he chooses over 20 different kinds of ability. If he wishes to be a completely well-rounded individual, he would assign 50 units to each of the 20 abilities. Or, he might select the 10 kinds of ability that he thinks most important and assign 100 units to each, neglecting completely the other 10 kinds of ability because they seem to him to be unimportant. Or, at the extreme, as a kind of talent gambler, he might stake his whole 1000 units on one kind of ability and neglect the other 19 completely. Which of these ways of distributing his total talent fund would be best for the individual?
>
> A parallel question can be asked from the point of view of society. Suppose that society rather than the individual decides how the 1000 units will be distributed. Which would best serve society: to assign 50 units to each

of 20 different kinds of ability, 100 units to each of 10 kinds, or the whole 1000 units to a single ability.

. . . From the standpoint of society, the best way to distribute talent is to take maximum advantage of differences in aptitude, interest, and motivation by having each individual concentrate on the thing he can do best. Instead of having the 1000-unit man distribute his ability 50 units on each of 20 kinds of ability or 100 units on each of 10, have him concentrate the whole 1000 units on a single ability. . . . Have one man be the best he can possibly become in one line and another the best he can possibly become in another line. Thus we would have the best physicist, the best poet, the best mathematician, and the best dramatist possible. The total value of the talents so distributed would be incomparably greater than would be the value of the same number of units of talent spread more uniformly over the different men and the different abilities involved.

Wolfle recognizes that for the individuals themselves, decisions are not so simple and that conflicts of values must often be resolved. "The eminent young mathematician has to help care for the children, occasionally to repair the lawn mower, and take his turn in helping to run the affairs of the local Boy Scout troop." Persons of all degrees of specialization are able to live useful and satisfying lives. What Wolfle's discussion brings forcibly to our attention is that there is a place in our society for persons of uneven development and that psychologists, educators, and administrators should develop and improve educational and social strategies to guarantee the development and utilization of their talents.

Vocational psychologists have been concerned with two kinds of situation in which special aptitudes must be evaluated. One is the *selection* situation where the task is to choose the most promising available person for a job. The other is the vocational *counseling* situation where the task is to choose the most promising job for a person. Although these situations are superficially similar, and the same test and interview methods have been applied in both, there are actually important differences between them. Many tests profitably used to select workers are just not good enough for conseling. The reason is that errors in judgment are of much more concern to us in one situation than in the other. In many selection situations such errors are not too important. Let us say, for example, that of the office clerks Mr. Henry hires in the course of a year 75 per cent are successful without the use of any tests at all. A testing program that can increase his percentage of good choices to 85 per cent will save the company money and make for better attitudes among the workers. He need not worry too much about the 15 per cent who still do not make good or about the equally large number that his tests have rejected, some of whom might actually have been more satisfactory than the girls he chose. But in a counselor's office where Lloyd Everett is trying to decide whether to major in journalism or engineering, much is at stake for him personally. If an engineering aptitude test misclassifies 25 per cent of the students who take it, Lloyd should know this fact and take it into consideration when he makes his decision. The fact that the test is "right" 75 per cent of the time leaves him still doubtful as to whether he is one of the majority for whom it predicts correctly the later course of events or one of the minority for whom it does not. It is because *all* existing aptitude tests make these errors in prediction that reputable psychologists in vocational counseling positions refuse to let final decisions as to what individuals should do with their lives rest on tests alone. Since these limitations vary from test to test, the task of drawing valid conclusions from a combination of several of them presents formidable difficulties.

Besides this distinction between kinds of situations in which tests are used there is another complication which must be clarified. It was easy to assume in the days when special tests for various aptitudes were first being developed that the individual differences they revealed were fixed ineradicable characteristics based, it might be, on differences in neural structure. But at the same time other psychologists were finding out more and more about learning and the *changes* that take place in human beings over long and short periods of time. Thus in regard to vocational aptitudes as with intelligence there has been a tendency for both research workers and technicians to separate into two camps—those who assume that abilities are relatively unchangeable and who emphasize the importance of *selection*, and those who assume that anybody can learn anything he wants to and who emphasize the importance of *training*. The truth lies somewhere in between, and is considerably more complicated than it would be if either of these extreme views were warranted. Success with some educational programs is more dependent upon having a certain pattern of abilities to start with than is success in other areas. Age makes a difference; so does motivation. There are certain general principles that are becoming apparent, but they are not as simple as many "consumers" of tests think they are. As we shall see later in this chapter, it is possible to combine selection strategies with training strategies to produce better results than can be accomplished by either alone.

CONVERGING LINES OF RESEARCH ON SPECIAL ABILITIES

Three main lines of research on special abilities were initiated during the first quarter of the twentieth century. They continued for some years quite independent of one another, and it was not until the 1940's that they began to converge. One of these lines of research is the use of factor analysis to break intelligence down into its component parts. We have considered this effort in some detail in Chapter 4. Another is the construction of increasingly discriminating school achievement tests to measure not just factual knowledge but different kinds of thinking and problem solving. We have called attention to this in Chapter 5. The third, which has not yet been discussed, is the search for so-called "aptitude" tests. In the 1920's vocational psychologists, in both England and the United States, initiated programs of research on mechanical aptitude (Cox, 1928; Paterson, et al., 1930). It was fortunate for their purposes that they began with this particular variety of special aptitude, because it has turned out to be easier to measure, analyze, and base decisions on than many other kinds of talent. Tests devised in these two research projects produced moderately high correlations with various criteria of success in mechanical pursuits. The way seemed to be clear for the systematic development of a series of valid tests to measure the basic kinds of ability required by various kinds of work.

The concepts and methods needed for such an undertaking seemed to be available. As in the case of intelligence, it was assumed that aptitudes were essentially *native* abilities not based on experience and training. The best way to validate a prospective aptitude test would be to give it to a group of subjects prior to training or job experience. At the end of some specified time, criterion measurements would be made to differentiate levels of competence or skill, and the test scores correlated with these criterion measures. If the correlation turned out to be significant and moderately high, the test could be considered valid. This concept of *predictive validity* has been the central idea in aptitude testing.

The orientation of the psychologists who did this kind of research was typically practical rather than theoretical, as contrasted with that of the psychologists who were concerned with factor analysis of intelligence tests. As soon as some evidence for the validity of an aptitude test had been obtained (and sometimes, unfortunately, while such evidence was anything but conclusive) norms were set up, usually on a percentile or standard-score basis, and the test was published to make it available for general use in selection and counseling situations. The use of aptitude tests to facilitate vocational decisions became standard practice in the 1930's.

As experience in the construction and use of such tests accumulated, the concept of "aptitude" took on a different shape, and the lines that had separated aptitude, achievement, and intelligence tests became more and more blurred. At present few psychologists believe that special abilities, any more than general intelligence, are based entirely on factors in the individual's makeup that are determined by heredity or present at birth. They would not deny the possibility that such hereditary differences exist. The point is that at the time we test him a person performs as he does because of something in the way in which his development has occurred up to this time. This development represents a complex interaction between his inborn and original behavior tendencies and the particular influences and opportunities for learning afforded by the situations in which he has lived. There is no way in which we can separate these two aspects.

This being the case, tests of what one has learned in school or at work can legitimately be used as aptitude tests if the purpose for which we use them is to predict future performance. In the Iowa Legal Aptitude Test, for example, two of the three parts consist of kinds of items commonly used in intelligence tests, verbal opposites and verbal reasoning, and the other part consists of items on legal information. Thus what earlier workers would have classified as intelligence and achievement items make up an aptitude test when put together in this way.

Probably the most successful attempt yet made to measure a special kind of aptitude by measuring a complex combination of traits was the Army Air Force research during World War II. *The Aviation Cadet Classification Battery* (Flanagan, 1947, DuBois, 1947) brought together motor skills tests, achievement tests in mathematics, and a personal history questionnaire and information test designed to measure interests and motivation. Each specific test in the battery was chosen because it added at least a little to the overall prediction of flying success. At each stage of the research enterprise, factor analysis was employed to help the investigators decide what it was that the better predictors had in common. They were thus able to improve the quality of their "hunches" about additional tests it might be profitable to try out. The results, shown graphically in Figure 21, were very impressive. The proportion of failures in primary pilot training was sharply reduced through the use of this battery of selection tests.

The concept of aptitude, as presently understood and applied, is much more complex than the one prevalent in 1930. The hope of developing a technology of aptitude measurement simple, accurate, and complete enough to enable each person to find out precisely the occupation for which he is best suited has all but disappeared. Psychologists and others can use tests of special ability as tools in the making of decisions but they must have a great deal of supplementary information about the tests and about the individuals with whom they are dealing if the use of test scores is to be justified by the soundness of its predictions.

THE VALIDITY PROBLEM

At the center of this complex reformulation of the problem of measuring special talents is the research on the validity of aptitude tests. At the beginning, investigators thought they knew how to demonstrate that a test was valid. As explained earlier, predictive validity was the objective, although concurrent validity (relationship to other measures of the same trait obtained at about the same time) often furnished supplementary

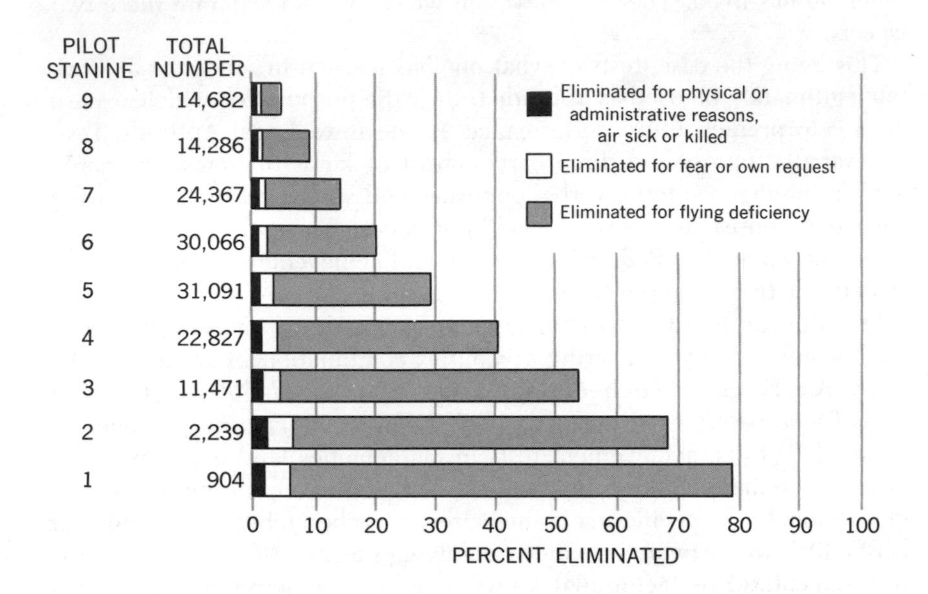

FIGURE 21

Percentage of Candidates Eliminated from Primary Pilot Training Classified According to Stanine Scores on Selection Battery

(Reproduced from Psychological activities in the training command, Army Air Force, by the Staff, Psychological Section, Fort Worth, Texas, in *Psychological Bulletin,* Washington, D.C., American Psychological Association, Inc., 1945)

evidence. What the person who constructed a new test was expected to do was to look for some measurable criterion of the ability in which he was interested. If the correlation between test scores and criterion measures in a group similar to the one for which the test was designed turned out to be statistically significant and reasonably high, the test was considered valid.

The complication arose when several validity coefficients for the same test became available. Often they bore no resemblance to one another, so that conflicting conclusions as to whether any test was or was not a valid measure of the ability for which it was named became the rule rather than the exception. Evidence with regard to this state of affairs, based on a survey of all available references, has been collected in a monograph by Ghiselli (1955). Figure 22 is a graphic portrayal of such conflicting evidence. Notice that between tests of mechanical principles and criteria of success in training for work as mechanical repairmen, correlations reported by 104 different investigators ranged all the way from —.30 to +.65. Evidently, groups, situations, or both, are different

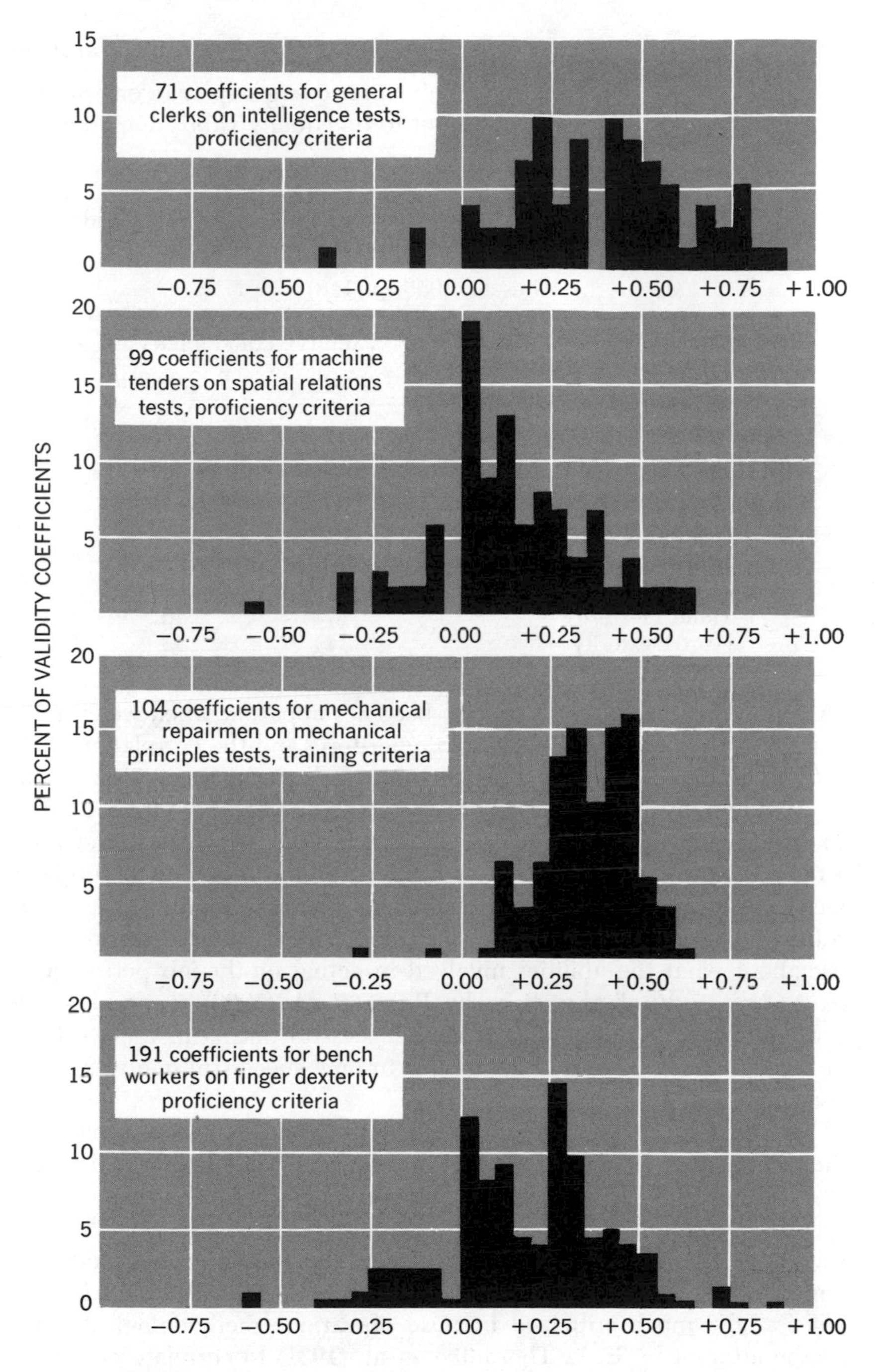

FIGURE 22

Range of Validity Coefficients for Several Varieties of Tests and Criteria

(Ghiselli, 1955)

enough so that a high correlation obtained for one group or in one place is no guarantee that the test will turn out to be equally valid in another.

TABLE 10
Differences between Validity Cofficients Based on Training and Proficiency Criteria for Complex Machine Operators

(Ghiselli, 1955, p. 118)

	VALIDITY COEFFICIENTS	
Test	*Training*	*Proficiency*
Intelligence	.34	.28
Arithmetic	—.08	.29
Spatial Relations	.36	.30
Perception of Details:		
Number Comparison	.42	.14
Name Comparison	.57	.22
Motor Abilities:		
Hand Dexterity	.40	.46
Arm Dexterity	.34	.33

A reason for some of this variation becomes apparent when we examine separately the correlations with *training* criteria and the correlations with *proficiency* criteria. There is little resemblance between them. Tests which tell us which persons are most and least likely to succeed with a training program are not the ones that give the best forecast of which persons will be the best and poorest workers once their training is complete. Table 10 gives some examples of these differences. Because training criteria are ordinarily easier to obtain than proficiency criteria, we often know very little about what the abilities involved in actual on-the-job performance are. As the study of physicians by Price, et al. (1963) reported in the previous chapter would suggest, how successful one is in the world of work may have little or no relationship to how successful one was in the classroom.

There have been some attempts at long-range prediction of proficiency criteria from tests of special abilities. Worbois (1951) compared 1948 and 1929 ratings of 75 electric-power station operators. The two sets of criterion ratings separated by a 19-year interval, correlated only .33. However, the test battery that had been used in the 1929 selection study still seemed to have appreciable validity in predicting the 1948 criterion. An earlier study, much criticized because of various methodological flaws, was the attempt by E. L. Thorndike, et al. (1931) to correlate criteria of occupational success evaluated in early adulthood with tests given during the school years. Most of the correlations turned out to be low and nonsignificant.

A similar long-range follow-up on a much larger scale was reported by

R. L. Thorndike and Hagen (1959) in the book *10,000 Careers.* The data for this investigation came from a search during 1955 and 1956 for 17,000 men who had taken the Air Force tests during a five-month period in 1943. It proved possible to locate more than 10,000 of them—hence the name of the book. The many and diverse occupations into which the men had gone were classified into 124 main categories. Seven different kinds of criterion scores were utilized: (1) monthly earned income; (2) number of persons supervised; (3) self-rated success; (4) self-rated job satisfaction; (5) vertical mobility; (6) lateral mobility; (7) length of time in occupation. The tests in the Air Force Battery were classified into five main groups: (1) general intellectual; (2) numerical fluency; (3) perceptual-spatial; (4) mechanical experience; (5) psychomotor. The correlations did not furnish evidence for the long-range validity of any of these varieties of test for predicting any of the seven occupational criteria in any of the 124 occupational groups. Because of the specialized nature of this aptitude battery (which had predicted very successfully the training criterion it was designed to predict, as indicated in a previous section) and this particular group of subjects, we must be cautious about accepting conclusions as overwhelmingly negative as the foregoing summary statement suggests.

Another sort of finding of the same research project was in some ways considerably more interesting than the correlational evidence. This was that many occupational groups were *differentiated* by their average scores on some or all of the tests in the battery, even though degrees of success within each occupation were not related to the scores. Thus the distinctive profile for accountants and auditors showed them to be definitely above the general average on numerical fluency and below it on mechanical ability. Architects, scoring at least at the average level on all the tests, were distinctively high on visual perception. Miners and drillers were almost half a standard deviation below the average of the total group in their general intellectual ability, but about three-quarters of a standard deviation above the group average on visual perception, mechanical, and psychomotor tests.

This differentiation did not hold for all occupations. Many showed rather flat profiles. For example, clergymen scored near the mean of the group in everything. Lab technicians also showed no unusually high or low scores. Painters and personal service workers averaged well below the group mean and sales engineers averaged well above it on all tests. It would appear that some occupations call for distinctive ability patterns, while others do not.

The authors called attention to one other aspect of the findings about group differences that must not be forgotten when we have practical applications in mind. The distinctive group profile represents averages, not individuals. Within each group a great deal of variability exists.

Figure 23 illustrates this fact. Some accountants are below average in numerical fluency. Some are above average in mechanical aptitude.

The most thorough study of occupational ability profiles that has been made so far was carried out some 25 years before the Thorndike and Hagen project, at the Minnesota Employment Stabilization Research Institute (Dvorak, 1935). The MESRI was an agency set up in 1931 to study economic and psychological aspects of unemployment. One of its undertakings was to test large numbers of employed and unemployed workers in various occupations. For each test standard-score norm tables were constructed based on a group of subjects chosen in such a way as to be representative of the whole urban employed population of Minnesota. In studying the pattern of scores for any individual or occupational group, standard scores based on these norms were used.

The tests sampled educational ability (usually called general intelligence), clerical ability, mechanical ability, and dexterity. The first comparison of profiles was between men office clerks and garage mechanics. Figure 24 portrays graphically the average-score profiles for the two groups.

Various statistical tests backed up the impression one gets from looking at these profiles that there was a significant difference in the pattern of

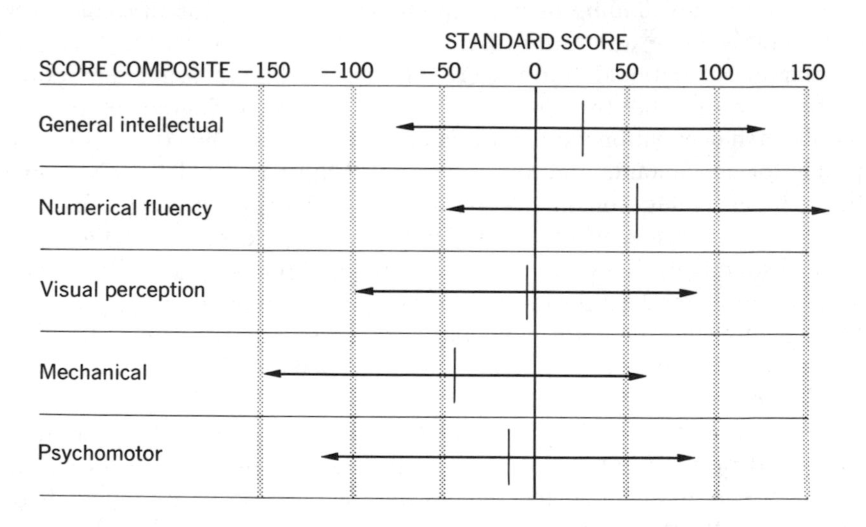

FIGURE 23

Score Composite Means and Standard Deviations for Accountants in the Air Force Follow-up Study

(Thorndike, L., and Hagen, E., *10,000 Careers*)

abilities. The clerical workers were considerably higher on the educational and clerical tests, somewhat higher on all the dexterity tests, but lower on the mechanical tests. Measures of overlapping indicated that only 3.7 per cent of the mechanics exceeded the median score of the clerks on the number-checking test, but 71.4 per cent of them exceeded the clerks' median on the spatial relations test. A supplementary analysis of groups of garage mechanics working in different places (Figure 25) showed that there was little or no difference in these patterns of abilities.

Another comparison was made between women office clerks and retail saleswomen (Figure 26). Again a marked difference was apparent. Not only did office workers tend to be higher in everything, but they were highest on the very test in which saleswomen were lowest, so that the profiles had an entirely different shape.

Dvorak also attempted to find out whether profiles of individual workers were sufficiently similar to the average profile for their occupation so that they could be classified by a person who knew nothing about the individuals except their test scores. Profiles of 90 employed women office clerks and 68 employed retail saleswomen were chosen at random from the research files and given to a vocational psychologist to sort into the two groups. His judgment turned out to be correct in 92.4 per cent of the cases.

Degree of success in the occupation seemed to be related to how *high* some or all of the scores were, rather than to their pattern. Figure 27 shows profiles for various groups of nurses where the A group was made up of those rated by their superiors as exceptionally capable, and the D and E groups made up of those rated definitely below average. The intelligence test and the two clerical tests differentiated the success groups most satisfactorily.

There was one other type of supplementary analysis which showed that these patterns of high and low abilities were not created by work on the job itself. In all work with aptitude tests it is important to have information on this point. For instance, if all the girls who work in an office for a time, regardless of their initial ability, become able to make high scores in tests like the Pressey Senior Verification and the Minnesota Clerical, then we would hardly be justified in using these tests to evaluate *aptitude* in girls who have not yet had this office experience. Dvorak assembled the evidence on this question for the specific tests used in this study and showed that training and experience in the kinds of work related to each test had a negligible effect in raising the scores.

Following this exceptionally thorough study, a similar investigation was made by Dodge (1935) in New York. The subjects were unemployed men and women who came to the Adjustment Service for guidance. Differences were in the same direction as in the Minnesota study, but they were less clear-cut, and there was so much variation from individual to individual

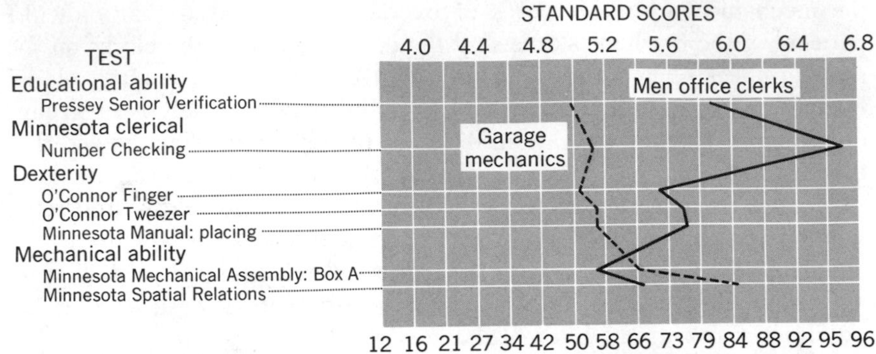

FIGURE 24

Occupational Ability Patterns of Men Office Clerks and Garage Mechanics

(Reprinted by permission of the University Press, University of Minnesota, from Dvorak, *Differential occupational ability patterns*, 1935)

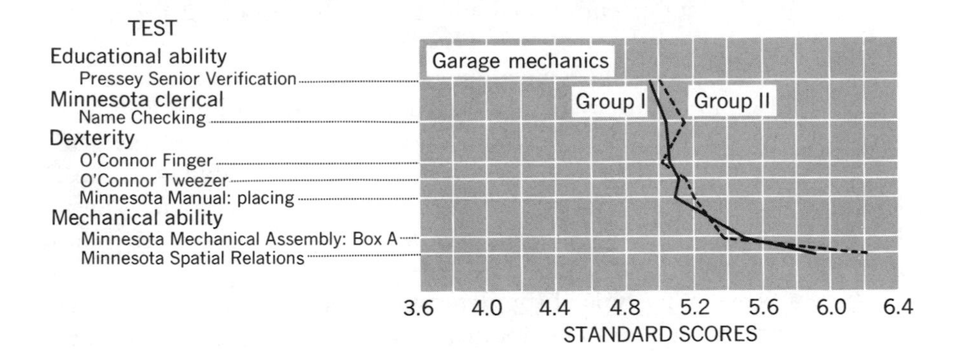

FIGURE 25

Occupational Ability Patterns of Men Garage Mechanics Employed in Two Different Places

(Reprinted by permission of the University Press, University of Minnesota, from Dvorak, *Differential occupational ability patterns*, 1935)

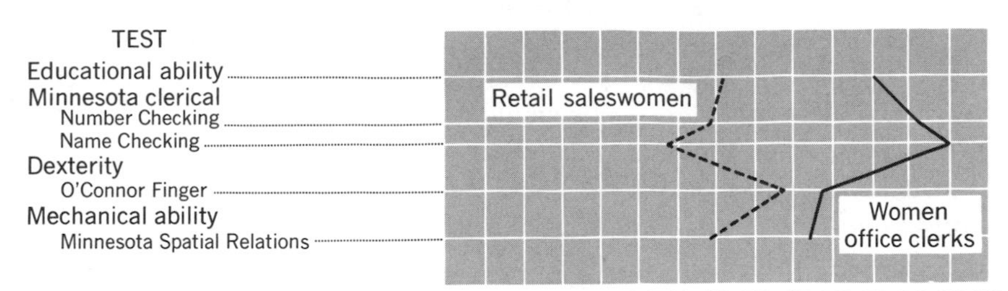

FIGURE 26

Occupational Ability Patterns of Women Office Clerks and Retail Saleswomen

(Reprinted by permission of the University Press, University of Minnesota, from Dvorak, *Differential occupational ability patterns*, 1935)

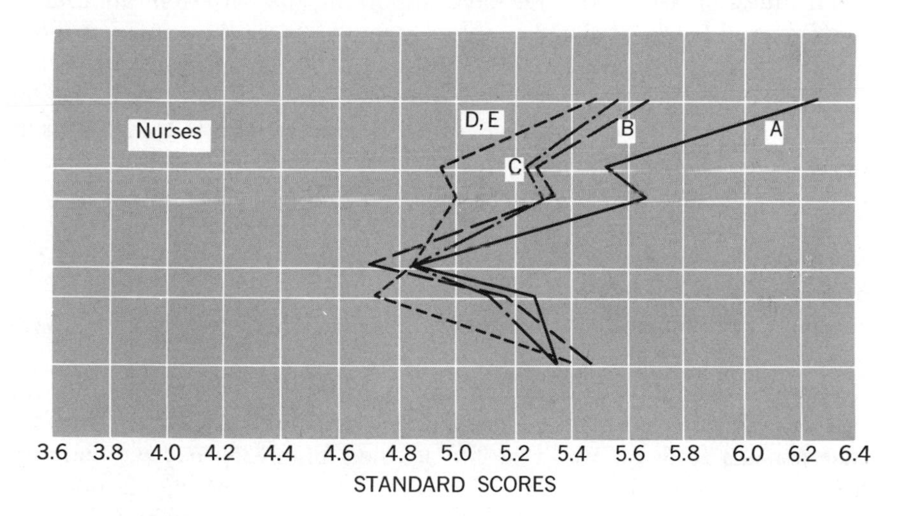

FIGURE 27

Occupational Ability Patterns of Four Groups of Nurses Rated for Success

(Reprinted by permission of the University Press, University of Minnesota, from Dvorak, *Differential occupational ability patterns*, 1935)

within each group that profiles would have been of very little use in vocational guidance. It is probable that the particular tests used in this research were not well chosen to bring out distinctive occupational characteristics. The omission of mechanical aptitude tests and the inclusion of the Bernreuter Personality Inventory might have served to blur any distinction that did exist. Dodge did, however, make one useful suggestion—namely, that *minimum* profiles would be of more value for guidance than *average* profiles. This idea is supported by Dvorak's findings that it was the general level of scores on differentiating tests that distinguished between successful and unsuccessful workers. The Employment Service psychologists have applied this idea in the procedure they have set up for the use of the General Aptitude Test Battery. In evaluating a candidate's fitness for a certain type of work, the counselor checks his test profile to see whether his scores on the tests which count for that occupation are above the minimum.

The question about which is more important, the pattern of abilities or their general level, is related to the controversy over the nature of intelligence as discussed in Chapter 4. Here as on the intelligence issue, the British psychologists have stressed the importance of all-round level of ability. In vocational as in academic situations they tend to think in terms of "g." Vernon (1950) has given us the clearest statement of this point of view. In referring to observations made in military personnel programs, he says, "The layman's notion that there exists a niche or special type of work ideally suited to the specialized aptitudes of each individual appeared to be much less true than the view that all types of work and all employees fall along a single high-grade to low-grade continuum." (Vernon, p. 122.)

He cited several types of evidence supporting this conclusion. One was just this general experience with military selection problems. The fact that persons from all walks of life learned highly specialized military duties as successfully as they did seemed to him to be significant. Just what sort of occupation they had previously been following, unless it happened to coincide exactly with what they were assigned to do in the Services, mattered very little. Retail tradesmen learned to be engine-room mechanics as easily as civilian machinists did. No type of previous mechanical experience seemed to have assisted radio or electrical mechanics in learning new jobs. Women with very nonmechanical backgrounds succeeded at skilled engineering jobs. The military psychologists were thus led to put a great deal more emphasis on school and work records showing stability and educational "drive" than on evidence of specific aptitudes. A more systematic type of evidence which Vernon presented came from factor analyses of job elements as assessed by occupational experts, training marks in Service schools, and objective measures of workshop ability. Each of these analyses showed a large general factor accounting for from 30 to 40 per cent of the variance in individual performance. It must be remembered, however, that the factor-analysis methods used were such as to maximize general factor loadings. Rotation might have produced an alternative interpretation, as in the case of intelligence measures.

However, it has become increasingly clear that in much of the American work carried through from the special-aptitude point of view there is also considerable support for the conclusion that general level of ability is important in occupational situations. When correlations between the different mechanical aptitude tests and the different parts of the Army General Classification Test were worked out for 5,000 men representative of the entire army population in age and educational attainments, the coefficients obtained were all high. Reading and vocabulary correlated with arithmetic to the extent of .81. Mechanical information correlated .77 with total score on the AGCT (Anastasi, 1948). We have noted in discussing the Minnesota studies that general level of scores was the factor that was related to degrees of success within an occupation. The work of Ghiselli and Brown (1951) showed that there is much more generality than specificity in what occupational tests predict. Spatial relations tests, for example, tend to correlate almost as highly with clerical as with mechanical criteria.

Now, however, an important postscript on this topic is in order. The decision to continue the search for efficient techniques to use in assessing special aptitudes and talents rests not so much on research findings as on the social factors analyzed at the beginning of the chapter. Increasingly our kind of society needs the services of large numbers of persons with highly developed talents. There simply are not enough *all-round* superior persons. While the correlations between different varieties of special aptitude are often *high,* they are not *perfect,* and any coefficient less than 1.00 represents a situation in which some persons are higher in one of the two distributions entering into the correlation than they are on the other. Thus we will always discover more "gifted" individuals if we judge them partly on the basis of special aptitudes than if we judge only on general intellectual level.

PROMISING RESEARCH DIRECTIONS

Faced with this challenge—the need for valid tests of special abilities and the evidence for serious deficiencies in the existing ones—what have psychologists proposed to do about it? There are several lines of research that constitute new approaches to the problem of measuring and thus discovering special aptitudes and talents.

One of these strategies for improving predictions from test data has been to study *specific* criterion situations one at a time and develop at the outset of an investigation a model of the type of person likely to succeed in it. Stern, Stein, and Bloom (1956)[1] reported tryouts of this method in various academic situations. Murray's introduction to this book affords one of the most vivid descriptions of what the method is:

> A little caricature might serve to sharpen our awareness of the step that has been taken by Professors Stern, Stein, and Bloom. Let us assume that the assignment is to predict grades in an English course given by Professor X. Responding to this challenge, psychologists of the old school would devote almost all their time to the construction of tests, let us say, of verbal facility, literary appreciation, and so forth, and combine these with a test of general intelligence to provide a measure of "aptitude for English studies." The authors of this volume, on the other hand, would start by obtaining as much information as possible about Professor X's tastes, especially the explicit and implicit standards that determine his grading of term papers and of final examinations. They would ask the Professor what special merits he saw in his best students and what particular objections he had to those he esteemed least. They would also conduct a systematic examination of the students who had received the highest grades in Professor X's course and those who had received the lowest. Then, on the basis of these and other data of the same order, the psychologists of this new school would compose a model of the type of personality that is most likely to receive high grades in Professor X's course. This model would constitute a target. Then, having clearly defined it, and not before, these psychologists would apply themselves to the task of selecting and devising instruments to measure the extent to which each applicant's personality approximates the model.

In the remaining chapters of the book, Stern, Stein, and Bloom reported several specific methods for constructing such models and using them in attempts at prediction. Their work was done in academic situations, and the special groups used in these research projects included theology students, teacher trainees, and graduate students in physics, as well as college freshmen. While the numbers in the subgroups intensively studied were small, the accuracy of the predictions was impressive. All six of the theology students, for example, and eight out of ten of the teacher trainees, were ranked by the assessors exactly as the faculty had independently ranked them. It is perhaps worthy of notice that the assessment in these studies rested heavily on noncognitive or personality measures rather than on the kinds of ability measures we have discussed so far. We will consider the special problems such testing involves in the next chapter.

One of the most comprehensive statements of this broadened view of human talents, in which the characteristics of particular situations are studied in relationship to the characteristics of particular persons is the

[1] G. G. Stern, M. I. Stein, B. S. Bloom. *Methods in personality assessment*. 1956. Used by permission of the Macmillan Company.

chapter by McClelland (McClelland, et al., 1958) prepared as an introduction to the report of the Committee on Identification of Talent set up by the Social Science Research Council. Table 11 summarizes the factors that must be considered in the study of talented behavior. Obviously any one research project cannot explore all of these determinants, but it would seem to be desirable that they all be kept in mind while such a project is planned.

Another important line of research that may serve to make existing aptitude tests better predictors of success in occupational situations is the work of Ghiselli (1956) on the "prediction of predictability." It rests on the observation that in any situation where a test is used to predict criterion scores, whether the correlation is low or high, some individuals perform as predicted, others do not. Ghiselli reasoned that it might be possible to identify these types at the time the test is given and then to use the test scores for predictive purposes only in the *appropriate* cases. To try out this idea, he administered to 193 taxicab drivers a short battery of motor-skills tests and an inventory of attitudes and opinions, which could be scored for "appropriateness of occupational level" and "interest in jobs involving personal relationships." The criterion, production during the first 12 weeks at work, was correlated with the motor-skills scores. The resulting r was only .259, far too low to contribute much to selection. What Ghiselli did, however, was to construct a regression equation, make a prediction for each man in the sample on the basis of his test score, and then compute the *difference* between this predicted score and the score the man actually made. Thus he was able to separate out two subgroups, one consisting of those for whom this difference was high and one consisting of those for whom this difference was low—the "unpredictables" and the "predictables." He then compared these subgroups on the attitude inventory and found that there was a significant difference between them on the "occupational-level" variable, but not on the "personal-relationship" variable. The predictable men were the ones who seemed to be satisfied with a relatively low occupational level. When a correlation was computed separately for the persons falling in the lowest third on the occupational level scale, it turned out to be .664, in contrast to the .259 that had been obtained for the group as a whole.

In later studies using other tests and other criteria (Ghiselli, 1960a and 1960b) he extended this procedure to demonstrate the possibility of differentiating a total group into subgroups, one of which is predictable on the basis of one test, the other predictable on the basis of another. These extra measuring techniques used to sort a total group out into subgroups differing in what can be predicted for them are called *moderator variables* (Ghiselli, 1963; Wallach, 1962). They increase the clarity of research findings in complex domains. They would appear to have many practical applications in education and industry once they are well understood.

TABLE 11.

Illustrative Analysis of the Determinants of Performance Considered "Talented" in Terms of Its Desired Effects

(McClelland, *et al.*, 1958)

A ANTECEDENT CONDITIONS *produce* →	B *A person with certain characteristics* *who interacts with* →	C *A situation with certain characteristics* *to produce performance with* →	D DESIRED OUTCOMES
Heredity	Abilities	Working conditions	Work efficiency
Cultural values	Emotional stability	Skills required	Occupational rank
Family structure	Values	Values required	School grades
Socio-economic status	Motives	Motives required	Salary earned
Parent attitudes	Characteristic modes of response (traits)	Stability required	Community service
		Type of persons in the situation	Good morale
			Successful leadership
			Social effectiveness
			Inclusion in *American Men of Science*

Another even more drastic reformulation of the aptitude testing problem is represented in the monograph by Cronbach and Gleser (1957). Here the task is conceptualized in terms of *decision theory* rather than correlational theory. Instead of attempting to discover how closely related a test is to a criterion, Cronbach and Gleser recommend that one analyze the contribution it makes to some specified decision that someone must make. These may be institutional decisions, such as whether to admit or not to admit an applicant to Medical School or whether to assign an army recruit to an electronics or a personnel training program. They may be individual decisions as when a high-school graduate chooses a technical school or a college. Test information to be utilized in such decisions need not be obtained all at once, but can be divided into segmented stages. Instead of administering a complete battery of tests to all candidates for a position, as has been customary following traditional test theory, a system of successive screens can be used. At each stage the alternative decisions are: (1) accept, (2) reject, (3) investigate further. What the Cronbach and Gleser monograph does is to classify decision problems on the basis of their formal characteristics and then to propose specific strategies suitable for handling each of these types of problem.

The three research trends we have discussed in this section: (1) careful analysis of situations as well as individuals; (2) differentiation of individuals in terms of their predictability; and (3) replacement of correlational theory by decision theory—have developed independently, but they are not unrelated to one another. So far they constitute programs for research rather than tested bodies of knowledge. But they justify some hope that in the future it will be possible to identify and develop the special aptitudes and talents of individuals more successfully than we have in the past. Dunnette (1963) has made a careful analysis of the varieties of research in personnel selection these new concepts generate.

AN INVENTORY OF APTITUDES AND TALENTS

In several special areas, enough significant research evidence has accumulated so that psychologists have a fairly clear picture of just what abilities are involved. Often the formulation of these is in factor analytic terms. In other cases tests are still classified according to the occupational criteria they were designed to predict. Let us look at a few of these aptitude domains.

1. *Mechanical*

From the time of the first systematic studies by Cox (1928) and Paterson and associates (1930) to the present, tests that research showed to be promising indicators of mechanical aptitude have fallen into a few major classes. The first type involves the perception and manipulation of spatial relations, the ability to visualize how parts fit together into a whole. The second type involves the comprehension of mechanical relationships, the recognition of tools used for various special purposes, and other similar items that are clearly based partly on experience. Other kinds of material have been used in some published tests of mechanical aptitude, but generally speaking, it is only the spatial visualization and mechanical comprehension tests that have shown any predictive validity for mechanical criteria. Factor analyses by Harrell (1940), Wittenborn (1945) and Guilford (1947, 1948) substantiate this conclusion.

2. *Motor Coordination*

Both vocational psychologists, who were mainly interested in the aptitude for rapid, well-coordinated arm, hand, and finger movements, and those who teach physical education and are interested in general physical fitness and athletic talent, have studied the abilities involved in skilled movements. One of the first things they discovered was that such abilities were apparently highly specific. The relationships seemed to be quite different from those encountered in the study of mental abilities, all of which correlated positively. Correlations reported by Seashore (1930) from a battery of motor skill tests are typical of what was generally found. These are shown in Table 12.

TABLE 12

Intercorrelations of Eight Motor Skill Tests

(Seashore, 1930)

TEST	ATAX	*P.M.*	*K.P.R.*	*S.D.*	*M.R.S.*	*P.P.*	*S.R.*	*B.S.P*
Ataxiameter	. .	.19	.12	−.15	.03	.16	.12	.15
Pursuitmeter	.19	. .	.29	.18	.17	.14	.09	.26
Koerth Pursuit Rotor	.12	.29	. .	.25	.40	.56	.33	.26
Serial Discrimeter	−.15	.18	.25	. .	.29	.33	.08	.32
Motor Rhythm Synchrometer	.03	.17	.40	.29	. .	.36	.63	.43
Pursuit Pendulum	.16	.14	.56	.33	.36	. .	.23	.44
Speed Rotor	.12	.09	.33	.08	.63	.23	. .	.38
Spool Packer	.15	.26	.26	.32	.43	.44	.38	. .

As factor analytic methods came into increasing use for analyzing such tables of intercorrelations, it became apparent that there were a considerable number of motor-skill factors. R. H. Seashore (1940) brought together the results of a number of such studies, including his own. He showed that the correlations between tests of reaction time, serial discriminative action, speed of tapping, pursuit coordinations, motor rhythm, and gross muscular coordination, and the factor loadings based on these correlations, could not be explained in terms of either the specific musculatures or the specific sense fields involved. He suggested instead that the group factors indicated *patterns of movement,* regardless of the particular musculature used in each performance.

During and after World War II, many more factor analyses of motor skills were made. Fleishman's work is the most important in this field. His most recent catalog of motor factors includes 15 separate kinds of ability in addition to gross body coordination and endurance (Fleishman, 1962). They are as follows:

1. Control precision.
2. Multilimb coordination.
3. Response orientation.
4. Reaction time.
5. Speed of arm movement.
6. Rate control.
7. Manual dexterity.
8. Finger dexterity.
9. Arm-hand steadiness.
10. Wrist-finger speed.
11. Aiming.
12. Strength.
13. Flexibility of muscle groups.
14. Energy mobilization.
15. Balance.

As the inventory of motor aptitudes has become more complete and accurate, however, more and more doubt has arisen about the usefulness of this line of research. The motor skills in which we are ultimately interested are those that have been developed and perfected through training and practice. Evidence has been accumulating that the separate aptitude factors, alone or in combination, do not contribute much to predictions of final performance. For example, in the study of the learning and retention of a perceptual motor skill designed to simulate the task of keeping an airplane on target, Fleishman and Parker (1962) found that only two factor scores were related to performance at any stage of the learning process and that these never accounted for more than 25 per cent of the variance. The correlations of the two aptitude scores with retention after an interval of no practice were negligible. Results of this sort make it appear unlikely that tests of aptitude factors are likely to show much validity as predictors of skills that must be *learned.*

3. *Clerical Aptitude*

The kind of test items most widely used to measure clerical aptitude are those requiring rapid checking of sequences of words or numbers. In the test that has led the field, the Minnesota Clerical Test, each item requires that the subject scan two identical or nearly identical names or numbers and place a check mark between them if they are exactly alike. In a sense it is a very easy task. Anyone who can read can accomplish it correctly.

One's score depends largely upon how fast he is—how many of these items he can complete in a specified amount of time.

Factor analyses have suggested that the special ability involved here is mainly perceptual speed, the knack of grasping details quickly. Since this is required in many kinds of paper work, tests of this type have shown significant though not always high correlations with many office-work criteria. Various investigators have also reported low to moderate correlations between clerical aptitude and general intelligence. Tests of learned skills, such as arithmetic and spelling, often add to the accuracy with which success in particular kinds of clerical situations can be predicted.

4. *The General Aptitude Test Battery*

With the increasing use of factor analysis to facilitate the task of unraveling the strands of separate abilities that enter into performance in work situations, the idea of using a battery of tests to measure many of these abilities at the same time had considerable appeal.

The United States Employment Service took the lead in developing such a test battery. For years they had been standardizing short tests to be used in various combinations to assess aptitude for a wide variety of specific occupations from File Clerk to Zig Zag Machine Operator (Stead, 1942). It was a natural step to make a factor analysis of the intercorrelations between these tests to ascertain how many separate abilities were involved and what they seemed to be (Occ. Anal. Div., 1945). So that the factors would not represent relationships peculiar to any one geographical area, nine separate analyses were made in widely separated parts of the country. A total of fifty-nine tests and 2,156 subjects were represented. Most of the same factors appeared repeatedly in different analyses. These were as follows:

O—General intelligence
V—Verbal ability
N—Numerical ability
S—Spatial ability
P—Perceptual ability as applied to geometrical figures or material requiring no formal educational background
Q—Perceptual ability as applied to words or numbers
A—Aiming ability. Accuracy or precision of movement
T—Time or speed
F—Finger dexterity
M—Manual dexterity
L—Logic or reasoning

These were assembled into a two-and-one-half-hour counseling battery which is widely used in employment offices throughout the country to identify the group or family of occupations for which an inexperienced worker shows the most aptitude.

A number of other counseling batteries based directly or indirectly on factor analysis have been put on the market. In many ways they are superior to the separate aptitude tests which for so long have been the stock-in-trade of school guidance workers and vocational counselors. There is one defect, however, that until it is corrected outweighs all these advantages. The evidence for their *validity* in predicting behavior in life situations outside the testing room is all too often lacking. It must of course be collected by the same laborious methods that are used with other aptitude tests. Before we can conclude that a boy who is high in S and P should enter an apprenticeship for a mechanical trade—or before we can allow *him* to draw such a conclusion from the tests alone—we must know that S and P scores derived from this particular battery are correlated with mechanical success. Criticisms of test batteries for inadequate validity data must always be made as of a definite time. Important information may be reported the day after the criticism goes to press. The point is simply that applied psychologists who contemplate the use of these tests in their own activities should be sure to scrutinize carefully the evidence that has been presented as to what criteria the scores have been shown to predict. And, as indicated in a previous section, evidence for the validity of all sorts of aptitude tests is complex and often conflicting, so that no one validity coefficient can tell us what we need to know.

5. *Musical and Artistic Talents*

Research on the abilities needed in the arts has constituted a special field, not very closely related to the research on other aptitudes. The work of C. E. Seashore (1939) set the pattern for much of the work on musical talent. The techniques he and his associates produced were essentially psychophysical measurements reflecting the fineness of an individual's discriminations of slight differences in pitch, loudness, time, timbre, and rhythm, and the accuracy of his immediate memory for musical phrases. There have been some attempts to test the more complex aspects of musical talent, such as judgment of the quality of musical phrases, discrimination of different intervals or different modes, or identification of the musical score of the selection one is hearing. Such tests, of course, are not applicable to persons who have not had some musical training. The predictive validity of musical aptitude tests has been consistently disappointing, and research interest in developing and evaluating such tests seems to have declined.

In the field of the visual arts, the tests to which most attention has been devoted have been those measuring esthetic judgment rather than production, although some attempts have been made to construct standardized tasks on which the subject's skill in drawing a design could also be assessed. While the available art tests usually show significant differences for groups of persons differing in their positions—art students *vs.* students in general, for example—the correlations of individual scores with criteria of achievement in the arts have not been impressive. Criteria for the judgment of what artists produce are even more difficult to obtain than criteria of success in other areas. Opinions of experts often differ greatly about how good a painting, a statue, or a person really is.

6. *Batteries of Tests for Selection of Professional Students*

One other variety of testing technique completes our inventory of the major attempts to measure aptitudes and talents. In an effort to increase the accuracy with which selection committees of college faculties could choose students likely to succeed in specialized professional training programs, for medicine, law, nursing, engineering, and several other fields, psychologists and test-construction agencies have put together batteries of subtests showing promising correlations with the professional training criteria. As explained in an earlier section, these are essentially achievement tests and are useful only in the case of an individual who has had the relevant preprofessional education. Medical aptitude tests draw heavily on knowledge of science. Legal-aptitude tests include questions drawing up legal information. Tests of this kind serve a useful purpose in supplementing what can be learned about would-be professional students from their application blanks and recommendations.

IDENTIFICATION AND USE OF SPECIAL ABILITIES—NEED FOR A NEW APPROACH

We have considered the clear social need for a technology to facilitate the identification of special kinds of talent and for counseling and placement procedures to help individuals find suitable settings in which to develop and utilize them. We have also surveyed the main varieties of existing tests and noted their inadequacies. (For those whose work involves the use of test information for vocational purposes, a much more complete discussion of the characteristics of specific tests can be found in the excellent volume *Appraising Vocational Fitness* by Super and Crites, 1962).

What applied psychologists, vocational counselors, and personnel workers need, if they are to carry out their tasks successfully, is not so much new tests or more information of the sort we now have about existing tests as a different set of concepts leading to other kinds of research. The basic question is "What can this person *do?*" rather than "How much of one or more hypothetical abilities does he *possess?*" By focusing their efforts on the second question rather than the first, psychologists have set for themselves a difficult if not impossible task, and there is no real reason why anyone should undertake it.

To be more specific, what one needs as a basis for answering the first question is not a validity coefficient showing the test-criterion relationship for all the persons in a group, but simply minimum scores for particular jobs or training programs. The main practical purpose aptitude tests could serve is to indicate what a person's *limits* are. If it is clear that Sam has more than the minimum amount of mechanical aptitude necessary for an apprenticeship in cabinet making, then his success in this training program will depend on other qualities of his own—motivation, work habits, and the like—and factors in the particular work situation he enters—the quality of the instruction and supervision, the congeniality of fellow workers, and such things. If it is clear that Martha discriminates pitches well enough so that she can play the violin at all, her final level of musical skill will depend upon things like how much she practices, how sensitive she is to musical phrasing, and what sort of teachers she encounters. In our attempts to validate aptitude tests we have ignored all the other influences that help to shape talent into developed skill. We must learn to think of aptitudes as *necessary* but not *sufficient* characteristics (Tyler, 1962).

This is not, of course, a completely new idea. Personnel psychologists have often presented research data on a selected program in the form of expectancy tables rather than correlation coefficients. From such a table, one can see what the effects would be of setting any given minimum score as a condition for entry into an occupation. The Air Force report shown in Figure 21 is a good case in point. The research staff that produced the General Aptitude Test Battery referred to above followed this procedure. The tests are designed to identify combinations of scores that are above the minima established for different occupations rather than to predict degrees of success within an occupational group. What has not been done heretofore, however, is to bring together a large amount of information of this kind for each of the varieties of aptitude discussed in this chapter.

If we are to build an adequate psychological foundation for all of vocational psychology, we must also emphasize research on how aptitudes and talents *develop*. In the cases of some individuals, the answer to the question "What can this person do?" might at present have to be "Nothing." But now that we no longer assume that aptitude tests measure pure native capacity, the possibilities for research on how various kinds of special ability can be produced through a learning or training process are almost unlimited. Fleishman's research program on motor skills, in which aptitude and training variables are considered simultaneously, constitutes an example of how such investigations can be designed.

The Cronbach and Gleser reformulation of test theory in terms of decision processes is compatible with both these recommended changes—an emphasis on minimum scores or thresholds and an emphasis on the development of abilities through training. The time is ripe for a new attack on problems related to the measurement of human talents.

SUMMARY

People differ from one another not only in general intelligence but in special abilities. With increasing social demands for high-level workers, it is increasingly important that special talents be recognized and developed. Aptitude tests have been used mainly for two purposes—selection and counseling. Not all tests usable in selection situations are suitable for counseling.

At first, achievement testing, aptitude testing, and the analysis of intelligence into its components constituted three independent lines of research. Recently they have converged, so that distinctions between the three kinds of test are now practical or historical rather than conceptual.

Aptitude testing has fallen into some disrepute in recent years because of the accumulation of negative and conflicting validity evidence. Profiles based on vocational tests differentiate occupations from one another, but individual test scores do not consistently predict the degree of success within an occupation.

Promising new research directions are suggested by Ghiselli's work on the prediction of predictability, Stern, Stein, and Bloom's work on analyzing criterion situations, and Cronbach and Gleser's reformulation of testing concepts in terms of decision theory.

Tests are available for mechanical aptitude, clerical aptitude, motor skills, musical and artistic talent, and complex combinations of characteristics involved in different kinds of professional training. Research in which thresholds or minima, rather than overall validity, are determined, and research in which training and testing procedures are combined are to be recommended.

CHAPTER 7

Individual Differences in Personality

WHEN A PERSON who has not been exposed to academic courses on the subject thinks about individual differences, he is more likely to be impressed with differences in personality than with differences in ability. It is evident to him that his children do not react the same way to the same training routines and to the maintenance of discipline; his friends differ in their degrees of dependability and sociability, and in their predominant moods. Success in work situations is to a large extent a matter of personal characteristics, such as how high a man's morale is, how consistently he can force himself to keep slogging along, how well he gets along with colleagues, and the like. In school, the best records are made by students who have other qualities in addition to intelligence—qualities like persistence, good study habits, and willingness to go along with established routines. From military classification to marriage counseling, in all types of situations where people live and work together, personality is constantly under scrutiny and being evaluated.

DIFFICULTIES AND COMPLICATIONS

It was only natural that when psychologists came on the scene they should try to apply to this vastly important domain of personal characteristics the same sort of quantitative concepts and techniques they had used to investigate individual differences in abilities. But this newer undertaking has been beset by a host of unforeseen difficulties and problems. To some extent these have been analyzed and overcome, but there is still considerable question about how generally successful the whole enterprise of quantifying personality differences has been.

The first of these special problems has to do with the definition of "personality." As we have seen in considering the research on intelligence, satisfactory definitions in psychology follow rather than precede the accumulation of research findings. However, it helps at the outset of a research undertaking to have some consensus about the nature of the characteristic to be measured. In the case of personality this consensus has not existed. The word has a variety of meanings and is interpreted in different ways under different circumstances. Guilford, for example, thinks of personality as a broad enough term to include all of an individual's traits, his physical characteristics, intellectual qualities, aptitudes and talents, as well as his temperamental qualities, interests, expressive behavior, and pathological symptoms (Guilford, 1959). Though in most psychology texts, a much narrower range of subject matter is included under the label "personality," for this is applied only to "noncognitive" traits, there is still a great deal of disagreement about how much and what the term should cover. If a person planning research on personality defines the concept too broadly, he finds it difficult to develop any sort of classification system from which fruitful hypotheses can be drawn. If he defines it too narrowly, he may leave out what some other workers consider to be essential aspects and thus end up with results that cannot be integrated with those of previous investigations.

As has been indicated in Chapter 1, type concepts for dealing with individual differences in personality appeared on the historical scene very early. Hippocrates and Galen used biological distinctions such as susceptibility to different diseases, or predominance of different "humors" as the bases for their classifications. More recently Kretschmer has presented a similar biological system, relating it, however, to susceptibility to mental rather than physical diseases. (We shall be considering it in Chapter 16.) For those more influenced by literature than by anatomy or physiology, Spranger's typology based on values—theoretical, economic, aesthetic, social, political, and religious—or the distinction William James made between tender-minded and tough-minded—has had more appeal. Psychologists, as well as the general public, have made a great deal of use of Jung's extravert-introvert classification.

Type concepts have an immediate popular appeal, and thus they probably still predominate in what might be called "folk" psychology. Manufacturers and advertisers often specify which of the several alternative varieties of their products are intended for each of several alternative types of person. Adolescents sort out their high school classmates by means of type categories their elders find incomprehensible. Fraternity and sorority members purport to be able to distinguish between the "Alpha-Beta" type and the "Gamma-Delta" type. Parents tend to use type concepts to describe individual differences in their children—the "athletic" type, the "little lady," or the "holy terror," for example. The fact that typologies do serve to simplify the complex realm of personality differences is undeniable. The fact that they are so diverse and usually so unsupported by objective evidence has led us to look beyond the verbal formulations themselves for the kind of evidence that separates the demonstratable from the merely plausible and at the same time, perhaps, discloses some degree of order.

Because it seemed to lend itself more readily to quantitative scaling, psychologists have generally preferred to organize personality differences around the concept of *traits* rather than the concept of types. This form of description also has its roots in nonscientific ways of characterizing personality. We say, for instance, that John is thoroughly honest, somewhat shy, and very kind and considerate. We make rough quantitative comparisons when we say that Ed is more sociable than Hugh, who in turn is more sociable than Roger.

The trouble with traits as the basic variables of personality research is that they are in some ways too narrow and in others too broad. So many separate characteristics have been distinguished from one another that the task of working out ways of measuring all of them would assume unmanageable proportions. Allport and Odbert (1936) reported that there are from 3,000 to 5,000 words in the language of a civilized people to describe personal qualities. It is obviously going to be impossible to measure personality in any complete way if in order to do so we must measure 3,000 traits. However, the proliferation of published personality "tests" indicates that psychologists have taken some steps in this direction. Hundreds of tests have been devised for traits that seemed important to someone. Leafing through a reference volume such as the *Mental Measurements Yearbook* (Buros, 1965) will give one some idea of their variety. There are tests for common-sense traits like self-reliance, friendliness and stability. There are tests for psychiatric-sounding traits like hypochondria and schizothymia. Some test-makers have preferred two-ended labels for a trait, such as nervous-composed, ascendance-submission, or "Bohemian unconcernedness *vs.* conventional practicality." The reader of either the Allport and Odbert list or the *Mental Measurement Yearbook* finds himself thinking, "But surely there aren't as many separate personality traits as all this. Surely there must be some simpler way of describing personality differences in people."

Yet in another sense, the traits the personality testers have been trying to measure are too broad rather than too narrow. They imply a consistency in the behavior of an individual from time to time and from situation to situation that observation of ourselves and others would lead us to question. Hartshorne and May (1928) years ago brought this fact to our attention in their discussion of the results they had obtained in attempting to measure such qualities as honesty, generosity, and self-control in children. A person who gets an average score for generosity may be generous to his playmates but not to his brother and sister, and he will probably be much more willing to give away some sorts of toys than others. What then does the score on generosity mean? The fundamental psychological facts are the ways he acts and feels in concrete situations.

His overall "generosity" score may actually cover up these basic facts and thus may be more misleading than helpful when we are trying to understand the boy. Because of this difficulty in the use of trait concepts, some psychologists have been inclined to abandon them and to try instead to develop ways of evaluating each person's unique way of organizing his own experience. For many practical purposes, however, trait evaluations with all their ambiguities seem to be more useful than more penetrating analyses of individual idiosyncracies. Trait concepts do make possible the comparison of one person with another.

Fortunately, as in the case of intelligence measurements, correlational techniques and the factor-analytic methods based on them have shown us how to bring some semblance of order into this confused realm. Traits are not completely separate and independent of one another, and some are much more fundamental than others in the structure of a personality. At their narrowest they merge into the myriad little characteristics of specific acts and experiences; at their broadest they become very much like what theorists of all the centuries have described as basic types. We shall take up these factor-analytic studies in considerable detail in later sections.

Another major difficulty has stood in the way of applying the sort of trait concepts used in ability measurement to personality study. As has been stressed in earlier chapters, tests for any kind of psychological characteristic have to be *validated* before we can be at all sure what they are measuring. As long as we are dealing with an ability of any kind, it is not too difficult to find some life situation in which different degrees of success seem to depend at least to some extent upon the postulated ability. Any correspondence between the degree of success shown by our subjects in the test and in the life situation constitutes evidence as to what our test is measuring. It is always difficult and often impossible to apply the same methods to personality measurements. What shall we use, for example, as a criterion for "optimism" or "determination"? There seem to be no life situations where success depends on the possession of either of these qualities to the extent that school success depends upon intelligence. If we rely upon the correspondence between test scores and ratings made by persons who know our subjects, we are pretty sure to be emphasizing outer appearances rather than inner realities. What we need for validation purposes are situations that will show what a person *is* rather than how he *appears.*

The one ready-made situation that test-makers in the field have had at their disposal is the psychiatric clinic or hospital. Psychotic and neurotic syndromes develop in some individuals, not in others. If we can think of these syndromes as the extremes of personality tendencies found to a lesser degree in many if not all normal people, we have a way of validating tests of some traits by ascertaining whether or not psychiatric patients obtain extreme scores on them. To a visitor from some other planet where psychologists have not been active it might seem a curious fact that we have so many more tests for maladjustment than for adjustment. We can measure neurotic tendencies much more successfully than leadership, delinquent tendencies much more successfully than altruism. One main reason for this state of affairs is that we have a means of validating the measurements in negative directions, an asset that we do not usually have for the positive traits. Furthermore, the practical demands for tests have come primarily from the agencies dealing with personalities that have proved to be in some way inadequate, and thus research has tended to center on their problems.

METHODS OF MEASUREMENT

1. *Ratings*

Quantitative research on individual differences in personality has made use of four principal methods. The first of these is *ratings*. Since most of us have become accustomed in everyday life to describing individuals in terms of traits such as sociability or dependability, it is easy to take the step to assigning numbers from 1 to 5 or from 1 to 7 to represent the strength of the given trait in a person. For practical purposes these ratings have never been superseded by more elaborate methods. When a store manager is trying to decide whether to employ Mr. Barnes, he is most interested in the kind of impression the man has made upon his previous employers. This is the sort of thing that ratings will tell him. They will not tell him much about the basic characteristics of Mr. Barnes—what his deepest desires and his system of values are like—but the employer does not *need* to know these things.

For the psychologist interested in personality theory, however, such knowledge is not only relevant but absolutely essential. When he studies ratings of observed traits, he finds that such data have a number of serious defects. For one thing, they are made by outsiders and thus represent the mask or the face a person shows to the world rather than the self behind the face. There is of course some relationship between these inner and outer selves—in many cases they appear to be much alike—but the relationship is complex and may differ from one person to another. Thus Mrs. Halliday keeps her windows shining clean and her furniture free from dust because she loves her husband and gets a deep satisfaction out of her role as homemaker. Mrs. Berwick does the same thing because she has irrational and obsessive fear of dust and disorder. Ratings of the two for cleanliness would be similar, but there is a world of difference in the personalities to which these similar ratings apply.

Furthermore, ratings inevitably have in them something of the personality of the rater as well as the person rated. Consequently, two sets of ratings of the same group of subjects often do not agree very well. Because of the shape life has imposed upon his perceptual apparatus, one rater sees some things in those he observes where another sees different things. No matter how hard we try to be objective, our own personalities affect the judgments we make of the personalities of others. When it is necessary to use ratings in a research study this defect can be corrected to some extent by using several judges and assuming that their idiosyncracies will cancel out in the general average. This procedure works more successfully for some traits than for others, and there are correlational techniques for testing its adequacy.

The apparent unreliability of ratings may arise from confusion about personality theory rather than from defects in the rating method itself. A clear theoretical orientation shows one what to rate. It seems quite apparent in the example given above that "cleanliness" is not really a personality trait, but a symptom of something else. It is because judges of personality start with different theories and interpret surface traits or habits in different ways that they come out with ratings that do not agree. In research settings where psychologists are proceeding according to clearly defined theoretical formulations, there is little difficulty in obtaining a satisfactory degree of agreement in ratings.

There is almost no limit to the kinds of traits that have been rated in studies of personality. Psychiatric ratings of patients have been used as basic data for correlational studies of syndromes or symptom-complexes, and as criteria for the validation of tests. Observers have been asked to rate the behavior of subjects in standard situations, their expressive movements, or their projective test protocols. Individuals in groups have been asked to rate one another, and ingenious ways of obtaining these judgments, the sociometric and "Guess Who" procedures, have been worked out. Statistical methods for handling all sorts of special rating problems have been developed. With all their defects, ratings have contributed much to our knowledge of personality.

2. *Questionnaires*

The second type of personality "measurement" that has been widely used is the questionnaire or self-report inventory. This requires that the subject answer questions about himself—what he does, what he likes and dislikes, how he feels. This method also has its defects, some obvious, some not so immediately apparent. The one usually noticed first is that the score depends to a large extent on the subject's honesty. Nothing can prevent him from saying "yes" to the questions having to do with good traits and "no" to those having to do with undesirable traits if he wishes to. This particular defect is more serious in practical situations where personality is being evaluated than it is in personality research. The applicant for admission to a professional school, for example, has a powerful motive *not* to be honest about his less admirable qualities, since he believes that his whole future depends upon his being allowed to obtain the professional training. The same person in a psychological laboratory may make a very satisfactory subject, particularly if conditions are set up to insure complete anonymity of results. In still another situation, one in which he is seeking psychotherapy, he may have a tendency to choose the *unfavorable* answers in order to prove that he does indeed need help. Such effects of the subject's interpretation of the test situation cannot all be classified as deliberate dishonesty. To a large extent they may be quite unconscious, a natural and unavoidable part of the total complex of motives that are operating. Some technical improvements in the construction of tests of the questionnaire type have obviated these difficulties to some extent. The widely used Minnesota Multiphasic Personality Inventory, for example, has special keys designed to indicate whether the person taking it was trying to show himself in a good or a bad light, and to correct the score for such tendencies. "Malingering" keys on various tests were developed during World War II. By paying attention to the way a person is *likely* to interpret a specific testing situation, a psychologist can avoid using inventories for purposes that are inappropriate. However, even when such precautions have been taken, there is still some residual doubt about the meaning of the answers to the questions. Even the score of a completely honest subject is somewhat ambiguous. Much human motivation is not accessible to conscious awareness. The answers we give to questions about ourselves doubtless have some relationship to unconscious motives, but they do not reveal such basic factors directly.

Since Cronbach first called attention to the phenomenon of *response set*, there have been many explorations of tendencies to answer test questions in certain ways, regardless of their specific content. Edwards (1957) demonstrated that a *social desirability* factor plays an important part in the scores individuals obtain on many personality questionnaires. Messick and Jackson (1961) demonstrated that *acquiescence*, the tendency to answer "yes" to questions about oneself or to go along with any opinion suggested, is one of these consistent response sets influencing test scores. On questions having to do with interests and preferences some persons say that they *like* the vast majority of the activities presented to them, whereas others show a predominance of *dislike* responses. When asked to indicate on a 5-point scale how strongly they agree with statements about attitudes and beliefs, some persons use the extreme categories, 1 and 5, to describe their own views, whereas others limit their responses to the middle ones, 2, 3, and 4. Enough has been discovered about these and other response sets to require that their possible effects must always be taken into consideration when we attempt to interpret the scores on personality inventories.

Whether or not answers can be taken at face value would not matter if we were in a position to validate personality tests against good outside criteria of the traits we seek to measure. We can if we like consider each "yes" or "no" answer (or each black mark on an IBM sheet) as a bit of behavior in response to a verbal stimulus. If it can be shown that it is related to other kinds of behavior, it is useful for personality evaluation. Thus if "I dislike black cats" is always answered "yes" by housewives and "no" by career women it becomes an index to whatever the personality trait or trait complex is that determines this choice of life pattern. This completely empirical approach has determined the choice of items in the Strong Vocational Interest Blank (to be discussed in more detail in the next chapter) and the Minnesota Multiphasic Personality Inventory. The reason it has not been used more often is that clear-cut criteria for sorting human beings into categories are scarce. Men and women, people in different occupational groups, and psychiatric patients with different diagnoses have so far furnished the more clear-cut groupings making possible the empirical selection of valid personality items. Whenever a research worker can identify a new kind of natural grouping, it then becomes possible to identify personality tendencies that go with it.

Another approach to the validation problem that has become increasingly popular is to correlate responses to test questions with *one another* rather than with outside criteria. By this means clusters of items can be found which hang together and thus seem to have some common root in personality. The term *factorial validity* is applied to traits discovered in this way, traits which do appear to have some consistency, generality, and stability. What must always be remembered, when we use tests that have been developed in this manner, is that there is no real evidence as to what the traits are or how they will show themselves in life situations. Perhaps they should always be called simply A, B, and C, or X-1, Y-2, and Z-3, rather than, for example, "dominance" or "introversion." Until some evidence of predictive validity is available for these tests, they cannot become a sound basis for practical judgments that must be made of students, patients, or applicants for jobs. It is clear that a high score on a group of items all *appearing* to measure dominance may reflect any one of a number of things—such as an unwillingness to admit shyness, a stereotype characteristic of a certain socioeconomic subculture, or the effect of a certain kind of schooling. If we use such scores to select salesmen or discussion leaders, we may choose the very persons who are likely to be least successful at such tasks. Factorial validation cannot be a substitute for tryout in life situations.

The concept of *construct validity* has been especially important in personality measurement for research purposes. Often the definition of a trait is based on some particular personality theory. In such cases a careful analysis of what has been said on the subject in which one is interested by Freud, Jung, or Rogers leads to hypotheses about expected relationships between sets of scores, or expected differences between experimentally determined groups. The researcher administers the set of test-items he has devised to measure the trait and analyzes the relationships or the group differences to find out whether or not they support his hypotheses. If they do, the test has acquired some construct validity. If they do not, either the test or the theory is faulty; there is no way of knowing which.

One other difficulty, in some ways more troublesome than any of the others we have discussed, characterizes personality measurement by questionnaire. In using as a score the number of items answered in a certain way, we make the assumption that more separate manifestations of a given trait mean a greater intensity or a larger amount of it. But is this necessarily true? Is a patient who has a variety of obsessive-compulsive symptoms really worse off than the one whose only abnormality is an overwhelming urge to set things on fire? Admittedly this is an extreme example. Probably in most cases a larger number of symptoms does indicate a greater degree of maladjustment. It would seem, however, that this limitation restricts the degree of validity that can be obtained for personality inventories even if all other validation problems can be solved.

A simple but penetrating analysis of the differences between the experimental conditions used in testing abilities and those used in testing personality has been made by Fiske and Butler (1963). When we measure ability we tell the subjects what their task is and motivate them to do their best. If we succeed in establishing these conditions for everybody, differences between individuals reflect differences in genuine ability. In testing personality, we do not tell the subjects what we are trying to find out, nor do we motivate them all in any standard way. Thus differences in their responses may mean any one of a number of things. Persons who make practical use of personality questionnaires in clinics, schools, and hospitals should always keep in mind these essential limitations.

3. *Projective Techniques*

During the 1940's and 1950's projective or expressive methods of personality evaluation became enormously popular among psychologists. The basic idea underlying them is simple: Since personality can be thought of as the consistent manner in which a man interprets and organizes his experience, the way to measure it is to present him with ambiguous nonstructured or partially-structured materials and note what he does with them. Literally hundreds of possible methods for doing this have been tried, and hardly a month passes that someone does not propose a new system. The leader of the procession, however, has been the Rorschach test with its ten inkblots for subjects to interpret.

The advantages of the projective methods are their flexibility and freedom, and the opportunity they afford for observing the person as a whole rather than trying to reconstruct him from separate trait scores obtained on separate tests. His intelligence and his emotions, his memories and his hopes, all coalesce in one of these protocols. Clinical experience has left little doubt that a sensitive, experienced interpreter can gain a large measure of intuitive understanding of an individual from his responses to projective tests. They have become indispensable in clinical work.

There are difficulties, however, when we try to use them as research instruments to help us understand the nature and organization of individual differences in personality. For one thing, quantification is a problem. To use results in regression equations or factor analyses we must have *scores* rather than qualitative descriptions. If we simply add answers of a given kind, as is often done in the case of Rorschach W, M, or FC responses, we are discarding the most distinctive and valuable contribution a projective technique has to offer, the opportunity of evaluation of each aspect of a record against the background of everything else in it. But if, on the other hand, we use this clinical approach, and ask the interpreter to *rate* the subject for introversion, ego strength, and anxiety, we have reverted to the very *trait* approach to personality that we hoped to avoid by using projective methods.

A more important source of ambiguity in research based on projective tests, as well as in their application in many practical situations, is the problem of validity. No less than in work with inventories it is essential that some evidence be forthcoming of a demonstrated relationship between test performances and behavior in real-life situations. Because a test like the Rorschach purports to cover such a broad range of personality qualities the question of its validity becomes very complex. It is not enough to show that skilled judges can match case histories and Rorschach records as a whole. We need to know something about the validity of each of the separate kinds of judgments. Do large numbers of movement responses show creative talent of some sort? If not, what do they show? Are all varieties of color response related to the same aspects of personality? Does a "small detail" score of 20 out of one hundred total responses mean the same as a score of 2 out of ten? Such are the questions that Rorschach validation research must take under consideration, and the other projective methods face similar problems.

4. *Behavioral and Physiological Tests*

There is still a fourth main type of personality evaluation which in spite of its long history has never come into general use. It can be labeled the *objective* method if we use "objectivity" as the measurement of something the subject *does* in a standardized situation rather than what he *says* he does. But the word "objective" has taken on so many shades of meaning in psychology that perhaps it is more accurate to characterize the methods falling under this heading as measurements of behavior or of physiological changes. What they have in common is that the subject is not asked to describe himself or to report on his own behavior. Thus all the problems related to response sets are bypassed.

One of the most ingenious collections of behavioral tests ever to be used in large-scale research was that assembled during the 1920's for the Character Education Inquiry reported in the three much-quoted volumes by Hartshorne et al. (1928, 1929, 1930). The tests for honesty, for example, included one in which children were placed in a situation where they would have an opportunity to copy answers from an examination key and one in which coins were left in boxes with the puzzles they were working. "Service" tests gave each subject opportunities to choose whether a score should count for himself or for the group and whether he should keep prized articles himself or give them away to less fortunate children. One of the inhibition tests required a subject to refrain from touching some interesting small object until his task was done.

Most recently two of the leading research workers in the field of personality have revived the interest in objective personality tests and developed some new techniques. R. B. Cattell (1948a) has attempted to get at such things as perseveration, fluency, speed of judgment, fluctuation of attitudes, and suggestibility. Eysenck (1947) has measured motor control, level of aspiration, persistence, and personal tempo. Both of these investigators have included in their test batteries physiological measurements such as dark adaptation and the psychogalvanic response. Their results and conclusions will be discussed a little later.

The reasons why these methods have been used less widely than ratings, questionnaires, or projective techniques are not hard to find. For one thing, in educational, industrial, and clinical settings, data like these cannot be obtained without great difficulty. Much of the testing must be done individually, complicated apparatus is often required, and hours of each subject's time may be needed. Furthermore, situations like many of those from which Hartshorne and May obtained their scores only occur in the presence of an individual's own social group. One test that attempted to assess personality traits objectively in a practical way by means of handwriting, the Downey "will-temperament" test (Downey, 1923), became very popular after it was first published but fell into disrepute when validity studies failed to support the author's statements as to what was being measured. There is at present no convenient way for a clinical worker or personnel man to evaluate personality through behavior. Even for research programs, tests of this type have certain disadvantages. Scores tend to be unreliable, as they are easily influenced by various chance determiners. Different tests which should logically be expected to measure the same trait show only low correlations with one another. The average intercorrelation for Hartshorne and May's nine tests of "deceitful behavior," for example, was only .227; for tests of "service," it was .201. Such findings led to doubt whether it was possible to get at broad personality traits in this way—whether, in fact, there were any such things as broad personality traits.

It was the development of the new and more powerful factor-analytic methods focusing on the *pattern* of the intercorrelations rather than their size that led psychologists to take another look at the objective test methods. They do have one great advantage over all the others, that a subject's scores are unbiased. Neither his own need to make a good impression nor the reputation he has among those who know him can influence them to any great extent. Traits identified by carrying out factor analyses of such scores might thus be expected to be more stable and less ambiguous than those identified by means of the other kinds of measurements.

In spite of the great diversity of measuring techniques and the many difficulties that beset all of them, some order has emerged in the domain of personality measurement. Some of the traits identified in research based on ratings and inventories have also turned up in the interpretations of projective protocols. Characteristics similar to those that differentiate neurotic from normal soldiers have been observed in school children. As statistical techniques for handling complex combinations of scores have been improved, it has become increasingly possible to analyze these relationships. Despite a good deal of confusion we have acquired some solid knowledge about a few basic personality traits.

BASIC PERSONALITY VARIABLES: NEUROTICISM

The first and broadest of the personality variables to be measured in many ways is general *neuroticism* or emotional instability. Much of the work of Eysenck reported in the three books *Dimensions of Personality* (1947), *The Scientific Study of Personality* (1952), and *The Structure of Human Personality* (1953b), has been directed to the definition and description of this trait by factor-analytic methods. The fact that it is defined in negative terms, as "neuroticism" rather than as some superior quality, is a natural result of the sociological fact mentioned above—that persons who get into difficulties requiring psychiatric help constitute a convenient group to use in validating personality tests. Eysenck has taken full advantage of this opportunity for validation. He has developed a procedure called *criterion analysis* to supplement the factor analysis of correlations between personality test scores and obtain evidence as to what the factors represent. After showing that the tests which come out with the highest loadings on the first, most general factor based on individual differences in normal nonpsychiatric subjects are the same tests that most clearly differentiate neurotic patients from people in general, he concludes that this particular set of tests measures a continuous variable which can reasonably be called "neuroticism" even in normal people. They differ from the patients not in any absolute, qualitative way, but simply by having less of the trait the tests measure. And some of them, of course, have more than others.

Eysenck and his associates carried on detailed research of various kinds with regard to this basic trait. They preferred, at least at first, to use "objective" tests to measure it—such things as motor dexterity, darkness vision, and body sway. The largest groups of subjects were normal and neurotic soldiers, but differences on the neuroticism factor showed up also in school children, mental defectives, students, and unskilled factory workers (Eysenck, 1952). Eysenck assembled considerable evidence that ratings, personality inventories, and the Rorschach test all measure this same trait along with whatever else they are measuring.

Such an interpretation makes good sense to clinical workers as well as experimentalists. Those who are familiar with the kinds of profiles obtained from scores on the Minnesota Multiphasic Personality Inventory, for example, know that the easiest thing to observe about an individual record is its general elevation. Factor-analytic studies have corroborated these impressions that separate symptoms of maladjustment tend to correlate, thus giving the impression that some individuals tend to be "worse off" in many or all ways than are others. The first judgment a skilled interpreter is likely to make of a Rorschach record has to do with the *degree* of personality difficulty it indicates. It has proved feasible to develop checklists of Rorschach characteristics in order to get a quantitative measure of neurotic tendency for use in diagnosis or research. Both the Munroe inspection method (Munroe, 1945) and the Bühler basic score (Bühler et al., 1949) are grounded in this kind of reasoning. Factor analysis of Rorschach scores has pointed to a factor that can reasonably be called neuroticism (Eysenck, 1952).

One of the most valuable contributions made by Eysenck's work of delimiting and defining this variable has been the clear separation of the tendency toward neurosis from the tendency toward psychosis or complete mental breakdown. Confusion over this issue has for years handicapped both the personality theorists and the applied psychologists who attempted to develop usable personality tests. The question essentially is, "Is a neurotic condition or syndrome a less severe manifestation of the same personality traits that lead to psychosis, or are two separate traits or dimensions involved?" The criterion-analysis procedure outlined above made it possible for the first time to answer the question unambiguously. The figures show (1952, Ch. 6) that neurotic and psychotic tendencies are two completely different dimensions of personality though both are continuous with traits existing in normal people. The nature of the proof involved in this rather complicated kind of statistical analysis is that the tests defining the neuroticism factor in normal individuals differentiate clearly between diagnosed neurotics and normals, but they do not differentiate at all between diagnosed psychotics and normals. Another quite different family of tests must be used to differentiate psychotics from normals.

The nature of the evidence that these two personality variables are independent of one another can be seen in Figure 28. It represents the

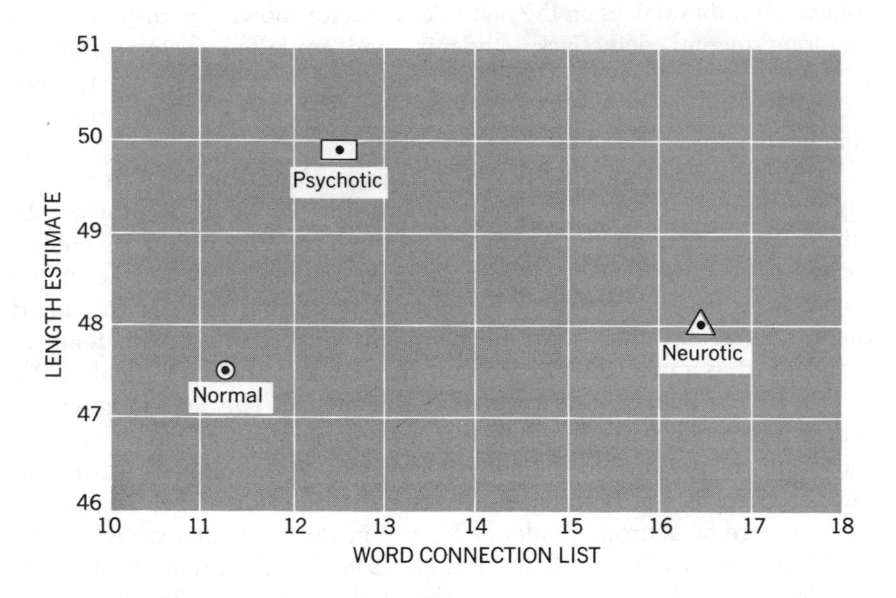

FIGURE 28

Differences in Average Scores Made by Neurotic, Psychotic, and Normal Subjects

(Reprinted by permission of The Macmillan Company from Eysenck, *The scientific study of personality,* 1952, p. 224)

average scores for the three groups on two tests. With regard to the Word Connection List, neurotics differ markedly from normals while psychotics make practically normal scores. But with regard to the test of Length Estimation, psychotics differ markedly from normals, whereas neurotics score at the normal level. This difference in the pattern of scores obtained from the two abnormal groups was apparent in most test combinations and showed up very clearly in the factor analyses based on the correlations. Because "neuroticism" and "psychoticism" are continuous variables, rather than all-or-none characteristics, a perfectly sane individual well within the normal range may show some behavior suggesting that of psychotic patients and some like that characteristic of neurotics. All of us probably have a certain amount of both traits as part of our basic human nature. Because the two tendencies are independent, we must not use the one as an indicator of the other. Eysenck would hold that the anxious, nervous man, or the girl who is subject to hysterical fainting spells is no more likely to be hospitalized for schizophrenia or manic-depressive psychosis than is the person without such neurotic symptoms.

There is one question growing out of the work on the neuroticism factor that has not been so satisfactorily answered. It is, "What is the positive or opposite end of this continuum?" "What is the meaning of unusual *freedom* from tendencies leading to a diagnosis of neuroticism?" It should be understood that it is the concept or its interpretation that gives us trouble rather than the test results themselves. On Eysenck's battery of objective tests there are some subjects in the normal group who are unusually free from worries, annoyances, and suggestibility. Who are these people, and how can we expect them to behave in real-life situations? What does "neuroticism" turn into at the opposite or "good" end of its distribution? This is of course the same problem that was discussed earlier in regard to personality measurement in general. We lack for subjects at the low end of the neuroticism scale the kind of criterion information that psychiatric study gives us for persons at the high end.

There are, however, some suggestive research leads. A number of investigators, working entirely with normal subjects, and applying factor-analytic methods to carefully obtained ratings of personal characteristics, have reported a factor the negative extreme of which is usually called "e" for "emotionality" and the positive extreme "w" for "will." The earliest of these studies was reported by Webb (1915). Ratings were made of two groups of students and four groups of children on 39 traits grouped under headings of "Emotions," "Self-qualities," "Sociability," "Activity," and "Intellect." Correlations were analyzed by Spearman's method, which as explained in a previous chapter identifies the most general factor first and then extracts factors of lesser scope from the residual correlations. As might be expected, the "g" factor, representing general intellectual ability, was the first thing to appear. It is the second factor, relatively independent of intelligence, that is of most interest to us here. Webb called it "w" and defined it as "consistency of action resulting from deliberate volition or will." Traits producing high "w" ratings are: tendency not to abandon tasks from mere changeability; tendency not to abandon tasks in face of obstacles; kindness on principle; trustworthiness; conscientiousness; and perseverance in face of obstacles.

Since 1915, something resembling this "w" factor has shown up again and again in quantitative personality studies, particularly those based on ratings. Burt (1939), who has made several such studies on children, has

volition – exercise of the will.

been most explicit about the meaning of the factor, which he called "general emotionality." At one extreme it represents neurotic instability, at the other dependability and persistence. P. E. Vernon (1953) would prefer to call the trait "dependability-undependability."

It would be easy to identify "w" with another trait arising from a quite different type of research, the Hartshorne and May character study described above (1928, 1929, 1930). They worked out for each child a variability score based on the standard deviation of his twenty-one scores on separate tests. These standard deviations can reasonably be considered measures of consistency or integration. Correlations between integration scores and various separate traits resemble those obtained by Eysenck and others for freedom from neuroticism (1953b, pp. 136–139). Maller (1934), who carried out a factor analysis of tests for honesty, cooperation, inhibition, and persistence, found that one general factor accounted for the correlations. It appeared to be the same as this "w" or integration factor. He described it as a "readiness to forego an immediate gain for the sake of a remote but greater gain."

It is impossible to be certain that a factor coming out of one study is identical with a factor coming out of another in which both subjects and tests are different. What is needed is some coordinated research in which various methods that have shown promise can be applied to the same groups. If it turns out, for example, that the *same children* get high scores on ratings defining Webb's "w" and tests defining Hartshorne and May's "integration," and low scores on tests defining Eysenck's "neuroticism," the nature of the underlying personality variable will be much clearer than it now is and we can proceed to find out what its sources are, how it affects behavior, and how amenable to change it is. We are a long way as yet from such certainty, and some pieces do not quite fit into the picture. The set of qualities we have been labeling "w" could as easily be seen as the obverse of psychotic as of neurotic trends, and the kind of person we label "psychopathic personality" would appear to be especially low in these character qualities. Yet Eysenck has shown that "psychoticism" is a separate trait from "neuroticism" and that the psychopaths too are different from neurotics (1952, p. 151). It would be possible to represent these facts geometrically by three axes meeting at a common origin as in Figure 29. The origin would then represent complete *freedom* from all these personality flaws. But what of the extension of each of the axes in the opposite direction as indicated by the dotted lines in the figure? Do they represent anything? Or is "normality" the most that can be achieved?

Eysenck himself has not moved in this direction. In his publications since 1953 he has been more interested in using his dimensional system to facilitate the exploration of other research questions. The system itself has not been changed or elaborated.

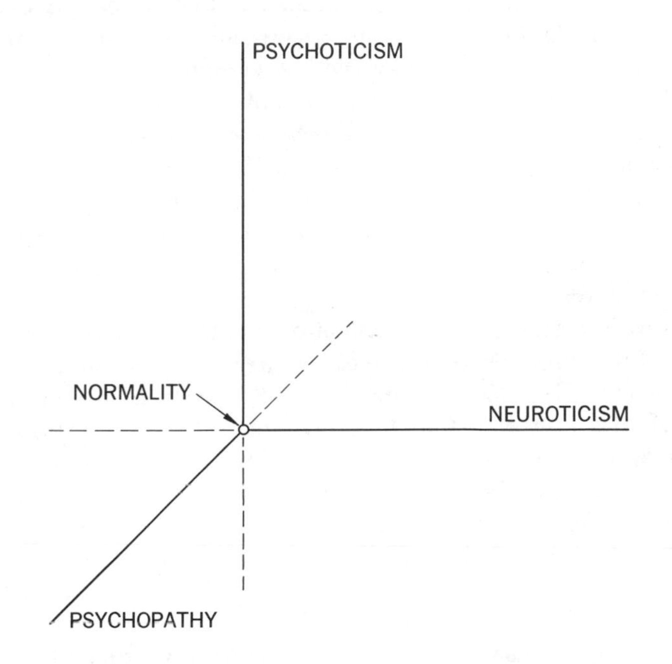

FIGURE 29
Hypothetical Relationship of Three Personality Dimensions

While there has been a considerable amount of discussion focusing on the concept of positive mental health, no quantitative research designed to delimit and clarify the concept has been reported.

BASIC PERSONALITY VARIABLES: EXTRAVERSION-INTROVERSION

There is another basic trait which has appeared again and again in the philosophical discussions and scientific investigations of personality. The terms *extraversion* and *introversion* were first used by Jung in his exposition of psychological types, but the distinction the words stand for had been made for centuries. "Extraversion" refers to the kind of outward orientation that makes a person highly aware of what is going on around him and causes him to direct his energy toward objects and people outside himself. "Introversion" is the opposite inward-turning tendency that makes a person sensitive to his own feelings and experiences and causes him to direct his efforts toward understanding them.

There has been much confusion over the terms and much misunderstanding. According to Jung's reasoning, extraversion and introversion are not mutually exclusive categories. Both trends are a part of everyone's psychological makeup, and if one of them is not in evidence in behavior he looks for signs of its unconscious operation. Furthermore, Jung did not equate extraversion with sociability as many psychologists have done. For Jung the introvert was not necessarily shy, seclusive, or socially maladjusted. When social behavior is used as the touchstone, introversion becomes confused with the neuroticism we have been describing. The lack of agreement between different theorists and different research workers as to the exact meaning of the terms makes for a situation in which psychologists use them with more hesitation than does the man in the street.

Work with personality questionnaires has made us very much aware of the fact that introversion-extraversion mean different things to different people. During the 1920's several different inventories were published by Laird, Heidbreder, Marston, Conklin, and others (see Symonds, 1931, pp. 195–205). Little evidence was adduced for the validity of any of these inventories, largely because of the difficulty of obtaining a usable criterion for the trait. Furthermore it became increasingly apparent that the different tests did not correlate very well with one another. It was quite possible for a person to come out as an introvert on one test, an extravert on another. P. E. Vernon (1938) found in summarizing correlations reported for various kinds of personality inventories that the average correlation between different tests of introversion was only .36 and that this figure was practically identical with the one obtained when introversion tests were correlated with tests supposedly measuring neurotic tendency. Such findings caused questionnaire assessments of introversion-extraversion to fall into disrepute. In fact, they caused a large number of psychologists to wash their hands of the whole concept.

Eysenck (1947), using objective personality tests and factor-analysis methods, came out with much more solid evidence that introversion-extraversion is a meaningful basic dimension of personality. He found first that the psychiatric diagnoses of neurotic patients were of two main types which he called *dysthymia* and *hysteria*. "Dysthymia" covers those conditions where the main feature is anxiety and depression, and seems to characterize introverted personalities. "Hysteria" covers the condition marked chiefly by physical conversion symptoms and by inability to work or to take responsibility, and is a disorder to which extraverts are subject. Patients in the two groups were clearly differentiated by many of their test performances. On "level-of-aspiration" tests, for example, subjects in the introverted group showed large discrepancies between the goals they set for themselves and their accomplishments, whereas the extraverts set their sights much lower and did not underestimate their past performances so much. On tests given to airplane pilots where precise organization of motor responses was required, the dysthymics (introverts) showed overactivity and restlessness, whereas the hysterics (extraverts) showed boredom and failure to concentrate on the task. In still a different sort of experiment, it was shown that extraverted patients were much more amused by cartoons than the introverted were, the greatest differences showing up on those with sexual themes. The fact that these same sorts of objective tests showed similar differences between persons who were within the normal range led Eysenck to think of introversion-extraversion as another personality continuum along which individuals, normal or neurotic, could be ranked. However, most of the studies he reported in which such tests were used in connection with practical problems—employability of the feebleminded, work adjustment of unskilled laborers, selection of students and of nurses—did not give much evidence for its utility (see 1952, Ch. 7). One interesting finding was that severe neurotics after the brain operation called leucotomy showed significant changes in the direction of extraversion. Since this is just what had been predicted about the effect of the operation, it constituted some evidence for the theoretical structure on the basis of which the prediction was made. We can sum up by saying that the research work of Eysenck and his associates furnished strong support for the idea of an introvert-extravert dimension in *neurotics,* but that the significance of the trait in normals remains somewhat uncertain.

Eysenck's work since 1953 on this dimension has been an attempt to identify its physiological basis. Viewing all of the basic dimensions as constitutional variables determined to a considerable extent by heredity (Eysenck and Prell, 1951; Eysenck, 1956) and reasoning from some of the postulates of Hull's learning theory, he hypothesized that the difference between extraverted and introverted persons arises from differences in excitatory and inhibitory potentials in the central nervous system. Persons high in neural inhibition are extraverted because of the fact that their experiences simply do not "resonate" long enough to support an interest in this inner life. Persons low in neural inhibition have persisting traces, so that the inward direction of attention characteristic of introverts is a natural result. Eysenck (1957) set up learning experiments designed to discover whether groups of dysthymics and hysterics, or groups of tested introverts and extraverts within the normal range differed in neural inhibition. His findings that the predicted differences did indeed occur have been questioned by others, so that as yet this particular aspect of Eysenck's theory has not been generally accepted.

There is one idea with regard to the introversion-extraversion continuum that has had wide currency and been discussed in hundreds of papers. It is the hypothesis that the contrasting psychiatric diagnoses of schizophrenia and manic-depressive psychosis represent the extremes of introversion-extraversion. According to this theory, the schizophrenics are exaggerated introverts, manic-depressive patients exaggerated extraverts. Often the idea has been tied in with the theories about the relationship between physique and temperament (Kretschmer, 1925) which we will take up in more detail in a later chapter. The best evidence on this question comes from Eysenck's study (1952, Ch. 6) of what he called the psychotic dimension. The subjects were 100 normal people and 100 psychotics, of whom 50 were manic-depressive and 50 schizophrenic. On the basis of the tests that he used he was able to obtain no evidence at all for the idea that the two psychotic states represent opposite ends of a single continuum. "Psychoticism" seemed to be a trait totally different from "neuroticism," but schizophrenics as a group differed from manic-depressives simply in being somewhat less "psychotic." One such study, however well designed, does not settle an issue of this magnitude. There is a real possibility that this particular battery of tests did not include the kinds of performance or expose the subjects to the kinds of situation that would allow differences between types of psychotics to show up. But negative findings like these should at least make us cautious about any conclusion that introversion and schizophrenia are different degrees of the same thing.

One way of summarizing the work on introversion-extraversion as a personality dimension is to say that it has been suggestive but not conclusive. Perhaps one barrier to progress here is the trait concept itself. The most promising recent work in this area, the development of the Myers-Briggs Type Indicator, has gone back to Jung's original formulation, in which introversion and extraversion are not traits or dimensions to be measured, but rather *directions of development.*

MORE COMPLEX FACTOR-ANALYTIC RESEARCH

British and American psychologists have differed in their approach to personality measurement just as they have in their work on intelligence. The factor-analytic methods used in Britain encourage interpretation in terms of a few broad characteristics such as neuroticism and introversion. The methods preferred in the United States lead to interpretations in terms of a much larger number of basic traits.

One main line of research here has been the analysis of correlations between item responses on personality questionnaires. The aim was to locate clusters of responses which could then be examined in an attempt to determine what tendencies they represented. Guilford and Guilford (1936, 1939a and b) and Martin (1945) made a number of such factor analyses of interitem correlations and came out with thirteen differentiable traits.

Subsequently Lovell (1945) factor-analyzed the correlations between total scores on these thirteen personality variables in a search for a smaller number of traits of broader scope which could be used in place of the thirteen to describe a personality. Four of these so-called "super-factors" seemed to account for most of the relationships. Another analysis of the Guilford data by L. L. Thurstone (1951b) produced seven major factors in place of the original thirteen.

Thus the question of just how many independent factors were represented in this comprehensive set of personality items has been a matter of some doubt. Another attempt to find out was made by Guilford and Zimmerman (1956). They first asked judges to classify the items, placing together those that seemed to be concerned with the same thing. They came out with 69 little tests of from two to eight items each, three variables for each of the original thirteen factors. They used as a 70th variable the sex of the subject. Using Lovell's sample of 126 men and 87 women, they ran a new factor analysis and found clear evidence for fourteen separate factors, the last one not readily interpretable. The final list included in the Guilford-Zimmerman Temperament Survey, now available in published form, is as follows:

G—General Activity
A—Ascendance *vs.* Submission
M—Masculinity-Femininity
I—Confidence *vs.* Inferiority Feelings
N—Calmness, Composure *vs.* Nervousness
S—Sociability
T—Reflectiveness
D—Depression
C—Emotionality
R—Restraint *vs.* Rhathymia (carefree disposition)
O—Objectivity
Ag—Agreeableness
Co—Cooperativeness, Tolerance

One trouble with work of this kind is that the answers subjects give to the questions in a personality inventory must necessarily be doubtful indicators of what their real personality traits are. There is a possibility that the Guilford factors represent different kinds of *test-taking attitude* rather than basic categories in experience or behavior. However, it is something to have shown that the things subjects are willing to say about themselves fall into these patterns. Corroboration is needed from other kinds of research before we can be sure that these are the basic dimensions of personality.

The work of R. B. Cattell, as reported in numerous journal articles and several books, is the most ambitious attempt anyone has made to combine factor analyses of ratings, questionnaires, and objective tests into an organized whole and to integrate the results with nonmathematical classifications of personality. The overall plan of his research program has been to identify basic factors from separate studies based on ratings, questionnaires, and objective tests, and then to apply all three methods to a single group in order to determine whether the same factors would show up for all three.

He started with ratings. The problem of *what to rate,* one of the continuing difficulties in personality study, was solved in an ingenious manner. His basic assumption is that language development over a period of many centuries has by now given us *words* for all the personality traits that are discernible in human beings. Thus if we include all the traits for which there are *names* we will have a list defining what Cattell calls the "total personality sphere." After identifying clusters of traits on this sphere, factor analysis should give us clues as to the source traits from which these clusters grow. Cattell took his basic list of trait names from the dictionary prepared by Allport and Odbert (1936), and suplemented it with names from psychiatric and psychological literature. In order to reduce the number to workable size, a psychologist and a student of literature went over the list carefully, grouping all synonyms together. Ratings were then obtained on 100 adults for each of these 171 characteristics. After this enormous number of ratings had been intercorrelated, traits were grouped into *clusters* by putting together those that correlated more than .45 with each other. By making some minor omissions it was possible to reduce the number of clusters to thirty-five. Then 208 male adults, representing quite a wide range of the population, were rated on each of the thirty-five variables. Correlations between these ratings constituted the raw material for the factor analysis. Twelve factors emerged from this analysis, reported in full in Cattell's 1946 book.

Since then, research activities of the Cattell group have proceeded in many directions. The studies using rating methods were replicated on different samples (R. B. Cattell, 1947, 1948a and b, 1950b,c,d). Other ways of correlating sets of scores with one another were employed to identify factors representing changes over time in a single person rather than factors representing what many persons have in common. (A. K. S. Cattell, R. B. Cattell, and Rhymer, 1947; R. B. Cattell and Luborsky, 1950). Different methods of measurement were tried, in addition to ratings.

Perhaps the most crucial phase of the Cattell research program was the attempt to match up factors obtained from questionnaires and from objective tests to see whether they corresponded to the factors based on ratings (R. B. Cattell and Saunders, 1950). The plan was to use the same 370 students as subjects in all the studies so that it would be apparent whether or not the same individuals stood high in a trait when it was measured in different ways. The unfortunate fact that many of these subjects dropped out of the project before it ended makes the final results somewhat ambiguous. On some of the objective tests the number dropped as low as 77, and only 35 finished all the special physiological measures. As the results stand, the factors from the three media do not really match up very well. Only three factors seemed to be the same for all three kinds of measurements, and because of the small N's involved in some correlations these were not too certain (Cattell and Saunders, 1950).

Each successive research undertaking has served to add some new factors to the previous list and to modify the description of what each dimension signifies about personality. A complete report of the findings, along with the results of similar analyses of motivational measurements and ideas about important personality problems that Cattell hopes this system of multidimensional measurements will eventually help to solve, can be found in his 1957 book, *Personality and Motivation: Structure and Measurement.*

The list of primary traits based on ratings or life history data includes:

A. Cyclothymia *vs.* Schizothymia
B. Intelligence
C. Ego Strength *vs.* Proneness to Neuroticism
D. Excitability
E. Dominance *vs.* Submissiveness
F. Surgency (optimistic enthusiasm) *vs.* Desurgency
G. Superego Strength
H. Parmia (parasympathetic immunity) *vs.* Threctia (threat reactivity)
I. Premsia (protected emotional sensitivity) *vs.* Harria (hard realism)
J. Coasthenia (cultural pressure conflict asthenia) *vs.* Zeppia (zestful co-operativeness)
K. Comention (conformity or cultural amenability) *vs.* Abcultion (abhorring and rejecting cultural identification)
L. Protension (projection and tension) *vs.* Inner Relaxation
M. Autia (autonomous, self-absorbed relaxation) *vs.* Praxernia (incapacity to dissociate feelings of inadequacy)
N. Shrewdness *vs.* Naiveté
O. Guilt-proneness *vs.* Confidence

Factor analyses based on questionnaire measurements offered some substantiation for the above factors and added several more:

Q_1 Radicalism *vs.* Conservatism
Q_2 Self Sufficiency
Q_3 Self Sentiment Control
Q_4 Ergic Tension, or Conflict Pressure
Q_5 Fantasy Tendency

Analyses of objective test results produced fewer good matches for the original source traits and a larger number of new traits than the questionnaire analyses did. It is the questionnaire approach that has been emphasized in more recent work. With the publication of the 16 P F test built to measure all but the last of the factors listed above (which have been given more commonplace names rather than the picturesque neologisms), and of similar personality questionnaires for high-school students and for younger children (R. B. Cattell and Gruen, 1953, 1954), this system of organizing variables has been made available for many kinds of research and application.

In evaluating the contributions made to our knowledge of personality by these highly complicated and time-consuming factor-analytic investigations, it can be said that while they have not as yet accomplished as much as they set out to do they have been of considerable value. They have not given us an unambiguous picture of personality structure in terms of which we can describe the chief ways in which one person differs from another. But they have given us new tools and new ideas with which to work. Time will disclose how useful these prove to be.

IDENTIFYING BASIC TRAITS WITHOUT FACTOR ANALYSIS

1. *Empirical Group Comparisons*

There are other approaches to the problem of identifying measurable personality traits. One of these is to assume that different kinds of psychiatric disability represent the extreme ends of distributions covering the normal range, and then to use these distributions as indications of what some of the important personality variables are. The most widely used personality test based initially on this assumption is the Minnesota Multiphasic Personality Inventory (MMPI). Each of the original clinical scoring keys is made up of items that differentiate significantly between patients with a specified diagnosis and normal persons. One trouble with accepting these as basic dimensions is that they have turned out to have rather high intercorrelations and thus represent fewer separate traits than the number of scores suggests. Comrey made a series of systematic attempts to clarify through factor analytic methods the underlying structure of personality traits represented in MMPI items (Comrey and Soufi, 1960). His factors have not come into general use as either a replacement of or a supplement to the clinical scales, however. For practical purposes, it does not seem to matter much whether the traits measured by a test are really separate and distinct from one another. In both the aptitude and the personality domains, tests developed empirically to serve specific purposes often lead to more accurate predictions of complex behavior than do the tests of pure factors.

2. *Analysis of Theoretical Systems*

Contrasted with both the factor analytic and the empirical techniques for identifying measurable personality traits is the method of scrutinizing some comprehensive personality theory in search of key variables. Freudian psychoanalysis, often used in this way, prompted attempts to measure "oral" traits (Goldman-Eisler, 1951; Blum, 1949; Blum and Miller, 1952) and "anal" traits (Sears, 1943). It provided the initial push of the far-reaching research on the "authoritarian" personality (Adorno et al., 1950). During the course of their work on anti-semitism and other varieties of prejudice it became apparent to these investigators that all of these prejudiced attitudes grew out of a common matrix which could be thought of as a personality type. A scale called the F-scale (pre-Fascism) was devised to measure the personality variable directly. A high scorer on this scale is characterized by: (1) repression rather than awareness of his own unacceptable motives; (2) externalization or projection which leads him to suspect and blame others and to avoid introspection; (3) conventionalism or conformity; (4) an orientation toward others in terms of power rather than love; (5) rigidity rather than flexibility. "Authoritarianism" seems to be independent of "neuroticism" and "psychoticism" since both low and high scores on the F-scale can be found among neurotics undergoing psychotherapy and among hospitalized patients. Vigorous research programs in many places have investigated the relationship of the trait to other aspects of personality and behavior.

A trait related to still another part of psychoanalytic theory is often used descriptively by clinical workers in their diagnoses of cases. It is usually called "ego-strength." The idea is somewhat related to a matter discussed earlier in the chapter, the need for concepts to represent positive aspects of the personality. The ego, as analysts see it, is the part of the person that copes with reality. Some individuals seem to have more of this coping ability than others do, so that they can endure large amounts of psychological stress. Barron (1953) selected the sixty-nine items from the Minnesota Multiphasic Personality Inventory that were related to success in psychotherapy and decided after inspection of the differentiating items that the scale was measuring ego-strength.

By far the most complex and influential of these theory-based systems of personality variables has been formulated by H. A. Murray and his associates at the Harvard Psychological Clinic (Murray, 1938). The theory is a synthesis of concepts distilled from the thinking of Freud, McDougall, Jung, Rank, Adler, Lewin, Allport, and others. They fall into three main categories: *need* (a large number of these, each a directional tendency in the person, *press* (a directional tendency in an object or situation operating upon the person), and *thema* (characteristic combinations of press and need). The Murray list of personality needs has been used again and again by investigators working with all sorts of assessment techniques. The terms n Achievement, n Affiliation, n Autonomy, n Order, and many others have become part of the basic vocabulary of personality researchers.

A quite different organized set of personality dimensions has been derived from a theoretical analysis of the *interpersonal* aspects of behavior as these are formulated in the writings of Karen Horney, Erich Fromm, and especially Harry Stack Sullivan. While a number of psychologists have worked with variables of this sort, the system was elaborated most thoroughly by a research group of the Kaiser Foundation and presented in a book by Leary (1957). There are two principal dimensions, *affection* vs. *hostility* and *dominance* vs. *submission*. Many other traits are located with reference to these main axes. A circle is used to show these relationships, and a particular person is characterized by the areas of such a circle in which his interpersonal behavior tends to fall. Figure 30 shows what this system is like. The Interpersonal Check List, designed to measure at least the outward and visible aspects of these characteristics, has constituted a useful tool in research projects of many kinds.

THE RETURN TO TYPE CONCEPTS

As mentioned at the beginning of this chapter, psychologists pretty generally turned away from the time-honored typologies for characterizing personality differences and directed their attention toward traits or dimensions instead. It was assumed that typologies were at best inaccurate, at worst downright unscientific.

Then Eysenck attempted to salvage the concept of *type* by setting up a hierarchical system in which a type is simply a higher-order trait. His idea is illustrated in Figure 31. It is based on the correlations that have been obtained for all sorts of personality measurements. Specific bits of bahavior show some consistency with one another, thus defining what Eysenck calls the *habitual-response* level. These habitual responses, in turn, are to some extent correlated, thus defining what we call *traits*. The traits too tend to group themselves into clusters which can be called *types*. Much of the confusion and many of the conflicting results coming from various quantitative studies disappear when we think in terms of such an organization. Factor-analytic methods like those used by most American investigators identify *traits* first but obtain *types* as second-order factors when trait measurements are correlated with one another. British factor-analytic methods locate *types* first, *traits* afterward. Ratings based on observed behavior usually stand for personal characteristics at the habitual-response level; questionnaire scores are more likely to be concerned with the trait level.

This orderly way of classifying personality characteristics has a good deal of merit. It suggests that eventually we might have such systematic procedures for describing individuals, for example, as the following:

FIGURE 30

Classification of Interpersonal Behavior into Sixteen Varieties. The Inner Circle Represents Adaptive Forms of the Behavior, the Middle Circle the Behavior It Tends to Evoke in Others, and the Next Circle the Rigid or Maladaptive Forms

(From *Interpersonal diagnoses of personality: a functional theory and methodology for personality evaluation.* Copyright, 1957. The Ronald Press Company)

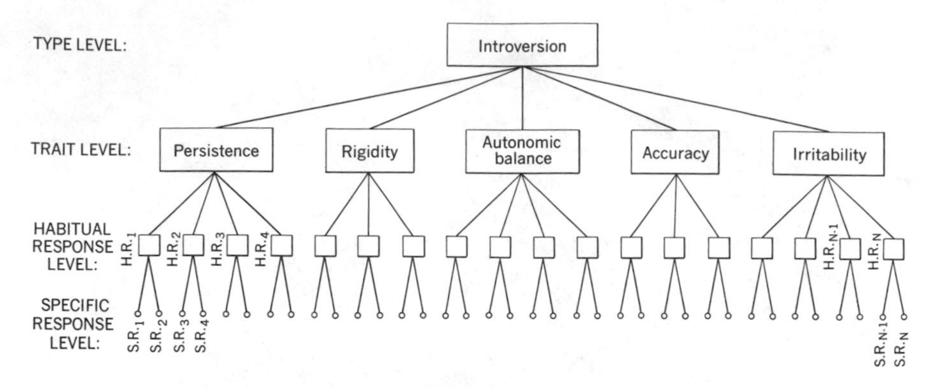

FIGURE 31

Diagrammatic Representation of Hierarchical Organization of Personality

(Reprinted by permission of The Macmillan Company from Eysenck, *Dimensions of personality*, 1947, p. 29)

> Henry M. is a man with an average amount of general stability or freedom from abnormal trends (type level). He tends to be introverted rather than extraverted (type level). Of the *traits* related to this type, however, he shows only shyness and subjectivity to a noticeable degree. In rigidity and irritability he is about average (trait level). Shyness is most marked in social groups involving both sexes and in meeting strangers. In classroom and business situations and on the speaker's platform he expresses himself without hesitation (habitual-response level).

But as time has passed since Eysenck first proposed this hierarchical system, it has seemed less and less satisfactory as a basis for research and practice. Perhaps its greatest weakness is the static character of the concepts. For a person is not only a combination of traits but a *process* in time. What he is becoming, the direction in which he is going, is inherent in what he is at any one period. This is especially apparent in the case of a child, but the constant movement in time characterizes adults as well.

In order to deal with this aspect of an individual's personality, some psychologists have been returning to the concept of type, but defining it not as the top level in a hierarchy of traits but rather as a *direction of development*. The penetrating discussion by Jung in his book *Psychological Types* (1923) has proved to be a source of fruitful hypotheses. In the *Myers-Briggs Type Indicator* (Myers, 1962) these have been developed into a usable assessment technique. We have already considered in some detail the best known of the Jungian distinctions, that between extraverted and introverted orientations. This difference in the direction of one's attitudes interacts with differences based on three pairs of contrasting functions. In the Myers-Briggs adaptation of Jung's ideas, these are: Sensation *vs.* Intuition, Thinking *vs.* Feeling, and Judgment *vs.* Perception. The Extraversion-Introversion index shows whether a person prefers to direct his mental activities toward the external world of people and things or toward the internal world of ideas and personal experience. The Sensation-Intuition index shows whether a person prefers to perceive his world in a factual, realistic way or to perceive possibilities partly created by his own imagination. The Thinking-Feeling index shows whether a person prefers to arrive at decisions by a logical impersonal process or by using personal and interpersonal subjective values. The Judgment-Perception index shows whether the subject prefers to take a judgmental attitude or an understanding, perceptive attitude toward people and situations.

The combination of these four kinds of differentiation produce sixteen types. In the research on the Myers-Briggs Type Indicator, interest has centered on the characteristics of groups of persons in each of these sixteen categories rather than on how high or how low the score is on any of the variables one measures in order to determine which of the two alternative approaches to life predominates. The *Manual* (Myers, 1962) summarizes a large number of studies in which predictions about the way in which certain groups in the population would score or behave were to some extent corroborated.

The question still remains, as in previous attempts to objectify or quantify the Jungian typology, whether these distinctions really demarcate mutually exclusive directions of development or simply represent the extremes of trait distributions. Much of the evidence Myers presents would be compatible with either trait or type concepts, although some results, such as the discontinuities and discontinuous regressions discussed in Chapter 9 of the *Manual,* do argue for a type interpretation. In a later presentation of research results, however, Stricker and Ross (1964) did not find positive evidence for dichotomous types. So it seems that the question is still open. At any rate, this instrument based on Jung's ideas constitutes a new attempt to identify *nonpsychiatric* personality characteristics. It promises to be useful in many practical life situations.

THE STABILITY OF PERSONALITY CHARACTERISTICS OVER TIME

Underlying all the research on individual differences in basic personality traits is the assumption that such traits are at least moderately consistent from day to day, month to month, or year to year. There has been only a limited amount of research on what we may call the stability problem, however, not nearly as much as the problem of IQ constancy has generated. During the 1950's and 1960's, results from several longitudinal studies of personality characteristics were reported. From these it is now possible to draw some limited conclusions.

Kelly (1955) reported on a retest during 1954–55 of 176 men and 192 women whom he had tested in the period 1935–38. The original investigation had been a study of 300 engaged couples. The average age of the men at that time was 26.7, of the women 24.7. Thus they were about 40 years old at the time of the followup. Correlations were significantly positive for all the kinds of personality measures used. For values, as measured by the Allport-Vernon instrument, they ranged from .32 to .60. On the Bernreuter personality test, the correlation for Self-confidence was .61, for Sociability .46. Correlations of about the same order of magnitude were obtained for interests as measured by the Strong test. It appears, then, that for adults after they have reached maturity, scores on personality tests tend to remain about the same over a 15–19 year period.

We can carry the question one step further and ask whether adolescent characteristics are stable. Evidence on this point (Tuddenham, 1959) comes from a followup in 1953 of 32 men and 40 women who had been subjects in the Adolescent Growth Study during the years 1932–39. (These were all the subjects who still lived in the San Francisco Bay area.) In this study ratings made on the two occasions, separated by some 14 or 15 years, were correlated. The original ratings on a large number of traits had been made by staff members at the time of the adolescent study. The followup ratings on the same traits were made by two psychologists each of whom had interviewed the subjects. Of the many correlations computed, 92 per cent were positive and only 8 per cent zero or negative. While the average stability coefficient was only .27 for males and .24 for females, a considerable number of the coefficients were statistically significant and as high as one could expect in view of the unreliability of the ratings on which they were based. In another followup based on this same study of adolescents, McKee and Turner (1961) found a number of significant correlations between ratings of basic "drives" made in 1940 and relevant scores on the California Personality Inventory given during the 1953–59 followup. So it would appear that there is a tendency for personality traits observable during adolescence to perpetuate themselves. Symonds (1961) contributed a little more evidence supporting this adolescence-adult stability.

The followup study covering the longest time period is that carried on at the Fels Institute (Kagan and Moss, 1962). During 1929–39 extensive data were collected on 89 subjects who became members of an experimental group at birth, using a wide variety of assessment methods. The Personality measures were grouped by periods: I. 0 to 3 years; II. 3 to 6 years; III. 6 to 10 years; IV. 10 to 14 years. Ratings based on these case materials were then correlated with adult ratings obtained during a followup in 1957, in which 71 of the original 89 subjects participated. Many of the correlations were significant, especially from Period III on. Some were fairly high. The most striking findings were in the areas of aggression, passivity, and independence. The most interesting aspect of these correlations, however, is the sex differences. In girls *passive reaction to frustration* is a highly stable characteristic. In boys it is not. Just the opposite tends to be true for aggression and competitiveness, which are stable for boys but not for girls. The authors discuss the significance of this sort of finding in some detail. Apparently a personality trait compatible with the standard sex role a young child must fit himself into is more likely to persist than a trait out of keeping with this role. We shall have more to say about this subject of sex roles in Chapter 10.

One more study of the stability of personality traits is worth mention because of the suggestion it gives that some traits originate in the earliest months of life. Escalona and Heider (1959) cooperated on a research attempt to predict what individual children would be like during their preschool years from case material that had been obtained in an intensive examination before the subjects were 8 months old. The opportunity arose when it was found that 31 children who had been subjects in the infancy study were several years later enrolled in a preschool group on which another research investigation was being conducted. What Escalona did was to go through the case folders on the subjects as infants and make as many specific predictions as she could about the kinds of behavior she would expect of each individual in the preschool situation. These were matched with actual descriptions of each child made independently by the other investigator to see how many were borne out by the facts. The results showed that about 66 per cent of the 882 predictions turned out to be correct or predominantly correct. Some traits were more predictable than others, and some children were more predictable than others. It is not possible to formulate any precise statement about the statistical significance of these results because one cannot determine what "chance" might produce in this particular predictive situation. But even the possibility that the roots of some kinds of personality manifestations are present within a few months after birth arrests our attention.

A large amount of evidence about the stability of all kinds of psychological traits has been assembled and organized by Bloom (1964). It is clear from his summary that in the personality area we need more and different kinds of evidence before any final conclusions can be drawn. Because of the prominence of developmental concepts in the leading personality theories, such evidence should be assembled.

SUMMARY

Individual differences in personality are very important to theory and practice, but their investigation has been hampered by various kinds of special difficulties. Even the term "personality" is defined in different ways by different psychologists. The number of traits that might be measured is unreasonably large. Criteria to be used in validating tests are difficult to find, especially for positive traits.

The major methods of assessment used in research on personality have been ratings, questionnaires, projective techniques, and "objective" tests. Each method has serious weaknesses.

The basic personality variables for which the most solid research support has been obtained are neuroticism or emotional instability and extraversion-introversion. The factor analytic work of Eysenck has contributed most to the clarification of these dimensions. Other, more complex systems based on factor analysis have been formulated by Guilford and Cattell.

Other workers have approached the task of identifying and measuring basic variables either by an empirical comparison of well-defined psychiatric groups with normals or by abstracting from a comprehensive personality theory. The Minnesota Multiphasic Personality Inventory is a product of the first approach, the Murray list of needs a product of the second. The Myers-Briggs Type Indicator represents a return to type rather than trait concepts.

Several follow-up studies have reported a statistically significant degree of stability for personality traits measured in adulthood, adolescence, and childhood. One study suggests that certain kinds of personality characteristics may originate during the first few months of life.

CHAPTER 8

Individual Differences in Interests and Values

THERE ARE IMPORTANT ASPECTS OF INDIVIDUALITY that seem to have little or nothing to do with the personality dimensions discussed in the previous chapter. It has not been customary to include vocational interests in discussions of personality, although they certainly constitute a part of one's personal life. But however we classify them, differences in interests and values have important practical and theoretical implications. As we think of our friends and associates or listen to the conversation of new acquaintances, what we are most likely to notice are expressions of interests and preferences. We can't help knowing, for example, that Mary Symonds, the thirteen-year-old daughter of our next-door neighbors, is tremendously interested in horses, and spends most of her weekends riding the horse her parents gave her for Christmas. We know that Mr. Sinnott, a successful banker, is strongly committed to "the American way of life" and the free enterprise system he identifies with it. We know that Laura Landis is a deeply dedicated social worker. Her whole life is organized around her work and the human purposes she sees it as furthering. As psychological theorists have turned their attention to the significance of choices and decisions in human affairs, the significance of interests and values as determiners and organizers of such decisions has been increasingly stressed.

As in so many instances throughout the short history of psychology, the main reason for classifying interest tests and personality tests in separate categories may be that they arose from independent lines of research. "Personality" tests originated as tools to be used by clinical psychologists in the diagnosis of psychiatric conditions. "Interest" tests originated as tools to be used by vocational psychologists in helping individuals find their way into suitable careers. As time has passed and research results have accumulated, both undertakings have broadened their scope so that they are not so far apart as they were at the beginning.

As long as the science of individual differences was conceived as a division of human knowledge that was to include only hereditary characteristics, interests and values did not seem to fall within its boundaries. Nobody seriously considers the possibility of genes determining scientific interests or religious values. To many observers, an individual's assortment of interests seems to represent a hodgepodge of miscellanea assembled from here and there, a collection that can perhaps be described but hardly ordered in any systematic fashion. It is often assumed that such traits are shallow and superficial in comparison with the kinds of traits that we have discussed in previous chapters, and that they are too changeable to permit any assessment. It has become increasingly apparent, however, that interests and values are *not* superficial and that they are less changeable than many "deeper" psychological traits. Furthermore, regularities about the way they are organized consistently show up. These lead to interesting theoretical generalizations. What started as purely practical research can now play an important part in the building of more comprehensive personality theory.

HOW INTERESTS ARE MEASURED

Much of what we know about occupational interest rests on work that has been done with the Strong Vocational Interest Blank. First published in 1927, this test has been given to hundreds of thousands of persons in both counseling and research situations. A large bibliography has accumulated.

The system of scoring used for the Strong, novel at the time the blank was first brought out, has become one of the most useful methods in personality measurement. What Strong did was to collect several hundred items of many kinds [1]—occupations, school subjects, recreational activities, self-ratings—and ask the respondent to mark each one indicating whether he liked it, disliked it, or was indifferent toward it. Each scoring key was constructed by tabulating the responses of a group of successful men in some one profession or occupation and comparing the percentage of this

[1] The adequacy of the original item pool is a matter of some importance in cases like this where such a large structure of research rests on a single foundation. It is very difficult to evaluate this. Fryer (1931) gives the clearest account of what happened during the early 1920's when work on interest inventories was getting started. About 1,000 items were collected in Yoakum's seminar at Carnegie Institute of Technology. Various people made up inventories for special purposes during the next few years. Items from the original pool were used, discarded, or replaced by new ones according to whether or not they seemed to be making any sort of occupational differentiation. There is no way now of determining what "universe" Strong's items represent. This does not matter so far as the practical uses of the blank are concerned, but it makes for ambiguity in our attempts to fit the results into any theoretical structure.

group endorsing each response with the percentage characteristic of men in general. Any response for which the difference in percentage was statistically significant became a part of the scoring key for this particular occupation. Weights were attached to items according to the size of the difference. In developing the "Engineer" key, for example, Strong found that 47 per cent of men in general as compared with 60 per cent of his engineers marked the first item of the blank, "Actor," D for Dislike. This led to the inclusion of the D response on "Actor" as part of the Engineer scoring key, with one point of credit. A little farther down the list, on the item "Author of technical book," 50 per cent of the engineers said L (Like) whereas only 31 per cent of the men in general gave this response. This greater difference meant that an L response to "Author of technical book" received three points of credit on the "Engineer" key (Strong, 1943, p. 75). The advantage of this variety of scoring key is that it has a certain amount and kind of validity built into it. We may not be able to describe in psychological terms what it is that distinguishes engineers from other men, but we know that there is *something.* In practical counseling situations, such empirical validity in a measuring instrument is a very valuable characteristic. By 1954, Strong had developed keys for forty-five different occupations. A women's blank with keys for twenty-five occupations had also been made available.

Scores based on item analysis have certain peculiarities that need always to be kept in mind. We do not know what kind of a measuring scale this technique gives us. On the Engineer scale, for example, the norms show that the average score for engineers is 112. If Harry Higgins comes out with a score of 200, what does that indicate about him? He seems to be much more like engineers than the average successful engineer is. This is a confusing, rather meaningless statement. What we must not conclude is that he has more interest *in* engineering than the average engineer, or that he is likely to be more *successful* than the average. There is no evidence at all that within any one occupational group, degrees of success are correlated with magnitude of Strong score. Some of the ambiguous results that have been obtained when interest tests have been correlated with other types of ability and personality measurements may arise from this basic ambiguity with regard to what sort of scale the measurements constitute.[2]

Strong himself centered most of his research around broad categories set up in such a way as to represent the degree of certainty one can feel that an individual really belongs to an occupational group. Strong's A

[2] Strong's long-term followup of men first tested in college, indicated that the size of the score is related to *remaining* in the occupation represented by the key in question. Men with scores well above the average for a norm group were considerably more likely to be found in an occupation corresponding to it twenty years later than were men who made just average scores on the scale (Layton [ed.], 1960, p. 185).

rating includes scores ranging all the way from a half standard deviation below the mean to the top of the distribution, thus covering the range over which it seems reasonable to say, "This individual unquestionably fits into this occupational group." "B+," "B," and "B−" stand for ranges of scores below the average for an occupational group, thus representing increasing amounts of doubt as to whether an individual belongs in it. What a "B" score means is that a person has *some* attitudes in common with men in the occupation, but other attitudes that are different. A "C" score indicates that he shows little or no resemblance to persons in this particular occupation. Research based on such letter grades, though it lacks the apparent precision of work with exact numerical scores, seems to rest on a sounder logical foundation.

Another widely used method for measuring interests is the Kuder Preference Record. It was developed in a different manner from the Strong. Kuder assembled a set of items representing diverse kinds of activity—such as "Visit an art gallery" or "Collect autographs,"—and gave it to about 500 college students. He examined their responses to see if he could find a group of items that seemed to cluster together. The first such group was the "Literary" scale. Using this as a starting point, he continued to use correlational methods of item analysis searching for another cluster of closely related items that would have little or no correlation with the first one. Having developed a second scale by this means, he repeated the procedure, seeking still another set of items that would correlate highly with one another but negligibly with *both* of the first scales. Since 1934 when the work on the Kuder blank began, scale after scale has been added in this manner. Since 1948, ten scoring keys have been available for the *Kuder Preference Record—Vocational.* They are: Outdoor, Mechanical, Computational, Scientific, Persuasive, Artistic, Literary, Musical, Social Service, and Clerical. In 1953, Kuder published the *Preference Record—Personal.* It is built in the same manner as the vocational blank, but the scales represent preferences for different kinds of personal or social activity, described as follows:

A. Preference for being active in groups
B. Preference for familiar and stable situations
C. Preference for working with ideas
D. Preference for avoiding conflict
E. Preference for directing others.

Still more recently (Kuder, 1959) Kuder has published a third instrument, the *Kuder Preference Record—Occupational.* For this he has used the preference type of item in which the person must choose which of three things he likes most and which he likes least, but he has developed scoring keys by comparing occupational groups with men in general, as

Strong did. Neither the *Personal* nor the *Occupational* tests have been used a great deal as yet, and the research with which we are concerned here has been based on the first of these three inventories, the *Kuder Preference Record–Vocational.*

When one carries on research with this Kuder test or evaluates research that others have done, it is important that he keep in mind the distinctive characteristics of the scores. For one thing, the validity of the test as a measure of characteristics actually involved in any occupation is not guaranteed. The fact that a set of items hangs together and that all these items appear to have something to do with mechanical types of activity tells us nothing about men in mechanical occupations. The process of validating a test like this is a long and difficult task. With the passage of time, more and more of the essential information is being accumulated. Each successive Kuder Manual has summarized it and users of the blank need to be familiar with it. Another point that must be kept in mind is that a person's score represents what he says when he is required to *make a choice* of the best- and least-liked activity in a group of three. Thus each of a person's scores is dependent upon all the others. It is the combination or profile that is meaningful rather than any one score taken singly. Embedded in a different set of choices, an individual's score on the Clerical scale, for example, might be considerably higher or considerably lower than it turns out to be in this particular context. The fact that scores obtained from the Strong and Kuder blanks represent different systems of measurement and that neither is a straightforward interval or ratio scale complicates research undertakings, whether we wish to relate either test to criteria of success or to determine the amount of agreement between them. The soundest procedure is probably to use the *judgment* made on the basis of the test as the experimental variable rather than to use test scores directly. Strong's letter grades and Kuder's reports of differential profiles for occupations are ways of accomplishing this purpose.

Since World War II another major research program on interest measurement has been in progress. The resulting *Minnesota Vocational Interest Inventory* is designed to identify interests characterizing different groups of *nonprofessional* men, such as electronics technicians, milk-wagon drivers, plumbers, retail salespersons, and others at skilled and semiskilled levels. In this test a preference-type item format was combined with a procedure similar to Strong's for differentiating each particular occupational group from a group of tradesmen-in-general. Clark (1961) has reported on the research of many kinds entering into the construction of this blank and its scoring keys.

There are several other interest inventories on the market, but none of them has been used in enough research investigations to require discussion here. There is, however, one sort of interest research, attempted sporadically ever since psychologists first began to measure interests in the 1920's, that does constitute a different approach altogether. It is the evaluation of interests by "objective" rather than "subjective" methods.

To do this requires that we set up some situation in which we can get an interest score from what a person *does* rather than from what he *says* about himself. The great advantage such objective tests would have is that scores on them could not be "faked." Some ingenious techniques have been proposed, but so far all of them have shown limitations which kept them out of common use. Information tests consisting of questions about processes and terms in different occupations or areas of knowledge certainly reflect interests, but they also measure general intelligence. It is difficult to separate one from the other. Tests of how much a person remembers from different passages he has been allowed to read once tell us something about his interests, but reading ability and general habits of concentration also help to determine such scores. Another method which has been tried is to show movies of work in progress in different occupational settings and then to gauge an individual's interest in such work by the amount he can recall when the showing is over (Super and Roper, 1941). Here too, other psychological characteristics besides interest probably figure, and the method has the further disadvantage that the large number of separate occupations there are in a modern industrial society make it impractical to show even short films of any considerable number of them. The Army Air Force psychologists during World War II did a considerable amount of research on objective-interest measures. Validity coefficients reported for these blanks were promising but not really satisfactory (about .3). More recently, this effort has been revived in England (Peel, 1959) in an attempt to differentiate children with P (practical) interests from children with A (academic) interests in order to improve the allocation of eleven-year-olds to secondary schools.

The majority of research workers and counselors have continued to use tests of the "subjective" or inventory type. We turn now to a summary of what we know about individual differences in interests on the basis of their experience with these inventories.

THE STABILITY OF VOCATIONAL INTERESTS

One of the most striking things that extensive research has shown is that the patterns of likes and dislikes identifying a person as a member of a certain occupational group are very stable aspects of his personality. Strong (1955a) accumulated follow-up data on a number of groups first tested during their college years and then retested many years later. The intervals were of different lengths for different occupational groups, the longest twenty-two years. Table 13 summarizes these results. When the set of scores originally making up a person's interest profile was correlated with the set of scores obtained after a long time interval, the individual correlations ranged from .67 to .88. For the groups with the twenty-two-year interval, the median *r*'s were .76 and .72. How close the relationship is seems to depend about equally on the length of the interval and the age of the subject at the time he first took the test. The high level of the correlations generally would suggest, however, that permanence in vocational interest pattern is the rule, not the exception.

Trinkaus (1954) reported results from a follow-up study of 308 Yale alumni about fifteen years after they first took the Strong test as college freshmen. Stordahl (1954) studied University of Minnesota students who had taken the Strong test two years before as high-school seniors. In both these studies, Strong's findings with regard to the stability of interest patterns was verified. Table 14 shows what Stordahl found with regard to letter grades. It can be seen that 60 per cent of the A's remain A after two years; 79 per cent of them are A or B+. The C's are even more stable, with 68 per cent remaining C and 83 per cent C or C+.

It is apparent from all these studies of interest stability, however, that there are *individual* differences with regard to it. Most persons change very little, but some few change a great deal. This fact shows up most clearly in studies of high-school students. Finch (1935), Taylor (1942), Carter (1940), Taylor and Carter (1942), and Dunkleberger and Tyler (1961) have shown that stability of interest pattern is the *rule* even for subjects as young as sixteen. But always in a few cases, the correlations between sets of scores obtained on two occasions turn out to be *negative;* in other cases they are so low that attempts to predict the later from the earlier interests would have been seriously in error.

Work on the Kuder has been less extensive, but here too there is some evidence that a fair amount of stability in obtained pattern is the rule rather than the exception. Reid (1951), testing college subjects, found a median correlation of .77 for sets of scores separated by a fifteen-month interval. Rosenberg (1953), with high-school subjects tested in the ninth grade and again in the twelfth, obtained correlations ranging from .47 to .75. Herzberg and Bouton (1954) reported similar correlations for intervals up to four years. In all these studies, as in the Strong studies, marked changes occurred in some individuals (Mallinson and Crumrine, 1952).

Many of the research studies on the long-range stability of vocational interests have attempted to find out what kinds of factors differentiate persons who show marked interest changes over the years from those who do not. This is a question that is obviously of considerable interest to counselors, who must often make judgments about whether or not a shift in the pattern of a client's interests can be expected to occur. Stordahl (1954) hypothesized that the Interest Maturity score on the Strong blank (the special score based on items differentiating fifteen-year-

TABLE 13

Permanence of Interest Profiles

(Strong, 1955, p. 64)

NO. OF SUBJECTS	COLLEGIATE LEVEL	DATES TESTED	INTERVAL	AGE AT TIME OF 1ST TEST	MEDIAN CORRELATION
50	Freshmen	1930-31	1	19	.88
50	Seniors	1927-32	5	22	.84
50	Seniors	1932-37	5	27	.86
50	Freshmen	1931-39	8	20	.72
50	Freshmen	1930-39	9	19	.67
50	Seniors	1927-37	10	22	.82
50	Freshmen	1939-49	10	28	.87
50	Seniors	1937-49	12	32	.88
50	Seniors	1932-49	17	27	.84
50	Business Graduates	1931-49	18	23	.74
50	Freshmen	1931-49	18	20	.72
50	Freshmen	1930-49	19	19	.72
228	Seniors	1927-49	22	22	.76
198	Graduates	1927-49	22	25	.72

TABLE 14

Change in Letter Grade Scores on the Vocational Interest Blank for 181 Boys Tested as High-School Seniors and Retested Two Years Later as College Students

(Stordahl, 1954)

TEST		RETEST						
LETTER GRADE	*N*	% *C*	% *C+*	% *B−*	% *B*	% *B+*	% *A*	TOTAL
A	804	2	3	6	10	19	60	100
B+	761	4	6	13	21	26	30	100
B	1,106	8	12	20	23	20	17	100
B−	1,394	19	16	24	20	12	9	100
C+	1,300	31	23	22	15	6	3	100
C	2,599	68	15	9	5	2	1	100

olds from twenty-five-year-olds) should help one make this judgment. But he found that the group of college men who had changed the most over a two-year period were not differentiated from those who had changed the least. L. A. King (1958), who retested in the spring 242 college freshmen who had taken the Strong the previous fall, also did not find that the IM score was related to change. Unrelated to it also were personal data such as age, socio-economic status, veteran status, or marital status, and ability and achievement measures, such as scholastic-aptitude test scores and grades in school subjects. Only certain aspects of the pattern of interest scores themselves turned out to show any relationship to changes. Some kinds of patterns seemed to be somewhat more stable than others.

Using the Kuder test, McCoy (1955) attempted to construct a special stability scale to differentiate between "changers" and "nonchangers." Unfortunately, this scale based on differentiations in one group did not differentiate in another used for cross-validation. McCoy did find, however, that scores above the 75th percentile and scores below the 25th were less likely to change than were scores within the middle range.

Another obvious possible reason for interest change would be occupational experience. This one has been investigated and seems *not* to be important. Strong has shown (1943, Ch. 15) that a person's interest pattern develops prior to the selection of an occupation, and is not much affected by subsequent work experience. There is some evidence in a study by Bordin and Wilson (1953), however, that curricular shifts in college freshmen are related in a rather complex way to interest changes on the Kuder test. The authors interpret this to mean that when the pressure of circumstances forces a change in an individual's self-percept, his measured interests change with it. There may also be internal personality factors that permit some persons to make these modifications in self-concepts and prevent others from doing so. Dunkleberger and Tyler (1961) found that boys and girls who showed most change in their pattern of Strong scores between the junior and senior years in high school tended to score higher on several of the scales of the California Psychological Inventory. The results suggested that the "changers" were better adjusted emotionally and intellectually than the "nonchangers." Perhaps we should think of interest shifts, especially in young persons, as indications of a sense of *freedom to change* rather than as *instability*.

THE PROBLEM OF FAKING

One possibility that must always be considered in research of various kinds on interest measurement as well as in practical situations where interest tests are used is that "faking" may have occurred. If a person has reason to suppose that some answers are more acceptable than others, the likes and dislikes he registers for items on the Strong or the choices he makes on the Kuder may reflect this attitude. When group testing is carried on in schoolrooms, it seems reasonable to suppose that some subjects may interpret the situation differently from others. Faking is always a possibility in selection situations.

Longstaff (1948) showed that Strong scores could be affected by deliberate attempts to "slant" them in certain directions. More recently Bridgman and Hollenbeck (1961) showed that college students were able to fake the Kuder test. Persons adopting the "salesman" applicant set obtained profiles of scores very similar to Kuder's norms for salesmen; persons adopting the "industrial psychologist" applicant set obtained profiles similar to the norms for industrial psychologists. The instructions to take this "applicant" set produced more striking changes in the responses individuals gave than did general instructions to make one's record look as "good" as possible.

At least one study suggests, however, that attempts to make interest scores look like those of persons in a particular occupation may have unexpected results. Kirchner (1961) compared the profiles of salesmen with five or more years of experience who took the Strong as part of a general validity study and thus had no reason for faking, with the profiles of salesmen who had taken the Strong at the time they applied for positions as salesmen and thus might have been trying to make their records look as suitable as possible. In 32 out of 96 comparisons there were significant differences between the two groups of salesmen but they were *not* on the sales scores, but rather on the scores in the office work and personnel areas. This came about because the applicants in trying to make a good impression tended to avoid dislike responses, whereas salesmen actually give a good many of these. We shall have more to say about the differential significance of L and D responses a little later.

Because the set a testee takes when responding to an interest test can influence his scores in ways not always predictable, it is important to control this factor as much as possible whenever such tests are used in research or practice.

THE PREDICTIVE VALIDITY OF INTEREST TESTS

Because of the practical orientation of the research on interest tests, studies of their predictive validity have been of considerable importance. Strong's long-range studies reported in detail in his 1955 monograph, *Vocational Interests 18 Years After College,* made it clear that measured occupational interests are tied in with the choice of a suitable occupation and the tendency to continue in it. Strong centered his follow-up work around the validation of four propositions (Strong, 1943, p. 388).

1. Men continuing in occupation A obtain a higher interest score in A than in any other occupation.
2. Men continuing in occupation A obtain a higher interest score in it than do other men entering other occupations.
3. Men continuing in occupation A obtain higher scores in A than do men who change from A to another occupation.
4. Men changing from occupation A to occupation B score higher in B prior to the change than in any other occupation, including A.

On the whole it can be said that all the follow-up studies support these propositions. The most extensive evidence has been obtained for physicians (Strong, 1952b) and engineers (Strong, 1952a), but the figures for the group in general appear to follow the same pattern (Strong, 1951a). The men who stay with a profession over a twenty-year period are found to have had higher interest scores for that profession when they were undergraduates than the men who have shifted away from the occupation at some time during the twenty years. It is to be remembered that the scores were obtained prior to their entry into the profession, so that we cannot say that they are based on experience with the work itself. There is a possibility that the occupational choices and shifts that the subjects made were influenced by their knowledge of their interest test scores, since they seem to have been given the results in return for their cooperation in filling out the blank (Strong, 1943, p. 389). It seems unlikely, however, that this knowledge could account for the correspondence between scores and ultimate occupational placement, since students do not ordinarily make their decisions on the basis of one set of test scores. Aside from this one point of doubt, the evidence for the validity of the Strong blank as a measure of some kind of motivation that enters into occupational decisions is impressive.

Berdie (1960) corroborated Strong's findings through an investigation of Strong scores the graduates of three professional curricula at the University of Minnesota had made when they were in 12th grade. There had been clearcut differences before they entered college between the groups who later became physicians, lawyers, and accountants. More than half of them had scored A or B+ on the scale for the profession they later entered.

Under some circumstances, however, it appears that interest scores do not predict occupational choice as well as this. McArthur (1954) in a follow-up study fourteen years after 60 Harvard students had taken the Strong test, compared the predictive efficiency of the test for boys whose earlier education had been in private secondary schools and boys whose earlier education had been in public high schools. Such groups roughly differentiate between upper-class and middle-class subjects. McArthur classified the prediction as a "good hit" if the occupation and the test score were closely matched, as a "poor hit" if there was some relationship

TABLE 15

Predictions of Occupation from Strong Scores for Middle Class (Public School) and Upper Class (Private School) Boys

(McArthur, 1954)

PREDICTION	*Public School*	*Private School*
Good hit	19	8
Poor hit	4	8
Clean miss	8	13

between them, and a "clean miss" if they seemed not to be related at all. Table 15 shows what he found. For the public-school subjects, the predictive validity of the Strong test is similar to that shown in previous reports. For private-school boys, the test apparently is of little or no value for predicting this occupational criterion. The reason is obvious. Among the private-school boys, where family traditions largely determine occupational choices, individual interests are not relevant.

Another study in which Strong scores failed to predict the specific occupation entered has been reported by Tucker (1962). In this case the subjects were all physicians, and the predictors were scores obtained ten years earlier in medical school on the four special scales for medical specialties that Tucker had constructed in order to differentiate the interests of surgeons, internists, pediatricians, and psychiatrists. The follow-up indicated clearly that the scores on the specialist scales did *not* predict the specialty chosen. The reason here seems to be a change in the nature of medical practice over the period in question. A much larger proportion of physicians now qualify as specialists than at earlier periods (75 per cent in 1960 as compared with 25 per cent in 1950). As the numbers have increased, the factors related to decisions to enter specialties have undoubtedly changed also.

Although such exceptions exist, we can say definitely that Strong scores tend to predict occupational choices and decisions, at least for middle-class men in occupations the nature of which remains fairly constant over the years. At least one study (Levine and Wallen, 1954) reports similar results for the Kuder. Does it follow from this relationship that interest tests can be said to be predictive of *satisfaction* in certain kinds of endeavor? The answer here is not quite so clear-cut. The correlations between interest scores and ratings of satisfaction with the jobs to which they point are rather low (.2 to .3) (Strong, 1955, Ch. 10). However, many factors besides how interesting a job is enter into one's feelings about it, as Strong points out in his discussion. Furthermore, the distribution of job satisfaction ratings has been curtailed to an unknown extent in this study of Strong's and the others similar to it, by the fact that the most dissatisfied members of each profession have left it before the time of the follow-up study. Perhaps a clearer, though less finely-differentiated indication that there is some relationship between interest and satisfaction comes from Perry's findings (see K. E. Clark, 1961, p. 92), as a by-product of some methodological research he was doing in the development of the Minnesota Vocational Interest Inventory, that Navy yeomen who answered "no" to the question, "Would you select any other Navy rate in preference to this one?" scored almost 22 points higher on the scale for yeomen than did those who answered "yes." The difference was clearly significant. A study by Lipsett and Wilson (1954) with the Kuder test points in the same direction.

The relationship between interest scores and various criteria of *success* in occupations and training programs is not very impressive. Whatever motivational characteristics interest scores may express, they are apparently fairly independent of the abilities making for success in a given occupation. Correlations between interest scores and occupational or educational criteria generally turn out to be low. In only one occupation, Life Insurance Selling, has it been clearly demonstrated that men with "A" Strong scores on the scale for the occupation earn higher incomes than those with the lower letter-grades (Strong, 1943, Ch. 19). The bulk of the evidence should make us very cautious about predicting success in a course or occupation from interest scores.

Here too, however, there are exceptions pointing to promising new directions for research. One of these is the Terman and Oden (1947) follow-up study of gifted children, to be discussed in greater detail in a later chapter. Almost twenty years after the subjects had first been studied as children, the 20 per cent of them who had turned out to be most successful were compared with the 20 per cent who had been least successful. (These were all subjects who had possessed IQ's of 140 or higher in childhood, so that the general intelligence necessary for success was known to be present in all cases.) One of the most striking differences found between the two groups was in their vocational interests. A significantly larger proportion of the successful were engaged in occupations for which the Strong blank gave them an A rating. Furthermore, there were a larger number in the unsuccessful group who failed to show any clear pattern of interests on the Strong and whose occupational record showed many shifts from one line to another (Terman and Oden, 1947, pp. 324–326).

Another kind of study of the relationship of interest scores to college scholarship was based on a rather complex hypothesis. Fredericsen and Melville (1954) separated a group of engineering students into "compulsive" and "noncompulsive" subgroups. The hypothesis was that in the case of compulsive (thorough, perfectionistic) persons, one would not expect much correlation between interests and grades, since they would be likely to work hard at whatever they do. In noncompulsive persons, however, one would expect a correlation between interests and grades to appear. Some might object to the means by which these investigators made the compulsive-noncompulsive judgment (by the use of the Strong Accountant scale and by a combination of vocabulary and reading speed scores). But the interesting result is that the predicted difference in correlations was found. The coefficients were about zero for the compulsive, whereas a number of them were .3 or higher for the noncompulsives. A repetition of this study some years later by Fredericsen and Gilbert (1960) produced similar results. These studies constitute interesting examples of how a moderator variable may be used to improve prediction.

Still another sort of special study suggests that interest scores are more predictive of success at some ability levels than at others. K. E. Clark, for example (1961, p. 86), found that in his group of electronics technicians, there was a fairly high correlation ($r = .47$) between interest and achievement for the subgroup whose intelligence scores were just below the mean for this specialty. It may be that where ability is marginal, interest plays a disproportionately important role in determining success or failure. Similarly, in two separate high-school situations Barrilleaux (1961) discovered that it was certain *combinations* of interest and aptitude scores that produced a disproportionately large number of outstanding science students. What he did was to rank each individual's interests from his Kuder profile and then tabulate the number of science students at each interest rank and aptitude level who met his criteria of outstanding performance. Table 16 shows the results in one of these studies in

TABLE 16

Relationship of Outstanding Science Achievement to Interest and General Intelligence

(Barrilleaux, 1961)

		IQ (California Test of Mental Maturity)			
		101-114		115-139	
RANK OF SCIENCE INTEREST	NUMBER OF CASES	NUMBER	PERCENT	NUMBER	PERCENT
1-3	50	26	50	24	88
4-6	44	25	44	19	58
7-10	43	26	15	17	24

which the criterion was a percentile of 85 or higher on the science test of the Iowa battery. The proportion of high-achieving students was exceptionally large (88 per cent) among those above 115 IQ with high science interests.

One other line of research attempting to relate interest measures to success ratings involves the construction of special scales by comparing groups of successful and unsuccessful workers rather than comparing occupational groups with men in general. V. W. Stone (1960), proceeding in this manner, constructed a scoring key for female shorthand students that correlated to the extent of .58 with success in this kind of work. Ghei (1960) by comparing successful with unsuccessful IBM workers on the Clark test (Minnesota Inventory) constructed a prediction key that correlated about .39 with supervisor's ratings in a new group of workers. Hughes and McNamera (1958) showed that predictor keys with satisfactory validity could be developed for different kinds of salesmen. The keys differentiating successful from unsuccessful men were specific to the particular groups for which they were designed. The scores the subjects made on the DP scale (data processing machine salesmen) were not related to the scores they made on the ET (electric typewriter salesmen) scale, and scores on both scales were *negatively* correlated with those obtained using Strong's salesman keys. Dunnette, Wernimont, and Abrahams (1964) showed that different groups of engineers can be differentiated, and that the patterns of correlations between scores on these separate engineer keys and various ability and personality variables differ quite markedly.

A rather unexpected finding of a relationship between measured interests and a quite different success criterion has been reported by Whitehorn and Betz. They compared physicians showing a high success rate in treating schizophrenics and physicians whose success rate was lower. Betz (1962) summarized the results of several of these studies. The A physicians differed significantly from the B physicians in their scores on four of the Strong scales (*not* the Physician, Psychiatrist, or Psychologist scales, as one might have expected). The A therapists consistently scored higher on Lawyer and CPA, lower on Printer and Mathematics-Science Teacher. On the basis of an item analysis, Whitehorn and Betz were able to select ten items, the responses to which enabled them to predict in new groups which persons would be the successful therapists. Their "hit" rate was from 67 to 83 per cent. What these investigators think these results indicate is that persons with a certain style or way of dealing with the world are more likely to succeed with schizophrenics.

Because of these various studies showing that under certain circumstances certain kinds of interest scores can be used to predict certain kinds of achievement criteria, it is necessary to modify what has generally been the conclusion about the relative independence of interests and abilities. One could almost conclude that it is possible to construct an interest test for any particular purpose for which one wishes to use it. It is well to remember, however, that the standard published tests scored in the ordinary ways do not permit such predictions. In counseling situations, it is necessary to measure interests and abilities separately.

THE PRINCIPAL INTEREST DIMENSIONS

From a practical standpoint some systematization of the knowledge about vocational interests has always been required. If vocational counselors had to think in terms of a specific interest pattern for each of the more than 30,000 separate jobs that have been identified and described, their task of helping an individual find a suitable occupation would be impossibly difficult. Hence it is thinking in terms of *families* of occupations, each characterized by a common interest pattern, that seems to be necessary. As in other fields, factor analysis has been brought to bear on the problem.

For a test constructed in the manner of the Kuder, the titles of the scales themselves constitute such principal dimensions. The items included in any one scale are there because they correlate with one another and do not correlate with scores on the other scales. The table of intercorrelations in the Kuder manual shows that on the whole these separate scores have turned out to be quite independent of one another. There are a few moderately high correlations (—.519 between Persuasive and Outdoor, for example, and .544 between Clerical and Computational), but the great majority of them are near zero. Evidence from factor analysis indicates that not quite all the separate scores are necessary, however. D. P. King and Norrell (1964), analyzing the scores of 464 male college freshmen, found that six factors would account for 85 per cent of the variance. They are:

1. Social Service
2. Engineering and Physical Science
3. Health Science
4. Outdoor-Technical
5. Verbal
6. Business-Artistic (job printer, interior decorator, architect).

Work done with the Strong and similar inventories of likes and dislikes did not furnish any ready-made system for classifying the kinds of interests we measure. Here the procedure has been to correlate the scores obtained by some representative group of people on all the various occupational scales and to examine these correlations for evidence of similarity between occupational scales. It is possible then to apply factor-analysis methods if we wish to do so. Strong has preferred to base his classification on the correlations themselves rather than on the factors derived from them. By including in each group the scales that correlate more than .60 with one another, he arrived at the following arrangement of men's occupations by groups: [3]

[3] Classification as it appears in *Manual for Strong Vocational Interest Blanks for Men and Women, 1959*. Consulting Psychologists Press, Palo Alto.

I: Artist, Psychologist, Architect, Physician, Psychiatrist, Osteopath, Dentist, Veterinarian
II: Physicist, Chemist, Mathematician, Engineer
III: Production Manager
IV: Farmer, Carpenter, Printer, Mathematics-Science Teacher, Policeman, Forest Service, Army Officer, Aviator
V: Y.M.C.A. Physical Director, Personnel Manager, Public Administrator, Vocational Counselor, Y.M.C.A. Secretary, Social Science Teacher, City School Superintendent, Minister, Social Worker, Physical Therapist
VI: Musician (performer), Music Teacher
VII: C.P.A. Owner
VIII: Senior C.P.A., Accountant, Office Man, Purchasing Agent, Banker, Mortician, Pharmacist
IX: Sales Manager, Real Estate Salesman, Life Insurance Salesman
X: Advertising Man, Lawyer, Author-Journalist
XI: President, Manufacturing Concern

The word "Group" is hardly applicable to III, VII, and XI, since each is made up of only one occupation. Whether there is actually something unique about these types of work, or whether it just happens that as yet no keys have been constructed for occupations similar to them, cannot be determined. In using the Strong blank in counseling, emphasis falls on Group I, which can be called a "Human-Science" type of interest; Group II, Physical Science; Group IV, Technical and Nonprofessional; Group V, Social Welfare; Group VIII, Business Detail; Group IX, Business Contact; and Group X, Verbal. Scales for measuring the interests of the group as a whole have been worked out in the case of Groups I, II, V, VIII, IX, and X.

Strong made a similar analysis of correlations for the women's blank. The fact that there are fewer separate occupational scales than for the men's blank makes the classification based upon correlations between them more uncertain. It is as follows, by groups: [4]

I: Artist, Author, Librarian
II: English Teacher
III: Social Worker, Psychologist
IV: Social Science Teacher, Y.W.C.A. Secretary
V: Lawyer, Life Insurance Saleswoman
VI: Buyer
VII: Business Education Teacher, Office Worker, Stenographer
VIII: Housewife, Elementary Teacher
IX: Home Economics Teacher, Dietician
X: Physical Education Teacher (high school)

[4] Classification as it appears in *Manual for Strong Vocational Interest Blanks for Men and Women, 1959*. Consulting Psychologists Press, Palo Alto.

XI: Occupational Therapist, Nurse
XII: Mathematics-Science Teacher
XIII: Dentist, Laboratory Technician, Physician
XIV: Musician (performer), Music Teacher

The thing which has always characterized the results obtained in counseling situations where the women's blank is used is that what appear above as Groups VII and VIII are by far the most common varieties of interest in girls. This pattern has been variously named "Nonprofessional interests," "Interest in working for the convenience of others," and "Interest in male association." Perhaps it might best be called "Typical Feminine Interests." The presence of this common core of similar likes and dislikes in the great majority of women and girls seems to constitute a factor differentiating feminine from masculine interests. No such standard set of attitudes has appeared in males. This sex difference may be one of degree, however, since there is a strong tendency for most high-school boys to score high on the Group IV scales, which we might call "Typical Masculine Interests."

Unfortunately there has been much less research on women's interests than on men's, so that many unanswered questions about how they are organized remain. We shall consider the matter in more detail in the chapter on Sex Differences.

When working with the Strong test or others for which scoring keys have been constructed in the same manner, we must always remember that the method itself maximizes *differences* between various groups and does not really give them a chance to show how much they are *alike*. When we include a Dislike response to the item "Auctioneer" in the key for engineering interest because it is chosen by 83 per cent of the engineers as compared with 65 per cent of the nonengineers, the use of the scoring key does not tell us how unpopular this occupation is with everybody, a fact which is readily apparent when we look at the percentages themselves. Strong's cautions about this (Strong, 1943, Ch. 6) have not had the attention they deserve. When we correlate the percentages themselves for any two different groups—figures like the 65 and 83 given above—we find that there is considerable agreement among groups in the rankings they give the various activities. Some things are popular with all, others unpopular. The correlation between percentages for twenty-five and fifty-five-year old men, for example, is .88. For college men *vs.* college women it is .74. For Engineers *vs.* Life Insurance men it is .68.

Another interesting finding with the Strong inventory is what has been called the "point-of-reference" phenomenon. If we compare physicians, lawyers, or ministers with men chosen as a representative sample of the great mass of American workers, we find that the scales developed in this way correlate very highly with one another. However, if we compare physicians, lawyers, or ministers with a group made up of men in the other *professions,* the scales we obtain are much more specific and do not correlate with one another to any great extent. Why is this? It seems to mean simply that professional men as a whole differ more from lower-level workers than physicians differ from lawyers. It is only when we leave out the lower-level men from our comparison group that the differences between specific professions get a chance to show up. This is where the "point-of-reference" concept comes in. From the standpoint of the unskilled worker, all professional men look alike. From a point closer to their own position, differences between them can be observed.

Strong worked almost entirely with business and professional men, so that the question of whether the interests of workers in lower-level jobs could be differentiated was not clearly answered until Clark published his results with the Minnesota Inventory. At the level of skilled mechanical, clerical, and sales activities, such differences have now been demonstrated. Just how many principal dimensions will be needed to account for the interest differences at this level is not as yet known.

The Strong, Kuder, and Clark inventories were developed mainly for practical purposes and there is no guarantee that they cover all the areas of human interests. Guilford, et al. (1954) carried out a factor analysis of the correlations between a large number of variables chosen with some care to cover as broad a range of types of motivation as possible. Variables like aggression and altruism were thrown into the initial correlation matrix along with business and mechanical interests. A liking for humor and a need for affection were included along with preferences for outdoor activity or social science subject matter. For each motivational variable, the score was based on ten items to which the subject was asked to respond. Two huge correlation matrices, 95×95, resulted from the administration of these tests to 600 airmen and 720 officer candidates. The size of the groups makes for dependability of the factor loadings. There turned out to be twenty-four factors for the airmen, twenty-three for the officers. Seventeen of them were common to the two analyses. They were named as follows:

A. Mechanical Interest
B. Scientific Interest
C. Adventure vs. Security
D. Social Welfare
E. Aesthetic Appreciation
F. Cultural Conformity
G. Self-reliance vs. Dependence
H. Aesthetic Expression
I. Clerical Interest
J. Need for Diversion
K. Artistic Thinking
L. Need for Attention
M. Resistance to Restriction
N. Business Interest
O. Outdoor-Work Interest
P. Physical Drive
Q. Aggression

It is interesting to note that the specifically vocational clusters of interests still separate themselves out, even where all the scores are statistically comparable and each item is included in only one original test. Factors A, B, D, I, and N are similar to Strong's groups and to Kuder's scales. For some factors the correspondence with previous interpretations of basic interests is not so close. Instead of getting separate factors for musical, artistic, and literary types of interest, for example, the two basic aesthetic factors show up as Aesthetic Appreciation and Aesthetic Expression.

R. B. Cattell and his co-workers have also concerned themselves with interests, but their approach has been from a different direction, and their results cannot easily be incorporated in the main stream of interest research (Cattell and Horn, 1963). The factors they come out with are what they call *ergs* (basic drives or *instincts* in the sense in which McDougall used the term) and sentiments (socially conditioned attitudes toward particular types of object or institution.) Examples are the Sex erg, the Fear erg, the Career sentiment, and the Spouse-sweetheart sentiment. Their system of factors represents also different ways of expressing these motivational forces, corresponding in part to the id, ego, and superego concepts of psychoanalysis.

THE RELATIONSHIP BETWEEN INTEREST AND PERSONALITY MEASURES

Researchers like Cattell and Guilford have hoped to incorporate interest measurement into a more inclusive theory of human motivation. To some extent, the practical interest-testers have also turned their attention to similar problems. There has been a considerable amount of correlational research attempting to link interests to other aspects of personality. Generally speaking, what we find when we examine research of this sort is a whole succession of near-zero correlations between interest tests and the personality inventories that have developed out of psychiatric thinking. No one kind of interest appears to be consistently related to *maladjustment* in any of its common forms. In the most extensive study of this sort, Cottle (1950) administered the Strong, the Kuder, the MMPI, and the Bell Adjustment Inventory to 400 male veterans and then made a factor analysis of the correlations between subscores. Of the seven factors that could be identified, none was common to both personality and interest tests.

Such a result is not completely convincing because of statistical artifacts. We have already mentioned the ambiguity with regard to the nature of the measurement system represented by scores on the Strong scales. Since each of the tests Cottle used differed in the way the scoring keys were derived, it is perhaps natural that the subscores of any one of them would correlate with one another more highly than they correlated with scores on another test. Furthermore, the fact that different scores obtained from any one blank are based on responses to some of the same items makes for some "built-in" correlation between them. It does not seem likely, however, that statistical artifacts account entirely for the failure to find relationships between interest scores and maladjustment.

A number of studies suggest that interests and personality adjustment may be linked together in more complex ways. Several studies have found that groups of neurotics tend to score higher than normals on the Kuder Musical and Literary scales, and lower than normals on the Mechanical scale (Steinberg, 1952). Drasgow and Carkhuff (1964) presented evidence based on 30 psychiatric patients variously diagnosed and in therapy from six months to two years, that scores on the Literary and Musical scales decreased significantly in cases where the treatment was successful.

Berdie (1943, 1945) showed that there were low but significant correlations between number of *dislikes* and maladjustment, and that neurotic soldiers could be differentiated from normal soldiers on this basis. More recently, M. J. Asch (1958), using a test especially constructed to reveal negative-response bias, demonstrated once more that the tendency to say "No" or "Disagree" is related to maladjustment and neuroticism.

Such results cannot be interpreted to mean that any Strong record on which a large proportion of the *dislikes* have been chosen is symptomatic of personality difficulty. Careful study of the responses on Strong's scoring scales reveals that *dislikes* are more important than *likes* in defining the pattern of the interests themselves. An unpublished study of Tyler's based on the Strong scores of 50 college boys indicated that scores based on *dislike* responses alone correlated more highly with full score than did scores based on *like* responses alone, for all the group scales and for occupational level. In the analysis reported by Tyler (1959a) of *like* and *dislike* patterns in Strong's group of 71 physicians retested after a 22-year interval, it was demonstrated that the tendency to obtain one's score on the Physician scale by choosing the L or the D responses included in it persists over this long period. Dislike responses are an important aspect of personality. We will turn to the question of what they may mean when we discuss interest development.

Another way of relating interests to adjustment is through the hypothesis that discrepancies of various sorts may be symptomatic of personality difficulties. Pool and Brown (1964) showed that for patients in a VA hospital discrepancies between Kuder and Strong scores in areas covered by both tests were significantly related to the number of high or deviant scores on the MMPI. Nugent (1961, 1962) presented some evidence that discrepancies between interests and aptitudes may be symptomatic of maladjustment.

It may be that some aspects of a person's interests are more closely related to his capacity for *coping* with anxieties and conflicts than to these difficulties themselves. Crites (1960) showed that, at least for the group of subjects over twenty-one years of age, ego strength as measured by Barron's scale was related to the extent of interest patterning (number of A and B+ scores).

The most consistent findings in relating interests to other aspects of personality have been correlations between interests and values. Sarbin and Berdie (1940) showed that scores on the Strong correlated significantly with scores on similar-appearing scales of the Allport-Vernon Study of Values. Ferguson, Humphreys, and Strong (1941) showed that factors derived from such correlations were defined by loadings based on both tests. In a review of psychological studies of values (Dukes, 1955), seven studies reporting consistent value-interest relationships were summarized.

There is another consistent finding running through the studies of interest-personality relationships. Interest patterns are linked in some way to social orientations. Dunnette, Kirchner, and de Gidio (1958) found evidence for this relationship, as have previous investigators. In the Dunnette study, 102 adults, employees of the Minnesota Mining and Manufacturing Company, were given three tests—the Strong Vocational Interest Blank, the California Psychological Inventory, and the Edwards Personal Preference Schedule. A number of significant correlations appeared, although most of them were fairly low. Persons scoring like sales, verbal, and personnel workers on the Strong tended to score higher than others on the Edwards scales for Need Exhibition and Need Dominance and on the CPI scales for Social Status, Socialization, and Social Presence. Persons scoring like scientists and skilled tradesmen on the Strong tended to be lower than average on these scales. What the results appeared to define was a main dimension extending from dominant, confident, sociable traits at one end to permissive, dependent, and individualistic characteristics at the other. A study of 727 Stanford male freshmen in which Strong scores were related to the Myers-Briggs Type Indicator discussed in the previous chapter (Stricker and Ross, 1962) reported findings of the same sort. Scientists tend to be introverts. Business and personnel men tend to be extraverts.

DEVELOPMENTAL RESEARCH ON INTEREST DIFFERENCES

Perhaps the most promising strategy for obtaining knowledge about these main lines of interest differentiation is to trace them back to their origins in childhood. Some years before the significance of vocational interest differences in personality structure was as clearly demonstrated as it is now, Tyler (1964) initiated a small-scale longitudinal study of the development of children's interests from 6 to 18. During the two-year period from 1946 to 1948, first-graders were administered a short, home-made interest inventory and a test of Primary Mental Abilities. Their personal characteristics were assessed by means of a sociometric procedure. Three years later, these subjects, now in fourth grade, were again assessed by means of an interest inventory, a test of Primary Mental Abilities, and a sociometric procedure. Other children now in the same school class as the original subjects were assessed at the same time. Follow-up studies of these children who entered the study as either first-graders or fourth-graders were planned for the eighth grade, 10th grade, 11th grade, and 12th grade. At each successive developmental level, measures of interests, personality, and special abilities appropriate to the age were obtained. Of the 287 subjects in the fourth grade sample, 145 continued in the group until the end of the study.

Analyses of the results for six-year-olds and nine-year-olds showed that the earliest type of differentiation to show up was the distinction between masculine and feminine kinds of activities. Even at the first-grade level, sex differences were apparent not only in the items preferred but also in the ways variables were related to one another. Among nine- or ten-year-olds, interest factors seem to represent concepts of the sort of person one ought or ought not to be. In boys, for example, the rejection of "sissy" behavior of all sorts seems to be one such factor; the rejection of "work" behavior seems to be another. In girls, the rejection of aggressive, violent kinds of activity acts as such an interest organizer.

It was evident also that it was mainly through *rejections* of some classes of activities that individuals developed their characteristic interest patterns. Nine- and ten-year-old children mark the "L" response for the great majority of items on an inventory appropriate for their age level. In order to distinguish between persons, we have to direct our attention to the minority of items upon which a fair number of *dislike* responses appear. The older and brighter children tend to mark more dislikes than the younger and the duller. Very young children are enthusiastic about almost any new toy, game, or experience. Adults do not even consider for themselves a large proportion of the activities available to them.

The most important analyses of the data obtained in this study involved the identification of groups of twelfth-graders whose interest profiles on the Strong test clearly showed acceptance or repudiation of certain patterns of interests representing ways of life, and then the identification of characteristics apparent at earlier stages in the lives of these individuals that could be thought of as early forms or precursors of such interest patterns. In one of these special comparisons, a group of boys with the interests of scientists was compared with the group who were most different from scientists. In another, a group of girls whose profiles showed some sort of career interests was compared with a group showing the typical feminine pattern referred to above. What the results showed, in general, was that these characteristic patterns of interest had begun to take shape by the eighth grade. In the data that had been obtained when the subjects were younger than this, the clearest differences appeared in the masculinity-femininity distinction. Boys who developed the interests of scientists had given "masculine" responses more consistently than had boys in the nonscientist group, even when they were first-graders. "Career" girls had chosen *less* feminine responses when they were first-graders than had the noncareer comparison group. It was interesting to note that it was the *early* masculinity-femininity that predicted the final interest pattern. The groups compared at the twelfth-grade level did not differ on the M-F variable, as measured by the Strong. Generally speaking, high and low abilities, social status, or sociometric status during childhood was not related to twelfth-grade patterns of interest.

Results of this kind led the investigator to a reformulation of the problem of what interest differences signify. Rather than looking upon interests as *traits,* we can view them as complex psychological *structures* controlling *choices* of the use one will make of his time. They indicate which of many possible directions he will take, which of many possible actions he will carry out. As yet we know very little about how such structures are developed, but the way is open for significant research. What such a shift from trait to structure implies for a general theory of human individuality will be discussed in the final chapter.

MAIN LINES OF RESEARCH ON VALUES

One result of the research on interest-personality relationships and of interest development has been to bring the concepts of *interests* and *values* into closer connection with one another. Until fairly recently, psychological research on values had not received a great deal of attention although Dukes (1955) did locate 211 studies of some aspects of the problem. Because the concept of "values" was complex and seemed somewhat "mentalistic," it was difficult to fit it into the structure of laboratory experiments or mental-testing projects. But in recent years, values have been taking on increased importance in discussions of such disparate topics as perception, politics, and career choice.

The instrument most widely used in psychological research has been the *Study of Values.* The original test, devised by Allport and Vernon, came out in 1931. The current revision, published in 1951, is by Allport, Vernon, and Lindzey. The six basic values this test is designed to measure came originally from the thinking of a German philosopher, Spranger (1928). They are as follows:

Theoretical—interest in the pursuit of truth by intellectual means.
Economic—interest in useful, practical things.
Aesthetic—interest in beauty and art.
Social—interest in helping people.
Political—interest in power or influence over people.
Religious—interest in mystical experience.

Research in which the *Study of Values* has been used has been concerned with differences between sex, socio-economic, ethnic, regional, and religious groups as well as occupational groups, with changes in responses under various circumstances, and with relationships to personality factors and behavior. In spite of its "armchair" origin, it has been a useful instrument for identifying aspects of personality not readily measurable in other ways.

A second major formulation of basic differences in values was proposed by the philosopher, Charles Morris (1956). His *Ways to Live* was based initially on a survey of orientations characterizing all of the world's major religions. This was supplemented by suggestions students made after responding to the test about alternative "ways" they considered preferable. Each "way" is represented by a descriptive paragraph. The subject is asked to rate each of them on a 7-point scale. They are as follows:

1: Preserve the best that man has attained.
2: Cultivate independence of persons and things.
3: Show sympathetic concern for others.
4: Experience festivity and solitude in alternation.
5: Act and enjoy life through group participation.
6: Constantly master changing conditions.
7: Integrate action, enjoyment, and contemplation.
8: Live with wholesome, carefree enjoyment.
9: Wait in quiet receptivity.
10: Control the self stoically.
11: Meditate on the inner life.
12: Chance adventuresome deeds.
13: Obey the cosmic purpose.

Morris and his associates have carried out a number of kinds of research on these ways of life, comparing students in different countries, relating the "ways" to social, psychological, and biological differences, and showing how they affect judgments of paintings (Morris, 1956). One interesting point is that the Morris system and the Allport-Vernon system appear to be quite independent of one another (Morris, 1956, pp. 109–111). This is because the Allport-Vernon classification is in terms of institutionalized social roles, whereas the Morris classification has to do with conceptions of the good life without institutional connotations. Because of this difference, it seems likely that the *Ways to Live* would not show as much correlation with Strong scores as Allport-Vernon results have shown.

Another major classification of values has been proposed by an anthropologist, Florence Kluckhohn (Kluckhohn and Strodtbeck, 1961). In some ways it is the most comprehensive of all. It starts with the premise that there are certain basic human problems every culture must face, and that there is a limited number of positions one can take with regard to each. These problems and the possible positions with regard to them are as follows:

1. Human nature	Evil, Neutral, Mixture, Good. Mutable, Immutable.
2. Man *vs.* nature	Subjugation, Harmony, Mastery.
3. Time	Past, Present, Future.
4. Activity	Being, Being in Becoming, Doing.
5. Relational	Lineality, Collaterality, Individualism.

These different value orientations can be studied in various behavior spheres—economic, religious, intellectual, for example. While the system is designed primarily for the comparison of cultures, there seems to be no reason that it cannot be used to differentiate individuals or subgroups within a culture.

The recent research on values most closely related to the work on interests is that of Super (1962). As one of the instruments to be used in a longitudinal study of the way career choices are made, he devised a preference-type inventory of fifteen values, which previous research had suggested might have occupational significance. They were as follows:

Intrinsic values: 1. Altruism, 2. Creativity, 3. Independence, 4. Intellectual stimulation, 5. Esthetics, 6. Achievement, 7. Management,
Extrinsic values-Rewards: 8. Way of life, 9. Security, 10. Prestige, 11. Economic returns,
Extrinsic values-Concomitants: 12. Surroundings, 13. Associates, 14. Supervisory relations, 15. Variety.

Super administered this *Work Values Inventory* to 88 of the ninth-grade boys whose careers he is following, along with the Strong blank, a projective measure of adjustment, an intelligence test, and various measures of background factors and achievement. A factor analysis of the intercorrelations between the 40 variables revealed ten factors. The most important finding for the purposes of this discussion is that measures of values and of interests produced loadings on the same factors. Three adjustment factors and one achievement factor were determined by other kinds of measures, *not* values or interests. Thus this confirms what some previous correlational studies had suggested—that what we measure as interests and what we measure as values overlap to some extent.

Consideration of this overlap leads to the question whether or not we are really dealing with two kinds of variable when we study interests and values? Could it be that the two terms are really names for the same thing? The answer to this will depend upon how we define the words "interest" and "value." In this as in the other areas, the progress of research has made it possible to produce more and more precise definitions. Jacob and Flink (1962) summarized a large number of efforts to delimit the definition of "values" in order to facilitate communication among researchers. The definition they proposed is as follows: "Values are normative standards by which human beings are influenced in their choice among the alternative courses of action which they perceive." They considered it important to distinguish "values" on the one hand from "beliefs" (existential propositions) and on the other hand from "impulses" (drives, needs, cathexes).

Another attempt to add precision to the concept of "values" was made by M. B. Smith (1963), He adapted a definition first presented by C. K. M. Kluckhohn so that it read: "Values are conceptions of the desirable that are relevant to selective behavior." In distinguishing "values" from similar but not identical concepts he says: "Personal values are attitudes. . . . But they are a special kind of attitude functioning as standards by which choices are evaluated. Personal values pertain to the *desirable,* the *preferable,* rather than to the merely *desired* or *preferred;* to the realm of 'ought' rather than to that of 'is' or 'want.'" (Italics mine.)

It is the word "normative" in the Jacob and Flink definition and the words "preferable" and "desirable" in the Smith definition that differentiate values from interests as measured by the Strong or Kuder tests. We have proposed that what these scores express are the personality structures controlling an individual's choices. It is apparent that these may or may not have the normative quality Jacob and Flink emphasize, the "oughtness" emphasized by Smith. The consistent but not very high correlations between the two kinds of measures could come about because some persons but not others make personal choices of activities on the basis of general concepts about what they ought to do, or that some personal choices but not others are controlled in this way. The distinction points the way to more penetrating research hypotheses. If there are important individual differences in the extent to which choices reflect values, the use of a moderator variable to distinguish the two types of subjects would constitute a significant improvement in research design. If in any one individual some choices are determined by values, others not, research designs that furnish information about *why* a subject likes, dislikes, or prefers each item, could be expected to shed new light on the whole problem.

Perhaps the time has come when the provocative findings from the psychology of interests and the psychology of values can be incorporated into a more comprehensive psychology of organized choices.

SUMMARY

Interests were investigated first by applied psychologists who needed to take them into consideration in vocational guidance. The Strong and the Kuder blanks, developed in different ways, have been very generally used. A large amount of work with the Strong blank over a long period of time has demonstrated that the characteristics that it measures are remarkably stable and that they reflect aspects of motivation that are important in a person's adjustment to his work. Results with the Kuder over a shorter period point to the same conclusions.

Correlational analyses have shown that there is a limited number of broad types of occupational interest rather than a large number of specific interest patterns. These would seem to be based on self-concepts or roles the person sees himself as playing rather than on experiences with work itself, since they appear before he enters any occupation. Interest scores of any type have not usually correlated to a significant extent with neuroticism or maladjustment, but they are consistently related to values.

Instruments for the measurement of values are based on philosophical analyses of the basic positions man can take toward life. The Allport-Vernon-Lindzey *Study of Values,* based on Spranger's *Types of Men,* and the Morris *Ways of Life,* based on a study of the world's religions, have been used more than any others in psychological research.

The relationships repeatedly found between interest and value measures, as well as the limited developmental evidence, suggest that what should be investigated are the general orientations or mental structures controlling an individual's choices and decisions.

CHAPTER 9

Individual Differences in Cognitive Style

WHILE RESEARCH ON PERCEPTION AND COGNITION has been carried on unceasingly since the days when the first psychological laboratories were established, it is only fairly recently that the investigation of individual differences has played much of a part in it. The possibility that the world might actually look, sound, and feel differently to different persons, that they might solve problems and form concepts in quite different ways, and that the same stimulating situation might carry different meanings for them was something investigators did not generally take into account.

EARLY WORK ON PERCEPTUAL DIFFERENCES

It is true that some early workers in the field of mental measurement had stressed differences in sensory and perceptual characteristics. Galton (1883) devised tests of weight discrimination and sensitivity to high tones, and tried to find out what forms the imagery of different subjects took. J. McK. Cattell and Farrand (1896) published the results from a group of 100 college students on a battery of tests that included a considerable number measuring perceptual differences—keenness of eyesight and hearing, color vision, perception of pitch and of weights, sensitivity to pain, and time perception. Jastrow (see Peterson, 1925) displayed a collection of psychological apparatus and tests at the Columbian Exposition in Chicago in 1893, and invited interested persons to take such tests. They included tests of cutaneous and kinesthetic sensibility, such as estimation of the distance of an unseen movement of one's finger and the estimation of a surface by touch, as well as the common measures of visual acuity, color vision, and speed and accuracy of movement. At about the same time, J. A. Gilbert (1897) gave similar perceptual and motor tests to several hundred children and compared them with measures of physical growth. Thus even before 1900 it had been demonstrated that accurate measurements of differences in perception were obtainable. Why then did interest in this line of investigation decline?

The reason seems to be that research in individual differences has a practical orientation and tends to be continued only when some possibility for application presents itself. Especially at the time when differential psychology was just getting started, differences in measured traits needed to be correlated with criterion measurements of some sort before anyone took much interest in them. The aim of the early mental-testers was to measure intelligence. When the evidence began to come in (Sharp, 1899; Wissler, 1901) that tests of this sort showed very little relationship to school success, the enthusiasm of psychologists for the whole mental-test movement was considerably dampened. Because tests of the kind that Binet and Henri (1896) had been recommending, tapping complex intellectual characteristics rather than perceptual sensitivities, stood up better under this kind of evaluation, they set the pattern for later work, and the attempt to measure perceptual differences was largely abandoned.

The rise of Gestalt psychology and its signal successes in clarifying the nature of perceptual processes probably served also to play down the importance of individual differences. Gestalt workers focused their attention on phenomena for which striking similarities between subjects are the rule—apparent movement, figure and ground, tendencies toward closure and "prägnanz," the constancy effects. Since the aim of much of this research was to enable them to make inferences about the nature of the brain as an electro-physical system, individual differences were not explored. The phenomena can be demonstrated in every person who carefully examines his own experience, and it is not necessary to use large groups of subjects in order to demonstrate their existence. Thus many crucial studies were done with small numbers of subjects and without benefit of the types of statistical treatment that would show us how much individual variation from the reported mean measures of performance actually occurs.

One perceptual characteristic the Gestalt psychologists had stressed lent itself to quantitative treatment much earlier than the rest—the constancy phenomenon. Thouless (1951) has summarized some of his own research on the constancy phenomena, for which he coined the new term *phenomenal regression*, work going back as far as 1932. It is to be remembered that "constancy" refers to the tendency we all show to react to objects in space in terms of their *known* size, shape, and color rather than in terms of the varying image that is projected onto the retina at different times. As material for differential psychology, this family of experiments has the advantage of permitting very accurate measurements. Just how much size constancy influences a subject's response can be determined by having him match a far object to a near one, after which the actual size of both objects and the distances to them can be accurately measured. Thouless showed that there were sizable, consistent differences in the matches made by different persons. Differences were significant at the .001 level. When the same group of twenty subjects was tested on two different occasions, the correlation between their scores was .876. In another study he showed that the correlation between size and shape constancy measurements for 53 subjects was .65, whereas the correlation between the means of the size and shape measurements and color constancy determinations for forty-five subjects was .58. All of these correlations are significant at the .001 level. There can be no doubt that some persons give evidence of the constancy effect to a greater degree than to others.

Other studies of the constancy phenomena confirmed Thouless in his conclusion that there are sizable individual differences, but left some doubt as to how consistent they are from one type of experimental situation to another. Lichte (1952) gave data for 50 students on shape constancy, measurements which showed a considerable range. The correlation of .88 and higher for sets of measurements on the same subjects taken a week apart showed that the differences are stable and accurately measurable as long as they are confined to this one type of task. But Sheehan (1938) who made three kinds of constancy measurements—brightness, shape, and size—on her 25 student subjects found only low correlations between the separate varieties, suggesting that the same persons are not necessarily object-oriented or stimulus-oriented in different situations.

An attempt to relate differences in shape constancy to something else was made by Ardis and Fraser (1957). They reported that the 12 university students who scored at the introverted extreme of a distribution of scores in an inventory designed to measure Thinking Introversion were significantly *less* subject to the constancy phenomenon than were the 12 subjects who scored at the extraverted end. They venture to explain the findings in terms of the greater amount of attention extraverts pay to the environment, as compared with introverts.

It was in connection with their investigation of the effects of attitudes, set, attention, or motivation upon perception that laboratory psychologists were most likely to find it necessary to take individual differences into consideration. In the earlier studies, such factors were usually thought of as something superimposed upon the standard experience of perception rather than as an inextricable part of it. Experiments were set up in such a way as to show that different verbal instructions can change the report subjects give of ambiguous figures, that indistinguishable pictures will more often be seen as food when subjects are hungry, or that experimentally induced frustration tends to disrupt the perceptual process. But it became increasingly clear that some set or attitude in the observer is *always* involved in a perception whether or not the experimenter takes any cognizance of it.

Gibson (1941) summarized a large number of experiments on "set" including those having a bearing on perception. A gradual extension of the meaning given to the term "set" becomes very apparent in this series of experiments. At first it was considered a temporary condition created in a subject by the experimenter's instructions. It was soon realized that what was perceived was dependent also on habits developed by past experience and on general expectations arising from the pattern of the total situation. The concept of "set" was extended to include all of these conditions in the perceiver. For the purposes of this discussion it matters little whether "set" is the most appropriate term. The recognition that there are these personal determiners of perceptual experience has opened the way to the investigation of individual differences with regard to them.

In particular it was the resurgence of interest in the relationship of *motivational* factors to perception, the "new look" in perceptual research, that led to the active contemporary work on individual differences which we shall take up later in this chapter. It coincided with a general shift of emphasis in differential psychology from the measurement of cognitive or intellectual traits to the measurement of temperamental or motivational traits. It is perhaps true that the early mental-testers abandoned too soon their search for relationships between perceptual differences and significant aspects of intellectual functioning. Some research during the 1950's suggest that there may be more rich ore in this vein than the first prospectors concluded that there was (Krech and Calvin, 1953). But the relationship between perceptual tendencies and personality characteristics seems to be even more striking. Enough significant findings have already appeared to warrant a thorough exploration of this terrain.

During the 1950's and 1960's cognitive processes have come in for extensive re-examination, and theorists have increasingly been thinking of perceptual processes as belonging in an enlarged and complex cognitive domain. M. D. Vernon (1957) in a carefully reasoned attempt to explain some of the findings in the research on perception, including individual differences, suggests that perception always involves a process of inference in order to "make sense" of what is perceived, a process ordinarily occurring so rapidly that we are not aware of it. In making such an inference, a person refers the new stimulating situation to already existing *schemata* he possesses. Minor incongruities will be overlooked, but major ones will initiate a reasoning process through which a satisfactory match can be achieved. Because some of these schemata develop out of experience common to everyone, people react alike to some kinds of perceptual situation. Because some are the result of particular experiences and training, individual differences in response to some situations are bound to occur.

Thus it is possible to incorporate individual differences in perception in theories about motivation, using concepts like "sensitization," "direction of attention," and the like, and in theories about cognition, using concepts like Vernon's "schemata." Perhaps the most interesting thing about this variety of research is the way in which it links concepts traditionally kept separate.

Although objective measurement of perceptual-personality relationships is a fairly recent development, theories about such relationships have a much longer history. A great many typologies have been constructed contrasting persons whose typical ways of experiencing the world differ in one way or another. They are too numerous for detailed consideration, but they do serve as sources of hypotheses and as materials that can be used to corroborate the evidence we get from objective studies. A good summary is available in M. D. Vernon (1952, pp. 247–256).

One of the most frequently recurring of these typologies contrasts the *analyzers* and the *synthesizers*. The analytic observer concentrates on details and tends to see separate parts. The synthetic observer sees the field as an integrated whole but may miss some of its details completely. Various workers cited by Vernon make mention of the fact that subjects spontaneously adopt one or the other attitude in experiments on psychophysical relationships, illusions, or comparisons of complex geometrical forms. Subjects seem to be most successful at a perceptual task when they adopt the attitude that is natural for them.

Another somewhat similar typology contrasts *objective* with *subjective* perceivers. The distinction here is between rigid, narrow consistency in the approach to a perceptual task—such as reading a few letters at a time but getting them all right—and fluctuating, broad inspection with considerable subjective interpretation of what is seen. There is some support for the idea that this may be related to other personality characteristics in the findings by Angyal (1948) that individuals with obsessional tendencies showed the objective pattern to tachistoscopic materials whereas persons suffering from anxiety or hysteria were more likely to show the subjective pattern.

Among children, *active* and *passive* perceivers have been differentiated. Whether this is really a distinction based on fundamental temperamental differences seems somewhat doubtful in view of the fact that several investigators have shown that the age of the subjects is an important consideration. Children become more active as well as more accurate in their perceptions as they get older. Hanfmann (1941), however, has noted that intelligent adult subjects approach the task of sorting the Vigotsky blocks into categories in different ways to which the *active* and *passive* labels might well be applied. (*Conceptual* and *perceptual* are the terms Hanfmann uses.) Some of the subjects work rationally, attempting to formulate hypotheses as to what the correct solution might be. Others proceed by trial-and-error, guided by their immediate impressions of the stimuli.

Still another differentiation of basic perceptual attitudes has been called *confidence* and *caution* by Bartlett (1932). The confident observer reports all he sees of a complex presentation in a single glance, often reporting details not actually present. The cautious observer gives a careful, hesitating report, including less detail than is actually present. Bartlett also differentiated between *evaluative* and *nonevaluative* attitudes.

One of the most inclusive of all the proposed typologies based on perception was that of Jaensch (1938). (See Frenkel-Brunswik, 1954.) He contrasted the "disintegrated" S-type, whose perceptions are unstable, irregular, and not firmly tied to reality, with the "integrated" J-type, whose perceptions are systematic, logical, and realistic.

Another perceptual typology that has appealed to a large number of European psychologists contrasts *color reactors* with *form reactors.* (See Eysenck, 1947, p. 220.) A great many ingenious experiments have been devised using stimulus materials that will trigger one response if the subject is most sensitive to color, and a different response if he notices the shape first. The theory has been that schizoid types of personality are form-conscious, whereas cycloid (manic-depressive) types are color-conscious. The evidence presented so far, however, does not establish this conclusion. We shall have more to say about this later.

Still another possible distinction is the one that has been made by Lowenfeld (1945) between *visual* and *haptic* types. The visually-minded person experiences the world primarily through his eyes. The haptically-minded person experiences the world primarily through touch and kinesthesis. In either case a person translates the experience that comes to him into the medium that suits him best. The haptic painter, for example, shows forms and textures in such a way that they can be sensed as if one were feeling them. The visual individual constructs in visual images some representation of what he encounters in the dark. Lowenfeld devised some ingenious tests that could be used to determine how strong each of the tendencies was and showed that there is a high degree of consistency in the verdict the different tests give on an individual.

The various perceptual typologies have been presented in some detail in spite of the fact that good quantitative evidence for their meaningfulness does not exist. They can still be considered sources of hypotheses, starting points for research. Let us look, now, at what some of this research has shown.

FACTOR ANALYTIC STUDIES

The first large-scale quantitative investigation of individual differences in perceptual characteristics was published by L. L. Thurstone in 1944. The monograph is interesting in the first place simply as a source of information as to how much individual variation occurs in the kinds of perceptual processes that have been so exhaustively studied by laboratory psychologists. As has been said, their own publications usually do not give us this information. Table 17, for example, gives the frequency distribution for the Gottschaldt Test, Form B, which turned out to be in several ways the most interesting test in the battery. It requires the subject to locate in a complex configuration a simple figure that he has been shown.

The study was designed to use the factor-analytic method as a way of exploring the perceptual domain. Thurstone hoped to find out how many different perceptual variables it would be necessary to postulate in order to account for the perceptual processes and to get some idea of the nature of the basic differences between individuals. He felt strongly that

TABLE 17

Scores of 186 Students on Gottschaldt Test B (Score represents the number of designs marked divided by the number of minutes required.)

(Thurstone, 1944a)

SCORES	FREQUENCY
.4- .7	5
.8-1.1	6
1.2-1.5	14
1.6-1.9	24
2.0-2.3	33
2.4-2.7	28
2.8-3.1	16
3.2-3.5	21
3.6-3.9	14
4.0-4.3	5
4.4-4.7	7
4.8-5.1	7
5.2-5.5	2
5.6-5.9	1
Over 6.0	3

it would be far more economical of time and effort to build our subsequent research on perception-personality relationships around variables identified in this way than to rest it on the typologies of the philosophical theorists or the intuitive categories of the practicing clinicians.

Forty tests were chosen to represent a wide variety of perceptual phenomena. Some were alternation tests, like the Necker Cube of which the near surface flops from front to back, thus restructuring the cube, as one watches it. Some were tests of closure, in which the subject's task is to see a clear simple figure under various distracting conditions. A number of well-known optical illusions were included. Response time and reaction time were measured in several tests. Several tests involved conflicts between color and form. Size constancy, shape constancy, and brightness constancy tests similar to those Thouless had used were included. The Rorschach test was also given, but only two scores, R, the total number of responses, and W, the number of organized wholes, were used in the analysis.

The subjects were 194 volunteers, mostly University of Chicago students. The customary procedures of intercorrelating all variables, extracting centroid factors, and then rotating these factors to simple structure, were employed. Because this was a pioneer study, and there was little previous information that could be used as a guide in the interpretation of the factors, Thurstone preferred to try to describe each in general terms rather than to pin it down by a specific name.

Eleven factors were identified mathematically, but only seven of them could be given the detailed examination from which some conclusions about the nature of the perceptual processes could be drawn. Of the eleven, one was a residual, apparently due to chance errors in the original correlation coefficients. One was what factor analysts call a doublet, carrying high loadings in only the two Rorschach scores. Another one was also a doublet linking two scores that were both derived from the same test, although logically they seemed to represent different things. One factor showed up in only the tests of the intelligence or cognitive type which had been carried over into this study from the previous work on primary mental abilities.

Of the seven that had some significance for perception, three seemed to represent different kinds of speed—the familiar *reaction time,* speed of *perception* (where stimuli were easily recognizable), and speed of *judgment* (where some decision had to be made about what had been clearly perceived). The findings of three separate speed factors rather than one was one of the interesting results of the study.

Two factors seemed to represent specific kinds of experimental material—in one case illusions, in the other case stimuli where alternations or reversals occur. There is evidence here that some persons are more subject to illusions than are others, and that the rate at which any of the alternating figures tends to reverse itself is a characteristic differentiating between individuals.

The most interesting of the factors from this analysis, and the ones that have stimulated most of the later research, were those concerned with *closure.* The Gottschaldt Test (called Concealed Figures in later studies) had fairly high loadings on both of these closure factors, but the tests that clustered with it showed a somewhat different pattern of loadings in the two factor columns. After discussing various possibilities as to what aspects of perceptual closure the two factors might represent, Thurstone tentatively described the first as *speed and strength of closure* and the second as *flexibility in the manipulation of several configurations.* (Closure refers to the act of grasping and retaining a clear, coherent pattern in the stimulus materials.) In a later discussion of these closure factors, after more work that was planned especially to throw light on their essential nature, Thurstone (1949) described them thus: "The first closure factor C_1 (speed of closure) seems to facilitate the making of a closure in an unorganized field, the second closure factor C_2 (flexibility of closure) seems to facilitate the retention of a figure in a distracting field."

Yela (1949) after reanalyzing some mental test data that had been presented by Alexander in 1935, identified the factor Alexander had called Z and had not been able to define very successfully as the now familiar *speed of closure* factor. His description of it is one of the clearest statements of what it involves:

> The subject will excel in this task if he can hold the given structure as a group of elements organized into a pattern and at the same time reproduce it quickly . . . or is able to perceive the figure that completes the unfinished configuration. At the beginning of the task the elements integrate themselves into changing configurations that interfere with the completion of the final pattern. In all cases the final structure is arrived at by quickly rejecting the patterns that do not lead to the correct configuration and by the ability to synthesize the units given into a meaningful whole.

There have been a number of studies in which attempts were made to find out what other psychological traits were related to these perceptual factors. From the first study on, there has been consistent evidence in the way the factor loadings were patterned that the *flexibility of closure* factor is related to reasoning ability (Botzum, 1951; Pemberton, 1952a). Hypotheses that one closure factor is linked with induction, the other with deduction, or that one represents "analytical," the other "synthetic" processes, are less well supported by the data. Pemberton (1952b) also showed that persons who are high on the first perceptual factor differ *temperamentally* from those who are high on the second. She used a number of inventories and self-ratings of interests and emotional characteristics. These were all brought together into ratings of eleven broad traits, such as "socially outgoing," "systematic," and "energetic and impulsive." Among this group of 154 subjects, mostly graduate students, those receiving high *speed of closure* scores tended to have high self-ratings on the traits "sociable," "quick in reactions," "artistic," "self-confident," "systematic," "neat and precise," and "dislike logical and theoretical problems." Those with high scores for *flexibility of closure,* on the other hand, tended to rate themselves "socially retiring," "independent of the good opinions of others," "analytical," "interested in theoretical and scientific problems," and "dislike rigid systematization and routine." This looks like another sort of typology and suggests in its general outlines the extravert-introvert classification that has been used in so many ways by so many people. It must be remembered, however, that the perceptual scores defining the traits Pemberton studied were *not* at opposite poles of one continuum, but were actually *positively* correlated. While the correlation was not high, it was still true that an individual with an outstanding score on *speed of closure* was less likely to be low on *flexibility of closure* than he was to be high. Thus, in the lives of actual people, we should expect many of the temperamental traits from apparently opposite clusters to occur together.

There is some limited evidence that individuals tend to maintain their relative positions on the *flexibility of closure* distribution whether the test they take is made up of visual or of auditory materials. White (1954), using 116 high school students as subjects, found that scores on the Concealed Figures and on the Hidden Tunes tests correlated as highly with one another as two visual tests of the factor.

Thurstone continued to explore various kinds of perceptual tests in the years that followed the publication of the 1944 monograph. He hoped to identify usable objective measures of temperament. (Objective is defined as in Chapter 7 to refer to what a subject *does* in some standardized situation rather than what he says about himself.) He assembled a considerable number of ingenious techniques, including projective methods, verbal association tests, and psychophysical discriminations, and explored in systematic fashion their relationship to temperamental traits (Thurstone, 1951 a, b, c, 1953). This work constitutes a source of ideas and research methods, even though it has not yet led to practical assessment techniques or a comprehensive theory.

FIELD-DEPENDENCE AND ITS PERSONALITY CORRELATES

Our current interest in individual differences in perception, as well as our knowledge about them, has been tremendously increased during the years since World War II as a result of a large-scale research program initiated at Brooklyn College by Asch and Witkin (1948) and reported in some detail in *Personality Through Perception* (Witkin et al., 1954) and *Psychological Differentiation* (Witkin et al., 1962). The investigation began when they discovered that there were large and consistent individual differences in the ability of college subjects to bring themselves to a vertical position when placed in a situation where visual cues were misleading.

There were three separate kinds of test situation. In the Rod-and-Frame Test, the subject sat in a darkened room where all he could see was a luminous frame surrounding a movable luminous rod. The frame could be tilted at any angle by the experimenter. The subject's task was to report on the position of the rod as it was moved a little at a time and to tell when it appeared vertical, disregarding the frame if he could. The angle between the setting of the rod the subject accepted as vertical and a line representing the true vertical constituted his score. In the Tilting-Room-Tilting-Chair Test, the subject sat in a small room in a special movable chair. The room could be tilted into any position and the chair could be tilted in either the same or in an opposite direction. Each trial started with different degrees of tilt. In some trials subjects were asked to manipulate the controls in such a way as to straighten the room. In other trials they were asked to straighten the chair. The angle made by one's adjustment with the true vertical again constituted his score. In the Rotating-Room Test the subject sat in a chair within a little room that was made to rotate around a circular track. Both chair and room could be tilted by various amounts, and the subject was required in some trials to straighten the room, in others to straighten the chair.

The perceptual trait that these research workers succeeded in defining clearly and measuring accurately by these methods was "the ability to keep an object isolated from compelling background forces." Subsequent work focused on a number of questions. How consistent are individuals from one sort of task to another with regard to this trait? How stable are their scores over a period of time? Can the same characteristic be measured by other methods—perceptual tests that do not involve bodily orientation as a basic variable, or personality evaluations of the kinds clinicians have been using? Can group differences be identified—between the sexes, between children of different ages, between hospital patients and normals? The method they followed was first to set up some hypotheses as to the correlations one would expect to get between this variable and some other—for example, Rorschach records or interview protocols—and then to see whether the obtained correlations supported the initial hypothesis.

Only the results that seem most important for the general understanding of the meaning of individual differences in perception can be summarized here. First of all, this perceptual trait is clearly a stable, consistent characteristic, and shows itself in a variety of ways. Odd-even reliability coefficients on the various tests ranged from .69 to .91. Test-retest coefficients were of about the same magnitude even when there was a one-year interval. A group of 32 men retested after three years obtained scores on the Rod-and-Frame Test that correlated .84 with their original records and scores on the Tilting-Room-Tilting-Chair Test that correlated .89 with the first ones. For a group of 30 women the three-year correlations were .66 and .89. Correlations between the *different* orientation tests were on the whole lower, but most of them were significant at the 1 per cent level. Table 18 shows these figures. Furthermore, the

TABLE 18

Intercorrelations Between Orientation-Test Index Scores (Number of cases: men = 46; women = 45)

(Witkin *et al.*, 1954, p. 66)

TEST	TILTING-ROOM-TILTING-CHAIR		ROTATING ROOM	
	Men	*Women*	*Men*	*Women*
Rod and frame	.64[a]	.52[a]	.25	.18
Tilting-room-tilting-chair			.51[a]	.62[a]

[a] Significant at less than 1 per cent level.

TABLE 19

Correlations Between Orientation and Embedded-Figures-Test Scores (Number of cases: men = 46; women = 45)

(Witkin *et al.*, 1954, p. 85)

	Men	*Women*
Rod-and-frame Index score	.64[a]	.21
Tilting-room-tilting-chair Index score	.60[a]	.51[a]
Rotating-room Index score	.36[b]	.39[a]
Orientation index (all three tests)	.66[a]	.46[a]

[a] Significant at or below 1 per cent level.
[b] Significant at or below 5 per cent level.

trait is not specific to bodily orientation situations. The Embedded Figures Test, a variation of the Gottschaldt Test discussed in reporting on Thurstone's work, correlated as highly with these scores as they correlate with one another. (See Table 19.) The kinds of measurements with which these scores did *not* correlate significantly turned out to be as helpful as the significant correlations in defining what the trait essentially is. It is only in tests that require subjects to keep one aspect of a complex perceptual situation isolated from its background that this particular trait shows up. The scores correlated significantly with success on a Two-

Hand-Coordination Test, for example, but not with measurements of body steadiness. The failure to get significant correlations with a test involving conflict between auditory and visual cues as to the location of a sound in space shows that something other than a simple preference for judgments based on visual impressions must be involved.

In a number of separate studies, ratings of field-dependence were made using data obtained by means of other well-known methods of studying personality—interview, Rorschach, Figure-Drawing, and Miniature-Toy Play Situation. These were correlated with orientation scores. As a whole, the results supported the hypotheses the authors had formulated with regard to the nature of the basic personality variable, although there is some possibility that knowledge of subjects' orientation scores might have biased the judgments made in interview and test situations. Each also *added* something to the total picture of "field-dependence" and the way it operates in a personality. The final description of the trait making for success in the orientation tests included three aspects: (1) *activity* in dealing with one's environment as opposed to passive acceptance; (2) *awareness* of one's inner life along with good control over impulses, and (3) *self-esteem* and self-acceptance.

Studies of children of various ages showed that the trait is related to maturity, though not in a clear-cut linear fashion. Thirteen-year-olds did better than eight- or ten-year-olds on all the tests, but the seventeen- and eighteen-year-olds on some tests made more errors than the thirteen-year-olds.

One of the most striking findings of all was that there were marked sex differences in all the kinds of samples tested—college students, children, hospital patients. Females seem to be markedly more field-dependent than males and thus less successful in these orientation tasks. These differences will be discussed in more detail in a later chapter when we are considering sex differences of all kinds.

A second book by Witkin and his co-workers (1962) reported a considerable body of new data, based mainly on ten-year-old children. At the outset, the authors presented what they referred to as the *differentiation hypothesis.* They explained it thus:

> Specifically the differentiation hypothesis proposes an association among the characteristics of greater or more limited differentiation . . . in each of several psychological areas: degree of articulation of experience of the world; degree of articulation of experience of the self, reflected particularly in nature of the body concept and extent of development of a sense of separate identity; and extent of development of specialized, structured controls and defenses.

The 64 ten-year-old boys who served as subjects in most of the studies were volunteers, mainly middle class and Jewish. For each subject a

Perceptual Index score based on the Rod-and-Frame Test, the Tilting-Room-Tilting-Chair Test, and the Embedded Figures Test was related to a variety of other tests chosen or constructed to measure the variables with which the differentiation hypothesis is concerned. There were three main varieties of research studies: (1) Studies of individual self-consistency, (2) Studies of the contributions of life experiences, particularly aspects of the family situation, to psychological differentiation, and (3) Studies of the stability of patterns during development and in adulthood. In each chapter relevant research done by others was assembled and combined with their own.

In general, the results supported the differentiation hypothesis as quoted above. Degree of articulation of experience of the world and the self appeared to be significantly related. Children differing in level of differentiation differed also in the kinds of controls and defenses they tended to use. The authors presented a considerable number of significant correlations, often fairly high, to support these conclusions.

One of the gaps in previous knowledge of this psychological variable that was to some extent filled in by this study is the matter of the relationship of psychological differentiation (or field independence, as it was previously labeled) to intelligence. Evidence was given that the Perceptual Index is related to three of the subtests of the Wechsler Intelligence Scale for Children (WISC)—Picture Completion, Object Assembly, and Block Design—but scarcely at all to the rest of the scale or to other verbal tests. The Figure Drawing rating, devised to measure "sophistication of body concept," showed the same pattern of relationship to the WISC.

Perhaps the most interesting material in the monograph is to be found in the chapters having to do with the mothers of the subjects in the study. Each of them was interviewed by someone who did not know what kind of scores her child had obtained and was classified in the group labeled IFD (interaction fostering differentiation) or the group labeled IID (interaction inhibiting differentiation). When point biserial correlations between mother's classification and child's Perceptual Index scores were computed in subgroups of children not used in developing the system for classifying the mothers, the coefficient was .82 in one group, .65 in the other. Some of the mothers' personal characteristics, especially self-assurance and self-realization, were related to children's perceptual scores and there were specific differences in the child-rearing procedures that had been used with "analytic" and "global" children. For example, mothers of field-dependent children used more coercive procedures, placed more stress on conformity, and pushed their children more consistently toward goals and standards set by the parents.

The investigators were able to report a considerable amount of additional evidence with regard to the stability of the traits measured by the

TABLE 20
Coefficients of Stability for Perceptual Test Scores: Children

(from Witkin, *et al.*, 1962, p. 375)

Age of Subjects	*Retest Interval*	*N*		BODY ADJUSTMENT TEST		ROD AND FRAME TEST		EMBEDDED FIGURES TEST		PERCEPTUAL INDEX	
		M	*F*	*M*	*F*	*M*	*F*	*M*	*F*	*M*	*F*
10-14	4 years	27	24	.58	.66	.56	.57	.51	.69	.64	.88
14-17	3 years	27	24	.68	.88	.82	.75	.95	.95	.87	.94
10-17	7 years	27	24	.31	.63	.49	.53	.48	.68	.50	.79

perceptual tests in adults and in children. Table 20 summarizes the findings for children. It is clear that most of these coefficients are fairly high, even over intervals of several years, and even for persons who were only ten years old at the time of the original test.

The results reported by the Witkin group have been criticized because of the small and nonrepresentative samples on which they were based. However, results obtained by others have generally tended to corroborate them. As indicated above, many such studies were summarized in the 1962 report. One of the most thorough of these investigations was the analysis of perceptual tests used in the assessment of 100 Air Force officers (Crutchfield, Woodworth, and Albrecht, 1958). Each man was scored on 600 personality variables. The number of significant correlations between the Embedded Figures Test and scores on various aspects of personality was unusually high, and in the direction one would have expected from Witkin's analysis.

Work continues in Witkin's laboratory and promises to tell us more, as time passes, about an important aspect of individuality. The longitudinal developmental studies should be particularly fruitful. Witkin (1964) has given us a general picture of the ongoing research program.

COGNITIVE CONTROL PRINCIPLES— THE MENNINGER FOUNDATION RESEARCH PROGRAM

What is in many ways the broadest and most comprehensive attack on the problem of individual differences in cognitive style has been in progress for some years at the Menninger Foundation. The theoretical framework for a whole series of experiments was initially explained in a symposium paper by Klein and Schlesinger (1949) and a chapter by Klein a little later (1951). Looking at personality from a functionalist point of view, one can see that an individual's perceptions have *adaptive* properties. "They are the means we have for fending off, choosing, and admitting stimulation from the outside world which, with free entrance, would traumatize and overwhelm us." In psychoanalytic terms, it is the *ego* that we study when we analyze a person's characteristic ways of perceiving, and broad perceptual attitudes can thus serve as clues to the whole *ego-control system.*

At the beginning, these workers used the term "perceptual attitude" or its German equivalent *Anschauung* as a label for these personal ways of coming to terms with reality. But it was soon clear that other cognitive processes besides perception were involved, and *cognitive control principle* seemed to be a more accurate label.

The first of these variables to be intensively studied was the *leveling-*

sharpening dimension. We shall consider in some detail the procedure for studying this, since it is also typical of the procedure for analyzing the others to which they turned later.

The first step was to use what had previously been observed as a basis for setting up hypotheses. The theoretical distinction between levelers and sharpeners is that "levelers" tend to assimilate new stimuli to an already dominant cognitive organization and thus not to be aware of differences between the new and the old, whereas "sharpeners" notice changes and keep successive stimulating situations separate from one another. If such a distinction between ways of dealing with the perceptual world exists, one would expect to be able to measure it in an experimental situation where subjects are presented with gradual changes in a pattern of stimulation. The experimental strategy was to select subjects clearly exemplifying the hypothesized tendencies on the basis of one experimental procedure and then try them out under a completely different experimental procedure to find out whether their tendency to respond in a certain way would show itself again.

For the leveling-sharpening study Holzman and Klein (1954) selected subjects who made extreme scores on the Schematizing Test and compared the two groups on measures of visual time error. What the Schematizing Test involved was presenting squares one at a time in random order in sets of five different sizes and asking the subject to judge the size of each. After he had had three trials on each square from the smallest set, the very smallest of the squares was removed and the next size larger introduced without the subject's knowledge. After three trials with each of these (in random order) the smallest square was again taken out and the next larger one substituted. This process of gradual shift was continued until a set made up of the five largest squares had been presented. For example, the first series of judgments might be made on squares with 2-inch, 3-inch, 4-inch, 5-inch, and 6-inch sides. The second set would consist of squares with 3-inch, 4-inch, 5-inch, 6-inch, and 7-inch sides. The final set would consist of 10-, 11-, 12-, 13-, and 14-inch squares. There were great differences in the accuracy with which subjects were able to *change* their size judgments as the general level of the squares being shown changed. In the experiment reported by Holzman and Klein (1954), nine extreme "levelers," subjects whose judgments were very inaccurate under these conditions, were contrasted with nine extreme "sharpeners" on a test of visual time error. This test required that the subject compare the brightness levels of stimulus lights with the brightness of a standard light which he had first been shown. Between the standard and the variable light stimuli, dark, dim, or bright interpolated lights were used on different trials. The hypothesis was that the "levelers" would be more confused by this interpolated stimulation, less able to keep the different stimuli separate, and thus would show greater "time errors." The results of the analysis of variance bore out this hypothesis and showed that differences were statistically significant even with this small number of cases. There were, however, large individual differences *within* each group. "Levelers" are not all equally good at the assigned tasks; neither are "sharpeners."

Holzman (1954) extended the study to three different sense modalities. Selecting 21 levelers and 22 sharpeners in the same way, by their success in judging the size of squares presented in sets that were gradually shifting in size, he tried them out on the same sort of visual test that had been used before, and also on auditory and kinesthetic tests of similar type. In the auditory test, subjects were asked to judge whether a comparison tone was louder or softer than a standard tone. In between the two, either a soft or a loud tone was interpolated. In the kinesthetic test, subjects judged whether a comparison weight was heavier or lighter than a standard. Between the two, light or heavy interpolated weights were used. As in the previous study, the analysis of variance showed that in all these tasks "sharpeners" made smaller errors than "levelers." Figures 32 and 33 show this graphically. The correspondence was far from perfect, so far as individuals were concerned, but the correlations were all positive. The rank-difference correlation between visual and auditory scores was .25. Between kinesthetic and auditory it was .66, and between kinesthetic and visual .50. Both the analysis of variance and correlational approach show that only a part of the differences between individuals in any one of these test situations can be accounted for by what all the tests have in common, but they do have *something* in common. It is the evidence for this common core which argues for the effect of a pervasive attitude or cognitive style.

Research since 1954 has proceeded in several directions. New cognitive control principles have been hypothesized, identified, and tried out in two or more experimental situations. Factor-analytic studies added new information about consistencies in the behavior of individuals in different test situations set up on the basis of the initial experiments (Gardner, et al., 1959) and indicated that at least some of the cognitive styles are related to intellectual abilities measured by familiar intelligence and aptitude tests (Gardner, Jackson, and Messick, 1960). Other studies were set up specifically to show whether a cognitive control principle was the same as or different from similar dimensions postulated by other investigators who based their work on other theories or techniques (Gardner and Schoen, 1962).

Besides *leveling-sharpening,* there are four other cognitive control principles for which evidence of one or more kinds has been obtained. One is *scanning.* The test by which it is usually measured is a size estimation task of some sort, in which the subject is required to match a variable stimulus (usually an adjustable circle of light) to a standard (usually a plain or complexly patterned disc). Persons who focus on the standard tend to overestimate its size. Those who scan the whole situation more broadly show much less overestimation. Gardner and Long (1962) showed that more extensive eye movements actually occurred in subjects whose test behavior classifies them as "scanners" than in others, and that one of Piaget's basic hypotheses—namely, that centration leads to overestimation of size (Piaget, 1961)—is supported by the results.

Another cognitive control principle is *equivalence range*. This is usually measured by an object-sorting test in which a subject is free to use as many or as few categories as he wishes. Individual differences are consistent and stable. Gardner and Schoen (1962) presented clear evidence that these differences were not related to intelligence or to the *capacity* for abstract thinking, or even to the *preferred level of abstraction*. There did turn out to be some significant correlations with Pettigrew's (1958) measure of *category width*, in which the subject chooses upper and lower extreme values to accompany an average value presented to him (e.g., the average width of windows).

Still another cognitive control principle is called *tolerance for unrealistic experience*. It can be measured by an apparent movement test in which the alternation rate of the stimuli can be varied. At low alternation rates, a subject typically sees static figures succeeding one another. At higher rates he sees a single figure moving from one place to the other. At still higher rates he sees two figures flashing on and off or flickering. The score used to measure this control principle is the range of alternation rates over which the illusion of movement occurs. Klein, Gardner, and Schlesinger (1962) showed that individual differences in this variable were general enough so that they could be identified in some of the characteristics of the subject's Rorschach records, and, to a lesser extent, in their reactions to stimuli seen through aniseikonic lenses (which distort the appearance of objects).

One other cognitive control principle about which less supplementary evidence has accumulated is called *flexible and constricted control*. It is measured by the Color-Word Test, in which after reading the names of colors, and naming actual colors presented in stimulus strips, the subject is presented with color names painted in conflicting colors (e.g., the word r-e-d printed in blue) and asked to name each color, ignoring the word. Since this control principle did not seem to define a separate factor in the study of individual consistencies referred to above (Gardner, et al., 1959), its status as a separate variable is a little more doubtful than that of the others.

In addition to these five control principles, the Menninger group has found evidence for the separate existence of the Witkin field dependence-independence dimension. They prefer the term *field articulation* for this variable.

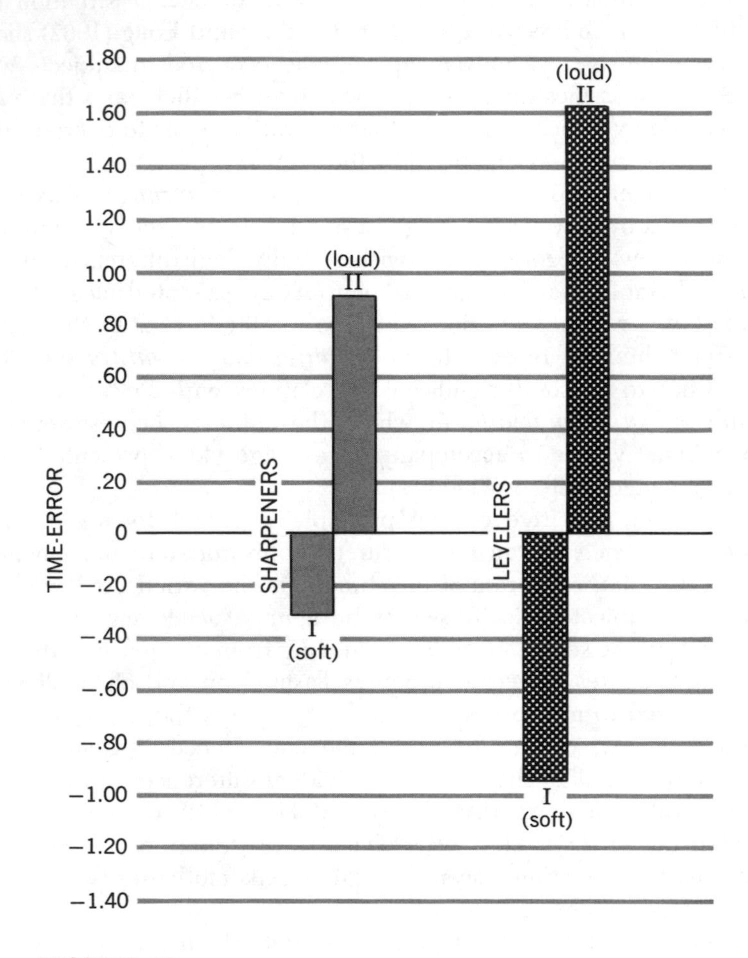

FIGURE 32

Differences in the Performance of "Levelers" and "Sharpeners" on a Test of Auditory Time Error under Two Conditions of Interpolated Field

(Holzman, 1954)

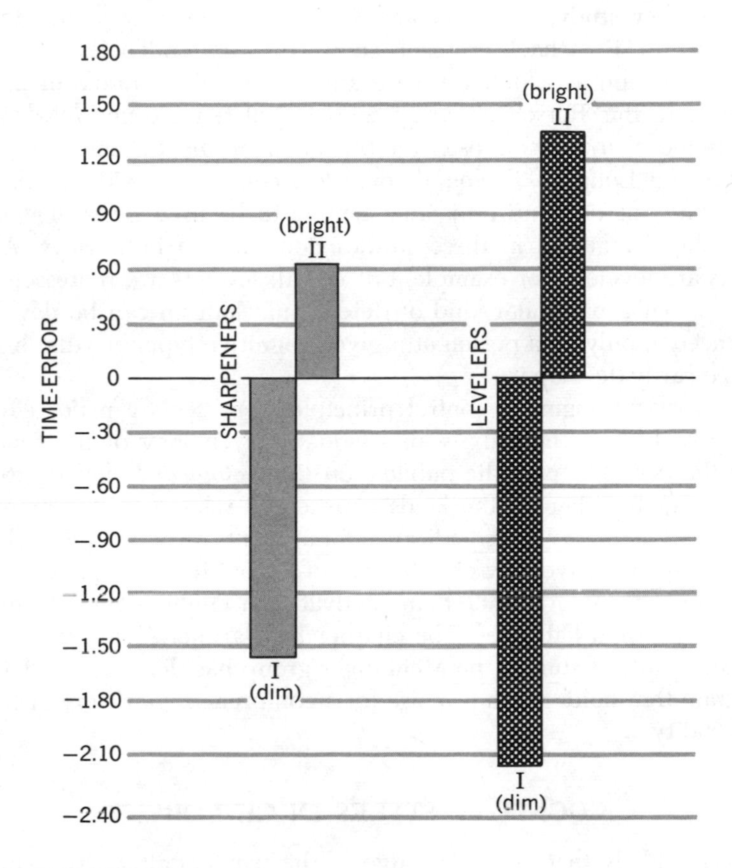

FIGURE 33

Differences in the Performance of "Levelers" and "Sharpeners" on a Test of Visual Time Error under Two Conditions of Interpolated Field

(Holzman, 1954)

One special line of research to which these investigations attached considerable theoretical importance explored the relationship of cognitive control principles to defense mechanisms. In a replication of a suggestive earlier study, Holzman and Gardner (1959) found that the six persons whose Rorschach protocols showed strong tendencies toward the use of repression as a defense were all *levelers*. The sample of 20 subjects used in this Rorschach study consisted of ten extreme *levelers* and ten extreme *sharpeners* chosen on the basis of the Schematizing Test. Gardner and Long (1962) found some less conclusive evidence that the defenses of isolation and projection tended to be used by *scanners*. The relationship suggested in these studies does not go both ways. All repressers are levelers, for example, but not all levelers are repressers. The theory is that a particular kind of defense mechanism can be developed if it is needed only by a person of a given cognitive type, but that he does not necessarily develop it.

This work on cognitive control principles represents a major effort to develop within psychoanalysis an adequate psychology of the functioning of the *ego*. The periodic publication *Psychological Issues* is attempting to bring together all the kinds of research related to this branch of psychoanalytic theory. Its significance for students of personality, whether they are psychoanalytically oriented or not, is that it is emphasizing adaptive, coping behavior rather than motivational conflicts and difficulties, assets rather than liabilities. The chapter by Gardner (1964) summarizes the many kinds of studies the Menninger group has done and is doing in a program that holds much promise for a comprehensive theory of human individuality.

COGNITIVE STYLES IN CHILDREN

It seems likely that our knowledge of the part cognitive styles play in the functioning of individuals will be advanced considerably by investigations of the way in which they originate in children. The intensive study of ten-year-olds by Witkin and his colleagues has already been discussed. Gardner and his colleagues also have developmental studies under way (Gardner, 1964). Their subjects are 60 children, now nine to thirteen years of age, who were studied in infancy by Escalona and at three subsequent stages of development by Lois Murphy.

At the Fels Institute, a number of studies of children of various ages have been carried on to explore the correlates of what these investigators call the *analytic* style of thinking. The first means used for identifying the style was a sorting test using drawings of human figures. The second was a test in which three pictures were presented at each trial, with instructions to select two of the three that "go together in some way." A person who selects "dog" and "cat" as similar because they are both animals shows an analytic approach. The person who combines "dog" with "doghouse" because one uses the other is not.

A monograph by Kagan, Moss, and Sigel (1963) reported significant stability coefficients for this variable over a one-year interval. The analytic attitude was correlated with the tendency to respond to nouns on a word association test by giving other nouns, and with scores on the nonlanguage portion of the California Test of Mental Maturity. It was also correlated with reaction time, the nonanalytic children being more active and impulsive. There were sex differences in the correlations, with stability coefficients higher for girls, correlations with other variables higher for boys. A cross-sectional comparison of age groups suggested that there are significant increases in analytic style with age among children, especially for boys.

In another report on a particular study, Lee, Kagan, and Rabson (1963) divided a group of 30 third-grade boys into two subgroups on the basis of the Conceptual Style Test described above. All IQ's in the group were above average, ranging from 105 to 134. The investigators presented the two groups, analytic and nonanalytic, with stimuli on the basis of which concepts could be discovered. As they had predicted, the analytic boys learned analytic concepts most readily; the nonanalytic boys learned relational concepts most readily.

On the basis of these preliminary reports one cannot say much about the over-all significance of this style difference in development nor can one be sure that it exactly parallels the differences analyzed in the other research programs we have discussed. But a beginning has been made on what may prove to be an important line of investigation.

IMPORTANCE OF THE RESEARCH ON COGNITIVE STYLES

We have discussed these experiments in considerable detail partly because the tests and the characteristics they are measuring are still unfamiliar to most readers. It is harder to see how a score is obtained on a tilting-room-tilting-chair test or a test requiring size judgments of squares in gradually shifting sets than it is to understand how an intelligence test is scored, simply because we have been exposed to intelligence tests again and again from our early youth on up. Furthermore, we are used to thinking of individuals in terms of IQ, reading age, or even cycloid-schizoid temperaments, whereas to evaluate them for speed of closure, equivalence range, or tolerance for unrealistic experience seems at first esoteric and farfetched. The experiments reported in this chapter lead us in a different direction from earlier work in individual differences.

They are worth considering carefully because of the relationships already demonstrated between the cognitive variables and a number of traits that have always been of the greatest interest to differential psychologists. On the cognitive side there is at least a slight possibility that experiments like these may help us out of some of the impasses we have run into in intelligence measurement. Perceptual scores seem to be related to some kinds of scores on our standard intelligence tests (Witkin, et al., 1962, Ch. 5). The work of Piaget showing how intelligence develops out of early perceptual "schemata" fits well into this framework.

On the other hand, these variables are clearly related to the traits we have been classifying as *noncognitive,* the motivational or personality traits. It is especially interesting that various approaches to personality theory can be reconciled by means of these concepts. While the dominant theoretical formulations by Klein, Gardner, and others have been couched in terms of psychoanalytic ego psychology, the ideas and research findings fit equally well into Adlerian "life-style" or Rogerian "self-concept" thinking. They even enable us to utilize the insights of typological theorists who have been beyond the pale in the eyes of emancipated scientific psychologists who demand the utmost in quantitative rigor in their work. Both Klein and Schlesinger (1949) and Frenkel-Brunswik (1954) were struck by the fact that the dimensions of personality they were revealing corresponded rather strikingly to the Jaensch integrate-disintegrate classification. The principal difference is that we have attached an opposite value judgment to the quality. Jaensch's integrated type, the simple man of action who scorns complexities and does not even see fine distinctions, appears here as the rigid authoritarian whom we think of as a real obstacle to the achievement of democracy. Frenkel-Brunswik's work relating intolerance of ambiguity to the complex syndrome that has been labeled the authoritarian personality points up the fact that an understanding of these cognitive styles may contribute to social psychology as well as to the psychology of the individual.

Work of this kind thus seems to occupy a strategic position in differential psychology. Not only does it tie together research being done in widely separated areas—intelligence measurement, clinical study of individual personalities, and research on basic social attitudes—but it suggests the possibility of measuring variables in which all of these psychologists are interested far more accurately than they can be measured by the techniques that have previously been used. The scores on these tests are *ratio* measurements, not the ordinal or interval scales we have had to content ourselves with in the other fields. The size of an angle, as in the Witkin experiments, or the error in size judgments, in those of Klein and Holzman, can be measured to any degree of accuracy we desire. The fact that the scale has a true zero point and equal intervals permits us to use any mathematical treatment we find that we need. (The success with which the experiments of the Menninger group have wrested unambiguous conclusions from small numbers of cases can probably be at least partially attributed to this fact.)

For all these reasons, it is fortunate that research on individual differences in cognitive styles is being pursued with vigor and enthusiasm.

SUMMARY

Psychologists were measuring individual differences in perceptual characteristics before the beginning of the twentieth century, but lost interest in the problem when simple perceptual measurements proved not to be indicators of general intelligence. Both armchair theorists and experimental workers proposed various typologies, however, with regard to perception—analyzers versus synthesizers, color-reactors versus form-reactors, and the like.

A series of factor-analytic studies during the 1940's delineated a number of factors having to do with perceptual speed, which seemed to be related to mental ability or aptitude of some sort. They also pointed with increasing clarity to two *closure* factors, speed of closure and flexibility of closure, which seemed to be related primarily to temperament.

A series of studies having to do with individual differences in the perception of the vertical under confusing conditions isolated a perceptual trait called *field-dependence* and showed it to be related to personality characteristics that have been evaluated by clinical techniques. A subsequent series of studies using ten-year-old children as subjects has shown how this trait, now defined more broadly and labeled *psychological differentiation,* is related to the individual's experience of the world and of the self and to the development of controls and defenses.

A series of experiments at the Menninger Foundation has identified a number of cognitive control principles—*leveling-sharpening, scanning, equivalence range, tolerance for unrealistic experience,* and *flexible-constricted control*—and analyzed their relationships to other variables. At the Fels Institute, the correlates of the *analytic* attitude in children are being explored.

The cognitive variables on which research has been done are of interest to psychologists who study abilities, personality, or social attitudes. They constitute a promising new approach to complex problems.

Part Three

VARIETIES OF GROUP DIFFERENCES

CHAPTER 10

Sex Differences

HISTORY OF THE PROBLEM

NO TOPIC IN PSYCHOLOGY is of more perennial interest than sex differences. Study after study, book after book, testify to the fact that research workers, writers, and readers consider the subject one of paramount importance. Partly this interest comes from the need men and women feel to understand one another. Many social problems having to do with marriage and divorce, education, and living and working conditions in general depend upon such knowledge for their successful solution. Partly the multiplicity of studies is perhaps just a matter of convenience. Any psychologist who is trying out a new laboratory procedure or standardizing a new test can easily compare the performance of males and females, since his subjects, however chosen, divide themselves into these two categories.

Although there had been many books containing theoretical discussions or general impressions on this topic even before 1900, quantitative research began at about the turn of the century and expanded very rapidly. The 25 references, only 10 of them directly psychological, that Dr. Woolley found to summarize in 1910 grew to the 327 that C. C. Miles covered in 1935. Much of the work done during this period was motivated by the desire to demonstrate that females are not inherently inferior to males. Over many centuries, in our culture and perhaps in most others, this had been the prevailing view. The fact that women were physically weaker than men had seemed to suggest an all-around weakness, which included mental traits. The primitive idea that in reproduction the male was the active, form-giving agent whereas the female furnished only soil and nourishment continued to affect attitudes long after research on the mechanics of heredity discredited it completely. But from 1900 on, the findings of the psychologists gave strong support to the arguments of the feminists. That differences between the sexes in mental abilities are small and that it is possible to account for such differences as there are on a sociological rather than a biological basis were the two conclusions that stood out. Differences between the sexes were minimized and overlapping of the two groups was stressed. Along with this emphasis on equality, however, a large amount of material showing differences in *patterns* of ability gradually accumulated.

During the 1930's the research emphasis shifted to the measurement of motivational and personality traits—interests, values, attitudes, emotional needs. The purpose of these studies was not to prove that females were *like* males, but rather to achieve a better understanding of the differences between the sexes upon which good relationships could be based. Many such studies were related directly or indirectly to psychoanalytic theory, postulating basic emotional differences determined by biological rather than social causes. One research strategy was to combine a great many separate items to which male and female subjects reacted differently into a masculinity-femininity scale. Such scales were constructed for a number of personality tests—the Strong, the MMPI, and the CPI, among others.

During the 1950's the emphasis changed once again. Research workers became interested in the developmental processes through which these characteristically male and female patterns of response are formed. The sociological emphasis on *sex roles* became salient, and *identification* emerged as an important concept. Psychologists began to plan investigations designed to show not just *how much* average difference in a certain trait, such as aggression, the two sexes showed, but also what other traits and external factors were correlated with this one in single-sex groups. It has become apparent that the way in which separate traits are linked together is very different for males and females. The clarification of these patterns of relationships, often through developmental studies, has constituted the central research task of the 1960's. A large accumulation of facts and figures on each of these successive research undertakings is now available. We shall try to sift out the principles and conclusions that have the most solid foundation.

SEX DIFFERENCES IN ACHIEVEMENT

Throughout these decades, while research attention has been focused on one aspect or another of the overall problem, one set of facts has persistently challenged the investigators. Why have women made so few major contributions to civilization? Why have women ostensibly achieved so much less than men? History has recorded the names and achievements of a large number of men but of only a very small number of women. Ellis (1904) in his study of British genius found only 55 women in his total group of 1,030 persons. J. McK. Cattell's (1903) list of the 1,000 most eminent persons in the world includes only 32 women, and some of these were distinguished by circumstances such as royal birth rather than by intellectual achievements of their own. Castle (1913) collected a list of 868 famous women down through the ages. The highest degree of eminence, as indicated by amount of space in biographical directories, characterized women whom circumstances rather than intrinsic merit had made prominent—sovereigns, political leaders, and mothers, wives, or mistresses of great men. More women attained eminence in writing than in any other profession. In the 1927 edition of *American Men of Science,* only 725 women were listed out of 9,785 entries, and out of the 250 names starred because of special eminence, only 3 were women. In spite of the great emphasis placed on science in our time, and of the encouragement and financial help given to both boys and girls to obtain college and graduate school educations, the proportions have not changed very much. If it is an indisputable fact that society produces, now and then, a Marie Curie, it is just as true that it does not repeat the performance at all frequently.

Even in fields traditionally assigned to women, the most eminently successful persons are likely to be men. Interest in the arts is accepted as a feminine trait, yet there are very few women who have distinguished themselves as creative artists. Even in dress-designing and interior decorating, the leaders in the field are men. Most of the world's cooking may be done by women, but the great chefs of all time have been men. Though acting is a field that has been open to women for a long time, the great playwrights and producers are men. Wherever we look we find this same preponderance of male leadership and high achievement. For the differential psychologist, this is a fact to be explained and a spur to the research that may eventually supply the explanation.

In contrast to this situation with regard to *adult* achievement, all studies of *school* achievement agree that girls consistently make better school records than boys. Differences of this sort have been reported from a wide variety of investigations, using various criteria of school success. It is recognized that girls are less frequently retarded and more frequently accelerated than boys. More of them receive high marks and fewer of them receive unsatisfactory marks. How large these differences typically are is shown in a survey by Northby (1958) of 12,826 students who graduated in 1956 from 83 Connecticut high schools (83 per cent of the total number of graduates in the entire state for that year). When the distribution of grade point averages was divided into tenths, the predominance of girls in the high categories and boys in the low ones was very striking. For example, the breakdown in the top tenth was 72 per cent girls, 28 per cent boys. In the bottom tenth it was 36 per cent girls, 64 per cent boys.

When batteries of achievement tests are used to evaluate school performance, the differences are less marked. For example, W. W. Clark (1959) compared boys and girls in grades 3, 5, and 8 on the California Achievement Tests, using a carefully chosen stratified sample of children from all 48 states. The six tests in this battery are Reading Vocabulary, Reading Comprehension, Arithmetic Reasoning, Arithmetic Fundamentals, Mechanics of English, and Spelling. There were only a very few significant differences. At all three grade levels, girls were better in spelling. Girls outscored boys in Mechanics of English at the 5th-and 8th-grade levels and in Arithmetic Fundamentals at the 8th grade level. This corroborates earlier studies in showing that even on standardized achievement tests, what differences there are tend to favor girls. Often, however, such studies have shown that boys score higher on some subtests. Girls typically excel in English, spelling, writing, and art, boys in arithmetical reasoning, history, geography, and science (see Terman and Tyler, 1954, for a summary of these studies).

Several main lines of explanation have been offered for these differences in achievement, both those in school and those in the world outside. They will simply be mentioned at this point and discussed in more detail as the other data on sex differences are analyzed. It is evident, to begin with, that it would be difficult to account for both kinds of achievement differences by any hypothesis of general intellectual inferiority or superiority. If women are, on the average, less intelligent than men, why do they consistently do better at school? If, on the other hand, they are brighter than men, why do they not continue to demonstrate the fact after school days are over? Cultural and social factors are often proposed in explanation of the difference in the number of great men and of great women. For only a very small fraction of recorded history have women been given anything like an equal opportunity to achieve, and the dice are still loaded against them to some extent. Differences in special aptitudes constitute a possible explanation of the disparity in school achievement. The fact that girls consistently do better in verbal tasks would make for feminine superiority on all sorts of school work involving reading, writing, or reciting.

Differences in rate of maturing are also sometimes used to explain the differences in school performance. Girls reach puberty, on the average, about two years earlier than boys. During the period preceding this change, they are taller, heavier, and more mature in their interests. This explanation has never appeared to be very convincing, in view of the large amount of evidence that mental and physical characteristics are related only very slightly, if at all. (See Chapter 16.) However, Ames and Ilg (1964), who compared sex groups made up of 33 boy-girl pairs, matched for IQ, age, and socio-economic status, found that at the kindergarten, first-, and second-grade levels, the girls scored significantly higher on four types of test that might be interpreted as measuring aptitude for school learning. W. W. Clark (1959) did not find such differences at the third-, fifth-, and eighth-grade level using the California Test of Mental Maturity, and they have not shown up in most previous comparisons. However, if the differences reported by Ames and Ilg are corroborated in studies involving larger numbers and more representative samples, they will tend to support the hypothesis that the greater maturity of girls at the age they enter school gives them a somewhat better start and thus leads to better scholarship throughout the school years.

Probably the most plausible explanation accounts for the sex differences in school achievement by relating them to differences in attitudes and personality traits. Docility and submissiveness, usually considered feminine traits, enable girls to make a better impression on teachers than boys do. Inevitably this will show up on report cards in other places besides the deportment column. And such traits would, to some extent, *prevent* their possessors from assuming positions of leadership in the world of affairs.

SEX DIFFERENCES IN TESTED ABILITIES

As long as psychologists considered that the intelligence tests they had devised were direct indicators of native intellectual abilities, they took some interest in comparing IQ's obtained by girls and boys. However, as their understanding of what it was that intelligence tests were measuring improved, they came to realize that the complex interaction of genetic potentialities with experience would tend to make boys superior in some kinds of test and girls superior in others. Since there was no way of deciding which varieties of items or subtests were inherently most valuable as intelligence indicators, the soundest policy seemed to be to balance the two types of test against one another so that the total score would not give an advantage to either sex. McNemar (1942) has explained how this was done in constructing the Stanford-Binet Test. Evidence that this procedure produces a scale on which large sex differences do not occur was contributed by two large-scale studies in Scotland, important because they were based on one of the most adequate samples that has ever been obtained in research of this sort (Scottish Council for Research in Education, 1939). All children in the whole country who were born on February 1, May 1, August 1, and November 1 in 1926 were singled out in whatever grade school they were attending and given Stanford-Binet tests. The average IQ's were 100.51 for the boys and 99.7 for the girls. The difference is not significant, and is about as small as one ever obtains between any two samples of any population.

A later Scottish study (Scottish Council for Research in Education, 1949) based on an equally good sampling, this time of children born in 1936, shows boys about 4 points higher on the individual test (Terman-

Merrill, Form L) and girls about 2 points higher on the group test. Both differences are statistically significant because of the large number of cases involved, but the fact that they are small and in opposite directions prevents them from lending support to a conclusion that either sex is superior.

The same situation as in the case of the Stanford-Binet Test—sex differences on some of the subtests, but none on total score—holds for the Wechsler intelligence scales, WISC and WAIS (Miele, 1958).

The exploration of special abilities has proven a more rewarding task than the search for absolute differences. The first of these, touched upon in the previous discussion of intelligence tests, is the consistent difference in verbal ability. From infancy to adulthood, females express themselves in words more readily and skillfully than males. Throughout the grades and high school, they obtain higher scores on verbal sections of intelligence tests and do better work in English courses. It is to be remembered in this connection also that among the women who have been distinguished for great achievements, a large proportion have been *writers* (Castle, 1913).

Most of the available evidence seems to indicate, however, that it is in verbal *fluency* (what Thurstone has called W), rather than in the grasp of verbal meanings (V) that females are superior. Hobson (1947) and Havighurst and Breese (1947) both found that girls of junior-high age were significantly higher on W but not on V of the Primary Mental Abilities battery. In the Hobson study boys actually averaged higher on V; in W there was no difference. Herzberg and Lepkin (1954) found senior high school girls were significantly higher than boys on W for all three ages they were considering: sixteen, seventeen, and eighteen. In this case the seventeen-year-old girls of all ages tended to get better scores on speed, but not on vocabulary or comprehension (Terman and Tyler, 1954). When we consider also the evidence that girls learn to talk a little earlier (Goodenough, 1927), are somewhat superior during the preschool years in articulation, intelligibility, and correctness of speech sounds (Wellman, et al., 1931), learn grammar and spelling more readily, and are less likely to be stutterers, we see it all supports the generalization that girls are more fluent from infancy on.

Comparisons of various groups of males and females on various tests, however, has also made it fairly clear that girls and women do *not* have larger vocabularies than boys and men do. In the study by W. W. Clark (1959) discussed above, girls and boys at all three grade levels (3, 5, and 8) made similar scores on the Reading Vocabulary test. Bennett, et al. (1959) reported very little difference between the sexes on either the verbal or the numerical aptitude scores of the Differential Aptitude Test battery designed for high school students. Dunsdon and Fraser-Roberts (1957) gave four oral vocabulary tests from leading intelligence scales to

2,000 English children, a 3 per cent random sample of all the children from 5 to 15 in Bristol. At all ages, the boys' norms averaged about one word *higher* than the girls'. In most of the comparisons that have been made on vocabulary, however, the sex groups have turned out not to differ significantly.

With regard to mathematical ability, male superiority is the rule. It shows up on the tests that require mathematical reasoning rather than on those that require simple computations. A number of studies of school achievement (Terman and Tyler, 1954) report significant differences in favor of boys in arithmetic tests requiring reasoning—what students call "story problems." At the lower age levels, kindergarten and below, where number tests involve simple counting or identification, and on tests for all age levels where only "mechanical" arithmetic is involved, differences do not appear. It is interesting to note that in two factor analyses of junior high school children (Hobson, 1947; Havighurst and Breese, 1947) males did not excel on N, the ability having to do with manipulation of numbers. It is *solving problems* with numbers that boys manage more successfully than girls.

In judgment and manipulation of spatial relationships, a consistent male superiority has been demonstrated. Tests of the form board type, requiring that pieces be fitted together quickly and accurately, have been widely used as performance tests of intelligence and as indicators of mechanical aptitude. From preschool levels to adult, males are in general more successful than females with this sort of task. They excel, also, in various related mechanical-aptitude measures, such as mazes (Porteus, 1918), puzzle boxes, and tests calling for the assembly of small objects. One of the tests in this field is the Mechanical Comprehension Test by G. K. Bennett, calling for the scrutiny of pictures representing mechanical relationships in order to answer questions about them. He reported a large and highly significant sex difference (G. K. Bennett and Cruikshank, 1942). There was not a single one of the sixty items on which women averaged higher than men. Among high-school students, only one girl in twenty exceeded the boys' average. Most of the studies using factor analysis have reported that males score significantly higher on the Space factor or factors, which seem to represent the most essential part of mechanical aptitude (Terman and Tyler, 1954).

Sweeney (1953) reported a series of experiments on a kind of sex difference that may be related to the differences we have been considering in both the mathematical and mechanical areas. He was interested in problem solving in general, and used a variety of problems in his various experiments. The subjects in this research were college students. Males were significantly superior on all problems requiring what he called *restructuring*, situations in which the person must discard his first system of organizing the facts he has been given and try out new approaches.

This difference between the sexes persisted even in groups that had been equated for general intelligence, verbal ability, mathematical ability, relevant knowledge, and various background factors. Taylor [1] presented some evidence that the difference is primarily a matter of *attitude* toward problems and is susceptible to training.

A study by G. M. Gilbert (1942) suggested that differential training may account for the sex difference that is customarily found on musical talent tests. Among the groups of men and women students in twelve Eastern colleges who had been given the Kwalwasser-Dykema music tests, subgroups based on the amount of training in music were formed. Women were superior to men when all subjects of both sexes were compared, but among the *untrained* there was no significant difference. Girls seem to be somewhat superior also on art ability, as it is commonly measured in the classroom (H. O. Barrett, 1950). To what extent this difference reflects differential training is not known.

In tasks involving manual dexterity—light, deft, swift movements of the hands—the advantage is again with girls and women. It is difficult to make any absolute generalization with regard to this sort of ability since the dexterities have been found to be highly specific, and a person who is skillful at one type of movement may be below average in another. But on several of the tests commonly used to predict success in various occupations requiring dexterity, the O'Connor Finger Dexterity Test, the O'Connor Tweezer Dexterity Test, and the Purdue Pegboard, the women average consistently better than men. (See test manuals.) It seems safe to conclude that in any industrial situation requiring dexterity and speed rather than strength, women workers, on the whole, can be expected to do at least as well as men, and in some performances they may do better. In sensory characteristics, such as hearing, eyesight, taste, and smell, sex differences are negligible, except for the fact that eye defects are less common in females than in males.

Most studies agree that females excel in rote memory. Memory tests in general use require the exact repetition of a group of digits or words immediately after presentation, the reproduction of geometrical figures that have been studied for a short time, or the recitation of a story or paragraph that has been read aloud. In all these types of test, female superiority is the general rule, although the differences are not very large (Havighurst and Breese, 1947). The direction of the difference is occasionally reversed in cases where the material to be remembered is more familiar or interesting to males or where it is of a quantitative nature (Duggan, 1950; Sommer, 1958). In amount and range of general information, men and boys usually turn out to be superior to girls and women (Miele, 1958).

[1] D. W. Taylor, Paper presented at the symposium on sex differences held at the meeting of the A.A.A.S. in Berkeley, Calif., December 27, 1954.

In the quick perception of details which constitutes the basic aptitude for clerical work of all sorts, women are definitely superior to men. Differences are large and unquestionably significant. Only 21 per cent of employed men clerical workers reach or exceed the median for women clerical workers on the widely-used Minnesota Clerical Test (see manual). Schneidler and Paterson (1942) summarized data from several sources showing that at all age and grade levels, only about 20 per cent of the males exceed the median for females. Sex differences in perceptual speed have been demonstrated on the WISC and WAIS coding and digit symbol tests (Gainer, 1962; Miele, 1958; Norman, 1953) and on the clerical aptitude section of the Differential Aptitude Tests (McGuire, 1961; Wesman, 1949).

One other type of sex difference which shows up with great clarity at the higher age and educational levels has to do with achievement in science. Some of the best evidence comes from reports on the Science Talent Search (Edgerton and Britt, 1944, 1947). Participation in this program was voluntary. Since each year two or three times as many boys as girls applied, one would have expected the girls to be far more highly selected. In spite of this fact, highly significant differences in favor of boys were obtained each year. These subjects were high-school boys and girls. At the grade-school levels, differences on achievement tests favor boys, but are less marked (Heilman, 1933). Primary and preschool studies have shown no sex differences in abilities that might seem to underlie science achievement, abilities like comprehending causal relationships (McAndrew, 1943). Increasing male superiority in science is something that develops as a part of the educational process. One might speculate that it is a matter of the same difference in attitude that shows up in the Stanford problem-solving experiments discussed above.

To summarize, males are clearly superior on tests of mathematical reasoning, spatial relationships, and science. Females are superior in verbal fluency, rote memory, perceptual speed, and dexterity. Some of these differences develop earlier and appear to be more fundamental than others.

In any discussion of *average* differences such as those that have been outlined, reference should again be made to the importance of noting *variability* as well as averages. In most of the abilities we have considered, differences between the *sexes* are so small, and differences between *individuals* of the same sex are so large that it is possible to find an individual who, regardless of his or her sex, will show almost any specified degree of any special ability. But distinction needs to be made between types of situation in which we may want to apply knowledge of human differences. If a *group* must be dealt with, as a whole, then average differences, even though small, may be highly important. For instance, if, because a nation is engaged in a war, one of its industrial plants finds it necessary to replace men with women workers throughout a whole department, and the personnel system and labor market conditions do not permit testing and selection, the difference between the two sexes *as a whole* on the type of task involved is decidedly worth knowing. If, however, the problem is to select *one* first-rate mechanical draftsman, then the sex of the applicants should not be the decisive factor. Although males usually excel in work of the sort, it is quite possible that one or more of the women among the applicants may be superior to any of the men. Group averages will not tell you what you want to know about individuals. The great Dr. Samuel Johnson was once asked, "Which has the most brains, man or woman?" His reply was, "Which man; which woman?" We cannot do better than to re-emphasize his remark.

One of the most plausible hypotheses that has been used to explain the difference in achievement between the two sexes makes use of the concept of variability. For a time, it enjoyed wide popularity and was often referred to as one of the basic truths about sex differences. According to this hypothesis, the principal way in which males and females differ has nothing to do with *averages*, but is a matter of range. Females are said to be clustered more compactly around the middle of the distribution with far fewer extreme deviates than males. Figure 34 shows graphically the way this hypothesis would represent the difference in intelligence between the two sexes.

Such a difference in the two distributions would explain very satisfactorily two indisputable facts. The first is the preponderance of males among eminent persons. The second is the surplus of males in institutions for the feeble-minded. Essentially, the theory holds that males are more likely to run to extremes; females tend toward mediocrity.

In 1922, L. S. Hollingworth published the first careful analysis of sex differences in numbers of feeble-minded in institutions, based on 1,000 hospital cases. The evidence pointed strongly to the conclusion that sampling factors, rather than any genuine sex difference, were at work. In the first place, the women, on the average, were older at the time they were institutionalized. This seems to mean that because of the less responsible and independent position they occupy in American life and perhaps because of their greater docility and submissiveness, feeble-minded girls are better able to make some sort of place for themselves both in their own homes and in their communities for a longer period of years than are feeble-minded boys. This explanation is strengthened by Hollingworth's further finding that the women in the institutions had lower IQ's than the men, on the average. In other words, a girl has to be *more* retarded than a boy does in order to be recognized as feeble-minded and sent to an institution. These and other data in this study indicated that percentages of institutional inmates are figures of questionable value as a basis for conclusions about the whole population. About 1914, there

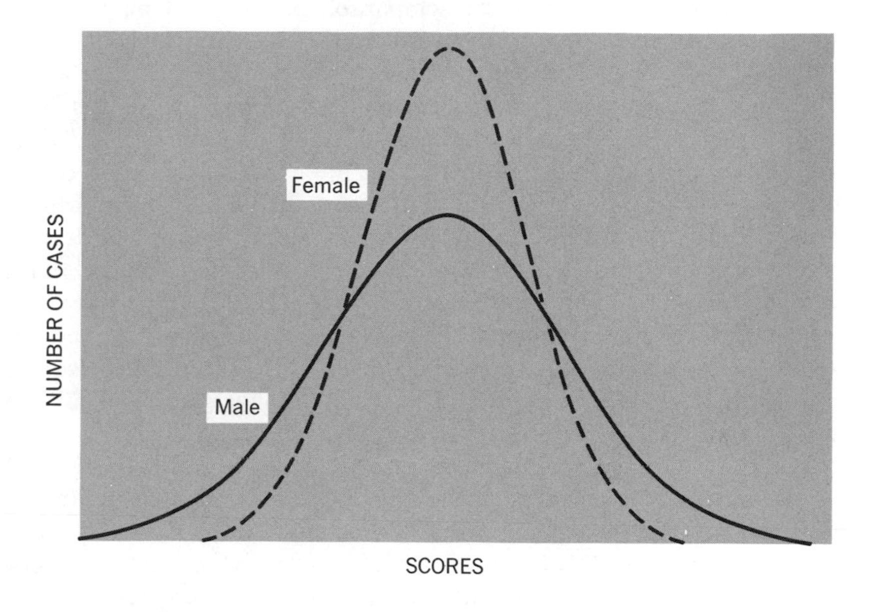

FIGURE 34

Hypothetical Distribution of Intelligence for the Two Sexes According to the Theory of Greater Male Variability

was a considerable increase in the percentage of girls in institutions, largely because a contemporary emphasis on eugenic factors (in this case restriction of parenthood) made it seem more important that potential mothers of the unfit be segregated. In summary, the argument for greater male variability based on findings at the *low* end of the intelligence distribution breaks down.

The most extensive information about the *high* end of the distribution came from Terman's famous study of gifted children (Terman, et al., 1925). A school population of 168,000 in grades three to eight which was sifted for children with IQ's of 140 or higher yielded 352 boys and 291 girls, a ratio of about 6 to 5. Witty (1930), on the other hand, found no difference in the proportions of boys and girls in his high-IQ group, and Lewis (1945), who selected the top 10 per cent from a population of 45,000 grade-school children in several hundred widely separated schools reported a sex ratio of 146 girls to 100 boys. The fact that he used a test the verbal content of which tends to favor girls and selected a larger proportion of the total group than Terman did may account for the discrepancy. But it illustrates the difficulty we encounter in trying to evaluate the hypothesis of greater male variability.

The student might think at first glance that this is a clear-cut statistical problem with an obvious statistical answer. But the many studies reporting the amount of variability for comparable male and female groups supply conflicting and inconclusive results. The main reason for this has been that until recently research workers could not agree as to whether they should use *absolute* or *relative* variability in a problem of this kind. Absolute variability is usually stated as a standard deviation and registers simply how much spread there is in the actual distribution of obtained scores. But the fact that in many kinds of measurement (height, for instance, or mechanical ability) women's averages are considerably lower than men's automatically cuts down the possible range of scores for them. Therefore, many research workers have held that if we want to consider variability alone, apart from averages, we must correct for this discrepancy by dividing each standard deviation by the *mean* or average of the group to which it applies. This gives us what is called CV, or Coefficient of Variability. Thus, for height, a standard deviation of 13 inches for a group in which the mean was 65 inches would be equivalent to a standard deviation of 14 inches for a group whose mean was 70 inches. Both would have the same CV. Fortunately for the progress of mental measurement, this is one controversy over method that has been quite conclusively settled. Although the CV has some merit for measurements like height that come in equal units starting from zero, it is never mathematically permissible to form a ratio by dividing figures that are *not* in these definite units. An IQ of 100 does not represent 100 units of anything, and a zero IQ does not mean zero intelligence. We have no real idea of what zero intelligence would be. Certainly a score of 56 on a test of mechanical aptitude does not represent 56 steps beyond just no mechanical aptitude at all. Consequently, for mental measurements, the use of relative variability is *never* justified, and we can rule out at one stroke all the conclusions based on it.

The McNemar-Terman summary (1936) is a compilation of significant results bearing on this problem. They found that for anthropometric measurements of all sorts, results varied from age to age, with adult men somewhat more variable than adult women. In educational achievement and in measurements of special aptitudes of all sorts, differences were very small and there was no consistent trend. On verbal intelligence tests, there was a consistent trend toward greater male variability. In twenty-nine out of the thirty-three comparisons they cited, the difference in standard deviations was larger than would be at all likely to occur in comparing different samples of the same sex. This trend is to some extent, however, dependent upon the type of test used, and some tests do not show it. The best evidence again came from the Scotch study already cited where sampling factors were absolutely controlled. The standard deviation for the boys was 15.88, for the girls 15.26. While the figure is higher for the boys, the difference is small. The hypothesis of the greater variability of the male will probably persist as long as no really decisive evidence shows up to disprove it. However, it does not rate as an important theoretical concept in current research on sex differences.

SEX DIFFERENCES IN PERSONALITY AND MOTIVATION

Interests and Values

It is when we move into the area of nonintellectual traits that we begin to find large psychological differences between males and females of all ages. First of all, their *interests* differ markedly. The most comprehensive research on interests was that carried out by Strong (1943). The method by which occupational scoring keys for the Strong blanks were obtained has been explained in a previous chapter. Sex differences were explored in a similar fashion. Strong tabulated item responses made by representative samples of men and women and attached scoring weights to those that showed large differences, thus obtaining an M-F (masculinity-femininity) key. In explaining this, he made a point that should always be remembered when interpreting results of studies in which this and similarly derived scoring keys are used. The procedure tends to *exaggerate* differences between groups, by scoring only the items on which differences occur. Actually there are many more ways in which men and women resemble one another in their interests than ways in which they differ. However, certain kinds of items repeatedly show large sex differences. The distinctly masculine interests show up on items having to do with: (1) mechanical and scientific activities, (2) physically strenuous, adventuresome activities; (3) legal, political, and military occupations, (4) selling activities, (5) certain forms of entertainment such as smokers, rough-house initiations, and chess, (6) certain miscellaneous preferences, e.g., for outside work over inside, for working for oneself, etc.

The distinctly feminine interests are indicated on items having to do with: (1) musical, artistic activities, (2) literary activities, (3) certain kinds of people, especially the unfortunate and disagreeable, (4) certain forms of entertainment, e.g., fortune-tellers, full-dress affairs, and movies dealing with social problems, (5) clerical work, (6) teaching, (7) social work, (8) merchandise, that is, looking at shop windows, displaying merchandise, etc., (9) certain school subjects, (10) miscellaneous characteristics. A more detailed description of the items thus classified can be found in Strong's book (1943).

When M-F scores based on these discriminating items alone were obtained for representative male and female groups, large and highly significant differences were found in all comparisons from adolescence to middle age. There was some overlapping between distributions, but very little. Only 3 per cent of adult men, for example, were more feminine in their scores than the average woman. No adult women were above the median for men, and only 1 per cent were above the 25th percentile.

It is to be expected, since this is the case, that men and women will also differ considerably in the scores they obtain on the occupational scales of the Strong test. This is found to be true. Women usually average considerably higher than men on the scales for occupations involving art, social service, and writing. Men score higher on the scales for science and business. Seder (1940) found, however, that if instead of comparing sample groups representing *all* men and women you chose groups of men and women in the same professions, the interests of the two sexes were practically indistinguishable. Men and women physicians, for instance, shared the same likes and dislikes. Men and women life insurance agents were likewise very similar. The interests of women doctors are probably more like those of men doctors than they are like those of housewives. More recently, Hornaday and Kuder (1961) have shown that the same conclusion can be drawn from the results obtained in giving the Kuder Preference Record—Occupational to groups of professional men and women. In most occupations the men and women scored alike.

In using the specially constructed Strong Vocational Interest Blank for Women, researchers and counselors have discovered another interesting fact. Whereas correlational studies of men's scores have revealed six main types of interests (see Chapter 8), similar correlational studies of scores obtained on the women's blank usually show that *one* type of interest pattern predominates so strongly over the others that very often it is the only thing that shows up. Crissy and Daniel (1939) who made one of the factor analyses that clarified this point called this interest factor, which appears to characterize as many as 90 per cent of graduating senior girls in high school, "Interest in Male Association." The name was chosen to represent what housewives, office workers, stenographers, and nurses have in common. It would be simpler and probably more correct to call the factor "Typical Feminine Interests," since it includes elementary teachers as well as housewives and office workers. It doubtless represents the general attitude and outlook of the woman who does not want a career for its own sake, but who is satisfied to pursue any pleasant congenial activity that offers itself until marriage, and perhaps afterward. One can get a fairly good idea of what it is by examining the content of one of the standard women's magazines—home, personal attractiveness, amusements, direct relationships with people. The comparative rarity of specialization of interests in women might well be one of the reasons for the dearth of high-level professional achievement which has been mentioned earlier.

Less extensive work with other tests has shown sex differences similar to those Strong has reported. On the Kuder Preference Record, boys average higher in the mechanical, scientific, computational, and persuasive areas, and girls average higher in the musical, artistic, literary, social service, and clerical areas (Traxler and McCall, 1941). On the Allport-Vernon Study of Values, men obtain higher average scores for theoretical, economic, and political values, indicating more interest in abstract ideas, more emphasis on practical success, and more desire for influence and power over others as goals for living. Women obtain higher average scores for aesthetic, social, and religious values, indicating more interest in art, more emphasis on religion, and more concern for the welfare of others as goals for living. Figure 35 shows these differences graphically.

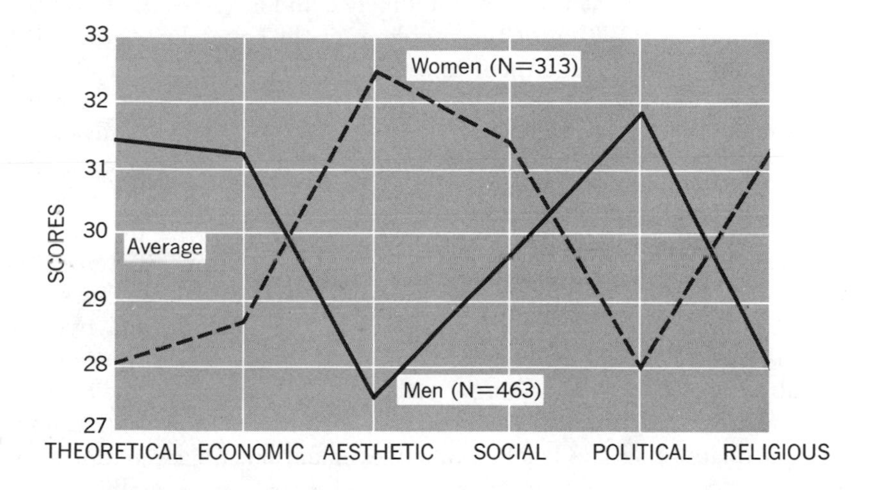

FIGURE 35

Composite Psychographs of Adult Men and Women on the Allport-Vernon Study of Values

(Allport and Vernon, 1931)

A large number of studies of children's interests by many methods have indicated that boys and girls show marked differences no matter how young they are. As early as the kindergarten years, boys engage in more active games calling for vigorous physical activity, whereas girls are more likely to enjoy dolls, paper activities, and games calling for skillful movements. In reading, movies, and radio girls show more interest in sentimental and domestic stories, whereas boys prefer adventure and violent action. When allowed to choose play materials, boys select building material and vehicles, whereas girls prefer articles of furniture and painting and modeling materials. (For a fuller discussion see Terman and Tyler, 1954.) There is no doubt about the fact that marked sex differences in interests develop very early. Comparisons of English with American children by Tyler (1956) and of Finnish with American children by Gaier and Collier (1960) indicate that these sex differences are much more salient than nationality differences, at least within countries representing Western culture.

ACHIEVEMENT MOTIVATION

It has been apparent for a long time to vocational counselors dealing with young people that girls do not put as much emphasis on professional or occupational success as do boys. Left to their own devices, a large proportion of boys are likely to make vocational choices in the professional areas, whether or not their level of intelligence and academic success warrants such a choice. With girls the problem for the counselors is often the opposite; how to encourage them to aspire to the positions their abilities would make possible. One of the techniques for measuring achievement motivation that has come into common use for personality investigations is the "Level of Aspiration" experiment. The subject is given a trial at some task, told his score, and then asked what score he will try for on the next attempt. It is interesting to note that results using this method have substantiated what had been observed about sex differences in occupational ambitions. Walter and Marzolf (1951) tested ten boys and ten girls at each of four grade levels, fourth, sixth, eighth, and twelfth, with the Rotter "aspiration board." Girls of all grade levels showed significantly lower "goal discrepancy" scores—that is, they set their sights lower—nearer to their actual performance. Differences in aspiration level were not related to grade level or to achievement on subject-matter tests. The lesser degree of ambition, if one can call it that, was equally characteristic of younger and older girls and of good and poor students.

In the most original and thorough study of achievement motivation done so far, that reported by McClelland et al. (1953), striking sex differences again appeared. The method used in all these experiments was to score for achievement motivation the stories written in response to pictures, both before and after subjects had been exposed to a sort of intelligence test presented in such a way as to stimulate achievement needs. Although statistically significant changes in responses to the pictures showed up in males under such circumstances, they were not apparent in females. An ingenious group of supplementary experiments served to show, however, that what the results indicated was not a lower general need for achievement in women, but rather that the needs they had were aroused in a different way. When *social* rather than *intellectual* acceptability was called in question by the situation set up between TAT test periods, achievement scores changed significantly in females but not in males. The authors thought that this difference might be related to the greater importance of dependence on others for women and independence of others for men. It also has obvious bearing on sex differences in professional achievement.

COGNITIVE STYLES

In the characteristic Witkin labeled *field dependence* or *psychological differentiation,* sex differences were very apparent. Table 21 shows how men and women scored on some of the Witkin tests (Witkin, et al., 1954). What they add up to is that women are less able to disregard the visual field in which the perceptual pattern they are trying to grasp is embedded. Supplementary experiments with tests which did not show sex differences served further to clarify the nature of the trait involved. It is not that females are less able than males to use stimuli coming from their own bodies. In the tilting or rotating room tests carried on *with eyes closed,* women did as well as men. The difference lay rather in their tendency to utilize a procedure the authors call "passive-acceptance"—to assume at the beginning that the room was upright even when it was tilted as much as 56° rather than to utilize all kinds of perceptual clues by means of which they could have *analyzed* the true situation. Develop-

TABLE 21

Sex Differences on Perceptual Tests

(Selected from Table 8.1, Witkin *et al.,* 1954, pp. 156-157)

		Men		*Women*		
TEST SITUATION	NATURE OF SCORE	N	SCORE	N	SCORE	P
Rod-and-frame (Series 1, body tilted)	Degrees deviation of rod from upright per trial	136	12.4	258	16.9	.01
Tilting-room-tilting-chair (Series 1a, room adjustment)	Degrees deviation of room from upright per trial	136	11.5	258	17.7	.01
Rotating-room (Series 1, room adjustment)	Degrees deviation of room from upright per trial	45	17.5	50	13.0	.05
Embedded figures	Mean time in seconds to locate simple figure in complex	51	39.8	51	58.2	.01

mental studies showed differences of the same sort even at the eight-year level, but they did not become marked enough to be consistently significant statistically until the adult years.

Another type of sex difference which is perhaps related to the Witkin findings was studied by Sandström (1953). He discovered the curious fact that if a subject in a completely darkened room is asked to point to a luminous spot of light, he finds it impossible to do this with any accuracy. The errors made by women were significantly greater than those made by men, and women were much more likely to show disoriented behavior. If Witkin's work indicates that females are more dependent on the surrounding field than males, Sandström's might be interpreted as evidence that they perform less well when no visual field is available and react in a more disturbed fashion to its absence.

The difference in problem-solving ability reported by Sweeney (1953), which he attributes to the difficulty women have in *restructuring* a situation, may also be related to the Witkin finding that the structure of the total situation influences females more than it does males. Milton (1957) showed that scores on a masculinity-femininity inventory were significantly related to success with this type of problem. Girls with more "feminine" scores were poorer problem-solvers than girls with more "masculine" scores.

Sex differences have shown up in another characteristic which can be classified within the general field of *cognitive style*. Pettigrew (1958) developed a questionnaire to measure Category Width. In each of its 20 multiple-choice items, the subject is given the average value of some category or dimension and required to select estimates of the largest and smallest members of the category. College women used significantly narrower categories than did college men. Since category width is related to some extent to mathematical aptitude, there is some doubt as to whether these sex differences represent anything more than the well-known difference in quantitative thinking. Kogan and Wallach (1964) hypothesized that a difference in attitude toward risk-taking is what is involved here. They set up some ingenious experiments for testing their hypotheses. The results are complex and will be presented in a later section of this chapter.

ADJUSTMENT AND MALADJUSTMENT

On various inventories of "neuroticism" or maladjustment, there is a tendency for women's averages to be closer to the maladjusted end of the scale than men's. On the Bernreuter Personality Inventory, for example, the norms show that women are more neurotic, less self-sufficient, more introverted, less dominant, less self-confident, and more socially dependent than men (Bernreuter, 1933). Sex differences of this sort, in contrast with the interest differences, do not appear in groups younger than the high-school age (Terman and Tyler, 1954). Does this mean that females become more neurotic or males less so as they grow up? This may be true, but an explanation which is at least plausible is that as males and females learn more about the places in life they are expected to fill, females become more willing than males to confess what their emotional difficulties are. However, one study by Darley (1937) seems to indicate that the difference may not be spurious. When college students who had been given tests for identifying maladjustment were interviewed by two experienced counselors, it was found that the excess of neurotic trends in women appeared even more markedly in the clinical diagnoses than in the test scores. Some other investigations of children by nonquestionnaire methods—fear responses, nervous habits, and so forth—suggest also that females may really be somewhat more unstable emotionally than males. It is interesting, for example, that thumb-sucking is more prevalent in girls than in boys during the preschool years (Honzik and McKee, 1962).

EMOTIONAL NEEDS AND EXPRESSION

Some studies have been based directly on psychoanalytic theory. Freud postulated psychological differences in the emotional needs of the two sexes arising from the physiological and anatomical differences between them. Blum (1949) devised a new sort of projective test specifically for the purpose of measuring the kinds of psychosexual variables that the analysts have discussed—oral and anal tendencies, castration anxiety, and the like. Having searched standard psychoanalytic textbooks for theoretical leads, he made specific predictions as to the direction of the sex differences that would appear in the various scores on the test. The most conclusive finding for our purposes was that for nine areas where it was possible to make such definite predictions, eight of the differences obtained from the responses of male and female college students were statistically significant in the predicted direction.

Another study utilizing a quite different approach also gives evidence for the kind of sex differences psychoanalytic theory postulates. Franck and Rosen (1949) asked their subjects, again college students, to make drawings from very simple stimuli, such as pairs of parallel vertical lines. They found that they could develop a scoring system for these drawings which differentiated between the sexes at a high level of significance. For instance, females tend to close in their drawings at the ends, males to leave them open. Females draw static objects, males moving things. Females draw flowers, rooms, and household furnishings, males vehicles and projectiles. It was such differentiations that formed the basis of the scoring system. The authors argued that most of the kinds of differences the test showed could not be explained on the basis of familiarity or environmental influence. Pokers as well as pans are household objects, but boys draw the former, girls the latter. Franck and Rosen considered the explanation to be rather that girls and boys differ in "body image," which, as they used the term, covered both structure and function. They explained how this general "body image" could constitute a set which could determine how an individual would deal with all sorts of ambiguous materials.

The subjects in these studies were college students, but the same sort of differences have been found in children of eleven, twelve, and thirteen. Erikson (1951) asked the children in the California Guidance Study to "construct an exciting movie scene" from building materials and objects supplied to them. Honzik (1951) analyzed the productions in terms of content, and found sex differences in interests—the preference of boys for blocks, vehicles, and people in uniform, the preference of girls for furniture and people in ordinary dress. But Erikson showed that the differences go beyond these content preferences which might be purely a matter of cultural influence. When he analyzed the way in which the same materials were used, he found that boys tended to produce high structures, ruins, and scenes suggesting sudden arrest of motion, whereas girls set up static, open enclosures such as rooms. Again, as in the Franck and Rosen study, there was internal evidence that this was not just a matter of familiarity, and some sort of "body image" theory fits in well with what was found.

When boys and girls are asked to choose the forms they like best, they tend to choose those that the foregoing studies would suggest are characteristic of the *opposite* sex rather than of their own. McElroy (1954) asked about 800 Scottish children whose ages ranged between nine and thirteen to select the preferred pictures from each of 12 pairs. In each pair, one picture was made up of curved lines (feminine), the other of straight, angular lines (masculine). There was a highly significant tendency for boys to choose the curved shapes and girls the angular shapes. Jahoda (1956) found the same tendency, although it was less marked, in African children. These findings can also be explained in terms of psychoanalytic theory.

AGGRESSION

Compatible with psychoanalytic theory, but explainable on other grounds as well, is the conclusion from a large number of studies that males are more aggressive than females. In the comprehensive bibliography prepared by Oetzel (1962) 30 studies based on observation, rating, experiments, projective techniques, and self-report inventories are included, with subjects ranging from preschool children to adults. In the great majority of these research reports, boys turn out to be significantly more aggressive than girls. In only a few cases are the differences too small to be significant. Only in cases where *verbal* rather than general or physical aggression is measured do girls come up with higher scores.

SOCIAL SENSITIVITY–RESPONSIVENESS TO PEOPLE

It is almost as universal a finding that females are more dependent upon people than males are. Here too a large number of research reports based on a variety of measuring techniques and subjects of all ages from preschool to adulthood could be cited (Oetzel, 1962). E. W. Goodenough (1957) reported that even at the age of two, girls showed more interest in persons than boys did, as judged from what they attempted to draw and what they talked about during the experiment. In studies using the Thematic Apperception Test, stories told by girls typically reflect more need for affiliation (Sanford, et al., 1943). Girls are usually found to be more suggestible than boys (Patel and Gordon, 1960). They are better than boys at simulating personality patterns characteristic of others in responding to questions on personality scales (Kimber, 1947; Noll, 1951). When one adds together all these miscellaneous kinds of evidence, the general conclusion that females are more personal than males in their orientation to life seems clearly warranted.

One of the most comprehensive analyses of masculinity-femininity made so far is the E. M. Bennett and Cohen study (1959). Their 1,300 subjects ranged in age from fifteen to sixty-four, and the age groups were weighted to produce a total distribution comparable to the 1950 census distribution. What each subject was asked to do was to choose sets of words that described him best and least well from a total of 300 words having to do with wishes, values, and the social environment. As Strong and Terman and Miles had pointed out years before, the choices made by men and women were more similar than different. The average correlation between the tabulations for the two sexes was .90. But there were characteristic differences on some of the words. After analyzing all of these differences in detail, Bennett and Cohen summarized the nature of the differences under five general principles. These can serve to sum up what has been found in many other studies as well as theirs. They are as follows:

1. Masculine thinking is a modification downward in intensity of feminine thinking.
2. Masculine thinking is oriented more in terms of the self while feminine thinking is oriented more in terms of the environment.
3. Masculine thinking anticipates rewards and punishments determined more as a result of the adequacy or inadequacy of the self while feminine

thinking anticipates rewards and punishments determined more as a result of the friendship or hostility of the environment.

4. Masculine thinking is associated more with desire for personal achievement; feminine thinking is associated more with desire for social love and friendship.
5. Masculine thinking finds value more in malevolent and hostile actions against a competitive society, while feminine thinking finds value more in freedom from restraint in a friendly and pleasant environment.

MASCULINITY-FEMININITY SCALES

A research approach that seemed for a time to hold great promise was to develop tests for measuring general masculinity-femininity in individuals of both sexes, tests consisting of specific items to which the responses of males and females had been shown to differ. The most thorough and comprehensive effort of this sort was that of Terman and Miles (1936). Their investigation had its origin years before in their discovery, while collecting information about gifted children, that boys and girls in the experimental group differed markedly from each other in certain ways. Using these items as leads, they tried out a large number of questions on male and female groups of various ages, selecting for their final assortment those which gave statistically significant differences between group responses. The result was the test that they called the Attitude-Interest Analysis Blank, a nondescripive title chosen so as not to give the individual taking it any clue as to its purpose. Seven types of item were included: Word Association, Inkblot Association, Information, Emotional and Ethical Response, Interests, Opinions, and Introversive Response. The authors gave abundant evidence that scores on this test produced large and statistically significant differences between men and women of all ages, occupational levels, and degrees of education. Terman and Miles reminded us, however, that the method they used tends to exaggerate sex differences because the large number of associations, interests, and opinions on which men and women do *not* differ were discarded in constructing the scale. However, the fact that such a set of items can be selected indicates that there are genuine differences between the sexes in our culture.

The nature of these differences was summarized by Terman and Miles as follows: [2]

> From whatever angle we have examined them the males included in the standardization groups evinced a distinctive interest in exploit and adventure, in outdoor and physically strenuous occupations, in machinery and

[2] Reprinted by permission from *Sex and Personality: Studies in Masculinity and Femininity* by L. M. Terman and C. C. Miles, Copyrighted 1936, by the McGraw-Hill Book Co., Inc.

> tools, in science, physical phenomena, and inventions; and, from rather occasional evidence, in business and commerce. On the other hand, the females of our groups evinced a distinctive interest in domestic affairs and in aesthetic objects and occupations; they have distinctively preferred more sedentary and indoor occupations, and occupations more directly ministrative, particularly to the young, the helpless, the distressed. Supporting and supplementing these are the more subjective differences—those in emotional disposition and direction. The males directly or indirectly manifest the greater self-assertion and aggressiveness; they express more hardihood and fearlessness, and more roughness of manners, language, and sentiments. The females express themselves as more compassionate and sympathetic, more timid, more fastidious and aesthetically sensitive, more emotional in general (or at least more expressive of the four emotions considered), severer moralists, yet admit in themselves more weaknesses in emotional control and (less noticeably) in physique.
>
> But we must define some of our terms more precisely, for instance, "aggressiveness" and "self-assertion." The evidence is for initiative, enterprise, vigorous activity, outdoor adventure; "aggressiveness" need not imply selfishness or tyranny or unfair attack. The compassion and sympathy of the female, again, appears from the evidence personal rather than abstract, less a principled humanitarianism than an active sympathy for palpable misfortune or distress. In disgust, in aesthetic judgment, and in moral censure, the evidence is rather for the influence of fashion and of feeling than of principle or reason. Our evidence need not imply the possession of a "truer" taste or a more discerning conscience (Terman and Miles, 1936, pp. 447–448).

It is plain from the data furnished by Terman and Miles that masculinity-femininity, as measured by their M-F scale, is no all-or-none trait. The various occupational groups differ, for instance. Among men, athletes and engineers have the most "masculine" averages; journalists, artists, and clergymen, the least "masculine." Among women, domestic employees are the most "feminine"; athletes and doctors, the least "feminine." Age groups differ also. Eighth-grade girls are more "feminine," eleventh-grade boys more "masculine" than any other age groups. Figure 36 shows of these differences graphically.

Individuals within any one of the occupational or age groups differ among themselves. What we have is a continuous distribution rather than an exact classification.

Terman and Miles reported in some detail a supplementary study in which they investigated the attitudes of male homosexuals, as shown by the M-F scale. They found a marked difference between the 71 classified as *passive* (those who customarily played female roles in homosexual relationships) and the 46 classified as *active* (those who customarily played male roles). The PMH group (passive male homosexuals) obtained significantly more feminine scores than the average, the AMH group (active

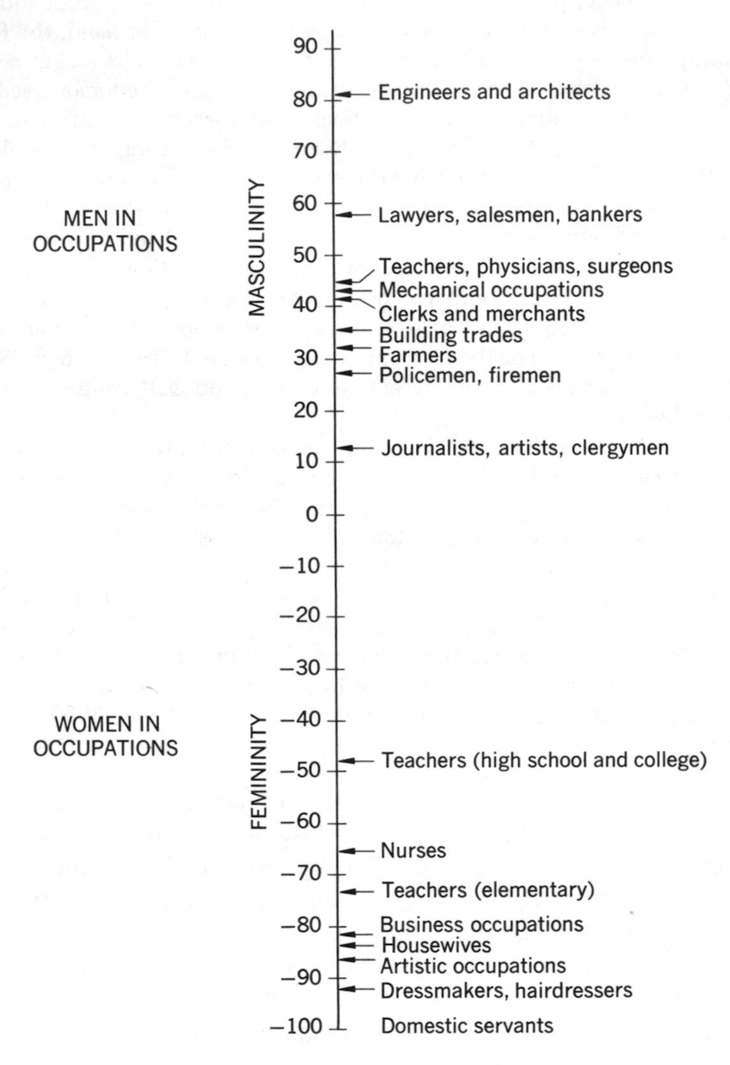

FIGURE 36

Mean M-F Scores of Various Occupational Groups

(Terman and Miles, 1936)

male homosexuals) slightly more masculine. All of the subtests with the exception of Exercise 4 (Emotional and Ethical Response) showed this characteristic femininity in the PMH group. It was most pronounced on Exercise 5 (Interests). The authors hastened to remind the reader that not all men who receive low M-F scores are inverts. They carried on some exploratory work with a special I (inversion) scale in which the weight attached to each item was based on the extent to which it differentiated between the PMH group and an average group of high-school boys. This item analysis showed, in general, that in the invert group, interests, attitudes, thought trends, and occupational preferences were characteristically feminine. Interest in art, music, and religion was common. Aggressiveness of all kinds was repudiated. Introvertive and psychoneurotic tendencies and excessive sex-consciousness also stood out in the invert group. Case studies of eighteen of the individuals, together with the fact that *physical* measurements did *not* differentiate the homosexuals from normals, led Terman and Miles to place the emphasis on environmental rather than constitutional factors in the development of homosexuality. It was characteristic of a number of these subjects that they grew up in a home where the mother was overaffectionate and the father was dead, or if alive, was cruel and autocratic. Many of them reported having been treated as a girl. An overemphasis on neatness and niceness of behavior and a lack of vigilance against seduction by older homosexual males also seemed to be involved.

Since Terman and Miles published their findings, a number of other M-F scales have been constructed. The Franck and Rosen drawing test discussed in an earlier section can be used in this way. There are M-F scales for many of the standard interest and personality inventories, such as the Strong, the MMPI, the CPI, and the Guilford-Zimmerman. Rosenberg and Sutton-Smith (1959) have developed an inventory of play and game activities that can be scored as an M-F test for children.

Research with these scales has clearly shown that masculinity-femininity is not a unidimensional trait. The separate parts of the Terman-Miles test show little correlation with one another. Shepler (1951) demonstrated that masculinity, as measured by the drawing completion test, was not the same as masculinity as measured by the Terman-Miles questionnaire. Ford and Tyler (1952) made a factor analysis of the correlations between subtests on the Terman-Miles blank, with groups of ninth-grade students as subjects. For the boys, two factors were clearly shown, one an emotional characteristic that could be labeled "Toughness" or perhaps "Insensitivity," the other an interest factor like that that we have described in connection with the Strong test. For the girls the first factor seemed to be "Sensitivity," the second an interest factor. The analysis for the girls also gave some evidence for a third factor which seemed to have to do with the acceptance of a feminine social role. Barrows and Zuckerman

(1960) found that there were only low intercorrelations (about .3) between scores on three commonly used M-F scales, the Strong, the MMPI, and the Guilford-Zimmerman. Their conclusion applies well to all the work in this area: "It seems apparent to the investigators that masculinity-femininity is not a clearly defined construct."

Because of this ambiguity about what any particular M-F scale measures, these scales have not turned out to be as useful in facilitating any sort of practical decisions about persons as it was once hoped that they would be. We must be very cautious about drawing diagnostic conclusions from M-F scores—more cautious, perhaps, than the average user of these tests realizes. As techniques for classifying subjects in some kinds of research investigations, general masculinity-femininity scales are of some value, but they are no longer an important focus of research interest.

SEX DIFFERENCES IN THE ORGANIZATION OF PERSONALITY

There is one kind of research finding that has been increasingly forcing itself upon the attention of those who investigate sex differences of any sort. Evidence is rapidly accumulating that the traits measured are *linked together differently* in the two sexes. It may well be that these differences in personality organization are more important than the differences in average score on the variables we have been considering.

Factor analyses of various kinds of test materials and various groups of subjects typically come out with discrepant factor patterns for males and females. Sometimes the factors justify the use of entirely different labels in each case; at other times, the numerical loadings do not agree. Gardner, et al. (1959) ran into this sex difference in their factor analysis of the cognitive-control principles discussed in the previous chapter. Diggory (1953) documented it for attitudes, Barratt (1955) for space-visualization factors, Bereiter (1960) for fluency.

H. G. Seashore (1962) collected from Psychological Corporation files a large number of validity coefficients based mainly on high school and college populations. He showed that there was a highly significant tendency for such coefficients to run higher for females than for males. His conclusion was: "Women are more predictable than men."

Other kinds of correlations, however, indicate that not all the differences in predictability are in the same direction. Weitz and Colver (1959) reported that better grades in college could be predicted for men who expressed a preference for a major field when they entered than for men who did not. For women this factor made no difference. Kagan and Moss (1962), in their investigation of the stability of personality traits from childhood to adulthood, found that correlations for some aspects of aggression at the two stages of life were higher for boys than for girls. The reverse was true in the case of passive-dependent behavior, where correlations were higher for girls than for boys. Similarly Tuddenham found that aggression was the most stable variable from adolescence to adulthood in boys, but social prestige was the most stable in girls. Dunkleberger and Tyler (1961) found more relationship between interest change and personality characteristics in high-school girls than in high-school boys.

Another set of discrepant correlations has to do with adjustment and popularity. Beloff (1958), for example, discovered that conforming women were lower than nonconforming women on neuroticism; the reverse was true for men. Iscoe and Garden (1961) found field dependence was related to popularity, positively for girls, negatively for boys. Livson and Bronson (1961) reported that social adjustment was related more to overcontrol of impulses in boys, but to impulsivity in girls. Gray (1959) observed that for boys perceived similarity to the father went with acceptance by one's peers, whereas for girls perceived similarity to the mother was related negatively to peer acceptance.

Concepts about maturity do not affect boys and girls in the same way. Sutton-Smith, Rosenberg, and Morgan (1963), using an inventory of play activities to analyze sex differences and growth trends, found that the perceived maturity level of the activities was a more important determiner of choices for boys than for girls. As boys get older they move on from games to sports and reject the things they see as childish. Girls continue to choose both immature and mature items.

Aggressive behavior has different concomitants and antecedents for boys and girls (R. R. Sears, 1961; Levin and Sears, 1956; Lansky, et al., 1961; and Becker, et al., 1962).

Underachievement in school follows a different course for the two sexes (Shaw and McCuen, 1960). Where it was present in boys, the pattern of low achievement, they found, began in the first grade and continued with little change throughout the school years. In contrast, the records of girls diagnosed in high school as underachievers showed that they had done well during the first five years of school and then changed suddenly.

What many of the developmental studies have found is that the same home influences, such as child-training methods and parental attitudes, affect boys and girls in different ways. Bronfenbrenner (1961), analyzing home influences related to responsibility and leadership in tenth-graders, found that the boys high in these traits tended to come from homes in which the mother was warm and nurturant and the father a moderately strong disciplinarian. For girls, strong paternal discipline made for irresponsibility, and nurturance and warmth were related more closely to dependency than to leadership. He concluded that the optimal balance of affection and control was different for boys and girls. Schaefer and Bayley

(1963) in a thorough analysis of longitudinal data from infancy through adolescence, reported that the mother's behavior seemed to be more closely related to her son's later characteristics than to her daughter's. They interpreted these results to mean "that girls' adjustment reflects more their current interpersonal situation while the adjustment of boys reflects more stable structures which have developed through their entire history of interpersonal relationships."

The most thorough and carefully designed research undertaking reported so far, which focused on the question of the different ways in which traits are related in the two sexes, is the Kogan and Wallach (1964) investigation of risk-taking tendencies. They divided their college subjects into subgroups not only on the basis of sex but also on the basis of whether their scores on tests of anxiety and defensiveness were above or below average. The results are far too complex to be summarized briefly, but they show clearly that males and females differ on *combinations* of factors more than they do on single variables. For example, the pattern of correlations for the two sexes between Number Judgments (the number of cards a subject looked at before he was willing to estimate the mean of the set) and Clues (the number of clues a subject needed to be given before he guessed the identity of a common object) is shown in Table 22. One can see that the patterns of relationship differed for males and females. For males, the highest correlation between these two measures of risk-taking occurred for subjects high on both anxiety and defensiveness. For females, the correlation for this particular subgroup was negligible. On the basis of distinctions like this the authors were able to separate out different kinds of cognitive and motivational factors affecting judgments.

Many more research findings could be cited to show that a major difference between males and females is to be found in the way the traits they manifest are organized or combined. Thus even things that look like the same sort of behavior in men and women may have different origins and different implications. It is this problem to which current theoretical discussions and research are directed. In studies of personality, sex has become an important *moderator variable.*

SEX ROLES AND THE DEVELOPMENT OF SEX-ROLE CONCEPTS

As in other areas of differential psychology, theoretical discussions of sex differences used to focus on the question whether these differences were determined mainly by biological factors or mainly by social influences. As interactive concepts of heredity and environment have replaced these "either-or" formulations, a more complex and sophisticated way of accounting for sex differences has emerged. The central concept

TABLE 22
Correlations between "Number Judgments" and "Clues"
(Wallach and Kogan, 1964)

Males

TEST ANXIETY	DEFENSIVENESS Low	DEFENSIVENESS High
Low	.17	.31
High	.41	.56

Females

TEST ANXIETY	DEFENSIVENESS Low	DEFENSIVENESS High
Low	.48	.34
High	.44	.10

is *sex role.* Every culture is organized around assumptions as to what these roles are, although anthropological studies like those of Margaret Mead (1935) show that they are differently formulated in different places and times. There are definite biological limits within which conceptions of sex roles can vary, however. In any society, it is women who must bear and nourish the children. Because of a society's concepts about sex roles, social influences on behavior must be thought of not only as direct constraints, such as discriminatory legislation and unequal educational opportunities, but also as influences operating from *within* each individual —internalized attitudes that determine what he or she learns and does, what he or she wishes and seeks. It is within this theoretical framework that much of the research on sex differences of the late 1950's and early 1960's was designed.

Some of these studies have attempted to discover what the generally understood concepts of sex roles are in our culture and how they affect development. Sherriffs and Jarrett (1953) and Fernberger (1948) showed that college students have definite, consistent beliefs about the ways in which men and women differ. Tuddenham (1951, 1952), using a reputation test in which the names of individuals in a child's own school room or play group are matched up with various traits, such as "Good at Games," "Show-off," or "Friendly," showed clearly that even among children in the early elementary grades there are consistent differences in the type of trait correlated with popularity. In boys' groups, such traits as "Real Boy," "Leader," "Good at Games," and "Takes Chances" make for popularity. Among girls, traits like "Quiet," "Not a Show-off," "Not Quarrelsome," "Doesn't Fight," are related more closely to popularity ratings.

McKee and Sherriffs (1957) discovered that even among university students, males are looked upon more favorably than females by subjects *of both sexes.* When asked whether men or women are more likely to manifest various favorable and unfavorable traits, 84 per cent of the girls ascribed more unfavorable traits to women. S. Smith (1939) had reported some similar findings based on a much younger group of subjects. Girls and boys in each age group from eight to fifteen were asked to vote whether boys or girls possess to a greater degree each of nineteen desirable and fourteen undesirable traits. The striking fact was that the older the groups were the more favorable all the ratings made by *both* sexes were to boys. This is the more remarkable when we remember that during these school years the girls are consistently behaving better, having less trouble, and getting better marks than the boys. It appears that sex-role concepts in the mid-twentieth century still assume male superiority.

The fundamental question to be answered through research is: How do these sex-role concepts *develop* in individuals? One research program on this problem has been concerned with both concepts and preferences in children of five, eight, and eleven (Hartley, 1960). When children were asked to sort activities, places, and objects into those appropriate for males and those appropriate for females, they "typed" them in very much the same way as adults do. Daughters of working mothers were somewhat less conservative in their views about the kinds of work women might do, but in general their attitudes agreed with those of the others.

Another series of studies has indicated that children tend to prefer or choose for themselves activities and objects which they consider are in agreement with accepted sex roles, but that there are interesting irregularities in the age trends. D. G. Brown (1956) devised a test to measure sex-role preference, the It test. The subject is first shown a picture of a child, drawn in such a way that it can be seen as either a boy or a girl. He then is asked to make choices for "It" from pictures of toys, games, activities, and other things. These pictures have previously been judged to be expressions of masculine or feminine sex roles in our culture. A child who chooses the masculine alternative at every opportunity makes a score of 84. One who chooses the feminine alternatives consistently scores zero. Most children score somewhere in between. The median for kindergarten boys was 71, for kindergarten girls about 38. These figures and some other data Brown reported suggest that girls are somewhat more likely to make masculine choices than boys are to make feminine choices. In simpler words, it is worse for a boy to be a "sissy" than for a girl to be a "tomboy." This is a conclusion upon which we cannot place too much weight, however. As Lansky and McKay (1963), and Brown himself in a later paper (1962), have pointed out, the projective properties of the It stimulus are not certain. Some boys think that It is a girl, and some girls think It is a boy. Thus their choices may not reflect their own attitudes.

Other investigations using the It test or similar techniques for discovering what children's preferences are have tried to relate them to various aspects of the child's situation. Fauls and Smith (1956) showed that children's choices tended to agree with the choices they thought their parents would make for them, but that boys were more likely to agree with perceived paternal preferences than girls were to agree with perceived maternal preferences. Hartup and Zook (1960) showed that even three-year-olds chose sex-appropriate pictures, and that such choices increased in frequency among four-year-olds. They also presented some evidence that increasing the similarity between the stimulus picture and the child subject by telling him that It was a child of his sex, or even giving It his name, increased the number of sex-appropriate choices.

Studies by Milner (1949) and by Rabban (1950) were concerned with the interaction of sex and social status in role formation. There is evidence from both these studies that it is the personalities of the parents and the nature of the children's relationship to them that affect the learning of these sex roles. The Rabban study also showed that concepts of sex roles develop in very young children, although there seemed to be some difference between the sexes and the social classes with regard to this. By the four- to five-year level, working-class boys showed an awareness of sex roles. Middle-class boys developed it about a year later. Middle-class girls were the slowest to develop a clear-cut sex-role concept.

Even clearer evidence about the ways in which sex-role concepts develop was furnished by a study reported by Sears, Pintler, and Sears (1946). In a standardized doll-play situation, three-, four-, and five-year-old children were scored for aggression. As in previous studies, there was a marked sex difference in the total amount of aggression shown. The next step was to compare the scores for children whose fathers were at home and children whose fathers were away in the Armed Services. The girls showed no difference in aggression whether they were from father-present or father-absent homes. But the boys from father-present homes were significantly more aggressive than the others. Differences were most pronounced in the three-year-olds. It would seem that by the age of three, boys whose fathers are at home develop a concept of masculinity permitting a considerable amount of aggression. Boys whose fathers are away develop the same concept, but more slowly. It is evident in their behavior by five but not by three.

During the decade from 1955 to 1965, considerable research interest centered on the concept of *identification* as the basis for sex-role learning. The word is somewhat ambiguous and is used in different ways by researchers using different theoretical frameworks. What they have in common are an interest in some measure of parent-child similarity and its correlates. Emmerich (1959) identified such similarities between the behavior of preschool children in a doll-play interview and the behavior of their like-sexed parents as perceived by them. (The perceptions were obtained from another part of the doll-play interview.) Strong (1957) reported significant father-son correlations in interests, and Lessing (1959) obtained similar mother-daughter correlations on the Kuder. Several studies by Mussen and various colleagues (Payne and Mussen, 1956; Mussen and Distler, 1959; Mussen and Rutherford, 1963) have been concerned with factors related to identification. The last of the three was perhaps most decisive. So far as theory is concerned, the psychoanalytic hypothesis that a boy identifies with his father out of hostility and fear of retaliation received less support than the hypothesis that a warm, affectionate relationship makes for maximum identification. Another interesting finding was that the development of masculine characteristics in boys was shown to be related not to the personality of the parents or to their encouragement of sex-typed activities, but rather to the *closeness* of the relationship. For girls the situation seemed to be different. Sex typing in girls was related to the mother's scores for nurturance, power, and self-acceptance, to the father's masculinity score, and to the amount of encouragement the father gave to "feminine" activities.

There have been two theoretical discussions of identification as a basis for sex-role differentiation that serve to reconcile some of the apparently puzzling results in the studies we have been reviewing. Lynn (1962) postulates basic sex differences in the nature of identification itself for the two sexes. Females are able to identify with specific aspects of the mother's role as they observe it directly. He calls this *mother identification.* Males, because they cannot observe most of the father's specific role behavior, must identify with a cultural stereotype of what is masculine. He calls this *masculine role identification.* Many of the specific differences between males and females that have been reported, such as differences in affiliation, field dependence, and problem-solving skills, fit neatly into the structure based on this distinction. The Mussen and Rutherford study, discussed in the previous paragraph, supports this theory with its evidence that a girl's femininity is related to her mother's personality characteristics, whereas a boy's masculinity is uncorrelated with his father's.

M. M. Johnson (1963) sets up the hypothesis that both girls and boys learn their differentiated sex roles from the *father*. The mother, because of the predominance of what sociologists call the "expressive" orientation (emphasis on feeling and personal relationships) in her own makeup, does not differentiate her treatment of boys and girls to any great extent. Both boys and girls tend to pick up "expressive" behavior from her. But the father, with his characteristically masculine "instrumental" orientation (the disciplined pursuit of particular goals) actually *teaches* the children to act like males or like females. Simply put, the boy child learns instrumental or masculine ways by trying to be a man as his father is, the girl child learns expressive or feminine ways by trying to be a woman who pleases her father. This theoretical formulation, like that of Lynn, accounts for puzzling discrepancies in the reported research, such as the Mussen and Rutherford finding that girls' femininity was related to fathers' masculinity. The Lynn and Johnson theories are not in conflict, as they refer to different aspects of the phenomena and concepts in question. Together they constitute a coherent explanation of a complex process.

The extent to which the marked differences in achievement we have noted at the beginning of this chapter grow out of differing concepts of sex roles is hard to estimate. In the long run, it would seem desirable that while formulating these roles in such a way that they are in harmony with biological facts, we should permit and encourage both male and female participation in all the varied activities which go into the making of our society. Art, business, education, and science are enriched by the distinctive contributions that both men and women can make (Mead, 1949). In the short run, however, individuals who fail to come to terms with the prevailing codes may be less happy than the ones who go along with them even when they are wrong. Seward (1945) asked college girls to fill out an attitude scale on sex roles in postwar society. She then compared on a number of psychological tests the fifteen who were the most liberal in their views with the fifteen who were most conservative. There was some evidence that the conservatives were somewhat happier and better adjusted than the liberals. Whether this was the cause or the effect of the sex-role differences would be hard to determine, but it illustrates the difficulties one encounters in thinking about changing such basic attitudes. As many writers on the subject have pointed out, the progress of science and the removal from the home of many kinds of work that were once done there makes the restriction of women's activities to home and family increasingly inappropriate. The wide range of abilities in both sexes makes it appear that sex typing of occupations is not appropriate either. But the *attitudes* that both men and women have grown up with fit these practices better than they do the actual economic and psychological facts, and too great a deviation from the accepted attitude makes for maladjustment. There lies a challenging problem.

SUMMARY

Interest in psychological research on the topic of sex differences has grown by leaps and bounds since 1900. Tabulation of statistical information about eminent individuals has brought into sharp relief the fact that high achievement is very rare among women. In school achievement, however, girls usually rank higher than boys. So far as tested abilities are concerned, there are some sex differences in the averages, but the distributions show a great deal of overlapping. Males tend to be higher in mathematical reasoning, spatial judgment, and science. Females average higher in verbal fluency, rote memorizing of most materials, perceptual speed, and dexterity. Careful analysis of what the distributions show has cast considerable doubt on the concept of greater male variability.

In interests, attitudes, and personality characteristics, much larger differences have been shown to exist, although even here there is considerable overlapping between distributions for the two sexes. Males show greater aggressiveness, females more symptoms of neuroticism and instability. Sex differences in likes and dislikes, in emotional and ethical attitudes, in the kinds of success that are desired, in cognitive styles, and in many other characteristics have been clearly shown.

Masculinity-femininity scales have been developed using items from all these areas that differentiate the sexes. These scales have been of some value for research purposes but have not been very helpful for practical purposes because of the multidimensionality of the trait.

Evidence has accumulated that it is in the relationships between variables that the most interesting and important sex differences appear. Developmental studies using the concepts of sex roles and identification are being used to explore these relationships.

CHAPTER 11

Age Differences

SEX AND AGE are the two *biological* factors that produce a natural sorting out of human beings into visible groups. These are kinds of differentiations everyone can see, and about which many people inevitably acquire definite opinions. The man on the street might formulate his ideas about age differences something like this:

> Everybody knows that young people are quicker than older ones—faster in their movements, quicker to learn new things. They're a lot more adventurous too, always wanting to try something new to get a new thrill. They are likely to be more radical, more hot-headed, less steady, than older people are. Men in their forties are slower, though their judgment is better. You don't find so many radicals among them, and they are a lot more settled in their attitudes. Old people are a little feeble, of course, though some of them manage to keep on working. They can't learn anything new very well, and they are often kind of tiresome because they insist on telling the same stories over and over, living in the past.

This is more or less the prevailing attitude, as we find it in ourselves and our friends. Unlike various other cultures such as the Chinese, ours has rather consistently emphasized youth as the golden age of life. Until recently America has been conspicuously a nation of young men and women. The sort of achievement we have admired most in the pioneer, the cowboy, or the self-made business man is the kind of thing that requires vigor, aggressiveness, and youthful energy. A good many of us have been conditioned to expect that all the years after the first twenty or so will be a prolonged anticlimax.

How much truth is there in such commonly held ideas? In what ways do the young, the middle-aged, and the old really differ? Firm knowledge about such matters can make useful contributions to economic and social policy—decisions about such things as retirement laws, community planning, and adult education. It can also be applied by each person individually as he tries to plan ahead how to get the most out of the years allotted to him.

In this chapter we will not concern ourselves with the differences between children and adults. The fields of child and adolescent psychology have been intensively cultivated and have developed a body of literature too large to be covered in a course on human differences in general. We shall confine ourselves here to the differences among adults at different periods of life.

PROBLEMS AND DIFFICULTIES

Of the problems discussed in Chapter 3, two have been special stumbling blocks in the path of research on age differences. The first of these is the problem of getting population samples that are satisfactorily representative. Growth studies of children have demonstrated the value of longitudinal rather than cross-sectional methods. In a longitudinal study the *same individuals* who form the initial sample are measured again from time to time. Thus the research worker knows that the groups of people he is comparing differ in age alone. Any change noted must be a change that comes with age. In a cross-sectional study, the measuring of different age groups is carried out at the same time, which means, of course, that the persons comprising each sample are not the same ones. We can never be sure in this type of research whether the differences between the ten- and the fifteen-year-olds are actually changes that come with age or whether the samples differ also in some other respects. It is obviously difficult to carry longitudinal studies through a large portion of the whole life span of any sample of adults. If we had information about the characteristics of a fairly large group of adults tested at twenty, and again at forty, sixty, and eighty, it would be of tremendous value in answering all sorts of questions. Obtaining this information, however, constitutes a project of such magnitude that even to begin it for a long time appeared impossible. Since World War II some studies of this type have been set up, and first reports from them are paying rich dividends in new knowledge.

In cross-sectional studies where groups of different ages are tested at the same time, the sampling difficulty is primary. Where are we to go to get a group of adults who will be as typical of the whole *adult* population as the sample of children we can find in some elementary schools is of the total *child* population? All organized groups of adults are *selected* in some pretty obvious fashion and none represents men and women as a whole. Church groups, luncheon clubs, labor unions, women's clubs, and inmates of homes for the aged constitute selected samples. Huge draft armies, like those of World War I and World War II give us more nearly representative samples of male America than have been obtained in any other way. It is to be noted that the first important comparisons of different age groups were made in a study of the test scores of officers in World War I. Had someone been able to persuade applicants for ration books to stay and be tested, we might have been able to get as adequate a sample of women, though it is doubtful whether it would ever have been possible to get all members of a large group to cooperate in such a plan. Investigators have solved the sampling problem more or less satisfactorily in various ways. We shall note what their solutions were as we proceed.

In longitudinal studies, there are sampling problems of a different kind. If we follow one group of subjects through their entire life span, death is certain to remove many of our subjects from the sample before they reach the age of eighty. Can we conclude that the age trends we find in those who live until the end of the study are similar to the trends that would have characterized the others had they survived? There is usually some loss of subjects for other reasons also in longitudinal research. Unless a large proportion of the subjects initially tested are located at the time of retests, selective factors may bias conclusions in unknown ways.

In both kinds of research there are measurement problems as well as sampling difficulties. A persistent question is: Are our tests equally fair to adults of all ages? A test is not a measuring rod but a standardized *situation* in which a sample of an individual's behavior may be taken. The psychological situation may not be the same for persons differing widely in age. To the child in school, any task is something to be completed as satisfactorily as possible. He has been subjected to a long training period in which he learns that the rewards come to him who does the assignments whether or not they look silly or pointless. The chances are that an adult long out of school will not react in this way. If the problem given him does not constitute a challenge, he sees no reason for struggling with it. If the questions are stated in childish terms or the materials give an impression of immaturity, the situation they represent for an adult is not the same as the situation they create for a child, and so our comparisons of their scores do not really tell us what we want to know. Recognition of the fact that age differences vary with the type of material used has led to some of the most significant work done in this area.

To call attention to these sources of error is not to say that research on age differences is of no value. The difficulties can be allowed for and dealt with in various ways. There are, for instance, ways of using the data one has to judge how representative of the original group a follow-up sample is. There are ways of assessing the attitude of one's subjects toward the tests they are taking and judging how comparable different age groups are in this regard. The point is simply that investigators should pay some attention to these matters, and that readers of their reports should make allowances for them as they try to draw general conclusions.

AGE DIFFERENCES IN GENERAL INTELLIGENCE

Cross-Sectional Studies

Some of the first evidence on the question of age differences in intelligence came from an analysis of World War I army test data (Yerkes, 1921). Enlisted men were almost all relatively young, but the 15,385 officers whose scores formed the basis of this study were men of all ages from eighteen to sixty. Table 23 shows the results obtained.

The steady decline in average score from the youngest to the oldest age groups is the most striking finding. There was, of course, a great deal of overlapping, and the variability *within* any one age group was far higher than the differences between the groups. Many sixty-year-olds did better than the average man of twenty. Many twenty-year-olds were below the average man of sixty. But the general trend was clear-cut and consistent.

Jones and Conrad (1933) also used Army Alpha to test practically the entire population of nineteen New England villages. They were able to get an unusually good sample of the population of all ages by giving free movies to which everyone was invited, and requesting the audience to take the intelligence test as well as a short test on the movie they had just seen. They found much the same general age trends as had the army psychologists. Figure 37 shows what their findings were.

The highest scores were made by persons between the ages of nineteen and twenty-one. With one exception, each age group, from here on up, scored a little lower than the preceding one, so that the average for fifty-five-year-olds was the same as that for eleven-year-olds.

Studies in Great Britain gave similar evidence of a decline in general intelligence level with the years. The most conclusive figures were those reported by Vincent (1952) who standardized a new verbal intelligence test on more than 7,000 civil service employees ranging in age from twenty-one to sixty. With the exception of one group, the forty-five to fifty-year olds, who scored unusually low, the other means showed a straight linear relationship with age, as Figure 38 demonstrates. Summarizing the age trends in most of the large-scale studies where some sort of general intelligence test had been used, Vincent showed that they agreed remarkably well. The mean annual decrement over this range from twenty to sixty was about .03 of a standard deviation, regardless of which test was used.

The Jones and Conrad study called attention to another fact that it seemed important to recognize. The rates of decline for the different

TABLE 23
Average Army Alpha Scores of 15,385 Officers in World War I

(Yerkes, 1921)

AGE	AVERAGE SCORE
Under 20	150
20-24	146
25-30	143
31-40	133
41-50	125
51-60	120

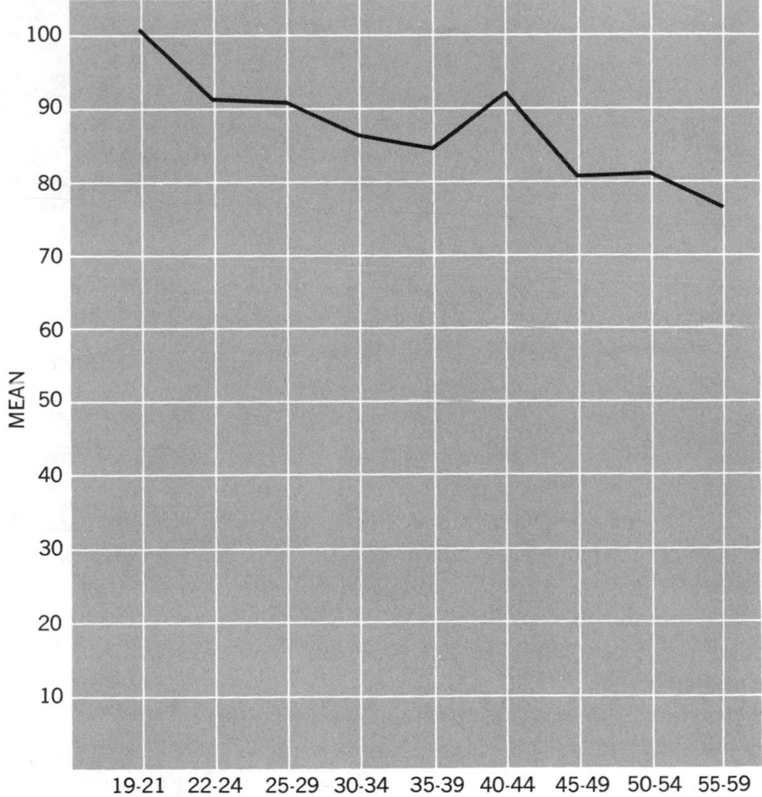

FIGURE 37
Age Differences in Scores on Army Alpha for Total Rural New England Sample

(Jones and Conrad, 1933)

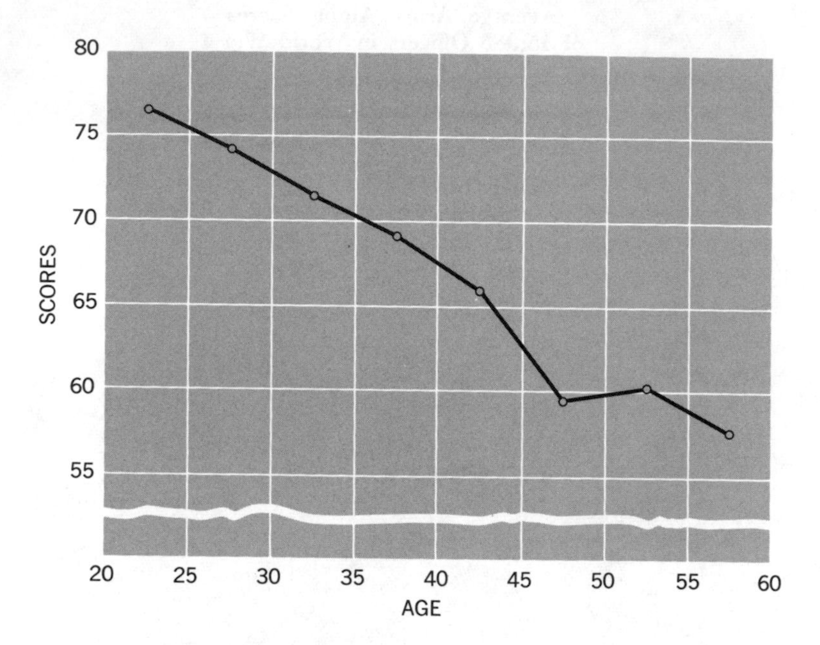

FIGURE 38
Relationship Between General Intelligence and Age in Adults
(Vincent, 1952)

varieties of mental ability measured by the eight subtests of Army Alpha were not the same. On Information and Vocabulary there was no decline until the age of sixty. The three subtests showing the *greatest* decline with age were Analogies, Common Sense, and Number Series. The one thing these three seem to have in common is the fact that they necessitate quick adaptation to *new* situations. This sort of differentiation in the age trends for different types of test item has been substantiated by all the later research.

In England, Foulds and Raven (1948b) using as subjects groups of adults of different ages employed in the same plant, showed that decline from age to age characterized the averages for the Progressive Matrices (a general intelligence test using geometric figures as material) but not the Mill Hill Vocabulary Test.

With the construction of the Wechsler-Bellevue Test for the measurement of adult intelligence, a considerable amount of material showing age trends in the different subtests became available. So far as total scores are concerned, Wechsler's standardization data showed the same trends as all the other studies (Wechsler, 1941). But consistent differences between types of test were reported in study after study of older men and women. The Information test showed the least age decrement, the Digit Symbol test the most. Fox and Birren's (1950) 50 subjects in the sixty to sixty-nine year range, chosen so as to be fairly typical of the population at that age, scored highest in Information, Vocabulary, and Comprehension, lowest on Digit Symbol, Picture Arrangement and Block Design. These results agree with those from previous studies. Whatever it is that the Digit Symbol test requires, it is the intellectual component that falls off most strikingly with age.

Factor analyses of the correlations between Wechsler subtests have suggested that the structure of mental abilities is somewhat simpler and less differentiated at the later ages (Balinsky, 1941; Green and Berkowitz, 1964). For older subjects, as for children, the subtests correlate with one another more highly than they do for intermediate age groups.

An unusually comprehensive study of the age trends for different kinds of ability was reported by Schaie (1958b). His subjects, 50 for each 5-year age period from twenty to seventy, were chosen from a large pool of members of a prepaid health plan and asked to participate. While the necessity for voluntary participation introduced some bias into the sample, it is probably more representative of the full range of economic levels in the population than the samples used in most previous studies. The intelligence test Schaie used was the Thurstone Primary Mental Abilities battery. The results are shown in Figure 39. It is apparent that the curves are of different shapes and that the decline is earliest and steepest for the Space and Reasoning factors.

A related problem of some practical and theoretical importance is the question of the extent to which the decline with age is a matter of *speed* rather than intellectual power.

A study by Lorge (1936) focused attention on this difference in age trends for speed and power tests. He used three age groups: twenty to twenty-five, twenty-seven and one-half to thirty-seven and one-half, and over forty. They had been equated on the C A V D test, a pure power test in which the individual is allowed to take as much time as he wants. Lorge then gave these same subjects Army Alpha, the Otis, and the Thorndike tests of intelligence, in all of which there is a considerable speed factor. The age groups which had been alike on the power test showed wide discrepancies on the speed tests, with the youngest subjects as usual getting the highest averages. On the basis of the discrepancy between the performance of his older subjects on the C A V D test and on speed tests like the Otis and Army Alpha, Lorge worked out a mathematical *correction* factor for loss of speed and applied it to the data of Miles and Miles and of Jones and Conrad. The effect of this correction for slowness was to wipe out the apparent decline in intellectual ability with increasing age. There is considerable question, of course, as to how valid such a mathematical treatment of scores is, but the focusing of

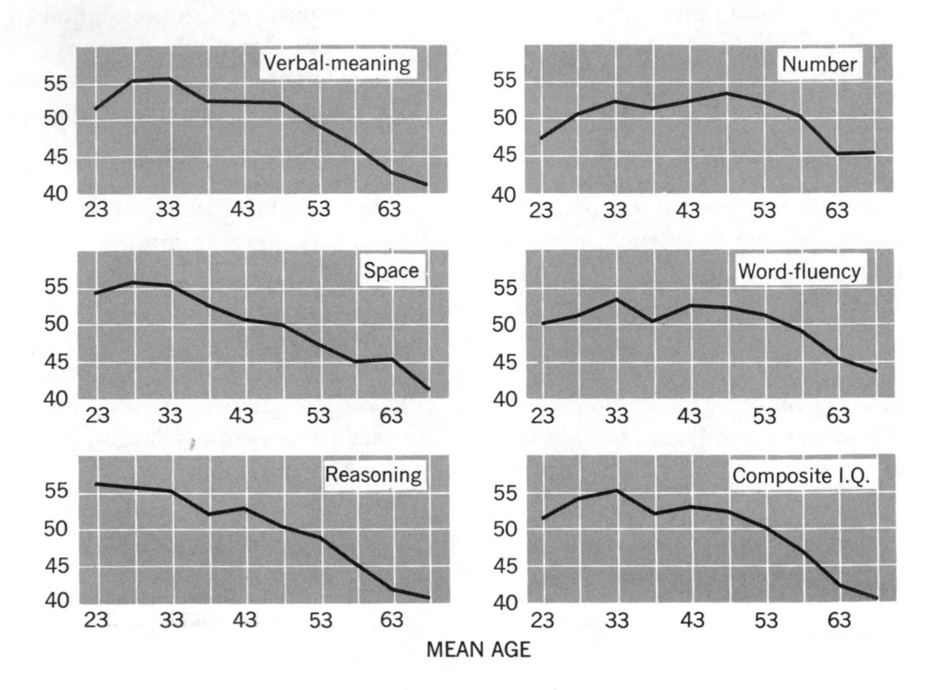

FIGURE 39

Age Changes in Primary Mental Abilities

(Schaie, 1958)

attention on the speed component of intelligence-test performance and its importance in age comparisons was a valuable contribution.

Study after study of one particular variety of test, *Vocabulary*, has shown no decline or even some increase in score with age, at least up to about sixty. Sorenson (1933) who compared 5-year age groups from fifteen to sixty-five, students in extension courses, reported higher vocabulary scores for the older groups. Christian and Paterson (1936) showed that for a group of parents and relatives of college students, the sixty to sixty-nine year group scored higher than any of the others. Heston and Cannell (1941), who tested a large number of rural men and women through the Farm Security Administration, found a slight persistent rise through fifty-five, a slight drop after that. Shakow and Goldman (1938), who equated all their age groups so that each constituted a representative sample of the educational attainment that was standard for the time in which the subjects were growing up, found that vocabulary level remained constant through the seventh decade and declined after that.

Thorndike and Gallup (1944) gave a short vocabulary test to the same representative sample of the American voting population that is used in the Gallup polls. Vocabulary level remained practically constant from twenty through sixty, declining slightly after that. Most of the samples in these various studies are nonrepresentative of the population in different ways. The fact that they all show the same trend is the impressive thing here.

Besides comparing age trends on different kinds of test, investigators have often compared groups with different amounts of *education*. Some have hypothesized that it would be mainly the uneducated whose intellects would become less keen in the later periods of life. The most comprehensive investigation of this and many other aspects of the study of age differences was the Stanford Later Maturity Study (Miles and Miles, 1932; W. R. Miles, 1933). In 1930, 863 persons ranging in age from ten through eighty-nine were tested. In 1932, another 1,600 persons were added. Subjects were obtained from clubs, lodges, and church groups by paying the organization for each individual they sent. This method of selection is well adapted to secure persons with an interested, cooperative attitude, but could hardly provide a representative sample of the population. This qualification must be kept in mind as we interpret the findings. One noteworthy feature was the inclusion of 190 of the *same* individuals in both the 1930 and 1932 studies. For these individuals actual *changes* in score over a two-year period could be ascertained. This was the first attempt anyone had made to get longitudinal data of the kind we will consider in the next section. Various results and conclusions from this major research project will be referred to in different parts of this chapter. On this particular question, whether rate of decline is dependent upon educational level, their findings can be seen in Figure 40. The shape of the curves for the different educational groups is the same. Elderly college graduates scored lower on the intelligence test than young college graduates, though the college-trained *individual* may remain above the grade school or high school average even to an advanced age.

Another study reported by Sward (1945) substantiated this finding. His subjects were all university professors. Forty-five men in the age range sixty to eighty were matched with men from the same departments in the age range twenty-five to thirty-five. The tests included many types of material often used in intelligence measurement—ingenuity, artificial language, synonyms and antonyms, symbol-digit, word meanings, number series, analogies, and arithmetic. On six of the eight tests there were significant differences in favor of the younger men. On only one, synonyms-antonyms, was there a significant difference favoring the older subjects. Again vocabulary showed up as the one kind of score not showing an age decrement.

The difference between groups with different amounts of education is

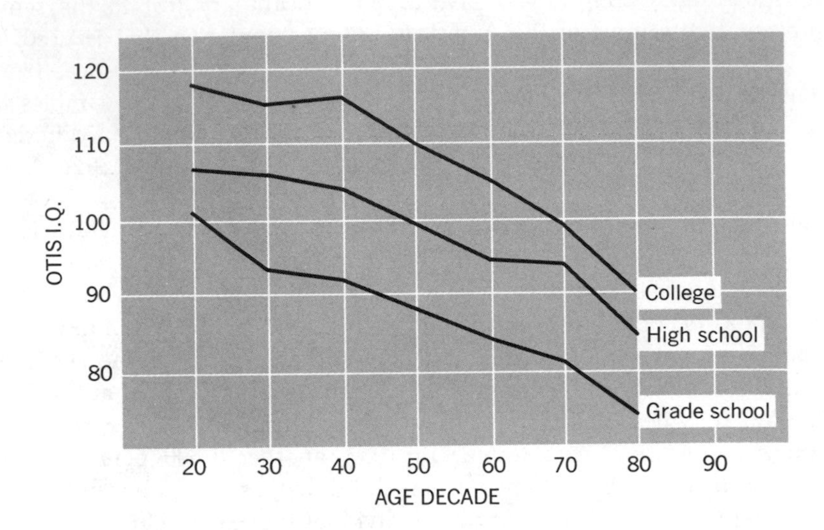

FIGURE 40

Age Differences in Intelligence Test Score for Groups Reporting Different Amounts of Formal Education

(Miles and Miles, 1932)

probably not in what happens at the later stages of life, but in what happens in *early* adulthood. Considerable evidence has accumulated that for persons who remain in school, tested intelligence increases into the early twenties, whereas for those who leave school, some decline may occur even in the teens. One such investigation was reported by P. E. Vernon (1948). He analyzed the scores of naval recruits between the ages of fourteen and twenty, obviously below the age when biological deterioration of any sort sets in. Measures of "g" showed some increases from fourteen to seventeen, but the increase was more marked in students than in those who had left school for work. Men in lower-level occupations showed decreasing averages from seventeen to twenty, whereas the scores of men in more intellectual types of work increased. Achievement scores in such areas as spelling and arithmetic fell off rapidly in those who left school at fourteen, but mechanical and spatial scores showed an increase even in persons who did not receive any technical education.

We can sum up the contributions of a large number of cross-sectional studies on age differences by saying that they pointed to a characteristic pattern of decline in mental ability from early adulthood on, a decline that is slight during the middle decades but becomes much more marked in old age. Verbal and highly practiced abilities appear to be maintained better and longer than nonverbal and problem-solving abilities, and the decline is much more noticeable in speed than in power tests.

Longitudinal Studies

In the 1950's, reports based on longitudinal investigations of age differences began to cast doubt on these accepted conclusions. The first of such studies was that of Owens (1953). What he did was to arrange for the retesting in 1949–50 of 127 males who had taken Army Alpha at the time they entered college thirty years before. Instead of scoring lower on the second occasion than they had on the first, this group averaged significantly *higher*. This was true for a number of the separate subtests as well as for total score. On no subtest had scores decreased significantly and in only three out of the eight was the increase only slight. Bentz (1953) reported some results over an eight-year interval that substantiated the Owens conclusions. His subjects were Sears Roebuck executives. Those who were thirty-five years or under at the time of the first administration of the American Council Psychological Examination showed significant *improvement* on retest. Bayley and Oden (1955) found that members of Terman's "gifted children" group and their spouses, who as adults took a high-level intelligence test twice, with about a twelve-year interval between the two administrations, also showed a significant increase over the period. Nisbet (1957) reported similar findings for a Scottish group of students in a teacher-training institution, first tested at tweny-two and then retested about twenty-four years later. Significant increases had occurred on thirteen of the fourteen subtests of the group intelligence measure. Campbell (1963), in connection with a follow-up of counseled university students and their matched controls twenty-five years after the counseling had occurred, discovered that these men and women also made higher scores on the college entrance test in 1962 than they had made in the 1930's.

This phenomenon does not seem to be restricted to college level populations. Bradway and Thompson (1962) retested in 1941 and again in 1956 persons who in 1931 were among the preschool children used in the standardization of the Terman-Merrill intelligence scale. These subjects too showed significant gains, amounting to about 11 IQ points, between the 1941 follow-up, when they ranged between about twelve and seventeen years of age, and the 1956 follow-up, when they were about twenty-seven to thirty-two years of age. Even the oldest of them had not, of course, reached the age of the subjects in the studies reported in the previous paragraph, and because of losses in the sample over the years, the average level of intelligence in the retested group was somewhat higher than that of the total representative sample of the population had been at the outset, but at least these findings justify us in ruling out the possibility that decline begins in the twenties or that only college-level persons fail to show it.

How shall we reconcile this apparent conflict between the results of cross-sectional and longitudinal studies? In the first place, we should keep in mind that they are not *entirely* conflicting. Some cross-sectional studies have also failed to find evidence for the beginning of a decline in general intelligence during early adulthood. Corsini and Fassett (1953) tested 1,072 adults entering San Quentin prison, classifying them in 5-year age groups from fifteen to seventy. The older groups made lower scores than the younger on most of the performance tests, as they usually do. But on most of the verbal tests, the older prisoners did not just equal the younger but actually excelled them. Those in their fifties made higher scores than those in their teens on Information, Comprehension, Arithmetic, and Digit Span. They were approximately equal on Similarities. There may, of course, have been selective factors at work. It would be gratifying to believe that a life of crime is attracting a less intelligent segment of our population now than it did in the days when the present middle-aged criminals were choosing their careers.

Ghiselli (1957) administered a general intelligence test to 628 adult subjects drawn from various sources, all persons who had had at least a year of college. He found no trend indicating either an increase or a decrease over the wide age spread from twenty to sixty. Hirt (1959) administered the General Aptitude Test Battery (developed for use in state employment offices) to 100 unskilled workers in each of 4 age groups, twenty-five to thirty-four, thirty-five to forty-four, forty-five to fifty-four, fifty-five and older. They were selected in such a way as to be representative of this segment of the working population, as employment agencies deal with it. While in all the abilities except Motor Coordination and Manual Dexterity there were declines at the later ages, the *peaks* came in the thirties rather than the twenties. In G (general mental ability) the peak was at about age thirty-seven. The fact that these more recent cross-sectional studies do not agree with those made in previous decades (note that the high point for Schaie's curve for Composite IQ, as shown in Figure 39, also occurred in the thirties) may indicate that the decline during early adulthood in former times can be attributed more to scarcity of intellectual stimulation in the lives people then lived than to biological changes in their nervous systems. Various lines of evidence to be considered in a later chapter have suggested that such intellectual stimulation has in fact increased. Kuhlen (1940) pointed out long before longitudinal studies made some rethinking necessary that it was premature to conclude that all of the reported differences between age groups could be attributed to the biological process of aging. By comparing certain kinds of age differences on tests with certain kinds of census data reflecting what the world had been like when the subjects of various ages were growing up, he showed that an explanation in terms of social and cultural change was at least a possibility. Perhaps we are safe in saying then that a decline in mental abilities setting in as soon as full maturity is reached is not occurring today and never really occurred. During the 1920's, 1930's, and 1940's, younger groups consistently scored higher than older groups because opportunities for individuals to develop in stimulating surroundings were constantly increasing.

When a group of subjects is tested only twice, as in the Owens study and several others, the fact that the second scores are higher than the first does not necessarily mean that a steady increase has been occurring throughout the whole interval. What could have occurred over a twenty-five-year period is an increase during a part of the time, perhaps for the first fifteen years, followed by a decrease during the remainder. If this were the case, the final scores might still be higher than the initial ones. As mentioned earlier, Miles and Miles retested some of their subjects after a two-year interval, but at an older age than the subjects Owens, Bayley, or Bradway worked with. They did find evidence for a decline of about the same magnitude as that indicated by the cross-sectional data. We have as yet very little longitudinal evidence about the actual *shape* of the age curves.

Glanzer and Glaser (1959) were able to report both cross-sectional and longitudinal data on the same group of men, 454 Air National Guard officers and 90 commercial pilots, ranging in age from twenty to fifty, who were given in 1955 a battery of ten tests previously shown to predict success with this kind of work. The main portion of the study was cross-sectional, and the typical low negative correlations between test scores and age were obtained. But because some of these men had taken four of the same tests in 1942–44, their scores over a ten- to twelve-year interval could be compared. Here the typical *longitudinal* results were obtained—the men scored significantly higher at the later ages than they had at the earlier time. The authors considered various possible explanations for this apparent conflict in the same study based on the same subjects. The one they judged most probable is that for a few years after the first testing, the subjects may have improved considerably because of both training and increasing maturity. Had they been tested at that time, the averages would have been higher than at any subsequent period. Thus even with some falling off after their peak performance, they would still be able to do better than they had at the beginning of their aviation training. What are involved in the group differences may be two sets of factors—first, the effects of learned skills and greater maturity, and second, the effects of aging after full maturity is reached.

The longitudinal studies we have cited earlier thus cannot prove that no decline has occurred at any time during the period of years the study covers. Furthermore, they do not supply any evidence on what may be happening during the years past middle age when more drastic declines had been suggested by cross-sectional research. One longitudinal investigation of a much older group has been reported by Berkowitz and Green

(1964). At a Veterans Administration facility, the Wechsler-Bellevue test was administered to 184 men who had taken it on some previous occasion from five to fourteen years earlier, and whose former scores were on record. The average age at the time of the first test was 56.32, and at the time of the retest 64.97. The second set of scores on these men indicated that there had been a significant though small *decrease*—from an IQ of about 101 to an IQ of about 98. This was true for both the verbal and the performance sections of the Wechsler test and for subjects whose initial scores had classified them as low, average, or high.

Summarizing, in brief, we can say that intellectual powers keep on increasing well into early adulthood if adequate educational stimulation is provided. Throughout the middle decades of life, they remain at about the same level, although their apparent stability may result from slight increases in some sorts of abilities and slight decreases in others. During the years from fifty on, some decline in most sorts of mental ability probably occurs, and during the seventies and eighties its effects are clearly apparent. Here as in all other areas we have explored, individual differences are very great and may often outweigh the effects of age, even among the very old.

AGE DIFFERENCES IN SPECIAL ABILITIES

In making decisions about the employment of older workers it is often important to know which special abilities decline with age. Miles and Miles, in the Stanford Later Maturity Study, made an admirably complete survey of many measurable traits. They included tests of vision and visual perception, tests of dexterity and motor coordination of different parts of the body, a test of judgment, in which positions of objects were determined from scale size, tests of memory for new materials, and an ingenious test of imagination by means of kinephantoms or shadow pictures. Some of the results are shown in Table 24. The highest group averages for each set of scores is arbitrarily given a value of 100 and the others indicate percentages of this standard comparison figure.

From this table it can be seen that motor skills, contrary to common opinion, are not the earliest to mature and the quickest to decline. In all motor abilities included in this study, the peak came in the eighteen- to twenty-nine-year group rather than in the adolescent group, while the thirty- to forty-nine-year group averaged almost as high. Even in the fifty- to sixty-nine-year group there was only a negligible decline, although it was very noticeable in subjects beyond seventy. Judgment also, as measured in this study, held up fairly well in to the advanced ages. The earliest to mature and to begin its decline was visual perception.

Since the time of the Stanford Later Maturity Study there have been numerous other reports of decreasing perceptual efficiency as age progresses. Braun (1959) summarized a large number of these studies, not

TABLE 24
Average Performance of Different Age Groups on Various Tests *
(Miles, 1933)

PERFORMANCE	*B* (*10-17*) %	*C* (*18-29*) %	*D* (*30-49*) %	*E* (*50-69*) %	*F* (*70-89*) %
Visual Perception	100	95	93	76	46
Motor Skills					
Rotary	90	100	97	89	72
Reach and Grasp	92	100	98	88	70
Finger Extension	87	100	98	99	71
Foot Reaction	85	100	96	94	71
Comparison and Judgment	72	100	100	87	69

* 100 indicates highest group average. Others are stated as percentages of this.

only in visual perception but in auditory, gustatory, olfactory, cutaneous, and kinesthetic perception as well. Special kinds of perceptual tasks, such as identifying ambiguous figures, perceiving concealed figures, and judging weights and lengths of lines were also included. Two clear conclusions emerged. One is that the loss with age is not simply a matter of loss of sensitivity in the sense organs. It appears that it is in the central rather than in the peripheral aspects of the perceptual task that the impairment occurs, and that the more complex is the judgment required, the more the difference between age groups shows up. Providing eye glasses or hearing aids does not correct impairment. The other generalization is that, as in the case of intelligence, there is some general speed factor that may be responsible for these differences. Birren (1956) has placed special emphasis on this finding.

Decline with age in motor skills is obviously related to declines in perceptual processes because skilled movements must be guided by perceptions. The question one might raise in this connection is why the decline in skills is so *slight* (see Table 24). In 1946 a research program was initiated at Cambridge University in England to study intensively the ways in which persons of different ages accomplish skilled tasks. Two books by Welford (1951, 1958) report many of these experiments. What these research workers have been doing is to *analyze* complex skills into their component parts, and to determine not only how successful people in different age groups are in coping with the tasks set for them, but just *how* they do them. Studies were made of both "manipulatory" skills such as throwing at a target and "mental" skills like solving an electrical problem. The investigators timed separately the different portions of the sequence of things that had to be done, and studied the separate time curves they obtained from persons of different ages. This project has shown rather conclusively that the *methods* by means of which older individuals accomplish a skilled act change even more than the scores for the whole performance do. The older individual distributes his time differently from the younger. In general, the results show that the time needed to grasp the meaning of the stimulus-situation, and decide what to do in it increases more than the time required to carry out the movements themselves. In a study by Szafran (1951), in which the subject was asked to point at the target whose position corresponded to that of a light presented to him in a stimulus panel, older men were slower to initiate movement, and kept the pointer on the bullseye longer. The time required for the actual movement of the pointer was the same in all age groups. Under another experimental condition in which red goggles made it impossible for a subject to *see* anything in the room except the filament of the stimulus light, it was the time spent searching for the target that increased significantly in older subjects.

The results of this long series of experiments are far too extensive to be reported in full. Welford (1959) has provided a good one-chapter summary. What is most significant about them is that they have suggested some new theoretical conceptions of what may be taking place as age progresses. Couched in terms of information theory, what both the perceptual and motor deficits seem to mean is that the "signal-to-noise" ratio in the nervous system decreases. It is more difficult for an older person to grasp a particular stimulus, especially if it is at all complex. He becomes confused. To some extent, he can compensate for these changes by concentrating on accuracy and taking more time to survey a situation before he reacts to it. This is just what many of the Cambridge experiments show that the older subjects do. Under circumstances where such compensatory responses are not possible—tasks performed under time stress or in dim light, for example—the performance of older subjects deteriorates markedly. The practical implications of these research findings are optimistic rather than discouraging. If a work situation can be re-designed to cut down on confusion, if the worker can be left a certain amount of freedom to distribute his time in his own way over various parts of the task, and if optimum lighting can be provided, older workers can be expected to do about as well at skilled tasks as younger workers.

In sheer physical strength, there is a falling off with age, but it is perhaps not as great as is commonly assumed. M. B. Fisher and Birren (1947) compared the age curves they obtained for 552 male industrial workers with those reported by previous workers. They all correspond fairly closely. The peak comes in the decade of the twenties. Decline is gradual during the next forty years, until by the age of sixty the average is about 16.5 per cent less than the average for the twenty-year-olds.

In comparing learning efficiency for subjects of different ages, the earliest widely quoted study was that of E. L. Thorndike and associates (1928). (It is to be remembered here that learning ability is *not* synonymous with intelligence. Our intelligence tests measure learning ability *only* for complex, abstract sorts of material, and recent work indicates that they do not predict very well the *rate* at which even this type of material will be learned. See Chapter 4.) Thorndike used a great variety of tasks and materials. His much-publicized verdict was that adults between the ages of twenty-five to forty-five learn at nearly the same rate and in nearly the same manner as they would have learned the same tasks at fifteen to twenty.

Another study was carried out by F. L. Ruch (1934) as a part of the Stanford Later Maturity Study. He was most interested in the differences between *types* of tasks in respect to the ease with which they could be learned by young, middle-aged, and old individuals. Results supported Thorndike's findings that the older subjects learned a little less readily than the younger, and that the deficit increased with age. It was more marked in tasks involving interference with old habits than in tasks in which old habits could be used. For instance, it was relatively easier for the older subjects to learn to follow with a stylus a moving object seen directly than one seen in a mirror. It was relatively easier for them to learn pairs of words that had a meaningful relationship to each other than to learn nonsense materials or false multiplications.

In a study by Hanes (1953), the efficiency of what he called "perceptual learning" was investigated. Subjects were 180 prison inmates divided into three age groups: twenty to thirty-four, thirty-five to forty-nine, and fifty to seventy. They were asked to remember three kinds of material presented in a tachistoscope: correct arithmetical statements (e.g., $6 \times 3 = 18$), incorrect statements (e.g., $20 \div 5 = 7$), and nonsense statements (e.g., $14{:}3 = 12$). Following Ruch's conclusions, his hypothesis was that the learning of false materials would show the greatest difference between age groups, the learning of true materials the least difference, and the learning of nonsense materials an intermediate amount. These hypotheses were not confirmed by the results. There was a consistent decline with age for all three types of material, and the nonsense material seemed most difficult for the older groups. The author's report suggests, however, that this particular procedure may have tested sheer speed of perception rather than learning, and if so, this general decline in everything is just what previous studies would have led us to expect.

Actually, there has not been any really definitive research about age changes in the ability (or abilities) to learn. As Jerome (1959) explains in his chapter on this subject, three factors, difficult to control, have made it impossible to draw unambiguous conclusions about what differences in age groups mean. These are motivation, speed of performance, and physiological status. Unless we can be sure that the subjects we are comparing are equated for all of these things, we are not able to say that a less satisfactory performance on the part of the older group really represents a change in the essential "modifiability" to which we are referring when we talk about learning.

There has been a good deal of interest in the question of memory decrement among older people. A study by J. G. Gilbert (1941) was directed at discovering how great is the decline in memory ability as applied to various sorts of tasks. She compared 174 subjects, aged sixty to sixty-nine, with an equal group aged twenty to twenty-nine who had been paired with them for vocabulary on the Stanford-Binet test. (Vocabulary is being used in much current work as an indication of the intellectual *level* the individual has attained, regardless of whether he functions efficiently at that level or not.) How the subjects were selected was not specified. As in previous studies, the average differences in all the memory tests were significantly in favor of the younger group, but there were marked variations in the extent of these differences. Older people were very nearly as good as younger on simple repetitions of a series of digits forward or backward. They were considerably inferior on learning paired unrelated words or Turkish-English vocabulary. It is interesting to note also that the most intelligent sixty-year-olds showed less decline than the average. The finding that complex materials revealed more differences between age groups than did simple materials is in agreement with the work on perception and motor skills.

In summary, the conclusions that can be drawn with regard to age differences in special abilities are:

1. A gradual decline in all types of measurable ability sets in after thirty but does not become marked until well after fifty.
2. Sensory and perceptual abilities decline most and also earliest.
3. Motor abilities hold up well until late middle age, but there is a change in the methods by which tasks are done.
4. Performance in various kinds of learning experiments declines with age, but it is not clear whether actual ability to learn is impaired.
5. With regard to all these things there are wide individual differences, so that in any age group there will be some persons superior to the average for groups much younger.

Finally, we should keep in mind that the work on special abilities has all been of the cross-sectional variety. Longitudinal studies might change these conclusions—or they may not. In any case we shall hope they will be made.

AGE DIFFERENCES IN PERSONALITY

By far the most thorough investigation of all aspects of the interests of adults we owe to Strong (1943). Data which he accumulated on men ranging in age from fifteen to fifty-nine made possible a thorough analysis of changes in likes and dislikes over this age range. The main conclusion that can be drawn from Strong's tables is that interests change very little throughout the entire adult life-span. There is surprising stability in the pattern of likes and dislikes that the individual shows even during adolescence. What changes there are are more likely to come between the ages of fifteen and twenty-five than between twenty-five and fifty-five. Only a few special sorts of items show any consistent trend when the figures for twenty-five-year-olds are compared with those for fifty-five-year-olds. Liking for activities and occupations involving writing shows a slight decrease. Liking also decreases for items suggesting change or interference with established habits and customs. In this connection, however, it is interesting to note that fifteen-year-old boys also show less liking for change than do the twenty-five-year-old men, who seem to be the group who are in this sense least conservative. In the words of Strong's summing up:

> The primary conclusion regarding interests of men between twenty-five and fifty-five years of age is that they change very little. When these slight differences over thirty years are contrasted with the differences to be found among occupational groups, or between men and women, or between unskilled and professional men, it must be realized that age and the experience that goes with age change an adult man's interests very little. At twenty-five years of age he is largely what he is going to be and even at twenty years of age he has acquired pretty much the interests he will have throughout life.

With regard to age trends in other personality traits, less can be said with certainty. In the Stanford Later Maturity Study there were very few significant differences between age groups in scores on the Bernreuter Personality Inventory. There was some tendency for dominance scores to be lower in older men, but there was a great deal of individual variability. Older people reported more handicaps and more feelings of inferiority. Psychiatrists have noted that older people show more feelings of anxiety and guilt, more intolerance and conservatism, and increasing tendencies toward regression, or the repetition of childish adjustment techniques. Since a psychiatrist's patients are by no means representative of the population as a whole, too much weight cannot be placed on this sort of evidence. It is true, however, that older persons are more likely than younger to have *need* for a psychiatrist's services. As individuals age, they become more vulnerable to illnesses of various sorts that bring mental deterioration along with them.

In discussing the general problem of the relationship of aging to life adjustment, Kuhlen (1959) summarized first the various systems of thinking about life-stages, the general pattern of expansion followed by restriction that characterizes the course of life. He then summarized the evidence bearing upon three hypotheses regarding adjustment: (1) the relationship between adjustment and age is essentially curvilinear—that is, shows first an increasing and then a decreasing trend; (2) under normal conditions there will be no over-all change in adjustment level as age progresses, but there will be shifts in particular adjustment areas; (3) the differences between older and younger age groups are essentially differences in susceptibility to stress and threat. Some evidence from data based on interviews, questionnaires, and projective tests supports each of these hypotheses, but the correlation of all measured adjustment variables with chronological age tends to be low. Kuhlen proposed a dynamic theory of aging in which one would think of personality characteristics not as the *result* of an aging process but rather as important variables affecting the aging process itself. One large-scale and intensive research project carried out in Kansas City (Peck, 1959) found that the aging process did not appear to affect mental health, except perhaps for a slight "dip" in the fifties, which for many persons are years of transition.

Since the steady increase in the number of aged individuals in our population has become recognized as a challenging social problem, the search for factors differentiating between successful and unsuccessful adjustment in old age has become a focus of much research effort. There are too many detailed findings from these comparisons of successful with unsuccessful "adjustees to old age" for more than a brief report here. The Kuhlen chapter (1959) summarizes them well. In general, the conclusions from such studies are that in addition to health and economic status, psychological factors like continued participation in employment or hobbies, the maintenance of family and social ties, and the existence of positive attitudes toward self and toward the future, favor good adjustment.

However, these relationships may not be quite so simple and obvious as they look at first. One major community study (Kutner, et al., 1956) showed that some of these relationships differ at different socio-economic levels. Visiting friends and children, for example, seems to be related to high morale at the lower levels but not at the higher. The report of another community study (Cumming and Henry, 1961) presents evidence that not continued participation but rather a progressive *disengagement* may be essential for successful aging. Reichard, Livson, and Petersen (1962) in a report on a study of 87 working-class men, aged fifty to eighty-four, initiated by Frenkel-Brunswik, add another idea to the discussion of the problem of what makes for successful aging. Cluster analyses of correlations between individuals in a successful group and in an unsuccessful group, based on 115 rated personality variables judged from intensive interviews, revealed three main types of successful aging, and two main types of unsuccessful aging, as well as several individual patterns. The three varieties of men who seemed to be aging well were the *mature* men (those who were realistic, flexible, at ease with themselves and others), the *rocking-chair* men (those who welcomed old age because it freed them to indulge passive-dependent needs that had been present all through their lives), and the *armored* men (those whose defenses against anxiety worked so well that they continued to function smoothly, at least as long as they "kept active." The two main varieties of poorly adjusted men were the *angry* men, who were bitter and inclined to blame others for all their troubles, and the *self-haters,* whose feelings of inadequacy and worthlessness led to depression. It appears that no easy and common-sense generalizations about policies favorable to good adjustment in old age are going to be sufficient.

One fact has been thoroughly documented—that good adjustment during this period of life is *possible.* Pressey (1957) collected numerous case studies of persons who keep on living rich rewarding lives regardless of advancing age. In our concern about the problems of aging we may overlook such cases—and they are apparently not at all rare. Another facet of this same research program is revealed in a report by Demming and Pressey (1957) in which they show that it is possible to construct a mental-ability test (in this case a test of practical information) on which old persons score significantly higher than comparable groups of young persons.

We can conclude, then, that personality and adjustment difficulties are not *inevitable* accompaniments of the biological process of aging. They are rather the product of the situations in which aging people find themselves, and their reactions to those situations. There is consequently a growing interest in old-age counseling. A pioneer in this endeavor was Dr. Lillian Martin who, upon retirement from Stanford University at the age of sixty-five, started a clinic for old people in San Francisco. In such centers, evidence has been accumulating that when adjustment has been disturbed by unfavorable circumstances, it is still possible to recreate constructive attitudes. You *can* teach an old dog new tricks.

THE CONCEPT OF DEVELOPMENTAL STAGES

With the increasing tendency to explain human differences related to the biological variables of sex and age in terms of *roles* to be played, there has been increasing interest in the concept of life-stages—periods qualitatively as well as quantitatively different from one another, so that the psychological traits appropriate at one stage may be useless or detrimental at another. This is not a new idea. Its most famous proponent is Shakespeare.

> All the world's a stage,
> And all the men and women merely players.
> They have their exits and their entrances;
> And one man in his time plays many parts,
> His acts being seven ages.
>
> *As You Like It,* Act II

The idea of life stages was taken up in earnest at the University of Vienna in the 1930's. Charlotte Bühler's *Der Menschliche Lebenslauf als Psychologisches Problem,* published in 1933 and revised in 1959, set forth what has been one of the most influential theories about the stages of life. Frenkel (1936) reviewed in English some of the same ideas, and sketched what was being done in Vienna to obtain research evidence on problems related to the "course of life" through analyses of biographies of famous and ordinary persons.

The Vienna researchers postulated five principal stages:

1. *Childhood,* during which period the child lives at home and is dependent on his family.
2. *Self-determination,* from seventeen to about twenty-eight, during which period the person engages in exploratory and preparatory activities through which he discovers what he wants to do with his life and establishes his independence.
3. *Stabilization,* from about twenty-eight to about fifty, during which the person does his most important work and carries major responsibilities.
4. *Decline,* from about fifty to sixty-five, a transition period during which the person evaluates what he has accomplished so far and comes to terms with the fact that life is limited.
5. *Retirement,* typically occurring at about sixty-five, during which the person gradually restricts his activities, loosens his ties, and develops acceptance of his past life, now irrevocably completed, and acceptance of the fact of death.

Bühler's division of life into these stages was based partly on biological factors, partly on social factors. Especially in recent publications (Bühler, 1962), she has postulated four basic tendencies: *need-satisfaction, self-limiting adaptation, creative expansion,* and *the upholding of the internal order.* The successive life-stages are characterized by changes in the relative predominance of these tendencies. Individual differences in their relative strength exist at all ages.

Havighurst (1953) has also proposed a series of life-stages with the emphasis mainly on specific *developmental tasks* to be accomplished at each stage. He too distinguishes between early adulthood, middle age, and old age. The tasks he lists for middle age are things having to do with carrying responsibility, helping the young, and supporting the old. The tasks he lists for old age have more to do with adjusting to decrements within oneself and the loss of loved ones.

One of the most influential "life-stage" formulations has been Erikson's (1950, 1959). He characterizes the successive periods in terms of the psychological quality, attitude, or skills that they require. The basic challenge for the adolescent is *identity vs.* identity diffusion. For the young adult it is *intimacy vs.* isolation. For the middle-aged it is *generativity vs.* self-absorption. For the aged it is *integrity vs.* despair.

The investigators at the University of Vienna in the 1930's initiated psychological studies of three aspects of the "Lebenslauf" or "course of life." These were the: (1) activities and events characteristic of each successive stage; (2) inner experiences at each stage; and (3) productivity at each stage. Following publication of the reports in German at that time, very little further was accomplished with regard to the first two of these aspects, especially for the middle periods of life. Super and his associates have been studying both events and experiences of the exploratory period in their career pattern study (Super, et al., 1957) and reports from this project about what happens to men in their late teens and twenties will eventually be forthcoming. Several of the studies of aging mentioned in the last section, notably Cumming and Henry (1961) have directed attention to the special psychological characteristics of the final period. The time is ripe for research on the long stretch of years in between.

One part of the Vienna program mentioned above has been very thoroughly carried out. Lehman has devoted his attention to the question of productivity as it varies during the course of life. His book *Age and Achievement* (Lehman, 1953) contains an enormous collection of information about the ages at which men and women have made their creative contributions to civilization. His method was to take a standard reference book which distinguishes and dates the outstanding contributions in a particular field, then to list these works and accomplishments and if necessary have them rated for importance by present-day authorities in the subject, and after that to ascertain the age of the person who made each contribution. Results are reported in graphs like Figure 41 showing the relative numbers of great works produced by men of each age range. (The figures are corrected to allow for the decreasing number of persons still living in each successive age group.) This way of presenting the data has the advantage of showing at a glance both the *peak* years, when the largest volume of work was done, and the *spread* or the range of ages at which eminent achievement has occurred.

For a great many fields, Lehman's figures show similar age distributions. The peaks come during young adulthood. For several fields they are as follows:

Games and Sports (baseball players, pugilists, auto racers)	25–29
Science (chemistry, physics, inventions)	30–34
Literature (poetry)	25–29
Literature (fiction)	30–39
Literature ("Best Books")	40–44
Medicine and Surgery	35–39
Philosophy	35–39

There seems to be little difference from one period to another or from one country to another (Lehman, 1954).

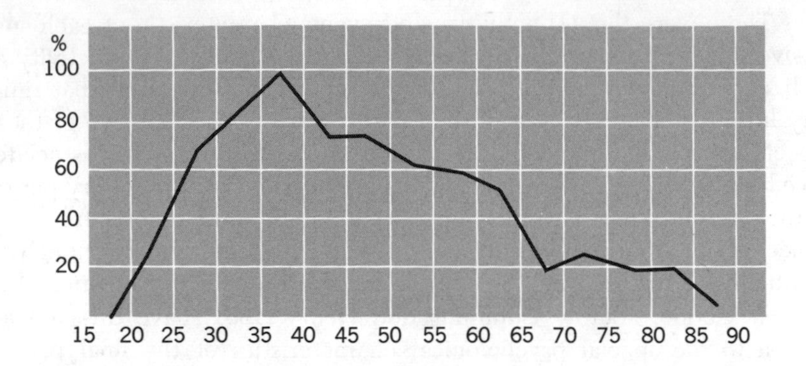

FIGURE 41

Ages at Which Great Paintings Were Produced. The Highest Figure Has Been Assigned a Value of 100 Percent and the Others Rendered Comparable

(Lehman, 1942)

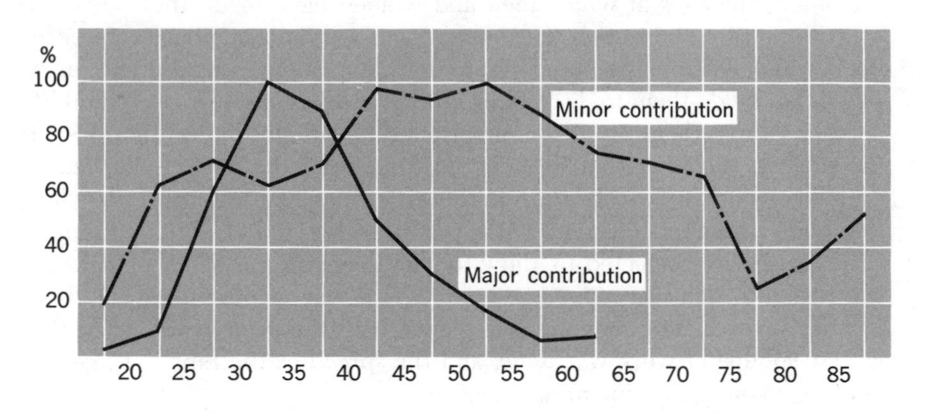

FIGURE 42

Relationship of Age to Rate of Production of Major and Minor Contributions to Chemistry

(From Lehman, H. C. The chemist's most creative years. *Science,* 1958, 127, No. 3308, 1213–1222)

In a later study of the 2,500 ablest of the world's chemists (Lehman, 1958) another important finding emerged. The curve for outstanding contributions to chemistry has its peak in the early thirties, but the curve for relatively minor contributions shows a much later peak and almost no falling off until the seventies. Figure 42 shows these results in graphic form.

We must be careful to avoid unwarranted conclusions about what Lehman's productivity curves mean. Lehman has reminded his readers on many occasions that they represent a complex of psychological and sociological factors impossible to unravel at present. Do the trends represent a decline in mental ability making high achievement increasingly difficult after "life begins at forty"? Do they mean that there are important changes in motivation as life proceeds? Do they mean that our society is organized in such a way that the middle-aged individual is too much involved in various other duties to give his time and attention to creative work? Adams (1946) showed that different causes seemed to operate in different cases such as—prolonged ill health, administrative duties, change of occupation. It is important for us to remember that great work has been produced by persons of all ages. Goethe was over eighty when he wrote *Faust,* Part II. Adams quotes a sentence from a letter written by F. D. Drewitt years ago which sums up about all we know here: "Humans vary, as apples do, some ripen in July, others in October."

In applying the knowledge we have about age differences, we should never lose sight of the factor of *overlapping* from one age group to the next. Reaction time, for instance, is one function which declines with age, yet Miles showed that 25 per cent of the seventy-year-olds were as quick as the average for the whole group. If a job requires fast reaction time, many men of seventy can qualify for it more satisfactorily than many men of twenty. The curves that have been shown are *group* curves. They show you nothing about any specific individual. The same principle that was emphasized for sex and race differences applies here also. Differences between the individuals in a group far outweigh the differences between *averages* of groups.

Statistics show that, for better or worse, the average age of our population is increasing. To clear the way for youth so that as much as possible can be accomplished during the years before forty, to establish social conditions that will keep mental vigor at its maximum throughout the life span and encourage continued achievement, to select persons for jobs on an individual rather than an age basis, to furnish clinical services that will maintain good adjustment in the middle-aged and old—these are some of the tasks which challenge us. More research is urgently needed. Meanwhile let us make good use of that which we have.

SUMMARY

While opinions about age differences are common, research on them has presented some special difficulties. Representative samples are almost impossible to obtain, and tests suitable for one age group may not be suitable for another. Longitudinal studies, which are now more numerous than they used to be, are more conclusive than cross-sectional studies, but our conclusions still rest largely on cross-sectional evidence.

Cross-sectional studies of the performance of different adult age groups on intelligence tests indicated a decline from the twenties on, with the magnitude of the decrement depending to a large extent on the type of task involved. Scores on vocabulary tests and tests involving elementary-school subject matter stayed up throughout middle age. Scores on performance tests and tests requiring rapid adaptation to new situations declined markedly. Speed tests declined more than power tests.

Longitudinal studies have typically shown increases rather than decreases in most of these types of test, at least into the fifties. Evidence for a decline in the sixties and seventies has been obtained in longitudinal as well as cross-sectional research.

In the field of special abilities and aptitudes, the greatest decline is for perceptual tasks of all kinds. Motor skills are maintained fairly well throughout middle age. Learning and memorizing are somewhat less efficient with advancing age, especially the learning of skills that involve the breaking of old habits. Personality differences between various age groups are slight, and the possibility of excellent adjustment for older persons has been demonstrated.

For most types of outstanding achievement, the peak years come before forty, although persons of all ages have produced masterpieces and important ideas.

CHAPTER 12

Race Differences

THE PROBLEM OF RACE DIFFERENCES and especially of their implications for a democracy has in our time taken on a new urgency. Within the United States, traditional assumptions about the nature of such differences and their bearing upon national policy have been challenged as never before in our history. On the world scene, the struggle of peoples, who used to be labeled "primitive" or "uncivilized," for independence, respect, and participation in the affairs of an emerging world society is a social movement of major importance. What people have been taught to believe and what they really know about race differences affects many aspects of their lives—how they vote, how they run their businesses, how they dispose of their property. In this area of human concern, it is especially important to act on the basis of the best evidence we have, even though that evidence is incomplete and in many ways inadequate. We shall try to summarize it here.

PROBLEMS AND DIFFICULTIES

As has been pointed out, the research investigator of human differences does not start his work in a vacuum. His task is usually not simply to make a beginning in a field where nothing is known, but to check up on convictions that are held with dogmatic certainty. Nowhere is this situation more evident than in the field of race differences. Up to the beginning of this century, there was scarcely a dissenting voice in the general consensus among persons of European descent that definite mental differences in the various races paralleled their obvious physical differences, and that the white race was unquestionably superior to all the others. G. O. Ferguson, in his monograph (1916), cited many such opinions. The eminent British scientist and pioneer in the field of differential psychology, Sir Francis Galton, held that if one postulated sixteen grades of mental ability between Aristotle and the lowest idiot the average Negro would be about two grades or one-eighth the total distance below the average white. Another common view, expressed by Tylor (1881), Odum (1910), G. Stanley Hall (1905) and others, was that adult Negroes were inferior to adult whites because their mental development stopped earlier. Whereas white children continued to grow mentally throughout adolescence, Negro children stopped short at about the age of twelve. Most writers on the subject agreed that it was in the so-called higher mental processes—such as reasoning, attention, foresight, and judgment—that these differences were most marked. Many were willing, however, to concede that in sensory and motor characteristics, keenness of the senses, quickness of response, and perception of slight details, some of the more primitive races excelled our own. Portrayal of the Indian scout in fiction embodies this opinion.

In general, the total effect of research done so far on the race-difference problem has been a *decrease* in the certainty with which it is possible to hold to such a conclusion, and an *increase* in the influence of alternative formulations. However, during the present crisis over desegregation, the older theory has in some quarters been revived and vigorously promoted. In his monograph prepared by commission of the Governor of Alabama, *The Biology of the Race Problem*, George (1962) has brought together biological and psychological evidence which to him warrants conclusions that Negroes as a group are inferior to Caucasians, and that this inferiority rests basically on hereditary factors not susceptible to change through improvement in education or social conditions.

Professor George is a reputable biologist, and his conclusions have the support of some reputable psychologists, notably H. E. Garrett, but these two scholars do not speak for the majority of the members of their professions. In 1963, the Committee on Science in the Promotion of Human Welfare of the American Association for the Advancement of Science discussed the issues raised by George and those who have joined him in what amounts to a crusade and presented cogent reasons for rejecting their conclusions. The difficulty arises from the fact that, to quote the committee report (AAAS, 1963):

> The total problem is enormously complex, and contains within itself a series of successively broader sub-problems: the biological mechanism of inheritance of individual characteristics, such as blood type, which can be measured precisely and objectively; the variability of such characteristics within specific population groups of various sizes in different environments; the problem of measuring more complex characteristics, such as "intelligence," by procedures which distinguish between innate ability and the effect of cultural factors; the influence of particular social factors on the expression of potential innate characters in the individual; the effects of interactions among groups whose members come in contact with each other

through education, immigration, social mobility, and inter-marriage. These problems differ greatly in their accessibility to precise scientific investigation and in their relevance to the issue of Negro civil rights.

Let us look at some of these special problems in more detail. The first is that almost never are we able to carry out our psychological studies on *pure* races. Race is essentially a biological concept. The fact that a group of persons now living had in the remote past a common ancestry means that they have a number of physical characteristics in common, characteristics that set them off from groups of other remote ancestry in the same way that dachshunds are distinguished from cocker spaniels. The number of places on our globe where one may encounter pure races of human beings, in this sense, is extremely limited, and as transportation and communication facilities expand and penetrate into remote regions of the world, there will be even fewer of them. To add to the difficulty, in the places where we find groups of people who seem to belong to a single racial group, such as the "true Negroes" of western Africa, our common varieties of psychological test are not applicable. We cannot ask these individuals the questions in the Binet Scale and expect meaningful answers. Even if we should translate the questions into their language, so many of them refer to objects and experiences that are totally unfamiliar to Africans that their responses would still be of no use to us. Performance tests of intelligence are less obviously dependent on a certain standard background of experience and information, but it is still possible that scores on them are affected by subtle factors like motivation, attitude, and experience with tools and pictures and toys.

When we compare racial groups living in the same country and speaking the same language, such as Negroes and whites in the United States, the difficulty of classification becomes an important consideration. Wherever races have lived in close proximity for many decades, considerable race mixture has occurred. This means that we will have within any so-called racial group individuals showing all different degrees of the physical characteristics that once differentiated this race from others. It may prove difficult or impossible, in such a case, to assign an individual *scientifically* to one race or the other. Anthropologists have given considerable attention to identifying the physical characteristics on the basis of which useful classifications of races can be made. The traditional criterion has been skin color, and the most widely used classification of human beings into the white, black, and yellow races, with red and brown races as possibly separate from these, is based upon it. Other physical characteristics, however, are more reliable indicators of racial origin than is color. The pigmentation of the eyes and the color and texture of the hair show race differences. Measurements can be made of the shape of the cross-section of a hair which will show whether it approximates the round shape characteristic of straight-haired races or the flat shape that makes it kinky or woolly. Gross bodily dimensions such as stature and breadth of shoulders show significant differences from race to race. Cranial and facial measurements are also useful differentiating data. Genetically, all these racial traits seem to be determined by genes that vary *independently,* so that almost any combination of physical traits may occur in an individual whose ancestry includes persons of more than one race. As long as a racial group remains isolated, the traits will all seem to go together inevitably because the mother and father who endow their child with a set of genes for the typical skin color of his race will also pass on to him the genes for the other typical physical characteristics. They have no other kind to give him. When there has been an admixture of genes from another race, however, this will not be true. Negroes, for instance, are, as a whole, relatively dark-skinned, long-limbed, and woolly-haired; but we have all seen so-called Negroes in this country who have long limbs but light skins and straight hair, and so on. It is difficult in many cases to decide whether a person is or is not a Negro.

A caution with regard to racial classification systems based on anatomical measurements has arisen from the findings of Boas (1911), Hirsch (1927), and Spier (1929) that such characteristics once thought to be entirely determined by heredity, are subject to environmental influence. Children born in the United States are significantly different in these measurements from children of the same race and nationality born elsewhere, perhaps because of differences in nutrition and type of infant care. Thus we must recognize that our racial classifications are not clear-cut exact representations of facts about human groups, but only rough approximations to some biological differentiation assumed to have a genetic origin in the far-distant past and not yet entirely wiped out by migration and intermarriage.

Many biologists and anthropologists hold today that the most satisfactory means of differentiating between races is to compare the *distributions* for representative samples of the groups in question with regard to traits known to have a genetic basis (W. C. Boyd, 1950). Blood types have been the factors most commonly used in this way. If we look at the figures for three varieties of Americans, for example, we find that they distribute themselves as follows:

U. S. Whites	45 % O	41 % A	10 % B	4 % AB
U. S. Negroes	44.2% O	30.3% A	21.8% B	3.7% AB
North American Indians (Sioux)	91 % O	7 % A	2 % B	0 % AB

If we use this method as a basis of classification we do not get clear-cut divisions. Chinese and Negroes differ less from white Americans than Poles differ from Frenchmen. Furthermore, it is obviously impossible to classify just one single *individual* by such methods. For any given person with a moderately dark skin and B-type blood, for example, how are we to know whether he belongs to the 22 per cent of the Negro race or to the 10 per cent of the white race whose blood is of this variety? Nevertheless, for analyzing the relationships between populations and tracing the migrations of the past, this study of distributions has been most helpful. The general concept it represents is an important basis for all our thinking about race. There is no absolute difference. The characteristics human beings show are the same. It is only the proportions that differ biologically.

There is still another vexing question related to the interpretation of research findings on race differences in a country like the United States. Historical and economic factors have produced a social structure in which persons of different races are exposed to quite different environmental influences throughout their lives. If anatomical proportions are not entirely determined by heredity, most psychologists agree that mental abilities and personality traits are even less so. Consequently, before we can answer the question as to whether there are fundamental biologically-determined mental differences between races, we must either make the proper allowance for the effects of unequal education and socio-economic status, or we must find groups of subjects of the races to be compared who have not been exposed to these inequalities but who still are representative of their respective populations. In order to do the first of these things, we need to know a great deal more than we do now about the specific effects of all sorts of environmental influences on mental development, the subtle factors such as the emotional responsiveness and the goals and values of the family, as well as the obvious factors such as material standard of living and amount and quality of education. To do the second is practically impossible. We cannot find, in this country, sizable groups of whites and Negroes for whom environmental influences have been equal in any scientifically adequate sense of that term.

As explained in an earlier chapter, psychological tests were not designed or constructed for the purpose of measuring differences between groups, but rather for comparing individuals with one another, within a group all of whose members have heen exposed to similar experiences. When we use our available tests for comparing group averages, it is incumbent upon us to set up a research program, so that, little by little, the nature of the factors underlying the obtained group differences will be clarified. This is what has been going on in American psychology for four or five decades. Because of this long procession of special studies, an investigator in 1964 does not interpret his findings in the same way that an investigator in 1924 would have interpreted them. It is this kind of scientific progress that such spokesmen for racial inequality as George and Garrett do not sufficiently take into account.

Practical-minded psychologists, however, have not let the fact that Negroes in the United States are not a pure race deter them from comparing groups of persons classified as Whites and Negroes, since the social classification itself is the phenomenon around which questions of policy revolve. If a child lives in a Negro district and is considered a Negro by his classmates, the research worker includes him in his Negro group. But we must remember that by following this method of classification we limit the scope of the theoretical conclusions we can draw from it.

There is still another sort of difficulty, inherent in the statistical techniques we use. One can never really *prove* the null hypothesis; one can only *dis*prove it with varying degrees of probability. Thus we could never prove conclusively that races are equal, no matter what kinds of evidence we assembled. What we can do is to identify inequalities and then to analyze their sources. If our society is dedicated to the ideal of equal opportunity for all its citizens, our task becomes the elimination of these sources of inequality. This is the real long-range value of research on race differences, not the discovery of evidence to be used in arguments pro or con on the status quo. The decision to promote equality of opportunity in the social order is an ethical decision and does not stand or fall according to whether scientists furnish indisputable proof that biological equality exists.

EARLY RESEARCH ON SENSORY AND MOTOR DIFFERENCES

Some of the earliest work in race differences was designed to discover whether there were differences in vision, hearing, smell, reaction-time, and motor control between the so-called "primitive" races and our own. In the early 1900's, reports were published of an anthropological expedition to the Torres Straits, giving the results of psychological tests of sensory and motor abilities of the natives (*Reports,* 1901–1903). In 1904, Woodworth (1910) tested 300 persons representing many primitive races at the St. Louis World's Fair. American Indians, Negritos from the Philippines, Malayan Filipinos, Ainus from Japan, Africans, Eskimos, Patagonians, and Cocopa Indians all were included in his group of subjects. There turned out to be very little difference between the sensory and motor abilities of any of these people and those of average white subjects. Indians and Filipinos were somewhat above the white norms for vision, but in hearing the averages of all the primitive groups fell somewhat below the white average. Circumstances might well account for these differences. The greater use of the eye for comparatively unnatural types of activity on the part of white men might be expected to impair their vision to some extent. The greater emphasis on cleanliness and hygiene and the freedom from some forms of injury incurred under primitive conditions should give the white man, in general, a better-functioning ear. Woodworth noted also that stimuli such as watch ticks and clicks would be less familiar to the primitive subjects. In keenness of smell, all groups were very much alike. The one most important sensory difference Woodworth noticed was in regard to the sense of pain. Greater pressure on the skin was required to produce a report of pain in the primitive than in white subjects. This may, however, represent a difference in what subjects understand "pain" to mean. In tests of color-matching, tapping, illusions, and handedness, no differences were apparent.

The only test similar to our present intelligence tests that Woodworth had at his disposal in those early years of the twentieth century was the Seguin Form Board test, in which a set of blocks of various shapes were to be fitted as quickly as possible into the holes where they belonged. Such tests are still widely used as nonverbal indicators of somewhat complex mental processes, though it is no longer held that they measure exactly the same abilities as tests based on language. On these tests, most of Woodworth's subjects did about equally well and made scores about equal to those of white subjects. A few groups, however, the Igorot and Negrito from the Philippines, and the Pygmies from the Congo, were very much lower than the average. About this finding, Woodworth comments:

> If the results could be taken at their face value, they would indicate differences of intelligence between races, giving such groups as the Pygmy and Negrito a low station as compared with most of mankind. The fairness of the test is not, however, beyond question; it may have been of a more unfamiliar sort to these wild hunting folk than to more settled groups (Woodworth, 1910, p. 181).

The investigation of sensori-motor differences is no longer considered an important research problem. Goodenough (1936), reanalyzing the Torres Straits and St. Louis Exposition data, brought out the fact that psychologists may have abandoned this line of investigation too soon. Differences in visual, auditory, and cutaneous sensitivity, as reported in these early studies, may have some significance even though they are small. Since such traits can be measured directly and not by inference, as intelligence must be, there is merit in her suggestion that investigation of them be continued. However, there is increasing evidence from other research fields that it is not the efficiency of the sense organs themselves so much as it is the *use* people have learned to make of them that varies from group to group. The blind, for instance, do not have a more delicate touch sense than do their seeing neighbors, but their *learning* of a certain kind is more advanced. They have learned to make *discriminations* that are much finer than ordinary persons customarily need. The feats of Commando troops during World War II are as spectacular as anything Cooper's Uncas could boast, showing that white men can learn the Indians' keenness and control if they are maximally motivated by knowing their lives depend upon it and if they are placed in the right learning situation.

Very little has been done so far to determine whether there are racial differences on the more complex kinds of perceptual traits we have discussed in Chapter 9. There is one study by Thouless (1933) in which 20 students from India were compared with 49 British students in what he called "phenomenal regression," but which is ordinarily called perceptual constancy—the tendency to perceive an object in terms of its known physical size and shape rather than its actual projection on the retina. There was a difference between the English and the Indians, significant at the .001 level. The Indians saw things more as the retinal image would be, the English more as the object itself was known to be. Thouless advanced the hypothesis that this difference might account for the lack of perspective in Oriental art.

That perceptual differences can be cultural in origin is suggested by Thompson's (1951) report that children from three different American Indian tribes differed in their characteristic responses to Rorschach blots. The Papago tend to see vague wholes, the Navajo obvious detail, and the Hopi differentiated, organized wholes.

The investigation of perceptual differences between races and cultures may again become an important line of research. So far, however, the large majority of studies have been concerned with differences in the complex mental abilities tapped by intelligence tests.

THE MEANING OF NEGRO-WHITE INTELLLIGENCE DIFFERENCES

The major research problem in this field in the United States has been the search for the sources of the differences between Negro and White distributions on intelligence measures. There is no question about the existence of these differences and no doubt about their statistical significance. It is unnecessary to go into this topic in detail, as a summary of all the important studies is now available in a book by Shuey (1958) in which more than 200 investigations are summarized. On both individual and group tests, the averages for Negro and white children of all ages from the preschool age on up, and the averages for adults tested during both world wars have consistently been found to differ by 10 to 20 IQ points, and fewer than 25 per cent of the Negro group have typically scored above the median for whites.

Negro-white comparisons have shown some other consistent trends. For one thing, the smallest differences occur at the youngest ages. The higher the school grade in which the tests have been given, the greater the difference between Negro and white averages has turned out to be. Many examples could be given of this finding, but the most recent illustrates it best, because the samples of the respective populations were more representative than samples obtained in previous studies. Kennedy, Van de Riet, and White (1963) administered the 1960 revision of the Stanford-Binet scale and the California Achievement Test to 1,800 Negro elementary-school children in five southeastern states—Tennessee, Alabama, Georgia, South Carolina, and Florida. In each state they chose three representative counties, one metropolitan (large city), one urban (small city), and one rural. In each county, representative schools were selected for testing, and at each school, a random selection of children at each grade level from one through six were chosen. All the evidence indicated that the families of these children matched the Negro population from which they were drawn in most socio-economic characteristics.

The overall comparison of the performance of this Negro group with the Terman and Merrill norms for white children is shown in Figure 43. As in many earlier studies, the mean is about 20 points lower than the

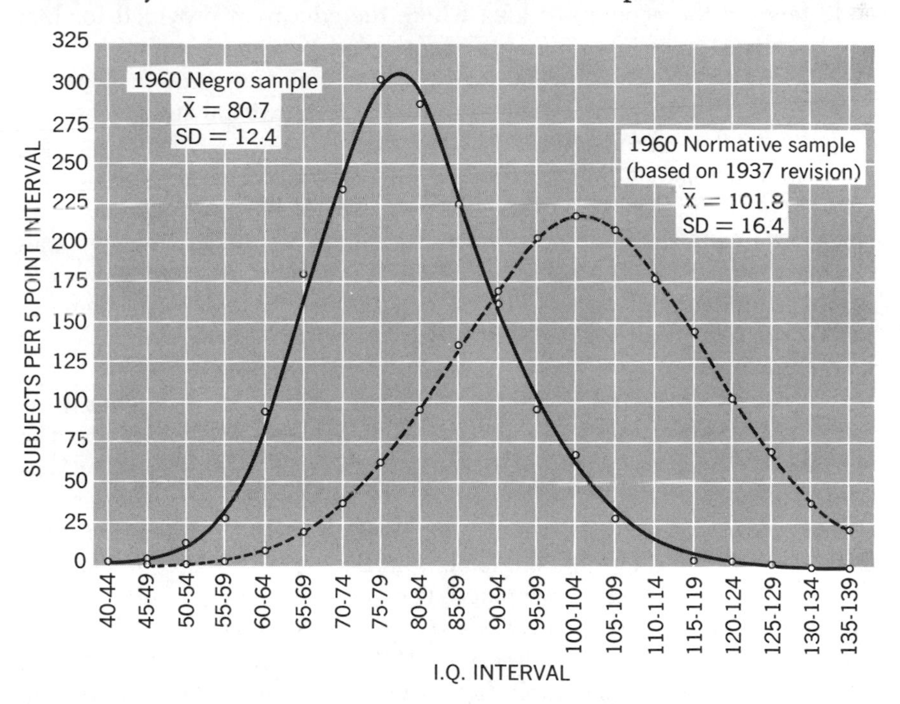

FIGURE 43

IQ Distribution of Negro Children in Five Southeastern States Compared with Terman-Merrill Normative Sample

(Kennedy, Van de Riet, and White, 1963)

mean for the white children. The standard deviation is also lower, indicating more of a bunching up of scores around the mean. But the most important fact disclosed by this study is the age trend, as shown in Table 25. Even if we leave out those below six and over twelve, who are younger or older than the boys and girls usually found in the first six grades, the drop from an IQ of 84 for six-year-olds to 75 for twelve-year-olds is a conspicuous finding. Deutsch (1964) has also emphasized this "cumulative deficit" phenomenon.

The Kennedy, Van de Riet, and White investigation was not designed to throw any new light on the general problem of race differences but rather to produce norms for the Stanford-Binet scale and the other tests used in the study, norms that would make it possible for guidance workers to do a more adequate job of assessing the ability of the Negro school child in our Southeastern states at the present time. But it also provides a sort of maximum estimate of the extent of the handicap the typical Negro child faces in the geographic area where the education provided for him has been least adequate. The most convincing hypothesis to account for the IQ decrease is that the normal amount of mental growth does not occur from year to year without stimulating educational influences. We shall discuss it at more length later.

Another consistent finding running through all of the research is a *geographical* difference. Negro groups in the North score higher than Negro groups in the South. The entering wedge for questioning the conclusion that the differences in test score represented true differences in "native" intelligence was a series of geographical reanalyses of some of the World War I Army data. Table 26 shows what was discovered in this kind of analysis.

It is clear that several groups of Northern Negroes made higher averages on the Army test than several groups of Southern whites. The meaning of these comparisons between Northern Negroes and Southern whites was again widely discussed after the publication of the pamphlet, *Races of Mankind,* by Benedict and Weltfish (1943). Montagu (1945), Garrett (1945a, b, c, and d), and Alper and Boring (1944) have reanalyzed the data from different viewpoints. The results of their efforts can be summed up in two generalizations: (1) Northerners consistently scored considerably higher than Southerners of the same race; and (2) whites consistently scored considerably higher than Negroes of the same region. Whether the comparisons are made on the basis of Alpha scores alone (verbal test), or the combined scale, these generalizations as to what the *facts* are hold true. How they should be *interpreted* is another matter upon which there is as yet no universal agreement.

Similar differences between groups of Negro school children from the North and from the South were also found. Peterson and Lanier (1929), for example, found that Negroes in Chicago and New York scored

TABLE 25
Stanford-Binet IQ Mean and Standard Deviation for Negro Children in Different Age Groups

(Kennedy, Van de Riet, and White, 1963)

Age	*Number*	*IQ Mean*	*SD*
5 years	19	86.00	6.40
6	227	84.43	12.48
7	243	81.71	11.80
8	302	80.88	12.04
9	281	80.10	12.08
10	299	80.10	12.68
11	279	80.63	11.98
12	109	75.48	11.34
13	30	65.23	10.45
14	9	66.11	7.35
15	1	58.00	
16	1	51.00	
All Ages	1,800	80.71	12.48

TABLE 26
Average Scores on Army Alpha for Negro Soldiers from Three Northern States and White Soldiers from Three Southern States

(Benedict and Weltfish, 1943; N's added by Garrett, 1945a)

WHITES			NEGROES		
State	*N*	*Median Alpha Score*	*State*	*N*	*Median Alpha Score*
Arkansas	618	41.0	New York	850	44.5
Kentucky	832	41.0	Ohio	152	48.8
Mississippi	665	40.8	Illinois	578	46.9

significantly higher than Negroes in Nashville on several kinds of intelligence tests.

Two sorts of explanation were at first formulated to explain North-South differences, the *selective migration* hypothesis and the *educational opportunity* hypothesis. According to those who stressed the first of these hypotheses, it was reasonable to suppose that there had been a continual draining off of the most alert, capable, and ambitious of the Negroes from the South into Northern cities where their opportunities were greater and their handicaps less marked. Consequently on any test of intelligence they could be expected to make higher scores than Negroes who had remained in the South. The chief weakness of this hypothesis was that it failed to explain why the scores of *whites* in Mississippi, Kentucky, Arkansas, Georgia, and the other Southern states were so low in comparison with the national averages. There has, of course, been some white migration out of these states also, but it is not clear that there has been any more of it than there has been from New England or the Midwest. The second hypothesis, held by those who explained the results in terms of educational and cultural influences, emphasized the fact that ranks of the states for scores on Army Alpha corresponded rather closely to their ranks for economic level and educational efficiency as judged by such indices as the percentage of daily school attendance, percentage of children attending high school, and the average per capita expenditure for education (H. B. Alexander, 1922).

The obvious way to find out which of these alternative explanations fits the facts better was to find out whether the IQ's of Negro children actually increased after they moved to the North and entered Northern schools. It was Klineberg (1935) who first set up an investigation to test these alternative hypotheses. It consisted of a number of related studies on various phases of the problem. In one of them, school marks (expressed in percentile ranks) for children who moved away from three Southern cities were compared with the marks of those who stayed behind. Results were inconsistent and showed no general trend. Thus the average percentile rank for Birmingham migrants was about 45, whereas the Nashville average was 54. This obviously did not look like selective migration, although advocates of this interpretation countered with the objection that school marks are known to be highly unreliable indices of mental ability, and differences would have to be very marked to show up at all in this type of comparison.

Klineberg also obtained data on groups of New York twelve-year-old children who had lived in the city for various lengths of time. While there was some variation in the results from school to school and some discrepancies in what different tests showed, the general trend was fairly clear. The longer a group had lived in New York, the higher the average

TABLE 27

Results of Studies by Klineberg and Associates Comparing Groups of Negroes in New York with Different Lengths of Residence Stanford-Binet

(Klineberg, 1935)

INVESTIGATOR		LENGTH OF RESIDENCE					
		Less Than 1 Year	*1-2*	*2-3*	*3-4*	*More Than 4 Years*	*Northern Born*
Skladman	N	20	20		19	20	28
	IQ	81.8	85.8		90.3	94.1	98.5
	S.D.	9.14	7.91		8.42	12.6	9.47
Wallach	N	24	23	21	24	26	49
	IQ	80.5	84.0	85.9	85.1	87.1	85.2
Rogosin	N	18	17	19	22	21	50
	IQ	82.6	84.5	83.0	85.9	87.7	89.3

IQ turned out to be. Table 27 shows the results obtained in three studies using the Stanford-Binet.

The Klineberg studies furnished some definite evidence as to the effect of improved environment in raising the average test score of a group. The ambiguity that remained arose from the fact that we did not know whether any one of the schools in which the investigators worked, or all of them taken together, were representative of the total Negro population of New York. As the figures stood there was as much fluctuation from school to school as from North to South. The New York-born children, for instance, in the Wallach study had an average IQ of 85.2, whereas the children with less than a year's residence in the Rogosin study, averaged 82.6, only 2.6 points less. What did these large differences between Negro *schools* in the North mean?

The picture became clearer as a result of a later study carried on in Philadelphia by Lee (1951). He obtained convincing evidence of the relationship between IQ and periods of time spent in Northern schools. The number of cases in each group was considerably larger than in the Klineberg study, ranging from 100 to 400. The same children were tested repeatedly after increasing periods of residence. Thus the effects of extraneous sampling fluctuations were ruled out. Still another feature of the study that turned out to be of special interest was the breakdown of the Northern-born group into those who had and had not attended kindergarten. Table 28 gives the results obtained with the Philadelphia Tests of Mental and Verbal Ability.

The lower part of the table shows a fairly consistent increase in scores

TABLE 28
Mean IQ's on Philadelphia Tests of Mental and Verbal Ability
(Lee, 1951)

GROUP	*N*	GRADE IN WHICH TEST WAS TAKEN *1A*	*2B*	*4B*	*6B*	*9A*
Philadelphia-born who attended kindergarten	212					
Mean		96.7	95.9	97.2	97.5	96.6
SD		14.3	14.8	15.0	13.9	14.2
Philadelphia-born who did not attend kindergarten	424					
Mean		92.1	93.4	94.7	94.0	93.7
SD		13.8	14.4	14.6	14.1	15.1
Southern-born entering Philadelphia school system in grades:						
1A	182					
Mean		86.5	89.3	91.8	93.3	92.8
SD		13.2	13.3	14.1	14.5	13.6
1B-2B	109					
Mean			86.7	88.6	90.9	90.5
SD			15.2	13.6	14.4	16.1
3A-4B	199					
Mean				86.3	87.2	89.4
SD				15.3	14.8	13.7
5A-6B	221					
Mean					88.2	90.2
SD					15.1	14.7
7A-9A	219					
Mean						87.4
SD						14.3

whether it is read from left to right or from bottom to top. Southern-born children averaged about 87 when they entered the first grade and about 93 when retested in the sixth grade and in the ninth grade. Southern-born children who entered Philadelphia schools at the junior-high level (bottom right corner) tested at about 87, whereas those who had had some Philadelphia schooling averaged about 90, and those who had had all their schooling there averaged about 93. This could not be explained on the basis of simply increasing familiarity with the test, since neither group of Philadelphia-born Negro children showed the increase. Lee carried out the necessary statistical tests to prove that these trends were clearly significant at the 1 per cent level.

One of the most interesting comparisons shown in Lee's tables is that between kindergartners and nonkindergartners. At each testing period, those who had attended kindergarten averaged higher than those who had not. The difference was only about 3 IQ points (96.6 versus 93.7 at the time of the last test) but was significant and always in the same direction. Lee made no attempt to explain it. It could arise from either selective factors in kindergarten enrollment or a genuine effect of kindergarten training on intellectual functioning. It is the possibility of the latter interpretation that has been most stimulating to later researchers.

One other aspect of the Lee research is also especially worth noting. A number of the subjects took the Chicago Tests of Primary Mental Abilities and the Minnesota Paper Form Board as well as the general intelligence test. With the single exception of the Memory factor (M), on which the various subgroups did not differ, all of these special kinds of ability measurement showed exactly the same trends as did the general test—increasing scores with increasing length of residence, and higher scores for those who had attended kindergarten than for those who had not.

The Klineberg and Lee research findings showed quite conclusively that Negro IQ's increased significantly under favorable educational circumstances. But can all of the difference between Negro and white averages be explained in this way? There have been a few studies suggesting that something more than just "schooling" is involved. One of these was reported by Tanser (1939) from Kent County, Ontario. The ancestors of the present Negro population there moved to the region before the Civil War, in the days of the "underground railroad." Negro and white pupils have attended the same schools since 1890. Tanser tested all Negro pupils in grades one through eight in one urban and seven rural schools, using white pupils in the same schools as comparison groups. The results are shown in Table 29. On all tests, language and nonlanguage alike, Tanser found a 15 to 19 point IQ difference between white and Negro groups.

Another study in which environmental factors were more nearly equalized than is customary is the one by Bruce (1940). Her work was done in a locality in South Virginia where the economic level of both whites and Negroes was unusually *low*. It thus furnished a complement to Tanser's at the other end of the scale. The subjects given the group test of intelligence (Kuhlmann-Anderson) were 521 white and 432 Negro children from nine matched pairs of schools. Their ages ranged from 6.0 through 12.9. Out of this number, 86 whites and 72 Negroes were selected as a representative group to be given individual tests, the 1916 Stanford-Binet and the Arthur Performance Scale. The results were as follows:

	White IQ	*Negro IQ*
Kuhlmann-Anderson	88	72
Stanford-Binet	90	76
Arthur	94	77

TABLE 29
Negro-White Comparisons on Four Intelligence Tests
(Tanser, 1939)

TEST	*N*	WHITE *IQ Mean*	WHITE *IQ S.D.*	*N*	NEGRO *IQ Mean*	NEGRO *IQ S.D.*
National Intelligence Test	386	103.6	16.5	103	89.2	15.9
Pintner Non-Language Test	387	110.9	19.0	102	95.2	13.3
Pintner-Cunningham Primary Test	155	97.6 *	....	54	82.8 *	....
Pintner-Paterson Performance Tests	211	109.6	22.4	162	91.0	19.0

* These averages are medians rather than means, and no variability figures are given.

As would be expected in a backward region of this sort, all IQ's were considerably below average, but the Negroes were 14 to 17 IQ points lower than the whites. This, of course, might mean that the Negroes were even more retarded environmentally than were the whites—that the whites were poor, but the Negroes even poorer. To obtain further evidence as to whether this possibility might explain the results, Bruce used the Sims Score Card, a method of evaluating economic level, to pick out a *paired group* of white and Negro children, presumably of equal economic status. These comparisons also indicated a definite differential, not quite so large, but still significant.

	White IQ	*Negro IQ*
Kuhlmann-Anderson	83	73
Stanford-Binet	86	77
Arthur	89	77

From 9 to 12 IQ points still separated Negro from white performance. Bruce reported one other significant finding. The difference between races was about equally marked for all kinds of material used in the tests. Negroes were no more handicapped on tests based on general information than on those involving new situations. They were no more handicapped on speed tests than on power tests. The differences characterized all the types of task that we include in intelligence scales.

One other much more recent study also compared Negro and white school children living under similar circumstances, at least so far as education is concerned. McQueen and Browning (1960) compared the intelligence and school achievement of 71 Negro pupils living in a small Northern city with that of 71 white pupils matched with the Negro subjects on age, sex, grade, years in school, residential area, and father's occupation. The city is one which has had a stable Negro population and completely desegregated schools for some time. The differences on both the Kuhlmann-Finch intelligence test and the Stanford Achievement Test turned out to be statistically significant but not large enough to have much practical significance. The average IQ for whites was 101, for Negroes 95. An examination of the marks teachers had given these children in school showed that in the lower grades there was a slight difference in favor of whites, but in the upper grades there was no difference.

There has been a good deal of controversy over the Tanser and Bruce results, which have been used to support the conclusion that there is *some* basic hereditary difference between the Negro and white races—that not all of the differences can be attributed to educational and other environmental differences. But this argument has never seemed very convincing to most social scientists. Reviews by Dreger and Miller (1960) and by Klineberg (1963) suggested other possible reasons for the differences. They can be included under two main headings. First, there is some doubt as to whether tests designed for white subjects are altogether adequate measures of Negro intelligence. Second, some developmental influence other than educational and socio economic handicaps may be having a consistently depressing influence on the mental growth of Negro children. Writers on the subject do not always distinguish between these two possible explanations but they are really quite different and imply different policies for bringing about improvement. If it is the tests that are at fault, all we need to do is to develop more adequate testing procedures. But if some subtle developmental influence is operating we must identify and remove it before Negroes will be able to achieve their full potential.

A number of possibilities have occurred to those who blame test inadequacies for the persistent race differences. Some have insisted that most tests are too *verbal* for people whose percentage of illiteracy is high. Others have questioned the emphasis on *speed* which they say fits poorly with Negro temperament. Still others have questioned whether the *motivation* of Negro and white groups is actually comparable, especially when tests are given by a white examiner. Evidence on all these points is scanty and somewhat hard to interpret because it comes from many different age groups and locations. We might ask ourselves first, is there any evidence that Negroes may achieve more than their test scores would lead one to predict? Here the report of Stalnaker (1948) on the Pepsi-Cola scholarship program has some bearing. In order to be sure that Southern Negro high-school students would have an opportunity to participate in the program, its sponsors awarded scholarships to the highest-scoring Negro applicants in each state even if they ranked considerably below the level of the white students to whom awards were made. Stalnaker reported that 55 out of the 59 Negro students chosen in this way were succeeding under competitive conditions at first-rate colleges. In general, however, the bulk of the studies covering the whole intelligence range rather than just this upper segment indicate that Negroes show the same deficiencies in their school work that they do on the intelligence tests themselves.

On the question of the appropriateness of verbal tests, there is at least one study, reported by Anastasi and D'Angelo (1952), which showed that among five-year-old preschool children in a day-care center, the Negroes were slightly lower than the whites on measures of sentence length and structure but not on the Goodenough Draw-a-Man Test. The fact that the sex differences on the language ratings were in an opposite direction for the two racial groups (Negro boys higher than girls, white girls higher than boys) made some sort of cultural explanation seem reasonable. Goodenough (1926), however, had encountered as much retardation on the Draw-a-Man Test as was being found on verbal tests, and in the normative study in the five Southeastern states to which reference has been made in an earlier section, the Goodenough showed the same increase in Negro retardation with age as the Stanford-Binet had shown (Kennedy and Lindner, 1964). In general, Negro-white differences have shown up whatever special variety of test has been used. Coppinger and Ammons (1952) found that their Negro grade-school subjects averaged about two years below the white norms on the picture vocabulary test. Hammer (1954) found his Negro subjects were somewhat higher on the language section than on the nonlanguage section of the California Mental Maturity Scale. McGurk (1953), after having his test questions sorted into "cultural" and "noncultural" categories by 78 judges, found that there was more difference between groups of white and Negro high-school students who had been equated for age, school attendance, curriculum, and general socio-economic level on the "noncultural" than on the "cultural" items. It is also worth noting that recent studies like that of McQueen and Browning (1960) have been finding a narrower gap between Negro and white averages than older studies typically did. If the tests we are using were basically unsuited to Negro special abilities or temperament it seems unlikely that Negroes would be improving their performance over the years in this way.

Explanations of racial differences as nothing but differences in test-taking motivation have not been supported by most of the evidence. Motivation does not seem to make that much difference. Maller and Zubin (1932) and Benton (1936) did not get significant increases in group intelligence-test performance by introducing rivalry, or offering prizes. Klugman (1944), using the Stanford-Binet test and money incentives, also failed to produce a significant improvement. His subjects included both white and Negro children. G. F. Boyd (1952), who used a level-of-aspiration procedure with groups of white and Negro children in a Northern, nonsegregated school, found that the Negroes showed significantly higher aspiration levels than the whites of the same intelligence level. Canady (1936) who investigated specifically the effects of "rapport," the relationship between a Negro subject and a white examiner (again in a Northern, nonsegregated school, however), found that while there was a slight tendency for children to score higher when tested by an examiner of their own race, in general the pattern of gains and losses upon retest was comparable with what is usually obtained when a racial factor is not involved. The hypothesis of Hammer (1954) that Negro children are handicapped in intelligence tests by a severe degree of "neuroticism" is not convincing. His measure of neuroticism consisted of ratings of the drawings the children made of a house, a tree, and a person, and such drawings are themselves at least as closely related to intellectual as to motivational characteristics.

Although it has been often mentioned as a possible basis for differences in score, it seems very doubtful whether a general speed factor enters in. Rhodes (1937), Lambeth and Lanier (1933), and Moore (1941) all failed to get significant Negro-white differences in psychomotor speed when the task was a simple one, although Peterson, Lanier, and Walker (1925) and Klineberg (1928) had noted a certain indifference to speed in some Negro groups.

The administration of tests to minority-group children in such a way that the results will be valid indicators of their abilities does pose special problems. The Society for the Psychological Study of Social Issues has developed a set of *guidelines* to help with this task (SPSSI, 1964).

To summarize, there is little or no evidence that the Negro-white differences remaining after socio-economic and educational influences have been at least roughly equated can be dismissed as purely an artifact of the testing situation. If we assume that it does represent some real difference in the course of development through which the intellectual characteristics of human beings take shape, we are led to consider research findings suggesting what some of these developmental differences might be. New theories about the way in which intelligence develops give some clues about what to look for. Hebb (1949) presented a very fruitful new concept when he discussed the effect of early *perceptual* learning on intellectual development. Piaget (1947) analyzed successive stages in the intellectual development of children starting with early sensory-motor development. Hunt (1961) combined these ideas with concepts based on cybernetics and information theory and produced a coherent account of the way in which the experience of the growing child enters into his intellectual development. Restructuring the problem of Negro-white intelligence differences along the lines opened up by these theories, what we need to know is what is actually *learned* by Negro and white individuals at successive developmental stages, especially the early ones. We do not at present have any data bearing directly on this issue, but we can get at it obliquely by looking at some kinds of evidence we do have.

First of all, there have been several studies attempting to find out which specific kinds of items in the tests Negroes tend to do poorly on in comparison with whites. Some of these studies have used as subjects groups of institutionalized criminals or delinquents who could be matched with one another in various ways and compared. At first glance, they might seem to be very unrepresentative subjects, but actually there are advantages in using them rather than such groups as school children or college students. We can be more certain that at least some of the environmental and motivational factors that are hard to control are constant for white and Negro subjects. Machover (1943) compared a group of 50 Southern Negroes who had migrated to New York after the age of sixteen with a group of New York-born Negroes matched with them for scores on the Comprehension and Similarities tests of the Wechsler-Bellevue scale. The Negroes from the South were most inferior to the New York Negroes on the Digit Symbol, Block Design, and Picture Arrangement subtests. The combination of these suggests some sort of *perceptual* defect. The culturally restricted group seems not to get the meaning of the stimulus material as clearly somehow as the group with the better educational background. In this study where all groups were initially matched by Comprehension and Similarities scores, differences between Northern Negroes and whites were small. It was the one type of difference between Southerners and Northerners that stood out. Franklin (1945) and De Stephens (1953) have given the Wechsler-Bellevue Test to delinquent Negro boys and have also reported special deficiencies on the Block Design and Digit Symbol subtests. Both these studies agree that Negro subjects are deficient also on the Arithmetic and the Picture-Completion subtests. Picture Completion would fit in with the hypothesis of a perceptual defect. Clarke (1941), who compared white and Negro delinquent boys on the Stanford-Binet Test, found that when the two groups were matched for overall IQ, the Negroes were superior to the whites on Dissected Sentences, Memory for Sentences, and Vocabulary, but inferior to them on Arithmetical Reasoning, Repeating 5 Digits Reversed, and Picture Absurdities. This agrees with the two previous studies in pointing to some special difficulty with numbers. The Picture Absurdities Test again involves perception of visual material.

A study by Davidson et al. (1950), whose subjects were white and Negro psychoneurotics matched for age and intelligence level, showed a similar pattern of differences on the Wechsler-Bellevue Test, with Negroes scoring lower on Arithmetic and on all the performance subtests. The authors interpret this as a culturally-conditioned difference in psychomotor speed. In view of the fact that the largest single subtest difference is on the Picture Completion Test, which is not ordinarily a speed test at all, it would seem more reasonable to interpret these results also as differences in some kind of perceptual ability and in skill with numbers. While a study by Woods and Toal (1957) comparing equated groups of white and Negro adolescents on the subtests of the Revised Army Beta leads to somewhat different conclusions, with Negroes scoring higher on perceptual tests like Digit Symbol and Visual Comparison, the bulk of the evidence, scanty as it is, suggests some inadequacy in perceptual development. There has been a series of reports in which performances on the Colored Raven Progressive Matrices have been compared. This is a test in which the respondent must perceive a pattern and then fit a missing piece into it. Higgins and Siners (1958) found that large groups of seven- to nine-year-old Negro and white children in a low socio-economic area who did not differ on the Stanford-Binet scale did show significant differences on the matrices, with the Negroes scoring lower. Sperrazzo and Wilkins (1958) found the same sort of race differences on the Colored Raven Progressive Matrices in a group of 480 school children. A reanalysis of the data (Sperrazzo and Wilkins, 1959), after dividing the subjects into three subgroups on the basis of socio-economic status, showed that the Negroes in all the subgroups scored lower than the whites on this test.

So far as perceptual defect is concerned, there is some indirect evidence suggesting that training of an appropriate sort at an appropriate time can correct it. In the Lee study cited above, the fact that Negro children who had been to *kindergarten* consistently scored higher than the others fits in with the idea that perceptual training makes a difference. Relevant too is a report by Tomlinson (1944) indicating that preschool Negro children scored significantly higher on the Binet than their older siblings did, and one by F. Brown (1944) reporting Negro averages almost as high as white for Minneapolis kindergarten children.

Two studies show clearly that perceptual discrimination can be *trained* and that Negroes benefit particularly from such training. Eagleson (1937) trained his 50 white and 50 Negro subjects, all high-school students, to move a marker into a position that would bisect the length of a bar. After each trial the subject was told how much in error he was and in which direction. Whites were considerably superior in the first trial, but as the experiment progressed the difference constantly diminished. Eagleson concluded, "Since training has been found to decrease the average error, the difference between the two groups for the first setting may be interpreted to mean that the white group had had more experience in this kind of activity than the Negroes at the beginning of the study." One wonders if the same conclusion would not apply with equal cogency to the other perceptual differences we have been outlining.

Boger (1952) shows that perceptual training can influence scores on group intelligence tests. His subjects were Negro and white primary school children, about 50 of each, in small rural Virginia schools. Two group intelligence tests were given in January and the same ones again in May. In the intervening months, half of the children, both white and Negro, were given practice periods with problems involving visual perception, discrimination, and spatial relations. The materials included scrambled comic strips, hidden picture puzzles, designs to be copied, and the like, and gave practice in following directions, noting details, detecting likenesses and differences, and coordinating hand and eye movements. The results showed significant increases in most of the tests for the experimental but not for the control groups, and the Negroes gained more than the whites. While the white children who had had the experimental program still scored higher in May (average IQ 101 on the Language section and 106 on the Nonlanguage section of the California Test), the Negro averages had come up to 84 on the Language section and 98 on the Nonlanguage. Retests the next October showed that gains had been maintained.

The hypothesis of a perceptual handicap originating in the meagerness of early childhood surroundings but perhaps remediable at later age levels if it can be identified is certainly not *established* from data available so far. The most that can be said for it is that it accounts for some research findings not easily explainable in other ways. There may be other deficiencies arising out of early experience also. While the comparisons of subtests we have cited do not suggest that the Negro handicap shows up primarily on verbal tests, there is some evidence pointing to language differences of a more pervasive and subtle sort than those tapped by the questions asked on intelligence tests. Newton (1960) described a syndrome encountered in substandard college freshmen. She called it *verbal destitution.* It consists of:

(a) Frequent inaccuracy in the use of standard English word inflections;
(b) Immature vocabularies composed principally of Anglo-Saxon and Middle-English content and functional words;
(c) Frequent mis-pronunciation of words;
(d) Rate utilization of descriptive or other qualifying terms;
(e) Usage of simple sentences and sentence fragments almost exclusively in discussions;
(f) Almost total inability to understand figurative language.

It is obvious that a defect of this sort, along with the narrow range of concepts Newton reported is likely to accompany it, might completely incapacitate an individual for college work. Newton made some recommendations for overcoming this condition but did not report how successful they were.

With a younger age group in the fourth, fifth, and sixth grades, Carson and Rabin (1960) found that the three groups of children, Northern Whites, Northern Negroes, and Southern Negroes, differed in *level of communication* on the Full Range Picture Vocabulary Test, even when they were matched for verbal comprehension, as indicated by their scores on the test itself. Deutsch (1964) has been making an intensive study of differences in language development associated with race, with socio-economic status, or with both, in an attempt to account for the cumulative deficit or increasing retardation that occurs as Negro children grow older. By measuring many aspects of language, he has identified a complex of deficits similar in many ways to the one Newton noted in college students. It involves syntax as well as word meanings, and communication as well as comprehension. Deutsch has also been interested in particular kinds of differences between Negro and white families, such as the frequent absence of the Negro father, that might influence children's development.

Evidence of the kinds we have been considering leads to an emphasis on *early* education to correct developmental trends likely to prevent full use of subsequent educational opportunities. Deutsch at the Institute for Developmental Studies, New York Medical College, Strodtbeck at the Social Psychology Laboratory, University of Chicago, and Gray and Klaus at the Peabody College for Teachers in Nashville, are among those who have carried out pilot projects on the effects of preschool education. Preliminary results have been encouraging. Gray and Klaus (1963) reported IQ increases of five to ten points in children attending summer nursery schools. Similar gains have been registered in the Chicago and New York studies. It is too early to say what the effects of this experience on the later school achievement of the subjects will be, but this will be analyzed and reported as time passes.

One study is especially suggestive because it seems to indicate that a comparatively small difference in the treatment of Negro children early in their school careers may have a rather large effect. Brazziel and Terrell (1962) set up an experimental group of 26 Negro first-graders using three similar first grades as control groups. The experimental treatment consisted of two full days of registration in which the parents discussed the children with the teacher, while the children became acquainted with the school situation and with one another, and afterward a six-week period of "readiness" training for the children, aimed at the development of perception, vocabulary, word reasoning, and the ability and will to follow directions. Along with this training went six weeks of meetings and conferences with the parents. At the end of the period these children scored at the 50th percentile on the readiness test (just average for their age) as compared with scores at the 16th, 14th, and 13th percentiles in the three control groups. On an intelligence test administered in the spring the average IQ of the experimental group was 106.5, suggesting that their gains had been maintained.

Preschool projects have been undertaken in many parts of the country. Educators are also trying to find out to what extent it is possible to overcome developmental handicaps at a later stage of the individual's school career. More and more, this problem is being conceptualized as the problem of *cultural deprivation* rather than of race differences, a problem growing out of slum living, irregular family structure, a dearth of stimulation, and inadequate opportunity for intellectual growth. The book edited by Passow (1963) makes available a wealth of information about these ideas and programs.

For such projects as for the preschool investigations, more time must pass before decisive results are available. The preliminary report on the New York demonstration guidance program by Wrightstone (1960) indicated that verbal IQ's increased from 95.6 to 102.5 in one junior high school and that there were corresponding gains on academic achievement, conduct, and aspirations. If progress in these educational directions continues, much more information about important practical and theoretical issues should be available to us in the decades to come.

In making practical applications of research findings on race differences, we must always remember one all-important fact: A difference between *averages* tells us nothing about what to expect of any given *individual* in either group. IQ's of white children range all the way from a hypothetical zero to a very occasional 200. The same can be said for Negro children. M. D. Jenkins (1948) summarized studies of gifted Negro children documenting the fact that IQ's as high as 200 have been found among Negro children in the public schools. It is important for such individuals themselves and for society that their exceptional abilities be developed and used for the good of all.

One of the minor problems taken up in many of the studies of race differences is the relationship between intelligence-test scores and amount of white blood. In most investigations, Negroid characteristics such as skin color, width of lips, or width of nostrils have been used as criteria of mixed ancestry. The Ferguson study already cited, using a subjective classification based largely on skin color, reported that the larger the proportion of white blood, the higher the score on the analogies and the completion tests. Peterson and Lanier obtained positive relationships between intelligence-test scores and lightness of skin in their Nashville group, but found no relationship between test scores and Negroid characteristics in their New York group. Klineberg found no relationship between skin color and other Negroid characteristics and either intelligence or length of residence in New York. Tanser, classifying his subjects on the basis of information supplied by Kent County residents, found that the mixed bloods did somewhat better on the National Intelligence Test than did the full bloods and that the larger the proportion of estimated white blood, the higher was the score. It is probably best, however, to draw no conclusion with regard to this problem. Just what mixture of genes has determined the racial characteristics of any present-day American Negro, is, as we have said, an unanswerable question. Herskovits (1928) has shown that in selected groups of Howard University students whose ancestry is quite definitely known, the variability of any one of the racial traits commonly used as criteria is so great as to render it a very unreliable indicator of degree of mixture. He has also shown that within the Negro group, a process of *social* selection on the basis of skin color has occurred. To the extent that groups of higher social level have greater educational and cultural advantages, some correlation between skin color and test score might occur entirely apart from racial factors. There is certainly no evidence for the opinion held by many people that hybrids are *less* able than persons of pure race. But there is also no clear conclusive evidence that mixed bloods are more intelligent than pure Negroes.

NEGRO-WHITE PERSONALITY DIFFERENCES

One might expect that the central position of problems of race relations in American society would have generated a large amount of research on race differences in personality and temperament. But this has not been the case. There are stereotypes and popular conceptions of Negro traits, but almost no dependable evidence. In his introduction to the number of the *Journal of Social Issues* in which some approaches to the study of Negro-American personality were presented, Pettigrew (1964) explained some of the reasons. The methodological problems that arise in this field are even more difficult than they are in research on race differences in abilities. Added to the ambiguities and inadequacies characterizing all the personality "tests" and assessment techniques in common use—deficiencies discussed in some detail in a previous chapter—are the special motivational problems arising out of the attitude a Negro subject may have to a white interviewer or examiner (or even to a Negro interviewer if highly personal questions are asked). There is also the further difficulty of getting really comparable groups to work with. Pettigrew commented on our lack of an adequate social psychological theory of Negro personality from which meaningful hypotheses might be drawn.

The few studies in which personality tests of the general adjustment variety have been administered to white and Negro groups have shown Negroes on the whole to be more maladjusted. Because these studies suffer from all the methodological shortcomings noted above, it is not possible to draw any conclusions from them. More objective evidence pointing in the same direction is the significantly higher rate of hospitalization among Negroes than among whites for almost all the major mental disorders (Frumkin, 1954). But this may be a socio-economic rather than a race difference. The differential susceptibility to mental illness in different social classes will be discussed in the next chapter.

There have been a few scattered comparisons of vocational interests (Strong, 1952, 1955b). In general, comparable groups of Negro and white professional men seem to be much more alike than different, and it is not clear what such differences as have shown up mean.

There has been one ambitious study of Negro personality (Karon, 1958). The subjects were drawn from a nationwide Gallup poll sample used in standardizing the Tomkins-Horn Picture Arrangement Test. By making two kinds of group comparison on the many personality variables for which this same objective-projective test can be scored, a comparison between Northern whites and Southern Negroes and a comparison between Northern Negroes and Southern Negroes, the investigator tried not only to identify differences between the racial groups one would expect to differ most markedly but also to draw conclusions about the extent to which "caste sanctions" had produced these differences. His reasoning was that if the Northern Negroes made "better" scores than the Southern Negroes on the same variables as Northern whites did, such differences could be attributed to the caste sanctions prevailing in the South rather than to genetic factors. The results turned out to be in this direction. Both the Negro-white differences and the North-South differences were most marked on variables having to do with the expression and control of aggression. This kind of difference is what would have been predicted from reports of psychotherapists on the special personality difficulties of Negro patients (Kardiner and Ovesey, 1951). Negroes, especially those living in the South, respond to questions on personality tests as they respond to the free interview situation in therapy, by denying aggressive motivation of all kinds, to "choke back anger," as Karon puts it. There were a few other less striking differences that could be seen as an outgrowth of this one. Karon has been criticized for generalizing his conclusions further than the data warrant. (The title of the book *The Negro Personality* is overly broad as a label for the results reported.) However, it is perhaps worth noting that even with more representative samples than are usually obtained, no personality differences emerge that cannot be readily explained by the social conditions under which Negroes live. The case for basic temperamental differences based on race still has no evidence to support it.

RESEARCH ON THE AMERICAN INDIAN

A number of studies have reported the scores of Indian children on intelligence tests. Pintner (1931), summarizing available research up to about 1930, reported IQ's ranging from 69 to 97. Since these were based on different tests, the only general statement that was warranted is that Indians as a group average considerably lower than whites on standard intelligence tests. There is another significant fact, however, which came out especially in the study by Jamieson and Sandiford (1928). Although their 717 Indian subjects could all speak English, and some of them came from homes where only English was spoken, they obtained very much better scores on nonverbal than on verbal tests of intelligence. Average IQ's on the two verbal tests used, the Pintner-Cunningham and the National Intelligence Test, were 78 and 80. On the Pintner-Paterson Performance Scale and the Pintner Nonlanguage Test the average IQ's were 92 and 97, differing very little from the 100 which is average for white children. Differences in cultural factors as well as language would seem to be reflected here.

Such an interpretation received further support from the study by Dennis (1942) on Hopi children. The test he used was the Goodenough Draw-a-Man Test. For young children in our culture, scores on this test have a rather close relationship to scores on the standard Stanford-Binet intelligence tests. Dennis's subjects, 152 Hopi children ranging in age from six to ten, obtained an average IQ of 108.3—several points *higher* than the white children's average. He attributed this superior showing to special practice, arising from the attention given the human figure in Hopi decorative arts. The fact that it was the boys, not the girls, whose scores were outstanding, fits in with this interpretation, since the boys are the ones who from early childhood are trained in the arts for which the tribe is famous. Havighurst, Gunther, and Pratt (1946) also showed that several groups of Indian children averaged higher than whites on the drawing test, and that Indian boys tended to do better than Indian girls. It may be that this test is for such groups more of an *achievement* test, showing what has been *learned* about drawing the human figure, and less of an intelligence test than it is in our culture.

Studies of the Indian like those by Tanser and Bruce of the Negro, equating economic and educational advantages for the two races, have not been made. Therefore, it is impossible to make any definite statement as to the source of average differences. It can be said with considerable certainty that Indian averages are considerably below white averages on tests involving a high degree of abstraction and the understanding of verbal concepts. In tests involving reasoning *in terms of concrete materials* and manipulation of spatial relationships, there is some evidence that the two races do not differ. In making use of these findings, we should remember that it is the abstract, verbal test materials that afford us our best prediction of school success, so that we should expect Indians as a group to be less well adapted than whites to the kind of school work customary in our civilization. We should also keep in mind as always the variability of the two distributions, so that we do not place too much stress on averages. Some individual Indians are far above the white averages on all sorts of intelligence tests; some individual whites have scores as low as those of the lowest Indians.

RESEARCH ON CHINESE AND JAPANESE

In contrast with the findings for Negroes and for Indians, investigations of Chinese and Japanese intelligence have shown them to be little below the white averages, in spite of language handicaps. Pintner (1931) in summing up available studies, reported IQ's on Binet tests running from 85 to 98, with all work on nonlanguage tests showing that Orientals were equal to or above the American norms. Since there was no study in which economic level, educational advantages, and selective factors had been controlled, these findings may indicate only that the culture from which Japanese and Chinese school children come is intellectually more closely related to our own than the Negro and Indian cultures are. The fact that Oriental children can be expected to do about as well as American children in school work is the principal practical conclusion which is justified. Again the factor of variability should be kept in mind. Chinese and Japanese individuals vary all the way from idiot to genius.

RESEARCH ON NATIONALITY DIFFERENCES

During the 1920's, after the Army test results had been published, there was a flurry of research on the comparative intellectual level of the various nationalities whose people had been immigrating to this country in large numbers. Army data, as analyzed by Brigham (1923), ranked the nationalities in order ranging from North Europeans who were highest to South Europeans at the bottom. The two groups at the top, English and Scottish, were nationalities for whom English is the native language. Various people have reported similar findings for children of foreign-born parents in American schools. A good summary of this work is to be found in Pintner (1931, pp. 459–462). In most of these investigations Jewish, English, and Scotch have ranked somewhat above American norms, Irish, Germans, and Scandinavians have been about average, and South Europeans and Mexicans have been below American norms. Goodenough (1926) published results from 2,457 public-school children who were given the drawing test described above. Since this test is completely nonverbal, the factor of whether or not English had been spoken in the child's home would not be expected to affect the scores, although, as the studies of Indians have subsequently shown, other environmental factors may. The general hierarchy was similar to that in the other studies—Jewish at the top, English and Scotch about average, Mexicans, Indians, and Negroes at the bottom.

The tendency of Jewish groups, from whatever European country they originated, to score at or above the American average has been apparent in all the studies of nationality differences. Since they would have the same language handicap as other groups growing up in foreign-speaking homes, this is a significant fact. Brill (1936), summarizing available studies up to 1936, criticized them all on the basis that neither socio-economic level nor language handicap had been controlled. What evidence there is, however, seems to warrant the conclusions that Jewish children in Great Britain and the United States are at least equal to non-Jewish children of similar socio-economic status, and that they are superior to most other foreign-born groups. Perhaps one reason for this superiority is the motivation arising from the emphasis on intellect in Jewish culture.

There has been little research interest since the 1930's in comparing scores made by different nationality groups on intelligence tests. It was apparent by that time that there were so many uncontrolled variables in such studies that no valid conclusions could possibly be drawn from them. Brigham, who in 1923 proposed the theory that Nordic, Alpine, and Mediterranean "races" differed in intelligence, basing his conclusion on the World War I army results, publicly abandoned this theory in 1930 when psychometric research had demonstrated the unsoundness of the assumption that all the tests used in the military program were measuring the same trait. Klineberg (1931) found no evidence for a Nordic-Alpine-Mediterranean hierarchy when he gave a performance test to children from a large number of villages in different parts of Europe on their home ground.

It was concluded that the reason immigrants from the North of Europe had averaged higher than immigrants from the South of Europe was that they constituted different samples of the parent population. A study by Franzblau (1935) produced some direct evidence for this conclusion. The subjects were approximately 300 school girls in each of four groups, Danes in Denmark, Italians in Italy, Danish-Americans, and Italian-Americans. Socio-economic levels for the four groups were equated as well as possible. A nonlanguage test was used, the International Intelligence Test. There was no statistical evidence that the Danes and the Italians in Europe differed at all, although the Danish-Americans received significantly higher scores than the Italian-Americans.

One other study bearing on both race and nationality differences is worth mentioning. S. Smith (1942) tested the public-school population of Honolulu with ages between ten and fifteen in 1924, and again in 1938. Three kinds of test were used: nonverbal, spoken English and printed English. The interesting fact is that differences between pairs of racial groups were highly significant both in 1924 and 1938 and that the rank order of the races was about the same on the two occasions. (For convenience, *race* is used in this report to include some groups better classified as nationalities.) High-scoring races both times were the Korean, Chinese, Japanese, and white. Low-scoring races were the Portuguese, Hawaiian, and Puerto Rican. The effect of the educational system that had been in effect during the fourteen-year interval had been to raise the averages for *all* these groups but *not* to reduce the differences between them. In fact, groups scoring high in 1924 showed more improvement than did groups scoring low. This study tells us no more about the intelligence of the population in the countries from which these groups originally came than the others that have been cited, since selective factors are unknown and probably unknowable. But it does strongly suggest that, whatever their source, we cannot expect differences between groups in the population to be completely eradicated by improving the education of all.

Cross-cultural research exploring differences between national groups in attitudes, beliefs, interests, values, and other personal characteristics has continued, but it is usually considered to fall within the domain of social rather than differential psychology. Perhaps eventually, as we abandon the assumption that pure "native" intelligence and talent is measurable, most of the results reported in this chapter will be thought of as data bearing on the important general problem of how culture influences individual development. There is much to be learned here.

SUMMARY

Research on psychological differences between races is extraordinarily difficult. Added to the problems of classifying individuals correctly are problems of selecting measuring instruments equally fair to all groups and allowing for the differences in environmental influence that race prejudice has created. Psychologists have in many cases short-circuited these problems simply by ignoring them. Consequently, what we often have are data on groups classified according to current social custom based on tests that may or may not be suitable.

Under these circumstances, average scores made by Negro groups on intelligence tests are consistently and significantly lower than those made by white groups in the same places. The fact that Northern Negroes score significantly higher than those in the South, and that averages increase with attendance at Northern schools, shows that deficiencies in education are involved, at least to some extent. The effect on mental development of restricted educational and cultural surroundings in early childhood has not yet been satisfactorily analyzed, but it has become an active research area, and preliminary results suggest that enrichment at the preschool level may bring about striking changes in developmental trends.

There is no evidence of personality differences between Negroes and whites that cannot be accounted for in terms of social structure in the United States.

Indians also score considerably below the white norm in both verbal intelligence and school achievement tests. There is evidence, however, that some groups of them are about as high as whites on nonverbal tests, and may score even higher on types of performance in line with their special training and experience. Chinese and Japanese groups usually score near the white norms.

Among immigrants to this country and their children, mental-testers in various places have found that a hierarchy exists, with Jews, Scandinavians, Germans, and English-speaking groups at the top, and South Europeans of all nationalities at the bottom. Two studies done in Europe have served to discredit the hypothesis that this constitutes a Nordic-Alpine-Mediterranean racial hierarchy and to explain the findings in terms of selective factors that brought persons from different strata of the European population to the United States. Interest in this research problem has declined since the 1930's.

CHAPTER 13

Social Class Differences

THE CLASS STRUCTURE OF AMERICAN SOCIETY

During the 1940's a series of research reports made Americans aware of the fact that they lived in a class society. It came to the unaware as something of a blow, as unwelcome and rather shocking news. True, novelists had often written about persons who encountered family opposition because they wished to marry outside their own circle, and high-school students had been known to complain that cliques dominated the social life of their school etc. But these were not thought to be the standard or prevailing state of things in America, the land of opportunity where by tradition every man willing to work hard and save could make a fortune, and anyone who really aspired to lead could win political prominence.

What the social scientists who presented these reports had done was to proceed in the same manner as anthropologists who study primitive societies. They went to live in the communities they proposed to analyze. After making friends with as many people as possible so that people trusted him and felt free to talk to him, the investigator interviewed a great many individuals of all ages and used the information they gave him as a basis for his analysis of the social structure around him. Large-scale research of this sort was carried on by Warner and Lunt in a New England community which they called *Yankee City* (1941); by Davis, Gardner, and Gardner in a southern community which they labeled *Old-town* (1941); and by Warner, Havighurst, and Loeb, in a midwestern community which they christened *Midwest* (1944). The Lynds' work on *Middletown* (1929, 1937) and West's *Plainville, U.S.A.* (1945) contributed information from other sections of the Midwest. The criteria these investigators used in determining what class an individual belonged to and what classes his community contained were those that revealed unequivocally which people were accustomed to associate freely with one another. The social clique was the basic unit. People were considered to be of the same class if they normally (a) ate or drank together as a social ritual, (b) freely visited one another's families, (c) talked together intimately in a social clique, or (d) married into each other's families. All these investigators were impressed with the high degree of agreement that all informants showed as to just where any given individual belonged in the social hierarchy.

In the Eastern cities, Yankee City and Oldtown, six distinct classes could be differentiated: upper-upper, lower-upper, upper-middle, lower-middle, upper-lower, and lower-lower. The two upper classes contained only a small fraction of the population, but they occupied the most influential positions, received the largest incomes, and lived in the "best" parts of town. The distinction between them was based on family. A person was considered to be in the upper-upper class only if, in addition to having wealth and position, he also belonged to one of the old established families. In the communities of the Midwest and Far West studied so far, the distinction between the two upper classes is typically nonexistent or unimportant, so that the number of classes reduces to five (and often to four). The upper middle class is made up of business and professional men who are leading citizens in community activities but lack wealth and social prestige. The lower middle class persons are predominantly minor clerical or retail workers who live in smaller homes nearer the "wrong" part of town. The distinction between "upper-lower" and "lower-lower" is based largely on moral considerations. "Upper-lowers," though poor, are honest and ambitious. "Lower-lowers" are considered shiftless, dirty, and disorderly.

Classifying the population in this way produces a very skewed distribution with the mode much nearer the lower than the upper end. In the study by Havighurst and Janke (1944) the proportions by class were as follows:

A Wealthy families (2 per cent of population) upper class
B Professional men, officials, and leading business men (6 per cent of population) upper-middle class
C Small business men, lesser professional workers, some skilled workers, white-collar workers (37 per cent of population) lower-middle class
D Semi-skilled workers and laborers, hard-working and respectable people (43 per cent of population) upper-lower class
E Lowest occupational groups with poor reputation in the community (12 per cent of population) lower-lower class

In a later report on another Midwestern city, called River City for research purposes, Havighurst, et al. (1962) reported the following proportions:

	Male	*Female*
A. Upper and upper middle	9 per cent	9 per cent
B. Lower-middle	26 per cent	27 per cent
C. Upper-lower	37 per cent	40 per cent
D. Lower-lower	28 per cent	24 per cent

One must keep this skewness in mind as he considers all kinds of reported class differences. Even if there were several times as high a *proportion* of talented persons in the upper-middle class as there were in the upper-lower class, for example, the absolute *number* of talented individuals would be higher among the upper-lower than the upper-middle class. At a time when talents are in demand, a society cannot afford to ignore the large reservoir of potential ability in its lower classes.

The task of analyzing the class structure of any community has been facilitated through the publication by Warner, Meeker, and Eells (1949) of the monograph *Social Class in America,* which describes in detail two methods that can be used to make such an analysis. The first, which they call *Evaluated Participation,* requires that a number of persons in the community be interviewed. What these informants say about other individuals, the categories in which they place them, the designations they use for these categories (such as "upper crust" or "poor whites"), the nature of the institutions with which they are identified, and several other kinds of information are used. The second, and much simpler, method gives what they call an *Index of Status Characteristics.* It was found that an excellent prediction of the class positions of individuals in a group could be made by assessing four characteristics and giving them approximate weights. The four were: (1) Occupation, (2) Source of income (inherited wealth, salaries, welfare, etc.), (3) House type, and (4) Dwelling area. The correlation between the *Evaluated Participation* and the *Status Characteristics* indices was .97. The *Index of Status Characteristics,* usually abbreviated *ISC,* has been used in many research studies to quantify the social status variable.

Occupation, by itself, is a reasonably good index of class position. Long before the analyses of whole communities to which we have referred, psychologists were using this way of evaluating what they called *socioeconomic status.* The results of these studies generally agree with those in which a more comprehensive analysis of class position has been made. We will consider them together in the various sections of this chapter.

Social class is primarily a sociological concept, and sociologists have explored in some detail its relationships to income, school attendance and adjustment, membership in organizations of many kinds, leisure activities, church affiliation, health and disease, methods of child-rearing, and political power. Nosow (1962) has given us a convenient summary of the empirical findings. In this chapter we shall examine only those parts of the general field of research which have been cultivated mainly by psychologists or are of particular interest to them. But we must keep in mind that the study of social class phenomena is an interdisciplinary undertaking and anthropologists, educators, economists, and political scientists, as well as sociologists and psychologists, are involved in it.

DIFFERENCES IN MENTAL ABILITIES

From the early days of the intelligence-testing movement to the present, one investigator after another has reported consistent differences between the average IQ's of groups at different socio-economic levels. When the more precise ways of dividing subjects into social classes became available, children from these classes were compared. Some of the most detailed information came from the *Midwest* project (Havighurst and Janke, 1944; Janke and Havighurst, 1945). What the investigators did was to select batteries of tests to be given to ten-year-olds and sixteen-year-olds in the city. The battery for ten-year-olds included the Stanford-Binet, the Cornell Coxe (a nonverbal test of intelligence), the Iowa Silent Reading, the Minnesota Paper Form Board (measuring judgment of spatial relationships), an adaptation of the Minnesota Mechanical Assembly Test for boys and a new mechanical-assembly test of their own devising for girls, the Porteus Mazes, and the Goodenough Drawing Test. For sixteen-year-olds the battery included the Stanford-Binet, the performance tests from the Wechsler-Bellevue Scale, the Iowa Silent Reading, the Minnesota Paper Form Board, and the two assembly tests. The aim was to include both verbal and nonverbal tests of intelligence along with tests of the more specialized reading and mechanical aptitudes. There were no children from the upper or upper-middle classes in the ten-year-old group. For the sixteen-year-olds, these two classes were combined to give nine cases altogether. One of the good features of the study was that practically the entire population of ten-year-olds was included, and evidence was given that the 29 sixteen-year-olds who had to be left out because of inaccessibility or failure to cooperate did not differ to any extent in IQ from the rest. Thus the effects of unknown selective factors are not distorting the results. Tables 30 and 31 show the means on the tests for the various social status groups.

The authors gave also the standard deviation and total range of scores for each group. Statistical tests showed that differences between the two lowest groups were the most significant for the ten-year-olds. It is to be noted that these differences showed up on *all* tests except the paper-form board and the mechanical-assembly test for boys. Among the sixteen-year-olds the differences between the A-B group and the others were the most significant. Again they showed up consistently on *all* tests except the mechanical assembly for boys. Contrary to an opinion that has often been

TABLE 30
Means of Social Status Groups on Psychological Tests—Ten-Year-Old Children

(Havighurst and Janke, 1944)

Social Status	N	Stanford-Binet	Cornell Coxe	Goodenough	Iowa Silent Reading	Paper Form Board	Mech. Assem.	Mech. Assem.	Porteus Maze
							T-Score		*Mental Age*
		IQ	*IQ*	*IQ*	*Score*	*Score*	*Boys*	*Girls*	
C	26	114	116	107	99	22.5	52.5	56.0	12.7
D	68	110	110	102	99	21.3	49.2	49.5	12.8
E	16	91	96	91	88	15.7	46.9	41.3	10.4

TABLE 31
Means of Social Status Groups on Psychological Tests—Sixteen-Year-Old Children

(Janke and Havighurst, 1945)

Social Status	N	Stanford-Binet	Wechsler Bellevue	Iowa Silent Reading	Paper Form Board	Mech. Assem.	Mech. Assem.
						Boys	*Girls*
A B	9	128	118	58.0	44	46.8	62.1
C	44	112	109	51.0	40	51.6	52.0
D	49	104	102	48.9	31	48.8	48.5
E	13	98	103	45.6	31	53.0	45.9

stated, the class differences were *not* more marked on verbal than on non-verbal tests. Since scores on the Minnesota Mechanical Assembly Test have been shown to depend partly on familiarity with the items, it seems likely that this factor explains why differences on it alone are not significant. Lower-status children may actually have a greater opportunity to try tasks of this kind.

Havighurst and Janke also analyzed differences between boys and girls, and between urban and rural children. The sex differences were very slight and not statistically significant. There was a consistent tendency for urban children to do better than rural on intelligence and reading tests, but most of the differences were not large enough to be clearly significant, with this number of cases. It is the class differences that emerge as the most clear-cut findings. Even here, not too much weight can be placed on one study, especially when it includes only a small number of cases.

A later study in the same community by Schulman and Havighurst (1947) reported similar results for vocabulary. Using a test that enables one to estimate the total vocabulary of the person who takes it, they found that differences between Classes B, C, D, and E were again significant at the 5 per cent level. The average estimated vocabulary for Class B subjects was 45,600 words as against 28,800 for Class E subjects. Again the differences between boys and girls and between urban and rural subjects were not significant.

In the River City study (Havighurst, et al., 1962) the relationship of intelligence to social class was reported in a slightly different way. The scores on a composite measure, obtained by averaging standard scores on several tests, were divided into four quartiles. The proportion of the members of each class falling into each of these four divisions was then determined. The results are shown in Table 32. It is clear that here also there is a sizable relationship between the two variables. It amounts to a correlation of .34 for boys and .28 for girls.

TABLE 32

Percentage of Each Social Class in River City in Each Intelligence Quartile (Tests given in sixth grade.)

(Havighurst, *et al.*, 1962)

INTELLIGENCE QUARTILE	SOCIAL CLASS A	B	C	D
	Male			
IV (High)	33%	26%	16%	11%
III	48	27	28	16
II	19	31	26	32
I (Low)	0	16	30	41
Number of Cases	22	62	91	62
	Female			
IV	62%	44%	19%	7%
III	14	25	28	20
II	5	20	30	40
I	19	11	23	33
Number of Cases	21	64	94	58

Another study based on adults rather than young people showed similar results. Schaie (1958a), in the course of his investigation of age differences, to which reference has been made in a previous chapter, compared groups of men equated for age (average 45.5) but differing in occupational level. The four socio-economic groups were skilled labor, clerical and sales, managerial and proprietary, and professional and semiprofessional. The test used was the Primary Mental Abilities battery. The results clearly indicated a difference between occupational groups in general intellectual level. Differences in the shapes of the profiles of special abilities for the different groups were not significant. The superiority of upper over lower groups was most marked on the Verbal-meaning, Reasoning, and Word-fluency subtests.

The relationship of measured intelligence to socio-economic level is one of the best documented findings in mental-test history. From the time when Decroly and Degand (1910) first called attention to the fact that children in more favored economic groups made scores higher than Binet's norms, one investigator after another has called attention to the differentiation of test scores by occupation. When the army psychologists tested large groups of men in World War I, they were impressed with the hierarchy of average scores running from professional men at the top to day laborers at the bottom. Figure 44 shows the trend.

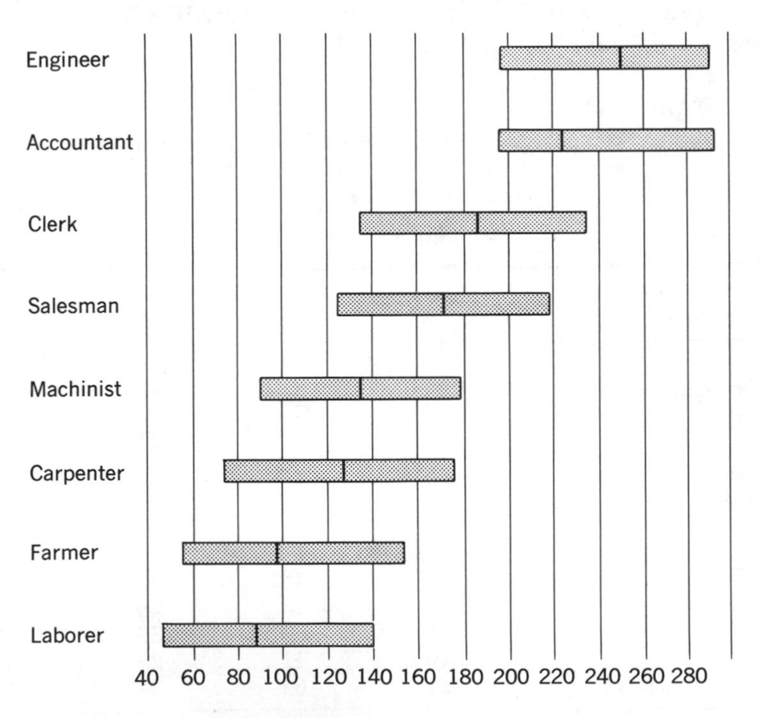

FIGURE 44

Scores on Army Alpha Obtained by Soldiers in World War I Who Reported Various Preservice Occupations

(Yerkes, 1921)

Similar findings for World War II, based on the scores of 18,782 white enlisted men of the Army Air Forces Air Service Command, were reported by Harrell and Harrell (1945). Table 33 shows these results. A more detailed analysis of the AGCT scores of over 80,000 white enlisted men in the Army, a representative sample made up of about 2 per cent of the total at the time, was published by Stewart (1947). It revealed the same hierarchy.

The trends were the same in the figures from both armies. The average score for men in the professions was at least one standard deviation unit above the mean. (In the AGCT test, the mean was 100 and the standard deviation 20.) Office workers and business men averaged from one-half to one standard deviation above the mean. People in the skilled trades showed averages about at the mean. Semiskilled workers were slightly below the mean, unskilled workers definitely below. In studying these figures, however, one must not forget the factor of individual differences within each group. The teamsters, the group with the lowest average in Table 33, had at least one man with a score of 145, far above the professional average. In general, the standard deviations showed a greater variability in the groups at the *bottom* of the scale than among those at the top. Educational requirements for professional and white-collar positions may account for this fact. It is not likely that a moron will ever be able to qualify as an engineer, lawyer, or accountant. However, it is quite possible for a brilliant man to be working as a truckdriver, lumberjack, or miner. Another interesting fact can be noted if we examine the scores representing the bottom of the range in the last column of Table 33. The variation in *low* scores for occupations was much greater than in average or high ones. This was true for occupations at the top of the hierarchy as well as those at the bottom. Table 33 shows, for example, that it was possible for a man to be a teacher, draftsman, or pharmacist even if his intelligence score was about one and one-half standard deviation units below the mean. (The low score for teachers was 76.) No engineer or chemist scored below 100. Evidently some jobs have a definite lower limit whereas others do not.

Simon and Levitt (1950) published some figures showing the same sort of hierarchy for the Wechsler-Bellevue Test, although the fact that their 8,000 subjects were not selected to constitute a representative sample of the employed population keeps us from putting too much confidence in the occupational averages themselves. Foulds and Raven (1948a) demonstrated the same differentiation between occupational levels in Scotland. Here the men were all employees of the same company, a plant manufacturing photographic equipment. The most important extra information we get from both these studies is that occupational differences in intellectual level are not confined to one sort of test material. They occur on both verbal and performance tests, both vocabulary and non-verbal rea-

TABLE 33

Mean GCT Standard Scores, Standard Deviations, and Range of Scores of 18,782 AAF White Enlisted Men by Civilian Occupation

(Harrell and Harrell, 1945)

OCCUPATION	N	M	MEDIAN	STANDARD DEVIATION	RANGE
Accountant	172	128.1	128.1	11.7	94-157
Lawyer	94	127.6	126.8	10.9	96-157
Engineer	39	126.6	125.8	11.7	100-151
Public-Relations Man	42	126.0	125.5	11.4	100-149
Auditor	62	125.9	125.5	11.2	98-151
Chemist	21	124.8	124.5	13.8	102-153
Reporter	45	124.5	125.7	11.7	100-157
Chief Clerk	165	124.2	124.5	11.7	88-153
Teacher	256	122.8	123.7	12.8	76-155
Draftsman	153	122.0	121.7	12.8	74-155
Stenographer	147	121.0	121.4	12.5	66-151
Pharmacist	58	120.5	124.0	15.2	76-149
Tabulating-Machine Operator	140	120.1	119.8	13.3	80-151
Bookkeeper	272	120.0	119.7	13.1	70-157
Manager Sales	42	119.0	120.7	11.5	90-137
Purchasing Agent	98	118.7	119.2	12.9	82-153
Manager, Production	34	118.1	117.0	16.0	82-153
Photographer	95	117.6	119.8	13.9	66-147
Clerk, General	496	117.5	117.9	13.0	68-155
Clerk-Typist	468	116.8	117.3	12.0	80-147
Manager, Miscellaneous	235	116.0	117.5	14.8	60-151
Installer-Repairman, Tel. & Tel.	96	115.8	116.8	13.1	76-149
Cashier	111	115.8	116.8	11.9	80-145
Instrument Repairman	47	115.5	115.8	11.9	82-141
Radio Repairman	267	115.3	116.5	14.5	56-151
Printer, Job Pressman, Lithographic Pressman	132	115.1	116.7	14.3	60-149
Salesman	494	115.1	116.2	15.7	60-153
Artist	48	114.9	115.4	11.2	82-139
Manager, Retail Store	420	114.0	116.2	15.7	52-151
Laboratory Assistant	128	113.4	114.0	14.6	76-147
Tool-Maker	60	112.5	111.6	12.5	76-143
Inspector	358	112.3	113.1	15.7	54-147
Stock Clerk	490	111.8	113.0	16.3	54-151
Receiving and Shipping Clerk	486	111.3	113.4	16.4	58-155
Musician	157	110.9	112.8	15.9	56-147
Machinist	456	110.1	110.8	16.1	38-153
Foreman	298	109.8	111.4	16.7	60-151
Watchmaker	56	109.8	113.0	14.7	68-147
Airplane Mechanic	235	109.3	110.5	14.9	66-147
Sales Clerk	492	109.2	110.4	16.3	42-149
Electrician	289	109.0	110.6	15.2	64-149
Lathe Operator	172	108.5	109.4	15.5	64-147
Receiving & Shipping Checker	281	107.6	108.9	15.8	52-151
Sheet Metal Worker	498	107.5	108.1	15.3	62-153

TABLE 33—(Continued).

OCCUPATION	N	M	MEDIAN	STANDARD DEVIATION	RANGE
Lineman, Power and Tel. & Tel.	77	107.1	108.8	15.5	70-133
Assembler	498	106.3	106.6	14.6	48-145
Mechanic	421	106.3	108.3	16.0	60-155
Machine-Operator	486	104.8	105.7	17.1	42-151
Auto Serviceman	539	104.2	105.9	16.7	30-141
Riveter	239	104.1	105.3	15.1	50-141
Cabinetmaker	48	103.5	104.7	15.9	66-127
Upholsterer	59	103.3	105.8	14.5	68-131
Butcher	259	102.9	104.8	17.1	42-147
Plumber	128	102.7	104.8	16.0	56-139
Bartender	98	102.2	105.0	16.6	56-137
Carpenter, Construction	451	102.1	104.1	19.5	42-147
Pipe-Fitter	72	101.9	105.2	18.0	56-139
Welder	493	101.8	103.7	16.1	48-147
Auto Mechanic	466	101.3	101.8	17.0	48-151
Molder	79	101.1	105.5	20.2	48-137
Chauffeur	194	100.8	103.0	18.4	46-143
Tractor Driver	354	99.5	101.6	19.1	42-147
Painter, General	440	98.3	100.1	18.7	38-147
Crane-Hoist Operator	99	97.9	99.1	16.6	58-147
Cook and Baker	436	97.2	99.5	20.8	20-147
Weaver	56	97.0	97.3	17.7	50-135
Truck Driver	817	96.2	97.8	19.7	16-149
Laborer	856	95.8	97.7	20.1	26-145
Barber	103	95.3	98.1	20.5	42-141
Lumberjack	59	94.7	96.5	19.8	46-137
Farmer	700	92.7	93.4	21.8	24-147
Farmhand	817	91.4	94.0	20.7	24-141
Miner	156	90.6	92.0	20.1	42-139
Teamster	77	87.7	89.0	19.6	46-145

soning. This result agrees with Schaie's finding that level, rather than pattern, of abilities is the differentiating factor.

When children are classified on the basis of their fathers' occupations, the same sort of differentiation is apparent. There have been dozens of reports emphasizing this finding, and their unanimity makes it unnecessary to point them out individually. Typical figures are those cited by McNemar (1942) from the data collected in the standardization of the Terman and Merrill revision of the Binet Test. Special efforts were made to insure that this sample would be representative of the total white population of the United States. Table 34 gives IQ's for children classified according to their fathers' occupations.

Children of professional men averaged highest, children of farmers and day laborers lowest, and the others somewhere in between. There was, of course, much overlapping between adjacent groups. However, the author pointed out that only about 10 per cent of the day laborers' children exceeded the mean for the professional men's children, and only about 10 per cent of the professional group fell below the general average. Stupid children can be and are born to parents of all levels, but they are much *less common* in those of higher economic status. Similarly, unskilled parents may have unusually bright children, but not many of them do. Terman and Merrill also brought out the fact that the difference was as marked among the youngest age group, those from two to five and a half, as it was among the oldest, fifteen to eighteen. They considered this important because in the case of the younger ones the environmental differences had had a much shorter time to influence the scores. However, recent emphasis on the special significance of *early* experience makes this a less convincing argument against an environmental interpretation of the differences than it seemed at the time this work was done. A thorough survey of a large number of studies, all showing the same trend, was published by Loevinger (1940).

A useful synthesis of five large-scale studies of intelligence and occupational level was made by D. M. Johnson (1948). He made the figures for different tests comparable by using their means and standard deviations to put all the distributions onto the same scale as the Stanford-Binet. Treated in this manner, the averages from the different studies in this country and Great Britain show a remarkable amount of agreement, as indicated in Table 35. The largest discrepancies are at the highest level. It might well be that Cattell's group was more highly selected than the American samples. It would be expected that the averages for the children of professional parents would fall somewhat below the averages for the parents themselves, because of regression toward the mean. Aside from these readily explained irregularities, the table gives a clear picture of the occupational hierarchy. We must remember, however, that these are *average* figures. The variability within each group cannot be ignored.

TABLE 34

Mean IQ's of Children According to Fathers' Occupations

(McNemar, 1942)

FATHERS' OCCUPATIONAL CLASSIFICATION	CHRONOLOGICAL AGES 2-5½	6-9	10-14	15-18
I Professional	114.8	114.9	117.5	116.4
II Semi-professional and Managerial	112.4	107.3	112.2	116.7
III Clerical, Skilled Trades, and Retail Business	108.0	104.9	107.4	109.6
IV Rural Owners	97.8	94.6	92.4	94.3
V Semi-skilled, Minor Clerical and Business	104.3	104.6	103.4	106.7
VI Slightly Skilled	97.2	100.0	100.6	96.2
VII Day Labor, Urban and Rural	93.8	96.0	97.2	97.6

TABLE 35

Estimated Average IQ's for Different Occupational Levels

(Johnson, 1948)

	Children			*Adults*	
STUDY CLASS	TERMAN-MERRILL	DUFF AND THOMPSON	ARMY ALPHA	CATTELL	AGCT
I Professional	116	115	123	132	120
II Semi-professional Managerial	112	113	119	117	113
III Clerical, Skilled Trades, Retail	107	106	108	109	108
IV Rural Owners, Farmers	95	97	97	–	94
V Semi-skilled, Minor Clerical	105	102	101	105	104
VI Slightly Skilled	98	97	98	–	96
VII Day Laborers	96	95	96	–	95

When scales are used to measure socio-economic status, the relationship to intelligence can be expressed in correlational terms. We have already referred to one such scale, the *Index of Status Characteristics*. There are many others, some based primarily on occupation, and some on the amount and kinds of furniture and equipment the home contains. One, developed by Gough (1948a and b, 1949b) is made up of personality items known to correlate with status, such as literary-aesthetic attitudes, social poise, and freedom from positive, dogmatic opinions. Correlations between socio-economic status, as measured by such scales, and intelligence, as measured by any of our common tests, usually turn out to be about .30.

It is an interesting fact that when subjects are asked to rank occupational titles on the basis of prestige, these rankings tend to follow the pattern of the intelligence differences. People of many sorts, at different places and times, *agree* remarkably well on these prestige ratings. Deeg and Paterson (1947) in 1946 asked for rankings of twenty-five occupations from four groups of subjects: (1) college freshmen and sophomores, (2) college juniors, seniors, and graduate students in a vocational psychology class; (3) seniors in an academic high school. The occupations on the list had been used by Counts (1925) in 1925 for a similar study. Table 36 shows the prestige rankings given in the two studies separated, as they were, by an interval of over twenty years.

TABLE 36

Comparison of Social Status of Twenty-five Occupations Obtained in 1925 and 1946 *

(Deeg and Paterson, 1947)

OCCUPATIONS	RANK ORDER BY COUNTS 1925	RANK ORDER BY DEEG AND PATERSON 1946
Banker	1	2.5
Physician	2	1
Lawyer	3	2.5
Supt. of Schools	4	4
Civil Engineer	5	5
Army Captain	6	6
Foreign Missionary	7	7
Elem. School Teacher	8	8
Farmer	9	12
Machinist	10	9
Traveling Salesman	11	16
Grocer	12	13
Electrician	13	11
Insurance Agent	14	10
Mail Carrier	15	14
Carpenter	16	15
Soldier	17	19
Plumber	18	17
Motorman	19	18
Barber	20	20
Truck Driver	21	21.5
Coal Miner	22	21.5
Janitor	23	23
Hod Carrier	24	24
Ditch Digger	25	25

* The ranks are based on the median rank assigned to each of the occupations by 450 persons in 1925 and by 475 persons in 1946. The occupations are listed according to the rankings obtained by Counts in 1925. The correlation (*rho*) between the two rankings is .97.

It is interesting to note that in spite of a depression, a war in which unprecedented numbers of workers went into industry, and a flourishing vocational-guidance movement, the rank orders on the two occasions were strikingly similar. The professional men still stood at the top. The unskilled and service occupations stood near the bottom. Welch (1949), using the same list of occupations, found that the ranking given them by 500 students in an Indiana teachers' college was similar enough to give a correlation of .98 with the Deeg and Paterson ranking. Hall and Jones (1950) obtained a very similar prestige ranking in England for 30 occupations chosen to represent the entire range. Medical Officer, Company Director, and Solicitor (lawyer) were ranked highest; Barman, Dock Laborer, and Road Sweeper stood at the bottom. All groups agreed on this prestige ranking—men and women, old and young, upper and lower classes. Himmelweit et al. (1952) showed that English adolescents agreed with the adults on the ranking of eight occupations taken from the Hall and Jones list. Burchinal (1959) obtained a correlation of .97 between two scales based on different methods of construction, and standardized on different samples of the population, with an interval of from six to nine years between the periods during which the two scales were developed. Apparently our concepts of the relative desirability of different occupations are highly stable parts of our thinking.

The relationship between intelligence and status or occupational level is not confined to any one nationality. Several British reports have already been mentioned. Livesay (1944) has shown that in Hawaii the average intelligence-test scores of high-school seniors are related to the income level of their parents. Sirkin (1929) found the same sort of relationship in the Soviet Union between intelligence scores of elementary-school pupils and the occupational and educational level of their parents. In this country, Robinson and Meenes (1947) have shown that the relationship holds for Negroes as well as whites. In the Netherlands, Van der Giessen (1960) reported that among 1,200 workers in a large Dutch industry, scores on four of the tests in the General Aptitude Test Battery, G (general), V (verbal), N (numerical), and S (spatial) were related to work level.

Besides showing that both men themselves and their children are differentiated according to occupational level, research has also shown specifically that intelligence-test scores made by children can be used to *predict* their later occupational level. Ball (1938) determined in 1937 the occupational rating on the Barr scale of 219 men who had been given the Pressey Mental Survey Test in 1918 or in 1923. For the 1923 group the correlation between test score and occupational level was .57; for the 1918 group it was .71. Both these figures show a substantial relationship, more pronounced where the interval was longer.

With all of this evidence pointing to a relationship between social status and intelligence, there is one group in the population for whom it does not seem to hold, namely, *infants* under a year or a year and a half of age. Furfey (1928), for instance, found no tendency for babies from homes scoring low on the Chapman-Sims Scale for measuring socio-economic status to be inferior in mental development to those from more favorable environments. Bayley and Jones (1937) found that during the first eighteen months intelligence-test scores and ratings on the California Socio-Economic Index were not significantly related. Irwin (1948) reported that infants in professional and white-collar families differed significantly from those who were being reared in laboring-class homes in the number of different types of sound they used and the frequency with which they used them. But these speech or language differences were statistically significant only after the eighteen-month level, not before.

More recently Hindley (1962) reported some results from a longitudinal study of English children now in progress. Eighty children, fairly representative of the London population, were each tested four times, at six months, at eighteen months, at three years, and at five years. On the first two occasions the Griffiths scale, designed for very young children, was used. On the last two occasions, the test was the Terman-Merrill revision of the Binet. On the basis of the four scores it was possible to compute a regression line for each child and to compare the slopes to make an accurate evaluation of changes that occurred. At six months and at eighteen months, no class differences appeared. But from then on, the children from the higher social levels *gained,* those from the lower social levels *lost.* There were interesting sex differences also, with the tendency to gain or lose according to which social class the family belonged to showing up earlier in girls than in boys. This study suggests that the relationship between intelligence and social class does not begin to appear until the second or third year of life.

We cannot say for sure what this failure to demonstrate a relationship in the earliest months of life means, because we are not at all sure that the infant tests measure the same trait that other so-called intelligence tests do (see Chapter 4). But it is an interesting finding to keep in mind as we try to account for all of the research results in this area.

WHAT DO SOCIAL CLASS DIFFERENCES MEAN?

As we have seen, the evidence leaves little room for dissent about the existence of social class differences in measured intellectual abilities. The controversy is about what they *mean.* It is important that we draw the soundest conclusions we can about this because of the influence such conclusions have on social policies in a country that proclaims the ideal of equality of opportunity and seeks the maximum development of all its citizens.

This controversy, like many others, has been a part of the more general heredity-environment discussion. Stated in an oversimplified manner the question becomes: Are people poor because they are dull, or are they dull because they are poor? It seems quite probable that some of the differences between social classes do rest on differences in genetic endowment. The situation here is different from the race difference question, because of the fact that mobility from class to class can and does occur, whereas movement from the less privileged to the more privileged race is prevented by physical barriers. If a society could be so organized as to provide absolute equality of opportunity, we might expect the persons of each generation to sort themselves out, the most able rising to the top, and the least able sinking to the bottom of the heap. As things are today it is difficult to account for the wide range of IQ's *within* a social class (or within a single family, for that matter) without postulating differences in genetic endowment. How is it possible, otherwise, for a boy from a lower-class family, aided by none of the advantages educated parents and a cultured neighborhood provide, to graduate from a first-rate college, become a successful author or scientist, and make social contributions of the highest order? It is more difficult to account for the *variability* of the social class distributions on the basis of environmental factors alone than it is to account for their *means*. Burt (1959) has been one of the most articulate spokesmen for this point of view. In this paper concluding a series on class differences, he comments on both the difference between classes and the wide variation within classes and cited some evidence suggesting that a great deal of interchange between classes in each generation is in fact occurring in Great Britain, probably at least partly on the basis of ability.

But even if class differences might be accounted for on the basis of heredity, most psychologists have not been content to dismiss the topic by settling it in this way. Two lines of thinking have emerged as they tried to analyze what else may be involved. The first starts from the hypothesis that our present intelligence tests are not really measuring the potential ability of lower-class children. As a consequence, lower-class children are consistently and repeatedly underestimated and discriminated against. If this is the case, the remedy should be to devise more adequate tests.

The second line of thinking rests on hypotheses about the importance of early experience on general intellectual development. Lower-class children are "underdeveloped" when they start school because of cultural deprivation during the preschool years, and the differences between those who start out in the more or less privileged groups widen as the years pass. If this is the case, the remedy is to provide for all children those early educational experiences upon which later development depends.

A considerable amount of evidence has now accumulated around the first of these hypotheses—that the tests are unfair. The most thoroughgoing investigation was carried out under the auspices of the Committee on Human Development at the University of Chicago. Results were published in a monograph by Eells et al. (1951). In this large-scale study, a number of standard intelligence tests were administered to all the nine- and ten-year-olds and all the thirteen- and fourteen-year-olds in a small Midwestern city, subjects whose social position had been identified by means of the Index of Status Characteristics. High-status groups were then compared with low-status groups, item by item, on all the tests. The main finding, the one which the author considered the principal support for his hypothesis of test unfairness, was that some items showed a much greater status difference than others. Only 37 per cent of the items for the nine- and ten-year-old group, however, and 9 per cent of them for the thirteen- and fourteen-year group showed differences which were too small to be significant at the 5 per cent level. In general, verbal items seemed to show more status difference than did nonverbal items, but there were many exceptions.

Do these findings really indicate that the tests are unfair, or could they be interpreted equally well as evidence for status differences of a more fundamental kind? In the report on the many separate analyses made during the course of the research, there are some facts pointing toward the second alternative. For one thing, there were only 19 items out of 334 at the younger level and 3 out of 324 at the older level for which the difference between high- and low-status nonethnic Americans did not favor the high group *to some degree*. Had the number of subjects been larger, all the other differences, though small, might also have been statistically significant. If the experience of the groups had been qualitatively different, one might have expected that some types of item would have favored the low-status children. Secondly, in a number of cases, a-priori judgments about items on which status differences would have been expected because of differential familiarity with the content were not supported. Familiarity seemed not to be the most important determiner of success on test items. Thirdly, the factor that did seem to be important in producing large status differences on both right and wrong alternative answers was the quality of *abstractness* in the item itself. This we have discussed as an aspect of intelligence in Chapter 4. Low-status children had more trouble with similarities items, for example, and showed more of a tendency to choose literal interpretations of proverbs. Out of the 25 items Eells chose for special consideration because of the large status differences they showed, 12 cannot be accounted for on the basis of *any* reasonable hypothesis as to how the environments of the two groups differ. Scrutiny of these items (Eells et al., pp. 316–317) suggests, however, that they require of the subject either a complex classification or the following of complex directions. This sounds like "g."

More definitive evidence on this "test unfairness" hypothesis has come in as the Davis-Eells Games, the test of problem-solving ability growing out of the research project we have been considering, has been used with various groups of children. While it is a common finding that lower-status children do somewhat better on this test than they do on standard intelligence tests, it seems that socio-economic differences may still persist when it is used (Angelino and Shedd, 1955), that it does not enable poor readers to score any higher than they do on other tests (Justman and Aronov, 1955), and that it ranks urban children higher than rural children and boys higher than girls (Tate and Voss, 1956). But the main reason it has not found a larger place in school-testing programs is that its validity is in doubt. None of the evidence so far has led to a clear idea of what its scores might be used to predict. Noll (1960) reported, for example, that while the Davis-Eells and the Otis tests produced similar means and standard deviations in each grade where they were given, and while the Davis-Eells showed almost no correlation with socio-economic status, whereas the correlations with the Otis were much higher, the big difference between the two instruments was with regard to their correlation with school achievement as measured in Grades three and four by the California Achievement Test. The Otis correlations with this criterion were .85 and .80. The corresponding correlations for the Davis-Eells were .20 and .38. If we think of intelligence tests as indicators of scholastic aptitude, the Davis-Eells test does not seem to belong with such tests.

Hiss (1955) reported that he had constructed an individual test that eliminated the customary difference between high- and low-status white children, aged six to ten, and still correlated as highly with reading achievement as standard tests do. This, of course, is the kind of instrument that would be useful in schools. But so far no such test has been developed for general use, and the bulk of the evidence using "culture-free" tests does not lead to a conclusion that we can account for social class differences on the basis of test bias alone. Haggard (1954) concluded from a study in which he investigated several variables at once—practice, motivation, revised items, and reading *vs.* being read to—that the difference between midlle-class and lower-class groups was complex, and that the so-called "middle-class bias" could not be removed by simply revising present types of test item.

Two other studies can be cited as having some bearing on this matter of the complexity of the class differences as related to test performance. Mitchell (1956) carried out separate factor analyses of the correlations between several different intelligence tests in a high-status and a low-status group of eleven- and twelve-year-old children. The principal finding was that the whole factor pattern was simpler and the first centroid factor (which can be considered an estimate of "g") accounted for more of the variance in the low-status group than in the high-status group. The high-status children showed more *differentiation* of abilities than the low-status children did. Findley and McGuire (1957) compared the performance of middle- and lower-class subjects who had been *equated* on intelligence on a sorting test measuring the ability to form abstract concepts. They used materials equally familiar to all subjects. The middle-class subjects were superior. This suggests, as did the large scale study by Eells, et al. (1951) cited above, that it is not lack of familiarity but inability to deal with abstractions that constitutes the lower-class handicap.

Thus while we cannot conclude that "middle-class bias" in intelligence tests is of no importance, we can say with some assurance that the differences lie deeper than this. The second type of hypothesis—that environmental factors, especially those operating during the early years, affect the growth of intelligence—must be seriously explored. Some suggestive studies have been cited in the previous chapter. A more detailed theoretical treatment will be presented in Chapter 17. At this point it is sufficient to say that we still do not know what it is that matters most about lower-class surroundings in the early years, nor the extent to which handicaps incurred during these years can be remedied at later stages. Some of the imaginative and stimulating educational programs recently organized in lower-class areas should eventually provide answers to many of the questions that puzzle us (Passow, 1963).

DIVERSITY WITHIN CLASSES

Although the meaning of the differences between the averages of the various social classes on intelligence tests is not completely clear, the existence of great variability within each class is not open to question. As Table 33 shows, the AGCT scores of machine-operators ranged all the way from 42 to 151. With a standard deviation of about 16 points, the Stanford-Binet IQ's of the children of day laborers, reported in Table 34 with an average of 96, could be expected to range from about 48 to about 144. From many points of view, the fact that there are high and low individuals in every social class is more important than the fact that the means differ.

During the 1950's and the 1960's, as the demand increased for intelligent, educated men and women to do the specialized work of our complex modern society, the challenge to provide more opportunities for the development of talented lower-class children became greater and greater. As has been indicated before, even though the proportion of gifted children is not as great at low as at high social levels, the number of such children is very great because of the large total membership in the class itself. Even with the inequalities in opportunity that have existed in the past, a larger number of our college graduates come from the laboring class than from the higher classes, as Table 37 shows (Wolfe, 1954). Although 43 per cent of the children of professional men graduate

TABLE 37
Estimated Distribution of College Graduates Classified by Occupation of Father

(Wolfle, 1954)

	Distribution of 1,000 Children	*Percentage of Each Class Graduating*	*Number of Graduates per 1,000 Population*	*Percentage of Graduates*
Professional and Semiprofessional	65	43%	28	22%
Managerial	128	19	24	19
Sales, Clerical, Service	158	15	24	19
Farm	162	6	10	8
Skilled and Unskilled Labor	487	8	39	31

From D. Wolfle. *America's Resources of Specialized Talent.* Reprinted by permission of Harper & Row.

from college, as compared with only 8 per cent of the children of laborers, out of every thousand children 39 from laboring class families eventually graduate from college as compared with 28 from professional families. This is because there are more than seven times as many laborers as professional men in the population.

Surveys generally show that more talent is being "wasted" because of failure to obtain advanced education at the lower than at the upper-occupational levels. A considerable proportion of bright lower-class children do not go to college. Many do not finish high school. Bingham (1946) summarized figures from testing done during World War II which showed that of the men classified Grade I on the AGCT (more than 1½ standard deviations above the mean) only about one-fourth were college graduates and 5,000 had not even finished grade school. Sibley (1942) analyzed 23,000 school records of Pennsylvania children who had been in the sixth grade in 1926 or 1928. Their subsequent school progress was related to *both* IQ and father's position. As far as college was concerned, the most intelligent individuals had a 4 to 1 advantage over the least intelligent, but those from the highest occupational levels had a 10 to 1 advantage over those from the lowest. It was usually assumed, when such figures began to appear, that lack of money was the principal reason for school drop-outs among bright students. Although finances are undoubtedly a factor, scrutinies of what the class structure means to adolescents, Hollingshead's *Elmtown's Youth* (1949), for example, or Havighurst and Taba's *Adolescent Character and Personality* (1949), suggest that continuing in school is partly a matter of emotional attitudes and motivation.

Berdie's (1954) survey of Minnesota high-school graduates is one of the best of many that have delineated this problem. It appears that the loss of talent is greatest not at the *top* ability level represented by the top 10 per cent of the students, but at the next lower ability level, represented by about the top third of the students. The student who scores very high on tests is quite likely to get to college regardless of his family background. The student who has enough ability to do college work that is adequate but not outstanding is likely not to attend unless he comes from an upper-level family. Other factors also affect college attendance. Girls are less likely to attend than boys, unless they come from professional families. Young people from farm areas are less likely to attend than those from cities. A more recent survey in Minnesota (Berdie and Hood, 1963) showed that there had not been much change in the relationships between going to college and family and community variables in the years between 1950 to 1961. The relationship of college-going to social class was also explored in some detail in the River City longitudinal study to which reference has been made (Havighurst, et al., 1962). In England too the predominance of middle-class students over lower-class students in the secondary schools that lead to the University has been noted (Floud and Halsey, 1957).

URBAN-RURAL DIFFERENCES

A class distinction that cuts across the occupational hierarchy we have been considering in the previous sections is the urban-rural differentiation. The relationship of intelligence-test scores to this factor has been pointed out repeatedly by a wide variety of investigators in many different parts of this country and of Europe (Pintner, 1931, pp. 251–253). Figures cited by McNemar (1942) from the Terman and Merrill standardization data can be considered fairly typical of what is generally found. These are shown in Table 38.

Suburban averages are almost identical with urban averages, as would be expected from the fact that the suburbs are populated almost exclusively by city people. Rural children average about 10 or 11 IQ points lower at all ages except the lowest, for which the difference is only about 5 points. Terman and Merrill's sampling of the rural population was less complete and representative than that of the urban population. They feel, however, that if it had been more satisfactory, the differences they found would have been even more marked.

School surveys indicate that rural children score lower than city chil-

TABLE 38
IQ Data for Urban, Suburban, and Rural Children
(McNemar, 1942)

	(Age—2-5½)			*(Age—6-14)*			*(Age—15-18)*		
	URBAN	SUB-URBAN	RURAL	URBAN	SUB-URBAN	RURAL	URBAN	SUB-URBAN	RURAL
N	354	158	144	864	537	422	204	112	103
M	106.3	105.0	100.6	105.8	104.5	95.4	107.9	106.9	95.7
σ	15.7	16.1	15.4	14.7	16.8	15.5	16.5	15.7	15.9

dren on tests in the various school subjects. There is little information as to how they compare on tests of special aptitudes. Shepard (1942) compared 104 children in two Kansas cities with an equal number of New York City children, using paired groups matched for occupational level of the parent, chronological age, sex, and place of birth (native or foreign). Besides the Otis test of intelligence, he included in his battery two tests calling for judgment of spatial relations, a mechanical assembly test, and a musical-aptitude test. Results showed that New York children were superior on the Otis test, and Kansas children were superior on the spatial and mechanical tests. On the music test, the Kansas children were slightly higher, but the difference was not statistically significant. There is some doubt as to the weight that should be given this study as an indicator of typical urban-rural differences, since the Kansas group would be considered *rural* only by a New Yorker! This is because in Kansas, a population of 12,000 constitutes a fair-sized city. It may be that regional rather than urban-rural differences are involved.

There is no argument among social scientists as to the *existence* of urban-rural differences in test scores; the controversy centers around what they mean. Again we encounter in discussions of this problem a hereditarian explanation and two types of environmental explanation that are not always clearly distinguished from one another. No one explanation will account for all the research findings. From the hereditarian viewpoint, *selective migration* is the important factor in urban-rural differences. It is assumed that the most able individuals from farms and small towns are the ones most likely to move to the cities. Among those who prefer to stress environmental differences, some try to show that the intelligence tests we commonly use are not fair to country children and thus the results tell us nothing about their actual intelligence. Others hold that there are real differences in intellectual ability, but that they arise from the educational handicaps under which rural children often grow up.

So far as selective migration is concerned, direct evidence for its occurrence is somewhat scarce, but there is some. One study is by Gist and Clark (1938). High-school students in a number of rural communities in Kansas were given the Terman intelligence test in 1922–23. In 1935, information was obtained on 2,544 of these individuals to determine whether or not they had migrated. Over 70 per cent of them had left their home towns, 38 per cent having moved to urban communities. Table 39 shows how the moving was related to IQ. It should be read down the columns rather than across the rows.

TABLE 39
IQ Distribution of Migrants and Nonmigrants
(Gist and Clark, 1938)

IQ	PER CENT OF GROUP MOVING TO CITIES	PER CENT OF GROUP REMAINING IN COUNTRY
105 and over	26.97	17.46
95–104	33.82	29.87
Under 95	39.21	52.66

Of the group that moved to the city, about 27 per cent had high IQ's, and about 39 per cent had low IQ's. Of the group that remained in the country the corresponding percentages were 17 and 53. For persons in the average group the difference was small. Statistical tests showed all these differences to be highly significant. The authors noted also a tendency for the migrants to large cities to be significantly superior to the migrants to small cities and for the nonfarm rural residents to be superior to the farm group. Less extensive studies showing the same trend for several small towns in the South are on record (Mauldin, 1940; G. A. Sanford, 1940). On the other hand, Klineberg's extensive research (1938) tended to minimize the importance of migration. He obtained intelligence- and achievement-test records for the children of migrants from rural regions in New Jersey. Scores were expressed in percentiles based on the total group taking the same test from the same teacher. The average percentile rank for the whole group of migrants was 47.5, which is just a little under the 50 which would be average for the whole population. In other words, these results showed no tendency for the bright to leave and the dull to stay. Unfortunately there is a considerable amount of purely seasonal migration in this particular region in connection with the harvesting of crops, and it was not possible to distinguish the temporary from the permanent migrants. It seems likely that the reasons for migration are very complex and differ from place to place. Consequently nothing can be said with any certainty about the relative intelligence of people who leave rural for urban areas. What we need are a number of studies in different parts of the country similar to that of Gist and Clark. It would then be possible to determine how widespread and universal selective migration is.

The best evidence for the hypothesis that rural children score lower because of environmental handicaps comes from a group of studies that have demonstrated an *increasing* deficit in rural children as they grow older. If we could depend upon the adequacy of Terman and Merrill's rural sample, we would have some evidence for this in Table 38. In the two- to five-and-a-half year group, the average IQ for farm children was almost 101. At the later ages it was more than 5 points lower. As has been said, McNemar felt that the rural sample was not complete enough to warrant any definite conclusion. However, there are a number of special investigations of children in isolated areas that unmistakably show this same trend. Among the best known are those of Gordon (1923), who tested canal-boat and gypsy children in England. While these are not rural samples of the population, the isolation and the lack of educational advantages constitute the same sort of handicap that farm children face. It was estimated that the canal-boat children attended school only 5 per cent of the total school year, the gypsy children only 35 per cent. The average Binet IQ for the entire group of canal-boat children was 69.6. For the 82 gypsy children it was 74.5. There was a marked, consistent tendency for the older children to get the lower scores. The correlation between age and IQ was —.755 for the canal-boat children, —.430 for the gypsies. When different children from the same family were tested, the older one almost invariably obtained a lower IQ than the younger one did.

In this country, similar work was done on children from southern mountain regions. N. D. M. Hirsch (1928) who examined 1,945 school children in various mountain regions in Kentucky using the Pintner-Cunningham and the Dearborn group tests of intelligence found the following average IQ's:

Age	5–6	7	8	9	10	11	12	13	14	15 and up
IQ	86.6	85	81.1	79.2	78.6	77.2	75.4	73.1	74.6	81.1

A general downward trend is apparent, the rise in the top category being attributable to the inclusion in the sample of a number of high-school students, who were a select group in these communities. Sherman and Key (1932) gave a number of tests to children living in four remote hollows in the Blue Ridge Mountains and in one small village in this region. Again there was a consistent tendency for the older children to get lower scores. Asher (1935) tested mountain children in southeastern Kentucky. On the Myers Mental Measure, IQ's declined from 83.5 at age seven to 60.6 at age fifteen. Wheeler (1942) in 1940 gave the Dearborn Intelligence Test to over 3,000 children in East Tennessee, repeating a testing program which had been carried out in 1930. During the ten-year period there had been a great improvement in educational and cultural opportunities in this area. The results showed that the average IQ for the region had increased about 10 points, from 82 to 92. There was, however, almost exactly the same tendency for IQ to decrease with age. In 1930, the decline had been from 95 at age six to 74 at age sixteen. In 1940, the decline was from 103 at age six to 80 at age sixteen.

These findings are usually interpreted as supporting the second of the environmental hypotheses outlined above, the hypothesis of educational handicap, but they may also point to the first. If the fact that tests are devised by professional persons using content appropriate to city children is responsible for the urban-rural differentiation, then we might expect that the factor should operate more strongly at the upper age levels where test scores are more dependent on vocabulary, general information, and skills acquired in school. It is impossible to decide between the two interpretations on the basis of the facts that have been presented. Shimberg (1929) worked specifically on the problem whether the content of tests enters into rural-urban differences, using information tests of her own devising. Each test consisted of twenty-five items of general information chosen from a much larger number, and scaled or arranged in order of difficulty according to the percentage of children who could pass it in the group to which it was originally administered. For one test, a group of city children was used in this preliminary scaling; for the other, a group of country children. The two tests were then administered to large numbers of urban and rural children. The important finding was that farm children showed a consistent superiority over city children on Information Test B, the one scaled on rural subjects. Interestingly enough the superiority of city children on the urban scale was not so marked. The fact that this was purely an information test limits the conclusions that can be drawn from the study as to intelligence-test materials in general, though Shimberg makes the point that general information plays a part in many of the tasks set by most intelligence tests. Jones, Conrad, and Blanchard (1932) also showed that the difficulty indices of the items in the Stanford-Binet Test, determined from the percentage of children passing each one, were different for rural subjects in New England than for the urban subjects on which the 1916 revision was standardized. The rural group was most inferior on three types of test items: (1) tests involving the use of paper and pencil; (2) tests involving experience with coins, street-cars, etc.; and (3) distinctly verbal tests.

There are a few research findings, however, that point in the reverse direction and prevent us from attributing all urban-rural intelligence-test differences to this familiarity factor alone. Klineberg (1931) in a European study found rural children consistently inferior to city children. The tests he was using were entirely nonverbal, and it is difficult to see how the content could have given the urban groups any great advantage. Since they were *timed* tests, a temperamental factor of speed of response might have been involved, but there was little clear evidence for this. Another bit of conflicting evidence comes from the 1932 Scottish survey cited earlier. The striking fact (Scottish Council, 1939) is that there were *no* urban-rural differences. The figures are as follows:

	N	*Mean*	*SD*
The Four Cities	319	100.86	15.29
The Industrial Belt	393	99.19	16.18
The Rural Areas	162	100.92	14.52
More Isolated Rural Areas	47	101.79	13.13

The one factor that would appear to be most important in explaining why a kind of difference found in the United States and various parts of Europe did not appear in Scotland is that the educational opportunities in Scotland were completely equalized. Schools in the country were just as good as the city schools.

The matter is complicated still further by the fact that the later Scottish survey, in which all children born on six selected days in 1936 were given Binet tests eleven years later, did show city children slightly but significantly ahead of country children. The urban mean was about 105 as compared with a rural mean of about 101. (Scottish Council, 1949, p. 53.) It may be that conditions had changed. It is also possible that the 1937 Terman-Merrill Revision of the Binet Test which was used in this study favors city children a little more than did the 1916 Stanford-Binet, which was used in the previous one. At any rate, differences in Scotland are apparently much smaller than in many other places where such comparisons have been made.

In accounting for urban-rural differences, then, no one type of explanation seems to account for *all* the facts. It seems more reasonable to conclude that a combination of causes has produced the findings. Many tests probably penalize rural children to some extent. This would need to be analyzed for each individual test to determine how large a handicap it imposes. Simply to include rural children in the group on which the *norms* are based does not solve the problem, since it is the selection and scaling of the test *items* that are at fault. The Scottish study strongly suggests that one or both of the other two factors producing differences outweigh this one in importance. It may well be that the relative importance of selective migration and educational handicap varies in significance from place to place and from study to study. *Some* selective migration has been shown to occur. *Marked* educational deficiencies have been shown to characterize some rural regions, and their relationship to lowered test scores at the older ages has been well documented. We can sum up by stating that country children, almost everywhere they have been tested, obtain lower averages on intelligence tests than do city children. There seems to be no one simple explanation for this fact.

With the increasing urbanization of the United States, psychologists have become less interested in this problem than in the problem of class differences within the urban population. It has some practical significance, however, in that it contributes to the educational difficulties with which some city schools are struggling. Among recent migrants to any one of our large cities, there are sure to be many children representing all three of the conditions that tend to produce below-average aptitude for education—Negro race, lower-class status, and rural background. It is useful for teachers to know what the concomitants of these factors are likely to be, whether we understand how they operate or not.

CLASS DIFFERENCES IN PERSONALITY TRAITS

General observation would suggest that there are wider differences between social classes on personality characteristics of various kinds than on measures of ability. What objective evidence do we have that this is true?

There is a considerable body of evidence for significant class differences in interests, attitudes, and values. Strong (1943) found that one of the most clear-cut differentiations he was able to make was that between professional and laboring men. L. E. Tyler (1941) showed that high-school girls taking a college preparatory course, who represent middle and upper social classes, differed in a number of respects from those in other high-school curricula. They were less hampered by traditional views as to "woman's place," more tolerant in their attitudes toward minor types of misconduct, less fearful. Mosier and Kuder (1949) developed five preference scales having to do with personal characteristics rather than work activities, and showed that these differentiated between men employed in different types of occupations. E. L. Phillips (1950) was able to develop three scales for the measurement of upper-, lower-, and middle-class attitudes by putting together items that differentiated significantly between junior high-school pupils classified into the three groups. Gough's (1948a) status scale mentioned in a previous section was constructed in much the same way. His analysis of the types of items to which upper- and lower-status groups respond differently is particularly helpful in understanding the nature of the differences. He lists five categories of items on which class differences occur:

1. Literary-esthetic attitudes. (Upper classes show more.)
2. Social poise, security, self-confidence. (Upper classes show more.)

3. Denial of fears and anxieties. (Lower classes show more.)
4. "Broad-minded," "emancipated," and "frank" attitudes toward moral, religious, and sexual matters. (Upper classes show more.)
5. Positive, dogmatic, and self-righteous opinions. (Lower classes show more.)

Public opinion surveys on political and economic issues have shown significant differences between classes on many specific points. Many of them can be summed up by saying that people at the lower occupational levels seem to be more concerned with *security,* people at the upper levels with *advancement.* J. W. McConnell (1942) found that wage-earner and white-collar workers in New Haven, Connecticut, differed in their attitudes about jobs, politics, family relationships, and education. The white-collar worker thought of his job as a way of getting ahead and expected to move up into a better one; the wage-earner's chief concern was with safeguarding what he had. The white-collar worker wanted a government that would be efficient but not curtail individual initiative; the wage-earner wanted a government that would protect his economic security and raise his standard of living. Wage-earners characteristically married earlier than white-collar workers and showed less freedom in choosing mates from classes other than their own. White-collar workers were more likely than wage-earners to see education as a means of advancement. A. W. Jones (1941) reported that different groups in the population—business leaders, technicians, farmers, teachers, office workers, factory workers, and a number of others—showed highly significant differences in their attitude toward property rights. Business leaders averaged at almost the maximum score so far as respect for corporate property rights was concerned, whereas union members showed very little of this attitude. Kinsey et al. (1948) indicated that there were class differences among males but not among females in sex practices that sizable proportions of interviewees thought to be wrong.

A comprehensive analysis of attitude differences on various matters was presented by Centers (1949). He showed that classes differ in job satisfaction, in aspirations for their children, in opinions about the place of women in society (lower groups less liberal), and in the reasons they give as to why some persons succeed more than others. Centers (1950, 1951) has also been particularly interested in what interviewees say when asked to *identify* the class to which they belong. He has shown that though there is a clear-cut relationship between occupation and class identification, this is by no means a perfect correlation. Most people whose jobs classify them in what we have been calling the lower classes say that they belong to the "working class," but some in each group answer "middle" and some "upper" to such a question. Both the overlapping between classes in the kinds of responses public opinion analysts get to all their questions and this evidence that people do not always identify their own class the way the analysts do serve to remind us that the lines we have been discussing throughout this chapter are not sharply drawn.

One interesting sideline to our present topic is McArthur's comparison of upper-class with middle-class boys (McArthur, 1955). Using the Kluckhohn formulation of the possible value orientations a person can take with regard to five basic human problems, he formulated hypotheses concerning the differences one would expect to find between the middle and upper classes. He then compared the responses of Harvard freshmen coming from public schools with the responses of those who had come from private schools on five stories they had written about pictures in the Thematic Apperception Test. All of his hypotheses were supported at adequate significance levels. Middle-class boys proved to be more oriented toward the future, upper-class boys toward the past. Middle-class boys were more interested in *doing*—making money, achieving fame, etc.—whereas upper-class boys were more interested in *being*—living up to family standards, etc. Upper-class sons tried to emulate their fathers, middle-class sons to escape from their fathers' domination. Since the number of upper-class families in the population is so small, there has been less research on their traits than on those of the other classes. McArthur's ingenious studies constitute practically all the research we have on the topic.

One special hypothesis that has perhaps generated the most discussion of any in its area and stimulated a considerable amount of research as well, is one that grew out of joint efforts of social anthropologists and psychoanalysts to account for class differences in personality traits by relating them to class differences in methods of rearing children. Davis (1943) and Davis and Havighurst (1946) proposed that class differences in methods of "socialization" would naturally lead to differences in behavior. Davis described what happens at various levels of Negro society, but many observers have thought that his generalizations apply equally well to white social-status levels. The chief difference he pointed out was that the lower-class child is not taught to inhibit his aggressive and sexual impulses, as is the middle-class child. He seeks immediate gratification rather than deferred satisfaction. Milner's (1949) intensive analysis of 30 adolescents at the middle-status levels seemed to point to some "group-typical" characteristics that fitted in with the hypothesis that in the training of middle-class children, inhibition and conformity had perhaps been overly emphasized.

Knapp et al. (1959), who developed a test in which subjects make preference judgments about different Scotch tartans, found that preferences for closely knit designs and somber colors correlated positively with occupational level. Subjects from lower-level families tended to prefer open designs and highly saturated colors. These differences supported the hypotheses about the oversocialization of children in the middle and lower classes, since they suggested that middle-class children express feelings less directly and exercise more self-control.

Another bit of evidence in the same direction was the finding by Alper, Blane, and Abrams (1955) that four-year-olds from the middle and lower classes reacted differently to finger paints. Middle-class children were more anxious about smearing the paints around. These investigators too attributed the differences to socialization practices in the two classes, particularly, in this case, earlier and more severe toilet-training in the middle class.

One of the most comprehensive explanations of the relationship of personality variables to social class was the related group of studies of inner conflict and defense carried out at the University of Michigan from 1951 through 1955 (Miller and Swanson, 1960). The subjects were junior high-school boys chosen in such a way as to control many of the variables that often make class comparisons ambiguous, variables such as intelligence, age, ethnic background, and intactness of family. These investigators found support for many of the hypotheses they had drawn from psychoanalytic theory about socialization practices. Working-class mothers were more likely to use corporal punishment and either concrete rewards or no rewards at all. Middle-class parents were more likely to use "psychological" methods of discipline. Weaning was earlier, toilet-training more coercive in the middle classes. As Freud would have predicted, these differences resulted in more repressive kinds of defenses, along with more planning and self-control, in middle-class children, and to more direct behavioral expressions of anger and anxiety in working-class children.

The differences between classes found in any of these studies were not very large, and they seemed to be complicated by relationships to factors other than social class, such as sex and intelligence. The whole hypothesis has come in for serious questioning since the middle 1950's because of a failure to find the sort of differences in socialization practices between middle- and lower-class parents that had been reported in the earlier studies (Sears, Maccoby, and Levin, 1957; Littman, Moore, and Pierce-Jones, 1957). It may be that as information about desirable child-training practices has been widely disseminated, mothers from different social classes have become more alike in their methods.

There is a possibility, however, that there still may be differences in the way middle- and lower-class mothers actually behave toward their children, even if they give an interviewer similar reports on what they do. One study suggests this. Walters, Connor, and Zunich (1964) observed how lower-class mothers acted in a special test situation. At the beginning the mother was told that her preschool child had not done very well in a previous testing situation. Comparing the behavior of these lower-class mothers with the behavior of middle-class mothers previously observed by Zunich (1962) the investigators noted that the lower-class mothers did less contacting, directing, interfering, and teaching. These differences in the amount of active stimulation and supervision given the child, if they are found to characterize other situations as well as this one, may be more influential in producing personality differences than the psychoanalytically oriented socialization variables previously studied.

Not much has been found when personality questionnaires or inventories have been used in social class comparisons. Auld (1952) summarized a large number of separate studies using a variety of so-called personality tests. In many cases, no difference between classes at all appeared; in many others, it was small and not statistically significant. S. B. J. Eysenck (1960) analyzed data obtained from a representative sample of the English population in the standardization of the Maudsley Personality Inventory. The typical sex differences were apparent but social class differences were negligible.

There is one type of research that has produced striking evidence for class differences in mental health—namely, large-scale psychiatric surveys of specified groups or areas. R. E. Clark (1949) classified 12,168 male first-admissions to mental hospitals in the Chicago area into nineteen large occupational groups. Age-adjusted rates were calculated for each. What we might call "rate of breakdown" for each occupation was then correlated with some of the other figures characteristic of it. Highly significant correlations were obtained. Among white patients, for example, income-level correlated —.83 with "rate of breakdown," prestige level —.75. For Negroes the coefficients were somewhat lower but still strongly negative: —.53 for income, —.60 for prestige. The same kind of relationship held when figures for the various diagnostic categories were analyzed separately, with the one exception of manic-depressive psychosis, which apparently occurred with about equal frequency at all occupational levels.

A still more comprehensive study was undertaken in New Haven, Connecticut, and reported by Hollingshead and Redlich (1958). In this investigation, all residents of New Haven and its suburbs who received any kind of treatment in the city or elsewhere between May 31 and December 1, 1950, constituted the experimental population. It thus included persons treated in physicians' offices as well as patients in public and private hospitals. A five-step classification of socio-economic level was used. Results showed in an unequivocal way that psychiatric difficulty was much more common the farther down the social scale persons were (see Table 40). Furthermore, there were clear-cut class differences in both type of disorder and kind of treatment. At the two upper levels, almost two-thirds of the patients were diagnosed as neurotic, about one-third as psychotic. At the lowest level, only 10 per cent were given the neurotic label, 90 per

TABLE 40
Class Status and the Distribution of Patients and Nonpatients in the Population

(Hollingshead and Redlich, 1958, p. 199)

CLASS	PERCENTAGE OF THE PATIENTS	PERCENTAGE OF THE NONPATIENTS
I (High)	1.0	3.0
II	7.0	8.4
III	13.7	20.4
IV	40.1	49.8
V (Low)	38.2	18.4
Total	100.0	100.0

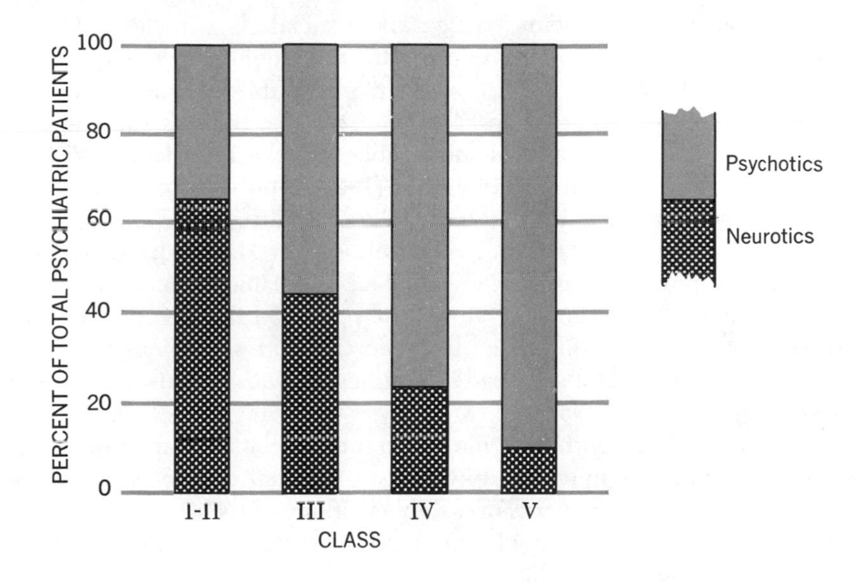

FIGURE 45
Percentage of Neurotics and Psychotics among Total Psychiatric Patients—by Class

(Hollingshead and Redlich, 1958)

cent the psychotic label (see Figure 45). Schizophrenia was eight times as prevalent at the lowest level as at the two upper ones. The majority of patients at the two upper levels received psychotherapy, the majority at the lowest level no treatment at all except hospitalization, or organic therapy of some sort. These differences in diagnosis and treatment are not of course independent of one another, and may arise partly from the fact that neurotic states of mind are more likely to be recognized by upper-class individuals than by those in lower classes, who in any case could not afford psychotherapy. The one thing about which these studies leave little doubt is that there is a highly significant *negative* relationship between social level and mental illness.

CHANGING VIEWS OF CLASS DIFFERENCES

As one reads what is being written about social class in the 1960's, he gets an impression of an orientation toward the whole problem somewhat different from that characteristic of what was published on the subject during the two previous decades. In the first place, there is some indication that the differences are less noticeable and the lines less rigid than they used to be. Peck and Havighurst (1960) reporting on varieties of character encountered in the children of "Prairie City" found less evidence of differentiation on the basis of social class than Havighurst and Taba (1949) had reported in an earlier study of the same community. Havighurst et al. (1962) in their preface to the report on the River City study called attention to the difference between this and a previous report on another community, Hollingshead's *Elmtown's Youth*, published in 1949. Classes no longer seem so fixed. Mobility is occurring in both directions. For a working-class youth, it is more a matter of choice than it once was whether he embarks upon an upward occupational course or seeks the increasingly attractive rewards of a stable working-class life.

But there is one fraction of our population to which the foregoing generalizations about the loosening of social class boundaries and the reduction in social class handicaps seems not to apply. It is the group classified in all the foregoing studies as *lower-lower*. Thus to some extent, the problem of class differences has become in the United States the problem of *poverty*. There is a hard core of families that do not benefit from the rising standards and increased opportunities that the other classes enjoy. We can see evidence of this in Table 40. It is only in Class V that the proportion of patients is very much greater than the proportion of patients in the population. Statistics on crime and delinquency, unemployment, school dropouts, and many other things show the same pattern.

At this level the problem merges with the problems relating to race differences discussed in the previous chapter. It is even more because such a large proportion of Negroes belong to this lower-lower class that they constitute a social problem than because they are colored.

The research question is rephrased as: Why should this one section of the American population be so cut off from the culture and values characterizing the majority? The key concept is now thought to be *cultural deprivation.* Taba (1964) has described the characteristics embodied in this concept—low levels of aspiration, skills and habits not suitable for getting along in school, undifferentiated mental structure because of stimulus deprivation, language deficiencies, and the lack of adequate cognitive skills. The schools in many cities are making an all-out effort to overcome some of these deficiencies (Passow, 1963). If these efforts are successful, the United States may move much closer to its ideals of equal opportunity for all and develop a class structure that gives structure and diversity to society and yet does not prevent the full development of individuals.

SUMMARY

Sociologists have devoted considerable attention to the analysis of the class structure of our contemporary American society. Studies in different parts of the United States have shown that five or six distinct levels can usually be differentiated. The upper classes are numerically small but command a considerable amount of prestige. Studies in Midwestern communities showed that the social-status groups differed in average level of intelligence. This finding fits in with the occupational differences in intelligence which have been reported again and again since the test data for soldiers in World War I first became available. There is a definite relationship between average intelligence and average occupational level, although among individuals in any given occupation there is a wide intelligence range. Probably both innate intellectual differences and environmental handicaps are involved in producing it.

Another intelligence difference that has been consistently reported is the tendency of urban groups to score higher than rural groups. Of the types of explanation that have been proposed to account for this finding, the hypotheses of selective migration and educational handicaps seem most reasonable. It seems likely that both factors affect results and that their relative influence varies from one location to another. The fact that test questions and tasks are not equally fair to rural and urban children is another explanation, but the finding that in some places farm children score as high as city children would lead us to discount the importance of this factor as compared with others.

Social class differences in personality are less well delineated through research. There are some clear-cut differences in interests and attitudes. The hypothesis that middle- and lower-class children differ in motives and defenses because of differences in child-rearing methods was supported more clearly by the research done before 1955 than by recent studies. Psychiatric surveys have shown highly significant differences with regard to many aspects of mental illness and health.

In general, class lines seem to be growing less distinct as time passes, but the special problem of a lower-lower class with multiple handicaps persists. Major efforts to understand and correct the *cultural deprivation* that seems to be responsible for this problem are now being pushed.

CHAPTER 14

The Mentally Retarded

CHANGING CONCEPTS

PROBABLY NOWHERE ELSE in the psychology of individual differences have there been as many changes in concepts and general orientation to research and practice as in the field of mental retardation. The overall shift has been from a very pessimistic view of the condition to a moderately optimistic view. This is apparent in the successive labels under which persons in this category have been classified. For many years the term *feeble-minded* was used. Then there was a gradual shift to *mental deficiency*. By the middle 1960's, *mental retardation* had come into general use. The older terms are still employed, of course, and some diagnosticians attempt to distinguish between *retarded* and *deficient*, or *deficient* and *defective*, or *retarded* and *feeble-minded*, but the general trend seems to be to use the more neutral descriptive term *retarded* to apply to all the persons whose developmental status is seriously below normal levels, regardless of how the condition originated.

If we go back much further into recorded history we find long periods during which some *supernatural view* of all mental abnormality prevailed. Persons who were mentally ill were thought to be possessed by demons driving them from within. Idiots have in some places received special veneration as purehearted children of God, unsullied by the evil of the world. In other times and places they have been thought to be the victims of witchcraft.

Although it had been advocated as early as the fifth century B.C. by the Greek physician Hippocrates, the *medical* view of abnormality did not become common until the nineteenth century. Mental deficiency was at last recognized as a disease, to be treated by physicians in the same spirit in which they would treat inadequate development of a leg or an arm or a lung. Much work on treatment was done in the early nineteenth century by Itard, in France. He was interested in determining how much could be done for the so-called wild boy of Aveyron.[1] This child, discovered at the age of eleven or twelve in a French forest, had apparently grown up like an animal with no human influences. Itard spent five years attempting to train the boy in human ways of thinking and acting, giving up the task finally because there seemed to be no prospect of bringing him up to normal. The general conclusion has been that the "wild boy" was probably a feeble-minded child to begin with, and the comparative failure of protracted treatment methods served to make physicians less optimistic about *curing* mental deficiency.

But the method that Itard used, later developed and systematized by Seguin, who in 1837 founded the first school devoted primarily to the education of the feeble-minded, has constituted a major contribution to education. He called it the physiological method. It was aimed at the development of the mental faculties and functions directly rather than at the imparting of knowledge or information. Under this system each sense was trained separately. The pupil was taught to make finer and finer discriminations in vision, hearing, touch, and even taste and smell. He was given special training in movements and coordinated actions such as cutting, folding, and using tools. He was trained in attending, memorizing, and imagining. With advancing knowledge of the way the mind works, psychologists no longer thought of intelligence as a composite of faculties that could be separately trained. They gave up hope of making seriously retarded individuals normal by such methods as these. Seguin's methods have continued to be used however to enable an individual who is limited in the more complex intellectual abilities to make the best use of those assets that he has. Incidentally, the form board that Seguin devised for training his pupils to recognize and use geometrical shapes became one of our standard performance tests of intelligence for the lower mental-age levels.

With the development of intelligence tests, the *psychometric* view of mental deficiency became common. It was apparent from the study of test-score distributions like those shown in Chapter 2 that while persons who had been classified as feeble-minded on other grounds almost invariably scored low, no definite and absolute dividing line could be set between normal and subnormal. To many psychologists the most reasonable procedure seemed to be to set some arbitrary boundaries which would not be strictly adhered to in classifying individuals. Because it seemed to fit in best with observations of how well persons managed to make an adjustment in society, an IQ of 70 was usually set as the bottom of the normal range. This standard was originally based on the 1916 Stanford-Binet test, but it seemed to work fairly well with the later individual tests of similar type. (Undoubtedly the figure has often been

[1] See the *Wild Boy of Aveyron*. By Jean-Marc-Gaspard Itard. Trans. by G. & M. Humphrey. 1962.

applied wrongly to IQ's derived from test distributions showing quite different standard deviations from the Binet.)

It has been customary to distinguish three *grades* or *levels* of mental deficiency, and these also have been recast in psychometric terms. Persons in the lowest group are called *idiots.* Even when their mental development is complete, they are never able to care for their personal needs, guard against common physical dangers, develop speech, or master simple occupational tasks. Persons in the next higher group are called *imbeciles.* They are capable of caring for their personal needs, guarding themselves from danger, and mastering simple routine tasks. They learn to speak, but show a marked poverty of ideas, and seldom learn anything from the ordinary school curriculum or acquire any but the simplest occupational skills. People at the highest level among the mentally deficient are called *morons.* They are capable of supporting themselves, at least under favorable circumstances, though they often lack judgment about handling their finances and meeting their responsibilities. They learn to read and write, but the only meanings they can grasp are the more literal and concrete ones. Abstract concepts such as truth, integrity, or suspicion mean little or nothing to them.

In IQ terms, the classification that has been most commonly used (and was even written into some state laws) is that which Terman set up in 1916:

Dullness, rarely classifiable as feeble-mindedness	80–90
Borderline deficiency, sometimes classifiable as dullness, often as feeble-mindedness	70–80
Moron	50–70
Imbecile	20–50
Idiot	Below 20

Psychologists who worked with the retarded were always reluctant to use figures like these as the sole basis for decisions about individuals with regard to institutionalization, placement in special classes, and the like. The distribution of IQ's varies somewhat from test to test, and all scores are to some extent unreliable. More tenable than a strict psychometric view of what constituted feeble-mindedness was a concept as much *sociological* as psychological.

Most of the subsequent sociological definitions and classifications grew out of the criterion of social adequacy set up in England in the Mental Deficiency Act of 1913 and its subsequent revisions. According to this view a person is feeble-minded if he lacks the mental ability to manage his own affairs with ordinary prudence. Doll (1946) enlarged and refined this concept, defining the feeble-minded as those individuals "who are socially incompetent because of serious degrees of intellectual subnormality resulting from subnormal psychosomatic development." The concept involved four essential attributes: social incompetence, intellectual retardation, developmental arrest, and constitutional deficiency. If any one of these factors was missing, the condition was judged to be something other than feeble-mindedness. A satisfactory diagnosis was to be based on a consideration of the individual's mental level, his developmental history, his social adjustment up to this time, his personal characteristics, his aptitudes and skills, and as much supplementary information as was available. Doll emphasized the importance of this kind of thorough diagnosis in individual cases and cautioned that the label "feeble-minded" should not be used unthinkingly.

To aid in measuring these social attainments with something like the precision with which the purely intellectual characteristics could be evaluated, Doll (1953a) devised a type of scale similar to the Binet tests, but measuring *social* rather than mental age. The Vineland Social Maturity Scale is made up entirely of items having significance for adjustment in society. For example, at the III–IV year level, such things as "buttons coat or dress," "helps at little household tasks," and "washes hands unaided" are included. At the IX–X year level we find such things as "cares for self at table," "makes minor purchases," and "goes about home town freely." Although performances of this sort are correlated with intelligence as ordinarily measured, the relationship is far from perfect, and some children are further advanced in these social skills than they are in intellectual abilities of an abstract nature.

A variant of the sociological view of feeble-mindedness was proposed by McCulloch (1947), who argued convincingly that mental deficiency is essentially an *administrative* concept related to our institutions more closely than to anything else. These special homes, schools, and colonies have been set up to take care of persons who show gross social incompetence with mental retardation. Individuals are committed to them for different reasons, and practice varies somewhat from time to time. McCulloch held that our important task was to improve the kinds of treatment given in such institutions in order to be able to increase the social competence of those placed in them until it was above the tolerance level of the community. With this as our objective it is not so essential to define precisely the sorts of persons the institution should serve. Thus in reaching a decision in a particular case, a doctor or social worker might judge a child mentally deficient simply because it appeared that a school for the mentally deficient in his community would be able to help him.

All of these viewpoints—the supernatural, the medical, the psychometric, the sociological, and the administrative—have some influence on our thinking about mental retardation today. From the time of the demonological explanations there have survived to our own time some inarticulate fears and anxieties about the unknown—feelings that there is something mysterious or monstrous about subnormal people. From the days of the predominantly medical explanations there have been carried over both uncomfortable feelings about psychological taints, and a body of knowledge about treatment for those conditions that do have definite physical causes. A mother once asked a psychologist if there was any danger involved in letting her little boy play with an imbecile child in the neighborhood. "Is there any chance," she asked, "that Joe might catch what Jerry has?" Obviously hers is a misunderstanding of the medical concept. The psychometric view has influenced the legislation that has been enacted in many states to provide special institutions and educational programs. Even where it is not the sole or principal basis for diagnosis, an intelligence test constitutes a valuable check on subjective judgments of a kind that are often very difficult to make. Sociological and administrative views are very influential in the planning of institutions and rehabilitation programs.

With these varying approaches to definition and diagnosis, it is not strange that there should be a considerable amount of ambiguity about how many mentally retarded persons there are in the population. In providing for classes of people with special needs, one of the first questions legislators, educators, or public officials are likely to ask is: How large a group are we going to have to provide for? It has never been possible to answer this question precisely. But there have been several large-scale surveys set up to attempt to reach a good estimate, and one of their findings has proved particularly stimulating to those who are trying to understand and grapple with the whole problem.

It is possible to say with some assurance on the basis of these large-scale surveys in England and America that the proportion of the population diagnosed as mentally retarded varies with age, that it is much higher during the school ages than at either the preschool or the adult level, and that it is highest of all in the age group bounded at its upper limit by the legal school-leaving age. In England, the highest proportion, 25.6 per thousand, occurs in the ten- to fourteen-year group. In a study made in Baltimore, the proportions were high both for this group (43.6 per thousand) and for the fifteen- to nineteen-year group (30.2 per thousand), reflecting apparently the somewhat higher school-leaving age in the United States (O'Connor and Tizard, 1956, p. 22). In contrast, both the English and American figures show only about one per thousand for the zero to four age group and about eight per thousand for the 20–29-year group. As Masland, Sarason, and Gladwin put it (1958, p. 303), "this means that children who have actually been considered retarded and intellectually inadequate in almost two out of three cases cease to be so identified as soon as their school obligations are outgrown and can therefore be presumed to have made some sort of satisfactory adjustment." Follow-up studies to be discussed in the next section show that this is exactly what happens in the majority of cases. They do make satisfactory adjustments. Thus the problem with which we are concerned takes on a new aspect. Specifically and more precisely, the deficiency consists of inability to profit by education, as this is ordinarily provided in schools.

Surveys of persons who have been institutionalized for mental deficiency turn up new complications. For one thing, many more boys than girls are placed in such institutions, and factors other than intellectual differences seem to be involved. Boys are more likely to be seen as a threat of some sort to the community and therefore "put away." Tizard, et al. (1950) found that more than half the cases in a group of high-grade institutionalized males with which they were working had IQ's above 70, regardless of which test was used. In this institution a considerable number of IQ's in the neighborhood of 100 were discovered. The natural question, then, is, "Why are they here?"

Out of thinking of the kinds we have been summarizing has evolved the new official definition adopted by the American Association of Mental Deficiency (Heber, 1959) which differs in several ways from Doll's definition of feeble-mindedness quoted on page 367.

> Mental retardation refers to subaverage general intellectual functioning which originates during the developmental period and is associated with impairment of adaptive behavior in one or more of the following: (1) maturation, (2) learning, and (3) social adjustment.

Gone are the specifications that the condition must involve permanent developmental arrest or social incompetency and that it must be of constitutional origin. Some workers have felt that the new definition is too broad and open, and have expressed some concern that they might be expected to take on the 15 to 25 per cent of the school population who have some sort of learning or adjustment difficulty. Blatt (1961) suggested some minor changes that could be made to clarify these matters and proposed a recommendation reflecting the real practical significance of this shift in definition, that we "assume, as an ideational tool, that the functionally retarded are capable of achieving typical functioning."

FOLLOW-UP STUDIES OF RETARDED INDIVIDUALS

Perhaps the most influential factor that led to a more optimistic view of the prospects for the retarded was a series of follow-up studies of persons in the 50–70 IQ range that demonstrated achievement of a more satisfactory level of adjustment by these individuals than educators and social workers would have dared predict for them when they were children. The nature of the predictions that were usually made before this evidence entered the picture is revealed in an amusing and eloquent way in the account Wembridge (1931) gave of the difficulties faced by the inhabitants of "Moronia." The following excerpt is typical:

> It was my duty at one time to interview a young man, Flora's mental counterpart, on trial for the murder of a policeman. The little fellow had been part of a hold-up party, in which he was either the cat's paw for cleverer members of the group, or had misunderstood directions, or was too drunk to know what he was doing—or any one of several explanations, none of which could he give himself. He was gentle and good-natured, simple and entirely vague as to the whole affair, for which he was later electrocuted. Even the bailiff, inclined to be severe over the murder of an officer on duty, looked at the mild little murderer with some misgivings.
>
> "It seems hard that policemen must be at the mercy of stupid little fellows like David, and hard that the first notice any one takes of David is to electrocute him," I remarked.
>
> The bailiff peered at him in doubt, "Can I do anything for ya, Dave?" he inquired gently, but murmured in an aside, "He ain't got a chancet. He shot him all right and before witnesses, and that gets the chair."
>
> Then he puffed away down the corridor shaking his head, while Dave smiled pleasantly and remarked, "I'm off the booze, all right. Excuse my necktie." The policeman's widow, and Dave's widow, the policeman's orphans and Dave's orphans, the arrest, the trial, the chair—all because Dave could not exercise the foresight and imagination which he did not possess, respect the law which he could not grasp, and think quickly in a new emergency when he could not think at all. His children will go through the same routine, and we all foresee it—all but Dave. He meditates upon his necktie, and then is seen no more.
>
> Of course, the real victims of such tragedies are the children. Many are the remedies that have been suggested—none, perhaps, adequate. Certainly none has been adequately tried. Early discovery of morons is granted as desirable, but what then? Reduction of the number of their offspring is also regarded by most people as desirable. But by what means? Segregation? That means money from the taxpayers. Sterilization? That means fright, opposition, and general panic. No granting of marriage licenses? That means the elimination of something which the moron is only too ready to do without. Birth control? Illegal, or morons cannot understand it, or it is irreligious —or what you will. Education of the feeble-minded for unskilled labor? Does that solve the problem of the delinquent tendencies of children reared by a moron mother? And so it goes. In the mean time they multiply. Today they compose from five to ten per cent of the population of the United States—according to how dull they must be to be included.
>
> As Flora, Lucille, and Chuck advance in age from twenty to forty, their escapades become less amusing, and even the most callous reporter does not consider them suitable for his pages. They are doing as well as they can, considering their training, their talents, their temptations, and the heavy burdens laid on their weak shoulders. But they and their pale babies are recognized as disasters. They are still subject to the same diseases and healed by the same means as we. Their children die from epidemics like

> flies, but they pass their germs on to our children before they go. Their children see ours in automobiles, and steal them from us. Our girls must dress in fashion, and so must theirs, even though our boys pay the bills. All of them flock gladly toward any frivolity or indecency which we commercialize. And ever the grim chorus chants, monotonously in the background—"The villainy you teach us we will execute, and it shall go hard but we will better the instruction."
>
> It is too dreadful and too stern a refrain for such frail little clowns as Chuck and Flora, and their children. And in the final tragedy, who are the villains and who the victims—They or We? (Wembridge, 1931, pp. 18–21.)

The results of the follow-up studies now make it abundantly clear that in spite of the handicap of low intelligence, as measured by our customary tests, the great majority of morons who have been given special training in school make good after they get out. Results have been reported from a good many different places and covering various periods of time as different from one another economically as were the depression, war, and postwar years. The study covering the longest period was one carried out in Nebraska. Baller (1936) in the first follow-up of "opportunity room" students managed to locate 95 per cent of the group, all over twenty-one at the time of the study. He compared the figures for this "under-70" IQ group with those for a high-normal group, IQ 100 to 120. He found that only 7 per cent of these so-called feeble-minded had been placed in institutions. Educationally they had, of course, done far less well than the normal group, having completed an average of four to five grades as compared with the normals' twelve to thirteen. (Nevertheless it is interesting to note that *one* of the low-IQ girls did manage to get through high school at the age of twenty-two.) In marital status, the mentally retarded girls had the same score as the normal controls, 59 per cent married. For the boys there was a substantial difference, only 33 per cent of them having married as compared with 52 per cent of the normal group. The subnormal were producing more children, a situation that could be attributed at least partially to the fact that the subnormal girls had married younger. Court records for the subnormal group were several times as frequent as for the normal (25 per cent *versus* 4 per cent in juvenile court, 18 per cent *versus* 6 per cent in police court) but the large majority had had no court record of any kind. The employment record of the subnormals was not as satisfactory as that of the normals, but 83 per cent of them had been self-supporting at least part of the time. Whether or not individuals were making satisfactory adjustment seemed to depend upon factors other than IQ. For girls marriage was the differentiating factor, and personal appearance and domestic training were important insofar as they led to it.

This Nebraska research project takes on special interest because of a second follow-up reported by Charles (1953), made when the subjects had reached an average age of forty-two. Again a remarkably high proportion of the original group were located, over 73 per cent. Only nine individuals were at that time in institutions, an even lower number than in 1935. The death rate had been somewhat high for this age group, 25 out of the 151 who could be traced having died, and deaths by violence or accident had been more common than in the population at large. A larger proportion of the group now had police records (60 per cent of the males), but the citations were largely for minor violations. Both the marriage rate, 80 per cent, and the average number of children, two, were now *lower* than the national average for the general population. As in 1935, 83 per cent were at least partially self-supporting, and their records showed that as the general economic situation had improved there had been decreasing need for relief. The jobs at which they were working covered a wide range of skill and salary levels. They were by no means all in the lower brackets. The kind of homes they lived in also varied quite widely. Detailed case studies showed a variety of kinds and degrees of adjustment. For the most part, their children were doing satisfactory work in school. The study confirmed the major conclusion of the first one—that special-class students on the whole become useful citizens.

Another large-scale study by Kennedy (1948) pointed in the same direction. This was a survey carried out in 1944–47 on morons who had been identified in a census of defectives taken in 1937. The group of 256 morons was compared with a group of 129 nonmorons matched with them for characteristics other than intelligence—such as age, race, sex, nationality, and father's occupation. The average age of the subjects at the time of the follow-up was 24.5. There were some significant differences between the two groups in work success, antisocial activity, social participation, and leisure interests. But there was a notable absence of significant differences in most other respects. On marital adjustment and on economic indices such as income, staying on the same job, and receiving agency relief, there was little or no difference. Seventy-five per cent of the morons were self-supporting, more than a fifth of them received top ratings by their employers, and about four-fifths of them had no court record.

Other studies of lesser scope corroborated these conclusions. Hegge (1944) found that during the war years of 1941–42, 88 per cent of the 211 parolees from Wayne County Training School were employed in fairly permanent jobs on which they made from $40 to $60 weekly. Muench (1944) located after an eighteen-year interval 18 individuals who had been rated mentally deficient by tests given in 1925. All of them were working, making from $38 to $55 per week, and showed no special problems. McIntosh (1949) discovered from a questionnaire sent to 1,000 graduates of a Canadian trade school for "nonacademic" boys that almost 98 per cent were working, and that the wages they were making were comparable with those of industrial workers as a whole. Even those whose initial IQ's had been below 60 were now self-supporting in 76 per cent of the cases. Mullen (1952) told of a rather informal follow-up carried out by a committee of Chicago teachers of the handicapped indicating that not more than 15 per cent of the group were unemployed. She also cited reports from Detroit, Cleveland, and the U.S. Department of Labor which gave similar figures for a number of other cities and various time periods. O'Connor (1953) reported similar findings in England. There is a remarkable uniformity in all these publications. Mentally deficient persons who have had the benefit of special-class training make a good occupational and social adjustment, and the less intelligent within this limited range do as well as the more intelligent. It is their characteristics other than IQ that distinguish between the successful and the unsuccessful. It should be borne in mind that all of these follow-up studies deal with individuals who received some sort of special training. They do not tell us anything about people who fail to receive such education. On the other hand, they do not, of course, prove that it was the training that produced the good results.

One of the most controversial questions growing out of these follow-up studies was whether or not these subjects had actually become more intelligent as a result of their experiences in school and in the world of work. Now that we have largely abandoned the notion of an IQ that remains constant from infancy to adulthood, this dispute has lost much of its sharpness, but some practical implications remain. The one study about which most controversy raged was that of Schmidt (1946). The follow-up study of what persons trained in 254 experimental centers in Chicago were doing five years after the study ended was not very different from the others we have considered. On the whole, the social and vocational adjustment of the group was very satisfactory. What did seem to be out of line with previous investigations, however, was Schmidt's report that the mean IQ of the group had risen from 52 to 89, so that about 86 per cent of the subjects scored at the "dull" or "normal" rather than the "feeble-minded" level. The critical evaluation of the report made by S. A. Kirk (1948) pointed out a number of ambiguities and possible inaccuracies in Schmidt's figures.

There have been at least a few other studies, not subject to these criticisms, indicating that under some conditions the IQ's of mentally retarded persons do show a moderate increase. Some of the most convincing data come from the Nebraska follow-up study by Charles (1953) which was cited above. Twenty-four of these subjects were given a Wechsler-Bellevue Test. The mean IQ's were: Verbal, 72; Performance, 88; Full, 81. Here also we have scores which fall in the dull-normal rather than the feeble-minded range. Charles concluded that the original scores were probably in error, but it would seem equally reasonable to assume that some genuine improvement had occurred, since their satisfactory adjustment in the community supports such a view.

Kephart (1939) also reported striking IQ changes following a special educational program. Sixteen boys, aged fifteen to eighteen, whose initial IQ's ranged from 48 to 80, were placed in an experimental group for a kind of training different from that which had been previously tried. They were given problems to work on and required to develop their own methods of solving them. After the training period, it was found that the average IQ on the Stanford-Binet Test had risen from 66 to 76. All except one of the boys had gained. However, one feature of the training makes for some doubt as to the meaning of the change. Subjects were taught to detect absurdities and illogical parts in material presented to them. Since a number of the Binet items are of this type, the increase may have reflected merely an improvement in the quality of the answers to this particular kind of question. In that case it might or might not indicate improvement in reasoning ability of other sorts. An analysis of the data to show what items improved from one testing to the next would have been helpful.

A negative note was sounded by Hill (1948) who reported what he found when he retested 107 special-class pupils in Des Moines after a lapse of about three years and nine months. The educational program for such pupils was described as being quite similar to Schmidt's, but its effects on IQ in the Hill study were negligible. There was practically no change at all in the mean, and downward shifts were as common as those in an upward direction.

One possible way of accounting for the different results obtained in different studies might be to check the ages of the subjects at the time the special educational programs were set up. It is interesting to note that the largest gains have been reported for *adolescents*. Thus even in the Hill report, all of the average changes for groups over ten years old at the time of the first testing *were* in a positive direction. It could be that in these children who develop slowly, *readiness* for academic training comes several years later than it does in the average child. If so, it would be advisable to postpone attempts to teach them to read, write, and figure until they reach the preadolescent years. This is simply a hypothesis rather than anything that has been proved however. There is not enough clear evidence to enable us to decide the matter.

Another hypothesis about IQ change is the one we examined in the previous chapter—that very *early* experience is most likely to produce an acceleration in growth rate. For this hypothesis there is some research support. In one research program (Skeels and Dye, 1939; Skeels, 1942) thirteen young children ranging in age from seven to thirty months were placed in a home for the feeble-minded. Initial IQ's ranged from 35 to 89, with the mean 64.3. In the "home," they were placed in the wards to be cared for by feeble-minded girls who were willing to lavish a great deal of attention on them, play with them, etc. According to Skeels, this turned out to be an exceptionally stimulating psychological environment for it gave the infants an opportunity to handle many kinds of play materials and try out all sorts of activities. After a few months of this treatment (varying in length from individual to individual) all of the children showed IQ increases of from 7 to 58 points, with a mean increase of 27.5. The average IQ of the group after the "psychological prescription," as he calls it, was about 92. Eleven of the thirteen were then placed for adoption in fairly good homes. Two and a half years later, their average IQ was about 96, showing that gains had been maintained. The contrast group consisted of twelve children who were kept in an orphanage with no special treatment at all. Their average IQ went *down* from about 87 at the beginning to about 61 at the end of the experiment. The increase for the one group and the decrease for the other are both statistically significant. The one difficulty that stands in our way when we try to draw conclusions from these figures, however, is that all the children were so young at the time of the first test that it could not under normal circumstances be considered a good predictor of later test results (J. E. Anderson, 1940). Furthermore, there is the statistical phenomenon called *regression toward the mean,* which signifies in simple terms that in successive testings errors tend to correct themselves. We know that there is some error in every test score. If it happens that a person scores lower than he should the first time through such chance factors, he is likely to score somewhat higher on the next occasion when chance factors are no longer working in his favor. Conversely, a score that is unduly high the first time is likely to be lower at the next testing. Since in the Skeels studies the contrast group averaged fairly high for orphanage children and the experimental group unusually low, they cannot be considered statistically comparable. Some increase in the low IQ's and decrease in the high ones can be accounted for on the basis of regression alone.

It seems unlikely, however, that by recourse to statistical artifacts one can explain away *all* of the improvement Skeels reports. Happily a much more carefully controlled study by S. A. Kirk (1958) showed that preschool education for the mentally retarded in institutions and in the community produced acceleration of growth rate in 70 per cent of the children. The improved level of functioning was maintained after the subjects entered regular schools. No comparable increase was found in control groups who did not participate in the special program.

Perhaps *either* early stimulation or deferred special education is better for retarded individuals than the common practice of sending them to ordinary schools at the typical age for school entry. Inability to cope with a curriculum designed for normal children could have discouraging effects on such a child's whole educational career.

In all our thinking about IQ changes, caution is advisable. We must keep in mind for practical purposes that the optimism that has arisen in some quarters with regard to the "curability" of mental deficiency is not justified. In comparison with the whole range of IQ's in the population, the amount of upward shift in even the studies reporting the most striking results is only moderate. Retarded children may perhaps become less retarded; they do not become brilliant. Morons can manage to support themselves in the community; they do not and cannot enter professional schools or become community leaders. Most parents of retarded children must come to terms with the realization that there is nothing that can be done that will enable these boys and girls to catch up with normal children.

RESEARCH ON PRACTICAL QUESTIONS

Once society began to take responsibility for the care and treatment of the mentally retarded, all sorts of questions arose as to policies and procedures. Psychologists carried out various kinds of research designed to answer some of these questions, or at least to provide evidence that could contribute to answers. Usually the subjects in these investigations were patients or residents of institutions for the feeble-minded. It has become increasingly clear that institutionalization itself has definite effects on people, so that in interpreting research findings, there is often some doubt as to whether what we find is due to retardation, institutionalization, or both.

One of these research questions has to do with whether the course of development throughout the successive stages of life is the same for the retarded as for persons of higher intelligence. There is some evidence that their IQ ratings tend to *decrease* with age throughout the childhood and adolescent years instead of remaining approximately the same (Kuhlmann, 1921; Sloan and Harman, 1947). The lower the IQ, the *earlier* mental growth ceases. Kuhlmann summarized these trends for 639 patients tested repeatedly over a period of ten years. The idiots showed no increase in mental age after fifteen. Imbeciles reached their ceiling at fifteen or sixteen, morons at seventeen, and borderline cases at eighteen. C. W. Thompson (1951) furnished some figures filling in the last part of the age curve. Her study of 137 subjects who originally had Binet IQ's of 50 to 69 when tested at sixteen or afterward showed a decline that set in considerably earlier than it does in normal subjects. Thompson chose types of test material that have been most useful for showing differences between age groups in investigations like those reported in the preceding chapter. Morons in their thirties were significantly lower than morons in their twenties on all ten tests. On only four of them has any difference between normal twenty-year-olds and thirty-year-olds been reported.

Curves for the morons leveled off after thirty in much the same way that curves for normal groups of adults have often been shown to level off after sixty. For these feeble-minded subjects, as for normals, there was no difference between successive age groups on the vocabulary test. Thompson tied these findings in with medical studies which indicate that the feeble-minded have a shorter life span and an accelerated aging process. The picture suggested is one of a weaker organism growing more slowly and for not so long, and deteriorating more rapidly after the peak is reached. The qualifications mentioned at the beginning of this section apply here, however. Studies of noninstitutionalized morons like that of Charles (1953) do not show this phenomenon of early peak and decline. Selective factors related to institutionalization rather than low intelligence by itself may be involved, or the institutional environment may have a depressing effect on intelligence.

Furthermore, even in institutions, not all individuals follow this pattern. Satter and McGee (1954) made a careful study of 24 cases they labeled "late developers," contrasting them after 20 years of residence in a training school with a control group of residents in the institution who had had the same initial IQ's when first tested at the age of eleven. At thirty-one, the "late developer" group averaged 18 points higher on the Binet, 21 points higher on the Wechsler. Actually they would no longer have been considered retarded according to a psychometric criterion, as their Wechsler IQ's were: Verbal, 77; Performance, 98; Total, 86. They were also clearly superior to run-of-the-mill cases in the control group on clinical tests of abstract ability and general maturity. The "late developer" group contained some organic cases and some with no evidence of brain damage. The only piece of information available at the time they were institutionalized that might have been used to predict their unusual growth was the fact that they were superior even then on some of the verbal and quantitative tests of the Binet scale, although their total IQ had averaged only 63. Studies like this one remind us that there is still an element of mystery about mental growth in individuals. Predictions must be checked against later performance. They are not always accurate.

Another research question leading to generalizations of considerable importance to practical workers has been, "How *general* is the handicap? Are the feeble-minded equally deficient in all respects?" A part of the answer to these questions is furnished by the well-documented accounts of *idiots-savants,* persons who gave striking evidence of having some one talent developed to an extreme degree. The report of Scheerer et al. (1945) on L., the eleven-year-old boy with an IQ of 50, who was so phenomenally good at numbers, was taken up in the chapter on intelligence. A number of equally arresting examples of mechanical aptitude, musical or artistic talent, and ability to memorize have been described.

An unusually interesting case study of an idiot-savant was reported by

Anastasi and Levee (1959). This thirty-eight-year-old man, the son of a well-to-do family, who had incurred brain damage from epidemic encephalitis in infancy, had a Binet IQ of only 67, but he had two exceptional talents—a phenomenal memory and very high musical aptitude. After a single reading of a two-and-one-half-page passage, he could reproduce it, word for word, even though he showed no real grasp of the abstract ideas it contained. He remembered accurately the times and places of past events, and could give dates of birth, marriage, and death for many historical characters. He was an excellent pianist, and took his playing very seriously, practicing from six to nine hours a day. He could read at sight or play by ear, and was considered to have outstanding ability by a considerable number of renowned musicians who had heard him.

Such special talents, in memory or in one or the arts, while rare, are more frequently encountered in the retarded than are aptitudes for the more common kinds of occupations. In general, persons whose IQ's are low tend to be below average on other test performances. Sloan (1951) compared 20 feeble-minded with 20 normal children on a test for six kinds of motor proficiency (ability to make skilled, coordinated movements). The feeble-minded were significantly inferior on all of them and showed the greatest handicap on the complex tests calling for the most integrative activity. At the adult level, Cantor and Stacey (1951) tested 175 mental defectives, IQ 42–82, with the Purdue Pegboard, and found that they averaged considerably below the norm for men in general. Tobias and Gorelick (1960) obtained similar results. In England, Tizard et al. (1950) gave some portions of the General Aptitude Test Battery to 104 males at the moron and borderline level. They scored below average on all four factors—spatial aptitude, form perception, dexterity, and motor speed. It is interesting to note that they were more deficient in motor speed than in anything else. Their mean was about two and a half standard deviation units below the reported norms for this, whereas for spatial aptitude it was only one standard deviation below. Ellis and Sloan (1957) reported a correlation of —.48 between mental age and reaction time for 79 mentally retarded cases.

A comprehensive study of the performance of 284 retarded children in special classes in public schools on a battery of motor skills tests relevant to physical education (Francis and Rarick, 1960) indicated that the retarded were from two to four years behind normal children in these skills. The correlations with IQ were positive, indicating that the degree of motor retardation was related to the degree of mental retardation, but the relationships varied from test to test and from age to age. They were higher for boys than for girls. The fact that several independent studies point up the motor deficiency of persons diagnosed as feeble-minded should be kept in mind, since it is not in line with what many people think. It is common opinion that persons who cannot work with their heads will be good at working with their hands. Unfortunately this is not true.

A more hopeful aspect of these studies of special aptitudes in the feeble-minded is the *variability* of their distributions with regard to any of these measurements. The average may be low, but some individuals do very well indeed. Cantor and Stacey showed, for instance, that on the different subtests of the Purdue Pegboard, from 4 per cent to 28 per cent of the feeble-minded scored above the general average. Tizard et al. found that a sizable fraction of their group had high enough scores on one or more of the special tests so that they would have good prospects for employment. Perhaps we can paraphrase Orwell's "All animals are equal, but some are more equal than others," by saying that in most mentally retarded persons, "All special abilities tend to be low, but some are lower than others."

One type of study indirectly related to this work on special aptitudes has sought to find out what *aspects* of intelligence are most and least deficient. The most thorough of these studies is the one by Magaret and Thompson (1950), who made an item by item analysis of the responses of mental defectives given the Stanford-Binet Test. They then compared these tabulations with those obtained from both average children and superior children who were younger in years than the feeble-minded group, but had the same *mental* age. As had been suspected, the pattern of successes and failures was somewhat different for the low-ability group. They were better at some things, poorer at others. The items they did least well with, however, were those that McNemar (1942) had shown to be the best measures of "g." In other words, the most serious deficiency of the mentally deficient individual is lack of general intelligence! On questions calling for more practical knowledge and less abstract reasoning, they did somewhat better.

Sloan and Raskin (1952) reported an ingenious study which showed that the answers adult mental defectives give to some kinds of questions reflect greater maturity, practicality, and realism than the answers given by children of comparable mental ages. For example, the question, "If someone gave you an elephant, what would you do with it?" prompted a majority of the feeble-minded subjects to think of ways of getting rid of it, whereas the majority of normal children seemed not to realize the practical difficulties they would incur if they tried to keep the animal. Pattern analyses using tests like the Wechsler-Bellevue have usually shown that mentally deficient groups do relatively better on the performance subtests than on the verbal subtests. All of these findings can be roughly summarized in the statement that the feeble-minded, though their overall mental ages would classify them with children, may differ from children in having somewhat more ability to deal with concrete materials and practical situations than their mental age would lead us to expect.

In spite of the fact that in most cases retardation tends to be general rather than specific, rehabilitation studies have indicated that persons so classified are fairly promising candidates for rehabilitation services. O'Connor and Tizard (1956) have reported several related studies made in England, showing that many such institutionalized persons are capable of useful work, that active rather than "laissez-faire" supervision leads to better performance, that substantial improvements in literacy can be made even with short periods of instruction, and that the work records of subnormal boys do not differ substantially from those of boys with average IQ's on unskilled jobs.

In the United States, Cowan and Goldman (1959) compared twenty mentally retarded clients given vocational training by a rehabilitation agency with twenty control subjects, tested but not trained. The criterion of satisfactory performance was to hold a paying position for at least twelve months. Twelve of the trained subjects met this standard, in contrast to four of the untrained group. This was a highly significant difference.

RESEARCH ON THEORETICAL QUESTIONS

Until fairly recently, mentally retarded subjects were seldom used in experiments designed to increase our knowledge of psychological processes. Since about 1955 there has been a tremendous upsurge of interest in this type of research. An excellent compendium of information about these undertakings is the *Handbook of Mental Deficiency,* N. R. Ellis (Ed.), 1963. Many theoretical hypotheses can be tested more readily by observing the behavior of mentally retarded persons than by using either animals or normal human beings as subjects.

One of the earliest of these lines of research was the attempt to test hypotheses drawn from Kurt Lewin's brilliant theories with regard to *rigidity.* According to Lewin, an individual's personality, as he grows toward maturity, becomes increasingly differentiated into separate "regions." The "boundaries" between these regions, he held, become thicker or less permeable with age. Kounin (1943) reasoned that because of his poor potentialities for development, a feeble-minded person does not develop a very complex or highly differentiated mental structure. But the boundaries between regions might change in the same manner as they do for a normal person. In this case there should be differences in the behavior one observes when he sets up experimental situations requiring a shift from one sort of reaction to another—differences between normal and subnormal subjects, and differences between older and younger subjects. In some ingeniously designed experiments, Kounin obtained results supporting Lewin's theory and supporting the general observation that feeble-minded persons are more content than normals to repeat the same simple act over and over again, and are less bothered than normals by competing desires and tendencies.

Considerable controversy developed over the interpretation of these experiments and over the general conclusion that the retarded are more rigid than normal subjects of the same mental age. Zigler (1962) and his associates produced some fairly definitive evidence that differences in motivation rather than differences in rigidity account for the results of Kounin's experiments and those that have followed. Because of the social deprivation from which patients in institutions have suffered, they are more susceptible to the kind of social reinforcement an experiment brings. Thus they are willing to try harder and continue longer at whatever task a friendly experimenter asks them to do. Other strands in the complex motivational pattern of the retarded that determines what things are "reinforcing" for them have also been unraveled. Along with their positive attitude toward the experimenter, retarded subjects are likely to have a negative and suspicious attitude toward people in general, based on unpleasant past experiences. Changing this attitude results in a stronger experimental effect than occurs in normal children. Still another motivational component is the superiority of tangible over intangible rewards for the retarded. Zigler stressed the practical as well as the theoretical implications of this re-evaluation of the conclusion that the retarded are inherently more rigid than normals. According to this newer view, one would attempt to understand the behavior of a retarded individual in the same way as he attempts to understand the behavior of anyone else—by looking at his intellectual qualifications or level of mental development and at the environmental conditions that determine his motivation.

Another theoretical research question has to do with the nature of the learning process in the retarded. This issue has been clouded by the common interpretation of measured intelligence as general learning ability. The assumption that learning ability is the characteristic that intelligence tests measure would naturally lead one to expect that very little progress would be made by low-scoring individuals. Actually, as we have shown in the chapter on intelligence, the two terms are far from synonymous, and most of the evidence shows IQ to be quite unrelated to the *rate* at which learning takes place and to the *amount* of material learned. Until recently research investigation of learning in the feebleminded has not had the attention its practical importance warrants. McPherson (1948) located eleven experimental studies, the earliest one reported in 1904. In a second survey a decade later (McPherson, 1958) only fourteen additional studies were located. Since that time there have been many times that number of investigations. They are important for our understanding of the nature of intelligence as well as for our understanding of the retarded.

One of the most significant series of studies of learning in retardates was that of Zeaman and House (1963). They studied discrimination learning by means of a technique developed by Harlow for use with animal subjects. The apparatus makes it possible to present to the subject a tray displaying two stimulus objects, one of which has a reward hidden under it. The subject's task is to choose the "right" one. In different experiments the discriminations the subject must make are between forms, colors, positions, patterns, or anything else the experimenter has chosen to investigate. The most striking results reported by Zeaman and House are presented in Figure 46. It is apparent that the learning curves for the two

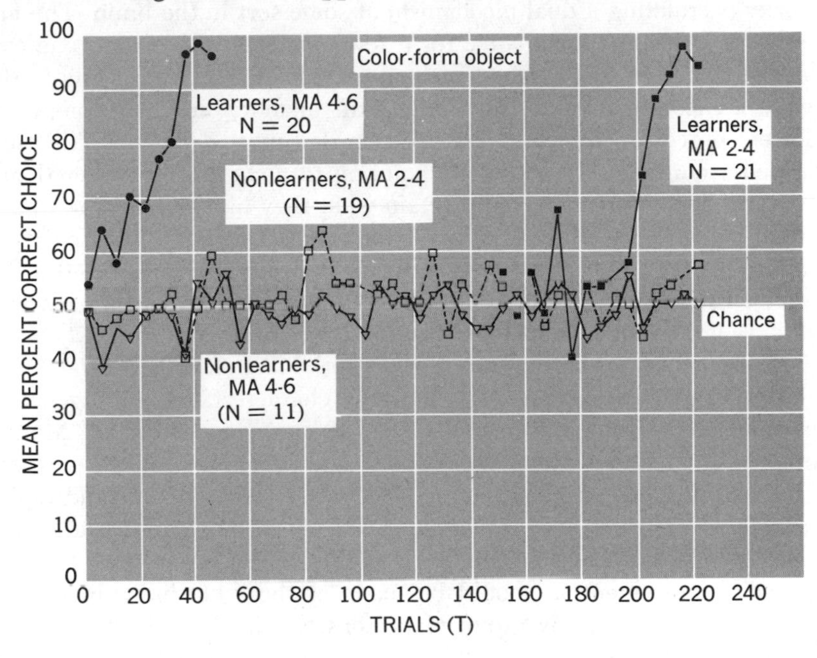

FIGURE 46

Effects of Intelligence on Discrimination Learning

(From Zeaman, D. and House, B. J. The role of attention in retardate discrimination learning. In N. Ellis, *Handbook of mental deficiency*. Copyright, 1963, McGraw-Hill Book Company. Used by permission)

MA groups do not differ in shape *once improvement begins.* The difficulty experienced by the low MA group shows up in the learning curve as a long period of chance performance in which no improvement from trial to trial occurs. The experimenters think that "the length of the initial flat chance-level stages of the performance curves is controlled primarily by an attention process, while the final, sharply rising portion of the curves is largely indicative of instrumental discriminative learning." They go on to analyze this difference, setting up a theoretical model in mathematical terms to account for it. In simple terms, what the low-ability person needs is some guidance at the outset as to which aspect of what for him is a confusing perceptual situation he is required to attend to if he is to succeed with the problem. This has obvious practical implications for persons concerned with the education or training of the mentally retarded. Later experiments reported in the Zeaman and House chapter suggest some ways of doing this.

Still another promising line of theoretical research is reported in the Ellis chapter of the *Handbook* (Ellis, 1963). It grows out of physiological theories postulating a dual mechanism of some sort in the brain. The first one keeps a memory trace alive for a few moments; the second one controls the storage of such traces for long periods of time. According to this theory immediate memory and long-term memory are two completely different processes. In which are the retarded most deficient? Ellis summarized a number of experiments pointing to a short-term rather than a long-term deficiency. Retardates retain what they have learned as well as normal persons do. What is difficult for them is to keep instructions or stimulus materials in mind long enough to learn anything in the first place. This is another conclusion which if supported by further research will have important practical implications for training.

These experiments corroborate earlier work like that of Woodrow (1917) pointing to the inaccuracy of definitions characterizing intelligence as "learning ability" and the mentally retarded as "slow learners." Motivation, attention, immediate memory—these and perhaps many other aspects of the learning process must be analyzed if we are to understand how it occurs at different levels of intelligence. The most important variable does not seem to be slowness vs. speed.

Finally, some mention should be made of the wide individual differences existing within any group of persons classified as "feeble-minded" or "retarded." Chipman (1946) called attention to these differences within a homogeneous psychometric group by writing up case studies of actual persons. The progress of research has made for less stereotyping of the group as a whole, and more attention to each person as a distinctive human being, whether he is a candidate for rehabilitation or a subject in an experiment.

PERSONALITY DIFFERENCES IN THE FEEBLE-MINDED

The emphasis on viewing each mentally retarded person as an individual with his own unique combination of assets and liabilities rather than simply as a typical example of a diagnostic category has been accompanied by new interest in the personalities of low-ability people. It would be difficult to say which was cause and which effect, but the influence of this whole new trend on our thinking is very apparent to anyone who examines the literature in this field since World War II.

Some of this emphasis seems to be related to the increasing use of projective tests, especially the Rorschach and the Thematic Apperception Test. The personality inventories that have played such an important role in investigations of normal, psychotic, and neurotic persons never figured very prominently in work with the feeble-minded, since low reading ability and a very limited stock of word meanings usually made it impossible for such persons to answer the questions on such blanks. Projective tests can of course be administered to low-ability subjects as easily as to those whose intelligence is normal. From the time of Rorschach's first publication to the present there have been a considerable number of reports on their use with the feeble-minded. These have been well summarized by Sarason (1953).

One major aim, the primary one in Rorschach studies, was to develop more adequate methods of *diagnosis*. Psychologists had long been dissatisfied with psychometric diagnosis based exclusively on the Binet and similar tests. They welcomed the chance to utilize diagnostic signs from another quite different procedure in making difficult decisions as to whether a person was or was not feeble-minded. Certain characteristics of their Rorschach responses did seem to be typical of low-ability subjects. Their total number of answers tended to be low. They gave few finely-differentiated, well-organized whole responses. They were less accurate than average in their perception of the form of each blot and found it difficult to integrate form with color. Human-movement responses were scarce, and the range of content represented by their answers was narrow. It was thus possible to make a list of indicators of feeble-mindedness and use it in diagnostic work.

The problem that arose when this procedure was followed was that a certain number of individuals who would clearly be considered feeble-minded on the basis of both intelligence tests and behavior did not show these Rorschach signs. There was considerable variability in the distributions for the feeble-minded, as there is for normals. What should we conclude with regard to such a person when his Rorschach record gives no sign of mental abnormality? One answer proposed by Jolles (1947), Sloan (1947), and others, is that what appears superficially to be feeble-mindedness might really be an emotional disturbance preventing the individual from utilizing his ability. Such a condition was labeled *pseudo-feeble-mindedness*. According to this view, such persons should not be treated as cases of genuine deficiency, but should be given some sort of psychotherapy in order to remove the handicaps that interfere with efficient functioning. There has been a good deal of clinical evidence pointing to the desirability of such a diagnostic category, but as the outlook for treatment of genuinely retarded persons has improved, the distinction between the "pseudo" and the "real" condition has become less important in practice. A thorough discussion of this problem can be found in Benton (1956).

What the Rorschach studies clearly show, and what is still more apparent in work with the TAT and similar picture-story tests, is that there are large individual differences in personality within the retarded group, and that problems and anxieties are common (Sarason, 1953). We are becoming increasingly aware that the indirect effects of a mental handicap and its accompanying circumstances may be as important as the deficit itself. It is especially likely that there have been inadequate parent-child relationships in such cases, from which anxiety, feelings of guilt and hostility toward others, discouragement, and depression are very likely to develop. It was a surprise to many psychologists to find in the mental defective evidence of a rich fantasy life and an internal struggle with many of the same problems that plague us all (Beier et al., 1951).

Both the possibility of pseudo-feeble-mindedness and the realization that mentally defective persons have emotional problems have led to some emphasis on psychotherapy for persons in this group. Axline (1949) reported that some retarded children gain as much as 20 IQ points as a result of play therapy. Other children do not show this increase in intelligence. Presumably the high gainers are the so-called pseudo-feeble-minded rather than the genuinely low. The case that Sarason (1953) makes for psychotherapy rests on the fact that it can help the person, whether or not the diagnosis of feeble-mindedness was correct in the first place, to overcome his behavioral handicaps and change his crippling emotional attitudes.

PROGRESS IN DIAGNOSIS

Another trend that through the years has characterized research on the characteristics of the feeble-minded as a group has been an increasing *differentiation* of diagnostic categories. The first distinction that became apparent—although it was not generally made until the nineteenth century—was that between *subnormality* and *abnormality*. Even yet in the eyes of the common-sense observer there is little distinction between the person who has "lost his mind" and the person who has never had one. Professionally and scientifically, however, we now differentiate very sharply between psychotic conditions on the one hand and mental deficiency on the other. We realize that many psychotic patients are highly intelligent, even when their bizarre associations caper off in strange directions. The fact that a person can be *both* subnormal *and* maladjusted to the point of neurosis or psychosis, as discussed in the previous section, does not mean that the two conditions are the same.

The next kind of differentiation to become common separated out various clinical types of feeble-mindedness. We shall not go into detail about them here, since their diagnosis and treatment are primarily medical problems, though they do have psychological aspects. The *Mongolians,* so-called because of slanting eyes giving them a superficial resemblance to the Mongolian race, the *intracranial birth-lesion* cases, where motor symptoms such as paralyses, tremors, and incoordination accompany the mental deficiency, the *microcephalics* with their small heads of a characteristic "sugar-loaf" shape, the *hydrocephalics* whose skulls are unusually large because of pressure from cerebrospinal fluid within the brain, and the *cretins,* who were cases of extreme thyroid deficiency in infancy, are the most common of these special varieties, but there are many other rarer conditions which are met in medical practice.

Whenever research is able to identify a specific cause for a specific type of feeble-mindedness, it opens up possibilities for treatment or prevention of that particular condition. The evidence presented by Yannet and Lieberman (1944) that incompatibility between mother and fetus with regard to the Rh factor in the blood may be the cause of mental defect in from 3 to 4 per cent of institutional cases is an example of work of this sort. Similar analyses of particular kinds of hereditary anomalies have occurred in the case of phenylketonuria (Allen, 1958) and mongolism (LeJeune, Turpin, and Gautier, 1959). Such discoveries have made some cases treatable if recognized in time. They also suggest ways of preventing some kinds of deficiency.

The great majority of persons now classified as mentally retarded, however, do not show any clearly differentiating clinical characteristics. They are what Sarason called "garden-variety" mental defectives. If their families show a high incidence of deficiency they are usually classified as "familial." If there is no such family history they are simply labeled "undifferentiated." Whether this group will ever be split up into subtypes to be separately diagnosed and treated is very doubtful. Even the distinction that for a time appeared to be useful in the planning of treatment procedures, the differentiation of *exogenous* cases (externally caused) from *endogenous* cases (internally or naturally caused) does not seem to be as important or as easy to make as it was anticipated it would be. (See Maher, 1963.) It is perhaps more fruitful to think of the undifferentiated mentally retarded as merging with the *culturally deprived* we have considered in the two previous chapters and to try to discover ways of accelerating their growth rate as much as possible. (See Sarason and Gladwyn, 1958.)

The effect of both the precise diagnosis of etiological types and the developmental view of undifferentiated cases is to make any general label—*feeble-minded, deficient, retarded,* and the like—unnecessary. This increasing tendency to think of persons as individuals regardless of their intellectual level is not the least important of the outcomes of a half century of research.

SUMMARY

Concepts of mental retardation have changed continuously over the years. The present official definition, adopted in 1959 by the American Association of Mental Deficiency, emphasizes impairment of adaptive behavior originating in the developmental period. Unlike some previous definitions it does not specify that the condition must be permanent or involve complete social incompetence.

A number of follow-up studies have provided evidence that the majority of mentally retarded persons who are given special schooling make satisfactory adjustments in their communities, supporting themselves and keeping out of trouble. There is evidence that measured IQ for some of these persons increases over the years, although it does not ordinarily rise above the dull normal level.

In general, mentally deficient individuals are comparable in intellectual achievement to children of equal *mental* age. The two groups differ, however, in some respects, and both special abilities and personality characteristics may vary a great deal among persons of the same IQ level. It has been clearly demonstrated that the feeble-minded can learn, and the feasibility of using psychotherapy and rehabilitation procedures has been demonstrated.

Studies undertaken to test theoretical concepts have indicated that what has been called rigidity in the retarded arises from motivational rather than intellectual sources. Other research programs have pointed to a deficiency in selective attention rather than rate of learning, and in short-term memory rather than long-term retention of what is learned.

Several specific kinds of mental retardation have been brought under control by identifying genetic or biochemical causes. The majority of undifferentiated cases can often be understood as extreme examples of "cultural deprivation" and treated accordingly.

CHAPTER 15

The Gifted

THE ENIGMA OF GENIUS

DOWN THROUGH THE CENTURIES, long before scientific psychology existed, men pondered over the enigma of genius. How does it come about that in each generation a few individuals tower above their fellowmen to such an extent that they almost seem to be members of some superhuman species? Why are they so often unrecognized until long after their death? Why are their personal lives often erratic and apparently disorganized? Does it make a difference whether a person of genius is adequately supported by his society, or will real genius overcome every obstacle? These and dozens of other questions have been discussed by philosophers and by people in general throughout the history of civilized man.

Two particular questions caught the attention of psychologists and stimulated early research efforts. One has to do with the relationship between genius and psychosis, or at least abnormality. It is commonly believed that there is something queer or abnormal about genius. In part this belief grows out of a "sour-grapes" attitude, the self-satisfaction that comes from proclaiming "Maybe I'm no genius, but thank God, I'm normal!" That men of genius are especially prone to show pathological characteristics has been seriously asserted by thoughtful men from the time of Aristotle. The most influential exponent of this view was the Italian criminologist, Lombroso (1896). In *The Man of Genius,* he gave example after example of famous men who showed various kinds of abnormality. Other eminent writers, such as Lange-Eichbaum (1931) and Kretschmer (1931) also emphasized the close relationship between genius and psychopathology. Witty and Lehman (1929, 1930) cited many additional examples lending support to the theory. Among writers they cited Poe, Byron, Dowson, Heine, Sappho, Shakespeare, and Oscar Wilde as persons who were driven by inner frustrations and conflicts. Poe's own eloquent words which they quote constitute a clear statement of the belief in the essential instability of genius:

> I am come of a race noted for vigor of fancy and ardor of passion. Men have called me mad; but the question is not yet settled, whether much that is glorious, whether all that is profound, does not spring from disease of thought, from moods of mind enacted at the expense of general intellect.

What are we to make of this sort of evidence? The soundest procedure seems to be to adopt the same standards and methods of making a judgment that we have used in previous chapters. Anecdotes and individual cases prove nothing except the almost unlimited variability of the human race. Of course there have been insane men of genius, but is the proportion of abnormal individuals among geniuses significantly higher than it is in the population as a whole? Of course even the sane men of genius behave strangely at times, but so do we all. Are instances of peculiar behavior any more frequent among them than among ordinary people? Psychologists feel obliged to challenge theories like those of Lombroso and Kretschmer in the name of empirical science, admitting, however, their value as sources of specific hypotheses which can be subjected to statistical tests.

Another perennially interesting question has to do with the relative weights to be assigned to personal and social factors in high achievement. There are numerous instances of inventions propounded simultaneously by two or more people working independently just when the time has become ripe for their appearance. Thus we have a Bell-Magendie Law and a James-Lange theory of the emotions, the hyphen indicating that neither of the two men can carry exclusive claim to priority. Many sociologists have stressed the fact that social influences are at least as important as constitutional endowment in the production of high achievement. William James (1927), in an essay first published in 1880, took exception to the extreme sociological and geographical views that had been propounded by Herbert Spencer and Grant Allen. His thesis was that the function of society and the geographical environment is not the *production* of genius but its *selection.* By fostering and increasing the influence of certain types of man, and by destroying what is incompatible with itself, a given environment makes certain achievements possible, but it does not produce the men capable of making them. The logic of James' reasoning is still an impressive answer to those who would insist that "the age makes the man." The argument as to whether the age makes the man or the man makes the age is a part of the general controversy over heredity *versus* environment. In its extreme form it has largely died down. The question is now one of *relative* importance and *specific* environmental influences. Is it possible, for example, for a mediocre man to be catapulted to greatness if the pressure of unusual circumstances is strong enough? Are there "mute, inglorious Miltons" who find no outlet at all for abilities of a high order? What kinds of family and school situations discourage and thwart genius? In what surroundings does it thrive and flower? We shall examine what evidence there is on these points later in the chapter.

When psychologists set out to study genius scientifically, it seemed to them that there were basically two approaches. One would be to select individuals who are unquestionably eminent and collect as much information about them as possible. The other would be to pick out children of unusual promise and follow their development. The investigator adopting the first of these plans can do various things. He can collect statistical data showing both the biological and the sociological characteristics of the settings in which the unusual individuals appear. He can study biographies and attempt to analyze and classify the psychological characteristics of the individuals themselves. The most elaborate refinement of this biographical method is the method of historiometry used by Cox (1926) in her epoch-making study. She not only noted and tabulated but managed to *quantify* the evidences of high ability that were available in the biographies of great men, so that an estimate of their childhood intelligence in terms of the lowest IQ that could reasonably account for their precocious achievements became possible. If one starts from the other direction and studies children who may some day become great, he may either make complete case studies of individuals in their early years to be kept on record for future reference, or he may obtain mental measurements from large groups of promising children and analyze their present and later achievements as well as other group characteristics.

Difficulties are encountered in either of these enterprises. If one chooses to study eminent persons, the first essential is to find a sound criterion for selecting those to be studied. Unless this is satisfactorily done, and unless a fairly comprehensive list of persons who satisfy this criterion is obtained, the kind of sampling errors that have been criticized in Lombroso and in Kretschmer can easily be made. Individual cases whose lives support any kind of theory toward which one leans may be found. The safest criterion is some objective indication of the amount of attention each person's achievements have commanded, such as the amount of space devoted to him in the standard biographical dictionaries. Another kind of criterion is based on ratings by experts in the field of the individual's achievements, so that chemists rate chemists, musicians rate musicians, writers rate writers, and so on. It is of course true that this sort of selection gives us *eminence* rather than ability as such, but it is wholly defensible to use eminence as a sort of operational definition of genius. While it may be that some individuals who merit very few lines in a biographical dictionary have more exceptional qualities than persons of greater fame, it is appropriate for the research worker to judge them as they are judged by society.

In order to be sure what the judgment of society about them is, however, it is usually desirable to let some time elapse after their careers are over. Many men who stand out as important figures in their own day are completely forgotten twenty years afterward. This means that we apply sounder criteria of eminence when we study great men who are no longer living than when we try to study contemporary examples of so-called genius. Thus another difficulty arises, because the biographical data available on great men of the past are incomplete. Often just the information that would be most useful to the psychologist is missing from the record. Biographers are likely to stress the periods in a person's life when his most important work was going on. The psychologist is most interested in the circumstances and the motivation leading up to that work. Consequently the study of eminent persons as a research method is limited in its scope. Only certain types of information, and those often not the most crucial, can be discovered this way.

The difficulties attendant upon longitudinal studies of gifted children are of other sorts. Probably the main one is the necessity for including in the initial sample an extremely large number of children in order to be sure that among them there will be at least a moderate number whose achievements later, as adults, are of very high quality. Furthermore, in these as in other longitudinal investigations, the original data are limited by the technological level of psychological science at the time they were collected. Thus by the time such a study ends, it will be pretty certain that questions are being formulated that cannot be answered by referring to the materials on hand. Fortunately, problems of these sorts did not deter psychologists like Terman from initiating their important research.

While these two approaches—the statistical and biographical study of eminent persons from the past and the longitudinal studies of gifted children—make up the bulk of what psychologists have done in this field, two new lines of investigation have opened up during the 1950's and 1960's. One is the preparation of searching case studies, based on intensive interviews and many kinds of personality assessment, of outstanding persons of our own time. Because of the tremendous prestige of science at the present time, such case studies have most frequently been of scientists, but there have been some studies of artists and writers as well. The other special kind of research that has flourished during the middle decades of this century is the study of creativity. We shall look now at research findings from all four of these main types of investigation.

STATISTICAL AND BIOGRAPHICAL STUDIES OF EMINENT INDIVIDUALS

There have been a number of statistical surveys of the data on record about famous persons since Galton (1952) began this type of research in 1869. Some of them centered chiefly on the biological information which might throw some light on Lombroso's theory of the prevalence of degeneracy and pathology in men of genius. Their results on the whole do not support any such conception. They show, for example, that the average age of the fathers of American men of science at the time of the subject's birth was thirty-five (J. McK. Cattell, 1915, 1917a and b). The parents thus tend to have been in the prime of life when the child was born. The great man is more likely to be the first-born than any other member of the family. He is most likely to come from a family in which there have been other eminent individuals. In Galton's study, for instance, the 977 eminent men had a total of 739 eminent relatives. Great men as a whole seem to be more vigorous than the average. C. C. Miles and Wolfe (1936) analyzed biographical data on fifty representative geniuses to get ratings of their mental and physical health during childhood. They showed that the distribution of ratings was at least as favorable as that for children in general. Only 2 per cent showed definitely frail health, only 8 per cent serious mental and emotional weakness. There was a difference between imaginative geniuses and men of action. Among the poets and artists there was a higher percentage of instability than among the statesmen and leaders. On the whole, however, no relationship between genius and mental pathology was demonstrated. Adams (1946) noted that the average life span for scientists born since 1600 has been considerably longer than the typical life span of their contemporaries.

Galton and many later writers stress the evidence supporting a hereditary theory of genius. Into outstanding families are born superior children from among whose number will come our outstanding men and women. Critics of this viewpoint have been quick to point out that in families like the Huxleys and the Adamses it is not just the germ plasm that is superior. In such a home a child receives physical care, mental stimulation, educational advantages, and motivation to high achievement far beyond the average. As has been said above, surveys of the biological facts about genius discredit the Lombroso theory of degeneracy and give evidence that the hereditary endowment of the great man is superior. They do not prove, however, that his good endowment is *all* that matters.

Out of the surveys of eminent men has come also considerable sociological information. Eminent persons are much more likely to come from the higher than from the lower occupational levels of the population, as Table 41 shows.

Certain regions are much more likely than others to produce eminent persons, as Table 42 shows; but with the passage of time, the relative proportions from different parts of the country change. This might be a result of either migration of first-rate families to the newer regions or the improvement of educational facilities in these areas.

More important than any of these miscellaneous facts about great men is the definite evidence that they were highly intelligent from early child-

TABLE 41

Occupational Distribution of Fathers of 282 Eminent Men and Women of all Countries

(Cox, 1926)

OCCUPATIONAL LEVEL	PERCENTAGE
Professional and nobility	52.5
Semiprofessional, higher business and gentry	28.7
Skilled workmen and lower business	13.1
Semiskilled	3.9
Unskilled	1.1
No record	0.7

TABLE 42

Numbers of American Men of Science Born in Eastern and Midwestern States, 1903 and 1932

(Cattell, 1933)

	NUMBER OF CASES (PER 1,000 ENTRIES)	
PLACE OF BIRTH	*Data Gathered in 1903*	*Data Gathered in 1932*
Massachusetts	134	72
Connecticut	40	16
New York	183	128
Pennsylvania	66	48
Illinois	42	88
Minnesota	4	32
Missouri	14	40
Nebraska	2	20
Kansas	7	32

hood on. There are, of course, famous anecdotes, for example, about the little Mozart composing music at five, playing for the emperor at six, and writing an opera at eleven. Sir Francis Galton's letter to his sister, written the day before his fifth birthday, in which he catalogs his accomplishments, is deservedly well known:

My dear Adele:

I am four years old and I can read any English book. I can say all the Latin substantives and adjectives and active verbs besides 52 lines of Latin poetry. I can cast up any sum in addition and can multiply by 2, 3, 4, 5, 6, 7, 8, 9, 10.

I can also say the pence table. I read French a little and I know the clock.

FRANCIS GALTON

February 15, 1827

But there are other cases of men like Edison who were reported by their teachers to be dull in school. Thus a great need was felt for a systematic attempt to bring together information and to translate into quantitative form as much about the childhood mental characteristics of geniuses as could be found, a task which was accomplished by Cox (1926) an associate of Terman. The subjects were 301 persons objectively rated as outstandingly eminent. As much biographical information as possible was brought together for each of them, and three experienced psychologists estimated the lowest IQ that would be required to account for what he was able to do at specified ages. It is interesting to notice that the more information there was available about individuals, the higher the rated IQ's turned out to be. Superior mental ability, of the type we are identifying readily in children today by means of intelligence tests, characterized *all* of these eminent individuals without exception. No individual was rated below average on the basis of available childhood information. The average for each type of leader considered, e.g. statesman, writer, artist, was above 140. For most of them it was 160 or above. These results encouraged Terman and other psychologists to undertake their research on gifted children, because they strongly suggested that the leaders of tomorrow are to be found among the gifted children of today.

Cox also rated other characteristics besides intellectual ability for her sample. The same background of high family occupational level noted by Galton and others appeared in this study. Breadth, intensity, and kind of interests also distinguished these persons from other children. They were more likely than average persons to have demonstrated strong intellectual interests in childhood. Their ratings for character and personality were also above average, as Table 43 shows.

Such ratings can be criticized because of their subjective nature. Psychologists, it may be argued, knowing that the persons they were rating had been outstanding in achievement, might be prejudiced in their favor in evaluating all these traits. Biographers of the eminent do probably record more of their good traits than of their bad ones. However, despite these objections this work at least suggests strongly that genius involves a complex of favorable personality characteristics as well as a high degree of ability.

STUDIES OF GIFTED CHILDREN

In 1922, Terman et al. (1925) embarked upon the most ambitious developmental study that had ever been attempted. Its object was a direct attack upon this problem of "genius." The method of this research project was essentially simple: first to canvass a given region (in this case, the state of California) in order to locate all the children who had demonstrated in school ability of a very high order; second, to collect as much

TABLE 43

High Personality-Trait Ratings of One Hundred Geniuses in Childhood

(C. C. Miles, 1954)

(Ratings are averages of two raters on a seven-point scale, +3 to −3, when 0 is the assumed average of the general child population.)

Trait	Rating
Intellectual Traits:	
Mental work devoted to routine studies	1.7
Independence of thought	1.8
Keenness of observation	1.9
Strength of memory	2.0
Quickness of apprehension	2.0
Originality, creativeness	2.1
Profoundness of apprehension	2.3
Mental work devoted to special pursuits	2.4
Social Traits:	
Trustworthiness	1.7
Conscientiousness	1.7
Wideness of influence	1.7
Intensity of influence on intimates	2.0
Self-traits and Motivation:	
Desire to be a leader, to impose his will	1.7
Correctness of his own self-appraisal	1.7
Correctness of self-appraised special talents	2.0
Belief in his own powers	2.0
Force of character as a whole	2.0
Devotion of effort toward distant goals	2.0
Strength of will in perseverance	2.3
Persistence in the face of obstacles	2.3
Steadfastness of effort	2.5
Desire to excel in efforts	2.6

information as possible about the abilities and personal traits of these children; third, to make follow-up studies every few years to find out what they were accomplishing. Two groups of questions can be answered by such research. First, what, generally speaking, becomes of gifted children? How well do they maintain their early superiority? Second, *which individuals* from this selected group accomplish work of the quality that will rank them with the geniuses we have been considering? How do such individuals differ from the others? Is there any way we could have identified them in childhood? Conversely, what do the failures among the group seem to lack? Is it characteristics of the individuals themselves or the handicapping effects of bad environment that hold them back?

The initial investigation, reported in *Genetic Studies of Genius,* Vol. I, was based on 1,000 preschool and elementary-school children and 300 high-school pupils with IQ's of 140 or above. Teachers' judgments as well as IQ's were used in making the initial selection. The first important follow-up study, reported in *Genetic Studies of Genius,* Vol. III (Burks et al., 1930), was made seven years later. The next follow-up, reported in the *Thirty-ninth Yearbook* of the National Society for the Study of Education, was made in 1935–36. A summary of the whole project to date and a detailed report on the follow-up studies made in 1940 and in 1945 was published in *The Gifted Child Grows Up* (Terman and Oden, 1947). This was particularly important since it showed what had happened to the subjects after they had grown up, left school, and begun their careers. Still another follow-up study, *The Gifted Group at Mid-Life* (Terman and Oden, 1959), came out after Terman's death. It continued the survey of the accomplishments of the subjects up to 1955, and reported some interesting "second-generation" information about the intelligence of the offspring of the gifted group. In due time we shall probably have a still later report.

The first important result of this work was a usable body of knowledge with regard to gifted children as a group. Since this group included about nine-tenths of the highest IQ's in a population of 250,000 public-school children, its size and completeness made the findings unusually dependable. In the first place, statistics about the *families* from which the children came showed striking similarities to those that had been accumulated about the historically eminent men and women. There was the same preponderance of high occupational level, 31 per cent having fathers belonging to the professional class, 50 per cent to semiprofessional and business occupations, 12 per cent to skilled labor, and 7 per cent to semiskilled or unskilled occupations. (It is to be remembered in evaluating such figures that there are many *more* nonprofessional than professional men in the population. The fact that 31 per cent of these children came from professional homes is noteworthy because not more than 5 to 10 per cent of the employed population is classified at this level. However, high IQ's do occur at all levels, as the 7 per cent whose fathers were laborers show.) The educational level of the fathers and mothers of the gifted children was considerably higher on the average than that of the general population. The frequency of insanity in their families was much below the average for the general population. Parents tended to be above average in general health and in the prime of life at the time the children were born. The gifted child was more likely to be the first-born than to occupy any other position in the family.

In physical and developmental characteristics, the gifted group showed a consistent superiority. Their averages at each age exceeded the age norms for children as a whole in a wide variety of anthropometric measurements, including height, weight, general physical development, and muscular energy. The gifted children were superior to the average in the rate at which they had learned to walk and talk. Puberty was reached somewhat earlier than normal. General health, as determined from physicians' ratings, was better than average, and symptoms such as headaches, stuttering, and nervousness were relatively uncommon. Of course there were wide individual differences in all these respects; but the old stereotyped picture of the child prodigy as a weak, sickly, frail little youngster with a vastly overdeveloped brain was demolished completely.

Their educational accomplishments were particularly outstanding. About 85 per cent of the children had skipped one or more half-grades, and their teachers thought that some 80 per cent were eligible for still further promotion. Their school work was most superior in subjects like debating, history, composition, literature, grammar, general science, geography, civics, reading, and arithmetic—subjects that require verbal comprehension and abstract reasoning. They were least superior in subjects such as physical education, art, and shop work. (The gifted child is actually at a disadvantage in the ordinary schoolroom in these things, since the physical and muscular development on which complex coordinations depend is not correlated to any significant extent with mental development. Thus the fact that he is likely to be from six months to several years *younger* than the average child in the *grade* means that he may appear deficient in these skills, even when development is normal or above for his *age*.) The stated preference of the gifted children for different kinds of school work showed the same trends as their accomplishments, though they were also inclined to give the same high preference ratings to games and sports as normal children do. Versatility rather than one-sidedness was characteristic of these bright children. Achievement tests showed high scores in *all* subject-matter fields.

The gifted children showed a wide range of interests and an active play life. Their play interests were quite similar to those of average children, except that they tended to prefer games that are favorites among children somewhat older than themselves, as might be expected from their greater mental maturity. The greatest contrast between gifted and average children was with regard to reading and other distinctively intellectual interests. They had learned to read unusually early, often with little or no instruction. They read more than twice as many books as the average children of the same age, and included in their lists much more good literature, such as poetry and drama, science, history, biography, and travel. They made twice as many collections as average children, and these were more likely to be of scientific interest and value.

In many character and personality traits, the group was considerably superior to the average. Table 44 shows some of the comparisons between gifted and control children on various rated traits. It is at once apparent that the greatest differences occur in the *intellectual* traits and in the motivation that leads to achievement. In most social traits the two groups do not differ. On tests of emotional adjustment there is a highly significant difference in favor of the gifted group. Though all sorts of individual patterns are represented in the group, the general tendency is plainly for good personality development to accompany high intelligence.

Fortunately there have been enough other studies of gifted children by various persons in other parts of the country to make it plain that Terman's findings are not unique nor limited to the California group of children. In New York, in Chicago, in Kansas City—wherever the investigations have been made, the same general superiority of the children with high IQ's has been apparent.

The heart of this kind of research, however, is not in the initial survey, but in the follow-up studies. What becomes of children like this as they grow up and take their places in society? Terman's first follow-up was published in 1930 as Vol. III of *Genetic Studies of Genius* (Burks et al., 1930). Since the subjects were about six years older than they had been at the time of the first testing, most of them had moved from elementary school to high school or from high school to college. One fact stood out as of paramount importance from the data collected in this first follow-up: in the large majority of cases the educational superiority of the group was being maintained. There was a slight drop in both average IQ and average achievement quotient $\left(\frac{\text{Test Age}}{\text{Chronological Age}}\right)$, to be explained at least partly on the basis of the phenomenon of regression toward the mean. When one selects for initial study a group far above the general average, any part of the high scores that is the result of chance errors in an upward direction is likely to be corrected at the time of the next testing, thus producing a slight decrease in the average score. One suggestive finding, however, was that the loss in IQ for the girls was 14 points as compared with only a 3-point decrease for the boys. Changes in either developmental rate or intellectual motivation seemed, in the case of the girls, to have supplemented those due to regression alone. But even in cases where a considerable decrease had occurred, the individuals were still well above average. The mean Stanford-Binet IQ was 143 for the boys and 135 for the girls. More students than before were now accelerated in school. School records showed consistently high achievement in all academic subjects. Character ratings and personality test scores were still high. With regard to the main finding of this study, the tendency for superiority to be maintained throughout the school years, data from other parts of the country have supported the Terman findings.

The next two follow-up reports (Terman and Oden, 1940, 1947) furnished a wealth of information about the subjects up to the age of approximately forty. Much of it can be summarized around a number of research questions to which the investigators turned their attention. First,

TABLE 44

Teachers' Ratings of Gifted and Control Children on Various Personality Traits *

(C. C. Miles, 1954)

TRAITS IN WHICH GIFTED CHILDREN DIFFER LITTLE FROM CONTROL CHILDREN		GIFTED		CONTROL	
		Boys	*Girls*	*Boys*	*Girls*
Fondness for groups	M	6.2	5.6	6.1	5.9
	SD	2.1	2.2	2.1	2.0
Freedom from vanity	M	5.9	5.4	6.1	5.6
	SD	2.7	2.3	1.9	2.0
Sympathy	M	5.8	5.2	6.3	5.7
	SD	2.1	2.1	1.8	1.8
Popularity	M	6.4	5.7	6.5	6.2
	SD	2.0	2.0	1.8	1.9

TRAITS IN WHICH GIFTED CHILDREN DIFFER SIGNIFICANTLY FROM CONTROL CHILDREN		GIFTED		CONTROL	
		Boys	*Girls*	*Boys*	*Girls*
Leadership	M	6.3	5.8	7.2	7.0
	SD	1.9	2.0	2.1	2.2
Desire to excel	M	4.2	3.6	6.1	5.6
	SD	2.2	1.9	2.4	2.0
Conscientiousness	M	4.8	4.0	6.2	5.4
	SD	2.5	2.2	2.3	2.2
Common sense	M	4.2	4.1	6.2	5.9
	SD	1.9	1.9	1.8	1.8
Perseverance	M	4.4	4.1	6.4	6.1
	SD	2.1	1.9	2.2	2.0

TRAITS IN WHICH GIFTED CHILDREN DIFFER LARGELY AND SIGNIFICANTLY FROM CONTROL CHILDREN		GIFTED		CONTROL	
		Boys	*Girls*	*Boys*	*Girls*
Desire to know	M	3.5	3.9	6.3	6.2
	SD	1.9	2.1	2.0	2.1
Originality	M	4.4	4.5	6.8	6.9
	SD	2.1	2.1	1.9	1.9
General intelligence	M	3.1	3.1	6.4	6.2
	SD	1.6	1.8	1.9	1.8

* Smaller numbers indicate superior ratings.

was the superior intellectual status still maintained? Getting an answer to this question was not so simple as it might appear at first glance. The tests on the basis of which the IQ's of the subjects were determined in childhood have much too low a "ceiling" for superior adults. It was necessary for Terman and his associates to develop a new and very difficult test called the Concept Mastery Test, and to give this along with better-known tests to college students in order to arrive at statistical estimates of the IQ's to which its scores correspond. Their final conclusion concerning the gifted group was that there had been some slipping back toward the average intelligence level. Whereas the whole group had originally averaged 3.2 standard deviations above the general mean, at this time their average was about 2.1 standard deviations above the population average.

R. L. Thorndike (1948a) using a different type of "bridge" between the Concept Mastery scores and the norms for the general population, arrived at an even lower figure. He estimated that Terman's group had declined to about 1.7 standard deviations above the general population. Only about half of this drop can be accounted for by the regression effect. The rest is not due to chance. When all this has been said, however, the important fact remains that the group as a whole was still very high. Translating the facts into percentile terms, Thorndike showed that half the group would still have scored above the 95th percentile and the other half would have spread out between the 75th and 95th percentile points on a test designed for the general population. There would have been no low or even no average scores. The report of Bayley and Oden (1955) that retests on the Concept Mastery Test after a ten-year interval showed an increase in score would seem to suggest that what drop there was in some subjects must have occurred during the school years rather than later.

A second question had to do with the physical and mental health of the group. Results of the later follow-up studies corroborated those of the earlier ones in showing predominantly good health and adjustment. While about 5 per cent were now rated seriously maladjusted, 80 per cent showed no emotional difficulties whatever. Comparison figures for people as a whole are not obtainable, but this incidence of adjustment difficulties appeared to be low rather than high.

A third question can be, "Had the group as a whole been successful in life?" Here the answer was outstandingly positive. School success was as marked at the later as at the early stages. About 90 per cent of the group had entered college, and more than two-thirds of them had graduated. Graduate study leading to advanced degrees, outstanding scholastic records, and election to honorary societies had been common. Participation in extracurricular activities and a considerable amount of self-support had accompanied this academic success. The fact that there had been some failures and many mediocre records, however, serves to indicate that the possession of high intelligence does not by itself guarantee such favorable outcomes.

The occupational status of these young adults was also very satisfactory, whether evaluated by general level attained or by income. The percentage of unemployment was far lower than that in the general population. Approximately 71 per cent of the gifted men were in professional or higher business fields as compared with less than 14 per cent of California males as a whole. There was a marked sex difference in this area, however. Occupational level and income were both much lower for the women than for the men in the group.

A fourth set of questions had to do with marriage and family life. The marriage rate was as high as it is for the population as a whole, and the evidence indicated that both marital happiness and sexual adjustment were slightly more satisfactory than they are in available comparison groups. Their spouses were intelligent also, but did not score quite so high on the Concept Mastery Test as did the subjects themselves. The average IQ for the children who had been born to them so far was 128.

Perhaps the most illuminating part of this study was a comparison of the 150 individuals rated most successful (Group A) with the 150 rated least successful (Group C). (The C individuals were not necessarily failures by general standards, but they had not lived up to the promise of their childhood years.) A number of significant differences showed up, although the two groups overlapped so much with regard to each characteristic that it would not have been possible to predict for any individual child whether or not he was to be successful. In Group C, intellectual level had dropped since high-school days so that these subjects were at the time of the follow-up significantly lower than the others on the Concept Mastery Test. Ratings on desirable personality characteristics—self-confidence, perseverance, integration toward goals, absence of inferiority feelings, and even common sense—averaged lower for the C's, whether they were made by wives, parents, or by themselves. There were more cases among them whose scores on the Strong Vocational Interest Test did not match career choices. Both slight and serious maladjustments were far more common among them. But it was the variables included under "Family Background" that showed the largest differences. Far more of the A's than of the C's had come from homes of high occupational and educational status. There was a significantly larger proportion of broken homes in the background of the C's, and divorces among the C subjects themselves were twice as numerous as among the A's. This study furnished striking evidence that background and motivational factors are very influential in determining how effectively high intelligence will be utilized.

A report that this is true even during the school years was presented by Lewis (1941). Lewis' study also was part of a large research project in which the 10 per cent scoring highest on the Kuhlmann-Anderson intelligence test and the 10 per cent scoring lowest were singled out for special scrutiny. Since the total sample included almost 50,000 grade-school children from 310 communities in 36 states, the results had the statistical reliability obtainable with large numbers. In this particular comparison, high-ability children whose scores on school achievement tests averaged at least a year lower than their mental ages were contrasted with those whose achievement was at least a year higher than their mental ages. The groups differed in much the same ways that Terman and Oden's A and C adult groups did. Ratings made by their teachers prior to any of the testing showed the overachievers to be more dependable, original, and self-reliant. They possessed more intellectual interests, as in reading, collecting, and music. A larger proportion of them came from the professional classes, and fewer of them from semi-skilled and unskilled occupational classes.

One side issue on which Terman and his co-workers attempted to get information was the question whether acceleration in school is really as unsatisfactory a way of handling gifted children as many administrators and teachers believe it to be. The comparisons of those who had been accelerated from two to four years with the others indicated that there had been no unfavorable effects. Upon all the indicators of social adjustment and mental health the accelerated individuals ranked high. Pressey (1949) made a number of related studies of the same problem and came to the same conclusion. There were of course individual exceptions, but as a whole the underage students were superior in both social adjustment and educational achievement.

Since the publication of these comprehensive studies of the effects of acceleration, evidence has continued to accumulate in support of this policy. Nevertheless, educators continued to oppose it, even during a period when resources of space and of personnel were barely sufficient to handle a steadily increasing school population. In one of his last important summaries of his work and ideas, Terman (1954) wrote: "It seems that the schools are more opposed to acceleration now than they were thirty years ago. The lockstep seems to have become more and more the fashion, notwithstanding the fact that practically everyone who has investigated the subject is against it."

Perhaps during the decade after Terman wrote these words the tide may have turned. New organizational plans, such as the nongraded elementary school, rapid progress sections in the high schools, and provisions for college credit by examination, have been helping to loosen up the rigid structure to which Terman referred.

In *The Gifted Group at Mid-Life,* the results of the still later follow-up studies, those made in the 1950's, were reported. They indicated that the members of the gifted group, some three and a half decades after their initial selection, were still maintaining their superiority in health, adjustment, intelligence, career success, and contributions to society. Among the men, 86 per cent were working at the professional or semiprofessional level, and only 1 per cent were engaged in semiskilled work (none in unskilled labor). Many of them were listed in *Who's Who* and *American Men of Science;* some had acquired international reputations. Altogether they had published more than 2,000 scientific and technical papers, 60 books and monographs, 33 novels, 375 short stories, novelettes, and plays, 60 essays, critiques and sketches, and 265 miscellaneous articles, as well as hundreds of news stories, editorials, and radio, television, and motion picture scripts. They had taken out at least 230 patents. While the women did not report so many easily identifiable achievements, there were many eminent individuals among them, and there were evidences that the others had lived stimulating and productive lives.

As before, some individuals fell short of these high standards, but no special attempt was made in this study to analyze the ways in which they differed from the others. Three or four men were clearly failures, and another 80 or 90 fell far below the level of the group as a whole.

The study of families of the gifted subjects was a special feature of this follow-up. By this time 93 per cent of the men and 89.5 per cent of the women had married. Slightly over a fifth of them had been divorced one or more times, a figure that is still lower than the proportion of marital failures in the population as a whole. Of these divorcees, 86 per cent remarried. More than 85 per cent of all married subjects rated their marriage as above average in happiness. The average number of children per family was 2.4, and the average IQ for the 1,525 children whom it was possible to test was 132.7. While this is lower than the average had been for the gifted children themselves, it is still about two standard deviations above the population mean. Of a total of 2,452 offspring, only 13 were known to be mentally retarded.

The studies of Terman and the Stanford group have told us much about children who score high on intelligence tests. There is some question as to how much bearing they have upon the question that interested the earlier research workers most, the origin and meaning of genius. One would not, of course, expect anywhere near all of the high-scoring children to attain the distinction for which this term might properly be reserved. In Galton's ingenious scale for evaluating eminence, even the lowest level of eminence—that represented by successful English judges and bishops—was defined as the point reached by only one in 4,000 of the general population. The rare, really illustrious characters of history he placed above the point reached by only one in a million. However, as one reads the thumbnail sketches of the eminent scientists, writers, and professors in the Terman and Oden volumes, it does not seem at all impossible that a few of them will leave a permanent impress on their society.

It was unfortunate that the word "genius" was used as a label for high-IQ children at the time the Terman study began. We no longer use the term in this way.

Some investigators, notably Hollingworth (1942), became especially interested in the rare children with extremely high IQ's, 180 and above. She assembled some fascinating case material on those she had an opportunity to study. In many of these extremely high individuals, creativity and originality had been evident even in early childhood. The following excerpts from the report on Child D, whose IQ was 184, illustrates this kind of achievement: [1]

> *Imaginary land.* From the age of about four years to about the age of seven, D was greatly interested in an imaginary land which he called "Borningtown." He spent many hours peopling Borningtown, laying out roads, drawing maps of its terrain, composing and recording its language (Bornish), and writing its history and literature. He composed a lengthy dictionary—scores of pages—of the Bornish language. The origin of the words *Borningtown* and *Bornish* is not known. It seems possible that D's imaginary land may have arisen out of the mystery of being born.
>
> *Gift for music.* D has had piano lessons for several years, and he has displayed remarkable ability to deal with the mathematical aspects of music. He composed music before he had any instruction in playing musical instruments. He read certain booklets which came with Ampico and decided to compose. He can compose music which he cannot himself play.
>
> *Gifts for form and color in drawing.* D's talent for color, for drawing and design, has been marked from the time he could wield a pencil. His drawings, paintings, and designs would fill a book by themselves.
>
> D loves color, and one of his favorite playthings has been a sample folder of silk buttonhole twists of three hundred shades. Between the ages of eight and nine years he would go over and over these, classifying the colors in various ways, scoring them for beauty, and naming them to satisfy his appreciation of them. Some of these names will give an idea of his appreciation:
>
> | | |
> |---|---|
> | spotted pale | spoiled pink |
> | darkling green | soft light pink |
> | shame blue | meadow beauty pink |
> | dark darking green | cat black |
> | regular green | royalest red |
> | paper white | apron blue |
> | alien white | beau yellow |
> | feeling blue | visitor's green |
>
> One of his favorite games (aged eight to nine years) was to assign a numerical value to each of the 300 shades and then to list them for "highest honors." "Royalest red" nearly always won in these contests.
>
> *Originality* of new concepts and new words. From earliest childhood D has felt a need for concepts and for words to express them that are not to be

[1] Quoted by special permission from *Children Above 180* by L. S. Hollingworth. Copyright, 1942, by Harcourt, Brace & World, Inc.

FIGURE 47
Musical Composition Produced by Child D at Age 8 Years 7 Months
(Hollingworth, 1942, p. 124)

> found in dictionaries. His occupation in this field he calls "wordical work." Some examples are recorded by his mother in the following note dated December, 1916.
>
> "Was having his dinner and being nearly finished said he didn't care to eat any more, as he had a pain in his actum pelopthis. He explained that his actum pelopthis, actum quotatus, serbalopsis, and boobalicta are parts of the body where you sometimes have queer feelings; they don't serve any purpose. He said he also had a place called the boobalunksis, or source of headaches; that the hair usually springs out from around the herkadone; that the perpalensis is the place where socks end, and the bogalegus is the place where legs and tummy come together. He also named one other part, the cobaliscus or smerbalooble, whose function is not explained. The definitions are exactly as he gave them in each instance."
>
> *Invention of games.* D has invented many games. To illustrate this aspect of his mental capacity, there are his designs for three-handed and four-handed checkers. D held that these would be better games than two-handed checkers because they are more complicated. A description of the games invented by D, together with his mathematical calculations concerning the chances and probabilities in each, would fill many pages. (Hollingworth, 1942, pp. 123–127.)

Hollingworth felt that activity of this sort bore much more resemblance to adult genius than the ordinary sort of school work does. So far, however, it has not been reported that any of her small group of eminent children has attained a high degree of adult eminence. (D, whose childhood achievements are catalogued above, died in 1938 at the age of twenty-eight.) It seems likely now that the quality distinguishing Child D from other bright children is *creativity* rather than intelligence. We shall turn to the special research on creativity later in the chapter.

Terman and Oden (1947) also included a special chapter on a group of 47 men and 34 women singled out for special study because their childhood IQ's had been 170 or above. The best general summary of the findings is that this subgroup later differed in no essential way from the group as a whole. The percentage of successful achievement among them was a little higher both in school and in occupational life, but there was no sharp dividing line. These investigators came to feel that above 140 IQ it is not the intelligence level that determines the degree of creativity and that there is no particular advantage in an IQ of 180 over one of 140.

Hollingworth (1940) also pointed out that the tendency for good personality adjustment to accompany high intelligence was not as apparent for the extremely high individuals as for the moderately high. Probably the optimum IQ range for good adjustment is from 130 to 150. Above that level certain problems arise which Hollingworth classified as follows: (1) problems of physique (being weaker and smaller than their classmates and thus susceptible to bullying); (2) problems of adjustment to occupation (preferring self-direction to direction by others); (3) problems involved in "suffering fools gladly" (difficulty in getting along with teachers and classmates who are inferior to them intellectually); and (4) problems created by isolation (the impossibility of finding friends with their own interests and goals). All of these problems are most acute when the child is of elementary-school age; after he gets into the secondary school and college, the intellectual level of those around him is more nearly equal to his own. Witty (1940) also called attention to the fact that some gifted children who appear satisfactorily adjusted when first tested increasingly develop undesirable trends in the direction of either laziness or cynicism.

Terman and Oden's report does not show any clear tendency for the very high subjects to be less well-adjusted adults than the rest. It is interesting to note, however, that the 1928 ratings, made when the children were in their middle teens, did show a significant difference in this direction, a difference which was greater for the girls than for the boys. Even at the time of the 1940 rating, almost twice as many of the women in the high group as in the total group were seriously maladjusted. Although the number of cases comprising this percentage is small, it does seem to point to the possibility that the girls with unusually high IQ's may have more adjustment difficulties than do the boys. The fact that differences appeared most clearly in the 1928 follow-up rather than earlier or later would suggest that children of this sort who tend to have some trouble during adolescence manage to overcome it successfully.

With the progress of research on the gifted child, more and more emphasis has been placed on proper handling and training. We cannot safely assume that because a child's intelligence is high, he will sail through life more easily than his classmates. The average elementary-school curriculum suits him little better than it does the retarded. If he is to develop to the limit of his potentialities—and society has a tremendous interest in seeing that he does—he should get enough special attention to enable him to make the most of his intellectual powers, develop habits of work and concentration, and maintain adequate contacts with his fellow men. It was this emphasis on identifying and nurturing the talents of gifted children that characterized much of the research of the 1950's. Special programs and projects, symposia at professional meetings, books, journal articles, and speeches reflected and stimulated a vastly increased public interest in bright children. All of us, living in a complex society where "brains" are at a premium, must see that for the individual's own sake and for the sake of society, it is important that latent talents be given an opportunity to develop.

STUDIES OF LIVING SCIENTISTS

Because of the importance of scientific work during World War II and in the postwar years, public attention was focused on the need for scientists. The questions raised were more practical and concrete than those growing out of people's interest in the general problem of genius. What combination of abilities does it take to make an outstanding scientist? What motives and personality traits enter into his choice of career? Why are some men more productive than others?

The first important series of studies in this area was carried out by Roe (1951a, 1951b, 1953). Her subjects were biologists, physicists, psychologists, and anthropologists, in each case men who it was agreed were among the most eminent, perhaps *the* most outstanding persons in their respective fields. Though the numbers were small (about 20 in each professional group) the methods of study she employed were very intensive, focusing on personality characteristics, family backgrounds, and motivation. Biographical material and information about attitudes were obtained from interviews. The Rorschach and the Thematic Apperception Tests were given and analyzed. A new high-level intelligence test made up of verbal, spatial, and mathematical sections was administered. Information from all these sources was brought together in a case study of each individual. It is these case studies themselves rather than any of the summary figures that are the most interesting part of the Roe monographs. They show how diverse and individual these men were.

It is difficult to summarize such data in any meaningful way. The subjects, biological, physical, and social scientists, most often came from professional and middle-class homes. In many cases some event occurred during childhood that led to a feeling of *apartness*—something like the death of one parent, a serious illness, or a physical handicap. There seemed to be no general pattern for the choice of a vocation. Some decided early, others much later. In some cases a teacher was very influential; in others childhood hobbies developed into adult work. The possibility of doing research was a decisive factor in many cases. The projective-test protocols and the interview data suggested that these were not particularly well-adjusted groups, in our ordinary sense of the term. There appeared to be a considerable amount of basic insecurity, with work itself serving as an adjustment technique in many cases. The social scientists differed somewhat from the physicists and biologists in that they were more concerned about human relations. They volunteered more biographical information and gave twice as many Rorschach responses. On the whole, however, individual differences far outweighed group differences.

As was expected, there were some group differences in the pattern of abilities shown on the V S M intelligence test (Verbal, Spatial, Mathematical). Interestingly enough, there was a considerable range of total scores on this test. This indicated that while these men were all high in general intellectual ability, some were much higher than others. Furthermore, the ones with the lower scores were just as successful as the higher ones. This corroborated Terman and Oden's conclusion that above a certain level differences in intelligence are not related to success.

Eiduson (1962) made a similar intensive study of 40 living research scientists. The data were obtained from the Rorschach and Thematic Apperception Tests and from clinical interviews. A considerable number of variables were rated by clinicians and compared with the ratings of business men and artists who had been studied in the same manner. The findings agreed with Roe's in many respects. Eiduson too found a great diversity of personality patterns, but among them there were some common threads. The interview reports they gave of their childhoods showed that these men, like the artists but not like the businessmen, had had very little personal contact with their fathers, and that, while many of them held ambivalent attitudes toward their mothers, it was clear that their mothers' influence had directed them toward achievement and education. All of them had shown high intellectual ability at an early age. As in Roe's group, almost all had undergone periods of isolation, either through illness or through physical or psychological circumstances. Most of them had turned away from their families during adolescence more decisively than most young persons do. A drive toward work was one of the principal things they had in common. While it constituted a balance wheel that kept other drives and conflicts under control, it was not a neurotic defense mechanism but an urge to *find out* things—to explore the unknown. They evaluated themselves against an ideal image of the scientist as a lonely searcher, an image that Eiduson thinks may be becoming less and less appropriate in the kind of scientific world where research is now done.

The fact that scientists do in fact play different kinds of roles in the work they do was brought out by Gough and Woodworth (1960). In connection with a large-scale investigation of creative scientists, writers, and architects, forty-five professional research scientists from three industrial laboratories were brought together for a three-day assessment program at the Institute of Personality Assessment and Research at the University of California. Each person was asked to sort 56 personality items in a special set prepared to describe research scientists, showing by his sorting the extent to which each item described him. This made it possible to correlate each person's item placements with those of each of the other subjects and to do a factor analysis of these correlations. The resulting factors consisted of sets of persons representing particular types. The authors labeled them as follows: (1) the zealot; (2) the initiator; (3) the diagnostician; (4) the scholar; (5) the artificer; (6) the esthetician; (7) the methodologist; and (8) the independent. Similar types emerged when forty honor students in the School of Engineering were analyzed by the same procedures.

Probably the most comprehensive analysis of the childhood characteristics of scientists that has ever been made was Terman's (1954) examination of the records of the 800 men in the California gifted group in order to identify factors differentiating between those who became scientists and those who entered other fields of work. Out of about 500 items of information, including test scores, ratings, and biographical data, only 108 items differentiated at the 5 per cent level of significance. The majority of these items had something to do with *interests*. Scores on the Strong test showed the clearest pattern, but interest in science as rated in childhood by parents, teachers, or the children themselves also showed up with high frequency on the records of those who later became scientists.

All these studies seem to show that the things scientists have in common besides high intelligence are interests, values, and self-images. In other personality traits, such as needs, defenses, and psychiatric symptoms, they are very different from one another. They tend to be independent, autonomous persons influenced more by their own thinking than by social pressures.

Eiduson's (1958) study of artists was similar in design to her later study of scientists. Forty artists from the fields of literature, theatre, music, and painting were compared with twenty-five businessmen on the basis of data obtained from interviews and Rorschach and TAT tests. As indicated above, they were later compared with scientists also. The variables that distinguished the artists from the businessmen had more to do with thinking and motivation than with emotions and temperament. Like the scientists, the group of artists was not characterized by any particular kinds of needs, conflicts, or defensive structures. What they did seem to show was sensitivity to experience and an ability to loosen the controls over their thinking and to reorganize their perceptions. These characteristics have shown up as important aspects of creativity, which has been the focus of much research attention since about 1955.

RESEARCH ON CREATIVITY

It would be a more complex task than can be undertaken here to trace the historical origins of this sudden surge of research interest in problems to which sporadic attention had been given since the beginning of the century. One important factor has been the work of Guilford and his associates at the University of Southern California through which the full complexity of the structure of intellect became strikingly apparent. We have referred in Chapter 4 to this program of factor analytic research and the three-dimensional model of intellectual abilities resulting from it. Even before the model had taken its final shape, it was recognized that some of the ingenious tests these workers were constructing to measure special varieties of high-level aptitude and the factors resulting from them were more likely to be related to creative thinking than the typical intelligence tests are. In particular, the tests of *divergent* as contrasted with *convergent* thinking, tests calling for the production of multiple possible solutions rather than single correct answers, appeared promising. Measures of fluency and flexibility also fit into the pattern. Guilford (1957) discussed the relationship of these mental abilities to creative work in the arts after several comprehensive factor analyses had been made (Guilford, et al., 1951, 1952). He concluded that the factors most clearly involved in creative thinking were those that had been labeled originality, redefinition, adaptive flexibility, spontaneous flexibility, associational fluency, expressional fluency, word fluency, ideational fluency, elaboration, and probably some evaluation factors. (Details about the nature of these factors and the ways they are measured can be found in Guilford, 1959, but their titles are descriptive enough to suggest their general nature.) This analysis made it possible to produce batteries of tests for creativity to be used in industrial and educational settings.

Since 1955 many branches have sprouted on the tree of creativity research. The two most relevant to our purposes in this chapter and in this book as a whole are the study of "creative" children and the search for differences between groups of creative and noncreative adults.

Much research on creativity in children of different ages is now under way. Two of these programs have at present writing been reported in sufficient detail to permit a close scrutiny of their results. Getzels and Jackson (1960, 1962) administered five creativity tests, some of them adapted from Guilford's battery, along with a standard intelligence test, to students from the sixth through the twelfth grades of a private school. The general level of intelligence and achievement was high. Two special groups were selected for intensive study, one consisting of persons scoring in the top 20 per cent on creativity but not on intelligence, the other consisting of persons scoring in the top 20 per cent on intelligence but not on creativity. The investigators found that even though there was a 23 point difference in IQ between the two groups (High Creativity, 127; High Intelligence, 150), they were equally superior in academic performance as measured by standard achievement tests. Striking differences were found, however, in indicators of motivation, values, personality, and background factors. The High Creativity students were less oriented toward success in life and more toward self-expression. In story telling and picture completions they evidenced freer fantasy, more humor, more playfulness, more violence. They expressed interest in unusual careers rather than typical ones. A number of significant differences in the homes from which they came showed up in responses to a parent questionnaire and interview. Children in the High Creativity group tended to come from somewhat less well educated, less "bookish" homes (e.g., business rather than university teaching reported as father's occupation) and to have received less supervision from their mothers. The authors incorporate what seems to be the essence of these motivational differences in one sentence. "The high-IQ adolescent may be seen as preferring the anxieties and delights of safety, the high-creativity adolescent the anxieties and delights of growth." (Getzels and Jackson, 1960, p. 17.)

Research of a similar design, but with younger and less highly selected children in a greater variety of schools has been carried out by Torrance (1962, 1964). The same sorts of differences also emerged there. Children scoring high on the creativity tests initiated more ideas than the others did in small group situations that involved creative problem solving. They produced drawings and stories characterized by humor, playfulness, and originality. They were often considered by classmates and teachers to have wild or fantastic ideas. In five out of seven schools where comparisons between High-IQ and High-Creativity children were made, the groups did not differ on standardized achievement tests. In this, as in the Getzels and Jackson study, however, there was evidence that teachers tend to prefer highly intelligent children to highly creative children.

One new kind of information contributed by Torrance and his Minnesota colleagues was that creativity in children seemed to fluctuate during the elementary-school years. After a peak at four and a half, there was a drop at five, the age when children enter kindergarten. During the first, second, and third grades there was a rise again, with another slump in the fourth grade. Recovery in the fifth and sixth grades was followed by a decline at the seventh-grade level. Torrance believed that this developmental curve reflected discontinuities in the American culture rather than basic biological trends.

One interesting fact has turned up again and again in these and other studies. There is only a very low relationship between these creative abilities and intelligence as ordinarily measured. Getzels and Jackson reported correlations ranging from .12 to .39 between IQ and their various creativity tests. Torrance found that the Minnesota battery of creativity tests correlated from .16 to .32 with various intelligence tests in various elementary schools. He mentioned, however, that correlations tended to be larger at the lower levels of ability than at the higher. He proposed that we think in terms of a concept of "thresholds of ability," a concept attributed to John E. Anderson. This is the hypothesis that there exists a cut-off point in the IQ distribution above which further increments of IQ make very little difference in performance. Several lines of evidence would suggest that this occurs at an IQ of about 120, and that the most favorable combination for achievement may be an IQ of at least 120 along with a considerable development of the creative thinking abilities that are independent of intelligence. To summarize and perhaps oversimplify: if a child scores below average on an intelligence test, it is not likely that he will score very high on tests of creativity either. But if he scores high on an intelligence test, he may or may not show aptitudes for creative thinking as well.

In drawing practical conclusions from this line of research, we must always remember that the *predictive validity* of these so-called creativity tests has not yet been demonstrated. We do not have the kind of evidence about what becomes of children who score high on them that Terman's long-continued research has given us about the children with high IQ's. But it is clear that these tests measure some sort of aptitude or talent not revealed by ordinary intelligence tests. As time passes, we will hope to have more information about what such talent is good for.

The other branch of creativity research that is especially important to the psychology of individual differences consists of studies in which groups of adults known to be creative are compared with other groups not distinguished for creativity. The studies by Eiduson already cited, in which artists and scientists were compared with businessmen, can be considered to fall in this category if we are willing to grant that the businessmen are a noncreative group. Probably a more justifiable design, if creativity is essentially what one wishes to assess, is that which was used in a series of projects at the Institute of Personality Assessment and Research at the University of California. Intensive studies were made there of carefully selected groups of writers, scientists, and architects. In each case the first step was to obtain from their peers nominations of outstandingly creative members of the profession. On the basis of this information a group of highly creative persons and a group of representative practitioners could be set up. Persons from these groups were invited to spend a few days at the assessment center on the Berkeley campus. There they took tests, talked to interviewers, and participated in a variety of group procedures.

Data obtained in this way were used to compare persons in the whole professional group with people in general, and to compare the more creative with the less creative members of the profession. The findings are too detailed to be summarized briefly, but a few findings bearing directly on the questions considered in this chapter can be singled out. One is that interests and values showed consistent relationships to creativity. On the Strong, creative persons tended to score high on Psychologist, Architect, and Author, and low on the business and subprofessional scales. On the Allport-Vernon-Lindzey, creative persons in all specialties tended to score high in aesthetic and theoretical values, low in economic values. Groups of "high-creative" males tended to score above average in femininity as measured by interest tests. They preferred complex to simple drawings and produced complex rather than simple designs when they were given materials to order in their own way. On the Myers-Briggs Type Indicator, the one thing all creative groups had in common was an *intuitive* orientation as contrasted with the orientation toward *sensation*.

What this meant was that they tended to perceive *possibilities* rather than *facts.* Creative persons also tended to score low on tests of conformity, although they were not necessarily nonconformists in their behavior. Some of the results suggested that creative persons experience more psychological difficulties, more conflicts between motives and values, than average persons do, but that they have enough *ego strength* to manage this turbulence.[2]

THE COMPLEXITY OF THE PROBLEM OF GENIUS

The intensive study of highly creative persons, as it has been carried on at IPAR, brings us back to the question of genius with which the chapter started. All the kinds of research we have considered have contributed to our present understanding of the problem. While we still do not understand what produces genius, we are now at least able to discard obviously untenable hypotheses and formulate sounder ones.

In the first place, we are now in a position to say quite definitely that high intelligence, defined as the quality measured by tests like the Binet, is a *necessary but not a sufficient* characteristic of genius. In other words, all geniuses are highly intelligent, but not all highly intelligent individuals are geniuses. Unless a person has a high degree of the ability we call intelligence, the chances of his producing any work of immortal significance are negligible. But even if he does have a brilliant intellect, he still may fail to make a mark in the world. Why?

For one thing, there is now abundant evidence that some kinds of intellectual ability are not measured to any extent by standard intelligence tests and that these may be essential for creative work. Genius then may be partly a matter of special aspects of thinking that we are only beginning to discover how to assess.

Besides this, we can fill in from our knowledge of case studies and biographies a catalogue of some other characteristics that appear to be involved in high achievement. One is certainly *special* talent of some kind. What little evidence there is indicates that gifted children are not much more likely than average children to be talented in art, music, or mechanics, though they often stand out in scientific and writing activities (Wilson, 1953). But unless they happen to have some outstanding talent or interest, some basis for specialization, they will fall short of the highest levels of achievement. Every college counselor is familiar with the case of the high-ability student who finds it extremely difficult, almost impossible, to choose a major. If he forces himself to choose on a purely arbitrary basis, such a person is likely to continue to try to cultivate the talents he

[2] Summary of IPAR findings based on summary in *Carnegie Corporation of New York Quarterly,* July, 1961, Volume 9, Number 3.

has had to pass by. The line between the versatility which is an asset and the diffuseness of effort which is a liability is often a very fine one.

Another essential is powerful motivation of some sort. It is in this sense that Lombroso and Kretschmer were partly right—that a stormy inner life akin to psychotic or neurotic disturbances may underlie great achievements. But while the creative worker may show some symptoms of mental ill health, he is distinguished also by a powerful ego adequate to control conflicting drives and impose order on chaotic experience. For some kinds of creative workers, especially scientists, curiosity furnishes the driving force. Some problem engages the person's attention early in his career, and from then on he channels his life into a search for its solution. The one thing a creative person will not settle for is an easy way out of the struggles of life—security through conformity.

Other qualities are desirable supplements to these essentials. Galton emphasized physical stamina, and many others have called attention to the protracted difficult labor required for all tremendous achievement. Many eminent men have, however, been sickly and frail, so that health would not seem to be a primary characteristic. Good habits of *work* are an advantage also. Many a promising writer has fizzled out because he could not bring himself to write regularly; many a brilliant would-be scientist fails because he never can organize his time in a way that leaves him free to do the necessary experiments. But the fact remains that there are lazy, unsystematic people who turn out inspired creative work from time to time, so that good work habits also are a supplementary rather than an essential characteristic. One might go on adding to this list indefinitely traits that would be desirable for a genius to have and that selected individuals do show to a high degree.

Probably the most important practical outcome of all the research in this field is the fact that we now know more than before about how to identify promising children and how to provide situations in which their talents can be brought to fruition.

SUMMARY

Since the earliest research on individual differences, psychologists have been interested in the nature and origin of genius. Different kinds of research have predominated at different periods.

During the first phase, statistical surveys of eminent individuals showed that, contrary to widely held popular opinion, such persons are likely to be stronger and more vigorous than the average man. They come predominantly from the upper occupational classes and from regions where a high level of education prevails. The analysis of biographical information shows that they were highly intelligent from childhood on and that they are superior to the average in character and personality traits.

Studies of gifted children have shown that they too are superior to the average in health and physical size and strength, that they come predominantly from the upper occupational levels, and that their play life and range of interests, their character and personality traits are superior to the average. Early academic superiority is maintained throughout the school years. The follow-up studies of Terman's original group make it clear that the great majority of the gifted have been successful in their chosen occupations, though few if any have as yet achieved work of genius quality. Hazards in the way of the satisfactory adjustment of gifted children, particularly those with the extremely high IQ's, have become apparent, and our schools are now trying various methods for meeting the special problems of this group.

A third approach, prominent during the 1950's, was to make case studies of outstanding living scientists, and to a lesser extent, of artists as well, searching for common factors underlying their achievements. While scientists differ from each other more than they resemble one another in most personality traits and in childhood experiences, they do have in common high intellectual ability, the exposure to some circumstance that isolated each of them for a time and led him to develop his own particular resources, and an overpowering interest in their work and commitment to it.

With the development of tests to measure kinds of intellectual ability not used in intelligence tests, especially the ability to do divergent thinking, research comparing highly creative with highly intelligent children was undertaken. While the two groups did not differ in measured school achievement, they differed quite markedly in attitudes and styles of self-expression. Studies of highly creative adults have pointed to some of the same special kinds of motivation—interest in the theoretical and aesthetic rather than the practical, free expression of fantasy, and strong, often conflicting, drives and values regulated by strong ego-controls.

The body of research evidence which has accumulated would lead us to conclude that high intelligence, though essential to genius, is not synonymous with it. Special abilities, motivation, habits of work, and probably many other factors must become teamed up in the production of outstanding achievement.

Part Four

FACTORS PRODUCING DIFFERENCES

CHAPTER 16

The Relationship of Mental to Physical Characteristics

INTRODUCTION

PROBABLY NO BELIEF has been more tenaciously held among people of all times than the conviction that it is possible to judge an individual's mental characteristics by the way he is put together physically. Novelists describe the build, facial shape, coloring, and clothes of their characters in such a way as to accentuate the inner qualities which they assume are expressed by these things. Intelligent men and women who "pooh-pooh" the idea of fortune-telling in general still feel that "there may be something in this palmistry or phrenology." Books explaining personality in terms of the glands obtain wide and enthusiastic acceptance. Employment interviewers develop their own systems of judging prospective employees by their appearance. Habits of thinking in such terms are ingrained in our language in such expressions as "high-brow," "long-headed," or "thin-skinned."

The investigation of these relationships is an important scientific problem. It *is* advantageous for us to be able to make good sight judgments of people. Hundreds of life situations require us to make the attempt. But here, as in so many other areas covered by differential psychology, it is important to remember that a *wrong* judgment is worse than a suspended judgment or no judgment at all. The trouble with most of our rule-of-thumb methods is that they may lead us to make serious errors. It is the task of the psychologist to check up on what the popular beliefs are and then to discover what physical characteristics, if any, really *are* related to mental ability and personality.

There are special reasons why people's conclusions on this subject are likely to be faulty. The scientist along with the man in the street is susceptible to these errors and must constantly guard against them. First, human beings are very prone to base their beliefs on a few outstanding instances and to neglect the much more numerous examples that do not support them. It is this tendency that keeps superstitions alive and active. The untrained observer is likely to remember the one person he knows who broke a mirror just the night before his house burned down and to forget that mirror factories are constantly turning out replacements for other broken mirrors in houses still standing. Similarly, if a person has one intellectual friend with a high forehead or one timid associate with a receding chin, his opinions tend to be determined or confirmed by his contact with these cases.

Second, attitudes and prejudices with which people approach their personal relationships or their scientific research actually enter into their judgments of mental characteristics. Even if the man with the receding chin is possessed of more than the average force of character, he is likely to be adjudged a weakling until he proves himself otherwise. The slim, aristocratic-looking boy may get better marks in school for the same quality of work than his pudgy neighbor does. The sales manager who thinks size is related to aggressiveness may rate the tall salesmen on his staff higher than the short ones. In scientific research, wherever evaluation of personality is based on *ratings* by other people, we must watch out for this source of error. Only when tests are used, does it cease to be important.

Third, any unusual physical characteristic may appear to carry personality characteristics along with it because of the way in which its possessor sees *himself*. These *indirect* effects of physical characteristics on personality can easily be confused with direct causal relationships. Careful study, however, will always show the difference, since in a group of people, examples will occur in which the same physical trait is associated with mental traits that are quite opposite. Take, for instance, the case of the weak, undersized child handicapped in infancy by a long illness. He may be shy, withdrawn, and retiring. On the other hand, he may try to compensate for his weakness by being noisy and troublesome in school and terrorizing younger children. These indirect effects of physical characteristics on personality are highly important, but there is nothing constant about them that we can use to help us make sight judgments of people. Only detailed study of an individual will show what his physical endowment means to *him* and how he is reacting to it.

Fourth, it must be remembered that relationships holding at the extremes of the distribution of human characteristics do not necessarily hold throughout the average range. There are numerous pathological conditions that produce abnormal personality characteristics, but unless conditions really *are* pathological, no abnormalities appear. Idiots of the microcephalic variety have extremely small heads. This does *not,* however, warrant a conclusion that the smaller your head is, the nearer you are to idiot status. The cretin's feeble-mindedness, along with definite physical symptoms, arises from an extreme thyroid deficiency; but that fact tells us nothing about the relationship of thyroid functioning to intelligence within the normal range. Extreme cases of various kinds often do suggest hypotheses which we may check by research. In themselves they do not *prove* anything about people in general. With these cautions in mind, we can proceed to the discussion of what the research workers have found.

BODY STRUCTURES AND INTELLIGENCE

A tremendous amount of detailed research in which careful measurements of various structural and anatomical characteristics were correlated with scores on intelligence tests can be summarized in a single brief statement: the correlations are too low to be of any practical significance. Paterson (1930) brought together the findings of the early studies, findings constituting conclusive evidence for this conclusion. Nothing in later correlational investigations has changed it, although the work on constitutional types to be discussed in a later section suggests that a different formulation of the problem may be of some value.

From the days of Porter's (1895) pioneer investigation of 35,500 St. Louis school children on to the present time, evidence has been amassed that what correlation there is between body size and intelligence is positive rather than negative. Such coefficients seldom exceed .2, however, and probably .1 is a more typical figure. The most likely explanation seems to be that families in which good intellectual development occurs also stimulate good physical development, and vice versa. Some evidence that the link is of this sort was furnished by Laycock and Caylor (1964), who compared physical measurements of 81 gifted children (average IQ 141) with the measurements of 81 of their nongifted siblings (average IQ 109). Under these circumstances, when the high and the average IQ subjects came from the same families, no significant differences in their physiques were found.

Correlations between other aspects of physique and intelligence test scores have also consistently turned out to be low. Some investigators have worked with height-weight ratios, some with head measurements, some with facial characteristics. Some have used maturity indices such as X-ray photographs of the hand and wrist. Paterson's 1930 book is an excellent source of detailed information about all of these unsuccessful attempts.

DISEASES AND PHYSICAL HANDICAPS

Another research area where low correlations of no practical significance have repeatedly turned up is the study of the relationship of physical impairments of various sorts to mental functioning. The general, common-sense opinion is that the way one feels has a good deal of influence on how well one thinks. Time after time students explain their inadequate performances on examinations in terms of the cold from which they are suffering or the sleep that they failed to get the night before. Teachers are taught to observe closely the physical defects shown by their pupils and to expect better school work, once these are corrected. Thus the trend of the research evidence in this area is likely to be somewhat surprising to people.

A number of studies have indicated that most kinds of physical defects bear little or no relationship to intelligence. A number of studies on malnutrition show that groups of undernourished children are fully as bright as those who are well fed. Defective teeth are just as common among the normal as among the dull. Children with diseased tonsils do not differ intellectually from those with normal tonsils, as Figure 48 strikingly shows.

There is some evidence from the early study by Ayres (1909–10) and

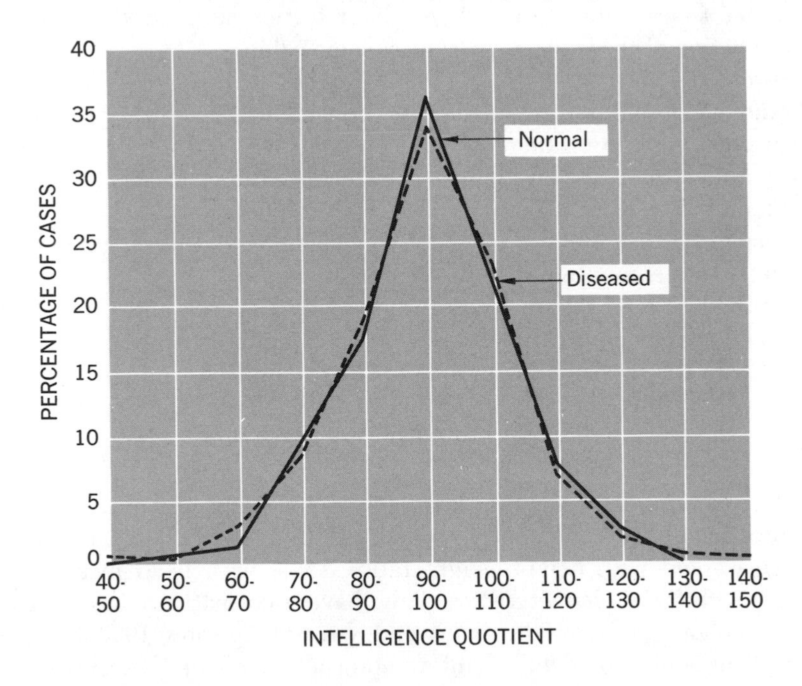

FIGURE 48

Frequency Distributions for Groups of Children with Normal and Diseased Tonsils

(Rogers, 1922)

the surveys by Sandwick (1920) and by Kempf and Collins (1929) that dull, normal, and bright groups of children are differentiated by total number of defects of all sorts, although some other school surveys (Mallory, 1922; Stalnaker and Roller, 1927; Westenberger, 1927) failed to substantiate these findings. Smillie and Spencer (1926) showed that lowered intelligence tends to accompany hookworm infestations. The average IQ for the very heavily infested cases in a hookworm "area" was 76.3, whereas for the children free from the condition it was 90.2.

The studies in which correlations have been computed between the *extent* of the defects and intelligence are more meaningful than the group comparisons. With few exceptions, these correlations have all run very low. Condition of teeth, nutritional status, condition of cervical glands and tonsils and adenoids all gave correlations of .15 or lower. (See Paterson, 1930, Ch. 6.) Since the data on which they were based were obtained by many different investigators working in a wide variety of places in England and the United States, we are justified in concluding that the relationship in general is low and insignificant.

The most reasonable explanation of whatever slight relationships have been found between physical defects and intelligence is in terms of the class differences we have already discussed in some detail. The poorer socio-economic groups have a larger number of uncorrected defects; they also average somewhat lower in IQ. The important correlation is the one between socio-economic status and intelligence, and we have already seen how difficult it is to analyze so as to show which is cause and which effect.

One other type of study has been carried out in connection with some physical defects. "Before-and-after" studies, designed to show whether or not the correction of a defect increases the intellectual level, are particularly interesting. It is important that a control group be used in this type of research to make sure that whatever change is noted arises from the elimination of the defect and not from some other unanalyzed factor in the situation. This has been done for malnutrition, for dental caries, and for tonsils. In general, such studies have shown the effect of the treatment on the IQ to be negligible (Paterson, 1930). Feeding a child well and attending to his teeth and tonsils do *not* make him brighter, whatever enthusiastic champions of public health measures may say. The physical benefits must be valued on their own merits.

Even the common belief that temporary illness depresses examination scores seems to be unwarranted. Some convincing evidence on this point came from a study made during World War I when it was necessary to test a group of men who had been recently inoculated for typhoid fever (Paterson, 1930, pp. 204–205). The average score for these 178 men was 67.7 as compared with an average of 67.1 for 7,167 men not recently inoculated. When the average score for those who reported that they were feeling the after-effects was compared with the average for those who were subjectively not affected, the figures turned out to be 67.4 and 67.9, so much alike that it must be concluded that the illness had no effect on the performance. It is still possible that certain *individuals* are so upset by their physical ailments as not to be able to concentrate on the tasks assigned them, and the good psychometrician is always on the lookout for such cases in individual testing. But, on the whole, regardless of what people may think of their own test performances, they are not necessarily handicapped when they do not feel well. Whether they would be able to carry on serious mental work for long periods of time under those circumstances is, of course, another matter, calling for a different kind of investigation.

The question whether longer periods of illness might have a depressing effect has also been considered. In a careful comparison between 101 children who had been stricken with poliomyelitis a year before the study began and a control group, E. L. Phillips, Berman, and Hanson (1948) found that there had been a 1.5-point drop in IQ for the polio group as compared with a 2-point increase for the controls. While the difference is statistically significant (at the 2 per cent level), it is too small to be of any practical importance. Harris (1950), who obtained ratings of 58 of these same subjects two years after their illness on a variety of personality traits, found that they were undistinguishable from the controls.

There seem to be only two kinds of physical handicap that have appreciable effects on mental functioning. The first is a disease or defect in the central nervous system itself, such as encephalitis lethargica. The other is a sensory handicap severe enough to reduce drastically the amount of stimulation a growing child receives from the world around him. It has become increasingly clear that mental growth depends upon this constant stimulation from the environment. Thus it is important to recognize such conditions as deafness and even minor hearing loss at an early age if a child's intellectual development is not to be impaired.

In summarizing all the work on the relationship of physical defects to intelligence, Paterson (1930) stressed the point that nature has thrown strong safeguards around the central nervous system, upon which intellectual functioning depends. Were it possible for any minor illness or injury to disorganize the thinking processes, which are our chief resource when in difficulty, it is probable that the human race would not have been able to endure the vicissitudes of existence as long as it has. This viewpoint makes the research findings seem reasonable. The general conclusions are that no physical condition except one that acts on the central nervous system itself has a serious effect on intellectual efficiency, at least for limited periods of time, and that no developmental handicap except one that severely restricts the individual's contact with his environment and his mastery of language has a serious effect on his IQ.

PHYSIOLOGICAL AND BIOCHEMICAL PROCESSES

As time passed, the research interests of psychologists shifted away from the kinds of problem we have just considered and focused more on the relations between our mental makeup and the functioning of physiological and biochemical systems in the body. It seemed reasonable to suppose that differences in some kinds of intellectual functioning might be linked to some aspect of these systems. It seemed an even more plausible hypothesis that personality differences might be based on such internal physiological factors.

Some psychologists attempted to relate differences in blood composition to personality differences. Several hypotheses were proposed: (1) that alkalinity is correlated with excitability; (2) that proportions of creatinine, phosphorus, and cholesterol are correlated with specific personality traits such as good-nature and perseverance; (3) that *variability* of blood composition from day to day is related to emotional instability. Results were inconclusive. One investigator, using a small number of cases, would find a trend in one direction; another with a different small group would find an opposite trend. The study by H. Goldstein (1935) demonstrated one of the reasons for this inconsistency. His subjects were nineteen college men. Each of them was given blood tests twice a week for ten weeks, and was asked to fill out the Bernreuter Personality Inventory and the CAVD intelligence test. The most striking finding was the great variability in the same individual from time to time. In all except one of the variables tested (cholesterol), there was as much variation in the twenty measurements of the same individuals as in one measurement for the nineteen individuals at any given time. For instance, the person whose blood was most alkaline one week might be average or even low in alkalinity the next week. The person who was very low in blood sugar on one trial might be fairly high the next time. What this means is that there is little prospect of getting significant correlations between blood concentrations taken at any single time and personality traits. There did seem to be a little evidence for the third hypothesis connecting blood variability with emotional instability, since individual variability from day to day was correlated to the extent of .41 with the neurotic-tendency score on the Bernreuter test. With an experimental group of only nineteen cases, however, it was impossible to be sure that this constituted evidence for an actual relationship.

Other research workers attempted to relate hormonal differences to personality differences. A fact that suggested the possibility of such correlations was the finding that glandular disturbances were unusually frequent in children with behavior problems. Lurie (1938), for instance, found in his analysis of 1,000 problem children that 20 per cent showed some glandular abnormality, and in 10 per cent this appeared to be a causative factor in the child's behavior. The thing that makes it difficult to attribute any specific personality trait to the functioning of a specific gland, however, is that quite different patterns of behavior may arise from the same apparent cause. Inadequate thyroid functioning usually produces a condition of sluggishness, dullness, and lack of energy. But some children with this same physiological defect show instead motor restlessness, destructiveness, and speech disturbances. The most likely explanation is that the behavior disorders are a *reaction or adjustment* on the child's part to the way he feels and his recognition of the fact that he is different from his fellows. They are thus indirectly rather than directly connected with the glandular disturbances. Since these patterns of adjustment are highly individual matters depending upon everything else in the person's experience, we would not expect to find general correlations between the physiological and the personality variables.

The relationship of sex-hormone production to various aspects of masculinity and femininity has also been a research topic of some interest. In general, as Beach (1948) has pointed out, the higher a species is in the evolutionary scale the more its sex behavior is determined by social factors and learning rather than by hormonal influence directly. However, there have been a few studies that suggested that some correlation between endocrine and personality measurements persist in human subjects. Sollenberger (1940) reported some relationships between the urinary excretion of male sex hormone and the interests and attitudes of adolescent boys. Stone and Barker (1939) showed that premenarcheal and postmenarcheal girls differed significantly in their interests. In both these studies, since the subjects were adolescents, the interest differences might have occurred, of course, as one consequence of their becoming aware of their own maturing, rather than as a direct consequence of the presence of sex hormones in the blood. It seems less possible to account in this way, however, for the correlation of .58 that Levy (1953) obtained between maternal behavior and duration of menstrual flow for 72 women whom he interviewed.

The one measurement of glandular functioning which, it appeared, might have some definite relationship to intelligence was basal metabolism. This is a measure of oxygen consumption in the body, which is closely related to the functioning of the thyroid gland. When basal metabolism is low, it is standard medical practice to resort to thyroid medication. It has, of course, been known for a long time that an extreme degree of thyroid deficiency early in life results in the type of feeblemindedness called cretinism. The question is whether children beyond the earliest years whose thyroid deficiency is less extreme will exhibit some degree of mental retardation. The strongest evidence for such a relationship came from two studies by Hinton (1936, 1939). He obtained under very carefully controlled conditions the basal metabolic rates for 200 orphanage and private-school children in the Chicago area. He then gave each one a Binet Test and an Arthur Performance Test to get both a verbal and a non-verbal index of intelligence. For the total group, aged six to fifteen, the correlations were as follows:

Binet IQ *vs*	BMR	.71
Arthur IQ *vs*	BMR	.74

Analysis of the figures by separate age groups showed coefficients in the .70's for all groups from six through eleven. Above that age they were considerably smaller. Hinton interpreted this to mean that the relationship holds most strongly during the childhood years of growth and is upset by the metabolic changes associated with adolescence. Other investigators have not obtained significant correlations between BMR and either measured intelligence or academic performance, but their subjects were older than Hinton's so that it is not clear whether the findings of the different studies are in conflict or not. Shock and Jones (1939) found no significant relationships between any of the physiological variables they measured, basal metabolic rate, blood pressure, pulse rate, and vital capacity, and scores on the Terman Group Test, but their subjects were adolescents. Yarbrough and McCurdy (1958) summarized several studies reporting near-zero relationships between basal metabolism and achievement for college students. Until or unless Hinton's study is repeated, the question must be considered to be still open.

Another physiological research area in which psychologists became interested was nutrition. The possibility of improving intelligence or personality by enriching the diet in one way or another is a very appealing one. The largest of the studies investigating the effects of dietary *deficiencies* was carried on during the war years by Keys et al., and reported in detail in their book *The Biology of Human Starvation* (1950). The 36 young men who underwent a radical decrease in food intake over a period of six months were subjected to all sorts of tests and examinations. In general, the result seemed to substantiate those obtained previously in showing that mental *abilities* changed very little. Drive and motivation, however, were markedly decreased, and marked neurotic characteristics appeared both in the subjects' behavior and in their responses to the MMPI test (Schiele and Brozek, 1948). It is interesting to note that neurotic manifestations differed from person to person and that there were marked individual differences in the capacity to withstand this stress.

There is some possibility that in younger children dietary deficiencies may impair mental functioning as well as personality, and that proper treatment may improve it. Examined superficially, results with regard to the B-complex vitamins seem to be conflicting. Guetzkow and Brozek (1946) and O'Shea et al. (1942), presented evidence that such deficiencies did not impair intelligence and supplementation did not improve it. R. F. Harrell (1947), on the other hand, in an unusually well-controlled study of 60 paired groups of orphanage children, showed that adding extra thiamin to the diet produced significant changes in intelligence test scores and in performance on tests of learning and visual acuity. Bernhardt et al. (1948), applying similar treatment to eleven-year-old children in Toronto, where identical twins were used as experimental subjects and controls, did not find any significant differences that could be attributed to the thiamin. Contradictory as they at first seem, taken as a whole these results make sense. The absence of any effect in the first two studies is explainable on the grounds that they used *adult* subjects. As we have noted previously, mental ability, once fully matured, is quite resistant to change. The difference between the two studies on children can be understood if we assume that the diet of Harrell's orphanage group was somewhat deficient at the beginning, whereas the Toronto children, living in their own homes, were probably well enough nourished so that the extra thiamin was neither needed nor utilized by their bodies. Most of the studies of IQ change in children following upon any sort of environmental change indicate that it is easier to produce IQ increases by improving unsatisfactory surroundings than by making an already good situation even better. This point will be considered in more detail in the next chapter.

Perhaps the most controversial of the research problems has been the attempt to improve the intelligence of feeble-minded children by giving large doses of glutamic acid. This is an amino acid which it was thought might be used by the brain in the synthesis of acetylcholine, a chemical playing an important part in nerve action (Gadson, 1951). The earlier studies, especially those by Zimmerman et al. (1948, 1951), were so loosely designed that their results could not be said to prove anything. As research reports on this topic multiplied, some cited significant increases, and others did not. Astin and Ross (1960) reviewed thirty-three of these conflicting reports and showed rather conclusively that the only studies in which positive results were obtained were those that had not used control groups for comparison purposes or those in which some other essential experimental control had been omitted. The well-designed studies uniformly produced nonsignificant results.

The measurement of electrical activity in the brain and recording it on the electroencephalogram or EEG opened up new possibilities of exploring physical-mental relationships. The most common research approach was to correlate some aspect of what is called "alpha activity" with intelligence. Alpha waves are those with a frequency of about ten per second, most characteristic of normal children and adults in a relaxed waking state. It was established by Travis and Gottlober (1936, 1937) that a person's brain waves do show individuality, can be identified with a high degree of agreement by different judges, and are consistent from day to day. Whether these individual differences in EEG are correlated with psychological traits of any sort, however, is less certain. Kreezer (1940) obtained correlations in the .30's between Alpha Index and mental age for Mongolian idiots whose mental ages ranged from 1.5 to 7.5 years. Since in these cases brain damage might produce both the abnormal EEG's and the feeble-mindedness, it is impossible to generalize from this special group to nonpathological cases. In a similar study in which the subjects were 46 familial mental defectives with no obvious physical pathology, Kreezer and Smith (1950) found that there was some correlation between Alpha Frequency and mental age, but it was too low for statistical significance. Knott, Friedman, and Bardsley (1942) reported a correlation of .50 between Alpha Frequency and IQ for 48 eight-year-old children, a coefficient which is statistically above the chance level. For twelve-year-olds, however, the correlation was only .12. The decrease here might be due to adolescent changes which upset the relationship. Generally speaking, investigators have not reported significant correlations between any aspect of EEG and intelligence for normal children.

There is some conflict in the results reported for adults. Shagass (1946) found no correlation between Alpha Frequency and intelligence in air-crew candidates. But Mundy-Castle (1958) found a correlation of .51 between Alpha Frequency and IQ for 34 South African adults. He interpreted this to mean that "central excitability" or "cortical conductivity" is directly related to intelligence, but there is insufficient evidence to permit such a conclusion to be drawn with certainty.

There is some possibility that the EEG may be related to personality characteristics. Reports from various clinics and schools indicate that a large proportion of behavior problem children have abnormal brain waves, many of them of an epileptiform nature. Attempts to correlate alpha activity with scores on personality inventories (Henry and Knott, 1941) have not met with much success. Saul, Davis, and Davis (1949) reported some very striking relationships between the EEG patterns of 136 adult patients and their predominant personality characteristics as these became apparent during psychoanalysis. (It is in line with all the evidence as to the persistence and distinctiveness of these EEG "brain-prints" that they did not change during psychotherapy.) The very passive individuals had high Alpha Indices. Women with strong masculine trends or maternal drives had low Alpha Indices. Frustrated, demanding, hostile, aggressive women had mixed or irregular records. These findings were reported in a descriptive way that made any check on the statistical significance of the relationships impossible, but the results are at least suggestive.

Great strides were made in electroencephalographic work after World War II through the use of new methods of analyzing the record of electrical activity in the brain into its components (W. G. Walter, 1953). Much of this work has been designed to throw light on brain functioning in general, but some attention has also been paid to the relationship of individual patterns to personality. In addition to types based on the predominance of the three principal types of waves—alpha, delta, and theta—Walter and his co-workers have set up distinctions based on the way in which a person's EEG record *changes* with stimulation. It is a familiar fact that alpha activity which is elicited from electrodes at the back of the head when the eyes are closed usually disappears when the eyes are opened, or when the person is requested to make some mental effort. But some individuals, according to Walter, show no alpha rhythm at any time. These turn out to be persons who think by means of visual imagery. The opposite type, in which alpha rhythms persist even when the eyes are open, includes those who tend toward auditory or kinesthetic rather than visual perceptions. Here again the detailed evidence is not presented, and much of the discussion is speculative, but the ideas are extremely interesting.

The most comprehensive attempt to analyze the relationships between certain aspects of brain chemistry and behavior is the program of research Rosenzweig, Krech, and their associates at the University of California have under way (Rosenzweig, Krech, and Bennett, 1960), using rats as subjects. The basic hypothesis is that the amount of acetylcholine, a substance known to be released at the synapse and to facilitate the transmission of the nerve impulse, is related to effectiveness in problem solving. The specific hypotheses guiding these research efforts have changed as the work has progressed, but the general trend of the evidence for this kind of relationship is positive.

There has been continuous progress over a period of several decades in research on individual differences in the functioning of the autonomic nervous system as a whole. Using indices that appeared promising from previous work, Wenger (1942) put together five measurements that would evaluate *autonomic balance,* or the extent to which sympathetic reactions, on the one hand or parasympathetic, on the other, predominate in a person's makeup. He showed that such scores were stable from day to day and that they distributed themselves in something like a normal distribution. He then looked for evidence with regard to psychological correlates of these scores. In a study of 87 children, aged six to thirteen, Wenger (1947) picked out the ten with extreme sympathetic scores, and contrasted them with the ten obtaining the extreme parasympathetic scores. One would expect the S group to be more reactive, excitable, unstable, and inhibited, the P group calmer, better nourished, and more phlegmatic. Using a number of indices of personality characteristics—ratings, personality test scores of the parents, and the like—Wenger made specific predictions with regard to the differences between his two groups. The differences turned out to be in the predicted direction for most of them, but only a few were of clear statistical significance with such small numbers. Inspection of the distributions indicated that it was only at the extremes that personality differences were unambiguously evident. For the bulk of the subjects with scores near the middle of the sympathetic-parasympathetic distribution, no predictions could be made. In a later large-scale study of Army Air Force men, Wenger (1948) used a number of methods for assessing the meaning in personality terms of scores for autonomic balance. One comparison was made in order to check the hypothesis that men with scores toward the sympathetic pole would show a tendency to become anxious in stress situations. Groups of men who had been returned from duty suffering from either operational fatigue or outright neurosis were compared with preflight cadets. As the hypothesis would have led us to predict, these anxious airmen scored significantly higher in sympathetic activity. The fact that other returnees did not differ from the cadets seemed to indicate that it was not simply exposure to combat that produced the difference. Another type of what might be called validation, in which autonomic balance scores were correlated with scores on personality inventories, was less successful. Some of the correlations were statistically significant, but they were all low. This state of affairs might reflect the inadequacy of the personality tests rather than the inadequacy of the physiological measure, but the doubt remains.

Another important finding in work on individual differences in autonomic functioning is that individuals show characteristic *patterns* of response. Lacey (1950) and Lacey and Van Lehn (1952) demonstrated the existence of such patterns and their consistency from one occasion to another. Terry (1953) made a factor analysis of twenty-two autonomic measures obtained from 85 male college students under rest and under mild stress conditions. There seemed to be evidence for three separate autonomic factors: conductance, heart period, and blood pressure. Later work (Lacey and Lacey, 1958) indicated that there were even more complex kinds of individual differences than had been recognized at first. Some persons showed the same pattern of response in different stress situations; others did not. While the individual patterns of response were generally consistent for a four-year period, some individuals were more consistent than others. The many aspects of this research program are conveniently summarized in Lacey (1959).

These individual differences in the pattern and amount of reactivity in the autonomic nervous system have also been examined in the longitudinal study of children at the Fels Institute (Sontag, 1963). A number of interesting correlations have turned up. For example, fetal activity in the eighth and ninth month correlates with social apprehension in nursery school. This measure of social apprehension at the age of two to five in turn correlates significantly with social apprehension at the age of twenty-two to twenty-five. Fetal heartrate lability correlates significantly (rho = .52) with heart rate lability at eighteen in the 12 cases available for comparison. Individual differences in cardiac response to stress were related to personal style. Strong cardiac reactors were more likely to react affectively to a picture story test and less likely to exhibit emotional control in social situations than the noncardiac reactors were.

It appears now that it may be possible to bring many of these findings together under the general heading of individual differences in *activation* (Duffy, 1962), or *arousal* (Fiske and Maddi, 1961), and that neurophysiological research, particularly the work on the reticular formation in the brain, may help to explain them. It is clear that such individual differences exist and that they affect behavior in many situations. A good summary is available in Duffy (1962, Chap. 10).

Simply to say that individuals differ in the sensitivity of their activation mechanism, however, is to leave out what may be an important part of the story. There is some evidence that the persons showing the greatest amount of *internal* activation show the least evidence of it in their behavior. H. E. Jones (1935, 1950) found that in young children reactivity as measured by the galvanic skin response (GSR) was not correlated with overt response to fear-producing stimuli. Similarly, among adolescents, those whose GSR's were most pronounced, the "internalizers" were rated higher than those with the low GSR's, the "externalizers," on many social traits such as being calm, good-natured, deliberative, cooperative, responsible, resolute, constant in mood. It was those with the low GSR response who were rated excitable and unstable.

A similar distinction was proposed on the basis of another physiological difference by Funkenstein, King, and Drolette (1954). "Anger in" subjects could be distinguished from "anger out" subjects. The behavioral differences were like those produced experimentally by two hormones affecting the autonomic system—adrenalin and noradrenalin.

BIOCHEMICAL INDIVIDUALITY

It may turn out that the most valuable contribution research on individual differences in physiological and biochemical reactions will make to further thinking is to turn our attention from traits studied one at a time to the patterns of characteristics which underlie the uniqueness of individuals. The person whose work has been most influential in this direction is R. J. Williams. In his books, *The Human Frontier*, 1946, *Free and Unequal*, 1953, and *Biochemical Individuality*, 1956, he has argued eloquently that the individual should be investigated simultaneously by scientists from many disciplines. In the last of these books, especially, he has assembled evidence showing just how marked the differences between individuals are. There is no such thing as a "normal" person, if one considers at the same time differences in digestive tracts, muscular systems, circulatory systems, numbers of different types of blood cells, and the many other things that can be measured. Because they have concerned themselves mainly with one of these systems at a time, medical men have assumed that most persons are somewhere near the norm, and that only a minority are deviant. Psychologists make the same error when they measure one trait at a time and apply normal curve statistics.

As a biochemist, Williams became especially interested in individuality with regard to (1) the composition of body fluids, such as blood, digestive juices, etc.; (2) the enzyme levels in tissues and body fluids; (3) the pharmacological responses to specific drugs; and (4) the quantitative needs for specific nutrients, such as minerals, amino acids, and vitamins. He and his students showed that individuals differ markedly in their metabolic patterns, as measured by what is excreted in the urine. Figure 49 shows the device by which Williams portrays biochemical individuality graphically. Individual A was unusually sensitive to potassium chloride, and showed a predominantly alkaline urinary reaction. Individual B, on the other hand, was most sensitive to creatinine, and showed an acid urinary reaction. Some of the difference persisted, even when the subjects were placed on exactly the same diet.

Psychologists would, of course, like to know what differences these unique patterns make in behavior. One study (F. J. King, Bowman, and Moreland, 1961) measured the amount of amino acids excreted in the urine and correlated these six measures with seven measures of intellectual capacities, using a statistical technique, canonical correlation, by means of which a whole set of scores can be correlated with another set, rather than dealing with only two variables at a time, as ordinary correlational techniques do. The subjects were 58 children ranging in age from eleven to sixteen. A sizable negative correlation (—.599) was found, indicating that those who excreted a large amount of the amino acids (and thus, by inference, had not metabolized them) were less bright than those who excreted a smaller amount.

A more extensive study, growing directly out of Williams' concepts, is one by Sanders, Mefferd, and Bown (1960). Their subjects were male college freshmen assigned to one of three comparison groups on the bases of their verbal and quantitative scores on the entrance examination. There were 30 in the Vq group (high on verbal, low on quantitative), 25 in the vQ (low on verbal, high on quantitative), and 29 in the VQ group (high on both). Besides comparing the groups on personality and achievement tests, these investigators analyzed 31 constituents of urine samples. A number of significant differences appeared, most marked for the Vq group. These boys were lower on 24 of the 31 constituents. It is not clear

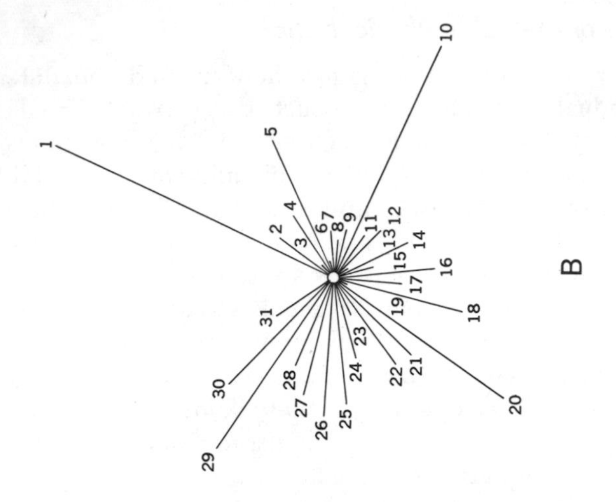

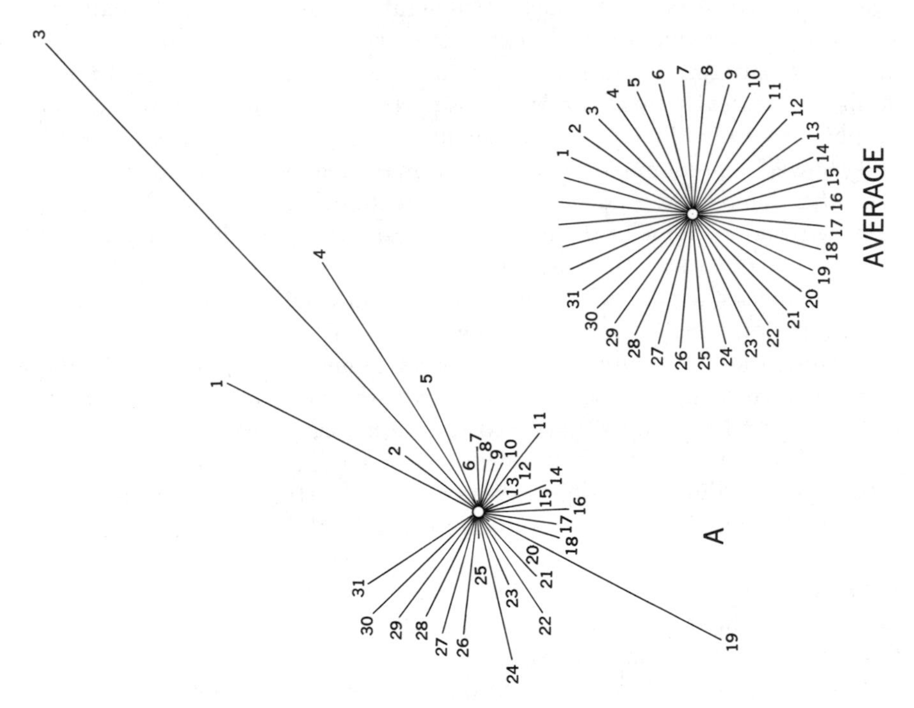

FIGURE 49

Physiological Patterns of Two Different Persons as Compared with a Hypothetical "Average" Person. Numbers 1–5 Represent Taste Sensitivity to Different Substances. Numbers 6–16 Represent Salivary Constituents. Numbers 18–31 Represent Urinary Constituents

(Williams, 1951)

why metabolic patterns should be related to ability patterns, but the fact that they are is interesting.

The study of biochemical individuality is a promising line of research for the future, since it is of great potential significance for human well-being. Williams puts it this way: [1] "Because biochemical individuality points the way toward individuality in the broadest sense of the word, it has profound implications not only in medicine, psychiatry, and psychology, but also in human relations, education, politics, and even philosophy."

CONSTITUTIONAL TYPES—PHYSIQUE AND TEMPERAMENT

Related to the foregoing kinds of research but branching off in a somewhat different direction is the age-old question as to whether people with different types of physique have different types of constitution that carry along with them distinctly different temperaments. This too is a very important question with potential implications for many areas of social planning. If distinctly different temperaments are identifiable, then, as Sheldon has so aptly pointed out, to house, clothe, feed, and educate them all the same way is sure to result in widespread maladjustment. Medical research has shown that there are important constitutional factors in susceptibility to various diseases. The long-thin types are more likely to get tuberculosis; the short-thick types develop high blood pressure and its attendant difficulties more easily. But our question is, "Are there psychological differences of any kind which consistently accompany differences in physical type?"

The work of Kretschmer (1925) was very important in stimulating discussion and research on the problem. He was interested primarily in what he could discover about the predispositions to psychoses of different kinds. A large proportion of the patients found in our mental hospitals are suffering from either manic-depressive psychosis, which is a cyclical condition characterized by extreme mood swings from excitement to depression, or schizophrenia, which is characterized by a withdrawal from reality, especially social reality, a cutting oneself off from the world outside and from one's fellow man. It is natural that a hypothesis should have developed that the manic-depressives are extraverted, emotionally responsive people who have eventually let these emotions run away with them completely, whereas the schizophrenics are the introverted, seclusive, lonely individuals who finally decide to live completely within themselves. Any observer of actual patients in a clinic or hospital knows that the differentiation is far less clear-cut than this explanation implies,

[1] From *Encyclopedia of Biological Sciences,* New York, Reinhold Publishing Corp., 1961.

but it seems to be true in a general way, and it has formed the basis for much thinking about the factors predisposing to psychotic breakdowns. Kretschmer's hypothesis was that the short-thick types of person whom he called *pyknics* are the ones with the extraverted personalities predisposing them to manic-depressive psychosis, whereas the long-thin types that he called *asthenic* or *leptosome* tend to be introverted and thus predisposed toward schizophrenia. He also postulated an *athletic* type with measurements intermediate between those of the pyknics and the leptosomes, and a *dysplastic* or mixed type in which the different parts of the body do not match. Kretschmer compiled data on over 4,000 abnormal cases and found interesting differentiations as shown in the following comparisons:

Body Type	*Schizophrenic*	*Manic-Depressive*
Pyknic and mixed pyknic	12.8%	66.7%
Leptosome and athletic	66.0	23.6
Dysplastic	11.3	0.4
Unclassifiable	9.9	9.3

Thus there appeared to be a strong tendency for manic-depressives to be pyknic in physique and for schizophrenics to be leptosome or athletic. Dysplasia was most likely to be associated with schizophrenia.

American investigations carried on by Wertheimer and Hesketh (1926) and by Burchard (1936) substantiated the general trend of the Kretschmer results. But there was one factor in all this work that was very difficult to control, namely, the *age* of the subjects. Schizophrenia is characteristically a mental disease of youth. The average manic-depressive is about ten years older than the average schizophrenic. Since most people become heavier as they grow older, it is natural that a group of people in their thirties should appear more pyknic than a group in their twenties. Garvey (1933), who matched his manic-depressive and schizophrenic patients by age, found almost complete overlapping in physical measurements for the two groups. Burchard (1936) found that at all ages there was some difference in body index between manic-depressives and schizophrenes, but that it was much less pronounced when age was controlled. These results left some doubt as to the relative importance of constitutional and age factors in the physical differences that had been shown to exist between the two abnormal groups.

Eysenck (1947, p. 85) pointed out other sources of confusion in the evidence and called attention to the fact that various subgroups of schizophrenics differed from one another in physique almost as much as schizophrenics differed from manic-depressives. His own work, reported in the same volume, showed that anxious, inhibited *neurotics* tended to be leptosomic, whereas hysterical, impulsive neurotics were closer to the pyknic end of the distribution. Schizophrenics did not differ from manic-depressives except with regard to chest *depth,* the front-to-back measurement. This interesting suggestion has never been corroborated by other research.

If any general conclusions are to be drawn, work on abnormal cases must of course be supplemented by work on persons within the normal personality range. Klineberg, Asch, and Block (1934) selected from a large group of male college students a group of 56 whose physical measurements combined into a Pignet Index [2] classified them as "pure" pyknics and 59 who could be called "pure" leptosomes. They gave them a number of psychological tests of intelligence, special abilities, and emotional adjustment. The two groups, which differed so sharply in physique, gave almost identical distributions for all the psychological traits. They were not differentiated mentally in any way.

Just about the time that most psychologists had come to the conclusion that the relationship between constitutional type and temperament was of no particular importance, within the normal range, at least, Sheldon et al. (1940, 1942, 1949) came out with an important new method and some challenging results. Sheldon's technique is to rate accurately the degree to which an individual shows each of three main *components* of physique and each of three main components of temperament. To shift the method from *types* to *components* might not seem to involve a very important change, but it served to distribute people along a sort of three-way continuum instead of forcing them into a small number of classes. The physical components were chosen after careful inspection of 4,000 photographs of nude males taken under carefully controlled conditions. The ratings could be made with complete objectivity by measuring in these photographs five different regions of the body. Sheldon et al. (1940) furnished norms to which such measurements could be referred.

The *temperament* components were chosen after an analysis of correlations between ratings of separate traits made on the basis of a series of twenty interviews with each individual. There appeared to be three and only three clusters of these basic traits. The three components of physique and their temperamental counterparts are as follows:

PHYSIQUE	TEMPERAMENT
Endomorphy—predominance of soft roundness in the body	*Viscerotonia*—predominance of relaxation and friendly, pleasure-loving traits
Mesomorphy—predominance of muscle, bone, and connective tissue	*Somatotonia*—predominance of vigorous, physical activity, adventurousness, and dominance

[2] Pignet Index = Height — (weight + chest circumference).

Ectomorphy—predominance of linearity and fragility

Cerebrotonia—predominance of intellectual, introverted trends

Each individual is rated from 1 to 7 on each of the three components and thus assigned a three-number combination. A great many such combinations are possible. Thus a 6 1 2 is slightly fatter and less muscular than a 5 2 2, since the figures representing the first and second components differ by one step. A 3 2 5 and a 1 3 5 are both predominantly ectomorphic, but the latter is more muscular and less "soft" than the former.

In the third volume (Sheldon, 1949), devoted primarily to biographical studies of 200 delinquent boys, Sheldon set up a third set of related dimensions each of which represented a pathological *deficiency* in one of the three basic components. He used the suffix "-penia" to characterize these negative traits: cerebropenia, visceropenia, and somatopenia. Their importance in the whole system as now formulated is that they are the *psychiatric* variables underlying different abnormalities. For example, the person with a high degree of cerebropenia might be expected to show delinquent or manic-depressive tendencies, since he would *lack* the control and inhibition that ordinarily keep such tendencies in check. The somatopenic individual, on the other hand, would be susceptible to hebephrenia, because he lacked the drive and energy necessary to carry on a normal life. The typical visceropenic would be a paranoid because of his lack of the soft, relaxed qualities.

The crucial question with regard to these three *sets* of variables is the extent to which they are related to one another. So far as normal individuals are concerned, Sheldon and Stevens (1942) presented two sorts of evidence. The first consisted of some unusually high correlations between temperament and physique ratings for 200 young males. They were as follows:

Viscerotonia *vs.* endomorphy	r = .79
Somatotonia *vs.* mesomorphy	r = .82
Cerebrotonia *vs.* ectomorphy	r = .83

The second kind of evidence, upon which the authors placed more weight, came from case studies of individuals, each of whom had been rated for adjustment and normality. These studies seemed to indicate that there was a much larger proportion of good adjustment and satisfactory achievement in cases where the somatotype and temperament agreed than in cases where they differed markedly. In other words, if you are a 4 2 5 and are satisfied to be an easy-going intellectual, you will probably get along all right. If you insist on trying to be an athlete or an Arctic explorer, maladjustment will be the inevitable outcome.

Validation of the hypotheses with regard to psychiatric conditions was attempted at Elgin State Hospital and reported by Wittman et al. (1948)

TABLE 45
Correlations Between Psychiatric Reaction Type Ratings and Somatotype
(Wittman, Sheldon, and Katz, 1948)

	AFFECTIVE	PARANOID	HEBOID
Endomorphy	.509	−.060	−.302
Mesomorphy	.468	.536	−.612
Ectomorphy	−.638	−.283	.542

TABLE 46
Correlations Between Psychiatric Reaction Type Ratings and Temperament Ratings
(Wittman, Sheldon, and Katz, 1948)

	AFFECTIVE	PARANOID	HEBOID
Viscerotonia	.733	.197	−.565
Somatotonia	.165	.688	−.456
Cerebrotonia	−.705	−.554	.808

and by Sheldon (1949). Wittman rated the case histories of 167 male patients on three main types of abnormal reaction which it was thought would correspond to the three "-penias" described above–affective (manic-depressive), paranoid, and heboid (hebephrenic) reactions. Sheldon, working independently, somatotyped the subjects and made a temperament rating for each based on his behavior in the somatotyping situation. The correlations were as shown in Tables 45 and 46. It is the *negative* correlations that have the most direct bearing on the hypotheses being tested, since *lack* of the component is assumed to be at the root of the difficulty. In general, they supported the theory, although there were a number of exceptions. Patients with affective psychoses (manic-depressive) did seem to lack ectomorphy and cerebrotonia. Hebephrenics did seem to lack mesomorphy and somatotonia. The paranoid component did not, however, show the expected negative relationship to endomorphy and viscerotonia. Sheldon felt that some modification of the original scheme was necessary, but that on the whole it was substantiated by the correlations.

To what extent can we accept the reported correlations in all these studies as evidence for the postulated close relationship between physique and temperament? In the psychiatric study by Wittman et al. (1948) care was taken to evaluate physique and diagnostic type *independently*, and the correlations were computed by a third worker who had seen neither the patients nor the case histories. Thus these correlations are probably free from the effects of initial bias. But this cannot be said for the evaluations of normal subjects. The psychologists who rated them on temperamental qualities were very familiar with the system of classifying physiques. It is almost an axiom in applied psychology that raters tend to see in people what they are prepared to see. Sheldon and Stevens pointed out that all possible precautions were taken to guard against this error. Temperament ratings were made before any physical measurements were taken. However, they admitted that an investigator who had learned to think of physiques in such terms as these would inevitably become aware of the somatotype as he talked with the subject. They stated that their knowledge of the error they were likely to make constituted a defense against it. They "looked for it suspiciously behind every bush in the psychological garden."

When we examine studies by other workers using the Sheldon variables, we find that significant correlations (though often much lower than those Sheldon reported) have usually been obtained when any sort of *ratings* were used as personality measures (Seltzer et al., 1948; Glueck and Glueck, 1950; Hanley, 1951; R. N. Sanford, 1953; Child, 1950). But when either psychological tests or objective measurements of characteristic psychological reactions have been used, few significant correlations have appeared (Child and Sheldon, 1941; Fiske, 1944; H. C. Smith, 1949; Janoff et al., 1950). One apparent exception to this rule, Coffin's study (1944) in which fairly high correlations were reported between values, as measured by the Allport-Vernon scale, and physique ratings, cannot be given much weight, since in this case the somatotype figures were based on self-ratings, not measurements, and the same self-concepts could have affected both these ratings and the answers to the Allport-Vernon questions.

One study by Wells and Siegel (1961) demonstrated clearly that definite opinions do exist about the kinds of temperamental and social qualities to be expected from persons of different physical types. Their group of 120 adult subjects consisted of equal numbers from the two sexes and equal numbers from three economic classes: middle, lower-middle, and upper-lower. They were asked to rate persons shown in four silhouette drawings, one an "average" physique, and one representing each of Sheldon's main types. The *endomorph* was rated fatter, older, shorter, more old-fashioned, lazier, less strong, less good-looking, more talkative, more warm-hearted and sympathetic, more good-natured and agreeable, more dependent, and more trusting. The *mesomorph* was rated stronger, more masculine, better looking, more adventurous, younger, taller, more mature, and more self-reliant. The *ectomorph* was rated thinner, younger, more ambitious, taller, more suspicious of others, more tense and nervous, less masculine, more stubborn, more pessimistic, and quieter. Most of these ratings are clearly in line with Sheldon's theory. Whether they represent a distillation of folk wisdom or are purely stereotypes with no factual basis cannot be decided from the data. If they do represent stereotypes, the doubt about the meaning of ratings of subjects in other research studies—subjects whose physiques are known—remains.

Nevertheless, the Sheldon system has continued to appeal to social scientists in several disciplines—anthropology, sociology, and medicine, as well as psychology—and various kinds of evidence have continued to accumulate. Glueck and Glueck (1956) not only found that delinquents were significantly more likely than nondelinquents to be mesomorphic in build but also suggested that the possession of psychological traits not characteristic of a person's physique might create an internal disharmony predisposing toward delinquency. Parnell (1958) located a great many suggestive relationships in various groups of British subjects. Most of these findings, however, were based on too few cases to be conclusive. He reported, for example, that mesomorphic women tend to have more children that nonmesomorphic, and a larger proportion of their children are boys. Mesomorphic university men are heavily represented in mining, medicine, dentistry, and mechanical engineering, whereas ectomorphs are likely to be found in physics, chemistry, mathematics, law, and liberal arts. Army pensioners, age fifty-six to eighty-four, who had survived the stresses of years of military life and were spending their declining years in Chelsea Royal Hospital, turned out to be mesomorphs in 86 per cent of the cases!

Probably the most important data Parnell reported came from a psychiatric and somatotype study of 100 children, who were assessed at seven years of age and again at eleven. Stability coefficients for the ratings of the components ranged from .48 (mesomorphy in girls) to .69 (ectomorphy in boys). A number of psychiatric ratings correlated with the physique ratings in the direction that would be predicted by Sheldon's theory. Anxiety, for example, correlated .60 with ectomorphy in boys, .42 with ectomorphy in girls. Again the fact that the psychiatric variables were rated rather than tested casts doubt on the conclusions.

The strongest support for the validity of the hypothesized relationships between body type and temperament in children has come from a study at the Gesell Institute at Yale (Walker, 1962) in which 125 two-, three-, and four-year-olds who had been carefully somatotyped, were rated by their nursery school teachers on 63 behavior scales. Out of 292 predictions of relationships to be expected on the basis of Sheldon's theory, 73 per cent were confirmed in direction, and 21 per cent were high enough correlations to reach the .05 significance level. In another study in this series (Walker, 1963), the ratings parents made of the same traits in their preschool children also turned out to correlate with somatotype ratings in the predicted direction, although most of the correlations were low. The fact that some of the correlations were in the direction opposite to that predicted suggested that rater biases were not responsible for the results.

There have also been some research attempts to set up systems of dimensions that would be superior to the Kretschmer-Sheldon system, but they have never really "caught on." One question that comes up again and again is whether there are three main types or really only two. The correlations between separate measurements or separate temperamental traits shown in Sheldon's tables raise this same question. They show that his three components are not actually *independent* of one another. The fact that endomorphy, mesomorphy, and ectomorphy correlate *negatively* with one another does not prove that they are independent. Independence produces zero, not negative *r*'s. The question naturally arises: "Would it not be possible to describe these same relationships in terms of two genuinely independent dimensions in place of three correlated ones?" [3]

Ekman (1951) suggested a simple workable scheme for reducing the Sheldon system to two dimensions. If we think of extreme ectomorphy as simply the *absence* of either endomorphic or mesomorphic trends, we can describe an individual physique by means of two digits rather than three. By specifying only a person's endomorphy and mesomorphy ratings, we can give all the information which Sheldon's three-digit label contains.

Rather than to remodel the Sheldon system, others have preferred to start out with measurements of individuals and attempt to establish the basic dimensions by factor analysis. A number of such studies were carried out in England, the largest of them based on measurements obtained from 2,400 RAF men (Burt, 1947). All of the studies agreed remarkably well in locating one general factor of *body size* that accounted for about 50 per cent of the variance in the measurements, and a second bipolar *shape* factor representing length *vs.* breadth. Various smaller factors, such as limb length *vs.* trunk length or bony breadth *vs.* fatty breadth, could also be distinguished, but their effects on the correlations between measurements were not very great. Eysenck (1947) presented some evidence that body size is negatively related to general personality weakness, whereas the length *vs.* breadth dimension correlates significantly with introversion-extraversion. All correlations were too low to be of much value in diagnostic work. There have been a number of other factor analyses of physical measurements, but no common pattern emerges from them. It is interesting that both Sills (1950) and Heath (1952) obtained factors that seem to correspond to the two dimensions Ekman proposed. Sills came out with separate factors for endomorphy

[3] Lubin (1950) showed that some of the combinations of correlations between Sheldon's temperamental traits are not just an inefficient way of describing the relationship but downright *impossible*. If we use accepted partial correlation methods and try to evaluate the relationship between two of these traits with the third held constant, we come out with an *r* larger than 1.00. Thus Lubin concluded that there must be computational errors in Sheldon's table.

and mesomorphy, both showing fairly high negative correlations with ectomorphy. Heath's two second-order factors seemed to represent the growth of fatty tissue and the development of bones. Howells (1952), who based his factor analysis on correlations between persons rather than between measurements, came out with a factor he calls *mass,* which is perhaps identifiable with the *body-size* factor discussed above, and two others that seemed to represent top-heaviness *vs.* bottom heaviness and trunk-face development *vs.* limb development. It is probably useless to seek for a common structure in these studies based as they are on different kinds of subjects and different specific measurements. The last word on dimensions of physique has not yet been said.

In spite of its imperfections, the Sheldon system for classifying somatotypes and temperaments has been the one most researchers seemed to prefer, perhaps because it corresponds to our intuitive evaluations of physique. Many psychologists now are inclined to conclude that there is a relationship between somatotype and temperament, but that the basis on which it rests is more complex than Sheldon hypothesized that it was. What an adult type represents is the culmination of a long period of development. There are individual differences in size and shape, activity and reactivity present at birth. Superimposed upon these are patterns influenced by several other kinds of factors. For one thing, children of different physical types undergo different kinds of social experience. The boy who is muscular and strong is likely to spend far more time in vigorous team sports than the boy who is either pudgy or slight in build. Furthermore, each child internalizes the social expectations of persons around him. If they view him as easy-going and good-natured, he is inclined to behave in that way. Thus his own self-concept adds its influence to his development in one direction rather than another.

This line of thinking makes all of the research findings on the relationship of physical to mental traits intelligible. Probably the reason that the *correlations* so often have turned out to be low is that the relationship varies from person to person. Barker et al. (1953) proposed a new term for the study of these complex relationships, *somato-psychology.* A person's size, shape, appearance, and strength help to determine the psychological situation in which he finds himself. They set limits to what he can do and serve as stimuli to himself and others. To understand their effects we must study the individual himself, not just his measurements and test scores. Somato-psychology has become a flourishing research field and a source of theoretical concepts for practical work in rehabilitation (Wright, 1960). Many studies have pointed out what some of these effects of a person's physique on himself and on others are (Stolz and Stolz, 1944; Levy, 1929, 1932; Jacobson, 1945; M. C. Jones and Bayley, 1950; R. Ames, 1957). This shift from a reliance on correlational methods to a study of complex relationships in individual cases represents an important change in our thinking about the problems with which this chapter is concerned.

SUMMARY

It has been conclusively demonstrated that all the relationships between anatomical characteristics, such as height, body shape, and head size, and intelligence, although *positive,* are so low as to be of no practical value whatever in judging people. Growth studies have demonstrated that physiological or anatomical age is unrelated to mental age. Physical handicaps, such as adenoids, dental caries, and malnutrition, apparently do not lower children's intelligence, and correcting them does not make the children brighter. Similarly, illness does not depress intelligence-test scores. With the exception of diseases such as encephalitis, which attack the central nervous system itself, and extreme sensory handicaps, such as total deafness, which decrease greatly the amount of stimulation the individual receives from the outside world, there is very little connection between physical conditions of any sort and intelligence.

Research on the relationship of biochemical and physiological functioning to intelligence and personality has led to two general conclusions: (1) that individuals differ in level of activation, and (2) that each individual has a unique pattern of biochemical and physiological characteristics.

The work of Kretschmer and others on the relationship of body type to psychosis showed that short-thick physiques predominated among manic-depressive patients and tall-thin physiques among schizophrenics, but that much if not all of this relationship can be accounted for by age differences in the two patient populations. Sheldon's system of somatotyping employing the concepts, endomorphy, mesomorphy, and ectomorphy for physiques, and viscerotonia, somatotonia, and cerebrotonia for temperaments now dominates this research field. The evidence for a relationship between physique and temperament is to some degree equivocal because of the possibility of an unconscious bias in ratings. A reasonable conclusion is that a relationship exists but that it varies somewhat from person to person because of a complex of developmental factors. The field of *somatopsychology* is concerned with these individual patterns of relationship.

CHAPTER 17

Environmental Factors Affecting Individual Differences

THE NATURE OF THE PROBLEM

THE MAJOR ISSUE UPON which theoretical and philosophical thinking about individuals has centered in the past is which is more important in their making—heredity or environment? The psychologists who carried out research and the clinicians and educators who applied their findings have taken strong positions on this issue. Pastore (1949b) showed that the convictions the leading contributors to the discussion expressed were likely to be tied in with generally conservative or generally liberal views on a variety of other matters. Typically, environmentalists have been liberals, holding fast to the optimistic assumption that under favorable circumstances, every individual is almost infinitely improvable. Typically, hereditarians have been conservatives, with pessimistic attitudes about the improvability of individuals through changed social conditions. Often they have been interested in eugenics, endorsers of plans designed to produce better human material.

The time has come, however, for all of us to break away if we can from what we like to think and examine the evidence from a neutral position. It should now be clear to all that if we say heredity *or* environment, nature *versus* nurture, we have already misstated the issue. With the exception of a few simple physical characteristics, such as eye color, that depend upon genetic endowment alone, all human traits in which we are interested are produced through an interaction of heredity *and* environmental influences. From plant and animal research there has come abundant evidence of the same sort of interaction. In corn, for instance, the outer tissue of the grain, the *pericarp,* shows variations in color. A certain dominant gene is known to produce red pericarp. This does not happen, however, unless the kernels are exposed to sunlight while they are maturing. If the husk had not been removed at the proper time in the ear's development, we would never have known that the genetic potentialities for red coloring were there. Canaries sing in their characteristic fashion because of the way their throats and nervous systems are built. But when Metfessel (1940) exposed these birds in their sound-proof cages to vibrato tones of a certain frequency, the sounds they learned to make resembled this pitch more than the one that is natural to the species. Birds put into cages with one another became more *alike* in their songs than were those reared alone. Thus a type of behavior that without question has a hereditary basis has been shown to be susceptible to considerable modification as systematic changes in the environment are made.

Still another example from animal research is the work which has been done on hoarding behavior in rats (Morgan, 1947). This seems to be a spontaneously occurring type of behavior that does not have to be learned. Adult rats placed in a situation where food pellets are available will hoard from five to twenty pellets a day in their home cages, eating only one or two. But there are a number of changes in environmental conditions that affect this behavior. Hoarding is increased by low temperatures, food deprivation, and frustration. It is decreased by placing lights in the home cage. Rats prefer the dark. Again we see that though the general pattern of behavior is determined by heredity, it is quite sensitive to environmental changes.

It is the sort of questions that Metfessel asked of his canaries and Morgan of his rats that we need to be concerned about with human beings. The most *usable* knowledge we can have with regard to any psychological characteristic is not what have been the relative contributions of heredity and environment to its make-up, but how amenable it is to change, and under what circumstances we can expect changes to occur. One of the commonest misconceptions here is the idea that only the innate characteristics are fixed and unchangeable, and that environmentally produced traits are modifiable at will. Neither part of the generalization is true. Hereditary tendencies can often be strikingly modified. Environmentally produced traits are often so firmly fixed that it is impossible to alter them. We all know of persons with hereditary susceptibility to tuberculosis who have built up strong vigorous bodies in which the disease never gets a foothold. On the other hand, much work with college-entrance tests has shown us that a freshman who is unusually weak in vocabulary will probably carry some degree of verbal disability throughout his adult years, even if it is plain that the deficiency grew out of an educational handicap during childhood rather than out of any innate lack of verbal intelligence. When our task is to decide whether a given individual belongs in college, whether a young man has enough mechanical aptitude to make good in the army program for training mechanics, or whether a person's interests are like those of scientists or of business men, we need not consider the heredity-environment issue at all. We have evidence as to the *permanence* of the traits in question, and that is all we need. We have come to realize that *all* traits, however they originate, somehow get built into the individual's nervous system. Since human beings show a considerable capacity for learning, most of these traits are susceptible to modification, but *both* heredity and previous experience set limits to its nature and amount. It is true that for long-range social planning over many generations we need to know as much as possible about the hereditary bases of important variables such as intelligence and emotional stability. There are a few practical problems such as those relating to the adoption of children for which direct information about the effects of heredity can be useful. But specific data about the development of children in good foster homes has met this need fairly well.

Loevinger (1943) has shown that the attempts which a number of psychologists have made to determine what *proportion* of the variance in some trait, intelligence for example, is due to heredity rest on unsatisfactory mathematical foundations. Investigators have come to see the desirability of shifting their focus from broad questions to narrower and narrower questions. The broad question whether environment produces any individual differences at all split first into questions like: *How much* difference can we expect a change of environment to make? *Which* traits are affected? *Which* aspects of the environment affect human development? Each of these has been further subdivided. For example, how much difference does preschool experience make in the development of middle-class children's intellectual abilities, social characteristics, emotional stability? How much difference does preschool experience make in culturally deprived children's development along these same lines? Which aspects of the preschool experience are responsible for the effects—the teacher, the physical surroundings, the social group? At what age does this kind of experience produce its maximum effect?

This shift from general to specific problems is the most salient aspect of current research on the effects of environment. It is obviously impossible to review any large proportion of it in this chapter. What is attempted here is a discussion of the kinds of research that were done on the broad problems through which it was demonstrated that environmental effects of some sort exist, and on the next lower echelon of problems designed to show what kinds of environmental influence it would be profitable to explore, along with a less complete presentation of some of the specific areas in which important research on limited questions is now being conducted.

STUDIES OF SEPARATED IDENTICAL TWINS

Infrequent as they are, the cases in which two monozygotic ("identical") twins have been reared in different homes constitute the most solid evidence we have that environmental differences can produce psychological differences in people.

In order to appreciate the crucial importance of such cases, we must remember that a pair of monozygotic twins presents us with the *only* kind of opportunity we ever have to study two individuals whose hereditary makeup is exactly the same. Persons with the same parents or the same ancestors do *not* necessarily have the same heredity. In fact, it is exceedingly improbable that they should. We each inherit only half our genes from either parent. The combination thus produced may be such as to develop *hereditary* characteristics quite different from those shown by either parent—characteristics that come to us *through* our parents from remoter ancestors. Thus differences between parents and children or brothers and sisters do not prove anything about the effects of environment. But differences between identical twins do, since in genetic makeup such individuals are exactly alike.

Identical or *monozygotic* twins are produced from a single fertilized ovum that separates into two parts at the time of the first cell division. The two individuals have the same assortment of genes. They may or may not be encased in the same protective membrane or chorion, so that birth records are not decisive in making a diagnosis as to whether they are truly monozygotic. What can be done, however, is to check a number of physical traits known to be determined by heredity, such as blood type, finger prints, hand and sole prints, hair texture, skin texture, and eye color. Since the probability that all these characteristics would be alike in two persons with different genetic makeup is equal to the *product* of the separate probabilities, the error in such a diagnosis is negligible, and it can be made no matter how old the persons are.

Several types of research have utilized twin subjects. We shall postpone until the next chapter the consideration of the studies that have compared the degree of resemblance in *monozygotic* twin pairs with the degree of resemblance in *dizygotic* or two-egg pairs. The latter are the so-called fraternal twins, who are no more alike in heredity than are ordinary siblings. Such studies are most useful for demonstrating the importance of heredity rather than of the environmental influences with which we are concerned here. The research we shall examine now deals with cases in which identical twins were separated while they were children and reared in different homes. These constitute a natural controlled experiment on the effects of environmental differences. Careful study of such cases should tell us something about *how much* difference environment makes in various outcomes, and *what features* of the environment are important in producing these effects.

TABLE 47

Differences Between Twins

(Newman, Freeman, and Holzinger, 1937, pp. 724, 344, as brought together by Woodworth, 1941, p. 19)

	FRATERNALS	IDENTICALS REARED TOGETHER	IDENTICALS REARED APART
Stature	4.4 cm	1.7 cm	1.8 cm
Weight	10.0 lb.	4.1 lb.	9.9 lb.
Binet IQ	9.9 points	5.9 points	8.2 points

TABLE 48

Correlations Between Twins *

(*Ibid.* pp. 97, 347)

	FRATERNALS	IDENTICALS REARED TOGETHER	IDENTICALS REARED APART
Stature	.645	.932	(.969)
Weight	.631	.917	(.886)
Binet IQ	.631	.881	(.767)

* Correlations not in parentheses corrected for age, and last figure corrected for range. (See Woodworth, 1941, p. 19.)

Newman, Freeman, and Holzinger (1937) made thorough, complete case studies of nineteen pairs of identical twins reared apart. The average difference they found, compared with the average differences in identical twins reared together and fraternal twins, are shown in Table 47, and the correlation between twin pairs are shown in Table 48. If we look only at these averages, we come out with the conclusion that environmental differences do not have much effect on intelligence. As would be expected on the basis of their hereditary similarity, identicals are more alike in everything than are fraternals. Differences between them are smaller; correlations between them are larger. At first glance it looks as though the pairs reared apart show more difference in Binet IQ than they do in height. For these subjects, the correlation for Binet IQ, .767, is considerably lower than the *r*'s for either height or weight. But Woodworth (1941) in his analysis of the results pointed out a factor the authors themselves seem to have overlooked—the error of measurement that is always involved in intelligence testing. The average variation in score when the same individuals are tested twice is about 5 IQ points. It would appear then that the average pair of identical twins reared together is almost as similar as are the two scores of a single person tested twice, and that those reared apart show a difference not very much greater. After allowing for chance errors, Woodworth estimated that the average IQ difference for identical twins reared apart was about 6 points. This can be compared with the average difference for identicals reared together, which was 3 points, and with the average difference for unrelated children from the same community paired at random, which was 15 points. What we can conclude from the figures is that environmental differences do operate to produce IQ differences in persons with exactly the same hereditary potentialities, but that differences thus produced are not nearly as large as those we find among children whose heredity is *not* alike.

Material assembled from the detailed case studies is more illuminating than the averages obtained from a group of pairs, particularly when we attempt to determine what it is about the environment that makes a difference in intellectual development. Table 49 contains Woodworth's summary of the evidence for the nineteen pairs, along with three other pairs that have been reported separately. It can be seen that in some individual cases the IQ differences were large, much larger than the average differences. It seemed natural to the investigators to ask themselves whether there was any evidence that the difference between the environments in which the two twins were reared was larger for these pairs than for the others. In order to get an answer to this question, they had five judges rate the social and educational quality of the environment for each person and estimate on a ten-point scale the amount of difference there was for each pair. Table 49 shows that educational factors were related to IQ differences. On the average, the IQ of the better-educated twin was 6 points higher than the other, a difference that was statistically significant. For the six pairs shown in Table 49 for which there was a *marked* difference in formal schooling, defined as four years or more, the average difference was 13 IQ points in favor of the better-educated twin. There was a correlation of .79 between the ratings for educational difference and the IQ differences. This analysis proved rather conclusively that educational influences can produce IQ differences in persons having the same heredity, but that it is the *large* rather than the minor environmental discrepancies that are important. The largest difference of all, listed first in Table 49, occurred in the case of a pair of girls, one of them reared in the backwoods with only two years of regular schooling, the other reared in a good farming community and given a college education. It is to be noted that the 24-point difference in IQ for this pair is still far less than the extreme differences we encounter in the population as a whole. We cannot explain the difference

TABLE 49

Some Data from Identical Twins Reared Apart *

(Newman, Freeman and Holzinger, 1937; Muller, 1925; Gardner and Newman, 1940; Saudek, 1934. Data brought together by Woodworth, 1941, p. 23)

				ENVIRONMENTAL DIFFERENCES			
CASE NUMBER	SEX	AGE AT SEPARATION	AGE AT TESTING	1. IN YEARS OF SCHOOLING	2. IN ESTIMATED EDUCATIONAL ADVANTAGES	3. IN ESTIMATED SOCIAL ADVANTAGES	IQ DIFFERENCE
11	f	18 mo.	35	14	37	25	24
2	f	18 mo.	27	15	32	14	12
18	m	1 yr.	27	4	28	31	19
4	f	5 mo.	29	4	22	15	17
12	f	18 mo.	29	5	19	13	7
1	f	18 mo.	19	1	15	27	12
17	m	2 yr.	14	0	15	15	10
8	f	3 mo.	15	1	14	32	15
3	m	2 mo.	23	1	12	15	−2
14	f	6 mo.	39	0	12	15	−1
5	f	14 mo.	38	1	11	26	4
13	m	1 mo.	19	0	11	13	1
10	f	1 yr.	12	1	10	15	5
15	m	1 yr.	26	2	9	7	1
7	m	1 mo.	13	0	9	27	−1
19	f	6 yr.	41	0	9	14	−9
16	f	2 yr.	11	0	8	12	2
6	f	3 yr.	59	0	7	10	8
9	m	1 mo.	19	0	7	14	6
Muller	f	1 mo.	30	9	?	?	−1
Gardner & Newman	f	1 mo.	19	0	2	?	−3
Saudek	m	1 mo.	20	0	?	?	−4

* The estimated differences in educational and social advantages are in "points" with a maximum possible of 50. From the case material each of five judges rated the environmental differences between every pair of twins on a scale of 10 points, and the figure given in the table is the sum of these five ratings. A minus sign before an IQ difference means that the twin who received the higher rating for educational advantages obtained the lower IQ.

between the retarded child with an IQ of 50 and the gifted child with an IQ of 180 in terms of educational influences alone.

The evidence assembled by Newman, Freeman, and Holzinger with regard to the effects of environment in producing *personality* differences in separated identical twins was less clear. The inadequacy of personality tests available in the 1930's imposed serious limitations on their analysis. The case studies included several examples of marked differences in superficial personality traits. The pair cited in the last paragraph was an instance of this. The college-educated schoolteacher was well-groomed and polished in her manners, whereas the backwoods girl was "all business without social charm or concern about how she impressed others." The authors had the impression, however, that there were basic temperamental traits in which the members of each pair of twins resembled each other despite the different environments in which they were raised. One sort of basic trait, for instance, appeared both in a young man from Tennessee, who was brought up in the mountains without benefit of much formal schooling and who had engaged in some illegal activity, and also in his twin brother, a high-school graduate who was a business man in a small town. Both were individualistic and stubborn. But in the way in which the traits were expressed they differed. Further evidence for some hereditary determination of basic temperamental characteristics will be presented in the next chapter.

The conclusions that can be drawn from the research on separated identical twins are: (1) Marked educational differences can produce substantial differences in measured intelligence; and (2) Intellectual differences in the population as a whole are too large to be accounted for in terms of environmental differences alone. Results would seem to justify a moderate optimism with regard to the social usefulness of a good educational system. It is quite possible that the intelligence level of the population as a whole can be moderately increased. What we are not justified in assuming is that dull individuals can be brought up to the level of the bright ones by some form of education.

Before turning our attention to other kinds of research, another sort of twin study should be briefly mentioned. Child psychologists have used the method of *co-twin control* to study maturation and learning. In such studies, one member of a twin pair is given specific training in a skill, such as climbing or manipulation of materials, and the other is left to develop at his own rate or given training at a later age. In general, such studies have shown that the simple skills develop by the appropriate ages whether training in them is given or not (Hilgard, 1933; Strayer, 1930; Gesell and Thompson, 1941). More complex functions, such as skating, jumping, or swimming show more of a training effect than do the simple reactions (McGraw, 1935). These studies have little direct bearing on the question with which we are principally concerned, however, since they do not supply evidence as to whether differences stemming from variations in training during infancy and early childhood can account for the relatively *permanent* differences we encounter in adults. In all these studies, the control twin had every opportunity to practice the skills involved in the experiment after the experimental period was over—and they were skills practically all normal children do practice a great deal. The environmental difference during the few days or weeks that the experiment lasted could hardly have been expected to have a great effect on the subjects' ultimate development. In fact, if there were a possibility of such effects, it would hardly be ethical to carry out such studies. These experiments have taught us more about maturation, as it occurs naturally in everyone, than they have about individual differences.

One co-twin study involved a much more drastic and prolonged difference between the way in which members of the pairs were treated. As a part of the study by Schmidt (1946), reported in a previous chapter, nine pairs of twins in the feeble-minded group were sent to separate schools. In each case the twin whose IQ was originally higher was assigned to the regular training program, whereas the lower one was placed in the special classes for the enriched school experience described in the monograph. Schmidt reported that the average IQ increased from 54 to 92 in the nine experimental twins during the three-year period. The controls dropped slightly, from 61 to 59. Case studies showed in a colorful way how much difference the new experience had made in the lives of those who participated in it. Unfortunately, in addition to the statistical criticisms that have cast doubt on the whole Schmidt study, there is another serious question that arises with regard to this part of it in particular. If these twin pairs were really identicals, as the author states that they were, how could they have been as different both in IQ and in other psychological traits as she described them to have been when the experiment began? It has been a universal finding that identical twins in the same home are more alike than this. If we can trust the reported figures, the fact that the twin who was initially lower in each case turned out to be much higher after the special training would be a fact of considerable importance, even if the pairs were not monozygotic. But can we trust them? The fact that in all the years since 1946 no other studies reporting a training effect anywhere nearly this large leads to definite skepticism.

CHILDREN IN FOSTER HOMES AND INSTITUTIONS

Because identical twins, especially those separated in infancy, are comparatively rare, it has seemed desirable to get supplementary data on the influence of the environment from other types of experiment. A number of excellent studies have been made of what happens to children adopted into good homes, but there are certain difficulties inherent in such research that make the interpretation of what they mean uncertain. If one could plan a simple "before-and-after" experiment in which a number of children were tested, then placed in good homes, then tested again after various lengths of time, the problem would be readily soluble. The trouble with such an apparently simple idea is that a great deal of evidence has been obtained in child psychology emphasizing the importance of the development that takes place during the *very earliest* years, whereas all the work in mental testing has shown us that an IQ that is reliable (in the sense of showing a high correlation with a retest some time later) and valid (in the sense of showing a high correlation with another test of intelligence or with school achievement) cannot be obtained in the case of an infant. Even for children two, three, and four years of age IQ's are not very satisfactory predictors of later mental ability. Therefore various compromise methods have had to be devised for the study of the effects of foster-home placement. The most satisfactory of these is to make an *estimate* on the basis of known facts about the children's parents as to the *average* IQ to be expected from a *group* under ordinary circumstances. It is then possible to test them after residence in good foster homes to find out whether or not their intellectual development has exceeded the estimates. Fairly sound estimates of the IQ in a group of children can be made from information about mother's or father's IQ, father's occupation, mother's or father's education, home ratings, and various other data. To predict the IQ of an *individual* by such methods would of course be highly unsound, but the averages of *groups* at different socio-economic and educational levels in the population are well known.

The factor of selective placement must always be considered when the results are interpreted. Child-placing agencies usually make an attempt to fit a child to the home. This tends to produce a small but consistent correlation between the children's intelligence and the intellectual quality of the foster home, a correlation that is *not* the result of the good environment but of the fact that child and home are matched to start with. For instance, illegitimate children may have brilliant fathers even if their mothers were not very bright. If a child of such a match is placed in a cultured, well-educated family, an observer, comparing his IQ with his real mother's, is likely to be tremendously impressed with the influence of a good environment. What the observer is not so likely to realize is that the child's brightness may be inherited from his intelligent father. The home may have nourished it rather than created it. In most of the large-scale investigations, there has been a good deal of discussion of the possible effects of selective placement on the results.

In one of the first important studies an attempt was made to find out simply how *successful* adopted children are. The New York State Charities Aid Association (Theis, 1924) undertook to check up on 910 persons more than eighteen years of age whom the agency had placed in adopted homes during childhood. They used a simple judgment of "capable" for persons who were managing their own affairs successfully, and attempted to relate the success or lack of success to factors on which the case records gave them information. The most important finding was that 77 per cent of the subjects could be described as capable. Only 10 per cent were delinquent or vicious. Popular notions that adopted children are likely to turn out badly were thus shown to be without foundation. There was a slightly higher percentage of capable individuals among the adopted's whose *own* families were good, but the majority of those whose own families were inferior also turned out well. Differences in economic level of the foster home were not related to success of the children, but differences in kind of care they received were. This study made a real and very practical contribution to the literature on adopted children.

In 1928, the National Society for the Study of Education published two important studies of foster children, one conducted by Freeman, Holzinger, and Mitchell (1928) at the University of Chicago, the other by Burks (1928) at Stanford. The Chicago group tested 401 adopted children and their foster parents and analyzed the results in various ways, trying to sort out the effects of environment from those of heredity alone. In one analysis, the correlation between the IQ's of *foster* siblings was .37. Since the correlation between IQ's of *real* siblings living in their own homes is usually in the neigborhood of .50 and the correlation between IQ's of unrelated children is .00, the value obtained represents a relationship of intermediate size, and would seem to show that just living in the same environment, though it does not make children as much alike as individuals in the same family, does to a limited extent make for similarity in their mental development. It was also found that there was a tendency for children adopted into the better homes to obtain the higher IQ's. The 114 children placed in good homes averaged 106.8; the 186 children placed in average homes averaged 96.4; the 101 children placed in relatively poor homes averaged 88.9. The correlation between cultural level and IQ was .48. Intelligence seemed to be related to the *age* at which the child was placed for adoption. Those who were young when adopted scored higher on the average than those who were older. Much of the significance of the comparisons between children adopted into homes of different economic and cultural levels hinges on the question of the extent to which selective placement could have operated in the group. If any attempt was made by the child-placing agencies to give superior children to superior foster parents, it would not, of course, be at all surprising that this group should get better-than-average scores when tested. The authors of the report considered this possible explanation, but they felt that the effect of what selection there was was negligible. The failure to produce any clear evidence on this point, however, left the interpretation of the results somewhat doubtful so far as differences in types of home are concerned.

Burks (1928), in California, compared a group of adopted children placed within the first year of life with a control group of "own" children matched with the adopted children for age and sex, and living in homes matched with the foster homes for locality and occupational level. From the information available about their real parents, she estimated the average IQ of the foster children's group at about 100. When they were tested at ages five to fourteen, their average IQ actually turned out to be 107.4. The mean IQ of the control children, however, was 115.1. The most reasonable conclusion is that a superior home can produce a moderate increase in a child's tested intelligence, but can not bring him to the level of individuals who have *both* superior heredity and superior environment on their side. Burks also computed correlations between IQ and various home characteristics, for both foster children and own children. For the foster children, these ranged from a low of .09 with foster father's IQ to a high of .29 with the rating of the home for cultural advantages. For the own children, all except the correlation with income were in the neighborhood of .50. It would seem that while there is a slight tendency for the intellectual level of adopted children to correspond to that of the home in which they are reared, it is not nearly so close a relationship as that which holds for children in their own homes.

The study by Leahy (1935) in Minnesota was similar in design to the Burks study, but even more carefully planned. Matched foster-child and control groups, 194 in each, were compared. The foster children were all illegitimate, all placed for adoption at six months or younger, and all from five to fourteen years old when tested. Leahy found evidence that there had been a certain amount of selective placement even when the children were adopted at such an early age. The social agency, knowing the real mother's education, took this into consideration when placing the child. The mean IQ of the group was 110, the same as that of the control children, and there was the same tendency in both groups for children in homes of higher occupational level to get higher scores. However, this was less pronounced in the case of the foster children, who ranged from an average of 108 in unskilled labor homes to 113 in professional homes, as compared with a range of 102 to 119 for the own children. Thus it seemed that the correspondence of child's IQ to father's occupation was less close in the case of the foster children; and selective placement, since it undoubtedly existed, might conceivably have accounted for what correspondence there was. Correlations of child's IQ with total home rating, based on occupation, economic condition, parental education, and material, social, and cultural level, were .23 for the foster children, and .53 for the own children. By this method also, a slight relationship between environmental advantages and child's mental level was indicated, but again we must remember that selective placement might have produced it.

These three major studies agreed in their findings that the intelligence of adopted children averages somewhat higher than that of children in homes of the educational level from which they come. They were also in essential agreement with the findings of the identical-twin research studies in which marked educational differences were shown to produce moderate IQ differences.

The middle-of-the-road conclusions about the effect of environment on IQ to which these studies led were challenged by a group of studies carried on over a period of years at the University of Iowa. Results up to 1940 were summarized in a paper by Skeels (1940). Several different kinds of evidence were presented, leading to the conclusion that the environment exerts a much larger influence than had been ordinarily attributed to it. In one study, children from very inferior homes were tested at the time of their entrance into an orphanage and the results classified by *age* of entrance. The figures show that the older the children were when they entered the orphanage, the lower their IQ's were. For children entering at the age of four, for instance, the average IQ was 92.6. For those who entered at twelve, it was only 81.6. This was taken to mean that continued residence in an inferior home has a progressive depressing effect on the IQ. It fits in with the results on the increasing retardation with age of isolated groups like the canal-boat and mountain children. In another study, 65 children from inferior homes were tested before and after foster-home placement. There was a consistent shift upward. The mean IQ of three-year-olds before placement was 98.5. A year later, upon re-examination, it was 104.2. One should note, however, that this difference was small.

The most important Iowa studies were those made of children placed for adoption in infancy (Skodak, 1939). As has been explained, valid intelligence test results cannot be obtained on infants. Consequently no tests previous to placement were possible. The first test was given, in each case, at the time the final papers were made out to legalize the adoption. The ages of the 180 children when the test was given ranged from one and a half to six, with a mean of two. A second test was given each of them a little over two years later. The mean IQ of the group at the time of the first test was 116. At the time of the second test it was 111.5. The distribution showed a predominance of superior children, with fewer cases in the dull-normal range than are customarily found. The crucial question is of course related to the thing that could not be measured, that is, the intelligence of the children to start with. The authors presented evidence that in occupational and educational level the true parents were definitely below average, so that below-average intelligence would have been predicted for the group of children as a whole. By the same criteria, the adopting parents were above the average of the population. Furthermore, children placed in the most superior adoptive homes turned out higher on the average than those placed in the less superior environments.

A follow-up study ten years later (Skodak and Skeels, 1949) corroborated the conclusions. For the 100 children out of the original 180 who could be located, the mean IQ was 107 on the 1916 Stanford-Binet Test, 117 on the 1937 revision. (The question as to which was the better measure to use here arose from the fact that on the one hand it seemed better to use the same test that was given at the beginning of the study, but on the other hand, the 1937 revision which came into use after the study began probably furnishes a better estimate of intellectual level, particularly in adolescents.) Whichever figure we take, it is clear that this group of adopted children still scored above the general average. Their average of 107 was 20 points higher than the average score that had been made by their true mothers when tested years before.

As one part of these various Iowa studies, a good many "family correlations" were computed. Skodak and Skeels in the paper just discussed reported practically zero correlations between child's IQ and education of the foster parent. The correlation of child's IQ with either the educational level or the IQ of the *true* parent increased as the children grew older. At the time of the second test, the mother-child correlation for IQ was .28. At the time of the fourth test it was .44. This seemed to show that children tended to approximate the intelligence of their true parents more closely as they grew up, whether they were living with them or not. Skodak (1950) ran some correlations on pairs of children in the same homes. For 41 pairs in which two adopted children lived in the same foster home, a surprisingly high *r* was obtained, .65. For 22 pairs consisting of one adopted and one own child in the same home, the correlation was .21. The author's conclusion was that adopted children in the same home come to resemble each other in intelligence as much as ordinary siblings do. (Sibling correlations usually turn out to be about .5.)

We must remind ourselves that it is impossible to extract any evidence about causes from correlations. They can only be suggestive of hypotheses. When we put together the bits of evidence summarized in the two previous paragraphs, the figures with regard to the *level* of intelligence reached by the foster children point to the importance of environmental influence, whereas most of the *correlations* suggest that the differences between individuals rest on an hereditary basis. The correlation between the IQ's of foster siblings could arise from selective placement rather than from the standardizing effect of the actual home environments. We can fit these facts in with findings from other types of research and say that the effect of improving the environment is to raise the level of the whole group involved but not to make the individuals in it any more *alike*.

The most controversial of these Iowa conclusions were those concerning the children of feeble-minded mothers. We have already discussed in a previous chapter the study of thirteen such children who evinced marked gains, averaging 27.5 IQ points, under the loving care of moron girls in an institution for the feeble-minded. In a later report, Skeels and Harms (1948) showed that groups of subjects selected from the total group on the basis of the fact that (a) their true mother's IQ had been under 75, or (b) their true father's occupational level was known to be very low, or (c) both these factors in combination, all averaged well above

100 when tested at the age of five. Skeels and Harms laid stress on their finding that an inferior social history did not seem to be as much of a handicap as one would expect it to be when favorable opportunities were given for intellectual development.

The criticisms that have been directed against these Iowa studies by other psychologists centered more on the conclusions and implications that had been presented than on the figures themselves. The IQ's of 105 to 117 reported in the various studies were not really a great deal higher than those which previous workers had obtained for adopted children. It has been widely agreed that adopted children average somewhat higher than the population as a whole. Some critics also questioned whether the true parents of many of the Iowa children were as inferior as the investigators reported that they were. The number of grades the mothers had completed in school was about as high as the average for the population at large. Furthermore, only 56 per cent of the fathers were located; it would seem possible that a fairly large number of superior individuals were among the total group. (The study by Skeels and Harms cited earlier does show, however, that even when the fathers are clearly inferior in occupational level, their children can turn out to be above average.) Finally there was evidence in the reports that the ever-present selective placement factor had operated. There was a correlation of .30 between the education of true and foster parents. It looked as though placement workers consciously or unconsciously had taken a child's family background into consideration in finding a suitable adoptive home for him, which, in many ways, is a sensible thing to do.

A more recent study by Wittenborn (1956), a follow-up of adopted children who had been examined before the age of five months at the Gesell Institute, attempted to obtain more finely differentiated information about the development of children in their adoptive homes. Of the 119 subjects in this study, 114 were eight, nine, or ten at the time the follow-up was made, and 81 were five years old. The children were tested and the children and mothers interviewed. Scores on such personality variables as dependency, aggressiveness, and sympathy were given the subjects on the basis of information obtained in the interviews. As in previous studies, the infant tests in the Gesell battery were not correlated with the children's intelligence at the time of the follow-up. Among the many correlations of child-parent characteristics, a considerable number were statistically significant although numerically low (mostly .20 to .30). These fell into two principal clusters. Child's intelligence level tended to be correlated with parent variables having to do with education and ambition for their child. Neurotic tendencies in the child, such as compulsiveness, overaggressiveness, and phobias were correlated with unsympathetic attitudes in the mother, such as tendencies to reject or punish the child. The results of this study agree with those of previous decades about the relationship of intelligence to educational advantages, and add suggestive information about the aspects of the home environment most clearly related to maladjustment.

On the whole, then, all these studies of foster children support our previous conclusions from research based on identical twins. Children do improve in IQ when stimulated by a marked improvement in educational environment. The improvement to be anticipated in any one case is, however, moderate. Nothing but disappointment can result from statements that lead foster parents to expect miraculous changes. Woodworth (1941, p. 68) stresses the point that these studies can be interpreted as showing us, not that hereditary factors have no effect on intelligence, but rather that the hereditary possibilities in many cases are greater than we thought they were. "If a child, from whatever parentage, develops superior intelligence, we know for certain that his heredity was good enough to make that achievement possible. We have simply been misjuding his heredity. The low economic and cultural level of his parents has misled us."

As the general effect of placing children in foster homes has been to improve their intellectual and emotional condition, so the general effect of keeping them in institutions has been to depress their level of development. In the 1940's a number of reports gave us details about serious adverse effects. Goldfarb (1943, 1944) compared a group of adolescents who had spent their first three years in an institution with a group similar in age, sex, and dependency status who had been placed in foster homes during their first three years. The comparison revealed striking differences in intellectual, social, and emotional characteristics. Institutionally reared children were lower in general intelligence, concept formation, memorizing, planning ahead, and language development. They were more anxious and aggressive than home-reared children. Many cases gave evidence of emotional impoverishment, coldness, and isolation.

A great deal of thought and much subsequent research has been directed at finding out what *aspects* of institutional life are so damaging to children. The facts that not all the children show these effects and not all institutions produce them complicate the problem. Many other situations involving separation of young children from their parents have also been studied. Yarrow (1964) has reviewed all the complex evidence on this subject. It appears now that general impoverishment of the surroundings, lack of perceptual and social stimulation, and absence of close relationships with adults are the main sources of the trouble, and that severe retardation can be avoided if these conditions are changed before it is too late. Children who come from very unfavorable home environments may actually gain rather than lose ground when placed in a stimulating institutional environment (Lewis, 1954). Vague concepts like "institutionalization," "hospitalism," and "separation from parents" are gradually giving way to more precise concepts likely to facilitate more penetrating research.

EDUCATION AND INTELLIGENCE

We have already reviewed in previous chapters several kinds of evidence that the measured intelligence of individuals or groups is related to some extent to their educational experiences. The fact that there are intellectual differences related to differences in amount of formal education even in subjects who initially tested alike, as Lorge (1945) showed, indicates that schooling does make a difference. Other studies such as those of S. Smith (1942) in Hawaii, Wheeler (1942) in East Tennessee, and Finch (1946) in two Midwestern states indicate that when there has been a considerable upward shift in the educational opportunities available in a region, the IQ level of the school population goes up accordingly. Tuddenham's (1948) finding that World War II men were considerably higher than World War I men on Army Alpha shows the same trend. Bloom (1956) showed that the national educational level continued to rise from 1945 to 1955.

We have considered the evidence for *handicapping* effects of inadequate environments in some detail in the chapters on race and social-class differences. It seemed reasonable to conclude that at least part of the difference between privileged and nonprivileged groups in the population reflects the retarding influence of poor environment on mental development.

Finally, the studies showing that many individuals originally labeled feeble-minded or mentally retarded become able to function as normal citizens in their communities after receiving the right kind of education constitute important testimony to the value of providing stimulating environments. Whether or not these persons were correctly classified as feeble-minded or might more properly have been labeled pseudo-feeble-minded, the school and the subsequent work experience it made possible changed them in a favorable direction.

In the 1930's, before the evidence for the susceptibility of the IQ to educational influences became as clear as it is now, investigators at the child-study laboratories of the University of Iowa embarked on a program of research centered on the hypothesis that enriching a child's environment could increase his IQ. The Iowa studies on adopted children that we have been looking at were part of this program. The other main division was a study of the effects of nursery schools. It seemed reasonable to suppose that if schooling makes a difference, the earlier its impact could make itself felt the greater would be its total effect on intellectual development.

There are some special difficulties in research of this sort. One of the most troublesome of these, when one tries to interpret the findings, is the nonrepresentativeness of the population in preschool samples. Nursery schools and day nurseries tend to enroll the children either of the well-to-do or of the poor. Children from social classes in between do not so often attend. Most of the nursery schools in college and university departments of psychology and child study charge a fairly high fee and enroll chiefly the children of professors and other professional men in the community. Nursery schools in settlement houses or community centers, on the other hand, are for the benefit of low-income families in which the mother finds it necessary to leave her home during the day in order to work and earn a living.

The Iowa investigators reported results from both types of school (Wellman, 1940). The work in the University of Iowa Nursery School involved first a comparison of IQ changes made from fall to spring, while school was in session, with the changes from spring to fall when it was not. The average gain during the first fall-to-spring period was 6.6 IQ points. After a small loss from spring to fall, those who continued in preschool made a further gain of 3.8 points the second year. For those who attended for a third year, there was very little further gain. A "diminishing-returns" tendency seemed to be operating. Paired groups of preschool and non-preschool children, matched for age and IQ, were also compared. The preschool group gained 7.0 points, and the non-preschool lost 3.9 points; the difference was statistically significant. A little evidence was presented that the advantage the preschool experience had given the children was maintained even up to the time of college entrance. In matched groups of 29 "grown-up" children, the ones who had attended preschool made an average percentile of 88 on the American Council of Education Test given at the time of college entrance, whereas the non-preschool group averaged 78. Since this difference was not statistically significant, however, it failed to prove the point.

The other major Iowa project was the establishment of a nursery school in an orphanage. The children came from underprivileged families, definitely below average in intellectual promise. The preschool itself was a novel and interesting activity superimposed upon a monotonous dead level of routine. An attempt was made to divide all children of preschool age into two matched groups, so that one could be given nursery-school experience and the other held as a control. The fact that children were constantly entering or leaving the orphanage, however, made it impossible to keep the groups matched very precisely during the three years that the experiment ran. Of the many publications by the investigators and their critics, the most dependable analysis of just what the study did show is to be found in the papers by Wellman and Pegram (1944) and by McNemar (1945). Wellman stressed the fact that the control group, lacking nursery-school experience, tended to *lose* significantly in

IQ. The preschool's effect was to counteract such losses and produce small gains instead. A certain minimal amount of exposure to the stimulating influences seemed to be required, since the figures showed no difference between the preschool group and the controls for less than 400 days of residence while the experiment was in progress, or for less than 50 per cent attendance at preschool. McNemar's critical analysis confirmed Wellman's conclusion with regard to gains during preschool and the relationship of gains to amount of attendance, but threw doubt on the conclusion that in the non-preschool group, losses were the rule. He showed that all of the apparent average loss was produced by eight extreme cases not typical of the whole group. However, there have been enough other studies before and since this one showing that deprived groups, especially those in institutions, do tend to decrease in intellectual level so that this is not an important criticism.

At the time the *Thirty-ninth Yearbook of the Society for the Study of Education,* which included the Iowa studies and nursery school studies from nine other places, came out in 1940, this kind of evidence was at odds with the views of most differential psychologists and it therefore touched off a barrage of criticism. At that time the "constancy of the IQ" was a dogma that seemed worth fighting for. And the Iowa studies were unquestionably vulnerable to criticism at many points. In some cases extreme IQ changes of 30 or 40 points had been selected for discussion from an experiment showing only a very moderate *average* change. In some cases the tendency of extreme scores to regress toward the mean on repeated testing had been ignored, so that losses in high-scoring children and gains in low-scoring children were accepted at their face value. In some cases IQ's based on different intelligence tests had been used interchangeably although they were not exactly comparable statistically. Furthermore, most of the non-Iowa nursery school studies had not reported similar IQ increases. A study by Page (1940) indicated quite conclusively that attendance at nursery school in one place at least did not give children higher IQ's than their non-preschool siblings at a *later* time, when they were all in elementary grades.

What was being overlooked in this whole controversy, by the Iowa investigators and their critics alike, was the difference in the two kinds of samples encountered in the nursery school populations. It was tacitly assumed by everyone at that time that if an environmental influence was effective it should be effective for everyone. Our increasing realization that this is not true—that the same situation affects different persons in different ways—is one of the chief gains in insight that we have made in the quarter-century of research since these Iowa studies of environmental influences. The fact that the gains Wellman reported in the orphanage study stood up even under McNemar's searching analysis suggests that we may be dealing in this case with a special psychological situation.

Nursery-school attendance coming as a tremendous enrichment of a drab, stultifying environment may have an effect that is much more drastic than the same experience added to the generally favorable situation that a good home provides. In the study of preschool education for the mentally retarded by Kirk (1958) and in the reports of pilot projects in various parts of the country on the value of preschool experience for the "culturally deprived," corroboration of Wellman's results has been obtained. The reopening of this line of inquiry after it had been neglected for some twenty-five years is one of the important developments of the 1960's.

EFFECTS OF EARLY EXPERIENCE

Two of the kinds of research problem we have been discussing, the effects of institutionalization and the effects of preschool education, can now be classified under a much more inclusive heading. Psychologists have become increasingly interested in the effects of early experience on later development and a large body of research information has accumulated. A good synthesis of these findings can be found in Thompson and Schaefer (1961). Interest in these problems has arisen from two theoretical sources: (1) the psychoanalytic concepts stressing the importance of the early childhood years in the formation of personality structure; and (2) the hypotheses of Hebb (1949) with regard to the importance of early perceptual learning for later mental development. The work of the ethologists on "imprinting" has also contributed something to thinking along these lines.

Animal subjects have been used in much of this research on the effects of early experience. It has been demonstrated that handling rats in infancy makes them better at learning mazes and more resistant to stress than nonhandled animals are at maturity. Dogs raised in isolation are more timid and excitable when they grow up than dogs raised normally. Thompson and Schaefer (1961) comment on these and many other experiments, and set up a framework within which the many aspects of the general problem can be organized. Such detailed questions arise as the following, to none of which satisfactory answers have yet been found: What type of stimulation is most effective with a certain species? At what age are its effects most pronounced? What kinds of effects occur under different circumstances?

It is the general direction of some of the findings that are of most interest to psychologists whose main concern is with people rather than with animals and with practical rather than theoretical knowledge. One consistent finding is that it is reduced *sensory* stimulation rather than reduced *motor* activity that tends to impair intellectual development (Thompson and Schaefer, 1961, pp. 87–88). Another is that the same environmental stimulation has different effects on subjects with different genotypes. We shall consider these findings in more detail in the following chapter. Still another suggestive finding is that there seem to be critical periods for the maximum effects of certain kinds of influences, but that to some extent at least the effects of early experience are reversible through experience provided later in life (Thompson and Schaefer, p. 86). All these generalizations from animal research must be checked to discover whether they are confirmed by studies with children before we can be sure they are applicable to human development and education. What the work so far has accomplished is to inject new vigor into developmental psychology and provide it with promising leads for research.

EFFECTS OF PRACTICE ON INDIVIDUAL DIFFERENCES

There is another cluster of research studies extending in a different direction from those having to do with environmental effects on intelligence and personality. Some psychologists have been interested in the question of what happens with regard to *variability* or the differences between individuals in a group of subjects who go through a series of practice trials on some specific skill? There is no question here about the amount of *average* change. Everybody improves markedly between the first trial and the last. But does practice involve a *leveling* or a *diversifying* trend? Are subjects more like each other after they have had this common experience, or does it serve to make latent differences between them more evident?

It can be seen that this question has important practical implications with regard to aptitude testing, industrial training programs, and education. If there is a tendency for all subjects to approach the same level of competence when adequate training has been given, then there is little point in developing elaborate testing programs to select persons for such training. In general, society is interested more in trained skills than in undeveloped talents, and thus it becomes especially important to identify the factors that account for differences in these finished products.

As in so many other areas of research, psychologists who initiated research on this question hoped to be able to obtain a general answer applicable to all kinds of material, persons, and situations. The typical design of an experiment was as follows:

1. A fairly large group of subjects is given an initial test on one or more measurable skills. A measure of central tendency and of variability is computed.
2. An interval intervenes during which all subjects are given equal amounts of practice in the given skill.

3. A final test equivalent in every way to the initial one is given. Central tendency and variability are again determined.

Early experiments planned in this way came up with conflicting results. In some, variability was shown to increase with practice; in others, it was shown to decrease. A more careful scrutiny of the methods could explain away most of these discrepancies. Anastasi (1934) in the introduction to the report on her carefully planned study analyzed the reasons for many of the discrepant findings. In the first place, measures of *absolute* variability—usually standard deviations—and of *relative* variability lead to different results. (The most common index of relative variability is the coefficient of variation, usually abbreviated CV, defined as $\frac{100\ \text{SD}}{\text{M}}$. Dividing by the mean makes an adjustment for the general level of performance.) As our understanding of the limitations of different kinds of numerical scales increased it became clear that the making of a fraction or ratio out of numbers on interval scales like most psychological test scores is not a legitimate operation. Thus the results of studies in which relative variability was used are usually meaningless. Secondly, Anastasi showed that

TABLE 50
Averages and Standard Deviations of Scores on First and Last Trials

(Anastasi, 1934)

	FIRST TRIAL		LAST TRIAL	
	Mean	*SD*	*Mean*	*SD*
Cancellation	40.63	6.78	59.60	7.88
Symbol-Digit	41.15	7.58	70.07	9.98
Vocabulary	39.06	6.84	59.28	8.87
Hidden Words	43.58	6.94	69.28	11.44

it makes a difference whether the time taken to complete a task or the number of units completed in a standard length of time constitutes the measure of proficiency. With regard to this difference it seems more reasonable to use amount scores, since they bear more resemblance to real-life situations. Time is a constant for all of us. It is the amount we accomplish in each twenty-four-hour period that varies. Thirdly, experiments give different results depending upon whether the practice during stage 2 is measured in number of practice trials or in time spent on the activity. Here again it seems more reasonable to use time spent as our measure of amount of practice, since this is the way the learning of real-life skills is usually organized—six hours a day in school, an hour a day at the piano, twenty hours a week on the football field.

With terms defined in this way, the evidence tends to show that individual differences *increase* with practice. Table 50, taken from Anastasi's study, is a good example of these trends. Results are shown for four different tests given to four different groups of about 120 college students. It can be seen that the groups as a whole showed considerable improvement, but that differences between individuals, as shown by the standard deviations, were larger at the end than at the beginning.

The development of more complex ways of designing an experiment, using analysis of variance methods, made it possible to analyze more precisely what happens to individual differences during a series of practice trials. Owens (1942a, b, c) gave his subjects, fifteen junior high school boys, a number of motor-skills tests.[1] He compared the variance associated with differences between *individuals* in the early trials, numbers 2, 3, and 4, with that in later trials, numbers 6, 7, and 8. The individual differences were slightly greater on the later trials, but the difference was not statistically significant. A large part of the variability at all stages, 82 to 85 per cent, was determined by individual differences rather than by practice differences. Garrett's (1940) experiment led him to a different conclusion. His subjects were college students doing tasks of an intellectual rather than a motor nature. He found that variability remained constant within the groups as the experiment progressed, and that practice was more significant than individual differences in its effect on total variability. The differences between the group's averages from trial to trial was greater than the differences between persons on any one trial. Hamilton (1943), who allowed groups of fifth-grade children to practice three different paper-and-pencil tasks, found that the proportion of the total variance that could be attributed to practice varied with the task and with the stage of proficiency that had been reached. In early trials, practice differences overshadowed individual differences. In later stages where improvement was slower, individual differences played a somewhat larger role.

The effect of these studies taken together has been to show us that like so many other broad general questions, the one that asks whether individual differences increase or decrease with practice cannot be answered with any generality once and for all. What we get in any given situation seems to depend on the homogeneity or heterogeneity of the group, the nature of the task, the length of the training period, and perhaps a number of other things. Tilton (1936) called attention to the importance of differential *forgetting* after an experiment is over as a source of individual differences. He summarized figures from thirty-nine sources, and they seemed to reveal a general tendency for standard deviations to increase, showing that differences between individuals were still greater after a

[1] Good experimental design made it possible to obtain from a relatively small number of cases dependable information as to the statistical significance of different factors.

fallow period than they were at the time practice trials ended. Burns (1937) stressed the importance of motivation in the subjects of the experiment, and Ewert (1934) reported one study in which under high motivation, variability increased with practice. In view of the complexity of the question, it seems that we must consider practice effects under the general heading of *sources of variability* and proceed to investigate their nature and extent for each specific trait in which we are interested.

There are two special questions in this area, however, that become important in a practical way to those who are using tests for purposes of selection. To what extent do the subjects in an experiment maintain their relative positions of superiority or inferiority in their group as practice progresses? Unless there is a fair amount of correlation between initial and final scores, the use of skills tests of any sort to select workers to be trained would seem to be unjustified. There is no point in hiring the individuals who score highest on a motor-coordination test, if the lower-scoring applicants are just as likely to get high scores after a period of training. Related to this is the question of identifying factors upon which *ultimate* proficiency rests. It is trained skills that count in the end, not aptitudes.

In general, a good foundation for personnel testing has been demonstrated in many reports showing positive correlations between initial and final scores in a variety of learning experiments. Those who are superior at the beginning maintain that superiority even during a period when all subjects are improving. Kincaid (1925) brought together the results of a number of early studies, and showed that the majority of the correlations between scores for first and last trials were above .60. In Anastasi's (1934) study, the initial-final correlations were as follows:

Cancellation	.67
Symbol-Digit	.30
Vocabulary	.51
Hidden Words	.82

It would seem then that we are quite safe in placing our bets on subjects who are initially high. However, the variation in reported correlations is also interesting. Hertzman (1939) focused attention on the way in which coefficients vary from group to group and from task to task. The most interesting fact he pointed out is that in cases where the practice period consists of a *short* series of trials, the correlations are higher than where it involves a *long* series. This suggests what some other research has pointed out more explicitly that over an extended practice period, a subject's performance changes qualitatively as well as quantitatively, and that by developing different methods of work he may change his position in the group to a significant extent.

Brief mention should be made of one question that has often been asked but cannot be adequately answered because of technical difficulties. It is the question as to who *gains* or improves most during practice in some sort of skill, the initially low individual or the one initially high? Many correlations have been computed between variable 1, *gain* scores obtained by subtracting the initial from the final score, and variable 2, the initial scores themselves. Taken at face value, such correlations seem to indicate that those poorer at the beginning improve more than those better at the beginning, since the vast majority of the correlations are *negative.* They cannot, however, be taken at their face value. The double dose of chance errors in gain scores, the fact that most tests have too low a *ceiling* to permit unlimited improvement in the better performers, and the unequal difficulty of test items, so that a gain of one point means something different at different levels of performance—all these things make gain scores very tricky to work with and put us on guard against conclusions based on them.

The best series of studies on the whole problem of factors that affect ultimate proficiency in learned tasks was carried out by Woodrow (1938a, b, c, d; 1939a, b; 1940). Some of the results have already been discussed in Chapter 4. The general procedure was to give a group of students a large number of practice periods on a variety of different tests. In addition, tests of intelligence and special aptitudes were administered at the beginning and at the end of the series of practice trials. Then the figures were analyzed by a variety of methods to ascertain what the essential relationships were. These analyses showed rather conclusively that it is not the *fast* learners who are highest at the end. It is rather the ones who *go on improving* for a long time who come out ahead. *Rate* of learning depends to some extent on the amount of practice the individual has had with similar material before the experiment began. The more previous practice he has had, the slower his progress will appear to be, since he enters the experiment at a later stage of the learning process, and learning curves always tend to show steeper climbs in the early than in the later stages. Therefore, to predict a person's ultimate score on the basis of the rate at which he improves during early stages of his training is not feasible. Final attainment depends to some extent on something that cannot be measured at the beginning, namely, the length of time over which improvement will continue. (This does not negate the fact discussed above—that correlations between initial and final scores are uniformly positive. We can to some degree predict a person's final score by looking at his initial score. The point is that such predictions are by no means perfect, and that a measurement of rate of learning at the beginning does not add anything to their accuracy.)

As has been mentioned in Chapter 4, Woodrow found that rate of learning was not correlated with the intelligence we measure by our tests. He considered also another hypothesis—that there is some general learning ability, not the same as the trait our intelligence tests measure, which affects the efficiency of all learning. This hypothesis too turned out to be untenable. Gains are specific. The individual who improves most rapidly on one type of skill may be slow or only average on another.

One of the most interesting of Woodrow's findings is that the *correlations* between tests are different after practice than they were before, and that factor analysis reveals a different pattern of loadings. This result suggests that subjects must accomplish the tasks after practice by methods that are different from those they used at the beginning. This often-neglected factor of *work methods* as a source of individual differences in manifest ability and accomplishment was emphasized also by Sargent (1942) and R. H. Seashore (1939). What seems to occur during a series of practice trials is that subjects stumble upon specific changes in their methods of doing a task which make more efficient performance possible. Most of us have had such experiences in connection with one or another special learning problem. The pianist working on a difficult sonata discovers that a change in the position of his hands makes it possible to execute a phrase smoothly and rapidly. A golf player learns to keep his eye on the ball instead of on the green in the distance where he wants it to go. Woodrow's changes in factor pattern fit in with common knowledge that learning is not simply a quantitative improvement in the rate at which the same thing is done, but a qualitative change in the psychological factors lying back of what is done.

Such results would suggest that we ought to investigate specifically the effects of *training* rather than practice alone on individual differences. It might be that by demonstrating to all members of a group the work methods that the best performers hit upon for themselves we could reduce the differences between individuals and raise the average level more than we do in most of our learning experiments. In practical situations, of course, music teachers, coaches, and efficiency engineers do this constantly. The fact that they do not succeed in bringing all their trainees up to the level of the highest ones shows that work methods are not the *only* factor involved in individual differences. But we need more research on *training* as contrasted with *practice* in order to determine how important a source of variability work methods are. This problem has become more susceptible to research since the development of programmed learning or "teaching machines." There is some evidence that working through a good program reduces individual differences with regard to the mastery of the information or principles it is designed to teach. Such a conclusion, if substantiated, would have important implications for education and training.

In considering all the kinds of evidence for environmental influences that have been discussed in this chapter, we should keep in mind one thing they do not show. They do not justify a conclusion that *all* differences between individuals arise from environmental factors *alone*. If this were the case, it is unlikely that we would ever have a brilliant writer coming out of the slums or a president from a log cabin in the backwoods. Such occurrences are only dramatic instances of what we find in every frequency distribution—that for a group coming from a standardized environment, whether its level is low or high, we obtain a wide range of individual scores. The more we have studied the effects of various aspects of environment on individuals, the more apparent it has become that persons will *differ* even when their environments are alike. We turn in the next chapter to the evidence that there is hereditary basis for such differences.

SUMMARY

Modern research workers have largely given up the argument about the relative importance of hereditary and environmental influences. They are concentrating instead on discovering how human characteristics can be changed in desirable ways. The study of identical twins raised in different homes has shown that environment, particularly its educational aspects, can have a measurable effect on intelligence. Studies of foster children have corroborated this conclusion. Adopted children tend to score, as a group, somewhat higher than children from low social levels who remain in their own homes. Children growing up in institutions such as orphanages have often, though not always, been intellectually or emotionally handicapped by the experience.

There is abundant evidence that improved education leads to higher intelligence. Preschools have produced some improvement in the intelligence level of orphanage children whose previous environment has been unusually sterile, though they seem to have had little effect on the mental development of children from good homes. Animal experiments have also demonstrated that early experience affects later development.

Studies designed to show the effect of a series of practice trials on individual differences in some specific skill have shown that such effects vary with many features of the learning situation, so that the question is not one that can be answered in general terms. There is enough correlation between initial and final scores to justify aptitude testing and prediction of final scores, but such predictions are only moderately accurate. Unpredictable individual differences in work methods show up during the course of learning, and some subjects continue to improve for a much longer time than others.

In all these kinds of research, there is evidence that environmental influences, whether they are as broad and general as schooling, or as narrow and well-defined as a series of ten practice trials in a dart-throwing experiment, affect the central tendency of the group being studied more than they do its variability. They produce *improvement* but not *uniformity*.

CHAPTER 18

The Hereditary Basis of Individuality

INTRODUCTION

ONE AIM OF THE PRECEDING chapter was to make it clear that there is no longer any scientific justification for a controversy over heredity *vs.* environment. To perpetuate this pugnacious dispute in our time reflects attitudes rather than evidence. Each individual constitutes a pattern of hereditary potentialities developed to a greater or lesser extent under the impact of various environmental influences. We have considered what some of these influences and their characteristic effects are. Now let us turn to the evidence about the part played by heredity in human differences. The facts reported in the previous chapter, collected and organized to show how environment changes people, still leave a large role for the hereditary differences we are now to turn to in more detail. The studies of twins indicate that even when they have been reared in different homes, identicals are much more *similar* in their mental abilities than are fraternal twins or ordinary siblings. Even the largest IQ difference reported, between the twins with the great discrepancy in education, is not nearly as large as the extreme differences we find among unrelated persons. The persistent tendency for foster children to resemble their real parents more than they resemble their foster parents supplies further evidence that hereditary differences are not eradicated by environmental influences. Learning experiments show that differences tend to persist even after long periods of standardized practice. Finally, the fact that individuals of the highest level of mental ability are constantly turning up even among the most underprivileged groups is most easily explained in terms of genetic differences. As has been indicated in previous chapters, we must be cautious in our conclusions as to the meaning of below-average scores that various underprivileged groups tend to make on intelligence tests—Southern Negroes, rural school children, unskilled laborers. But it is difficult to account in purely environmental terms for the *brilliant* Southern Negroes, farm children, and unskilled workers whom we have all encountered or read about. The fact is that no matter how uniformly good or poor their environments may be, whenever we measure the mental traits of a group we obtain a *distributed range* of individual scores. Although this of course proves nothing about heredity, it does constitute a starting point around which the evidence for genetic differences can be organized.

Recent years have brought phenomenal progress in the science of genetics. The mechanisms and chemical processes involved in hereditary transmission are better understood than ever before. Good discussions of these concepts and principles as they affect problems in which psychologists are interested have been presented by Fuller and Thompson (1960), Gottesman (1963a), and McClearn (1964). Research in genetics has taken a great deal of the mystery out of heredity. No longer do knowledgeable people think in terms of vague hereditary taints and gifts, as they have done throughout most of human history. It is true that we still know far less about the part heredity plays in human differences than we know about genetic differences in strains of corn, fruitflies, mice, or even dogs. But we can now understand *in principle* many processes we have not yet analyzed in detail, and this is a great advantage. Let us look, then, at some of the main varieties of evidence about genetic differences in tendencies toward various kinds of behavior.

ANIMAL EXPERIMENTS

That heredity sets limits to mental development is accepted by many people with so little question that it comes as a shock to realize that there was no real proof of the fact until recently. Watson caused a considerable stir when he stated that if he were given a dozen healthy average children to train from birth on, he would guarantee to make of each of them anything that anyone stipulated. This was a possible hypothesis, even if it was sensational, until the animal-breeding experiments proved conclusively that some kind of mental ability *could be inherited*. Breeding experiments on rats were first carried on by Tryon (1942) at the University of California and by Heron (1935) at the University of Minnesota. The learning behavior that had been most widely investigated in rats at that time was maze-running, and animals had been shown to differ widely. The plan of both the Tryon and Heron experiments was to select in the F-1 generation two groups of animals, those who made the best and those who made the worst maze scores. By breeding good maze-runners with each other and poor maze-runners with each other, groups of offspring were produced that differed to some extent in this ability. The process was continued generation after generation, environmental factors being kept as uniform as possible for all the animals. With each generation the groups drew farther apart, until by the F-8 in the Tryon experiment (see Figure 50) there was almost no overlapping and the poorest individual in the "bright" group was as good as the best individual in the "dull" group. Maze-running ability had been shown to depend on something that could be inherited.

Other workers bred strains of animals differing markedly in what might be called *temperamental* or *motivational* characteristics. Rundquist (1933) after twelve generations of selective breeding obtained groups of *active* and *inactive* rats. Active males averaged 123,000 revolutions of a revolving drum during a fifteen-day experimental period, whereas inactive males averaged only 6,000. C. S. Hall (1934, 1936, 1937) produced strains of rats differing in *emotionality,* and Hall and Klein (1942) showed that *aggressiveness* was a part of the complex of traits that was being inherited in the nonemotional, fearless strain.

At the time Tryon and Heron first undertook their work on "maze-bright" and "maze-dull" rats, many psychologists saw these characteristics as analogous to human intelligence. Trying these "bright" and "dull" rats out on other sorts of learning problems demonstrated that this interpretation was unwarranted. The "bright" rats were not good at everything, but simply at maze-running. The best evidence as to what the differences between the strains really meant came from a study by Searle (1949). He obtained 30 measurements for ten rats of each strain. Rats from each group showed a characteristic *pattern* of high and low scores, quite different for the two groups. The "dull" group did as well as the bright on many learning tasks that did not involve mazes. In general the "maze-bright" animals were "characteristically food-driven, economical of distance, low in motivation to escape from water, and timid in response to open spaces," whereas "dulls" were "relatively disinterested in food, average or better in water motivation, and timid of mechanical apparatus features." The striking thing about these differences was that they seemed to be of a *temperamental* or *motivational* rather than of a cognitive nature.

Another advance in the use of animal breeding techniques to investigate the genetics of behavior was made when Hirsch developed a method of applying them to *drosophila melanogaster.* This species of fruitfly has been a favorite organism for research in genetics because large numbers of subjects in successive generations can so quickly be obtained. Perhaps the most ingenious aspect of this research program initiated by Hirsch and Tryon (1956) was the identification and measurement of reliable individual differences in the behavior of these very simple organisms whose behavioral possibilities would at first sight seem very limited. The

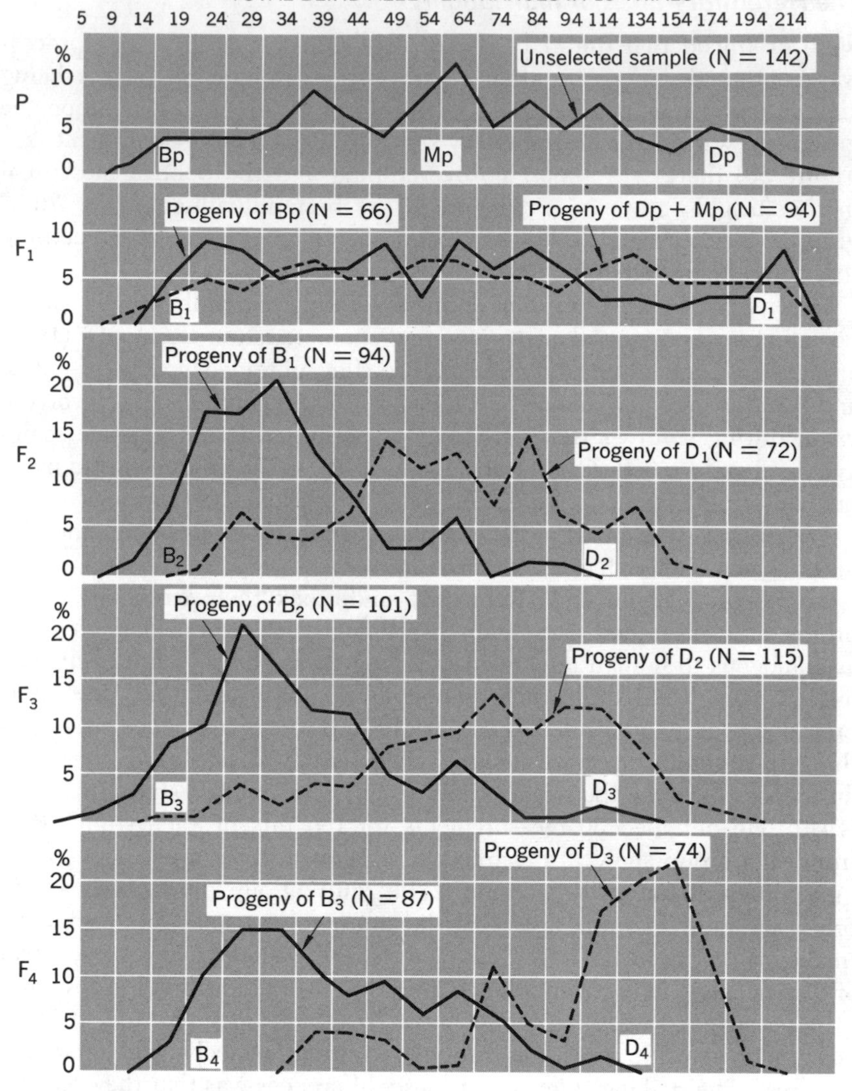

FIGURE 50

Differences Between Groups of "Maze-bright" and "Maze-dull" Rats in Successive Generations

(Reproduced by permission of the publishers from *Comparative psychology*, Revised Edition, edited by F. A. Moss. Copyright, by Prentice-Hall, Inc., 1934, 1942)

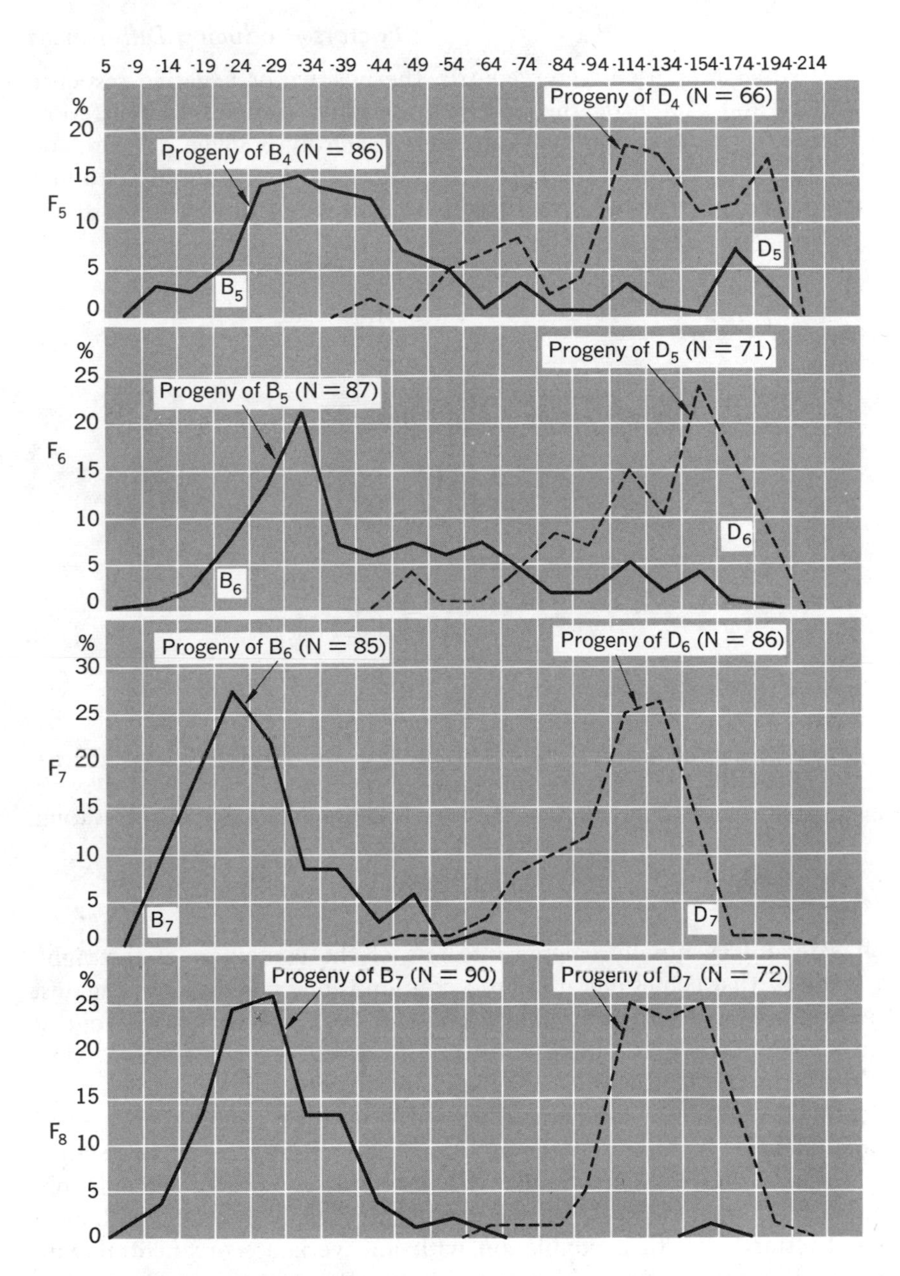

FIGURE 50 (continued)

Differences Between Groups of "Maze-bright" and "Maze-dull" Rats in Successive Generations

two variables they used were *geotaxis,* the positive or negative response to gravity, and *phototaxis,* the positive or negative response to light. Most of the work has been done with geotaxis. Each fly is given a "score" on this variable by means of the apparatus diagramed in Figure 51, a 10-unit vertical maze constructed from tubing. All flies enter the apparatus at the

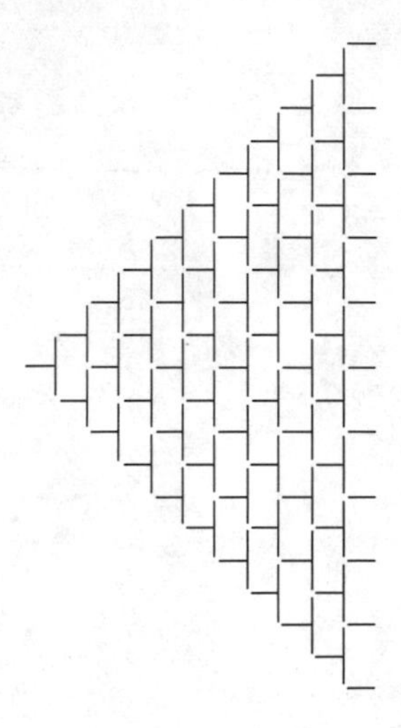

FIGURE 51

Diagram Showing the Structure of the Hirsch Drosophila Maze for Measuring Geotactic Tendency

(Hirsch, 1959)

left side and eventually emerge into one of the containers at the right. A "subject" that comes out at the top position is one who has gone against the pull of gravity at every choice point. A "subject" that comes out at the lowest position has gone with gravity at every choice point. Most subjects distribute themselves somewhere between these extremes, indicating that they have sometimes made the positive geotactic choice and sometimes the negative. The distribution obtained for flies on this simple behavioral variable is not unlike the distributions most commonly obtained for human subjects on psychological tests. Weiss (1959) showed that by starting with a population with an average score neutral with respect to gravity, she could produce in twenty generations of selective breeding specialized populations with opposite response tendencies. The "upwardly mobile" group of flies produced in this way showed negative geotaxis on about 80 per cent of its trials; the "downwardly mobile" group showed positive geotaxis on about 77 per cent of its trials. These results are comparable to those that others have obtained with rats.

With this basic technique for producing large numbers of subjects of a certain behavioral type, Hirsch and his co-workers have proceeded to investigate the mode of inheritance of the characteristic tested. A summary of this work and discussion of its significance can be found in Hirsch (1962). The details of these experiments designed to show how drosophila's three chromosomes determine the geotactic tendencies need not be discussed here. The general finding of considerable importance to differential psychology is that even this simple bit of behavior is inherited in a complex way. Simple Mendelian (dominant-recessive) relationships between one or two genes are ruled out as explanations. All three drosophila chromosomes affect the behavior.

Another kind of animal research in genetics consists in first producing by inbreeding over several generations pure strains of various kinds, and then examining behavioral differences between them on a variety of kinds of "test." Pure-bred dogs constitute a sort of natural experiment on inherited characteristics, and there have been some careful psychological studies of the differences between them. Stockard et al. (1941) showed that basset hounds differ from German shepherd and Saluki dogs in their reactions to conditioning experiments as well as in the activity and alertness evident in their behavior. Scott (1953) and Fuller and Scott (1954) reported on experiments conducted at the Jackson Memorial Laboratory. They showed that different breeds of dogs differ in many motivational characteristics, such as aggressiveness, timidity, and sensitivity to noise. Three kinds of learning situation that were used as "tests" of their abilities—leash-control training, discrimination training, and spatial orientation—showed clearly that some breeds excelled in one sort of thing, others in another. There was practically no correlation between scores on the different "tests." Furthermore, when measurements were made at different stages of the learning process it was apparent that methods of attack on a new situation differed from breed to breed. It was characteristic of beagles, for example, to make many errors at the beginning, to make very rapid progress at the second stage, and to come out with variable, nonrigid habits at the end.

Others have used mice in these studies of pure, inbred strains. McClearn (1961) showed that activity was related to genotype. Of more possible relevance to an urgent human problem is the evidence accumulated by Rodgers and McClearn (1962) that there are very large differences between strains of mice in the alcohol they consume under conditions permitting free choice of solutions of different concentrations. Furthermore, the strains liking alcohol increased their preference for it as time passed, so that by the third week of the study mice of this type were choosing 10 per cent solutions (about like table wine) far more frequently than any of the weaker solutions. Similarly strains showing an aversion to alcohol increasingly chose pure water in preference to any of the alcohol solutions as time passed.

Animal research on the genetics of behavior has made several important contributions to our general thinking about heredity, in addition to demonstrating that psychological differences have a hereditary basis. For one thing, they have indicated that *polygenic* theories postulating many gene determiners for each trait fit the facts better than theories attributing genetic effects to single major genes. The shift to polygenic explanations is one of the salient developments in research of the middle decades of the twentieth century. A second contribution from this source is to call attention to the fact that genetic differences show up in *patterns* of characteristics, some high and some low, rather than in levels of general ability. In human research, until fairly recently, so much emphasis was placed on differences in general intelligence that the possibility of such patterns was not considered as seriously as it might have been. Thirdly, the genetic differences shown in the animal studies seem to be more readily classifiable as *temperamental* characters than as ability. Here too, the emphasis in the human studies, at least until fairly recently, has been on abilities. Studies like those we have been considering have laid a firm foundation for the further study of behavior genetics. Much progress has been made; still more can be anticipated in the future.

FAMILY RESEMBLANCES IN INTELLIGENCE

The facts that constitute the evidence for heredity most obvious and convincing to the man on the street are the least convincing to the scientist. Resemblances between members of the same family can signify many things. However, since there have been many studies in which family resemblances were systematically explored, they can legitimately be used to supplement more conclusive types of evidence. The trouble is, of course, that in any family we have a mixture of hereditary and environmental influences which it is impossible to disentangle.

Students in the social sciences used not to get far before they encountered the Jukes and the Kallikaks. The Jukes were a New York family traced through seven generations of pauperism, feeble-mindedness, crime, vice, and disease. The "Kallikaks" consisted of two lines of descent starting at the time of the American Revolution from the union of Martin Kallikak with two different women. The descendants of one line, that from a feeble-minded girl's illegitimate son by Kallikak included a large number of feeble-minded and degenerate individuals. The descendants of Martin Kallikak and his lawful wife were predominantly normal, self-respecting citizens. Both these studies were widely quoted for a long time as evidence for the supposed fact that the serious effects of bad heredity could last through many generations. Of recent years, however, critics have pointed out that such a conclusion is not justified in view of the fact that the feeble-minded or degenerate parents furnished for their children such very unfavorable environments that they could not be expected to develop excellent human qualities whatever their heredity. It is impossible for us to determine whether the genes or the environments constituted the greater handicap.

Other workers have studied *correlations* between members of families and have set up various hypotheses as to what these might mean. Although members of a family do not have the *same* heredity, they are genetically considerably more alike than persons chosen at random from the general population. If in a fairly large number of family groups, we can get an estimate of the amount of intragroup resemblance that heredity alone would account for, then we can consider deviations from this trend as evidence of the effects of environment. The following hypotheses have been tried by one or more investigators:

1. If environment is an important factor in the production of intellectual traits, then correlation coefficients between siblings should be *lower* for these traits than for physical characteristics like eye color, height, and head measurements, which are thought to be almost entirely hereditary.
2. If environment is an important factor, correlations between like-sexed siblings should be higher than those between different-sexed siblings, since the environment is more closely similar for two brothers or for two sisters than it is for a boy and a girl in the family.
3. If environment is an important factor, correlations between siblings should be higher than correlations between parents and children, since the fact that they belong to the same generation would operate to make the siblings' environment more similar.
4. If environment is an important factor, correlations between mothers and children should be higher than those between fathers and children since the mother is more closely associated with the children during their early formative years.

Scattered evidence has been cited both for and against each of these hypotheses. So far as the first is concerned, practically all investigators agree that the intrafamily correlations for intelligence-test scores are of a magnitude comparable to those for structural physical traits. They are about .50 for both kinds of characteristics. Thus they furnish no evidence that intelligence is more dependent upon environmental influences than eye color or height is. The most thoroughgoing tests of the other three hypotheses are available in the work of Conrad and Jones (1940), who gave 997 individuals in 269 family groups the Army Alpha examination. None of the hypotheses outlined finds any support in their results. No clear trend with regard to like-sexed *vs.* different-sexed or mother-children *vs.* father-children correlations was apparent. The correlation between siblings was exactly the same as the correlation between parents and children: .49. The only conclusion we can draw is that if differences in

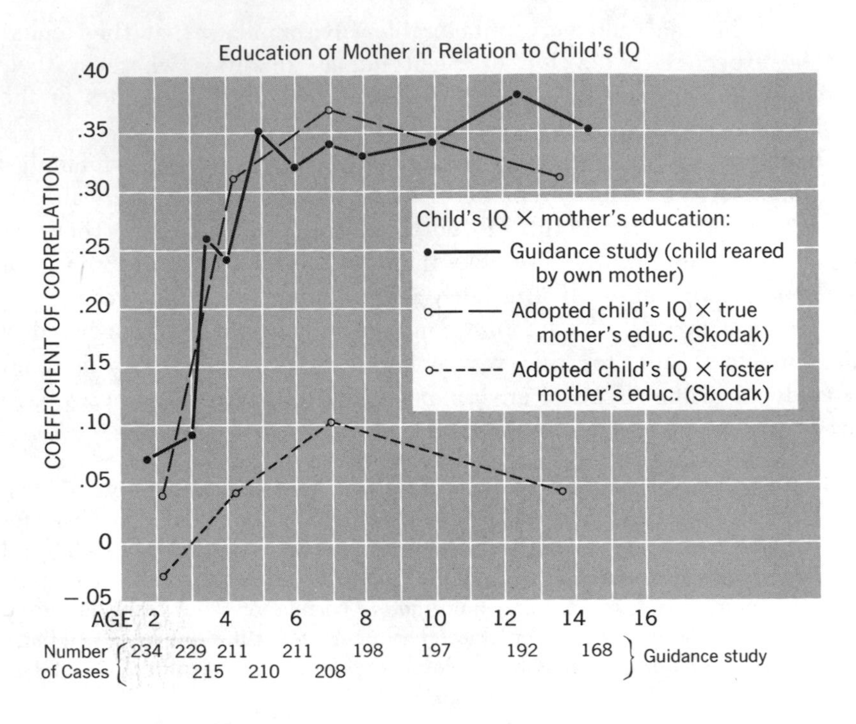

FIGURE 52

Correlations Between Mother's Education and Child's IQ at Successive Ages for Different Samples

(Honzik, 1957)

environment have a pronounced effect on differences in mental ability, we have not been able to demonstrate that fact by methods of this sort. Jones and Conrad show that correlations such as those they obtained *can be* accounted for on the basis of heredity alone. That they *are* actually based on genetic similarity must be established in some other way.

A more convincing kind of correlational evidence that environment does not account for all of the similarity between members of the same family has emerged from longitudinal studies, particularly the studies of adopted children. It is clear from many longitudinal studies that the resemblance between children and their parents in intelligence tends to increase as the children grow toward adulthood. The reason for thinking that this trend reflects hereditary rather than environmental determiners is that it occurs whether children are living in the homes of their true parents or not. Honzik (1957) brought such findings together from two

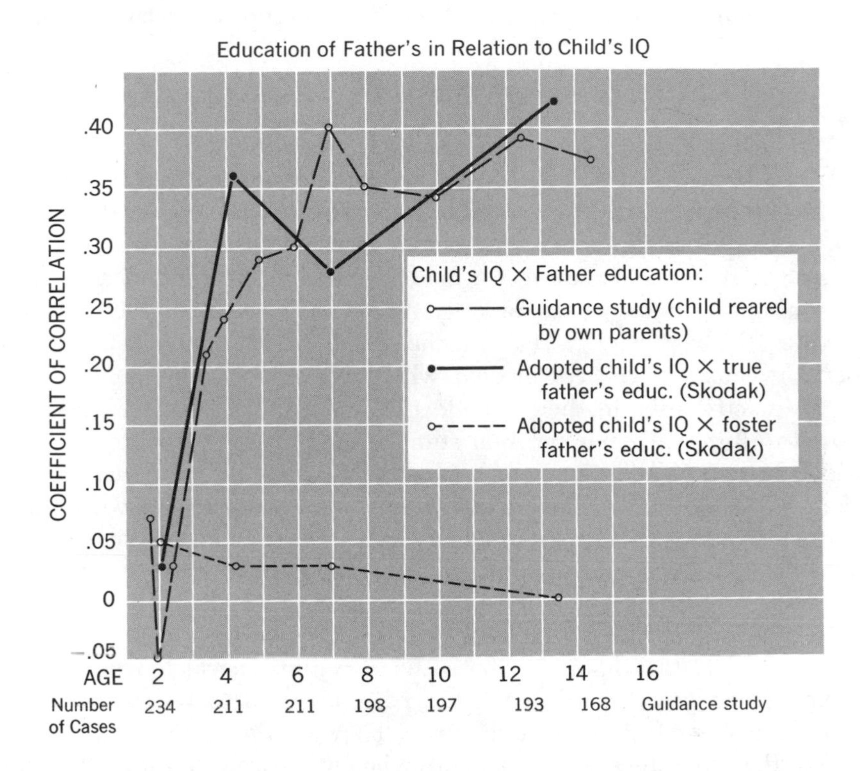

FIGURE 53
Correlations Between Father's Education and Child's IQ at Successive Ages for Different Samples
(Honzik, 1957)

very different longitudinal studies. Figures 52 and 53 show how closely the relationships between the intelligence of adopted children and the education of their *true* parents (which can be used as a rough indicator of the intelligence of these parents) follow the pattern of the relationships between child's intelligence and parents' education for children growing up in their own homes. In contrast, the relationships between child's intelligence and foster parents' education are very low. We must remember in this connection that the evidence cited in the previous chapter showed a very significant *average* increase in the intelligence of children adopted into good homes. But the individual differences within groups of such children are still related to differences in their true parents.

These family correlational studies were a more popular kind of research in the years when hereditarians and environmentalists were waging an all-or-nothing contest than they are now. Other kinds of research are more productive if we wish to get beyond the original question *whether* behavior tendencies are inherited to questions of *what* and *how.*

TWIN STUDIES

We have explained in the previous chapter why it is that work on identical twins produces the soundest evidence we have that environmental influences affect measured intelligence. The best evidence we have on the hereditary basis of human psychological traits also comes from twin studies. The use that is made of twin subjects differs according to which questions we are asking. As we have seen in the previous chapter, the best way to evaluate the effects of environment is to hold heredity constant. This can be done where two monozygotic twins, known to be exactly alike in their genetic possibilities, are separated and exposed to different environmental stimulation. The best way to evaluate the influence of *heredity* is to take subjects who have experienced the *same* environment but who are known to differ in genetic endowment and compare them with a group in which *both* heredity and environment are the same. This is commonly done by comparing the amount of difference between identical twin pairs with the amount of difference between fraternal twins or between siblings.

Two words that figure prominently in reports on such research are *concordance* and *discordance.* Twin pairs are said to be concordant if they both show a certain characteristic. They are discordant if one shows it and the other does not. In general, whenever it can be shown that the percentage of concordant pairs is much higher among identical than among fraternal twins, there is a sound basis for concluding that the trait in question has, in great part, at least, a genetic origin. There are some qualifications and difficulties that arise in connection with this type of research, but we will postpone consideration of them until we have examined the important findings.

As was shown in Table 47 in the previous chapter, IQ differences between identical twins are smaller than are IQ differences between fraternal twins. When they are reared together, identical twins tend to get scores on intelligence tests that are almost as similar as the scores one person gets when he is tested twice. Furthermore, the fact that the resemblances in IQ are as striking as the resemblances in height and weight suggests that intelligence may be as much dependent on the genes as these physical characteristics are.

It is the consistency of the twin resemblances from time to time and from place to place that is most impressive. Table 51 shows how much alike the correlations are in a large number of studies based on quite different population samples.

With the growth of interest in the measurement of aptitudes and

TABLE 51

Summary of Results of Studies of the Intellectual Resemblance of Twins

(Nichols, 1964)

STUDY	*MZ Twin Sets Intraclass Correlation*	*N*	*DZ Twin Sets Intraclass Correlation*	*N*	TEST
Holzinger (1929)	.88	50	.63	52	Binet IQ
Newman, Freeman, Holzinger (1937)	.91	50	.64	50	Binet IQ
Newman, Freeman, Holzinger (1937)	.92	50	.62	50	Otis IQ
Blewett (1954)	.75	26	.39	26	PMA Composite
Husen (1959)	.90	215	.70	416	Swedish Military Induction Test
Husen (1960)	.89	134	.62	180	Reading Achievement
Husen (1960)	.87	134	.52	181	Arithmetic Achievement
Erlenmeyer-Kimling and Jarvik (1963)	.87	Median of 14 Studies	.53	Median of 11 Studies	Various Intelligence Measures
Nichols (1964)	.87	687	.63	482	NMSQT Composite

special kinds of intellectual abilities, attempts were made to discover whether these also might have genetic roots. Brody (1937) found that the correlations between scores on the Minnesota Spatial Relations Test (a test of mechanical aptitude) were .28 for fraternal twins and .69 for identical twins. McNemar (1933) obtained correlations averaging about .43 for fraternal twins and .79 for identical twins on motor-skill tests.

When one wishes to compare the findings with regard to different traits measured in the same group of subjects, there is an advantage in computing a single *heritability index* (h^2) for each trait. Several different formulas for this have been proposed for use with different kinds of data. What this index is, essentially, is the ratio of the variance attributed to hereditary sources to the variance resulting from both heredity and environment. At one stage in the development of our knowledge in this area, it was customary to cite such figures as though they had some absolute value—to say, for example, that 85 per cent of the variance in intelligence comes from heredity, 15 per cent from environment. As we have come to understand the meaning of the interaction between heredity and environment more clearly, we have seen that it is not legitimate to do this. What the variance ratio turns out to be depends upon how similar in heredity the members of the group are and how uniform their environment is. A trait with an h^2 of .90 in one group and situation may show an h^2 of only .50 in another. But for comparing traits within a single specified group, particularly if it constitutes a good representative sample of a known population under normal environmental conditions, the heritability index is a useful technique.

It was used by Blewett (1954) in comparing the different abilities represented in the Primary Mental Abilities battery. The important finding here was that h^2 was higher for some of the factor scores than it was for the total measure of general mental ability. This suggests that in human beings, as in animals, what is inherited may be patterns of characteristics rather than an amount of a single general ability.

By far the largest body of information we have about the relative heritability of different kinds of measured psychological characteristic comes from the Michigan Twin Study (Vandenberg, 1962) in which 46 monozygotic pairs and 37 dizygotic pairs, all high school students in the Detroit area, were compared on a great variety of anthropometric, biochemical, and psychological measurements. Some significant heritability indices were found in each of the major areas the study was designed to explore, but there were more in some of these areas than in others. Table 52 shows what they are. Without knowing whether the tests selected for the study were equally representative of the domain in which they were classified we cannot be very certain about conclusions that some kinds of

TABLE 52

The Heritability of Various Kinds of Psychological Traits as Shown in the Michigan Twin Study

(Vandenberg, 1962)

AREA MEASURES	*Number of Measures*	*P Value*		*Number not Significant*	*Percentage Not Significant*
		.01	*.05*		
1. Primary Mental Abilities Subtests	17	3	8	6	35.3%
2. Motor Skills	14	6	2	6	42.9
3. Perceptual Tests	16	3	5	8	50.0
4. Cognitive and Achievement Tests	18	3	4	11	61.1
5. Sensory and Musical	24	4	5	15	62.5
6. Personality	28	5	4	19	67.9
All Measures	117	24	28	64	54.7

From S. G. Vandenberg. The hereditary abilities study: hereditary components in a psychological test battery. *Amer. J. Hum. Genet.* 1962, 14, 220–237. Reprinted by permission of Grune & Stratton, Inc.

things are more heritable than others, but the figures suggest that intellectual abilities have the largest hereditary component, personality characteristics the smallest. Inadequacies in personality tests may be responsible for some of this difference. Within the intellectual area alone, Vandenberg reported that the heritability indices for N (Number), V (Verbal), and W (Word Fluency) were significant at the .01 level and the index for S (Space) significant at the .05 level. R (Reasoning) and M (Memory) did not produce significant heritability indices.

The most extensive information about the part heredity plays in tendencies toward certain kinds of psychiatric difficulties has come from a large-scale study at the New York Psychiatric Institute under the direction of Kallman (1950). The work has been summarized at various stages. Probably the most useful of these inclusive presentations are in Kallman (1953) and Kallman (1959). The method is to start with a group of persons characterized by a certain diagnosis and then to locate and check up on their blood relatives. While much information has been accumulated about family members who show all degrees of relationship to the index cases, it is the figures for the twins that are most meaningful. Table 53 summarizes the concordance rates for monozygotic and dizygotic twins from the principal research studies that have been reported by Kallman and his associates.

The results for schizophrenia are most striking because of the large number of cases on which they are based. According to these figures, if one of a pair of identical twins has the disease, the chances are that eighty-six times out of a hundred the other twin has it also. The other fourteen who are not frankly schizophrenic are found to have schizoid personalities. Family comparisons for lesser degrees of relationship show much smaller percentages of agreement. As shown in Table 53 only 14.5 per cent of the fraternal twin pairs are concordant. Siblings of schizophrenics show about this same rate, as do children of one schizophrenic

TABLE 53

Concordance Rates in Monozygotic and Dizygotic Twins Summarized from Kallman Studies

(Hurst, 1952)

	MONOZYGOTIC		DIZYGOTIC	
	N	% CONCORDANT	N	% CONCORDANT
Schizophrenia	268	86.2	685	14.5
Manic-Depressive	23	95.7	52	26.3
Senile Psychosis	33	42.8	75	8.0
Involutional Psychosis	29	60.9	67	6.0
Homosexuality	40	100	45	11.5

parent. Where both parents are schizophrenic, however, about 65 per cent of the children develop the condition. Kallman believes the genetic mechanism involved here is inheritance by way of a single recessive gene producing a predisposition to schizophrenia. Along with this, however, some kind of constitutional "defense" system is inherited, and this seems to depend upon many genes. Thus the resistance to schizophrenia also varies from person to person. It is the evidence for the importance of these natural defense processes that keeps Kallman from taking a pessimistic view with regard to the disease. If we could learn what this defense process is like, we ought to be able to duplicate it, or at least strengthen it in persons whose family history shows them to be susceptible.

The results for manic-depressive psychosis also reveal far higher concordance rates for monozygotic than for dizygotic twins. Kallman thinks that the figures for this disease suggest the operation of a dominant gene whose action is somewhat irregular. The number of cases reported so far is not sufficient to warrant a definite statement. One minor fact of some interest in these studies, since it seems to show that the two mental diseases are quite different in their genetic origin, is that among monozygotic twin pairs there was not a single instance where one twin was schizophrenic, the other manic-depressive.

The evidence summarized in Table 53 with regard to the senile psychoses comes from a much larger study of senescent twin pairs. All twins obtainable in New York state who were sixty or over at the time the research began were studied in a variety of ways. In 1951, 2,500 such pairs had been observed for six years (Kallman, Feingold, and Bondy, 1951). Longevity figures showed that the life span was more similar for monozygotic than for dizygotic pairs. This adds to the considerable body of evidence that longevity itself has a hereditary basis. Physical similarities in the monozygotic pairs were pronounced even to an advanced age. Twins remained similar in size, developed wrinkles in the same places, and lost about the same amount of hair. Intellectual capacities were more similar for the identical than for the fraternal pairs, just as former studies have shown them to be in childhood and early youth. This suggests that the amount of deterioration in intelligence that comes with old age may depend upon the genes. A later report on the senescent studies after a twelve-year follow-up (Falek, Kallman, Lorge, and Jarvik, 1960) confirmed the earlier conclusions. One additional bit of suggestive evidence was also included. The men and women who lived longer had tested a little higher on the intelligence tests given at the beginning of the study than those who did not survive so long.

Kallman's study of male homosexuals was less successful than the others because of the difficulty in locating such subjects and obtaining their cooperation (Kallman, 1952). The findings did point in the same direction, since in cases where a subject was monozygotic the other twin always had a record of at least a moderate amount of homosexual activity. Kallman was convinced from what the men said that this complete concordance did not represent mutual influence. The practices were developed independently and often far apart, according to their reports. What Kallman thinks is inherited in these cases is some weakness, perhaps based on discrepant sex genes, which might be one cause of the failure to develop mature sex behavior. Much more evidence is needed before any more precise theory here can be formulated.

It is of some interest that there is one kind of psychiatric problem for which no evidence of genetic origin could be found—namely, suicide (Kallman, 1959).

Slater's research in England corroborated Kallman's conclusions with regard to schizophrenia (Slater, 1953). The concordance rate for 67 monozygotic twin pairs was 76 per cent; for 224 dizygotic pairs, 14 per cent.

There have been several investigations of the heritability of personality traits or tendencies in which personality was evaluated by means of tests. Some of these have already been mentioned (Newman, Freeman, and Holzinger, 1937; Vandenberg, 1962). Their evidence for the heritability of personality traits is not very striking.

Others have reported more significant findings. Eysenck and Prell (1951) searched the birth records of five boroughs in south London for the names of all like-sex twins born during the period 1935–37. Out of 130 pairs they located 68 and made careful tests to determine whether the pairs were of the one-egg or two-egg variety. They then administered the battery of tests by means of which the "neuroticism" factor is being measured in their research. (See Chapter 7.) The correlation between identical twins for neuroticism was .85. For fraternal twins the corresponding figure was .22. This constitutes just about the same amount and kind of evidence that neuroticism depends to some degree on heredity as that intelligence is genetically determined.

In a later study of 52 twin pairs, Eysenck (1956) reported that his second factor, extraversion-introversion, also had a hereditary basis. The correlation between identical twins in factor scores for this variable was .50, for fraternal twins −.33.

R. B. Cattell and his co-workers have investigated the heritability of the personality factors included in their list of basic traits. For questionnaire data on eleven to fifteen-year-olds, Cattell, Blewett, and Beloff (1955) found significant heritability coefficients for Factor A (cyclothymia *vs.* schizothymia) and for Factor H (adventurous cyclothymia *vs.* submissiveness). For fifteen-year-olds who took a battery of objective tests, only "comention" which they redefine as "corrigibility-incorrigibility," in addition to intelligence, showed clear evidence of heritability.

A similar study using the MMPI and the Cattell High School Personality Questionnaire with 34 monozygotic and 34 dizygotic twin pairs was reported by Gottesman (1963). The only factors from the Cattell battery showing up as significant in both the correlational and the heritability analyses were F (sober, serious, *vs.* happy-go-lucky) and Q_2 (group dependency *vs.* self-sufficiency). The MMPI showed more significant sections. The highest heritability index was found for Si (social introversion) but the indices were significant for D (depression), Pd (psychopathic deviate), Pt (psychasthenia), and Sz (schizophrenia) as well.

Attention was called in a previous section to the fact that animal studies have suggested that patterns of special abilities and certain kinds of temperamental traits are determined by heredity to a larger extent than any sort of general ability analogous to human intelligence. Research with human subjects has generally led to the opposite conclusion—that heredity plays a larger role in intelligence than in special abilities or temperament. It is not certain whether there is a real conflict here or whether the scarcity of dependable tests for use with human subjects in areas other than intelligence, and the fact that such tests have been used in a much smaller number of investigations explains the discrepancy. Burt (1958) after reviewing the evidence for the inheritance of mental ability, including the results of many studies of his own pointing in the same direction as the work we have cited, concluded that the emphasis on general intelligence is justified, not only on the basis of the evidence, but because of the practical importance of this trait in human affairs. It seems possible, however, that knowledge of the more differentiated and more elusive characteristics might be of even greater importance if we had it. At any rate, the research we have been considering gives some evidence that patterns of special abilities may have hereditary origins, along with such personality traits as neuroticism, schizoid tendencies, and extraversion-introversion.

Three important twin studies have been initiated in which many kinds of characteristics are being assessed for the same subjects. When they have been completed we may have clearer answers to many of the remaining questions, such as whether heredity influences general intelligence more than special abilities, or intellectual traits more than temperamental ones. In the Louisville Twin Study, Vandenberg (1964) has administered a large number of group and individual tests of all sorts of ability and personality characteristics to a fairly large number of twin pairs. The National Merit Scholarship research organization after identifying more than 1,500 twin pairs who took the NMS examination in 1962, has developed a valid method for diagnosing zygosity from questionnaire data, and is undertaking studies of general ability, special abilities, and personality (Nichols, 1964). At the Menninger Foundation, Gardner (1964) is carrying out an intensive study of 100 same-sex twins, age eight to nineteen, and their parents, including measurements of cognitive styles, personality traits, and all sorts of situational variables. He and his colleagues will make a special effort to get at interactions between hereditary and environmental factors, and moderator variables that affect the relationships of different factors in different groups and circumstances.

Twin studies constitute the most satisfactory method we have for investigating hereditary psychological differences in human beings. But they are not free from flaws. Pastore (1949a) and Rosenthal (1962) have pointed out some of these pitfalls and cautioned against oversimplified conclusions from the research on schizophrenia. Rosenthal (1959) showed that the disease may have different origins in different cases. He compared background information on the families of schizophrenics from discordant and concordant twin pairs. In cases where the patient was from a discordant pair (his twin did not have schizophrenia), the onset had been later, the prognosis more favorable. Such results suggest that environmental influences can by themselves produce schizophrenia, but that if they do it is not as serious as the hereditary variety.

One question that always arises in interpreting differences between identical and fraternal twin pairs has to do with whether the environmental factors that count most heavily in psychological developments are really equally similar for the two kinds of twins. As emphasis is placed on emotional rather than physical aspects of the environment, this becomes a factor of considerable potential importance. In many areas, such as intelligence, special abilities, and personality, there is a possibility that identical twins tend to be more alike than fraternals at least partly because they have lived through more nearly identical experiences. As one examines Kallman's figures for the major psychoses, however, it seems very improbable that the difference in concordance rates could have been produced entirely in this way. Psychogenic explanations of schizophrenia postulate an emotional trauma of such severity that it does not seem possible that one of two fraternal twins could escape suffering its effects, while the other, in the same family, did not. Even if some of the evidence for heredity reported from the type of twin study that compares monozygotic and dizygotic pair differences can be explained away when we examine environmental influences closely, it seems unlikely that all of it can be disposed of in this way.

Twin studies also involve biases which might lead us to *under*estimate the importance of genetic determiners. Price (1950) has called attention to two types of *prenatal* environmental influences that act differentially upon monozygotic twins. These may eventually produce behavioral differences between the two individuals which we mistakenly attribute to post-natal causes such as education and training. *Lateral inversions* are common in identical twin pairs. In such cases each twin is a mirror image of the other. If one is right-handed, the other is left-handed, and other characteristics may follow the same pattern. We do not know enough about these cases to know whether there is a possibility of some impairment of cerebral dominance in one twin that would tend to hamper him in his development. Price is inclined to stress more strongly a second kind of evidence, in which some factor affects monozygotic pairs developing in a single chorion or membrane differentially. Since in such cases the two individuals share the same circulatory system, there is a real possibility that a temporary imbalance may create a deficiency in oxygen supply or moisture for one twin at a crucial developmental stage. This could handicap him permanently, if only to a slight degree. In such a pair, differences that we measure years later in intelligence, neuroticism, or general vitality would be wrongly attributed to the external environment, and our conclusions about its influence would thus be in error.

The whole field of research on human heredity is beset with difficulties. Its importance, however, justifies the expenditure of large amounts of money and research ingenuity.

POPULATION TRENDS

As we have explained earlier, decisions about individuals and attitudes of pessimism or optimism concerning the future possibilities of any one person do not depend upon what we may conclude with regard to heredity and environment. If a trait is *modifiable,* and a good share of all human psychological traits are, improvement can be brought about through learning. When we understand anyone's weaknesses or special susceptibilities we can often anticipate their potentially harmful effects and so prevent the difficulties we have foreseen from occurring. So far as the *individual* is concerned, the progress of knowledge about both environmental and hereditary determiners of psychological traits fits in with a moderately hopeful outlook.

The significance of the research on heredity for many who have considered it is its implications for the future of the total population of our West European society. If the progress of science leads to a steady increase in that segment of our population somewhat lacking in intelligence and stability, the generations to come will face serious problems.

This possibility occurred to psychologists when they became aware of the sizable differences in average IQ between the various social classes. (See Chapter 13.) Social statistics consistently show that children from the so-called lower classes have more siblings than the middle and upper classes do. A differential of this sort, if maintained, could lead to a considerable drop in average intelligence in the course of a few generations.

A number of attempts have been made to predict from the figures just how great this decline is likely to be. Thomson (1946), on the basis of data from the Isle of Wight, presented the figures found in Table 54. They

TABLE 54

Data from the Isle of Wight Leading to a Prediction of a Decline in the Intelligence Level from One Generation to the Next

(Thomson, 1946)

(*a*) NUMBER OF FAMILIES	(*b*) NUMBER IN FAMILY	(*c*) AVERAGE IQ	(*d*) PRODUCT OF a x c	(*e*) NUMBER OF CHILDREN	(*f*) PRODUCT OF c x e
115	1	106.2	12,213.0	115	12,213.0
212	2	105.4	22,344.8	424	44,689.6
185	3	102.3	18,925.5	555	56,776.5
152	4	101.5	15,428.0	608	61,712.0
127	5	99.6	12,649.2	635	63,246.0
103	6	96.5	9,939.5	618	59,637.0
88	7	93.8	8,254.4	616	57,780.8
102	8	95.8	9,771.6	816	78,172.8
1,084			109,526.0		434,227.7
			Mean = 101.04		Mean = 98.98

illustrate clearly the way in which such predictions are made. Thomson showed, as have a number of others in Great Britain and the United States, that if we use a weighted average of the IQ level in families of different sizes as an indicator of what the IQ level will be in the next generation, we come out with a predicted drop of about 2 IQ points per generation. In correlation terms, studies with various groups of school children consistently gave negative *r*'s from —.16 to —.26 between intelligence and number of children in the family (Lorimer, 1952). In the Thomson study it was —.25.

The new material that has been contributed toward our thinking on this problem in the years since World War II has served to make the problem more puzzling than it was before. There have been several studies in which the same test has been given to school children in the same area after an interval of from seven to fifteen years. The largest and most complete of these is reported in *The Trend of Scottish Intelligence* (Scottish Council, 1949). The same kind of findings are reported by R. B. Cattell (1950a). Instead of the expected decrease in average IQ, these retest studies show a slight but significant increase. In the Scottish study it amounted to about 2 points for the fifteen-year period.

Both the negative correlations between children's IQ's and the sizes of the families from which they come and the failure of the results of large-scale testing programs to confirm the predictions based on them have generated a considerable amount of discussion. A thorough analysis of the whole problem, along with a summary of all the research findings, was made by Anastasi (1956). She showed that the apparent simplicity of the figures masks some hidden complexities. For one thing, a report by a school child on the number of siblings he has cannot be considered a valid indicator of family size, because many if not most of the children are reporting on *incomplete* families. If there were a tendency for lower-class parents to begin having children earlier and to have them in more rapid succession than middle-class parents do, the average number of siblings a lower class child reported would be higher than the number a middle-class child reported, even though the size of the families proved eventually to be the same. Some evidence suggests that when parents report on completed families the usual negative correlation between family size and intelligence is not obtained.

Probably a more important consideration in this whole controversy, however, is that the negative correlation itself may be caused by factors other than heredity. Anastasi pointed out what these factors could be and presented relevant evidence. One causal explanation is that the environment provided by the less intellectual parents is less conducive to the development of a high level of intelligence than the environment provided by the more intellectual parents. Another type of causal explanation, for which Nisbet (1953) has provided some correlational evidence, is that because children from large families have less contact with adults than children from small families do, they develop language facility more slowly, and this handicaps them when they take the customary verbal intelligence tests. Vernon (1951) has argued that intelligence tests cannot validly be used in population surveys.

One factor that may be of some eugenic importance is the finding that at the lower end of the intelligence distribution the reproduction rate falls off markedly. It has been known for some time that idiots and imbeciles seldom have children. Most of the idiots and imbeciles of each new generation come from normal or moron families. A follow-up study by Reed et al. (1954), in which family data were obtained on individuals who were inmates of the institution for the feeble-minded in Faribault, Minnesota during the period from 1911 to 1918, is interesting in this connection. The average IQ for the subjects in the original group was 38. For these institutionalized cases the reproduction rate was of course negligible. The new data reported by Reed et al. show that the *siblings* of these cases, who were probably dull but not feeble-minded, also failed to attain the reproduction rate necessary for replacement. The figures suggest the possibility that unfavorable genes like those making for mental deficiency tend to eliminate themselves.

The study of dysgenic and eugenic population trends is terrifically complex. Every change in any kind of social policy may alter them. There is some concern, for example, that the policy of treating psychotic patients in the community instead of institutionalizing them may lead to more marriage and child-bearing in schizophrenics and thus increase the number of persons with hereditary susceptibility to the disease. The realization of the complexity of these phenomena, however, has led to more caution about the adoption of policies supposedly based on eugenic considerations. There is no simple way to maintain and improve hereditary human quality.

CURRENT THINKING ABOUT HEREDITY AND ENVIRONMENT

At the end of these two chapters concerned with research on environmental effects and heredity, it seems worthwhile to consider what kind of general orientation toward human affairs is suggested by these diverse sorts of evidence they contain. Prevalent views have undergone a great change since the early years of the century when most of these research efforts began. A profound but very readable discussion of some of the major issues can be found in a little book by the eminent British zoologist Medawar (1960).

First of all, it no longer seems a legitimate aim of genetic research to eliminate all human defects in the hope of breeding a race of supermen. One reason is that the recognition of the polygenic transmission of most traits means that identifying the particular genetic combinations likely to produce either undesirable characteristics or special gifts is in most cases impossible. Major genes do account for some diseases and defects, and genetic counseling should make it possible to decrease the incidence of these. But this would not change the total composition of the human race very much. Another reason that Medawar points out is that even if it were possible to breed a race of persons homozygous for all desirable traits, this might not result in a superior population. There is evidence that heterozygosity itself is an advantage, especially for complex organisms who must adapt to changing conditions. The so-called "sickle-cell" trait is an example. It comes from a genetic factor resulting in the production of haemoglobin S in the blood rather than haemoglobin A. Persons who receive the gene for haemoglobin S from one parent have an inborn resistance to malaria. But persons who happen to inherit this gene from both parents usually die early in life of a blood disease called sickle-cell anemia. It is an advantage to a population in a malarial area to have most of its population heterozygous for the sickle-cell gene even though the price is a certain number of deaths from anemia. What is a genetic defect in a nonmalarial area is a genetic asset in an area where malaria is prevalent. There are undoubtedly many examples of similar complexities. What they suggest is that a gene pool producing a great variety of individual differences is the most likely to bring about a *society* able to flourish in many different environments. As Medawar puts it: "Human beings are committed to a genetic system which attaches a certain weight, perhaps great weight, to there being many different kinds of men."

How then shall we attempt to improve the human race? Medawar's recipe is essentially the same as that of Williams (1960), whose research on biochemical individuality was cited in earlier chapters: *Improve the environment.* But in order to do this we must recognize that different genotypes require different *kinds* of environment in order to flourish. Williams' research in nutrition, for example, has produced evidence for the almost literal truth of the statement that one man's meat is another man's poison. And if we are to develop optimum diets for different genotypes, why not develop optimum kinds of education as well?

It is here that some of the results from environmental studies mesh with those from genetic studies. Several investigations have proved that the effects of early treatments, such as handling or isolation, on different pure strains of mice are quite different (McClearn, 1963, pp. 466–467). This is true also for different breeds of dogs. Cooper and Zubek (1958) showed that for groups of rats classified as "brights," bred from many generations of good maze-learners, the effects on maze-learning of enriching the early environment were negligible, whereas for "dulls," bred from generations of poor maze-learners, the effects were very striking. (Enrichment for rats consisted in providing such things as ramps, swings, balls, slides, and a decorated cage wall.) Restricted environments had the opposite effect. "Bright" rats suffered from these conditions far more than "dulls" did. The whole experiment corroborates the results others have obtained in the preschool experiments discussed in the previous chapter. Preschools appear to improve the unpromising but to leave the superior unchanged in intelligence.

We are beginning to realize that a person's genotype establishes for him a *reaction range* rather than a single line of development. With regard to any desirable trait, how much of it he develops will depend upon which of many possible environments surrounds him during his growing years. To identify and understand many varieties of genotype in order to manipulate many kinds of environmental conditions intelligently—this is a basic purpose of research on heredity.

SUMMARY

The rapidly growing science of genetics has produced both factual knowledge and general principles that are of use in thinking about the development of human individuals.

Animal experiments have demonstrated that psychological traits, differences in motivation and temperament, and differences in the pattern of learning abilities, which may depend upon such motivation, as well as characteristics like susceptibility to stress and preference for alcohol, are inherited. With Hirsch's extension of selective breeding for behavioral differences to fruitflies, animal studies are beginning to throw light on the mode of inheritance as well.

The study of family resemblances is not very conclusive for understanding heredity, since differences as well as likenesses within the same family depend upon genes. In general, correlations for intelligence are as high as for physical traits, and there is clear evidence that children tend to resemble their parents in intelligence even when they have not been brought up by them.

The twin studies most crucial for the demonstration of the effects of heredity are those in which concordance and discordance rates are compared for identical and fraternal twins. The most striking findings have been in the medical and psychiatric fields. Identical twins are much more similar than are fraternals with regard to several mental diseases and length of life. The evidence is less clear for homosexuality.

Heritability studies using many kinds of psychological tests with the same group of subjects have typically shown that general intelligence is more heritable than special abilities and personality traits, though some evidence has accumulated that hereditary factors play a part in the case of all these traits.

Our increased understanding of heredity has led to a considerable interest in eugenics and to efforts to identify and check dysgenic trends in our population. Predictions that the average intelligence level will decline because of the negative correlations between IQ and family size have not been borne out when testing programs have been repeated in communities where tests had previously been given.

Out of all this research more complex concepts have developed about the contribution genetics can make to human welfare. Through identifying different genotypes we will eventually be able to provide better environments for different varieties of developing individuals.

CHAPTER 19

The Science of Human Individuality: Past and Future

THE SCIENCE OF HUMAN DIFFERENCES has reached a transitional stage. In a sense, of course, it has always been there, for the nature of scientific research is to transcend itself. But now in the mid-1960's there is some evidence that far more sweeping changes are in progress than have occurred during previous decades. Let us examine some of these trends and attempt to identify the quarters in which important findings are most likely to turn up during the years ahead.

MAJOR SHIFTS IN THINKING ABOUT HUMAN DIFFERENCES

The present structure of knowledge about differences between individuals rests on the methodological foundations laid by Galton, Binet, J. McKeen Cattell, Stern, and the other psychologists who initiated mental measurement. We have considered in some detail in our early chapters what these foundation procedures were: (1) Measuring one trait at a time; (2) Assigning each individual a number corresponding to his position in the group to which he belongs; (3) Exploring the meaning of a trait by relating one set of measurements to other sets of measurements; (4) Seeking to discern the source of the differences delineated in this way by designing appropriate experiments or developmental studies.

We have seen in the preceding chapters how the complexity of the data that investigators encountered led to complex variations of these basic strategies. Factor analytic methods, by means of which large matrices of correlations between traits could be transformed into smaller and more intelligible matrices of factor loadings, became increasingly necessary. Multiple regression procedures for predicting criteria important in practical life replaced attempts to find single tests that would be valid predictors of these criteria. Multivariate experimental designs in which the effects of several independent variables were explored simultaneously were increasingly used. Spatial concepts like *dimension* (Where is the individual located with regard to some hypothetical reference axis?) largely replaced concepts of amount or *capacity* (How much of some hypothetical trait does a person have, actually or potentially?).

Now the question arises whether we may have reached the limit of what can be accomplished with these methods. Tyler (1959) analyzed the problem in this way:

> Useful as this approach has been, I have found myself questioning more and more whether it is really adequate at this stage in the development of our science. For one thing, it does not *feel* quite right. Most people find it hard to think of themselves as points in *n*-dimensional space. Occasionally I encounter an unusually articulate student who reacts violently against the whole conception, and I think that at a lower level of awareness many of the others show a kind of passive resistance to it. For another thing, the system shows signs of becoming completely unworkable in the sense I have defined workability, because of the proliferation of dimensions. It looked for a time as though factor analysis would enable us to simplify it, but there are now so many factors and their relationships with each other are so complex that factor theory does not really constitute a simplification. But the most important reason I see for questioning the adequacy of this way of looking at things is that we are no longer making the progress with it that we have a right to expect. Correlations with criteria significant for theory or for practice are not going up very much. Seldom do we find a cross-validated multiple correlation with any criterion that exceeds .6. The addition of new dimensions and the increasing refinement in the ways we measure the old ones are not really "paying off" very well. The possibility is at least worth considering that we are approaching the limit of what can be done with this particular system.

Thus we are initiating changes in our views about the kind of theoretical concepts upon which quantitative research should be based.

But there is another sort of change in the orientation of investigators to the subject matter of differential psychology that is equally important. It has occurred so gradually that we have only recently begun to see it clearly. It is this. The search for grand universal principles has been abandoned. What we now seek are limited, contingent conclusions about specified populations in particular situations. Early workers viewed the normal distribution as a majestic law of nature; we see it now as a phenomenon occurring when data of a certain sort are processed in a certain way. Early workers sought to establish the universality of the principle that males are more variable than females; we no longer look on this as a problem of any particular interest or importance. Early workers made great efforts to discover the essential form of the mental growth curve; we now expect to find different curves for different individuals. Early workers hoped to be able to state precisely how much of the variation in every trait arose from hereditary factors; we now know that any absolute answer to this question is unattainable. Examples of such shifts in our thinking could be multiplied.

Besides cutting down the *size* of the questions we attempt to answer and the generalizations we attempt to reach, we have also made marked changes in our assumptions about the *permanence* of the characteristics we investigate. This change shows up most strikingly in research on the trait with the longest history—intelligence. Many particular kinds of research effort have been involved here—longitudinal studies of children who become brighter or duller over the years, animal studies of the effects of early experience on later behavior in learning situations, efforts to educate the mentally retarded, research and action programs to accelerate the intellectual development of the "culturally deprived." Instead of simply observing and measuring mental growth we are now trying in a variety of ways to find out how to stimulate it. The same kind of approach to the study of other abilities and personality characteristics is being adopted.

NEW CONCEPTS ARISING FROM RESEARCH

While these shifts in general approach to psychological differences were occurring, new concepts leading to improved research designs have been coming into use. One of these kinds of work is the analysis of differences in the *strategies* subjects use in dealing with experimental situations. It is strikingly exemplified in the work of Bruner and his associates on problem solving and concept formation (Bruner, Goodnow, and Austin, 1956). In a later volume, Bruner (1963) has noted how fruitful this approach has been in the study of the cognitive development of children (pp. 81–96). For example, in an experimental situation modeled on the game of "Twenty Questions," some children adopted what Bruner labeled a "constructionist" strategy, others a strategy of "passive reception." Which of these things a child was doing could be identified by the questions he asked. Jack, who started with a broad question the answer to which ruled out a large number of alternatives at once and then systematically narrowed down the scope of his questions to "close in" on the right answer, was employing a different strategy from Bill, who asked a series of unrelated questions.

The concept of individual differences in strategies for dealing with situations is useful in thinking about many of the problems taken up in this book, whether the investigators themselves used it or not. Cognitive styles can be considered as variables of this sort. Leveling and sharpening, focusing and scanning, and the rest can more readily be understood as strategies than as traits. The kinds of sex differences that appear in sex-role behavior, the kind of age differences Welford has discovered in the performance of complex tasks, and the differences between lower- and middle-class children in their dealings with environmental challenges are only a few of the varieties of research findings that might well be re-examined from this new point of view.

The concept of strategy has some real advantages over the trait concepts it has replaced in the areas where it has been used. For one thing, different strategies are not mutually exclusive, so that it is quite possible for a person to develop several alternative ones that he is capable of using in any given situation. What looks like inconsistency, considered as a personality trait, may mean that a person selects from his behavior repertory different alternatives on different occasions. Furthermore, strategies are in principle teachable, so that it seems possible that ability to handle many kinds of life situations might be markedly increased in an individual who learns to use a more effective strategy in place of a less effective one. Thus what is involved in a shift from *dimension* to *strategy* is more than a mere change of label.

Another important new research concept touched upon here and there in previous chapters is the concept of *moderator variables*. We encountered it first in Ghiselli's research on the "prediction of predictability" in the domain of special aptitudes and their relationship to occupational and educational criteria. These studies demonstrated that it was possible to identify moderator variables on the basis of which persons whose criterion performance was predictable could be distinguished from those whose performance was not predictable, or those whose performance was predictable from one set of facts could be distinguished from those whose performance was predictable from a different set of facts. The effects of this new concept on correlation and regression theory is likely to be profound. Personality research may profit even more than aptitude research from this new method of dealing with complex relationships. Here too, it might be profitable to re-examine some old problems from the new viewpoint. To take an example, one generalization that might be drawn from all of the work on sex differences is that sex is primarily a moderator variable and that it should always be used in this way in research designs where the purpose is to throw light on any aspect of personality. The work of Kogan and Wallach (1964) is the first example of a large-scale research undertaking in which the concept of moderator variables has been employed. There will undoubtedly be many others designed in such a way that "differences in the differences" for various groups of persons can be identified.

Research along these lines would be facilitated by the identification of some other moderator variables general enough to function in this manner in a number of different areas. In the Kogan and Wallach study, the moderator variables that proved to be important for risk-taking behavior were *anxiety* and *defensiveness.* It seems likely that such characteristics as these would be equally important in many other personality areas. Perhaps age, conservatism-radicalism, or verbal *vs.* quantitative intelligence, will turn out to be moderator variables influencing other relationships. The imposition of a new structure like this may enable us to make headway with many problems that standard correlational procedures have left unsolved. Fortunately the availability of high-speed computers now makes it possible to carry out the extra mass of computations such studies involve.

A third trend generating new ways of looking at human differences is the use of *idiographic* methods to obtain basic data upon which to base theoretical principles. The conflict between nomothetic and idiographic approaches no longer dominates our thinking. After years of neglect and disparagement the work of Piaget and his collaborators is coming to occupy a position of central importance. What distinguishes it methodologically from most other work in developmental psychology is that after detailed observations have been made of the behavior of individual children, one does not average their scores but, instead, distils theoretical principles from a consideration of those features that characterize the behavior of all. Longitudinal studies of children also exemplify this turning toward idiographic thinking. Their focus is on the individual child rather than the age group, the individual growth curve rather than the norms.

Still another new research direction comes from a reawakening of interest in *type* concepts. The research that uses the Jungian typology facilitated by the development of the Myers-Briggs Type Indicator has been mentioned in previous chapters. Much of the work on cognitive styles has been presented as a kind of typology. Research based on the Sheldon typology of physiques and temperaments is flourishing.

The way in which the new type concepts differ from the traditional ones is that they are more flexible. It is realized that types need not be considered either as inclusive or as permanent as they have often been in the past. We are no longer beguiled by the delusion that any simple system of classifying people will ever enable us to understand or to predict all of their behavior. For some purposes it may be convenient to classify an individual according to one set of type concepts. For other purposes another set may be more useful. The concepts of strategies and types are often used interchangeably.

Myers and Briggs look upon the distinctions they have formulated as differences in *direction of development.* For example, at some juncture in his life a person may choose, consciously or unconsciously, to pay more attention to his inner experience than to the objective details of his outer world, and thus develop in an introverted rather than an extraverted direction. The concept of types as general directions of development rather than as built-in predispositions makes them more usable in personality research.

A BLUEPRINT FOR A PSYCHOLOGY OF INDIVIDUALITY

Into what sort of overall theoretical structure can we organize the results of past research efforts while also providing space for new research undertakings of these different varieties? What would a sound and stimulating psychology of the individual really be like? We can begin to see the dim outlines of such a structure, although its complete shape is far from clear.

We need to distinguish at the outset between "Man" as a species, and "man" as an individual human being. For Man as a species the possibilities for development are almost unlimited. Murphy (1958) has discussed this proposition at some length. With the kind of anatomical, physiological, and neurological systems Man possesses, he can adapt himself to almost any environment, solve almost any problem. He can create and manage technological and social innovations in ever-increasing number and complexity. Each new situation into which Man moves, each new period of his history brings out aspects of human potentialities never recognized before.

In contrast, man as an individual is *limited.* This is not necessarily because he lacks any of the potentialities we attribute to the human species, but because he lacks *time*. Each individual human being thus constitutes a *selection* of a few characteristics to be developed, a selection from the vast range of possibilities initially open to him as a member of the human race. The nature of the selection occurring during each person's developmental history determines his unique individuality. And it is only through the intensive development of *different* possibilities by different individuals that the race as a whole can attain its full stature. *Man* is essentially a *plural* term.

How is this selection accomplished? It is the answer to this question that constitutes the subject matter of the psychology of human differences. A large part of the process is obviously influenced by factors not under the control of the individual himself. He begins with one particular fraction of the human gene pool, facilitating development in some directions, retarding it in others. He grows up in a particular family, in a particular city and country, at a particular period in history. By learning to talk a particular language, he selects some thought patterns, rules out others. The amount and kinds of play materials, companions, and attention from adults he encounters during his early years stimulate some kinds of growth and retard others.

Broad social policies, differing from one period to another, help to determine which human potentialities individuals will be encouraged and stimulated to develop. We are witnessing in our time one of these major policy changes. Because of the impact of automation on industry and the impact of agricultural technology on farming, society needs fewer and fewer persons with superior physical strength and manual skills, more and more persons with superior ability to manipulate symbols. Such a shift, striking at the structure of society, stimulates interest in projects such as the intensive preschool education of culturally disadvantaged children. It leads to the modification of school laws and programs in a way that will influence boys and girls to obtain more education than they would have spontaneously sought. The fact that every such change in policy means that a different assortment of human characteristics is being selected for emphasis, and that consequently other human potentialities are automatically being *de-emphasized* is not always realized. Some sorts of feelings about nature, for example, and the broad values related to them, will not occur as frequently in human society as they did when a large proportion of us grew up on farms. Some sorts of physical skills and the attitudes about the self related to them will not be represented in as many individuals as they were in the days when humanity depended upon the hard physical labor of the majority of adults. Education, when continued into the middle twenties, enables young people to develop some of their potentialities to a high degree, but it *inhibits* the development of others that would have flourished under circumstances requiring independent adulthood at fifteen.

Besides these kinds of selection imposed by circumstances, there is another process that is coming to play an ever more important part. From childhood on, a person's own *choices* determine to a considerable extent which possible courses of development are to be followed, which to be closed out. As American society has become more complex, and as child-rearing philosophies have changed so that a child's freedom to make decisions for himself is stressed at least as much as unquestioning obedience to his parents and other authorities, personal choices are becoming extremely significant—more significant than individuals often realize when they make them. It is now known, for example, that a decision to drop out of high school at fifteen or sixteen has a crucial negative impact on many aspects of a boy's or girl's later development, though the boys and girls themselves are often unaware of this. It is clear that means must be found to induce individuals to consider the developmental implications of the choices they make.

All of the emerging research concepts discussed in the previous section are more compatible with this new orientation than with the traditional theoretical framework of mental measurement. It is essentially an idiographic approach to human differences, though strategies, types, and moderator variables constitute useful techniques for putting together groups of individuals about which some one theoretical generalization can be made, and some particular sorts of hypotheses set up to be tested through experimental, developmental, or statistical investigations. It is not really paradoxical to strive for *general* conclusions about *unique* individuals.

Another way of describing this partially formulated theory of human differences is to say that it is basically a psychology of *development* rather than of *measurement.* Its graphic symbol would be not the *normal curve* but the *growth curve.* It would still be concerned with continuous distributions and stable characteristics, but it would be equally concerned with noncontinuous distributions and developmental discontinuities. We know a good deal about the changes in individuals that come about as a gradual increase in capacities, a gradual unfolding of personality tendencies. We know much less about the *sudden* changes that occur—things like religious conversion, the response to the challenge of a new and demanding position, or the pervasive effects of a genuine commitment to a movement or an ideal. These phenomena must be studied if individuals are to be understood.

The construction of such a psychology of human individuality is a task for the future. But the possibility of such a psychology was envisaged long ago. One of the earliest and perhaps the greatest of America's psychologists, William James, assigned a place of fundamental importance to the individual selective process we have been considering. He expresses the idea in this way:

> . . . the mind is at every stage a theatre of simultaneous possibilities. Consciousness consists in the comparison of these with each other, the selection of some, and the suppression of the rest by the reinforcing and inhibiting agency of attention. . . .
>
> . . . The mind, in short, works on the data it receives very much as a sculptor works on his block of stone. In a sense the statue stood there from eternity. But there were a thousand different ones beside it, and the sculptor alone is to thank for having extricated this one from the rest. . . . Other sculptors, other statues from the same stone! Other minds, other worlds from the same monotonous and inexpressive chaos! [1]

Or again:

> I am often confronted by the necessity of standing by one of my empirical selves and relinquishing the rest. Not that I would not, if I could, be both handsome and fat and well dressed, and a great athlete, and make a million a year, be a wit, a *bon-vivant,* and a lady-killer, as well as a philosopher; a

[1] James, William, 1890. *Principles of Psychology.* New York: Holt. Vol. I, pp. 288–289.

philanthropist, statesman, warrior, and African explorer, as well as a "tone-poet" and saint. But the thing is simply impossible. The millionaire's work would run counter to the saint's; the *bon-vivant* and the philanthropist would trip each other up; the philosopher and the lady-killer could not well keep house in the same tenement of clay. Such different characters may conceivably at the outset of life be alike *possible* to a man. But to make any one of them actual, the rest must more or less be suppressed. So the seeker of his truest, strongest, deepest self must review the list carefully, and pick out the one on which to stake his salvation. All other selves thereupon become unreal, but the fortunes of this self are real. Its failures are real failures, its triumphs real triumphs, carrying shame and gladness with them. This is as strong an example as there is of that selective industry of the mind on which I insisted some pages back. Our thought, incessantly deciding, among many things of a kind, which ones for it shall be realities, here chooses one of many possible selves or characters, and forthwith reckons it no shame to fail in any of those not adopted expressly as its own.[2]

Perhaps at long last we are now ready to build a structure of research and practice on the foundation William James laid.

[2] *Ibid.*, pp. 309–310.

Bibliography

A.A.A.S. Committee on Science in the Promotion of Human Welfare. 1963. Science and the race problem. *Science,* 142, 558–561.

Adams, C. W. 1946. The age at which scientists do their best work. *Isis,* 36, 166–169.

Adorno, T. W., Frenkel-Brunswik, E., Levinson, D. J., and Sanford, R. N. 1950. *The authoritarian personality.* New York: Harper & Row.

Alexander, H. B. 1922. A comparison of the ranks of American states in Army Alpha and in social-economic status. *Sch. and Soc.,* 16, 388–392.

Allen, G. 1958. Patterns of discovery in the genetics of mental deficiency. *Amer. J. ment. Defic.,* 62, 840–849.

Allport, G. W. 1937. *Personality: a psychological interpretation.* New York: Holt, Rinehart and Winston.

Allport, G. W., and Odbert, H. W. 1936. Trait-names, a psycholexical study. *Psychol. Monogr.,* 47, No. 1.

Allport, G. W., Vernon, P. E., and Lindzey, G. 1951. *Study of values.* Boston: Houghton Mifflin.

Alper, T. G., Blane, H. T., and Abrams, B. K. 1955. Reactions of middle and lower class children to finger paints as a function of class differences in child-rearing. *J. abn. soc. Psychol.,* 51, 439–457.

Alper, T. G., and Boring, E. G. 1944. Intelligence test scores of Northern and Southern white and Negro recruits in 1918. *J. abnorm. soc. Psychol.,* 39, 471–474.

American Personnel and Guidance Association. 1957. *The use of multifactor tests in guidance.* Washington: A.P.G.A.

Ames, L. B., and Ilg, F. L. 1964. Sex differences in test performance of matched girl-boy pairs in the five-to-nine-year-old range. *J. genet. Psychol.,* 104, 25–34.

Ames, R. 1957. Physical maturing among boys as related to adult social behavior: a longitudinal study. *Calif. J. educ. Res.,* 8, 69–75.

Anastasi, A. 1934. Practice and variability: a study in psychological method. *Psychol. Monogr.,* 45, No. 5.

Anastasi, A. 1948. The nature of psychological traits. *Psychol. Rev.*, 55, 127–138.

Anastasi, A. 1956. Intelligence and family size. *Psychol. Bull.*, 53, 187–209.

Anastasi, A., and D'Angelo, R. Y. 1952. A comparison of Negro and white preschool children in language development and Goodenough Draw-a-Man I. Q. *J. genet. Psychol.*, 81, 147–165.

Anastasi, A., and Levee, R. F. 1959. Intellectual defect and musical talent. *Amer. J. ment. Def.*, 64, 695–703.

Anastasi, A., Meade, M. J., and Schneiders, A. A. 1960. *The validation of a biographical inventory as a predictor of college success.* New York: College Entrance Examination Board.

Anderson, J. E. 1940. The prediction of terminal intelligence from infant and preschool tests. *Yearb. nat. Soc. Stud. Educ.*, 39 (I), 385–403.

Anderson, J. E. 1959. The use of time and energy. In J. E. Birren (Ed.), *Handbook of aging and the individual.* Chicago: Univ. of Chicago Press. Chap. 22.

Angelino, H., and Shedd, C. L. 1955. An initial report of a validation study of the Davis-Eells tests of general intelligence or problem-solving ability. *J. Psychol.*, 40, 35–38.

Angyal, A. F. 1948. The diagnosis of neurotic traits by means of a new perceptual test. *J. Psychol.*, 25, 105–135.

Ardis, J. A., and Fraser, E. 1957. Personality and perception: the constancy effect and introversion. *Brit. J. Psychol.*, 48, 48–54.

Asch, M. J. 1958. Negative response bias and personality adjustment. *J. counsel. Psychol.*, 5, 206–210.

Asch, S. E. 1936. A study of change in mental organization. *Arch. Psychol.*, No. 195.

Asch, S. E., and Witkin, H. A. 1948. Studies in space orientation: I. Perception of the upright with displaced visual fields. *J. exp. Psychol.*, 38, 325–337.

Asher, E. J. 1935. The inadequacy of current intelligence tests for testing Kentucky mountain children. *J. genet. Psychol.*, 46, 480–486.

Astin, A. W., and Ross, S. 1960. Glutamic acid and human intelligence. *Psychol. Bull.*, 57, 429–434.

Auld, F., Jr. 1952. Influence of social class on personality test responses. *Psychol. Bull.*, 49, 318–332.

Axline, V. M. 1949. Mental deficiency—symptom or disease? *J. consult. Psychol.*, 13, 313–327.

Ayres, L. P. 1909–10. The effect of physical defects on school progress. *Psychol. Clin.*, 3, 71–77.

Bailey, H. K. 1949. A study of the correlations between the group mental tests, the Stanford-Binet, and the Progressive Achievement Test used in the Colorado Springs elementary school. *J. educ. Res.*, 43, 93–100.

Balinsky, B. 1941. An analysis of the mental factors of various age groups from nine to sixty. *Genet. Psychol. Monogr.*, 23, 191–234.

Ball, R. S. 1938. The predictability of occupational level from intelligence. *J. consult. Psychol.*, 2, 184–186.

Baller, W. R. 1936. A study of the present social status of a group of adults who, when they were in the elementary schools, were classified mentally deficient. *Genet. Psychol. Monogr.*, 18, 165–244.

Barker, R. G. 1953. *Adjustment to physical handicap and illness: a survey of the social psychology of physique and disability* (2d Ed.). New York: Social Science Research Council.

Barratt, E. S. 1955. The space-visualization factors related to temperament traits. *J. Psychol.*, 39, 279–287.

Barrett, H. O. 1950. Sex differences in art ability. *J. educ. Res.*, 43, 391–393.

Barrilleaux, L. E. 1961. High school science achievement as related to interest and IQ. *Educ. Psychol. Measmt.*, 21, 929–936.

Barron, F. 1953. An ego-strength scale which predicts response to psychotherapy. *J. consult. Psychol.*, 17, 327–333.

Barrows, G. A., and Zuckerman, M. 1960. Construct validity of three masculinity-femininity tests. *J. consult. Psychol.*, 24, 441–445.

Bartlett, F. C. 1932. *Remembering*. Cambridge: Cambridge University Press.

Bayley, N. 1954. Some increasing parent-child similarities during the growth of children. *J. educ. Psychol.*, 45, 1–21.

Bayley, N., and Jones, H. E. 1937. Environmental correlates of mental and motor development: a cumulative study from infancy to six years. *Child Developm.*, 8, 329–341.

Bayley, N., and Oden, M. H. 1955. The maintenance of intellectual ability in gifted adults. *J. Geront.*, 10, 91–107.

Beach, F. A. 1948. *Hormones and behavior*. New York: Hoeber-Harper.

Becker, W. C., Peterson, D. R., Luria, Z., Shoemaker, D. J., and Hellmer, L. A. 1962. Relations of factors derived from parent interview ratings to behavior problems of five-year-olds. *Child Developm.*, 33, 509–535.

Beier, E. G., Gorlow, L., and Stacey, C. L. 1951. The fantasy life of the mental defective. *Amer. J. ment. Defic.*, 55, 582–589.

Beloff, H. 1958. Two forms of social conformity: acquiescence and conventionality. *J. abnorm. soc. Psychol.*, 56, 99–104.

Benedict, R., and Weltfish, G. 1943. *Races of mankind*. New York: Public Affairs Comm.

Bennett, E. M., and Cohen, L. R. 1959. Men and women: personality patterns and contrasts. *Genet. Psychol. Monogr.*, 59, 101–155.

Bennett, G. K., and Cruikshank, R. M. 1942. Sex differences in the understanding of mechanical problems. *J. appl. Psychol.*, 26, 121–127.

Bennett, G. K., et al. 1959. *Differential aptitudes tests manual* (3rd Ed.). New York: Psychological Corporation.

Benton, A. L. 1936. Influence of incentives upon intelligence test scores of school children. *J. genet. Psychol.*, 49, 494–497.

Benton, A. L. 1956. The concept of pseudofeeblemindedness. *Arch. Neur. Psychiat.*, 75, 379–388.

Bentz, V. J. 1953. A test-retest experiment on the relationship between age and mental ability. *Amer. Psychologist*, 8, 319–320.

Berdie, R. F. 1943. Likes, dislikes, and vocational interests. *J. appl. Psychol.*, 27, 180–189.

Berdie, R. F. 1945. Range of interests. *J. appl. Psychol.*, 29, 268–281.

Berdie, R. F. 1954. *After high school–what?* Minneapolis: Univ. of Minnesota Press.

Berdie, R. F. 1960. Strong vocational interest scores of high school seniors and their later occupational entry. *J. appl. Psychol.*, 44, 161–165.

Berdie, R. F., and Hood, A. B. 1963. Academic ability and socio-economic level of the home. (Paper presented to 13th Annual Conference, Statewide Testing Program, Univ. of Minnesota, Sept. 21, 1963.)

Bereiter, C. 1960. Verbal and ideational fluency in superior tenth grade students. *J. educ. Psychol.*, 51, 337–345.

Berkowitz, B., and Green, R. F. 1964. Changes in intellect with age: I. Longitudinal study of Wechsler-Bellevue scores. *J. genet. Psychol.*, 103, 3–21.

Bernhardt, K. S., Northway, M. L., and Tatham, C. M. 1948. The effect of added thiamine on intelligence and learning with identical twins. *Canad. J. Psychol.*, 2, 58–61.

Bernreuter, R. G. 1933. The theory and construction of the personality inventory. *J. soc. Psychol.*, 4, 387–405.

Betz, B. J. 1962. Experiences in research in psychotherapy with schizophrenic patients. In Hans H. Strupp and Lester Luborsky, Eds., *Research in psychotherapy,* Vol. 2. Washington, D.C.: American Psychological Association.

Binet, A., and Henri, V. 1895. La psychologie individuelle. *Année psychol.*, 2, 411–465.

Bing, E. 1963. Effect of childrearing practices on development of differential cognitive abilities. *Child Developm.*, 34, 631–645.

Bingham, W. V. 1946. Inequalities of adult capacity. *Eugen. News,* 31, 41–43.

Birren, J. E. 1956. The significance of age changes in speed of perception and psychomotor skills. In J. E. Anderson (Ed.), *Psychological aspects of aging.* Washington, D.C.: American Psychological Association, Pp. 97–104.

Blatt, B. 1961. Towards a more acceptable terminology in mental retardation. *Train. Sch. Bull.*, 58, 47–51.

Blewett, D. B. 1954. An experimental study of the inheritance of intelligence. *J. ment. Sci.*, 100, 922–933.

Bloom, B. S. 1956. The 1955 normative study of the *Tests of general educational development. School Rev.*, 64, 110–124.

Bloom, B. S. 1964. *Stability and change in human characteristics.* New York: Wiley.

Blum, G. S. 1949. A study of the psychoanalytic theory of psychosexual development. *Genet. psychol. Monogr.*, 39, 3–99.

Blum, G. S., and Miller, D. R. 1952. Exploring the psychoanalytic theory of the "oral character." *J. Pers.*, 20, 287–304.

Boas, F. 1911. *Abstract of the report on changes in bodily form of descendants of immigrants.* Washington: Government Printing Office.

Boger, J. H. 1952. An experimental study of the effects of perceptual training on group IQ test scores. *J. educ. Res.*, 46, 43–52.

Bolton, T. L. 1892. The growth of memory in schoolchildren. *Amer. J. Psychol.*, 4, 362–380.

Boring, E. G. 1923. Intelligence as the tests test it. *New Republic,* 35, 35–37.

Borow, H. 1945. A psychometric study of non-intellectual factors in college achievement. Ph.D. Thesis, Pennsylvania State College.

Botzum, W. A. 1951. A factorial study of the reasoning and closure factors. *Psychometrika,* 16, 361–386.

Boyd, G. F. 1952. The levels of aspiration of white and Negro children in a non-segregated elementary school. *J. soc. Psychol.,* 36, 191–196.

Boyd, W. C. 1950. *Genetics and the races of men.* Boston: Little, Brown.

Bradway, K. P., and Thompson, C. W. 1962. Intelligence at adulthood: a twenty-five year follow-up. *J. educ. Psychol.,* 53, 1–14.

Braun, H. W. 1959. Perceptual processes. In J. E. Birren (Ed.), *Handbook of aging and the individual.* Chicago: Univ. of Chicago Press. Chap. 16.

Brazziel, W. F., and Terrell, M. 1962. An experiment in the development of readiness in a culturally disadvantaged group of first grade children. *J. Negro Educ.,* 31, 4–7.

Bridgman, C. S., and Hollenbeck, G. P. 1961. Effect of simulated applicant status on Kuder Form D occupational interest scores. *J. appl. Psychol.,* 45, 237–239.

Brill, M. 1936. Studies of Jewish and non-Jewish intelligence. *J. educ. Psychol.,* 27, 331–352.

Brody, D. 1937. Twin resemblances in mechanical ability, with reference to the effects of practice on performance. *Child Developm.,* 8, 207–216.

Bronfenbrenner, U. 1961. Some familial antecedents of responsibility and leadership in adolescents. In L. Petrullo and B. M. Bass (Eds.), *Leadership and interpersonal behavior.* New York: Holt, Rinehart and Winston.

Brown, D. G. 1956. Sex-role preference in young children. *Psychol. Monogr.,* 70, No. 14.

Brown, D. G. 1962. Sex-role preference in children: methodological problems. *Psychol. Rep.,* 11, 477–478.

Brown, F. 1944. An experimental and critical study of the intelligence of Negro and white kindergarten children. *J. genet. Psychol.,* 65, 161–175.

Bruce, M. 1940. Factors affecting intelligence test performance of whites and Negroes in the rural South. *Arch. Psychol.,* No. 252.

Bruner, J. S. 1963. *On knowing: essays for the left hand.* Cambridge, Mass.: Harvard Univ. Press.

Bruner, J. S., Goodnow, J. J., and Austin, G. A. 1956. *A study of thinking.* New York: Wiley.

Bühler, C. 1959. *Der Menschliche Lebenslauf als Psychologisches Problem.* Göttingen: Verlag für Psychologie.

Bühler, C. 1962. Goal-structure of human life: model and project. *Psychol. Rep.,* 10, 445–446.

Bühler, C., Bühler, K., and Lefever, D. W. Copyright 1949. *Development of the Basic Rorschach Scores with manual of directions.* Berkeley: University of California Press.

Burchard, E. M. L. 1936. Physique and psychosis: an analysis of the postulated relationship between bodily constitution and mental disease syndrome. *Comp. Psychol. Monogr.,* 13, No. 1.

Burchinal, L. G. 1959. Agreement of occupational prestige as ranked by two empirical occupational prestige scales. *J. soc. Psychol.,* 50, 335–340.

Burgemeister, B. B. 1940. The permanence of interests of college women students. *Arch. Psychol.,* No. 255.

Burks, B. S. 1928. The relative influence of nature and nurture upon mental development. *Yearb. nat. Soc. Stud. Educ.*, 27 (I), 219–316.

Burks, B. S., Jensen, D. W., and Terman, L. M. 1930. *Genetic studies of genius*, Vol. III. The promise of youth; follow-up studies of a thousand gifted children. Stanford: Stanford University Press.

Burns, Z. H. 1937. Practice, variability, and motivation. *J. educ. Res.*, 30, 403–420.

Buros, O. K. (Ed.). 1965. *The sixth mental measurements yearbook.* Highland Park, N.J.: Gryphon.

Burt, C. L. 1939. The factorial analysis of emotional traits. *Char. and Pers.*, 7, 238–254, 285–299.

Burt, C. L. 1947. Factor analysis and physical types. *Psychometrika*, 12, 171–188.

Burt, C. L. 1949. The structure of the mind: a review of the results of factor analysis. *Brit. J. educ. Psychol.*, 19, 100–111, 176–199.

Burt, C. L. 1958. The inheritance of mental ability. *Amer. Psychologist*, 13, 1–15.

Burt, C. L. 1959. Class differences in general intelligence: III. *Brit. J. statist. Psychol.*, 12, 15–33.

Calvin, A. D., Tyrrell, S., Schultz, R. E., and Koons, R. G. 1958. The effect of exposure-time on the relation between perceptual organization and intelligence. *Amer. J. Psychol.*, 71, 573–577.

Campbell, A. A., and Hilgard, E. R. 1936. Individual differences in ease of conditioning. *J. exp. Psychol.*, 19, 561–571.

Campbell, D. P. 1965. A cross-sectional and longitudinal study of scholastic abilities over twenty-five years. *J. counsel. Psychol.*, 12, 55–61.

Canady, H. G. 1936. The effect of "Rapport" on the IQ. *J. Negro Educ.*, 5, 209–219.

Cantor, G. N., and Stacey, C. L. 1951. Manipulative dexterity in mental defectives. *Amer. J. ment. Defic.*, 56, 401–410.

Carroll, J. B. 1941. A factor analysis of verbal abilities. *Psychometrika*, 6, 279–308.

Carson, A. S., and Rabin, A. I. 1960. Verbal comprehension and communication in Negro and white children. *J. educ. Psychol.*, 51, 47–51.

Carter, H. D. 1940. The development of vocational attitudes. *J. consult. Psychol.*, 4, 185–191.

Castle, C. S. 1913. A statistical study of eminent women. *Arch. Psychol.*, No. 27.

Cattell, A. K. S., Cattell, R. B., and Rhymer, R. M. 1947. P-technique demonstrated in determining psycho-physiological source traits in a normal individual. *Psychometrika*, 12, 267–288.

Cattell, J. McK. 1890. Mental tests and measurements. *Mind*, 15, 373–380.

Cattell, J. McK. 1903. A statistical study of eminent men. *Pop. Sci. Mon.*, 62, 359–377.

Cattell, J. McK. 1915. Families of American men of science. I. *Pop. Sci. Mon.*, 86, 504–515.

Cattell, J. McK. 1917a. Families of American men of science. II. *Sci. Mon.*, 4, 248–262.

Cattell, J. McK. 1917b. Families of American men of science. III. *Sci. Mon.*, 5, 368–377.

Cattell, J. McK., and Farrand, L. 1896. Physical and mental measurements of the students of Columbia University. *Psychol. Rev.*, 3, 618–648.

Cattell, R. B. 1944. *A culture-free test: manual of directions.* New York: Psychological Corporation.

Cattell, R. B. 1946. *The description and measurement of personality.* New York: Harcourt, Brace & World.

Cattell, R. B. 1947. Confirmation and clarification of the primary personality factors. *Psychometrika,* 12, 197–220.

Cattell, R. B. 1948a. Primary personality factors in the realm of objective tests. *J. Pers.*, 16, 459–487.

Cattell, R. B. 1948b. The primary personality factors in women compared with those in men. *Brit. J. Psychol., Statist. Sect.*, 1, 114–130.

Cattell, R. B. 1950a. The fate of national intelligence; tests of a thirteen-year prediction. *Eugen. Rev.*, 42, 136–148.

Cattell, R. B. 1950b. *An introduction to personality study.* London: Hutchinson.

Cattell, R. B. 1950c. The main personality factors in questionnaire self-estimate material. *J. soc. Psychol.*, 31, 3–38.

Cattell, R. B. 1950d. *Personality: a systematic, theoretical and factual study.* New York: McGraw-Hill.

Cattell, R. B. 1954. Primary personality factors in the questionnaire medium for children from eleven to fourteen years old. *Educ. psychol. Measmt.*, 14, 50–89.

Cattell, R. B. 1957. *Personality and motivation structure and measurement.* New York: Harcourt, Brace & World.

Cattell, R. B., Blewett, D. B., and Beloff, J. R. 1955. The inheritance of personality. *Amer. J. hum. Genet.*, 7, 122–146.

Cattell, R. B., and Gruen, W. 1953. The personality factor structure of 11-year-old children in terms of behavior rating data. *J. clin. Psychol.*, 9, 256–266.

Cattell, R. B., and Horn, J. 1963. An integrating study of the factor structure of adult attitude-interests. *Genet. Psychol. Monogr.*, 67, 89–149.

Cattell, R. B., and Luborsky, L. B. 1950. P-technique demonstrated as a new clinical method for determining personality and symptom structure. *J. gen. Psychol.*, 42, 3–24.

Cattell, R. B., and Saunders, D. R. 1950. Inter-relation and matching of personality factors from behavior rating, questionnaire, and objective test data. *J. soc. Psychol.*, 31, 243–260.

Cattell, R. B., Stice, G. F., and Kristy, N. F. 1957. A first approximation to nature-nurture ratios for eleven primary personality factors in objective tests. *J. abnorm. soc. Psychol.*, 54, 143–160.

Centers, R. 1949. *Psychology of social classes.* Princeton: Princeton University Press.

Centers, R. 1950. Social class identification of American youth. *J. Pers.*, 18, 290–302.

Centers, R. 1951. Toward an articulation of two approaches to social class phenomena: II. The Index of Status Characteristics and class identification. *Int. J. Opin. Att. Res.*, 5, 159–178.

Charles, D. C. 1953. Ability and accomplishment of persons earlier judged mentally deficient. *Genet. Psychol. Monogr.*, 47, 3–71.

Chauncey, H. 1952. The use of the Selective Service College Qualification Test in the deferment of college students. *Science*, 116, 73–79.

Chen, T. L., and Chow, H. H. 1948. A factor study of a test battery at different educational levels. *J. genet. Psychol.*, 73, 187–199.

Child, I. L. 1950. The relation of somatotype to self-ratings on Sheldon's temperamental traits. *J. Pers.*, 18, 440–453.

Child, I. L. & Sheldon, W. H. 1941. The correlation between components of physique and scores on certain psychological tests. *Char. and Pers.*, 10, 23–34.

Chipman, C. E. 1946. Psychological variation within a homogeneous psychometric group. *Amer. J. ment. Defic.*, 51, 195–205.

Clark, K. E. 1961. *Vocational interests of nonprofessional men.* Minneapolis: University of Minnesota Press.

Clark, R. E. 1949. Psychoses, income, and occupational prestige. *Amer. J. Sociol.*, 54, 433–440.

Clark, W. W. 1959. Boys and girls—are there significant ability and achievement differences? *Phi Delta Kappan*, 41, 73–76.

Clarke, D. P. 1941. Stanford-Binet Scale L response patterns in matched racial groups. *J. Negro Educ.*, 10, 230–238.

Coffin, T. E. 1944. A three-component theory of leadership. *J. abnorm. soc. Psychol.*, 39, 63–83.

Comrey, A. L., and Soufi, A. 1960. Further investigation of some factors found in MMPI items. *Educ. Psychol. Measmt.*, 20, 777–786.

Conrad, H. S., and Jones, H. E. 1940. A second study of familial resemblances in intelligence, environmental and genetic implications of parent-child and sibling correlations in the total sample. *Yearb. nat. Soc. Stud. Educ.*, 39 (II), 97–141.

Cook, W. W. 1947. Individual trait differences in public schools with implications for school organization and curriculum development. *Teach. Coll. J.*, 19, 56–59, 67–70.

Cooper, R. M., and Zubek, J. P. 1958. Effects of enriched and restricted early environments on the learning ability of bright and dull rats. *Canad. J. Psychol.*, 12, 159–164.

Coppinger, N. W., and Ammons, R. B. 1952. The Full-Range Picture Vocabulary Test: VIII. A normative study of Negro children. *J. clin. Psychol.*, 8, 136–140.

Corsini, R. J., and Fassett, K. K. 1953. Intelligence and aging. *J. genet. Psychol.*, 83, 249–264.

Cottle, W. C. 1950. A factorial study of the Multiphasic, Strong, Kuder, and Bell inventories using a population of adult males. *Psychometrika*, 15, 25–47.

Counts, G. S. 1925. Social status of occupations. *Sch. Rev.*, 33, 16–27.

Cowan, L., and Goldman, M. 1959. The selection of the mentally deficient for vocational training and the effect of this training on vocational success. *J. consult. Psychol.*, 23, 78–84.

Cox, C. M. 1926. *Genetic studies of genius:* Vol. II. *The early mental traits of three hundred geniuses.* Stanford: Stanford University Press.

Cox, J. R. 1928. *Mechanical aptitude.* London: Methuen.

Crissy, W. J. E., and Daniel, W. J. 1939. Vocational interest factors in women. *J. appl. Psychol.,* 23, 488–494.

Crites, J. O. 1960. Ego-strength in relation to vocational interest development. *J. counsel. Psychol.,* 7, 137–143.

Cronbach, L. J. 1949b. "Pattern tabulation": a statistical method for analysis of limited patterns of scores with particular reference to the Rorschach test. *Educ. psychol. Measmt.,* 9, 149–172.

Cronbach, L. J. 1950. Studies of the group Rorschach in relation to success in the college of the University of Chicago: *J. educ. Psychol.,* 41, 65–82.

Cronbach, L. J. 1957. The two disciplines of scientific psychology. *Amer. Psychologist,* 12, 671–684.

Cronbach, L. J. 1960. *Essentials of psychological testing.* 2nd Ed. New York: Harper & Row.

Cronbach, L. J., and Gleser, G. C. 1957. *Psychological tests and personnel decisions.* Urbana: University of Illinois Press.

Cronbach, L. J., Rajaratnam, N., and Gleser, G. C. 1963. Theory of generalizability: a liberalization of reliability theory. *Brit. J. stat. Psychol.,* 16, 137–163.

Crutchfield, R. S., Woodworth, D. G., and Albrecht, R. E. 1958. Perceptual performance and the effective person. Lackland AFB, Texas *Personnel Lab. Rep.* WADC–TN–58–60. ASTIA Doc. No. AD 151–039.

Cumming, E., and Henry, W. E. 1961. *Growing old.* New York: Basic Books.

Curtis, H. A. 1949. A study of the relative effects of age and of test difficulty upon factor patterns. *Genet. Psychol. Monogr.,* 40, 99–148.

Darley, J. G. 1937. Tested maladjustment related to clinically diagnosed maladjustment. *J. appl. Psychol.,* 21, 632–642.

Davidson, K. S., Gibby, R. G., McNeil, E. B., Segal, S. J., and Silverman H. 1950. A preliminary study of Negro and white differences on Form I of the Wechsler-Bellevue Scale. *J. consult. Psychol.,* 14, 489–492.

Davis, A. 1943. Child training and social class. In R. G. Barker, J. S. Kounin, and H. F. Wright. *Child behavior and development.* New York: McGraw-Hill, Ch. 34.

Davis, A., Gardner, B. B., and Gardner, M. B. 1941. *Deep south.* Chicago: University of Chicago Press.

Davis, A., and Havighurst, R. J. 1946. Social class and color differences in child-rearing. *Amer. sociol. Rev.,* 11, 698–710.

Decroly, O., and Degand, J. 1910. La mesure de l'intelligence chez les enfants normeaux d'après les tests de Mm. Binet et Simon. *Arch. Psychol.,* Genève, 9, 81–108.

Deeg, M. E., and Paterson, D. G. 1947. Changes in social status of occupations. *Occupations,* 25, 205–208.

DeHaan, R. F., and Havighurst, R. J. 1957. *Educating gifted children.* Chicago: University of Chicago Press.

Demming, J. A., and Pressey, S. L. 1957. Tests "indigenous" to the adult and later years. *J. counsel. Psychol.,* 4, 144–148.

Dennis, W. 1942. The performance of Hopi children on the Goodenough Draw-a-Man test. *J. comp. Psychol.*, 34, 341–348.

DeSoto, C., and Leibowitz, H. 1956. Perceptual organization and intelligence: a further study. *J. abnorm. soc. Psychol.*, 53, 334–337.

De Stephens, W. P. 1953. Are criminals morons? *J. soc. Psychol.*, 38, 187–199.

Deutsch, M. 1964. *The role of social class in language development and cognition.* New York: Institute for Developmental Studies, Dept. of Psychiatry, New York Medical College. (Mimeographed.)

Deutsch, M., and Brown, B. 1964. Social influences in Negro-White intelligence differences. *J. Social Issues*, 20, 24–35.

Diggory, J. A. 1953. Sex differences in the organization of attitudes. *J. Person.*, 22, 89–100.

Doll, E. A. 1946. The feeble-minded child. In L. Carmichael (Ed.), *Manual of child psychology*. New York: Wiley. Ch. 17.

Doll, E. A. 1953. *The measurement of social competence: a manual for the Vineland Social Maturity Scale.* Minneapolis: Educational Test Bureau.

Donahue, W. T., Coombs, C. H., and Travers, R. W. M. 1949. *The measurement of student adjustment and achievement.* Ann Arbor: University of Michigan Press.

Doppelt, J. E. 1950. The organization of mental abilities in the age range 13 to 17. *Teach. Coll. Contrib. to Educ.*, No. 962.

Doppelt, J. E., and Bennett, G. D. 1951. A longitudinal study of the differential aptitude test. *Educ. Psychol. Measmt.*, 11, 228–237.

Downey, J. E. 1923. *The will-temperament and its testing*. New York: Harcourt, Brace & World.

Drasgow, J., and Carkhuff, R. R. 1964. Kuder neuropsychiatric keys before and after psychotherapy. *J. counsel. Psychol.*, 11, 67–69.

Dreger, R. M., and Miller, K. S. 1960. Comparative psychological studies of Negroes and whites in the United States. *Psychol. Bull.*, 57, 361–402.

DuBois, P. H. (Ed.). 1947. *The classification program.* (AAF Aviation Psychology Report, No. 2.) Washington, D.C.: Government Printing Office.

Duffy, E. 1962. *Activation and behavior*. New York: Wiley.

Duffy, E., and Crissy, W. J. E. 1940. Evaluative attitudes as related to vocational interest and academic achievement. *J. abnorm. soc. Psychol.*, 35, 226–245.

Duggan, L. 1950. An experiment on immediate recall in secondary school children. *Brit. J. Psychol.*, 40, 149–154.

Dukes, W. F. 1955. Psychological studies of values. *Psychol. Bull.*, 52, 24–50.

Dunkleberger, C. J., and Tyler, L. E. 1961. Interest stability and personality traits. *J. counsel. Psychol.*, 8, 70–74.

Dunnette, M. D. 1963. A modified model for test validation and selection research. *J. appl. Psychol.*, 47, 317–323.

Dunnette, M. D., Kirchner, W. K., and de Gidio, J. 1958. Relations among scores in Edwards Personal Preference Schedule, California Psychological Inventory, and Strong Vocational Interest Blank for an individual sample. *J. appl. Psychol.*, 42, 178–181.

Dunnette, M. D., Wernimont, P., and Abrahams, N. 1964. Further research on vocational interest differences among several types of engineers. *Pers. Guid. J.*, 42, 484–493.

Dunsdon, J. I., and Fraser-Roberts, J. A. F. 1957. A study of the performance of 2,000 children on four vocabulary tests. *Brit. J. statist. Psychol.*, 10, 1–16.

Dvorak, B. J. 1935. *Differential occupational ability patterns.* Minneapolis: University of Minnesota Press.

Eagleson, O. W. 1937. Comparative studies of white and Negro subjects in learning to discriminate visual magnitude. *J. Psychol.*, 4, 167–197.

Ebbinghaus, H. 1897. Über eine neue Methode zur Prüfung geistiger Fähigkeiten und ihre Anwendung bei Schulkindern. *Z. angewand. Psychol.*, 13, 401–459.

Ebert, E., and Simmons, K. 1943. The Brush Foundation study of child growth and development: I. Psychometric tests. *Monogr. Soc. Res. Child Develpm.*, 8, No. 2 (Whole No. 35).

Edgerton, H. A., and Britt, S. H. 1944. Sex differences in the Science Talent Test. *Science*, 100, 192–193.

Edgerton, H. A., and Britt, S. H. 1947. Technical aspects of the Fourth Annual Science Talent Search. *Educ. psychol. Measmt.*, 7, 3–21.

Educational Testing Service. 1952. *A summary of statistics on the Selective Service College Qualification Test of December 13, 1951, April 24, 1952, and May 22, 1952.*

Educational Testing Service Developments. 1953. 2, No. 1.

Educational Testing Service. 1958. *The SCAT-STEP supplement 1958.* Princeton: Educ. Test. Serv.

Edwards, A. L. 1957. *The social desirability variable in personality assessment and research.* New York: Holt, Rinehart and Winston.

Edwards, A. L. 1959. Social desirability and personality test construction. In B. M. Bass and I. A. Berg (Eds.), *Objective approaches to personality assessment.* Princeton, N.J.: Van Nostrand.

Eels, K., Davis, A., Havighurst, R. J., Herrick, V. E., and Tyler, R. 1951. *Intelligence and cultural differences.* Chicago: University of Chicago Press.

Eiduson, B. T. 1958. Artist and nonartist: a comparative study. *J. Person.*, 26, 13–28.

Eiduson, B. T. 1962. *Scientists: their psychological world.* New York: Basic Books.

Ekman, G. 1951. On the number and definition of dimensions in Kretschmer's and Sheldon's constitutional systems. In *Essays in psychology dedicated to David Katz.* Uppsala: Almquist and Wiksells.

Ellis, H. A. 1904. *A study of British genius.* London: Hurst.

Ellis, N. R. 1963. The stimulus trace and behavioral inadequacy. In Ellis, N. R. (Ed.), *Handbook of mental deficiency.* New York: McGraw-Hill. Ch. 4.

Ellis, N. R., and Sloan, W. 1957. Relationship between intelligence and simple reaction time in mental defectives. *Percept. Mot. Skills*, 7, 65–67.

Embree, R. B. 1948. The status of college students in terms of IQ's determined during childhood. *Amer. Psychologist*, 3, 259.

Emmerich, W. 1959. Parental identification in young children. *Genet. psychol. Monogr.*, 60, 257–308.

English, H. B., and English, A. C. 1958. *A comprehensive dictionary of psychological and psychoanalytical terms.* New York: Longmans.
Erikson, E. H. 1950. *Childhood and society.* New York: Norton.
Erikson, E. H. 1951. Sex differences in the play configurations of preadolescents. *Amer. J. Orthopsychiat.*, 21, 667–692.
Erikson, E. H. 1959. Identity and the life cycle. *Psychol. Issues,* 1, No. 1.
Erlenmeyer-Kimling, L., and Jarvik, L. F. 1963. Genetics and intelligence: a review. *Science,* 142, 1477–1479.
Escalona, S., and Heider, G. M. 1959. *Prediction and outcome.* New York: Basic Books.
Ewert, H. 1934. The effect of practice on individual differences when studied with measurements weighted for difficulty. *J. gen. Psychol.,* 10, 249–285.
Eysenck, H. J. 1947. *Dimensions of personality.* London: Routledge and Kegan Paul.
Eysenck, H. J. 1952. *The scientific study of personality.* London: Routledge and Kegan Paul.
Eysenck, H. J. 1953. *The structure of human personality.* London: Methuen.
Eysenck, H. J. 1956. The inheritance of extraversion-introversion. *Acta Psychol.,* 12, 95–110.
Eysenck, H. J. 1957. *The dynamics of anxiety and hysteria.* New York: Praeger.
Eysenck, H. J., and Prell, D. B. 1951. The inheritance of neuroticism: an experimental study. *J. ment. Sci.,* 97, 441–465.
Eysenck, S. B. J. 1960. Social class, sex, and response to a five-part personality inventory. *Educ. psychol. Measmt.,* 20, 47–54.
Falek, A., Kallman, F. J., Lorge, I., and Jarvik, L. F. 1960. Longevity and intellectual variation in a senescent twin population. *J. Gerontol.,* 15, 305–309.
Fauls, L. B., and Smith, W. D. 1956. Sex-role learning of five-year-olds. *J. genet. Psychol.,* 89, 105–117.
Ferguson, G. O. 1916. The psychology of the Negro. *Arch. Psychol.,* No. 36.
Ferguson, L. W., Humphreys, L. G., and Strong, F. W. 1941. A factorial analysis of interests and values. *J. educ. Psychol.,* 32, 197–204.
Fernberger, S. W. 1948. Persistence of stereotypes concerning sex differences. *J. abnorm. soc. Psychol.,* 43, 97–101.
Finch, F. H. 1935. The permanence of vocational interests. *Psychol. Bull.,* 32, 682.
Finch, F. H. 1946. Enrollment increases and changes in the mental level of the high school population. *Appl. Psychol. Monogr.,* No. 10.
Findley, D. C., and McGuire, C. 1957. Social status and abstract behavior. *J. abnorm. soc. Psychol.,* 54, 135–137.
Fisher, J. 1959. The twisted pear and the prediction of behavior. *J. consult. Psychol.,* 23, 400–405.
Fisher, M. B., and Birren, J. E. 1947. Age and strength. *J. appl. Psychol.,* 31, 490–497.
Fiske, D. W. 1944. A study of relationships to somatotype. *J. appl. Psychol.,* 28, 504–519.
Fiske, D. W., and Butler, J. M. 1963. The experimental conditions for measuring individual differences. *Educ. Psychol. Measmt.,* 23, 249–266.

Fiske, D. W., and Maddi, S. R. 1961. A conceptual framework. In D. W. Fiske and S. R. Maddi (Eds.), *Functions of Varied Experience.* Homewood, Ill.: Dorsey. Ch. 2.

Fjeld, H. A. 1934. The limits of learning ability in Rhesus monkeys. *Genet. Psychol. Monogr.*, 15, 369–537.

Flanagan, J. C. 1947. *The Aviation psychology program in the AAF.* (AAF Aviation Psychology Report, No. 1.) Washington, D.C.: Government Printing Office.

Flanagan, J. C., Dailey, J. T., Shaycroft, M. F., Gorham, W. A., Orr, D. B., and Goldberg I. 1962. *Project talent: design for a study of American youth.* Pittsburgh: University of Pittsburgh Press.

Flanagan, J. C., Davis, F. B., Dailey, J. T., Shaycroft, M. F., Orr, D. B., Goldberg, I., and Neyman, C. A., Jr. 1964. *The American high school student.* Pittsburgh: University of Pittsburgh Press.

Fleishman, E. A. 1962. The description and prediction of perceptual-motor skill learning. In R. Glaser (Ed.), *Training Research and Education.* Pittsburgh: University of Pittsburgh Press.

Fleishman, E. A., and Parker, J. F. 1962. Factors in the retention and relearning of perceptual-motor skill. *J. exp. Psychol.*, 64, 215–226.

Flood, J., and Halsey, A. H. 1957. Social class, intelligence tests, and selection for secondary schools. *Brit. J. Sociol.*, 8, 33–39.

Ford, C. F., and Tyler, L. E. 1952. A factor analysis of Terman and Miles' M-F Test. *J. appl. Psychol.*, 36, 251–253.

Foulds, G. A., and Raven, J. C. 1948a. Intellectual ability and occupational grade. *Occup. Psychol.*, London, 22, 197–203.

Foulds, G. A., and Raven, J. C. 1948b. Normal changes in the mental abilities of adults as age advances. *J. ment. Sci.*, 94, 133–142.

Fox, C., and Birren, J. E. 1950. The differential decline of subtest scores of the Wechsler-Bellevue Intelligence Scale in 60-69-year-old individuals. *J. genet. Psychol.*, 77, 313–317.

Francis, R. J., and Rarick, G. L. 1960. *Motor characteristics of the mentally retarded.* U.S. Off. of Educ., Coop. Res. Monogr. No. 1.

Franck, K., and Rosen, E. 1949. A projective test of masculinity femininity. *J. consult. Psychol.*, 13, 247–256.

Franklin, J. C. 1945. Discriminative value and patterns of the Wechsler-Bellevue Scales in the examination of delinquent Negro boys. *Educ. Psychol. Measmt.*, 5, 71–85.

Franzblau, R. N. 1935. Race differences in mental and physical traits studied in different environments. *Arch. Psychol.*, No. 177.

Fredericsen, N., and Gilbert, A. 1960. Replication of a study of differential predictability. *Educ. psychol. Measmt.*, 20, 759–767.

Fredericsen, N., and Melville, S. D. 1954. Differential predictability in the use of test scores. *Educ. psychol. Measmt.*, 14, 647–656.

Freeman, F. N., Holzinger, K. J., and Mitchell, B. C. 1928. The influence of environment on the intelligence, school achievement, and conduct of foster children. *Yearb. nat. Soc. Stud. Educ.*, 27 (I), 101–217.

French, J. W. 1940a. Individual differences in paramecium. *J. comp. Psychol.*, 30, 451–456.

French, J. W. 1940b. Trial and error learning in paramecium. *J. exp. Psychol.*, 26, 609–613.

French, J. W. 1963. Comparative prediction of college major-field grades by pure factor aptitude, interest, and personality measures. *Educ. psychol. Measmt.*, 23, 767–774.

Frenkel, E. 1936. Studies in biographical psychology. *Char. and Person.*, 5, 1–34.

Frenkel-Brunswik, E. 1954. Further explorations by a contributor to "The Authoritarian Personality." In R. Christie and M. Jahoda (Eds.), *Studies in the scope and method of "The Authoritarian Personality."* New York: Free Press (Macmillan). Pp. 226–275.

Frumkin, R. M. 1954. Race and major mental disorders: a research note. *J. Negro Educ.*, 23, 97–98.

Fryer, D. 1931. *The measurement of interests in relation to human adjustment.* New York: Holt, Rinehart and Winston.

Fuller, J. L., and Scott, J. P. 1954. Heredity and learning ability in infrahuman mammals. *Eugen. Quart.*, I, 28–43.

Fuller, J. L., and Thompson, W. R. 1960. *Behavior genetics.* New York: Wiley.

Funkenstein, D. H., King, S. H., and Drolette, M. 1954. The direction of anger during a laboratory stress-inducing situation. *Psychosomat. Med.*, 16, 404–413.

Furfey, P. H. 1928. The relation between socio-economic status and intelligence of young infants as measured by the Linfert-Hierholzer scale. *Ped. Sem. and J. genet. Psychol.*, 35, 478–480.

Gadson, E. J. 1951. Glutamic acid and mental deficiency—a review. *Amer. J. ment. Defic.*, 55, 521–528.

Gaier, E. L., and Collier, M. J. 1960. The latency-stage story preferences of American and Finnish children. *Child Develpm.*, 31, 431–451.

Gainer, W. L. 1962. The ability of the WISC subtests to discriminate between boys and girls of average intelligence. *Calif. J. educ. Res.*, 13, 9–16.

Galton, F. 1870. *Hereditary genius: an inquiry into its laws.* New York: D. Appleton and Co. (Republished by Horizon Press, New York, 1952).

Galton, F. 1883. *Inquiries into human faculty and its development.* London: Macmillan.

Gardner, R. W. 1964a. The development of cognitive structures. In C. Sheerer, Ed., *Cognition: Theory, Research, Promise.* New York: Harper & Row. Pp. 147–171.

Gardner, R. W. 1964b. The Menninger Foundation study of twins and their parents. (Paper presented at American Psychological Association, Sept. 9, 1964.)

Gardner, R. W., Holzman, P. S., Klein, G. S., Linton, H., and Spence, D. P. 1959. Cognitive control: a study of individual consistencies in cognitive behavior. *Psychol. Issues,* 1, No. 4. Monograph 4.

Gardner, R. W., Jackson, D. N., and Messick, S. J. 1960. Personality organization in cognitive controls and intellectual abilities. *Psychol. Issues,* 2, No. 4. Monograph 8.

Gardner, R. W. and Long, R. I. 1962. Control, defence, and centration effect: a study of scanning behavior. *Brit. J. Psychol.*, 53, 2, 129–140.

Gardner, R. W., and Schoen, R. A. 1962. Differentiation and abstraction in concept formation. *Psychol. Monogr.*, 76, No. 41 (Whole No. 560).

Garrett, H. E. 1938. Differentiable mental traits. *Psychol. Rec.*, 2, 259–298.

Garrett, H. E. 1940. Variability in learning under massed and spaced practice. *J. exp. Psychol.*, 26, 547–567.

Garrett, H. E. 1945a. Comparison of Negro and white recruits on the Army tests given in 1917–1918. *Amer. J. Psychol.*, 58, 480–495.

Garrett, H. E. 1945b. "Facts" and "interpretations" regarding race differences. *Science,* 101, 404–406.

Garrett, H. E. 1945c. A note on the intelligence scores of Negroes and whites in 1918. *J. abnorm. soc. Psychol.,* 40, 344–346.

Garrett, H. E. 1945d. Psychological differences as among races. *Science,* 101, 16–17.

Garrett, H. E. 1946. A developmental theory of intelligence. *Amer. Psychologist,* I, 372–378.

Garrett, H. E., Bryan, A. I., and Perl, R. E. 1935. The age factor in mental organization. *Arch. Psychol.*, No. 176.

Garrett, H. F. 1949. A review and interpretation of investigations of factors related to scholastic success in colleges of arts and science and teachers colleges. *J. exp. Educ.*, 18, 91–138.

Garvey, C. R. 1933. Comparative body build of manic-depressive and schizophrenic patients. *Psychol. Bull.*, 30, 567–568.

Gaw, F. 1925. A study of performance tests. *Brit. J. Psychol.*, 15, 374–392.

Geier, F. M., Levin, M., and Tolman, E. C. 1941. Individual differences in emotionality, hypothesis formation, vicarious trial and error and visual discrimination learning in rats. *Comp. Psychol. Monogr.*, 17, No. 3.

George, W. C. 1962. *The biology of the race problem.* New York: National Putnam Letters Committee.

Gesell, A., and Thompson, H. 1941. Twins T and C from infancy to adolescence: a biogenetic study of individual differences by the method of co-twin control. *Genet. Psychol. Monogr.*, 24, 3–122.

Getzels, J. W., and Jackson, P. W. 1960. *The gifted student.* U.S. Dept. of Health, Education, and Welfare, Cooperative Research Monogr., No. 2. Pp. 1–18.

Getzels, J. W., and Jackson, P. W. 1962. *Creativity and intelligence.* New York: Wiley.

Ghei, S. 1960. Vocational interests, achievement, and satisfaction. *J. counsel. Psychol.*, 7, 132–136.

Ghiselli, E. E. 1955. The measurement of occupational aptitude. *U. of Calif. Pub. in Psychol.*, 8 (No. 2), 101–216.

Ghiselli, E. E. 1956. Differentiation of individuals in terms of their predictability. *J. appl. Psychol.*, 40, 374–377.

Ghiselli, E. E. 1957. The relationship between intelligence and age among superior adults. *J. genet. Psychol.*, 90, 131–142.

Ghiselli, E. E. 1960a. The prediction of predictability. *Educ. Psychol. Measmt.,* 20, 3–8.

Ghiselli, E. E. 1960b. Differentiation of tests in terms of the accuracy with which they predict for a given individual. *Educ. Psychol. Measmt.*, 20, 675–684.

Ghiselli, E. E. 1963. Moderating effects and differential reliability and validity. *J. appl. Psychol.*, 47, 81–86.

Ghiselli, E. E., and Brown, C. W. 1951. Validity of aptitude tests for predicting trainability of workers. *Personnel Psychol.*, 4, 243–260.

Gibson, J. J. 1941. A critical review of the concept of set in contemporary experimental psychology. *Psychol. Bull.*, 38, 781–817.

Gilbert, G. M. 1942. 1942. Sex differences in musical aptitude and training. *J. gen. Psychol.*, 26, 19–33.

Gilbert, J. A. 1897. Researches upon children and college students. *Iowa Univ. Stud. Psychol.*, 1, 1–39.

Gilbert, J. G. 1941. Memory loss in senescence. *J. abnorm. soc. Psychol.*, 36, 73–86.

Gist, N. P., and Clark, C. D. 1938. Intelligence as a selective factor in rural-urban migration. *Amer. J. Sociol.*, 44, 36–58.

Glanzer, M., and Glaser, R. 1959. Cross-sectional and longitudinal results in a study of age-related changes. *Educ. Psychol. Measmt.*, 19, 89–101.

Glueck, S., and Glueck, E. 1950. *Unraveling juvenile delinquency.* New York: Commonwealth Fund.

Glueck, S., and Glueck, E. 1956. *Physique and delinquency.* New York: Harper & Row.

Goldfarb, W. 1943. Effects of early institutional care on adolescent personality. *J. exp. Educ.*, 12, 106–129.

Goldfarb, W. 1944. Effects of early institutional care on adolescent personality: Rorschach data. *Amer. J. Orthopsychiat.*, 14, 441–447.

Goldman-Eisler, F. 1951. The problem of "orality" and of its origin in early childhood. *J. ment. Sci.*, 97, 765–782.

Goldstein, H. 1935. The biochemical variability of the individual in relation to personality and intelligence. *J. exp. Psychol.*, 18, 348–371.

Goldstein, K., and Scheerer, M. 1941. Abstract and concrete behavior. *Psychol. Monogr.*, 53, No. 2.

Goodenough, E. W. 1957. Interest in persons as an aspect of sex difference in the early years. *Genet. psychol. Monogr.*, 55, 287–323.

Goodenough, F. L. 1926. Racial differences in the intelligence of school children. *J. exp. Psychol.*, 9, 388–397.

Goodenough, F. L. 1927. The consistency of sex differences in mental traits of various ages. *Psychol. Rev.*, 34, 440–462.

Goodenough, F. L. 1936. The measurement of mental functions in primitive groups. *Amer. Anthrop.*, 38, 1–11.

Goodman, C. H. 1943a. Factorial analysis of Thurstone's seven primary mental abilities. *Psychometrika,* 8, 121–129.

Goodman, C. H. 1943b. A factorial analysis of Thurstone's sixteen primary mental abilities tests. *Psychometrika,* 8, 141–151.

Gordon, H. 1923. *Mental and scholastic tests among retarded children.* Educ. Pamphlet No. 44. London: Board of Education.

Gottesman, I. I. 1963a. Genetic aspects of intelligent behavior. In N. R. Ellis (Ed.), *Handbook of Mental Deficiency.* New York: McGraw-Hill. Ch. 7.

Gottesman, I. I. 1963b. Heritability of personality: a demonstration. *Psychol. Monogr.*, 77, No. 9 (Whole No. 572).

Gough, H. G. 1948a. A new dimension of status: I. Development of a personality scale. *Amer. sociol. Rev.*, 13, 401–409.

Gough, H. G. 1948b. A new dimension of status: II. Relationship of the St scale to other variables. *Amer. sociol. Rev.*, 13, 534–537.

Gough, H. G. 1949a. Factors relating to the academic achievement of high school students. *J. educ. Psychol.*, 40, 65–78.

Gough, H. G. 1949b. A new dimension of status: III. Discrepancies between the St scale and "objective" status. *Amer. sociol. Rev.*, 14, 275–281.

Gough, H. G. 1953. What determines the academic achievement of high school students. *J. educ. Res.*, 46, 321–331.

Gough, H. G. 1957. *Manual for the California Psychological Inventory.* Palo Alto, Calif.: Consulting Psychologists Press.

Gough, H. G., and Fink, M. D. 1964. Scholastic achievement among students of average ability, as predicted from the California Psychological Inventory. *Psychology in the Schools,* 1, 375–380.

Gough, H. G., and Woodworth, D. G. 1960. Stylistic variations among professional research scientists. *J. Psychol.*, 49, 87–98.

Gray, S. W. 1959. Perceived similarity to parents and adjustment. *Child Develpm.*, 30, 91–107.

Gray, S. W., and Klaus, R. A. 1963. *Early training project: interim report, November, 1963.* Nashville, Tenn.: George Peabody College for Teachers. (Mimeographed.)

Green, R. F., and Berkowitz, B. 1964. Changes in intellect with age. II. Factorial analysis of Wechsler-Bellevue scores. *J. genet. Psychol.*, 104, 3–18.

Guetzkow, H., and Brozek, J. 1946. Intellectual functions with restricted intakes of B-complex vitamins. *Amer. J. Psychol.*, 59, 358–381.

Guilford, J. P. (Ed.). 1947. *Printed classification tests.* (AAF Aviation Psychology Report, No. 5.) Washington, D.C.: Government Printing Office.

Guilford, J. P. 1947. The discovery of aptitude and achievement variables. *Science,* 106, 279–282.

Guilford, J. P. 1948. Factor analysis in a test development program. *Psychol. Rev.*, 55, 79–94.

Guilford, J. P. 1950. Creativity. *Amer. Psychologist,* 5, 444–454.

Guilford, J. P. 1957. Creative abilities in the arts. *Psychol. Rev.*, 64, 110–118.

Guilford, J. P. 1959a. *Personality.* New York: McGraw-Hill.

Guilford, J. P. 1959b. Three faces of intellect. *Amer. Psychologist,* 14, 469–479.

Guilford, J. P., Christensen, P. R., Bond, N. A., and Sutton, M. A. 1954. A factor analysis study of human interests. *Psychol. Monogr.*, 68, No. 4.

Guilford, J. P., and Guilford, R. B. 1936. Personality factors S, E, and M, and their measurement. *J. Psychol.*, 2, 109–127.

Guilford, J. P., and Guilford, R. B., 1939a. Personality factors D, R, T, and A. *J. abnorm. soc. Psychol.*, 34, 21–36.

Guilford, J. P., and Guilford, R. B., 1939b. Personality factors N and GD. *J. abnorm. soc. Psychol.*, 34, 239–248.

Guilford, J. P., Wilson, R. C., and Christensen, P. R. 1952. A factor-analytic study of creative thinking. II. Administration of tests and analysis of results. *Univ. Sth. Calif. Psychol. Lab. Rep.*, No. 8.

Guilford, J. P., Wilson, R. C., Christensen, P. R., and Lewis, D. J. 1951. A factor-analytic study of creative thinking. I. Hypotheses and descriptions of tests. *Univ. Sth. Calif. Psychol. Lab. Rep.*, No. 4.

Guilford, J. P., and Zimmerman, W. S. 1956. Fourteen dimensions of temperament. *Psychol. Monogr.*, 70, No. 10.

Haggard, E. A. 1954. Social status and intelligence: an experimental study of certain cultural determinants of measured intelligence. *Genet. Psychol. Monogr.*, No. 49.

Hall, C. S. 1934. Emotional behavior in the rat: I. Defecation and urination as measures of individual differences in emotionality. *J. comp. Psychol.*, 18, 385–403.

Hall, C. S. 1936. Emotional behavior in the rat: II. The relationship between need and emotionality. *J. comp. Psychol.*, 22, 61–68.

Hall, C. S. 1937. Emotional behavior in the rat: IV. The relationship between emotionality and stereotyping of behavior. *J. comp. Psychol.*, 24, 369–375.

Hall, C. S. 1951. Individual differences. In C. P. Stone, *Comparative psychology* (3rd Ed.). Englewood Cliffs, N.J.: Prentice-Hall.

Hall, C. S., and Klein, S. J. 1942. Individual differences in aggressiveness in rats. *J. comp. Psychol.*, 33, 371–383.

Hall, G. S. 1905. The Negro in Africa and America. *Ped. Sem.*, 12, 350–368.

Hall, J., and Jones, D. C. 1950. Social grading of occupations. *Brit. J. Sociol.*, 1, 31–55.

Halstead, W. C. 1947. *Brain and intelligence.* Chicago: University of Chicago Press.

Halstead, W. C. 1951. Biological intelligence. *J. Pers.*, 20, 118–130.

Hamilton, M. E. 1943. The contribution of practice differences to group variability. *Arch. Psychol.*, No. 278.

Hammer, E. F. 1954. Comparison of the performance of Negro children and adolescents on two tests of intelligence, one an emergency scale. *J. genet. Psychol.*, 84, 85–93.

Hammond, K. R., and Householder, J. E. 1962. *Introduction to the statistical method.* New York: Knopf.

Hanes, B. 1953. Perceptual learning and age. *J. consult. Psychol.*, 17, 222–224.

Hanfmann, E. 1941. A study of personal patterns in an intellectual performance. *Char. and Pers.*, 9, 315–325.

Hanley, C. 1951. Physique and reputation of junior high school boys. *Child Develpm.*, 22, 247–260.

Harlow, H. F. 1949. The formation of learning sets. *Psychol. Rev.*, 56, 51–65.

Harrell, R. F. 1943. Effect of added thiamin on learning. *Teach. Coll. Contrib. to Educ.*, No. 877.

Harrell, R. F. 1947. Further effects of added thiamin on learning and other processes. *Teach. Coll. Contrib. to Educ.*, No. 928.

Harrell, T. W. 1940. A factor analysis of mechanical ability tests. *Psychometrika,* 5, 17–33.

Harrell, T. W., & Harrell, M. S. 1945. Army general classification test scores for civilian occupations. *Educ. psychol. Measmt.*, 5, 229–239.

Harris, D. B. 1950. Behavior ratings of post-polio cases. *J. consult. Psychol.*, 14, 381–385.

Hartley, R. E. 1960. Children's concepts of male and female roles. *Merrill-Palmer Quart*, 6, 83–91.

Hartshorne, H., and May, M. A. 1928. *Studies in deceit.* New York: Macmillan.

Hartshorne, H., May, M. A., and Maller, J. B. 1929. *Studies in service and self control.* New York: Macmillan.

Hartshorne, H., May, M. A., and Shuttleworth, F. K. 1930. *Studies in the organization of character.* New York: Macmillan.

Hartup, W. W., and Zook, E. A. 1960. Sex-role preferences in three- and four-year-old children. *J. consult. Psychol.*, 24, 420–426.

Havighurst, R. J. 1953. *Human development and education.* New York: Longmans.

Havighurst, R. J., and Breese, F. H. 1947. Relation between ability and social status in a midwestern community: III. Primary mental abilities. *J. educ. Psychol.*, 38, 241–247.

Havighurst, R. J., Bowman, P. H., Liddle, G. P., Matthews, C. V., and Pierce, J. V. 1962. *Growing up in River City.* New York: Wiley.

Havighurst, R. J., Gunther, M. K., and Pratt, I. E. 1946. Environment and the Draw-a-Man Test. *J. abnorm. soc. Psychol.*, 41, 50–63.

Havighurst, R. J., and Janke, L. L. 1944. Relations between ability and social status in a midwestern community: I. Ten-year-old children. *J. educ. Psychol.*, 35, 357–368.

Havighurst, R. J., and Taba, H. 1949. *Adolescent character and personality.* New York: Wiley.

Heath, H. 1952. A factor analysis of women's measurements taken for garment and pattern construction. *Psychometrika,* 17, 87–100.

Hebb, D. O. 1949. *The organization of behavior.* New York: Wiley.

Heber, R. (Ed.). 1959. A manual on terminology and classification in mental retardation. *Monogr. Am. J. ment. Def.*, 64, No. 2.

Hegge, T. G. 1944. The occupational status of higher-grade mental defectives in the present emergency. *Amer. J. ment. Defic.*, 49, 86–98.

Heilman, J. D. 1933. Sex differences in intellectual abilities. *J. educ. Psychol.*, 24, 47–62.

Henry, C. E., and Knott, J. R. 1941. A note on the relationship between "personality" and the alpha rhythm of the electroencephalogram. *J. exp. Psychol.*, 28, 362–366.

Heron, W. T. 1935. The inheritance of maze learning ability in rats. *J. comp. Psychol.*, 19, 77–89.

Herskovits, M. J. 1928. *The American Negro.* New York: Knopf.

Hertz, M. R. 1952. The Rorschach: thirty years after. In D. Brower and L. E. Abt, *Progress in clinical psychology.* New York: Grune & Stratton. Vol. I, Ch. 8.

Hertzman, M. 1939. Specificity of correlations between initial and final abilities in learning. *Psychol. Rev.*, 46, 163–175.

Herzberg, F., and Bouton, A. 1954. A further study of the stability of the Kuder Preference Record. *Educ. psychol. Measmt.*, 14, 90–100, 326–331.

Herzberg, F., and Lepkin M. 1954. A study of sex differences on the Primary Mental Abilities Test. *Educ. psychol. Measmt.*, 14, 687–689.

Hess, R. D. 1955. Controlling culture influence on mental testing: an experimental test. *J. educ. Res.*, 49, 53–58.

Heston, J. C., and Cannell, C. F. 1941. A note on the relation between age and performance of adult subjects on four familiar psychometric tests. *J. appl. Psychol.*, 25, 415–419.

Hieronymus, A. N. 1951. A study of social class motivation: relationships between anxiety for education and certain socio-economic and intellectual variables. *J. educ. Psychol.*, 42, 193–205.

Higgins, C., and Siners, C. 1958. A comparison of Stanford-Binet and Colored Raven Progressive Matrices IQ's for children with low socio-economic status. *J. consult. Psychol.*, 22, 465–468.

Hilden, A. H. 1949. A longitudinal study of intellectual development. *J. Psychol.*, 28, 187–214.

Hildreth, G. 1950. Individual differences. From W. S. Monroe, *Encyclopedia of educational research.* (Rev. Ed.) New York: Macmillan.

Hildreth, G. H., Bixler, H. H., et al. 1948. *Metropolitan Achievement Tests: manual for interpreting.* New York: Harcourt, Brace & World.

Hilgard, J. R. 1933. The effect of early and delayed practice on memory and motor performances studied by the method of co-twin control. *Genet. Psychol. Monogr.*, 14, 493–567.

Hill, A. 1948. Does special education result in improved intelligence for the slow learner? *J. except. Child.*, 14, 207–213; 224.

Himmelweit, H. T., Halsey, A. H. & Oppenheim, A. N. 1952. The views of adolescents on some aspects of the social class structure. *Brit. J. Sociol.*, 3, 148–172.

Hindley, C. B. 1962. Social class influences on the development of ability in the first five years. *Proceedings of the XIV International Congress of Applied Psychology,* Vol. 3, pp. 29–41.

Hinton, R. T., Jr. 1936. The role of the basal metabolic rate in the intelligence of ninety grade school students. *J. educ. Psychol.*, 27, 546–550.

Hinton, R. T., Jr. 1939. A further study on the role of the basal metabolic rate in the intelligence of children. *J. educ. Psychol.*, 30, 309–314.

Hirsch, J. 1959. Studies in experimental behavior genetics: II. Individual differences in geotaxis as a function of chromosome variations in synthesized *Drosophila* populations. *J. comp. physiol. Psychol.*, 52, 304–308.

Hirsch, J. 1962. Individual differences in behavior and their genetic basis. In E. L. Bliss (Ed.), *Roots of Behavior.* New York: Hoeber-Harper. Ch. 1.

Hirsch, J., and Tryon, R. C. 1956. Mass screening and reliable individual measurement in the experimental behavior genetics of lower organisms. *Psychol. Bull.*, 53, 402–410.

Hirsch, N. D. M. 1927. Cephalic index of American-born children of three foreign groups. *Amer. J. phys. Anthrop.*, 10, 79–90.

Hirsch, N. D. M. 1928. An experimental study of the East Kentucky mountaineers: a study in heredity and environment. *Genet. Psychol. Monogr.*, 3, 183–244.

Hirt, M. 1959. Use of the General Aptitude Test Battery to determine aptitude changes with age and to predict job performance. *J. appl. Psychol.*, 43, 36–39.

Hobson, J. R. 1947. Sex differences in Primary Mental Abilities. *J. educ. Res.*, 41, 126–132.

Hofstaetter, P. R. 1954. The changing composition of "intelligence": a study in T-technique. *J. genet. Psychol.*, 85, 159–162.

Holland, J. L., and Nichols, R. 1964. Prediction of academic and extra-curricular achievement in college. *J. educ. Psychol.*, 55, 55–65.

Hollingshead, A. 1949. *Elmtown's Youth*. New York: Wiley.

Hollingshead, A. B., and Redlich, F. C. 1958. *Social class and mental illness*. New York: Wiley.

Hollingworth, L. S. 1922. Differential action upon the sexes of forces which tend to segregate the feeble-minded. *J. abnorm. Psychol.*, 17, 35–37.

Hollingworth, L. S. 1940. Intelligence as an element in personality. *Yearb. nat. Soc. Stud. Educ.*, 39 (I), 271–275.

Hollingworth, L. S. 1942. *Children above 180 IQ*. New York: Harcourt, Brace & World.

Holtzman, W. H., and Brown, W. F. 1953. Study habits and attitudes in the prediction of academic success. *Amer. Psychologist*, 8, 369.

Holzinger, K. J. 1929. The relative effect of nature and nurture influences on twin differences. *J. educ. Psychol.*, 20, 241–248.

Holzman, P. S. 1954. The relation of assimilative tendencies in visual, auditory, and kinesthetic time-error to cognitive attitudes of leveling and sharpening. *J. Pers.*, 22, 375–394.

Holzman, P. S., and Gardner, R. W. 1959. Leveling and repression. *J. abn. soc. Psychol.*, 59, 151–155.

Holzman, P. S., and Klein, G. S. 1954. Cognitive system-principles of leveling and sharpening: individual differences in visual time-error assimilation effects. *J. Psychol.*, 37, 105–122.

Honzik, M. P. 1938. The constancy of mental test performance during the preschool period. *J. genet. Psychol.*, 52, 285–302.

Honzik, M. P. 1951. Sex differences in the occurrence of materials in the play constructions of preadolescents. *Child Develpm.*, 22, 15–35.

Honzik, M. P. 1957. Developmental studies of parent-child resemblance in intelligence. *Child Develpm.*, 28, 215–228.

Honzik, M. P., McFarlane, J. W., and Allen, L. 1948. The stability of mental test performance between two and eighteen years. *J. exp. Educ.*, 17, 309–324.

Honzik, M. P., and McKee, J. P. 1962. The sex difference in thumbsucking. *J. Pediatrics*, 61, 726–732.

Hornaday, J. A., and Kuder, G. F. 1961. A study of male occupational interest scales applied to women. *Educ. Psychol. Measmt.*, 21, 859–864.

Horst, P. 1957. Differential prediction in college admissions. *Coll. Board Rev.*, 33, 19–23.

Howells, W. W. 1952. A factorial study of constitutional type. *Amer. J. phys. Anthrop.*, 10, 91–118.

Hughes, J. L., and McNamara, J. J. 1958. Limitations on the use of the Strong sales keys for selection and counseling. *J. appl. Psychol.*, 42, 93–96.

Hunt, J. McV. 1961. *Intelligence and experience.* New York: Ronald.
Husen, T. 1951. The influence of schooling upon IA. *Theoria,* 17, 61–88.
Husen, T. 1953. The stability of intelligence test scores. *Acta Psychol.,* 9, 53–81.
Husen, T. 1959. *Psychological twin research. I. A methodological study.* Stockholm: Almquist and Wiksells.
Husen, T. 1960. Abilities of twins. *Scand. J. Psychol.,* 1, 125–135.
Irwin, O. C. 1948. Infant speech: the effect of family occupational status and of age on the use of sound types. *J. Speech Hearing Disorders,* 13, 224–226, 320–323.
Iscoe, I., and Garden, J. A. 1961. Field dependence, manifest anxiety, and sociometric status in children. *J. consult. Psychol.,* 25, 184.
Jacob, P. E., and Flink, J. J. 1962. Values and their function in decision-making. *American Behavioral Scientist,* Supplement, 5, No. 9.
Jacobson, W. E. 1945. First impressions of classmates. *J. appl. Psychol.,* 29, 142–155.
Jaensch, E. R. 1938. *Der Gegentypus.* Leipzig: Barth.
Jahoda, G. 1956. Sex differences in preferences for shapes: a cross cultural replication. *Brit. J. Psychol.,* 47, 126–132.
James, W. 1890. *The principles of psychology.* New York: Holt, Rinehart and Winston.
James, W. 1927. Great men and their environment. In *The will to believe and other essays in popular philosophy.* New York: Longmans. Pp. 216–254.
Jamieson, E., and Sandiford, P. 1928. The mental capacity of Southern Ontario Indians. *J. educ. Psychol.,* 19, 313–328, 536–551.
Janke, L. L., and Havighurst, R. J. 1945. Relations between ability and social status in a midwestern community: II. Sixteen-year-old boys and girls. *J. educ. Psychol.,* 36, 499–509.
Janoff, I. Z., Beck, L. H., and Child, I. L. 1950. The relation of somatotype to reaction time, resistance to pain, and expressive movement. *J. Pers.,* 18, 454–460.
Jastrow, J. 1891. Some anthropometric and psychologic tests on college students—a preliminary survey. *Amer. J. Psychol.,* 4, 420–428.
Jenkins, J. G. 1946. Validity for what? *J. consult. Psychol.,* 10, 93–98.
Jenkins, M. D. 1948. The upper limit of ability among American Negroes. *Sci. Mon.,* 66, 399–401.
Jepsen, V. L. 1951. Scholastic proficiency and vocational success. *Educ. psychol. Measmt.,* 11, 616–628.
Jerome, E. A. 1959. Age and learning—experimental studies. In J. E. Birren (Ed.), *Handbook of aging and the individual.* Chicago: University of Chicago Press. Ch. 19.
Johnson, M. M. 1963. Sex role learning in the nuclear family. *Child Develpm.,* 34, 319–333.
Jolles, I. 1947. The diagnostic implications of Rorschach's test in case studies of mental defectives. *Genet. Psychol. Monogr.,* 36, 89–198.
Jones, A. W. 1941. *Life, liberty, and property.* Philadelphia: Lippincott.
Jones, H. E. 1935. The galvanic skin reflex as related to overt emotional expression. *Amer. J. Psychol.,* 47, 241–251.
Jones, H. E. 1950. The study of patterns of emotional expression. In M. L.

Reymert (Ed.), *Feelings and emotions*. New York: McGraw-Hill. Pp. 161–168.

Jones, H. E., and Conrad, H. W. 1933. The growth and decline of intelligence. *Genet. Psychol. Monogr.*, 13, 223–298.

Jones, H. E., Conrad, H. W., and Blanchard, M. B. 1932. Environmental handicap in mental test performance. *Univ. Calif. Publ. in Psychol.*, 5, No. 3, 63–99.

Jones, L. V. 1949. A factor analysis of the Stanford-Binet at four age levels. *Psychometrika*, 14, 299–331.

Jones, M. C., and Bayley, N. 1950. Physical maturing among boys as related to behavior. *J. educ. Psychol.*, 41, 129–148.

Jung, C. G. 1923. *Psychological types*. London: Routledge and Kegan Paul.

Justman, J., and Aronov, M. 1955. The Davis-Eells Games as a measure of the intelligence of poor readers. *J. educ. Psychol.*, 46, 418–422.

Kagan, J. 1964. American longitudinal research on psychological development. *Child Develpm.*, 35, 1–32.

Kagan, J., and Moss, H. A. 1962. *Birth to maturity*. New York: Wiley.

Kagan, J., Moss, H. A., and Sigel, I. E. 1963. Psychological significance of styles of conceptualization. *Monogr. soc. Res. Child Develpm.*, 28, No. 2, 73–112.

Kagan, J., Sontag, L. W., Baker, C. T., and Nelson, V. L. 1958. Personality and IQ change. *J. abnorm. soc. Psychol.*, 56, 261–266.

Kallman, F. J. 1950. The genetics of psychoses. *Amer. J. hum. Genet.*, 2, 385–390.

Kallman, F. J. 1952. Twin and sibship study of overt male homosexuality. *Amer. J. hum. Genet.*, 4, 136–146.

Kallman, F. J. 1953. *Heredity in health and mental disorder; principles of psychiatric genetics in the light of comparative twin studies*. New York: Norton.

Kallman, F. J. 1959. Psychogenetic studies of twins. In S. Koch (Ed.), *Psychology: a study of a science*, Vol. 3. Pp. 328–362.

Kallman, F. J., Feingold, L., and Bondy, E. 1951. Comparative adaptational, social, and psychometric data on the life histories of senescent twin pairs. *Amer. J. hum. Genet.*, 3, 65–73.

Kardiner, A., and Ovesey, L. 1951. *The mark of oppression*. New York: Norton.

Karon, B. P. 1958. *The Negro personality*. Princeton, N.J.: Springer.

Kelly, E. L. 1955. Consistency of the adult personality. *Amer. Psychologist*, 10, 659–681.

Kempf, G. A., and Collins, S. D. 1929. A study of the relation between mental and physical status of children in two counties of Illinois. *U. S. Pub. Reports*, 44, 1743–1784.

Kennedy, R. J. R. 1948. *The social adjustment of morons in a Connecticut city*. Hartford, Conn.: Mansfield-Southbury Training Schools, Social Service Department.

Kennedy, W. A., and Lindner, R. S. 1964. A normative study of the Goodenough Draw-a-Man Test on southeastern Negro elementary school children. *Child Develpm.*, 35, 33–62.

Kennedy, W. A., Van de Riet, V., and White, J. C. 1963. A normative sample of intelligence and achievement of Negro elementary school children in the southeastern United States. *Monogr. Soc. Res. Child Develpm.*, 28, No. 6.

Kephart, N. C. 1939. The effect of a highly specialized program upon the IQ in high-grade mentally deficient boys. *Proc. Amer. Assn. Ment. Defic.*, 63, 216–221.

Keys, A., et al. 1950. *The biology of human starvation.* Minneapolis: University of Minnesota Press.

Kimber, J. A. M. 1947. The insight of college students into the items on a personality test. *Educ. Psychol. Measmt.*, 7, 411–420.

Kincaid, M. A. 1925. A study of individual differences in learning. *Psychol. Rev.*, 32, 34–53.

King, D. P., and Norrell, G. 1964. A factorial study of the Kuder Preference Record—Occupational, Form D. *Educ. Psychol. Measmt.*, 24, 57–64.

King, F. J., Bowman, B. H., and Moreland, H. J. 1961. Some intellectual correlates of biochemical variability. *Behav. Sci.*, 6, 297–302.

King, L. A. 1958. Factors associated with vocational interest profile stability. *J. appl. Psychol.*, 42, 261–263.

Kinsey, A. C., Pomeroy, W. B., and Martin, C. E. 1948. *Sexual behavior in the human male.* Philadelphia: Saunders.

Kirchner, W. K. 1961. "Real-life" faking on the Strong Vocational Interest Blank. *J. appl. Psychol.*, 45, 273–276.

Kirk, S. A. 1948. An evaluation of the study by Bernadine C. Schmidt entitled: "Changes in personal, social, and intellectual behavior of children originally classified as feebleminded." *Psychol. Bull.*, 45, 321–333.

Kirk, S. A. 1958. *Early education of the mentally retarded.* Urbana: University of Illinois Press.

Klein, G. S. 1951. The personal world through perception. In R. R. Blake and G. V. Ramsey (Eds.), *Perception: an approach to personality.* New York: Ronald. Ch. 12.

Klein, G. S., Gardner, R. W., and Schlesinger, H. J. 1962. Tolerance for unrealistic experiences: a study of the generality of cognitive control. *Brit. J. Psychol.*, 53, 41–55.

Klein, G. S., and Schlesinger, H. J. 1949. Where is the perceiver in the perceptual theory? *J. Pers.*, 18, 32–47.

Klineberg, O. 1928. An experimental study of speed and other factors in "racial" differences. *Arch. Psychol.*, No. 93.

Klineberg, O. 1931. A study of psychological differences between "racial" and national groups in Europe. *Arch. Psychol.*, No. 132.

Klineberg, O. 1935. *Negro intelligence and selective migration.* New York: Columbia University Press.

Klineberg, O. 1963. Negro-white differences in intelligence test performance: a new look at an old problem. *Amer. Psychol.*, 18, 198–203.

Klineberg, O., Asch, S. E., and Block, H. 1934. An experimental study of constitutional types. *Genet. Psychol. Monogr.*, 16, 140–221.

Kluckhohn, F. R., and Strodtbeck, F. L. 1961. *Variations in value orientations.* New York: Harper & Row.

Klugman, S. F. 1944. The effect of money incentive versus praise upon the reliability and obtained scores of the Revised Stanford-Binet Test. *J. gen. Psychol.*, 30, 255–269.

Knapp, R. H., Brimmer, J., and White, M. 1959. Educational level, class status, and aesthetic preference. *J. soc. Psychol.*, 50, 277–284.

Knott, J. R., Friedman, H., and Bardsley, R. 1942. Some electroencephalographic correlates of intelligence in eight-year- and twelve-year-old children. *J. exp. Psychol.*, 30, 380–391.

Koch, A. M. 1935. The limits of learning ability in Cebus monkeys. *Genet. Psychol. Monogr.*, 17, 164–234.

Kogan, N., and Wallach, M. A. 1964. *Risk-taking: a study in cognition and personality.* New York: Holt, Rinehart and Winston.

Kounin, J. S. 1943. Intellectual development and rigidity. In R. G. Barker, J. S. Kounin, and H. F. Wright, *Child behavior and development.* New York: McGraw-Hill. Ch. 11.

Kraepelin, E. 1895. Der psychologische Versuch in der Psychiatrie. *Psychol. Arbeiten*, 1, 1–91.

Krech, D., and Calvin, A. 1953. Levels of perceptual organization and cognition. *J. abnorm. soc. Psychol.*, 48, 394–400.

Kreezer, G. L. 1940. The relation of intelligence level and the electroencephalogram. *Yearb. nat. Soc. Stud. Educ.*, 39 (I), 130–133.

Kreezer, G. L., and Smith, F. W. 1950. The relation of the alpha rhythm of the electroencephalogram and intelligence level in the non-differentiated familial type of mental deficiency. *J. Psychol.*, 29, 47–51.

Kretschmer, E. 1925. *Physique and character.* New York: Harcourt, Brace & World.

Kretschmer, E. 1931. *The psychology of men of genius.* New York: Harcourt, Brace & World.

Kuhlen, R. G. 1940. Social change: a neglected factor in psychological studies of the life span. *Sch. and Soc.*, 52, 14–16.

Kuhlen, R. G. 1959. Aging and life adjustment. In J. E. Birren, *Handbook of aging and the individual.* Chicago: University of Chicago Press. Ch. 24.

Kuhlmann, F. 1921. The results of repeated mental reexaminations of 639 feebleminded over a period of ten years. *J. appl. Psychol.*, 5, 195–224.

Kutner, B., Fanshel, D., Togo, A. M., and Langner, T. S. 1956. *Five hundred over sixty: a community survey on aging.* New York: Russell Sage Foundation.

Lacey, J. I. 1950. Individual differences in somatic response patterns. *J. comp. physiol. Psychol.*, 43, 338–350.

Lacey, J. I. 1959. Psycho-physiological approaches to the evaluation of psychotherapeutic process and outcome. In *Research in psychotherapy.* Washington: American Psychological Association. Pp. 160–208.

Lacey, J. I., and Lacey, B. C. 1958. Verification and extension of the principle of anatonomic response stereotypy. *Amer. J. Psychol.*, 71, 50–73.

Lacey, J. I., and Van Lehn, R. 1952. Differential emphasis in somatic response to stress. *Psychosom. Med.*, 14, 71–81.

Lambeth, M., and Lanier, L. H. 1933. Race differences in speed of reaction. *J. genet. Psychol.*, 42, 255–297.

Lange-Eichbaum, W. 1931. *The problem of genius.* London: Kegan Paul.

Lansky, L. M., Crandall, V. J., Kagan, J., and Baker, C. T. 1961. Sex differences in aggression and its correlates in middle class adolescents. *Child develpm.*, 32, 45–58.

Lansky, L. M., and McKay, G. 1963. Sex role preferences of kindergarten boys and girls: some contradictory results. Paper presented at meeting of Midwestern Psychological Assn., May, 1963.

Laycock, F., and Caylor, J. S. 1964. Physiques of gifted children and their less gifted siblings. *Child Develpm.*, 35, 63–74.

Layton, W. L. (Ed.). 1960. *The Strong Vocational Interest Blank—research and uses.* Minneapolis: University of Minnesota Press.

Leahy, A. M. 1935. Nature-nurture and intelligence. *Genet. Psychol. Monogr.*, 17, 235–308.

Learned, W. S., and Wood, B. D. 1938. *The student and his knowledge.* New York: Carnegie Foundation for the Advancement of Teaching.

Leary, T. 1957. *Interpersonal diagnosis of personality.* New York: Ronald.

Lee, E. S. 1951. Negro intelligence and selective migration: a Philadelphia test of the Klineberg hypothesis. *Amer. sociol. Rev.*, 16, 227–233.

Lee, L. C., Kagan, J., and Rabson, A. 1963. Influence of a preference for analytic categorization upon concept acquisition. *Child Develpm.*, 34, 433–442.

Lehman, H. C. 1953. *Age and achievement.* Princeton: Princeton University Press.

Lehman, H. C. 1954. Men's creative production rate at different ages and in different countries. *Sci. Mon.*, 78, 321–326.

Lehman, H. C. 1958. The chemist's most creative years. *Science*, 127, 1213–1222.

LeJeune, J., Turpin, R., and Gautier, M. 1959. Le mongolisme, premier example d'aberration autosomique humaine. *Ann. Génétique*, 2, 41–49.

Lessing, E. E. 1959. Mother-daughter similarity on the Kuder vocational interest scales. *Educ. Psychol. Measmt.*, 19, 395–400.

Levin, H., and Sears, R. R. 1956. Identification with parents as a determinant of doll play aggression. *Child Develpm.*, 27, 135–153.

Levine, P. R., and Wallen, R. 1954. Adolescent vocational interests and later occupation. *J. appl. Psychol.*, 38, 428–431.

Levy, D. M. 1929. A method of integrating physical and psychiatric examination: with special studies of body interest, overprotection, response to growth, and sex differences. *Amer. J. Psychiat.*, 9, 121–194.

Levy, D. M. 1932. Body interest in children and hypochondriasis. *Amer. J. Psychiat.*, 12, 295–315.

Levy, D. M. 1953. Psychosomatic studies of some aspects of maternal behavior. In C. Kluckhohn and H. A. Murray, *Personality* (2nd Ed.). New York: Knopf. Ch. 6.

Lewis, H. 1954. *Deprived children.* London: Oxford University Press.

Lewis, W. D. 1941. A comparative study of the personalities, interests, and home backgrounds of gifted children of superior and inferior educational achievement. *J. genet. Psychol.*, 59, 207–218.

Lewis, W. D. 1945. Sex distribution of intelligence among inferior and superior children. *J. genet. Psychol.*, 67, 67–75.

Lichte, W. H. 1952. Shape constancy: dependence upon angle of rotation; individual differences. *J. exp. Psychol.*, 43, 49–57.

Lipsett, L., and Wilson, J. W. 1954. Do "suitable" interests and mental ability lead to job satisfaction? *Educ. Psychol. Measmt.*, 14, 373–380.

Littman, R. A., Moore, R. C. A., and Pierce-Jones, J. 1957. Social class differences in child rearing: a third community for comparison with Chicago and Newton. *Amer. sociol. Rev.*, 22, 694–704.

Livesay, T. M. 1944. Relation of economic status to "intelligence" and to the racial derivation of high school seniors in Hawaii. *Amer. J. Psychol.*, 57, 77–82.

Livson, N., and Bronson, W. C. 1961. An exploration of patterns of impulse control in early adolescence. *Child Develpm.*, 32, 75–88.

Livson, N., and Krech, D. 1956. Dynamic systems, perceptual differentiation, and intelligence. *J. Person.*, 25, 46–58.

Loevinger, J. 1940. Intelligence as related to socio-economic factors. *Yearb. nat. Soc. Stud. Educ.*, 39 (I), 159–210.

Loevinger, J. 1943. On the proportional contributions of differences in nature and in nurture to differences in intelligence. *Psychol. Bull.*, 40, 725–756.

Lombroso, C. 1896. *The man of genius.* London: Scott.

Longstaff, H. P. 1948. Fakability of the Strong Interest Blank and the Kuder Preference Record. *J. appl. Psychol.*, 32, 360–369.

Lorge, I. 1936. The influence of the test upon the nature of mental decline as a function of age. *J. educ. Psychol.*, 27, 100–110.

Lorge, I. 1945. Schooling makes a difference. *Teach. Coll. Rec.*, 46, 483–492.

Lorge, I. 1949. Trends in the measurement of achievement. In W. T. Donahue, C. H. Coombs, and R. W. M. Travers, *The measurement of student adjustment and achievement.* Ann Arbor: University of Michigan Press. Pp. 85–96.

Lorimer, F. 1952. Trends in capacity for intelligence. *Eugen. News*, 37, 17–24.

Lovell, C. 1945. A study of the factor structure of thirteen personality variables. *Educ. psychol. Measmt.*, 5, 335–350.

Lowenfeld, V. 1945. Tests for visual and haptical aptitudes. *Amer. J. Psychol.*, 58, 100–111.

Lubin, A. 1950. A note on Sheldon's table of correlations between temperamental traits. *Brit. J. Psychol.*, Statist. Sect., 3, 186–189.

Lurie, L. A. 1938. Endocrinology and the understanding and treatment of the exceptional child. *J. Amer. Med. Assn.*, 110, 1531–1536.

Lynd, R. S., and Lynd, H. M. 1929. *Middletown.* New York: Harcourt.

Lynd, R. S. 1937. *Middletown in transition.* New York: Harcourt, Brace & World.

Lynn, D. B. 1962. Sex role and parental identification. *Child Develpm.*, 33, 555–564.

McAndrew, M. B. 1943. An experimental investigation of young children's ideas of causality. *Stud. Psychol. Psychiat. Cathol. Univ. Amer.*, 6, No. 2.

McArthur, C. 1954. Long term validity of the Strong Interest Test in two subcultures. *J. appl. Psychol.*, 38, 346–353.

McArthur, C. 1955. Personality differences between middle and upper classes. *J. abnorm. soc. Psychol.*, 50, 247–254.

McClearn, G. E. 1961. Genotype and mouse activity. *J. comp. physiol. Psychol.*, 54, 674–676.

McClearn, G. E. 1964. Genetics and behavior development. In M. L. Hoffman and L. W. Hoffman, *Review of child development research*. New York: Russell Sage.

McClelland, D. C., Atkinson, J. W., Clark, R. A., and Lowell, E. L. 1953. *The achievement motive*. New York: Appleton-Century-Crofts.

McClelland, D. C., Baldwin, A. L., Bronfenbrenner, U., Strodtbeck, F. L. 1958. *Talent and society*. Princeton, N.J.: Van Nostrand.

McConnell, J. W. 1942. *The evolution of social classes*. Washington: American Council on Public Affairs.

McConnell, T. R. 1940. A study of the extent of measurement of differential objectives of instruction. *J. educ. Res.*, 33, 662–670.

McCoy, R. A. 1955. Stability and change of measured vocational interests of high school students. *Dissertation Abstr.*, 15, 85–86.

McCulloch, T. L. 1947. Reformulation of the problem of mental deficiency. *Amer. J. ment. Defic.*, 52, 130–136.

McElroy, W. A. 1954. A sex difference in preference for shapes. *Brit. J. Psychol.*, 45, 209–216.

McGraw, M. B. 1935. *Growth: a study of Johnny and Jimmy*. New York: Appleton-Century.

McGuire, C. 1961. Sex role and community variability in test performance. *J. educ. Psychol.*, 52, 61–73.

McGurk, F. C. 1953. On white and Negro test performance and socio-economic factors. *J. abnorm. soc. Psychol.*, 48, 448–450.

McIntosh, W. J. 1949. Follow-up study of one thousand non-academic boys. *J. except. Child.*, 15, 166–170.

McKee, J. P., and Sheriffs, A. C. 1957. The differential evaluation of males and females. *J. Person.*, 25, 356–371.

McKee, J. P., and Turner, W. S. 1961. The relation of "drive" ratings in adolescence to CPI and EPPS scores in adulthood. *Vita Humana*, 4, 1–14.

McNeil, J. D., and Keisler, E. R. 1961. Individual differences and effectiveness of auto-instruction at the primary grade level. *Calif. J. educ. Psychol.*, 12, 160–164.

McNemar, Q. 1933. Twin resemblances in motor skills, and the effect of practice thereon. *J. genet. Psychol.*, 42, 70–99.

McNemar, Q. 1942. *The revision of the Stanford-Binet scale*. Boston: Houghton-Mifflin.

McNemar, Q. 1945. Note on Wellman's reanalysis of IQ changes of orphanage preschool children. *J. genet. Psychol.*, 67, 215–219.

McNemar, Q., and Terman, L. M. 1936. Sex differences in variational tendency. *Genet. Psychol. Monogr.*, 18, 1–65.

McPherson, M. W. 1948. A survey of experimental studies of learning in individuals who achieve subnormal ratings on standardized psychometric measures. *Amer. J. ment. Defic.*, 52, 232–254.

McPherson, M. W. 1958. Learning and mental deficiency. *Amer. J. ment. Defic.*, 62, 870–877.

McQueen, R., and Browning, C. 1960. The intelligence and educational achievement of a matched sample of white and Negro students. *School and Society*, 88, 327–329.

Machover, S. 1943. Cultural and racial variations in patterns of intellect. *Teach. Coll. Contrib. to Educ.*, No. 875.

Magaret, A., and Thompson, C. W. 1950. Differential test responses of normal, superior, and mentally defective subjects. *J. abnorm. soc. Psychol.*, 45, 163–167.

Maher, B. A. 1963. Intelligence and brain damage. In N. R. Ellis (Ed.), *Handbook of mental deficiency*. Ch. 6.

Maller, J. B. 1934. General and specific factors in character. *J. soc. Psychol.*, 5, 97–102.

Maller, J. B., and Zubin, J. 1932. The effect of motivation upon intelligence test scores. *J. genet. Psychol.*, 41, 136–151.

Mallinson, G. G., and Crumrine, W. M. 1952. An investigation of the stability of interests of high school students. *J. educ. Res.*, 45, 369–383.

Mallory, J. N. 1922. A study of the relation of some physical defects to achievement in the elementary school. *George Peabody Coll. for Tchrs. Contrib. to Educ.*, No. 9.

Martin, H. G. 1945. The construction of the Guilford-Martin inventory of factors G-A-M-I-N. *J. appl. Psychol.*, 29, 298–300.

Masland, R. L., Sarason, S. B., and Gladwin, T. 1958. *Mental subnormality: biological, psychological, and cultural factors.* New York: Basic Books.

Mauldin, W. P. 1940. Selective migration from small towns. *Amer. sociol. Rev.*, 5, 748–758.

Mead, M. 1935. *Sex and temperament in three primitive societies.* New York: Morrow.

Mead, M. 1949. *Male and female*. New York: Morrow.

Medawar, P. B. 1960. *The future of man.* New York: Basic Books.

Meehl, P. E. 1954. *Clinical vs. statistical prediction.* Minneapolis: University of Minnesota Press.

Meili, R. 1946. L'Analyse de l'intelligence. *Archives de Psychologie,* 31, 1–64.

Meili, R. 1949. Sur la nature de facteurs d'intelligence. *Acta Psychol.*, 6, 40–58.

Messick, S., and Jackson, D. N. 1961. Acquiescence and the factorial interpretation of the MMPI. *Psychol. Bull.*, 58, 299–304.

Metfessel, M. 1940. Relationships of heredity and environment in behavior. *J. Psychol.*, 10, 177–198.

Meyer, W. J. 1960. The stability of patterns of primary mental abilities among junior high and senior high school students. *Educ. Psychol. Measmt.*, 20, 795–800.

Meyer, W. J., and Bendig, A. W. 1961. A longitudinal study of the Primary Mental Abilities Test. *J. educ. Psychol.*, 52, 50–60.

Meyers, C. E., and Dingman, H. F. 1960. The structure of abilities at the preschool ages: hypothesized domains. *Psychol. Bull.*, 57, 514–532.

Meyers, C. E., Orpet, R. E., Attwell, A. A., and Dingman, H. F. 1962. Primary abilities at mental age six. *Monogr. Soc. Res. Child Develpm.*, 27, No. 1 (Whole No. 82).

Michael, W. B. 1949. Factor analysis of tests and criteria: a comparative study of two AAF pilot populations. *Psychol. Monogr.*, 63, No. 3.

Michael, W. B. 1954. A suggested research approach to the identification of psychological processes associated with spatial-visualization factors. *Educ. psychol., Measmt.*, 14, 401–406.

Miele, J. A. 1958. Sex differences in intelligence: the relationship of sex to intelligence as measured by the Wechsler Adult Intelligence Scale and the Wechsler Intelligence Scale for Children. *Dissert. Abstr.*, 18, 2213.

Miles, C. C. 1935. Sex in social psychology. In C. Murchison (Ed.), *Handbook of social psychology*. Worcester, Mass.: Clark University Press. Ch. 16.

Miles, C. C. 1954. Gifted children. In *Manual of child psychology*. New York: Wiley.

Miles, C. C., and Miles, W. R. 1932. The correlation of intelligence scores and chronological age from early to late maturity. *Amer. J. Psychol.*, 44, 44–78.

Miles, C. C., and Wolfe, L. S. 1936. Childhood physical and mental health records of historical geniuses. *Psychol. Monogr.*, 47, 390–400.

Miles, W. R. 1933. Age and human ability. *Psychol. Rev.*, 40, 99–123.

Miller, D. E., and Swanson, G. E. 1960. *Inner conflict and defense*. New York: Holt, Rinehart and Winston.

Milner, E. 1949. Effects of sex role and social status on the early adolescent personality. *Genet. Psychol. Monogr.*, 40, 231–325.

Milton, G. A. 1957. The effects of sex-role identification upon problem-solving skills. *J. abnorm. soc. Psychol.*, 55, 208–212.

Mitchell, J. V. 1956. A comparison of the factorial structure of cognitive functions for a high and low status group. *J. educ. Psychol.*, 47, 397–414.

Montagu, M. F. A. 1945. Intelligence of northern Negroes and southern whites in the first World War. *Amer. J. Psychol.*, 58, 161–188.

Moore, J. E. 1941. A comparison of Negro and white children on speed of reaction on an eye-hand coordination test. *J. genet. Psychol.*, 59, 225–228.

Morgan, C. T. 1947. The hoarding instinct. *Psychol. Rev.*, 54, 335–341.

Morris, C. 1956. *Varieties of human value*. Chicago: University of Chicago Press.

Mosier, M. F., and Kuder, G. F. 1949. Personal preference differences among occupational groups. *J. appl. Psychol.*, 33, 231–239.

Moursy, E. M. 1952. The hierarchical organization of cognitive levels. *Brit. J. Psychol., Statist. Sect.*, 5, 151–180.

Muench, G. A. 1944. A follow-up of mental defectives after eighteen years. *J. abnorm. soc. Psychol.*, 39, 407–418.

Mullen, F. A. 1952. Mentally retarded youth find jobs. *Personnel Guid. J.*, 31, 20–25.

Mundy-Castle, A. C. 1958. Electrophysiological correlates of intelligence. *J. Pers.*, 26, 184–199.

Munroe, R. L. 1945. Prediction of the adjustment and academic performance of college students by a modification of the Rorschach method. *Applied Psychol. Monogr.*, No. 7. Stanford: Stanford University Press.

Münsterberg, H. 1891. Zur Individualpsychologie. *Centralblatt für Nervenheilkunde und Psychiatrie*, 14, 196–198.

Murphy, G. 1958. *Human potentialities*. New York: Basic Books.

Murray, H. A. 1938. *Explorations in personality*. New York: Oxford University Press.

Mussen, P. H., and Distler, L. 1959. Masculinity, identification, and father-son relationships. *J. abnorm. soc. Psychol.,* 59, 350–356.

Mussen, P., and Rutherford, E. 1963. Parent-child relations and parental personality in relation to sex-role preferences. *Child Develpm.,* 34, 589–607.

Myers, C. S. 1947. A new analysis of intelligence. *Occup. Psychol.,* London, 21, 17–23.

Myers, I. B. 1962. *The Myers-Briggs Type Indicator, manual.* Princeton: Educ. Testing Serv.

Myers, R. C. 1952. Biographical factors and academic achievement: an experimental investigation. *Educ. psychol. Measmt.,* 12, 415–426.

Neidt, C. O., and Merrill, W. R. 1951. Relative effectiveness of two types of response to items of a scale on attitudes toward education. *J. educ. Psychol.,* 42, 432–436.

Newell, A., Shaw, J. C., and Simon, H. A. 1958. Elements of a theory of human problem solving. *Psychol. Rev.,* 65, 151–166.

Newman, H. H., Freeman, F. N., and Holzinger, K. J. 1937. *Twins: a study of heredity and environment.* Chicago: University of Chicago Press.

Newton, E. S. 1960. Verbal destitution: the pivotal barrier to learning. *J. Negro Educ.,* 29, 497–499.

Nichols, R. C. 1964. The National Merit twin study. (Paper presented at American Psychological Association, Sept. 9, 1964.)

Nisbet, J. D. 1953. *Family environment.* Occasional Papers on Eugenics, No. 8. London: Cassell.

Nisbet, J. D. 1957. Symposium: contributions to intelligence testing and the theory of intelligence: IV. Intelligence and age: retesting with twenty-four years interval. *Brit. J. educ. Psychol.,* 27, 190–198.

Noll, V. H. 1951. Simulation by college students of a prescribed pattern on a personality scale. *Educ. Psychol. Measmt.,* 11, 478–488.

Noll, V. H. 1960. Relation of scores on Davis-Eells Games to socio-economic status, intelligence test results, and school achievement. *Educ. Psychol. Measmt.,* 20, 119–130.

Norman, R. D. 1953. Sex differences and other aspects of young superior adult performance on the Wechsler-Bellevue. *J. consult. Psychol.,* 17, 411–418.

Northby, A. S. 1958. Sex differences in high school scholarship. *School and Society,* 86, 63–64.

Nosow, S. 1962. Social correlates of occupational membership. In S. Nosow and W. H. Form (Eds.), *Man, work, and society.* New York: Basic Books. Ch. 15.

Nugent, F. A. 1961. The relationship of discrepancies between interest and aptitude scores to other selected personality variables. *Pers. Guid. J.,* 39, 388–395.

Nugent, F. A. 1962. Interest-aptitude congruency: a theoretical synthesis and a suggested method of investigation. *Pers. Guid. J.,* 40, 523–530.

Occupational Analysis Division, War Manpower Commission. 1945. Factor analysis of occupational aptitude tests. *Educ. psychol. Measmt.,* 5, 147–155.

O'Connor, N., and Tizard, J. 1956. *The social problem of mental deficiency.* London: Pergamon Press.

Odum, H. W. 1910. *Social and mental traits of the Negro.* New York: Columbia University Press.

Oehrn, A. 1889. *Experimentelle Studien zur Individualpsychologie.* Dorpater Dissertation. (Also published in *Psychol. Arbeiten,* 1895, 1, 92–152.)

Oetzel, R. M. 1962. Selected bibliography on sex differences. Stanford: Stanford University. (Mimeographed.)

Olander, H. T., Van Wagenen, M. J., and Bishop, H. M. 1949. Predicting arithmetic achievement. *J. educ. Res.,* 43, 66–73.

O'Shea, H. E., Elsom, K. O'S., and Higbe, R. V. 1942. Studies of the B vitamins in the human subject; mental changes in experimental deficiency. *Amer. J. Med. Sci.,* 203, 388–397.

Osler, S. F., and Fivel, M. W. 1961. Concept attainment: I. The role of age and intelligence in concept attainment by induction. *J. exp. Psychol.,* 62, 1–8.

Osler, S. F., and Trautman, G. E. 1961. Concept attainment: II. Effect of stimulus complexity upon concept attainment at two levels of intelligence. *J. exp. Psychol.,* 62, 9–13.

Otis, A. S. 1939. *Otis Quick-Scoring Mental Ability Tests. Manual of Directions for Alpha Test.* New York: Harcourt, Brace & World.

Owens, W. A., Jr. 1942a. Intra-individual difference versus inter-individual differences in motor skills. *Educ. psychol. Measmt.,* 2, 299–314.

Owens, W. A., Jr. 1942b. A new technic in studying the effects of practice upon individual differences. *J. exp. Psychol.,* 30, 180–183.

Owens, W. A., Jr. 1942c. A note on the effects of practice upon trait differences in motor skills. *J. educ. Psychol.,* 33, 144–147.

Owens, W. A., Jr. 1953. Age and mental abilities: a longitudinal study. *Genet. Psychol. Monogr.,* 48, 3–54.

Page, J. D. 1940. The effect of nursery-school attendance upon subsequent IQ. *J. Psychol.,* 10, 221–230.

Parnell, R. W. 1958. *Behaviour and physique.* London: Arnold.

Passow, A. H. (Ed.). 1963. *Education in depressed areas.* New York: Teachers College, Columbia University, Bureau of Publications.

Pastore, N. 1949a. The genetics of schizophrenia. *Psychol. Bull.,* 46, 285–302.

Pastore, N. 1949b. *The nature-nurture controversy.* New York: King's Crown Press, Columbia University.

Patel, A. S., and Gordon, J. E. 1960. Some personal and situational determinants of yielding to influence. *J. abnorm. soc. Psychol.,* 61, 411–418.

Paterson, D. G. 1930. *Physique and intellect.* New York: Century.

Paterson, D. G., Elliott, R. M., Anderson, L. D., Toops, H. A., and Heidbreder, E. 1930. *Minnesota mechanical ability tests.* Minneapolis: University of Minnesota Press.

Payne, D. E., and Mussen, P. H. 1956. Parent-child relations and father identification among adolescent boys. *J. abnorm. soc. Psychol.,* 52, 358–362.

Peck, R. F. 1959. Measuring the mental health of normal adults. *Genet. Psychol. Monogr.,* 60, 197–255.

Peck, R. F., and Havighurst, R. J. 1960. *The psychology of character development.* New York: Wiley.

Peel, E. A. 1959. The measurement of interests by verbal methods. *Brit. J. Statist. Psychol.,* 12, 105–118.

Pemberton, C. L. 1952a. The closure factors related to other cognitive processes. *Psychometrika,* 17, 267–288.

Pemberton, C. L. 1952b. The closure factors related to temperament. *J. Pers.*, 21, 159–175.

Peterson, J. 1925. *Early conceptions and tests of intelligence.* New York: Harcourt, Brace & World.

Peterson, J., and Lanier, L. H. 1929. Studies in the comparative abilities of whites and Negroes. *Ment. Meas. Monogr.*, No. 5.

Peterson, J., Lanier, L. H., and Walker, H. M. 1925. Comparisons of white and Negro children in certain ingenuity and speed tests. *J. comp. Psychol.*, 5, 271–283.

Pettigrew, T. F. 1958. The measurement and correlates of category width as a cognitive variable. *J. Pers.*, 26, 532–544.

Pettigrew, T. F. 1964. Negro American personality: why isn't more known? *J. soc. Issues*, 20, 4–23.

Phillips, E. L. 1950. Intellectual and personality factors associated with social class attitudes among junior high school children. *J. genet. Psychol.*, 77, 61–72.

Phillips, E. L., Berman, I. R., and Hanson, H. B. 1948. Intelligence and personality factors associated with poliomyelitis among school age children. *Monogr. Soc. Res. Child. Develpm.*, 12 (2).

Piaget, Jean. 1947. *The psychology of intelligence.* New York: Harcourt, Brace & World.

Pickrel, E. W. 1957. Levels of perceptual organization and cognition: conflicting evidence. *J. abnorm. soc. Psychol.*, 54, 422–424.

Pinneau, S. R. 1961. *Changes in intelligence quotient.* Boston: Houghton-Mifflin.

Pintner, R. 1931. *Intelligence testing.* New York: Holt, Rinehart and Winston. Ch. 20.

Plant, W. T., and Richardson, H. 1958. The IQ of the average college student. *J. consult. Psychol.*, 5, 229–231.

Pool, D. A., and Brown, R. A. 1964. Kuder-Strong discrepancies and personality adjustment. *J. counsel. Psychol.*, 11, 72–75.

Porter, D. 1959. Some effects of year long teaching machine instruction. In E. Galanter (Ed.), *Automatic teaching.* New York: Wiley. Pp. 85–89.

Porter, W. T. 1895. The physical basis of precocity and dullness. *Trans. Acad. St. Louis*, 6, 161–181.

Porteus, S. D. 1918. The measurement of intelligence: 653 children examined by the Binet and Porteus tests. *J. educ. Psychol.*, 9, 13–31.

Pressey, S. L. 1949. Educational acceleration. *Ohio State Univ. Bureau of Educ. Res. Monogr.*, No. 31.

Pressey, S. L. 1951. Potentials of age: an exploratory field study. *Genet. Psychol. Monogr.*, 56, 159–205.

Price, B. 1950. Primary biases in twin studies: a review of prenatal and natal difference-producing factors in monozygotic pairs. *Amer. J. hum. Genet.*, 2, 293–352.

Price, P. B., Richards, J. M., Taylor, C. W., and Jacobsen, T. L. 1963. *Measurement of physician performance.* (Report presented at American Association of Medical Colleges, Second Annual Conference on Research in Medical Education, Oct. 30, 1963.)

Rabban, M. 1950. Sex-role identification in young children in two diverse social groups. *Genet. Psychol. Monogr.*, 42, 81–158.

Razran, G. H. S. 1933. Conditional responses in animals other than dogs. *Psychol. Bull.*, 30, 261–324.

Reed, S. C., Reed, E. W., and Palm, J. D. 1954. Fertility and intelligence among families of the mentally deficient. *Eugen. Quart.*, 1, 44–52.

Reichard, S., Livson, F., and Petersen, P. G. 1962. *Aging and personality.* New York: Wiley.

Reid, J. W. 1951. Stability of measured Kuder interests in young adults. *J. educ. Res.*, 45, 307–312.

Reports of the Cambridge anthropological expedition to the Torres Straits. 1901 and 1903. Vol. II, Cambridge (Eng.).

Rhodes, A. 1937. A comparative study of motor abilities of Negroes and whites. *Child Develpm.*, 8, 369–371.

Rimoldi, H. J. A. 1948. Study of some factors related to intelligence. *Psychometrika,* 13, 27–46.

Rimoldi, H. J. A. 1951. The central intellective factor. *Psychometrika,* 16, 75–101.

Robinson, M. L., and Meenes, M. 1947. The relationship between test intelligence of third grade Negro children and the occupations of their parents. *J. Negro Educ.*, 16, 136–141.

Rodgers, D. A., and McClearn, G. E. 1962. Mouse strain differences in preference for various concentrations of alcohol. *Quart. J. Stud. Alcohol,* 23, 26–33.

Roe, A. 1951a. A psychological study of eminent biologists. *Psychol. Monogr.*, 65, No. 14, 1–68.

Roe, A. 1951b. A psychological study of physical scientists. *Genet. Psychol. Monogr.*, 43, 121–235.

Roe, A. 1953. A psychological study of eminent psychologists and anthropologists, and a comparison with biological and physical scientists. *Psychol. Monogr.*, 67, No. 2, 1–55.

Rogers, M. C. 1922. Adenoids and diseased tonsils, their effect on general intelligence. *Arch. Psychol.*, No. 50.

Rosenberg, B. G., and Sutton-Smith, B. 1959. The measurement of masculinity and femininity in children. *Child Develpm.*, 30, 373–380.

Rosenberg, B. G., and Sutton-Smith, B. 1960. A revised conception of masculine-feminine differences in play activities. *J. genet. Psychol.*, 96, 165–170.

Rosenberg, N. 1953. Stability and maturation of Kuder interest patterns during high school. *Educ. psychol. Measmt.*, 13, 449–458.

Rosenthal, D. 1959. Some factors associated with concordance and discordance with respect to schizophrenia in monozygotic twins. *J. Nerv. Ment. Dis.*, 129, 1–10.

Rosenthal, D. 1962. Problems of sampling and diagnosis in the major twin studies of schizophrenia. *Psychiat. Res.*, 1, 116–134.

Rosenzweig, M. R., Krech, D., and Bennett, E. L. 1960. A search for relations between brain chemistry and behavior. *Psychol. Bull.*, 57, 476–492.

Rotter, J. B. 1954. *Social learning and clinical psychology.* Englewood Cliffs, N.J.: Prentice-Hall.

Ruch, F. L. 1934. The differentiative effects of age upon human learning. *J. gen. Psychol.*, 11, 261–286.

Rundquist, E. A. 1933. Inheritance of spontaneous activity in rats. *J. comp. Psychol.*, 16, 415–438.

Sanders, E. M., Mefferd, R. B., and Bown, O. H. 1960. Verbal-quantitative ability and metabolic characteristics of college students. *Educ. Psychol. Measmt.*, 20, 491–503.

Sandström, C. I. 1953. Sex differences in localization and orientation. *Acta Psychol.*, 9, 82–96.

Sandwick, R. L. 1920. Correlation of physical health and mental efficiency. *J. educ. Res.*, 1, 199–203.

Sanford, G. A. 1940. Selective migration in a rural Alabama community. *Amer. sociol. Rev.*, 5, 759–766.

Sanford, R. N. 1953. Physical and physiological correlates of personality structure. In C. Kluckhohn and H. A. Murray, *Personality* (2nd Ed.). New York: Knopf. Ch. 5.

Sanford, R. N., et al. 1943. Physique, personality and scholarship. *Monogr. Soc. Res. Child Develpm.*, 8 (1).

Sarason, S. B. 1953. *Psychological problems in mental deficiency* (2nd Ed.). New York: Harper & Row.

Sarbin, T. R., and Berdie, R. F. 1940. Relation of measured interests to the Allport-Vernon Study of Values. *J. appl. Psychol.*, 24, 287–269.

Sargent, S. S. 1942. How shall we study individual differences? *Psychol. Rev.*, 49, 170–181.

Satter, G., and McGee, E. 1954. Retarded adults who have developed beyond expectation. *Train. Sch. Bull.*, 51, 43–55, 67–81, 237–243.

Saul, L. G., Davis, H., and Davis, P. A. 1949. Psychologic correlations with the electroencephalogram. *Psychosom. Med.*, 11, 361–376.

Schaefer, E. S., and Bayley, N. 1963. Maternal behavior, child behavior, and their intercorrelations from infancy through adolescence. *Monogr. Soc. Res. Child Develpm.*, 28, No. 3 (Whole No. 87).

Schaie, K. W. 1958a. Occupational level and the primary mental abilities. *J. educ. Psychol.*, 49, 299–303.

Schaie, K. W. 1958b. Rigidity-flexibility and intelligence: a cross-sectional study of the adult life span from 20 to 70. *Psychol. Monogr.*, 72, No. 9 (Whole No. 462).

Scheerer, M., Rothmann, E., and Goldstein, K. 1945. A case of "Idiot Savant": an experimental study of personality organization. *Psychol. Monogr.*, 58, No. 4.

Schiele, D. C., and Brozek, J. 1948. "Experimental Neurosis" resulting from semistarvation in man. *Psychosom. Med.*, 10, 31–50.

Schmidt, B. 1946. Changes in the personal, social, and intellectual behavior of children originally classified as feeble-minded. *Psychol. Monogr.*, 60, No. 5.

Schneidler, G. G., and Paterson, D. G. 1942. Sex differences in clerical aptitude. *J. educ. Psychol.*, 33, 303–309.

Schulman, M. J., and Havighurst, R. J. 1947. Relations between ability and social status in a midwestern community: IV, size of vocabulary. *J. educ. Psychol.*, 38, 437–442.

Scott, J. P. 1953. New directions in the genetic study of personality and intelligence. *Eugen. News*, 38, 97–101.

Scottish Council for Research in Education. 1939. *The intelligence of a representative group of Scottish children.* London: University of London Press.

Scottish Council for Research in Education. 1949. *The trend of Scottish intelligence.* London: University of London Press.

Searle, L. V. 1949. The organization of hereditary maze-brightness and maze-dullness. *Genet. Psychol. Monogr.*, 39, 279–325.

Sears, P. S. 1951. Doll play aggression in normal young children: Influence of sex, age, sibling status, father's absence. *Psychol. Monogr.*, 65, No. 6.

Sears, R. R. 1943. *Survey of objective studies of psychoanalytic concepts.* New York: Social Science Research Council.

Sears, R. R. 1961. Relation of early socialization experiences to aggression in middle childhood. *J. abnorm. soc. Psychol.*, 63, 466–492.

Sears, R. R., Maccoby, E. E., and Levin, H. 1957. *Patterns of child rearing.* New York: Harper & Row.

Sears, R. R., Pintler, M. H., and Sears, P. S. 1946. Effect of father separation on preschool children's doll play aggression. *Child Develpm.*, 17, 219–243.

Seashore, C. E. 1939. *Psychology of music.* New York: McGraw-Hill.

Seashore, H. G. 1962. Women are more predictable than men. *J. counsel. Psychol.*, 9, 261–270.

Seashore, R. H. 1930. Individual differences in motor skills. *J. gen. Psychol.*, 3, 38–66.

Seashore, R. H. 1939. Work methods: an often neglected factor underlying individual differences. *Psychol. Rev.*, 46, 123–141.

Seashore, R. H. 1940. An experimental analysis of fine motor skills. *Amer. J. Psychol.*, 53, 86–98.

Seder, M. A. 1940. The vocational interests of professional women. *J. appl. Psychol.*, 24, 130–143, 265–272.

Seltzer, C. C., Wells, F. L., and McTernan, E. B. 1948. A relationship between Sheldonian somatotype and psychotype. *J. Pers.*, 16, 431–436.

Seward, G. H. 1945. Cultural conflict and the feminine role. *J. soc. Psychol.*, 22, 177–194.

Shagass, C. 1946. An attempt to correlate the occipital alpha frequency of the electroencephalogram with performance on a mental ability test. *J. exp. Psychol.*, 36, 88–92.

Shakow, D., and Goldman, R. 1938. The effect of age on the Stanford-Binet vocabulary scores of adults. *J. educ. Psychol.*, 29, 241–256.

Sharp, S. E. 1899. Individual psychology; a study in psychological method. *Amer. J. Psychol.*, 10, 329–391.

Shaw, D. G. 1949. A study of the relationships between Thurstone Primary Mental Abilities and high school achievement. *J. educ. Psychol.*, 40, 239–249.

Shaw, M. C., and McCuen, J. T. 1960. The onset of underachievement in bright children. *J. educ. Psychol.*, 51, 103–109.

Shaycroft, M. F., Dailey, J. T., Orr, D. B., Neyman, C. A., Jr., and Sherman, S. E. 1963. *Project talent: studies of a complete age group–age 15.* Pittsburgh: University of Pittsburgh Press.

Sheehan, M. R. 1938. A study of individual consistency in phenomenal constancy. *Arch. Psychol.*, 31, No. 222.

Sheldon, W. H. 1949. *Varieties of delinquent youth.* New York: Harper & Row.

Sheldon, W. H., and Stevens, S. S. 1942. *The varieties of temperament.* New York: Harper & Row.

Sheldon, W. H., Stevens, S. S., and Tucker, W. B. 1940. *The varieties of human physique.* New York: Harper & Row.

Shepard, E. L. 1942. Measurements of certain nonverbal abilities of urban and rural children. *J. educ. Psychol.*, 33, 458–462.

Shepler, B. F. 1951. A comparison of masculinity-femininity measures. *J. consult. Psychol.*, 15, 484–486.

Sherman, M., and Key, C. B. 1932. The intelligence of isolated mountain children. *Child Develpm.*, 3, 279–290.

Sherriffs, A. C., and Jarrett, R. F. 1953. Sex differences in attitudes about sex differences. *J. Psychol.*, 35, 161–168.

Shimberg, M. E. 1929. An investigation into the validity of norms with special reference to urban and rural groups. *Arch. Psychol.*, No. 104.

Shock, N. W., and Jones, H. E. 1939. The relationship between basal physiological functions and intelligence in adolescents. *Psychol. Bull.*, 36, 642–643.

Shuey, A. M. 1958. *The testing of Negro intelligence.* Lynchburg, Va.: J. P. Bell.

Sibley, E. 1942. Some demographic clues to stratification. *Amer. sociol. Rev.*, 7, 322–330.

Sills, F. D. 1950. A factor analysis of somatotypes and of their relationship to achievement in motor skills. *Res. Quart. Amer. Ass. Hlth. Phys. Educ.*, 21, 424–437.

Simon, L. M., and Levitt, E. A. 1950. The relation between Wechsler-Bellevue IQ scores and occupational area. *Occupations*, 29, 23–25.

Simrall, D. 1947. Intelligence and the ability to learn. *J. Psychol.*, 23, 27–43.

Sirkin, M. 1929. The relation between intelligence, age, and home environment of elementary-school pupils. *Sch. and Soc.*, 30, 304–308.

Skeels, H. M. 1940. Some Iowa studies of the mental growth of children in relation to differentials of the environment: a summary. *Yearb. nat. Soc. stud. Educ.*, 39 (II), 281–308.

Skeels, H. M. 1942. A study of the effects of differential stimulation on mentally retarded children: a follow-up report. *Amer. J. ment. Defic.*, 46, 340–350.

Skeels, H. M., and Dye, H. B. 1939. A study of the effects of differential stimulation on mentally retarded children. *Proc. Amer. Ass. ment. Defic.*, 44, 114–136.

Skeels, H. M., and Harms, I. 1948. Children with inferior social histories; their mental development in adoptive homes. *J. genet. Psychol.*, 72, 283–294.

Skodak, M. 1939. Children in foster homes: a study of mental development. *Univ. Iowa Stud. Child Welf.*, 16, No. 1.

Skodak, M. 1950. Mental growth of adopted children in the same family. *J. genet. Psychol.*, 77, 3–9.

Skodak, M., and Skeels, H. M. 1949. A final follow-up study of one hundred adopted children. *J. genet. Psychol.*, 75, 85–125.

Slater, E. 1953. *Psychotic and neurotic illnesses in twins.* London: H. M. Stationery Office (Med. Res. Counc., Spec. Rep. Ser., No. 278).

Sloan, W. 1947. Mental deficiency as a symptom of personality disturbance. *Amer. J. ment. Defic.*, 52, 31–36.

Sloan, W. 1951. Motor proficiency and intelligence. *Amer. J. ment. Defic.*, 55, 394–406.

Sloan, W., and Harman, H. H. 1947. Constancy of IQ in mental defectives. *J. genet. Psychol.*, 71, 177–185.

Sloan, W., and Raskin, A. 1952. A study of certain concepts in high grade mental defectives. *Amer. J. ment. Defic.*, 56, 638–642.

Smillie, W. G., and Spencer, C. R. 1926. Mental retardation in school children infested with hookworms. *J. educ. Psychol.*, 17, 314–321.

Smith, H. A. 1949. The relationship between intelligence and the learning which results from the use of educational sound motion pictures. *J. educ. Res.*, 43, 241–249.

Smith, H. C. 1949. Psychometric checks on hypotheses derived from Sheldon's work on physique and temperament. *J. Pers.*, 17, 310–320.

Smith, M. B. 1963. Personal values in the study of lives. In R. W. White, *The study of lives.* Englewood Cliffs, N.J.: Prentice-Hall. Ch. 14.

Smith, S. 1939. Age and sex differences in children's opinions concerning sex differences. *J. genet. Psychol.*, 54, 17–25.

Smith, S. 1942. Language and non-verbal test performance of racial groups in Honolulu before and after a 14-year interval. *J. gen. Psychol.*, 26, 51–93.

Society for Psychological Study of Social Issues. 1964. *Guidelines for testing minority group children.* Supplement to *J. social Issues,* 20, No. 2. Pp. 129–145.

Sollenberger, R. T. 1940. Some relationships between the urinary excretion of male hormone by maturing boys and their expressed interests and attitudes. *J. Psychol.*, 9, 179–189.

Sommer, R. 1958. Sex differences in the retention of quantitative information. *J. educ. Psychol.*, 49, 187–192.

Sontag, L. W. 1963. Somatographics of personality and body function. *Vita Humana,* 6, 1–10.

Sontag, L. W., and Baker, C. T. 1958. Personality, familial, and physical correlates of change in mental ability. *Monogr. Soc. Res. Child Develpm.*, 23 (2), 87–143.

Sontag, L. W., Baker, C. T., and Nelson, V. L. 1958. Mental growth and personality development: a longitudinal study. *Monogr. Soc. Res. Child Develpm.*, 23 (2), 1–85.

Sorenson, H. 1933. *Adult abilities in extension classes.* Minneapolis: University of Minnesota Press.

Spearman, C. E. 1927. *The abilities of man.* New York: Macmillan.

Sperrazzo, G., and Wilkins, W. L. 1958. Further normative data on the Progressive Matrices. *J. consult. Psychol.*, 22, 35–37.

Sperrazzo, G. 1959. Racial differences on Progressive Matrices. *J. consult. Psychol.*, 23, 273–274.

Spier, L. 1929. Growth of Japanese children born in America and in Japan. *Wash. State Univ. Publ. in Anthrop.*, 3, No. 1., 1–301.

Spitzer, H. F., et al. 1947. *Iowa Every-Pupil Tests of Basic Skills: Manual.* Boston: Houghton, Mifflin.

Spranger, E. 1928. *Types of men* (trans. by P. J. W. Pigors). Halle: Niemeyer.

Stalnaker, E., and Roller, R. D., Jr. 1927. A study of one hundred non-promoted children. *J. educ. Res.*, 16, 265–270.

Stalnaker, J. M. 1948. Identification of the best Southern Negro high school seniors. *Sci. Mon.*, 67, 237–239.

Stead, W. H. 1942. *The occupational research program of the United States Employment Service.* Chicago: Public Adm. Serv.

Stead, W. H., Shartle, C. L., Otis, J. L., et al. 1940. *Occupational counseling techniques.* New York: American Book.

Steinberg, A. 1952. The relation of vocational preference to emotional adjustment. *Educ. psychol. Measmt.*, 12, 96–104.

Stern, G. G., Stein, M. I., Bloom, B. S. 1956. *Methods in personality assessment.* New York: Free Press (Macmillan).

Stern, W. 1900. *Über Psychologie der individuellen Differenzen* (*Ideen zur einer "Differenziellen Psychologie"*). Leipzig: Barth.

Stewart, N. 1947. AGCT scores of Army personnel grouped by occupation. *Occupations*, 26, 5–41.

Stockard, C. R., Anderson, O. D., and James, W. T. 1941. *Genetic and endocrine basis for differences in form and behavior.* Philadelphia: Wistar Institute Press.

Stolurow, L. M. 1960. Teaching machines and special education. *Ed. psychol. Measmt.*, 20, 429–448.

Stolurow, L. M. 1961. *Teaching by machine.* U.S. Dept. of Health, Education, and Welfare, Coop. Res. Monogr. No. 6.

Stolz, H. R. and Stolz, L. M. 1944. Adolescent problems related to somatic variations. *Yearb. nat. Soc. Stud. Educ.*, 43 (1).

Stone, C. P., and Barker, R. G. 1939. The attitudes and interests of pre-menarcheal and postmenarcheal girls. *J. genet. Psychol.*, 54, 27–71.

Stone, V. W. 1960. Measured vocational interests in relation to intraoccupational proficiency. *J. appl. Psychol.*, 44, 78–82.

Stordahl, K. E. 1954a. Permanence of Strong Vocational Interest scores. *J. appl. Psychol.*, 38, 423–427.

Stordahl, K. E. 1954b. Permanence of interests and interest maturity. *J. appl. Psychol.*, 38, 339–340.

Strayer, L. C. 1930. Language and growth: the relative efficacy of early and deferred vocabulary training, studied by the method of co-twin control. *Genet. Psychol. Monogr.*, 8, 209–319.

Stricker, L. J., and Ross, J. 1962. A description and evaluation of the Myers-Briggs Type Indicator. *Research Bulletin* 62–6. Princeton, N.J.: Educational Testing Service.

Stricker, L. J., and Ross, J. 1964. An assessment of some structural properties of the Jungian personality typology. *J. abnorm. soc. Psychol.*, 68, 62–71.

Strong, E. K., Jr. 1943. *Vocational interests of men and women.* Stanford: Stanford University Press.

Strong, E. K., Jr. 1951a. Interest scores while in college of occupations engaged in 20 years later. *Educ. psychol. Measmt.*, 11, 335–348.

Strong, E. K., Jr. 1951b. Permanence of interest scores over 22 years. *J. appl. Psychol.*, 35, 89–91.
Strong, E. K., Jr. 1952a. Nineteen-year follow-up of engineer interests. *J. appl. Psychol.*, 36, 65–74.
Strong, E. K., Jr. 1952b. Twenty-year follow-up of medical interests. In L. L. Thurstone (Ed.), *Applications of psychology*. New York: Harper & Row. Pp. 111–130.
Strong, E. K., Jr. 1952c. Interests of Negroes and whites. *J. soc. Psychol.*, 35, 139–150.
Strong, E. K., Jr. 1955a. *Vocational interests 18 years after college*. Minneapolis: University of Minnesota Press.
Strong, E. K., Jr. 1955b. Are medical specialist interest scales applicable to Negroes? *J. appl. Psychol.*, 39, 62–64.
Strong, E. K., Jr. 1957. Interests of fathers and sons. *J. appl. Psychol.*, 41, 284–292.
Super, D. E. 1942. *The dynamics of vocational adjustment*. New York: Harper & Row.
Super, D. E. 1949. *Appraising vocational fitness*. New York: Harper & Row.
Super, D. E. 1962. The structure of work values in relation to status, achievement, interests, and adjustment. *J. appl. Psychol.*, 46, 231–239.
Super, D. E., and Crites, J. O. 1962. *Appraising vocational fitness*. New York: Harper & Row.
Super, D. E., Crites, J. O., Hummel, R. C., Moser, H. P., Overstreet, P. L., and Warnath, C. F. 1957. *Vocational development: a framework for research*. New York: Teachers College Bureau of Publications.
Super, D. E., and Roper, S. 1941. An objective technique for testing vocational interests. *J. appl. Psychol.*, 25, 487–498.
Sutton-Smith, B., and Rosenberg, B. G. 1960. Manifest anxiety and game preference in children. *Child Develpm.*, 31, 515–519.
Sutton-Smith, B., Rosenberg, B. C., and Morgan, E. F. 1963. Development of sex differences in play choices among preadolescents. *Child Develpm.*, 34, 119–126.
Sward, K. 1945. Age and mental ability in superior men. *Amer. J. Psychol.*, 58, 443–479.
Sweeney, E. J. 1953. *Sex differences in problem solving*. Stanford: Department of Psychology, Stanford Univ. Tech. Report 1, Dec. 1.
Swineford, F. 1949. General, verbal, and spatial bi-factors after three years. *J. educ. Psychol.*, 40, 353–360.
Symonds, P. M. 1931. *Diagnosing personality and conduct*. Century Psychology Series. New York: Appleton-Century-Crofts.
Symonds, P. M., with Jensen, A. R. 1961. *From adolescent to adult*. New York: Columbia University Press.
Szafran, J. 1951. Changes with age and with exclusion of vision in performance at an aiming task. *Quart. J. exp. Psychol.*, 3, 111–118.
Taba, H. 1964. Cultural deprivation as a factor in school learning. *Merrill-Palmer Quart.*, 10, 147–159.
Tanser, H. A. 1939. *The settlement of Negroes in Kent County, Ontario*. Chatham, Ontario: Shephard Publ. Co.

Tate, M. W., and Voss, C. E. 1956. A study of the Davis-Eells test of intelligence. *Harv. educ. Rev.*, 26, 374–387.

Taylor, K. von. F. 1942. The reliability and permanence of vocational interests. *J. exp. Educ.*, 11, 81–87.

Taylor, K. von F., and Carter, H. D. 1942. Retest consistency of vocational interest patterns of high school girls. *J. consult. Psychol.*, 6, 95–101.

Taylor, R. G. 1964. Personality traits and discrepant achievement: a review. *J. counsel. Psychol.*, 11, 76–82.

Tempero, H. E., and Ivanoff, J. M. 1960. The Cooperative School and College Ability Test as a predictor of achievement in selected high school subjects. *Educ. Psychol. Measmt.*, 20, 835–838.

Terman, L. M. 1954a. Scientists and nonscientists in a group of 800 gifted men. *Psychol. Monogr.*, 68, No. 7.

Terman, L. M. 1954b. The discovery and encouragement of exceptional talent. *Amer. Psychologist*, 9, 221–230.

Terman, L. M., et al. 1925. *Genetic studies of genius:* Vol. I., *Mental and physical traits of a thousand gifted children.* Stanford: Stanford University Press.

Terman, L. M., and Merrill, M. A. 1937. *Measuring intelligence.* Boston: Houghton-Mifflin.

Terman, L. M., and Merrill, M. A. 1960. *Revised Stanford-Binet Intelligence Scale: Third Edition.* Boston: Houghton Mifflin.

Terman, L. M., and Miles, C. C. 1936. *Sex and personality: studies in masculinity and femininity.* New York: McGraw-Hill.

Terman, L. M., and Oden, M. 1940. The significance of deviates: II. Status of the California gifted group at the end of sixteen years. *Yearb. nat. Soc. Educ.*, 39 (I), 67–74.

Terman, L. M., and Oden, M. 1940. The significance of deviates: III. Correlates of adult achievement in the California gifted group. *Yearb. nat. Soc. Stud. Educ.*, 39 (I), 74–89.

Terman, L. M., and Oden, M. 1947. *The gifted child grows up.* Stanford: Stanford University Press.

Terman, L. M., and Oden, M. 1959. *The gifted group at mid-life.* Stanford: Stanford University Press.

Terman, L. M., and Tyler, L. E. 1954. Psychological sex differences. In L. Carmichael (Ed.), *Manual of child psychology* (2nd Ed.). New York: Wiley.

Terry, R. A. 1953. Autonomic balance and temperament. *J. comp. physiol. Psychol.*, 46, 454–460.

Theis, S. V. 1924. *How foster children turn out.* New York, State Charities Aid Association.

Thompson, C. W. 1951. Decline in limit of performance among adult morons. *Amer. J. Psychol.*, 64, 203–215.

Thompson, L. 1951. Perception patterns in three Indian tribes. *Psychiatry*, 14, 255–263.

Thompson, W. R., and Schaefer, T., Jr. 1961. Early environmental stimulation. In D. W. Fiske and S. Maddi (Eds.), *Functions of Varied Experience.* Homewood, Ill.: Dorsey. Ch. 4.

Thomson, G. 1946. The trend of national intelligence. *Eugen. Rev.*, 38, 9–18.

Thorndike, E. L., Bregman, E. O., Lorge, I., Metcalf, Z. F., Robinson, E. E., and Woodyard, E. 1934. *Prediction of vocational success.* New York, Commonwealth Fund.

Thorndike, E. L., Bregman, E. O., Tilton, J. W., and Woodyard, E. 1928. *Adult learning.* New York: Macmillan.

Thorndike, R. L. 1948a. An evaluation of the adult intellectual status of Terman's gifted children. *J. genet. Psychol.*, 72, 17–27.

Thorndike, R. L. 1948b. Growth of intelligence during adolescence. *J. genet. Psychol.*, 72, 11–15.

Thorndike, R. L. 1963. *The concepts of over- and underachievement.* New York: Bureau of Publications, Teachers College, Columbia University.

Thorndike, R. L., and Gallup, G. H. 1944. Verbal intelligence of the American adult. *J. gen. Psychol.*, 30, 75–85.

Thorndike, R. L., and Hagen, E. 1959. *10,000 Careers.* New York: Wiley.

Thouless, R. H. 1932. Individual differences in phenomenal regression. *Brit. J. Psychol.*, 22, 216–241.

Thouless, R. H. 1933. A racial difference in perception. *J. soc. Psychol.*, 4, 330–339.

Thouless, R. H. 1951. Individual differences in perception and their significance in psychology. In *Essays in psychology dedicated to David Katz.* Uppsala: Almquist and Wiksells.

Thurstone, L. L. 1938. *Primary mental abilities.* Psychometr. Monogr., No. 1. Chicago: University of Chicago Press.

Thurstone, L. L. 1944a. *A factorial study of perception.* Chicago: University of Chicago Press.

Thurstone, L. L. 1944b. Second-order factors. *Psychometrika*, 9, 71–100.

Thurstone, L. L. 1946. Theories of intelligence. *Sci. Mon.*, 62, Sup. 5, 101–112.

Thurstone, L. L. 1949. *Mechanical aptitude: III. Analysis of group tests.* University of Chicago Psychometric Laboratory Report, No. 55.

Thurstone, L. L. 1951a. *An analysis of mechanical aptitude.* Chicago: University of Chicago Psychometric Laboratory Reports, No. 62.

Thurstone, L. L. 1951b. The dimensions of temperament. *Psychometrika*, 16, 11–20.

Thurstone, L. L. 1951c. Experimental tests of temperament. In *Essays in psychology dedicated to David Katz.* Uppsala: Almquist and Wiksells. Pp. 248–262.

Thurstone, L. L. 1953. *The development of objective measures of temperament.* Chapel Hill, N.C.: Psychometric Laboratory Report No. 1.

Thurstone, L. L., and Thurstone, T. G. 1941. *Factorial studies of intelligence.* Psychometr. Monogr. No. 2. Chicago: University of Chicago Press.

Thurstone, T. G. 1941. Primary mental abilities of children. *Educ. Psychol. Measmt.*, 1, 105–116.

Tilton, J. W. 1936. The effect of forgetting upon individual differences. *Psychol. Monogr.*, 47, No. 2, 173–185.

Tilton, J. W. 1949. Intelligence test scores as indicative of ability to learn. *Educ. Psychol. Measmt.*, 9, 291–296.

Tilton, J. W. 1953. The intercorrelations between measures of school learning. *J. Psychol.*, 35, 169–179.

Tizard, J., O'Connor, N., and Crawford, J. M. 1950. The abilities of adult high-grade male defectives. *J. ment. Sci.*, 96, 889–907.

Tobias, J., and Gorelick, J. 1960. The effectiveness of the Purdue-Pegboard in evaluating work potential of retarded adults. *Train. Sch. Bull.*, 57, 94–104.

Todd, F. C., Terrell, C., and Frank, C. E. 1962. Differences between normal and underachievers of superior ability. *J. appl. Psychol.*, 46, 183–190.

Tomlinson, H. 1944. Differences between preschool Negro children and their older siblings on the Stanford-Binet scales. *J. Negro Educ.*, 13, 474–479.

Toops, H. A. 1926. Returns from follow-up letters to questionnaires. *J. appl. Psychol.*, 10, 92–101.

Torrance, E. P. 1962. *Guiding creative talent.* Englewood Cliffs, N.J.: Prentice-Hall.

Torrance, E. P. 1964. Education and creativity. In C. W. Taylor, *Creativity: progress and potential.* New York: McGraw-Hill. Ch. 3.

Travers, R. M. W. 1949. Significant research on the prediction of academic success. In W. T. Donahue, C. H. Coombs, and R. M. W. Travers, *The measurement of student adjustment and achievement.* Ann Arbor: University of Michigan Press. Pp. 147–190.

Travis, L. E., and Gottlober, A. 1936. Do brain waves have individuality? *Science*, 84, 532–533.

Travis, L. E. 1937. How consistent are an individual's brain potentials from day to day? *Science*, 85, 223–224.

Traxler, A. E., and McCall, W. C. 1941. Some data on the Kuder Preference Record. *Educ. Psychol. Measmt.*, 1, 253–268.

Trinkaus, W. K. 1954. The permanence of vocational interests of college freshmen. *Educ. Psychol. Measmt.*, 14, 641–646.

Trout, D. M. 1949. Academic achievement in relation to subsequent success in life. In W. T. Donahue, C. H. Coombs, and R. M. W. Travers, *The measurement of student adjustment and achievement.* Ann Arbor: University of Michigan Press. pp. 201–217.

Tryon, R. C. 1942. Individual differences. In F. A. Moss (Ed.), *Comparative psychology* (Rev. Ed.). Englewood Cliffs, N.J.: Prentice-Hall. Ch. 13.

Tucker, A. C., and Strong, E. K., Jr. Ten-year follow-up of vocational interest scores of 1950 medical college seniors. *J. appl. Psychol.*, 46, 81–86.

Tuddenham, R. D. 1948. Soldier intelligence in World Wars I and II. *Amer. Psychologist*, 3, 54–56.

Tuddenham, R. D. 1951. Studies in reputation: III. Correlates of popularity among elementary school children. *J. educ. Psychol.*, 42, 257–276.

Tuddenham, R. D. 1952. Studies in reputation: I. Sex and grade differences in school children's evaluations of their peers. *Psychol. Monogr.*, 66, No. 1.

Tuddenham, R. D. 1959. The constancy of personality ratings over two decades. *Genet. Psychol. Monogr.*, 60, 3–29.

Tyler, L. E. 1941. The measured interests of adolescent girls. *J. educ. Psychol.*, 32, 561–572.

Tyler, L. E. 1955. The development of "vocational interests": I. The organization of likes and dislikes in ten-year-old children. *J. genet. Psychol.*, 86, 33–44.

Tyler, L. E. 1956. A comparison of the interests of English and American school children. *J. genet. Psychol.*, 88, 175–181.

Tyler, L. E. 1958. The stability of patterns of primary mental abilities among grade school children. *Educ. Psychol. Measmt.*, 18, 769–774.

Tyler, L. E. 1959a. Distinctive patterns of likes and dislikes over a twenty-two year period. *J. counsel. Psychol.*, 6, 234–237.

Tyler, L. E. 1959b. Toward a workable psychology of individuality. *Amer. Psychologist*, 14, 75–81.

Tyler, L. E. 1962. Research on instruments used by counselors in vocational guidance. *J. counsel. Psychol.*, 9, 99–105.

Tyler, L. E. 1963. *Tests and measurements.* Englewood Cliffs, N.J.: Prentice-Hall.

Tyler, L. E. 1964. The antecedents of two varieties of interest pattern. *Genet. Psychol. Monogr.*, 70, 177–227.

Tyler, R. W. 1936. The relation between recall and the higher mental processes. In C. H. Judd (Ed.), *Education as cultivation of the higher mental processes.* New York: Macmillan.

Tylor, E. B. 1881. *Anthropology.* New York: D. Appleton and Co.

Uhlinger, C. A., and Stephens, M. A. 1960. Relation of achievement motivation to academic achievement in students of superior ability. *J. educ. Psychol.*, 51, 259–266.

UNESCO. 1952. *What is race?*

Vandenberg, S. G. 1962. The hereditary abilities study: hereditary components in a psychological test battery. *Amer. J. hum. Genet.*, 14, 220–237.

Vandenberg, S. G. 1964. The Louisville twin study. (Paper presented at American Psychological Association, Sept. 9, 1964).

Van der Giessen, R. W. 1960. De GATB in de bedrijfspsychologie de praktijk. *Ned. Tijd. voor de Psychol. in haar Grensg.*, 51, 472–496.

Vernon, M. D. 1952. *A further study of visual perception.* Cambridge, Mass.: Cambridge University Press.

Vernon, M. D. 1957. Cognitive inference in perceptual activity. *Brit. J. Psychol.*, 48, 35–47.

Vernon, P. E. 1938. *The assessment of psychological qualities by verbal methods.* London: H.M.S.O.

Vernon, P. E. 1948. Changes in abilities from 14 to 20 years. *Advanc. Sci.*, 5, 138.

Vernon, P. E. 1950. *The structure of human abilities.* London: Methuen.

Vernon, P. E. 1951. Recent investigations of intelligence and its measurement. *Eugen. Rev.*, 43, 125–137.

Vincent, D. F. 1952. The linear relationship between age and score of adults in intelligence tests. *Occup. Psychol.*, London, 26, 243–249.

Vogel, W., Raymond, S., and Lazarus, R. S. 1959. Intrinsic motivation and psychological stress. *J. abn. soc. Psychol.*, 58, 225–233.

Walker, R. N. 1962. Body build and behavior in young children: I. Body build and nursery school teachers' ratings. *Monogr. Soc. Res. Child Develpm.*, 27, No. 3 (Whole No. 84).

Walker, R. N. 1963. Body build and behavior in young children: II. Body build and parents' ratings. *Child Develpm.*, 34, 1–23.

Wallach, M. A. 1962. Commentary: Active-analytical vs. passive-global cognitive functioning. In S. Messick and J. Ross, *Measurement in personality and cognition.* New York: Wiley. Ch. 12, pp. 211–215.

Walter, L. M., and Marzolf, S. S. 1951. The relation of sex, age, and school achievement to levels of aspiration. *J. educ. Psychol.*, 42, 285–292.

Walter, W. G. 1953. *The living brain.* New York: Norton.

Walters, J., Connor, R., and Zunich, M. 1964. Interaction of mothers and children from lower-class families. *Child Develpm.*, 35, 433–440.

Warner, W. L., Havighurst, R. J., and Loeb, M. B. 1944. *Who shall be educated?* New York: Harper & Row.

Warner, W. L., and Lunt, P. S. 1941. *The social life of the modern community.* New Haven: Yale University Press.

Warner, W. L., Meeker, M., and Eells, K. 1949. *Social class in America.* Chicago: Science Research Associates.

Warren, J. M. 1961. Individual differences in discrimination learning by cats. *J. genet. Psychol.*, 98, 89–93.

Webb, E. 1915. Character and intelligence. *Brit. J. Psychol., Monogr. Suppl.*, 1, 3.

Wechsler, D. 1941. *The measurement of adult intelligence.* Baltimore: Williams and Wilkins.

Wechsler, D. 1950a. Intellectual development and psychological maturity. *Child Develpm.*, 21, 45–50.

Wechsler, D. 1950b. *The measurement of adult intelligence.* Baltimore: Williams and Wilkins.

Wechsler, D. 1952. *The range of human capacities.* Baltimore: Williams and Wilkins.

Weiss, J. M. 1959. The hereditary determination of individual differences in geotaxis in a population of *Drosophila Melanogaster.* Unpublished doctoral dissertation, Columbia University.

Weitz, H., and Colver, R. M. 1959. The relationship between the educational goals and the academic performance of women, a confirmation. *Educ. Psychol. Measmt.*, 19, 373–380.

Welch, M. K. 1949. The ranking of occupations on the basis of social status. *Occupations,* 27, 237–241.

Welford, A. T. 1951. *Skill and age.* London: Oxford University Press.

Welford, A. T. 1958. *Ageing and human skill.* London: Oxford University Press.

Welford, A. T. 1959. Psychomotor performance. In J. E. Birren (Ed.), *Handbook of aging and the individual.* Chicago: University of Chicago Press. Ch. 17.

Wellman, B. L. 1940. Iowa studies on the effects of schooling. *Yearb. nat. Soc. Stud. Educ.*, 39 (II), 377–399.

Wellman, B. L., Case, I. M., Mengert, I. G., and Bradbury, E. 1931. Speech sounds of young children. *Univ. Iowa Stud. Child. Welf.*, 5, No. 2.

Wellman, B. L., and Pegram, E. L. 1944. Binet IQ changes of orphanage preschool children. *J. genet. Psychol.*, 65, 239–263.

Wells, F. L., Williams, R., and Fowler, P. 1938. One hundred superior men. *J. appl. Psychol.*, 22, 367–384.
Wells, W. D., and Siegel, B. 1961. Stereotyped somatotypes. *Psychol. Rep.*, 8, 77–78.
Wembridge, E. R. 1931. *Life among the lowbrows.* Boston: Houghton Mifflin.
Wenger, M. A. 1941. The measurement of individual differences in autonomic balance. *Psychosom. Med.*, 3, 427–434.
Wenger, M. A. 1942. The stability of measurement of autonomic balance. *Psychosom. Med.*, 4, 94–95.
Wenger, M. A. 1947. Preliminary study of the significance of measures of autonomic balance. *Psychosom. Med.*, 9, 301–309.
Wenger, M. A. 1948. Studies of autonomic balance in Army Air Forces personnel. *Comp. Psychol. Monogr.*, 19 (101), 1–111.
Wertheimer, F. I., and Hesketh, F. E. 1926. The significance of the physical constitution in mental disease. *Medicine*, 5, 375–463.
Wesman, A. G. 1949. Separation of sex groups in test reporting. *J. educ. Psychol.*, 40, 223–229.
West, J. 1945. *Plainville, U.S.A.* New York: Columbia University Press.
Westenberger, E. J. 1927. A study of the influence of physical defects upon intelligence and achievement. *Cath. Univ. of Amer. Educ. Res. Bull.*, 2, No. 9, 1–53.
Wheeler, L. R. 1942. A comparative study of the intelligence of East Tennessee mountain children. *J. educ. Psychol.*, 33, 321–334.
White, B. W. 1954. Visual and auditory closure. *J. exp. Psychol.*, 48, 234–240.
Whitehorn, J. C., and Betz, B. J. 1960. Further studies of the doctor as a crucial variable in the outcome of treatment with schizophrenia patients. *Am. J. Psychiat.*, 117, 215–223.
Williams, R. J. 1946. *The human frontier.* New York: Harcourt, Brace & World.
Williams, R. J. 1953. *Free and unequal.* Austin: University of Texas Press.
Williams, R. J. 1956. *Biochemical individuality.* New York: Wiley.
Williams, R. J. 1960. Why human genetics. *J. Hered.*, 51, 91–98.
Williams, R. J. 1961. Biochemical individuality. From *Encyclopedia of biological sciences,* P. Gray (Ed.). New York: Reinhold.
Wilson, F. T. 1953. Some special ability test scores of gifted children. *J. genet. Psychol.*, 82, 59–68.
Wissler, C. 1901. The correlation of mental and physical traits. *Psychol., Monogr.*, 3, No. 6.
Witkin, H. A. 1964. Origins of cognitive style. In C. Sheerer (Ed.), *Cognition: theory, research, promise.* New York: Harper & Row. Pp. 172–205.
Witkin, H. A., Dyk, R. B. Faterson, H. F., Goodenough, D. R., and Karp, S. A. 1962. *Psychological differentiation.* New York: Wiley.
Witkin, H. A., Lewis, H. B., Hertzman, M., Machover, K., Meissner, P. B., and Wapner, S. 1954. *Personality through perception.* New York: Harper & Row.
Wittenborn J. R. 1945. Mechanical ability, its nature and measurement. *Educ. Psychol. Measmt.*, 5, 241–260, 395–409.
Wittenborn, J. R. 1956. A study of adoptive children. *Psychol. Monogr.*, 70 (1, 2, 3). pp. 1–115. (Whole Nos. 408, 409, 410).

Wittman, P., Sheldon, W. H., and Katz. C. J. 1948. A study of the relationship between constitutional variations and fundamental psychotic behavior reactions. *J. nerv. ment. Dis.*, 108, 470–476.

Witty, P. A. 1930. Study of one hundred gifted children. *Univ. Kans. Bull. Educ.* 2, No. 7.

Witty, P. A. 1940. A genetic study of fifty gifted children. *Yearb. nat. Soc. Stud. Educ.*, 39 (II), 401–408.

Witty, P. A., and Lehman, H. C. 1929. Nervous instability and genius: poetry and fiction. *J. abnorm. soc. Psychol.*, 24, 77–90.

Witty, P. A., and Lehman, H. C. 1930. Nervous instability and genius: some conflicting opinions. *J. abnorm. soc. Psychol.*, 24, 486–497.

Wolfle, D. (Ed.). 1954. *America's resources of specialized talent.* New York: Harper & Row.

Wolfle, D. 1960. Diversity of talent. *Amer. Psychol.*, 15, 535–545.

Woodrow, H. 1917. Practice and transference in normal and feebleminded children. *J. educ. Psychol.*, 8, 85–96, 151–165.

Woodrow, H. 1938a. The effect of practice on groups of different initial ability. *J. educ. Psychol.*, 29, 268–278.

Woodrow, H. 1938b. The effect of practice on test intercorrelations. *J. educ. Psychol.*, 29, 561–572.

Woodrow, H. 1938c. The relation between abilities and improvement with practice. *J. educ. Psychol.*, 29, 215–230.

Woodrow, H. 1939a. Factors in improvement with practice. *J. Psychol.*, 7, 55–70.

Woodrow, H. 1939b. The application of factor analysis to problems of practice. *J. gen. Psychol.*, 21, 457–460.

Woodrow, H. 1939c. The relation of verbal ability to improvement with practice in verbal tests. *J. educ. Psychol.*, 30, 179–186.

Woodrow, H. 1940. Interrelations of measures of learning. *J. Psychol.*, 10, 49–73.

Woodrow, H. 1946. The ability to learn. *Psychol. Rev.*, 53, 147–158.

Woods, W. A., and Toal, R. 1957. Subtest disparity of Negro and white groups matched for IQ's on the Revised Beta Test. *J. consult., Psychol.*, 21, 136–138.

Woodworth, R. S. 1910. Racial differences in mental traits. *Science, N. S.*, 31, 171–186.

Woodworth, R. S. 1941. *Heredity and environment.* New York: Social Science Research Council Bulletin 47.

Woolley, H. T. 1910. A review of the recent literature on the psychology of sex. *Psychol. Bull.*, 7, 335–342.

Worbois, G. M. 1951. Predicting long-range performance of substation operators. *J. appl. Psychol.*, 35, 15–19.

Wrenn, C. G. 1949. Potential research talent in the sciences based on intelligence quotients of Ph.D.'s. *Educ. Rec.*, 30, 5–22.

Wright, B. A. 1960. *Physical disability—a psychological approach.* New York: Harper & Row.

Wrightstone, J. W. 1960. Demonstration guidance project in New York City. *Harvard Educ. Rev.*, 30, 237–251.

Yannet, H., and Lieberman, R. 1944. The Rh factor in the etiology of mental deficiency. *Amer. J. ment. Defic.*, 49, 133–137.

Yarbrough, M. E., and McCurdy, H. G. 1958. A further note on basal metabolism and academic performance. *J. educ. Psychol.*, 49, 20–22.

Yarrow, L. J. 1964. Separation from parents during early childhood. In M. L. Hoffman and L. W. Hoffman (Eds.), *Review of child development research*, Vol. 1. New York: Russell Sage Foundation.

Yela, M. 1949. Application of the concept of simple structure to Alexander's data. *Psychometrika*, 14, 121–135.

Yerkes, R. M. (Ed.). 1921. *Psychological examining in the U. S. Army*. Memoirs of National Academy of Science, Vol. 15.

Zeaman, D., and House, B. J. 1963. The role of attention in retardate discrimination learning. In N. R. Ellis (Ed.), *Handbook of mental deficiency*. New York: McGraw-Hill. Ch. 5.

Zigler, E. 1962. Rigidity in the feeble-minded. In E. P. Trapp and P. Himelstein (Eds.), *The exceptional child: research and theory*. New York: Appleton-Century-Crofts. Ch. 10.

Zimmerman, F. T., and Burgemeister, B. B. 1951. Permanency of glutamic acid treatment. A.M.A. *Arch. Neurol. Psychiat., Chicago,* 65, 291–298.

Zimmerman, F. T., Burgemeister, B. B., and Putnam, T. J. 1948. The ceiling effect of glutamic acid upon intelligence in children and in adolescents. *Amer. J. Psychiat.*, 104, 593–599.

Zunich, M. 1962. Relationship between maternal behavior and attitudes toward children. *J. genet. Psychol.*, 100, 155–165.

INDEX